# Now Upon a Time

# Now Upon a Time

## A Contemporary View of Children's Literature

Myra Pollack Sadker
*American University*

David Miller Sadker
*American University*

Harper & Row, Publishers
New York  Hagerstown  San Francisco  London

Sponsoring Editor: Wayne E. Schotanus/Michael E. Brown
Project Editor: Renée E. Beach
Designer: Andrea C. Goodman
Production Supervisor: Will C. Jomarrón
Compositor: American Book–Stratford Press, Inc.
Printer and Binder: Halliday Lithograph Corporation

**Now Upon a Time: A Contemporary View of Children's Literature**

Library of Congress Cataloging in Publication Data

Sadker, Myra.
    Now upon a time.

    Includes bibliographies and index.
    1. Children's literature—History and criticism.
2. Books and reading for children.  I. Sadker, David
Miller, 1942-    joint author.  II. Title.
PN1009.A1S23        028.52       76-46423
ISBN 0-06-045693-0

This book is dedicated
to our daughters, Robin and Jacki;
and to Robin's Montessori School
and Jacki's nap time,
which made it possible.

# Contents

## 3    Save our planet—save ourselves    267

## 4    Approaches to working with children and books    360

## Appendixes    422

# Preface

In *Future Shock* Alvin Toffler writes:

Why . . . must teaching be organized around such fixed disciplines as English, economics, mathematics or biology? Why not around stages of the human life cycle: a course on birth, childhood, adolescence, marriage, career, retirement, death. Or around contemporary social problems? . . .

The present curriculum and its division into airtight compartments is not based on any well thought out conception of contemporary human needs. Still less is it based on any grasp of the future, any understanding of what skills Johnny will require to live in the hurricane's eye of change.*

The swift and profound changes that bombard and challenge the social fabric of our society call for an equally profound response in our approaches to preparing children for tomorrow's world. It is this urgent and critical need that motivated us to write this book.

Looking back, the roots of this text can be traced to our concern with sexism, an issue that affected our professional careers. Personal anguish was translated into research and writing concerned with the ramifications of sex bias in various aspects of education. It was natural that this concern would surface in our children's literature courses as we began to explore sex role stereotyping in children's books.

The topic excited our students and led naturally to the exploration of racism in children's books. Like Jefferson's "firebell in the night," other issues demanded our attention; we explored the way various topics such as sexuality, death, age, and ecology were treated in children's books, and as we brought these topics into our children's literature classes, we found that this approach caught the imagination and interest of our students. The crucial issues of our society and the needs of our students to cope effectively with these issues suggested

* Toffler quoted in *School: Pass at Your Own Risk*, Arthur Daigon and Richard Dempsey, Prentice-Hall, Englewood Cliffs, N.J., 1974, pp. 40–41.

a new approach to the teaching of children's literature, one that is reflected in this book.

*Now Upon a Time* is something of a departure from the traditional children's literature text. We have been selective in the books discussed, and sometimes we have chosen to discuss books because they are contemporary in mood or topic rather than because they exemplify all the elements of lasting literature. In discussing these books we have placed great emphasis on how a particular topic or issue is portrayed, and less effort on evaluating books in terms of the more traditional literary analysis. These literary characterstics are touched upon in this text, but the emphasis is on the issue and its potential impact on children. *Now Upon a Time* is meant to be a focused, manageable text, and not a comprehensive reference guide or compendium of the vast body of children's literature currently available.

To supplement this approach we have included extensive bibliographies at the end of each chapter. In our own courses we also use additional articles, book chapters, lectures, and student reports concerned with the other traditional areas of children's literature such as poetry, mythology and folklore, and nonfiction. It is our hope that we provide some insight into the world of children's books and help to motivate individuals so that they visit their libraries and read these books for themselves. It is also our hope that we help teachers consider some of the issues of deep concern to students and become aware of books that portray such topics and problems.

We have attempted to tie this text to the real world, to give it a practical thrust. From our own years of public school teaching we have experienced the need for textbooks that tie the theoretical with the practical. One way this can be accomplished is through a book's organization. Many of the chapters of this text fit neatly into curricular topics currently used in schools. The chapters on American minority groups, women, and ecology, for example, are important topics in elementary and secondary schools and can be put to good use by elementary, English, social studies, and science teachers, as well as by librarians and parents. Other topics, such as the treatment of divorce, age, and death in children's books, represent issues yet to be confronted in most schools or by many adults and are included in this book to encourage teachers and librarians to explore these new and critical frontiers.

Finally, in both a practical and theoretical sense, *Now Upon a Time* is in part a response to the rapidly changing world in which we live. For it is not only technological advances that seem to follow one upon the other, but falling social taboos, changing lifestyles, a new sensitivity to ethnic groups, a growing awareness of the role of women, and a heightened appreciation of our limited natural resources that promise a tomorrow radically different from today. Our society is moving so quickly, in fact, that the term *future shock* had to be coined for those of us unable to keep pace with the frequent changes that alter our lives. We hope that *Now Upon a Time* will map a journey through literature and highlight those books that may reduce the trauma of present and future shock for our children and help them gain greater understanding of themselves and of the world around them.

We would like to thank the many individuals whose help was invaluable in the creation of this book. The skill and patience of our typists, Shirley Pollack and Adelaide Jones, was indispensable as they typed and retyped drafts and revisions of the manuscript and bibliographies that seemed to need endless updating. Many of our students at American University, including Ellen Rosenberg, Connie Haje, Mary Beth Corman, Dennis Nutt, and Barbara Schifter, participated in the initial research for the book. We also express our appreciation for Abby Hunt's evaluative comments and her diligent compilation of the bibliography in the Appendix. Margaret Coughlin and Virginia Haviland's guidance at the Library of Congress was most helpful, as were the thorough and insightful comments of Patricia Cianciolo, in her reviews of the manuscript at various stages of its development. We also wish to thank Tommy Feldman of the Jewish Community Center, Rockville, Maryland, and Jerome Hershon and his colleagues at the Board of Jewish Education of Greater Washington for their reviews and suggestions. Our editors, Mike Brown and Wayne Schotanus were unflagging in their encouragement, and many knowledgeable librarians in Montgomery County, Maryland, and Washington, D.C., patiently helped us load our station wagon, time and time again, with stacks of recommended books. And we would like to thank the state of Maine for providing the serene retreat, without telephone and almost without mail service, where we hibernated to write this book.

M. P. S.
D. M. S.

# Acknowledgments

## Text

The authors and publisher gratefully acknowledge permission to reprint the following material:

From "New Novels for Juniors" by Jean A. Seligmann, *Newsweek*, March 4, 1974. Copyright Newsweek, Inc. 1974, reprinted by permission of the publisher.

From "Teen-agers Are for Real" by Susan Hinton, *New York Times Book Review*, August 27, 1967. Copyright 1967 by the New York Times. Reprinted by permission of the publisher.

From "The Kind of Books We Give Children: Whose Nonsense?" by Julius Lester, *Publishers' Weekly*, February 23, 1970. Copyright 1970 by R. R. Bowker Company. Reprinted by permission of the publisher.

From "If That Don't Do No Good, Well That Won't Do No Harm" by Sheila Egoff, *Library Journal*, October 15, 1972. Copyright 1972 by R. R. Bowker Company. Reprinted by permission of the publisher.

From "Writing for Children—With Respect" by Alice Bach *Publishers' Weekly*, February 24, 1975. Reprinted by permission of Joan Daves. Copyright © 1975 by Alice Bach.

From "Kids, Kulture, and Us" by Frank McLaughlin, *Library Journal*, October 15, 1972. Copyright 1972 by R. R. Bowker Company. Reprinted by permission of the publisher.

From "McLuhan, Youth, and Literature" by Eleanor Cameron, *Horn Book*, October 1972. Copyright 1972 by the Horn Book. Reprinted by permission of the publisher and the author.

From "Getting Inside Jazz Country" by Nat Hentoff, *Horn Book*, October 1966. Copyright 1966 by the Horn Book. Reprinted by permission of the publisher.

From "The Maturation of the Junior Novel: From Gestation to the Pill" by Lou Willett Staneck, *Library Journal*, December 1972. Copyright by R. R. Bowker Company. Reprinted by permission of the publisher.

From "Sexuality in Books" by Josette Frank, *Library Journal*, February 1973. Copyright by R. R. Bowker Company. Reprinted by permission by the publisher.

From "Sexuality in Books" by Barbara Wersba, *Library Journal*, February 1973. Copyright by R. R. Bowker Company. Reprinted by permission of the publisher.

From *Deenie* by Judy Blume. Copyright 1973 by Bradbury Press. Reprinted by permission of the publisher.

From "Tilting At Taboos" by Isabelle Holland, *Horn Book*, June 1973. Copyright 1973 by the Horn Book. Reprinted by permission of the publisher.

From *Charlie and the Glass Elevator* by Roald Dahl. Illustrated by Joseph Schindelman. Copyright © 1972 by Roald Dahl. Reprinted by permission of Alfred A. Knopf, Inc.

From "The Man He Killed" by Thomas Hardy, *Collected Poems of Thomas Hardy*. Copyright 1925 by Macmillan Publishing Co., Inc. Reprinted by permission of the publisher.

From *The Long Secret* by Louise Fitzhugh. Copyright 1965 by Harper & Row. Reprinted by permission of the publisher.

From "Books in the Classroom" by Donald Bissett, *Elementary English*, May 1974. Copyright 1968 by the National Council of Teachers of English. Reprinted by permission of the publisher.

From "Black Images in Children's Literature" by Marvis Wormley Davis, *Library Journal*, January 1972. Reprinted by permission of the publisher.

From "The 34th Man: How Well Is Jewish Minority Culture Represented in Children's Book Selection" by Leona Daniels in *Issues in Children's Book Selection*, edited by Lillian Gerhardt. Copyright by R. R. Bowker Company, 1973. Reprinted by permission of the publisher.

From "Censorship in the 1970's: Some Ways to Handle It When It Comes (And It Will)" by Kenneth Donelson, *English Journal*, February 1974. Reprinted by permission of the publisher.

From *The Students' Right to Read* by Kenneth L. Donelson. Copyright 1972 by the National Council of Teachers of English. Reprinted by permission.

From "The All White World of Children's Books" by Nancy Larrick in *Saturday Review*, September 11, 1965. Reprinted by permission of the publisher.

From "A Few Safe Assumptions About Censorship and the Censor" by Kenneth Donelson, *Peabody Journal of Education*, April 1973. Reprinted by permission of the publisher.

From the *Newsletter on Intellectual Freedom*, September 1972, American Library Association. Reprinted by permission of the publisher.

From "Acting for the Children" by James A. Harvey, *Library Journal*, February 15, 1973. Reprinted by permission of the publisher.

From "What To Do When the Censor Comes" by Kenneth Donelson, *Elementary English*, March 1974. Reprinted by permission of the publisher.

From "White Walls and High Windows: Some Contemporary Censorship Problems" by Kenneth Donelson, *English Journal*, November 1972. Reprinted by permission of the publisher.

From *Whispering Wind: Poetry by Young American Indians*, copyright © by The Institute of American Indian Arts. Edited by Terry Allen. Reprinted by permission of Doubleday and Co., Inc.

From "Evaluate Your Textbook for Racism, Sexism" by Max Rosenberg, *Educational Leadership*, November 1973. Reprinted by permission of the publisher.

"On a Sunny Evening," from . . . *I Never Saw Another Butterfly* . . . , Children's drawings and poems from Terezin Concentration Camp 1942–1944. Reprinted by permission of McGraw-Hill.

Nursery rhymes from *The Real Mother Goose* illustrated by Blanche Fisher Wright. Copyright 1916 by Rand McNally and Co. Renewed copyright 1944. Reprinted by permission of the publisher.

From "Some Day My Prince Will Come; Female Acculturation through the Fairy Tale," by Marcia Lieberman, *College English*, December 1972. Copyright by National Council of Teachers of English. Reprinted by permission of the publisher.

From "A Decade of Sexism in Readers," by Diane Bennett Gaebner, *Reading Teacher*, October 1972. Copyright by the International Reading Association. Reprinted by permission of the publisher.

From "Guidelines for Publications" by the NCTE Committee on the Role and Image of Women in the Council and the Profession," *Elementary English*, October 1973. Copyright by the National Council of Teachers of English. Reprinted by permission of the publisher.

From "Meg, Jo, Beth, Amy, and Louisa" by Elizabeth Janeway in *Only Connect: Readings in Children's Literature*, Sheila Egoff et al. (eds.) Copyright © 1969. Copyright by Paul R. Reynolds. Reprinted by permission of the publisher.

"Death of a Young Poet," *Washington Post*, March 19, 1974. Reprinted by permission of the publisher.

Three excerpts from "I Met Death One Clumsy Day" by Flora Arnstein, *English Journal*, September 1972. Copyright © 1972 by the National Council of Teachers of English. Reprinted by permission of the publisher and the author.

From "The Treatment of Death in Children's Literature" by Evelyn J. Swenson, *Elementary English*, March 1972. Copyright © 1972 by the National Council of Teachers of English. Reprinted by permission of the publisher and the author.

"Original Poems for Infant Minds" by A. Taylor and J. Taylor from "What Man Has Told Children About Death," by Thomas J. Schur, *Omega*, October 1971. Copyright by Baywood Publishing Company, Inc. 1971. Reprinted by permission of the publisher.

From "Stereotypic Family in Children's Literature" by Jean Zwack, *Reading Teacher*, January 1973. Copyright by the International Reading Association. Reprinted by permission of the publisher.

From "Advice to People, Generation Unknown" by Mike McCord in Anne Power and Carole Rush, "Youth in the Seventies; Socially Conscious or Self-Obsessed?" *Social Education*, April 1974.

Copyright by the National Council for the Social Studies. Reprinted by permission of the publisher and the author.

From "From Now to 1984," by Betty Bacon, *Wilson Library Bulletin*, October 1970. Copyright by the H. W. Wilson Company. Reprinted by permission of the publisher.

From *The Long Secret* by Louise Fitzhugh. Copyright 1965 by Harper & Row. Reprinted by permission of the publisher.

## Illustrations

Illustration by William Tracy, from *Phi Delta Kappan*, June 1971. Reprinted by permission of William Tracy.

From *On Mother's Lap* by Ann Scott. Copyright © 1972. Used by permission of McGraw-Hill Book Company.

Illustration by Emily Arnold McCully, from *Black Is Brown Is Tan* by Arnold Adoff. Pictures copyright © by Emily Arnold McCully. Reprinted with permission of Harper & Row Publishers, Inc.

*The Little Island* by Golden McDonald, copyright 1946 by Doubleday & Company, Inc.

Illustration by Ray Cruz, from *Alexander and the Terrible Horrible No Good Very Bad Day* by Judith Viorst. Text copyright © by Judith Viorst. Illustrations copyright © by Ray Cruz. Used by permission of Atheneum Publishers.

Illustration, copyright © by Martha Alexander. From the book *Emily and the Klunky Baby and the Next-Door Dog* by Joan M. Lexau. Reprints by arrangement with The Dial Press.

Illustration, copyright © 1971 by Robert Weaver. From the book *Me Day* by Joan M. Lexau. Reprinted by arrangement with The Dial Press.

Illustration by Garth Williams, from *Little House in the Big Woods* by Laura Ingalls Wilder. Pictures copyright 1953 by Garth Williams. Reprinted with permission of Harper & Row Publishers, Inc.

Copyright © 1973 by Peggy Mann, from *My Dad Lives in a Downtown Hotel*. Illustration copyright © 1973 by Richard Cuffari. Reprinted by permission of Doubleday & Company.

*The Wonderful Story of How You Were Born* by Sidonie Matson Gruenberg, copyright © 1952, 1953, 1959, 1970 by Doubleday & Company. Illustration by Symeon Shimin. Reprinted by permission of Doubleday & Company, Inc.

From Margaret Sheffield, *Where Do Babies Come From*, illustrated by Sheila Bewley. Copyright © 1972 by Sheila Bewley and Margaret Sheffield. Reprinted by permission of Alfred A. Knopf, Inc.

From *A Story, A Story* by Gail E. Haley. Copyright © 1970 by Gail E. Haley. Used by permission of Atheneum Publishers.

Illustration copyright © 1966 by Ronni Solbert. From *Favorite Fairy Tales Told in Sweden* retold by Virginia Haviland, by permission of Little, Brown and Company.

Illustration by Ben Shecter from *Grandpa* by Barbara Borack. Pictures copyright © 1967 by Ben Shecter. Reprinted by permission of Harper & Row Publishers, Inc.

Illustration by Ted Lewin from *Grandma Didn't Wave Back* by Rose Blue. Used by permission of the publisher, Franklin Watts, Inc.

Illustration by John Wallner. Cover of *A Figure of Speech* by Norma Fox Mazer. Copyright © 1973 by Norma Fox Mazer. Reprinted with permission of The Dial Press.

Reprinted by permission of G. P. Putnam's Sons, *Nana Upstairs and Nana Downstairs* by Tomie de Paola. Copyright © 1973 by Tomie de Paola.

Illustration copyright © 1971 by Peter Parnall. From *Annie and the Old One* by Miska Miles. By permission of Little, Brown & Company in association with The Atlantic Monthly Press.

Illustration by John Kaufmann from *The Empty Schoolhouse* by Natalie Savage Carlson. Pictures copyright © 1965 by John Kaufmann. Reprinted by permission of Harper & Row Publishers, Inc.

Illustration from *A Letter to Amy* by Ezra Jack Keats. Copyright © 1968 by Ezra Jack Keats. Reprinted by permission of Harper & Row Publishers, Inc.

From *Sam* by Ann Herbert Scott, illustrated by Symeon Shimin. Copyright © 1967. Used by permission of McGraw-Hill Book Company.

From *The Jazz Man* by Mary Hays Weik. Illustrations by Ann Grifalconi. Copyright © 1966 by Mary Hays Weik. Used by permission of Atheneum Publishers.

Illustration from *Stevie* by John Steptoe. Copyright © 1965 by John Steptoe. Reprinted by permission of Harper & Row Publishers, Inc.

Reproduced with the permission of Farrar, Straus & Giroux, Inc., from *Medicine Man's Daughter* by Ann Nolan Clark, jacket illustration by Donald Bolognese. Copyright © 1963.

Jacket cover of *Walk the World's Rim* by Betty Baker. Reprinted by permission of Harper & Row Publishers, Inc.

From *The Angry Moon*, retold by William Sleator. Illustration copyright © 1970 by Blair Lent. By permission of Little, Brown and Company, in association with The Atlantic Monthly Press.

Jacket illustration by Ken Dewey from *The Spirit of Cochise* by Elliott Arnold. Reprinted by permission of Charles Scribner's Sons. Copyright © 1972 Elliott Arnold.

From *Peter and Veronica*, copyright © 1973 by Marilyn Sachs. Illustrated by Louis Glanzman. Reprinted by permission of Doubleday & Company, Inc.

From *Mixed-Marriage Daughter* by Hila Colman. Copyright © 1968. Used by permission of William Morrow and Company, Publishers.

Reproduced with the permission of Farrar, Straus & Giroux, Inc., from *Mazel and Shlimazel* by Isaac

Bashevis Singer. Illustrated by Margot Zemach. Pictures copyright © by Margot Zemach.

Illustration from *Song of the Swallows* by Leo Politi. Reprinted by permission of Charles Scribner's Sons. Copyright 1949 Charles Scribner's Sons.

Reproduced with the permission of Farrar, Straus & Giroux, Inc., from *Pepito's Story*, by Eugene Fern. Copyright © 1960 by Eugene Fern.

From *Nilda* by Nicholasa Mohr. Copyright © 1973 by Nicholasa Mohr. Reprinted by permission of Harper & Row Publishers, Inc.

Reprinted by permission of Coward, McCann and Geoghegan, Inc., from *Mr. Charley's Chopsticks* by Doris Portwood Evans. Illustrations copyright © 1972 by Richard Cuffari.

Jacket illustration by Donald Carrick is reprinted by permission of Charles Scribner's Sons, from *Journey to Topaz* by Yoshiko Uchida. Text copyright © 1971 Yoshiko Uchida. Illustration copyright © 1971 Charles Scribner's Sons.

From Little Miss Muffet, *The Tall Book of Mother Goose*, illustrated by Feoder Rojankovsky, copyright 1942. Copyright renewed 1970 by Western Publishing Company, Inc. Reprinted by permission (Gratis).

From *The Real Mother Goose* illustrated by Blanche Fisher Wright. Copyright 1916, renewal copyright 1944 by Rand McNally & Company.

From *Alice's Adventures in Wonderland* by Lewis Carroll, illustrated by John Tenniel.

Illustration by William Pene du Bois from *The Magic Finger* by Roald Dahl. Illustrations copyright © 1966 by William Pene du Bois. Reprinted with permission of Harper & Row.

Illustration by Garth Williams, from *Charlotte's Web* by E. B. White. Copyright © 1952 by E. B. White. Reprinted with permission of Harper & Row Publishers, Inc.

Illustration by William Pene du Bois from *William's Doll* by Charlotte Zolotow. Pictures copyright © 1972 by William Pene du Bois. Reprinted with permission of Harper & Row Publishers, Inc.

From *Wump World* by Bill Peet. Copyright © 1970 by Bill Peet. Reproduced by permission of Houghton Mifflin Company.

From *The Little House* by Virginia Lee Burton. Copyright © 1969 by George Demetrios. Reproduced by permission of Houghton Mifflin Company.

Illustration from *Where the Wild Things Are* by Maurice Sendak. Copyright © 1963 by Maurice Sendak. Reprinted by permission of Harper & Row Publishers, Inc.

Illustration by Maurice Sendak, from *Let's Be Enemies* by Janice May Udry. Illustrations copyright © 1961 by Maurice Sendak. Reprinted by permission of Harper & Row Publishers, Inc.

Cover of *The Hating Book* by Charlotte Zolotow, illustrated by Ben Shecter. Harper & Row, Publishers, Inc. (1969).

Reprinted from *The Pushcart War*, © MCMLXIV by Jean Merrill, illustrated by Ronni Solbert, a young Scott Book, by permission of Addison-Wesley Publishing Company, Inc.

From *George and Martha* by James Marshall. Copyright © 1972 by James Marshall. Used by permission of Houghton Mifflin Company.

From *Frog and Toad Are Friends* by Arnold Lobel. Copyright © 1970 by Arnold Lobel. Reprinted by permission of Harper & Row Publishers, Inc.

From *Little Bear* by Else Holmelund Minarik. Illustrated by Maurice Sendak. Pictures copyright © 1957 by Maurice Sendak. Reprinted by permission of Harper & Row Publishers, Inc.

From *Curious George Gets a Medal* by Hans A. Rey. Copyright 1941 by H. A. Rey. Copyright renewed © 1969 by H. A. Rey. Reproduced by permission of Houghton Mifflin Company.

From *Petunia Takes a Trip* by Roger Duvoisin. Copyright 1953 by Alfred A. Knopf, Inc. Reprinted by permission of Alfred A. Knopf.

From *Lyle, Lyle, Crocodile* by Bernard Waber. Copyright © 1965 by Bernard Waber. Reproduced by permission of Houghton Mifflin Company.

From *An Anteater Named Arthur* by Bernard Waber. Copyright © 1967 by Bernard Waber. Reproduced by permission of Houghton Mifflin Company.

From *Anatole* by Eve Titus, illustrated by Paul Galdone. Copyright © 1956. Used by permission of McGraw-Hill Book Co.

From *The Story of Babar* by Jean de Brunhoff, translated by Merle Haas. Copyright 1933 and renewed 1961 by Random House, Inc. Reprinted by permission of Random House, Inc.

Reprinted by permission of Coward, McCann and Geoghegan, Inc. from *Millions of Cats* by Wanda Gag. Copyright 1928 by Coward-McCann, Inc.; renewed 1956 by Robert Janssen.

From *In the Night Kitchen* by Maurice Sendak. Copyright © 1970 by Maurice Sendak. Permission granted to reprint by Harper & Row Publishers, Inc.

From *Sylvester and the Magic Pebble* by William Steig. Copyright © 1969 by William Steig. Reprinted by permission of Windmill-Simon and Schuster Children's Book Division.

From *Ramona The Pest* by Beverly Cleary. Illustrated by Louis Darling. Copyright © 1968. By permission of William Morrow & Company, Inc., Publishers.

# Introduction: Issues in Children's Literature

### Realism and children's needs

A few years ago Patrick Merla, in a *Saturday Review* article, made some intriguing comparisons between literature for adults and literature for children. He noted that whereas adults seem to be reading about fantasy worlds and fictional never-never lands, children are becoming increasingly interested in books that are starkly realistic.[1] Here, for example, is the way a 1974 article in *Newsweek* describes this realism in the newer books for children.

Once upon a time, most books written for young people—aside from out-and-out adventure stories —were populated by cheerful white teen-agers whose biggest worries were how to get a date for the senior prom or whether the home team would win the Saturday night game. Not any more. A pandemic of realism has invaded young people's fiction, and adults who haven't taken a look at this genre since the pre-Kennedy years are in for a shock. In books with titles like "Dinky Hocker Shoots Smack!," "Diary of a Frantic Kid Sister," "My Dad lives in a Downtown Hotel," and "Mom, the Wolf-Man and Me," today's youthful heroes and heroines are smoking dope, swallowing diet pills, suffering mental breakdowns, worrying about homosexuality and masturbation, watching their parents squabble and split up, being battered by racial discrimination, confronting serious illness and even death. In short, they are doing things that real kids do.[2]

There is little doubt that some adults would indeed be shocked by these newer books, for they are quite different from the children's literature that characterized the first half of the twentieth century. Children's books in the earlier 1900s often described childhood nostalgically as a time of happiness and innocence, a time untouched by ugliness and hardship, a time in which children were immersed in the best of all possible worlds. The expectation that children's books should be characterized by pleasure and delight rather than problems and issues has led to adult perplexity, consternation, and worry about how to react to these newer books for children.

Not only parents and teachers but also authors and critics who write children's books or who write about them evidence conflicting opinions as to whether these books should mirror the totality of today's world or whether children should be protected from unpleasant or controversial topics. Some writers, for example, passionately insist that children's reading should reflect the reality around them, and they decry the omission of that reality as hypocritical and naive.

The world has not spared children hunger, cold, sorrow, pain, fear, loneliness, disease, death, war, famine or madness. Why should we hesitate to make use of this knowledge when writing for them?
*Mary Q. Steele, "Realism, Truth, and Honesty," The Horn Book, February 1971*

"He said his first word today—'relevant'!"

Teen-agers know a lot today. Not just things out of a textbook, but about living. They know their parents aren't superhuman, they know that justice doesn't always win out, and that sometimes the bad guys win. They know that persons in high places aren't safe from corruption, that some men have their price, and that some people will sell out. Writers needn't be afraid that they will shock their teen-age audience. But give them something to hang onto. Show that some people don't sell out, and that everyone can't be bought. Do it realistically. Earn respect by giving it.
*Susan Hinton, "Teen-agers Are for Real," The New York Times Book Review, August 27, 1967*

Perhaps one of these days, children's books will be concerned not only with fantasy and fairies, with nonsense and animals, but with ghettos, slums, wars, and drunks lying on sidewalks. As long as they don't, we train our children to be victims of the social environment which impinges on their consciousness everyday. We make them emotional and spiritual amputees. They see the pain and feel it themselves, quite often, yet we tell them that it does not exist, that they're too young to understand, that they shouldn't worry about it. In a world in which a child can be dead from an overdose of heroin at age twelve, Snow White is not only inadequate, it is in danger of being vulgar.
*Julius Lester, "The Kind of Books We Give Children: Whose Nonsense?" Publishers' Weekly, February 1970*

Still other critics and authors speak for a point of view that has been evident since the nineteenth century, one that Selma Lanes in *Down the Rabbit Hole* called the Peter Pan Principle. Those writers and critics who espouse this principle believe that too many books expose children to material they cannot cope with or even comprehend, and that we must be careful not "to ruffle that blanket of primal innocence with which all children enter the world."[3]

The position that we take in *Now Upon a Time: A Contemporary Approach to Children's*

*Literature* is that the concerns that children must face are real and vital, and today teachers are challenged to help children deal with issues that embroil our society and that range from divorce to death, from sexism to sex education, from ecological crises to the threat of nuclear obliteration. The reasons for this new awareness and concern among children vary from television to Dr. Spock, from the civil rights movement of the early 1960s to the Vietnam protests almost a decade later. Whatever the source of this new awareness, the situation that has been created is a challenging one for teachers, and it is our feeling that it is impossible and undesirable to isolate and protect students from the world around them.

Indeed, one way that teachers can help students confront and cope with the social issues that impinge upon and affect their lives is through the rich and powerful resource of children's literature. Most obviously, modern realistic fiction, those stories that present real children facing real problems, serves to reflect and crystallize contemporary experience for today's children. But in another sense the deepest issues that affect children are timeless; they cut across academic lines and lie at the heart of each literary genre. Consequently, not only contemporary realistic fiction but also fables and fairy tales, myths and poetry, historical fiction and modern fantasy have meaning for children of today and are able to clarify and give depth to the contemporary experience.

In advocating literature that may help children cope with contemporary issues and problems, we by no means underestimate the very special and crucial place that children's books that entertain and delight will always hold. We also are not ready to wish the Peter Pan Principle away to never-never land. Rather, we feel that use of realistic fiction demands increased adult knowledge about how children grow and develop, about their interests and needs, about the ways in which they respond to various topics. For example, we as adults must be knowledgeable of developmental stages that suggest how children at different age levels perceive their world—what they fear, what makes them laugh, when they are ready to learn about sexuality, how attitudes toward others different from themselves are formed, and how they conceive of death. Although it is hypocritical to deny children realistic books, it is also irresponsible to inundate them in a catalogue of complex topics without adequate understanding of what children are like and how they may react to such topics. In short, although Selma Lanes's "blanket of primal innocence" may no longer fit, we suggest that it is irresponsible to strip it away without making oneself aware of the potential responses of children.

## Realism and literary merit

Sheila Egoff, a noted author and critic, tells about a friend who claims that he first became interested in reading by poring over the exploits of football players as recounted on cornflakes boxes. From this humble beginning his reading career progressed to Schopenhauer and James Joyce. Egoff feels that such a progression is highly atypical and that the avid reader of cornflakes boxes is more likely to move on to Sugar Crisp boxes rather than to literary classics. She takes a strong stand concerning the need for children to read books of high literary quality:

The words of John Gardner can be applied to children's reading: The society which scorns excellence in plumbing because plumbing is a humble activity, and tolerates shoddiness in philosophy because philosophy is an exalted activity, will have neither good plumbing nor good philosophy. Neither its pipes nor its theories will hold water.

\*　　\*　　\*

I would suggest that we teachers and librarians abandon the principle of "if that don't do no good, well that won't do no harm." Instead we should take our cue from Matthew Arnold: "I am bound by my own definition of criticism: a disinterested endeavor to learn and propagate the best that is known and thought in the world."[4]

A number of critics have taken aim at the newer realistic books, commenting on their superficiality, their obsession with topicality and relevance, and their absence of literary quality. One critic dismisses many of them as no more than false sociology and bad literature. Another critic, Alice Bach, looks warily at the "relevance" in these books and comments:

Many writers (and publishers) are tempted to shout a message to the child, so he will *get* it, and this stridency kills genuine fiction. There are reviewers and librarians who expect the children's novel to perform a socializing function, to be a blueprint for adolescence, a guide on how to get through this uncertain time. And most important— and so it seems from the flurry of praise certain glib books receive from the media—is a book that provides the child with a tidy packet of reassuring answers for survival in our fast changing world.

Today's novels blurble on. . . . "It's all right to have an unmarried mother; it's not to worry that you had a homosexual dalliance; study hard and you can leave the ghetto behind you. . . ." A book about a biophysicist mom who swears at her kids can be just as flat and unreal as the much-maligned genre that described a dishwashing mom earnestly hemming her cheerleader daughter's tulle prom frock the night before the dance. It's the writer's vision that makes a book memorable, not the family situation. In children's novels, as in any fiction, it's what the writer does with his material that is of lasting importance.[5]

Bach warns that the current attention to *what* a book is about rather than *how* a writer handles his or her subject will be ultimately detrimental to the literary quality of children's books. Yet, despite the academicians' and the

critics' pleas for literary quality, there is evidence that some educators are not very informed or concerned about the level of literary quality in the books they give children to read. In fact, one study shows that only 64 percent of educators responding to a questionnaire felt that children's literature must fulfill the standards of excellence in writing.[6]

For the most part, children, whether seven or seventeen, are fed stories in school that are full of nice, good things. The seven-year-old probably reads many sterile stories about one insipid postman, policeman, doctor or fireman who is always smiling and appears only to exist to do good things. The seventeen-year-old gets a steady diet of the "good books" too. These, of course, are called classics, which for at least sixty percent of the students, serve only to bore, irritate, or intimidate them. My personal bias is that the main psychological outcome of studying Shakespeare is making a large percentage of high school students feel inferior about their own taste. We have also destroyed our chance of sensitizing students through literature.[7]

So writes Frank McLaughlin in an article, "Kids, Kulture and Us," and his comments probably reflect the feelings of disgruntled, frustrated teachers who find many of their students in reluctant confrontation with books of literary quality, groaning at the mention of Shakespeare and turned on, instead, by cornflakes boxes and comic books.

Such an antipathy is not the natural and necessary state of things. Each year there are increasingly large numbers of children's books of fine quality that do speak to children of today. It is important that all who work with children and their literature be aware of these books and of criteria for judging the literary quality of children's books. There seems to be general agreement by experts in the field that the same factors that determine literary quality in books for adults also determine literary quality in books for children, namely, plot, content and theme, characterization, and style and form.[8]

## Plot

Although many adult books are primarily concerned with the inner action of the characters' minds, as is often reflected in the stream of consciousness novel, most children's books are concerned with outer rather than inner actions. Plot is of primary importance to children, who want most of all to know what a story is about and if it is exciting and suspenseful. Quite simply, the plot tells what happens to the characters. In one form of plot development, there is usually conflict or a problem; the action builds in suspense until the climax, after which there is resolution or promise of resolution. In recent years episodic novels as well as unresolved plots have become more commonplace in children's literature. It is important that a plot does not rely on contrivance and coincidence; rather, it should evolve naturally from a given situation and a given set of characters.

## Setting

The setting provides a location and a time in which the story takes place. It may be a minor aspect of the story or it may pervade the story and create a mood that highlights the nature of the characters and the action in which they are involved. A specific locale may be created in detail, or it may be left deliberately vague so as to emphasize the universality of the characters, plot, and theme.

The way the setting is revealed is often an indication of the author's skill and talent. In some books the depiction of time and place emerges clumsily and conspicuously, whereas in others it is conveyed more subtly, perhaps through the natural dialogue of the characters, or through costumes or historical events of the times. In those books that depict a historical period, accuracy of time and place becomes a particularly important aspect of the setting.

## Theme

One bright student explained theme as, "What the book is about after you've forgotten what the book is about."[9] Theme is the story's central core, its underlying meaning aside from the action of the plot. For example, a book whose plot is about baseball might make a thematic statement about the debilitating effects of prejudice. Or a book apparently about the relationship of a child and a pet might have as its underlying theme the passage from childhood to maturity. A book's theme should be related to the concerns of young readers and should, without being overly didactic and moralistic, cause them to reflect on some aspect of the human experience.

## Characterization

It is a tribute to the importance of well-drawn characters that "Long after we have forgotten their stories, we can recall some of the personalities of children's literature."[10] An author can create his or her characters in a variety of ways: (1) through dialogue and a character's manner of speech, (2) through the ways a character acts and reacts in various situations, (3) through entering into the character's mind and learning of his or her private thoughts, and (4) through observing what others think and feel about the particular character.

A character should act in accordance with age, culture, and background, and there should be some consistency in his or her approach to life. If a character matures or regresses, there should be adequate motivation to account for these changes, and development should be sequential and believable rather than instantaneous and contrived. It is important that characacters emerge as highly realized individuals rather than as stereotypes and caricatures.

## Style

Style is each individual author's manner of expression, his or her unique adaptation of language to fit ideas. It involves an author's selection and arrangement of words, the length and pattern of sentences, and the use of rhythm and literary imagery. Style should be consistent with and appropriate to a story's characterization, theme, and plot, both reflecting and enhancing these elements.

In many respects it is unrealistic to expect that style in children's books can be as rich and sophisticated as that in fine adult literature. An audience of children does impose some limits on an author's manner of expression, restrictions such as controlled vocabulary or relatively short sentences. Many children also appear to dislike stories that are too heavily descriptive, preferring action to a more thoughtful quality. They also want conversations in their stories, and they often reject literary imagery that is outside their own experience.

## Authenticity

For those who feel it important that books provide children with an awareness and understanding of the issues and concerns that characterize their world, an authenticity to the nature of these issues becomes an extremely important critical principle. In a sense, authenticity involves the literary elements just described, but it includes another aspect as well —a social, psychological, and moral trueness to life. It is this critical principle with which this book is most concerned.

In the issues analyzed in this book the principle of authenticity, trueness to life, is often applied in attempting to evaluate the merit of an individual book or a group of books. For example, in the section "Life's Cycle," we analyze the way children's books portray various issues and groups; we look at the way adults are drawn, noting whether the portrayal is authentic or whether parents too consistently emerge as bumbling, ineffective, or even cruel figures. In another chapter we analyze the way the elderly are drawn, to assess whether their unique experience in our society is authentically conveyed, or whether in children's books their lives are idealized, exaggerated, or caricatured. We look at events that affect our lives and the lives of those around us—sexual experience, family upheaval, death—attempting to discover whether children's books depict these occurrences with authenticity or with condescension and avoidance. For some of the more controversial topics, we offer varying viewpoints as to whether these issues should be authentically portrayed in children's books or whether they have a place in children's literature at all.

## Other considerations

There are several other aspects that must be taken into consideration when one evaluates children's books. For example, different criteria must be used when analyzing different genres. Obviously, different evaluative principles must be relied upon, depending on whether one is looking at a picture book, a book of poems, a modern fantasy, a work of realistic or historical fiction. For example, art work is important in a picture book; the coherent and viable construction of an imaginary world may be an element to be evaluated in modern fantasy; and accurate portrayal of a given time period is obviously necessary in historical fiction.

Also, children's books should not be reviewed in isolation; rather, they must be assessed within a network of several related factors. For example, a particular book should be compared with other books that portray a similar topic or issue, and it should also be contrasted with other books written by the same author. And, of extreme importance, the book should always be assessed with children in mind. If children do not like a book they will not read it, no matter how much critical praise it has received. As John Rowe Townsend notes, "But if a children's book is not popular with children here and now, its lack of appeal may tell us something. It is at least a limitation, and it *may* be a sign of some vital deficiency which is very much the critic's concern."[11]

## Topical issues as reflected in children's books

This book is organized to reflect some of the ways that literature can connect children to life around them and can intensify their personal awareness of and their ability to cope with critical issues that comprise and test the very fabric of our society.

The book is divided into four major parts: I, "Life's Cycle"; II, "The American Mosaic"; III, "Save Our Planet—Save Ourselves"; and IV, "Approaches to Working with Children and Books." In the first three parts books appropriate for a wide range of ages, abilities, and interests are discussed, from the preschool years to adolescence. The first section, "Life's Cycle" analyzes the way children's literature portrays themes and issues that affect people at different developmental stages of their lives, such as family relationships, sexual development, aging, and death.

*Chapter 1: Family Matters.* Family bonds have always been considered to be deep and lasting, and they have provided the traditional backdrop against which children grow and mature. In this chapter we analyze the way

the family has been presented in children's literature, and we trace the differing images of family life that have appeared in children's books, a portrayal varying from a warm, close-knit group to a unit that is apparently beset by tension and upheaval. We discuss the increasing frankness with which authors of children's literature portray family problems ranging from divorce to conflict between parent and child and to total disintegration of the family unit.

*Chapter 2: Sex in Fact and Fiction.* As with family problems, issues related to sexuality are being treated more frankly and more explicitly in children's books than they have ever been before. Moreover, several topics once considered taboo now provide central themes for a number of recent books. In this chapter we discuss a range of children's books, from those providing sex information for children to those attempting to confront, through fiction, such controversial issues as premarital pregnancy and homosexuality. We also provide different viewpoints as to whether and when sexual topics of a controversial nature have a place in what children read.

*Chapter 3: Growing Old in the Literature of the Young.* In our society as people grow old, they too often experience a concomitant loss of dignity and of decent physical care, a lack at times so appalling that stories about the elderly in poverty or in criminally inadequate nursing homes frequently emerge in newspaper headlines. In this chapter we examine the profile of the elderly in children's books, and we analyze how books tell children what it means to grow old.

*Chapter 4: Facing the Reality of Death in Children's Literature.* Death is our society's last taboo. We mature with increasing awareness of death's inevitability, but we are often not able to speak of death directly, inventing instead phrases such as *passing on, meeting our maker, going to our eternal rest.* This chapter discusses the way children at various stages of development perceive death. It also analyzes the way death has been presented to children, from the Victorian obsession with death to the silence that has characterized the last fifty years, and to the recent attempts that books have made to help children comprehend and accept death's inevitability.

Part II, "The American Mosaic," is concerned with the way various minority groups have been portrayed in children's literature. Here the focus shifts from the stages of the individual life-span to the various groups that maintain their borders of unique separateness and still unite in a mosaic formation of American society. The first part of this section includes several chapters that deal with the portrayal in children's literature of ethnic minority groups, blacks, native Americans, Jewish Americans, Spanish-Americans and Asian-Americans. The second part analyzes the image of women in children's books.

*Chapter 5: The Black Experience in Children's Literature.* The portrayal of blacks in children's books is very uneven. There have been periods of blatant racism through stereotyping and omission, and some children's classics, such as *Mary Poppins, Charlie and the Chocolate Factory,* and even *Sounder* have been criticized for explicit or implicit racism. Currently there is increased interest and concern in a more positive and honest portrayal of the black American, and the chapter describes not only the stereotyped images but also some of the very fine books about black characters that have been published in recent years.

*Chapter 6: Native Americans in Children's Books.* The American Indian has never suffered from invisibility in books and movies and television shows for children. However, the image of the Indian, inevitably drawn by a non-Indian author, is crystallized in a few distorted and extremely demeaning caricatures. In this chapter we analyze these all too frequent stereotypes and we discuss several of the children's books that relate with accuracy and sensitivity the culture, history, and contemporary life of the native American.

*Chapter 7: Jewish Americans in Children's Books.* In contrast to the frequent portrayal of American Indian characters, the Jewish American has generally been omitted from the pages of children's books. We analyze the limited number of books that do portray the Jewish American experience, and we also discuss some of the powerful recent novels that convey what it meant to be a Jew during the holocaust of World War II.

*Chapter 8: Other Selected Minority Groups as Portrayed in Children's Books.* Chapter 8 offers brief accounts of the way children's literature has portrayed some of the other minority groups that make up America's cultural mosaic, those Americans who emigrated from Mexico, Puerto Rico, Japan, and China. Although the chapter in no way attempts to provide a comprehensive view of all minority groups, it does provide further insight into the nature of stereotyping and greater awareness of those books that do offer realistic and unbiased portrayals of selected minority groups.

*Chapter 9: Breaking Out of the Pumpkin Shell: The Image of Women in Children's Literature.* Recently children's literature has been heavily criticized for the frequent characterization of female characters as passive, insipid, and incompetent. In this chapter we discuss the nature of this criticism, point out some of these biased portrayals, and describe many of the fine nonsexist books that are currently available to children.

Part III, "Save Our Planet—Save Ourselves," deals with the way children's literature comes to grips with some of the crucial issues such as ecology and war that affect and threaten the future existence of life on space-ship earth. It also contains a chapter on humor in children's literature, for laughter certainly must be one way of keeping a sense of balance in critical and disturbing times.

*Chapter 10: Spaceship Earth: Ecology in Children's Literature.* Although anger and indignation about the havoc that men and women have created with their natural environment is an issue that has emerged fairly recently among adults, concern for the quality of the environment and the conservation of natural beauty has been a recurrent theme in children's literature. This chapter touches on such issues as our vanishing wildlife and ecological problems of an urban environment. There is discussion of the recent spate of children's books concerned with ecology and analysis of the too often polemical and one-sided presentation of the problem.

*Chapter 11: War . . . and Peace.* Our inhumanity to one another often emerges in violent conflict—between individuals, between groups, or between nations. Chapter 12 analyzes the impact that violence in the media and literature may have on children. It also reviews books that present children who, with aggressive impulses unchecked, confront and victimize one another through gang warfare. Finally, the chapter looks at some of the historical fiction that portrays children trying to cope with an adult world at war. Emphasis is placed on the fine recent books about World War II and also on those books that stress peaceful resolution of conflict.

*Chapter 12: Room for Laughter.* In the face of problems so devastating that their consequences boggle the mind, it is still within the human capacity to laugh. And indeed books that engender laughter seem to hold a special place in the affections of children. In this chapter we discuss the developmental nature of children's humor and some favorites, both new

and old, that have delighted children and have made them laugh.

Part IV, "Approaches to Working with Children and Books," raises some of the problems teachers may confront, ranging from how to deal with censorship to how to motivate children to read. In Chapter 13, "The Censorship Controversy," we discuss some of the issues and implications associated with censoring children's reading material, and we also suggest some logical steps teachers can take when selecting books so that their academic freedom and their students' right to read can be ensured. In the final chapter, "Creative Teaching with Literature," techniques are suggested for instruction in children's literature. Furthermore, ideas are given for tying children's literature into various aesthetic activities, including art, music, and creative writing. This section also includes a discussion of values clarification as well as a selection of values clarification exercises that can be used to help students, ranging from the elementary to the college years, clarify their feelings on many of the contemporary topics discussed in this book.

Throughout these various sections we have attempted to describe how various topics of contemporary concern are portrayed in books for children. Although realistic fiction has been stressed, many fantasies and humorous books are included in our discussions. Keeping in mind the controversy between those who advocate realism and those who insist upon the necessity of protecting children, we frequently present research showing how children at different developmental stages my perceive of or react to various controversial topics. Since there is also a need for greater adult awareness of fine books that deal with contemporary topics, we attempt to point out children's literature that is of high literary quality.

Although there is no research that definitively proves that literature helps children understand themselves and others and provides them with a means for coping with the complexity and reality of contemporary life, there are nevertheless many personal testimonials concerning the powerful impact of literature. For example, consider this statement by James Baldwin: "You think your pain and your heartbreak are unprecedented in the history of the world, but then you read. It was books that taught me that the things that tormented me the most were the very things that connected me with all the people who were alive or who had ever been alive."[12]

Literature deepens experience and ties the individual to the issues of the times and to other human beings. And it is this human connection that we have tried to emphasize in this text, this bond and sense of responsibility that is beautifully illustrated by Lloyd Alexander's comparison of two quotations. One was written in the second century B.C. by the Roman poet Terence: "I am a man; nothing human is alien or indifferent to me." The other was written in the late twentieth century by an unknown buttonmaker: "I am a human being, do not fold, spindle or mutilate."

Television likes to remind us, "We've come a long way, baby." But modern concerns have deep roots, and "between Terence and the buttonmaker, perhaps the distance isn't so great after all."[13]

## NOTES

1. Patrick Merla, "What Is Real? Asked the Rabbit One Day," *Saturday Review*, *55*, no. 4 (1972), 43–50.
2. Jean A. Seligmann, "New Novels for Juniors," *Newsweek*, March 4, 1974, p. 83.
3. Selma G. Lanes, *Down the Rabbit Hole*, New York, Atheneum, 1972, p. 78.
4. Sheila Egoff, "If That Don't Do No Good, Well That Won't Do No Harm," *Library Journal*, 97 (October 15, 1972), 97.
5. Alice Bach, "Writing for Children—With Respect," *Publishers' Weekly*, *207*, no. 8 (February 24, 1975), 66.
6. Laurel Ladevich, "Determining Literary Quality in Children's Literature," *Elementary English*, *51*, no. 7 (October 1974), 983–986.
7. Frank McLaughlin, "Kids, Kulture, and Us," *Library Journal*, 97, no. 18 (October 15, 1972), 3428.
8. Ladevich, op. cit.
9. Quoted in Stephen Dunning and Alan B. Howes, *Literature for Adolescents*, Glenview, Ill., Scott, Foresman, 1975, p. 205.
10. Charlotte S. Huck and Doris Young Kuhn, *Children's Literature in the Elementary School*, New York, Holt, Rinehart and Winston, 1968, p. 13.
11. John Rowe Townsend, "Standards of Criticism for Children's Literature," *Top of the News*, June 1971, pp. 385–387.
12. James Baldwin, quoted in *Reading Ladders for Human Relations*, Virginia Reid, ed., Washington, D.C., American Council on Education, p. 11.
13. Lloyd Alexander, "Identifications and Identities," *Wilson Library Bulletin*, *45*, no. 2 (October 1970), 144–148.

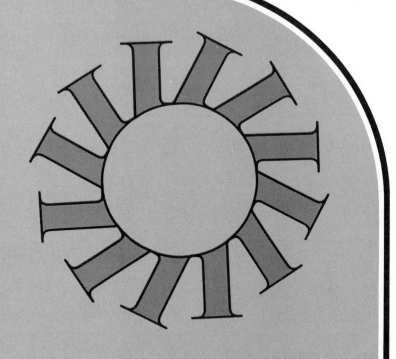

# Life's cycle

# 1
# Family Matters

There is a great need to view family life as "close and loving and loyal," as can be seen in the enormous popularity of "The Waltons," a television series based on the book *Spencer's Mountain* (1961). The Waltons are a rural family, encompassing both small children and grandparents, who love, struggle, and grow together during the Depression. They are a family with intimate knowledge of neighbors and those who provide services, from the local storekeeper to the doctor and teacher. Their values are rooted in honest labor, in the necessity of education, and in the crucial importance of loving and caring for members of the family and of the larger community.

This romantic and nostalgic view of happy American family life in times past contrasts with our common conception of a contemporary society that is colder and more frenetic, one in which shallow roots are repeatedly transplanted as families move from one community to another; in which families know more of cake mixes than of the fragrance of vanilla and more of manicured lawns than of their neighborhoods; in which family members communicate during television commercials and "station-wagon away" from each other on their way to nursery schools, teen clubs, bridge groups, and activities for senior citizens. In this time of shifting values and shifting locations, there is a great yearning to see the family as a snug harbor where we can be safely anchored in the certainty of our beliefs, sheltered in the security of loving ties that bind.

Although futurists predict that the family is alive and well in America and will remain so for some time to come, there is no doubt that it is a unit fraught with some tensions and one expected to cope with varying changes.[1] Ours is a society where the divorce rate is higher than it has ever been and where, in 1973, over 14 percent of children lived in homes with only one parent. Ours is a society where many children feel the tragic effect of drugs and the terrible reality of child abuse, which in 1973 resulted in over 50,000 deaths and 300,000 permanently injured children. Ours is also a society where sex-typed parental roles are changing; 1973 labor statistics indicated that in over 40 percent of two-parent families, both parents were in the labor force. Moreover, there are many indications that patterns of family life will be subject to further change as the birth rate continues to diminish. In short, today any generalization about family life is open to question.

Recently a neighbor and one of this book's authors took our preschool children to the library. Browsing through a collection of newer books, the author's neighbor discovered a picture book that portrayed a divorced family. Irate, she marched up to the librarian's desk and registered her complaint. We then drove to her attractive, suburban home, where she explained over coffee, "The world is such a harsh place with so many problems—drugs, death, divorce. I don't want my kids seeing that stuff or reading about it either. I want to protect them as long as I can."

It is the authors' position that children should not be overwhelmed with books that deal with family tensions and upheaval. However, we applaud the appearance of that picture book that portrayed a family where divorce had occurred, just as we recognize an individual parent's right to make a decision that material concerning divorce is inappropriate for his or her child. We firmly believe that books portraying the complexity of family life should be available to children, that children should meet in their literature not only such families as the Waltons, but also those families that struggle to cope with divorce and the many issues that generate conflict between parent and child.

For a child who has experienced some family tensions in his or her own life, it may be helpful to see these experiences reflected in literature.

And those children whose family lives are untroubled and harmonious may learn greater understanding and empathy as they vicariously experience family problems through the books they read. Divorce, single-parent homes, and generational conflicts are factors in family life today. Hiding from them will not make them disappear. Such behavior is a naive denial of life as it is. It is our position that educators, librarians, and those who work with children have the responsibility of providing reading material that presents a balanced picture of family life, one that includes the tensions and problems as well as the pleasures and joys.

In this chapter we examine how the family is portrayed in picture books and in fiction for children in the middle and upper grades. We look at some of the vivid portrayals of warm family life that have traditionally characterized children's books. We also examine the growing recognition in books for children that the family can be an explosive and a volatile unit as well as a tender and a loving one and that the traditional family patterns must make room for new and emerging life-styles.

## Family relationships in picture books

### Where the heart is

In picture books the family is most frequently drawn as a warm, safe haven where the young child is offered love and understanding. Many of these books focus on the affectionate relationship between mother and child. Ann Herbert Scott's *On Mother's Lap* (1972) portrays the love between an Eskimo boy and his mother. Michael delights in rocking back and forth, cuddled and secure on his mother's lap. He brings his doll, boat, reindeer blanket, and puppy, and there is room for all this on his mother's lap. However, when his baby sister begins to cry, Michael is worried that his mother will not be able to make room for both children. His mother easily manages to hold them both, rocking and cuddling her two children in the reindeer blanket. "You know, it's a funny thing," she whispers, "but there is always room on mother's lap."[2] The large, warm pictures beautifully complement the theme of this reassuring picture book.

Margaret Wise Brown's *The Runaway Bunny* (1942) also portrays the special relationship between mother and child. A little bunny tells his mother that he plans to run away, and she responds, "I will run after you, for you are my little bunny." For every runaway scheme he devises, she manages to think of a strategy to win him back. If he becomes a fish she will become a fisherman; if he becomes a rock she will become a mountain climber and climb to where he is; if he becomes a bird she will turn into the tree that he comes home to. Finally the little bunny says, "Shucks, I might just as well stay where I am and be your little bunny."[3] The dialogue is playful and the pictures imaginative.

The love and admiration a child feels for his or her mother is the theme of Betsy Reyher's picture book version of a Russian folktale, *My Mother Is the Most Beautiful Woman in the World* (1945). The story depicts a little girl and her mother and father as they work together in the fields. One day Varya gets lost; to find her mother she tells people that she is looking for the most beautiful woman in the world. When her mother is found the humble woman expresses the story's theme: "We do not love people because they are beautiful, but they seem beautiful to us because we love them."[4]

Love between father and child is also frequently depicted, as in Ruth Sonneborn's *Friday Night Is Papa Night* (1970). Mamma, Pedro, Manuela, Carlos, and Ricardo live in a small apartment in the city. The apartment is so tiny that Pedro, the youngest, has to sleep in the kitchen, but he does not mind because

there he can watch Mamma at her work. So begins this story of a warm Puerto Rican family as they prepare dinner and wait for Papa, who comes home only on Friday night because he must work at two jobs far away. The family waits, it gets dark, dinner time passes, the street lights go on, and still Papa does not come. Finally, late at night, Papa arrives, explaining that he had to help a friend who was sick. In the midst of the late-night chatter and affection, Papa opens his bag and distributes presents for the family. Pedro is certain that Friday night, Papa night, is the nicest night of all.

There are also some pleasant picture books depicting warm relationships between father and daughter. In Janice May Udry's *What Mary Jo Shared* (1966) a black child, Mary Jo, is shy about bringing something to share at her school's Show-and-Tell session. She con-

*On Mother's Lap*

siders bringing in her umbrella or perhaps the grasshopper that she caught, but nothing seems good enough. Finally Mary Jo hits upon the perfect idea, and she decides to share someone she loves very much and is very proud of—her father.

*Peas in a Pod* (1971), by Miriam Young, depicts a girl and her father who are just alike. They like the same thing for breakfast, they play music and cards together, and they go for long walks in the summer evenings. "Mother says we're like two peas in a pod, Daddy and I. Here we are, one big pea and one little pea— just alike."[5]

Family security is a theme in many picture books. Robert McCloskey is one author whose works are built on the theme of reassurance in family life. In the Caldecott winner *Make Way for Ducklings* (1941) a family of ducklings, competently led by their proud mother and aided by some friendly policemen, maneuvers its way across the narrow, crowded streets of Boston to meet the father in the Boston Commons. In *Time of Wonder* (1957), another Caldecott winner by McCloskey, the children's safe world is threatened by a hurricane, but their family makes preparations to meet the danger and they survive its threat. *Blueberries for Sal* (1948) presents a berry picking expedition in which a little girl and a bear cub temporarily get involved in a mix-up of mothers, a confusion that is quickly cleared up.

There are also numerous picture book portrayals of loving families in which moments of pleasure and joy emerge through life's daily routine. Arnold Adoff's *Black Is Brown Is Tan* (1973) captures the small special joys and intimacies of family living. There is an added dimension to this warm picture book since the family portrayed is an interracial one with a black mother, a white father, and their two children. The family reads together, cuddles and tickles one another, barbecues corn and

*Black is Brown is Tan*

chicken legs and hamburgers. A white grandmother and a black grandmother tell stories of long ago, and there is much shouting and puffing as the parents urge the children into bed. The pictures are warm and expressive and the text is lyrical. The book concludes:

> Black is brown is tan
> is girl is boy
> is nose is face
> is all the colors
> of the race
> is dark is light
> singing songs
> in singing night.[6]

Charlotte Zolotow's *The Sky Was Blue* (1963) emphasizes the special intimacies in family life, pleasures that continue despite the passage of time. A mother and her daughter look through an old album of pictures of past generations, and the little girl asks what life was like when her mother, her grandmother, and her great grandmother were young. The mother responds that someday the girl will be talking to her child like this and that "important things will always be the same."[7]

Lore Segal's *Tell Me a Mitzi* (1970) presents a sturdy, vigorous family of two parents and their children, Mitzi and Jacob. Whenever Mitzi wants a story of some past family adventure she says to her parents, "Tell me a Mitzi," and within the framework of her requests, three stories of family life emerge. In the first story Mitzi gets dressed early, changes Jacob's diapers, and brings him down to a taxi to go to their grandparents' house. When Mitzi realizes that she does not know where her grandparents live, she and Jacob go back upstairs. In the second story the parents and the two children all come down with colds and their grandmother comes over to take care of them; then the grandmother catches the cold and the family takes care of her. In the final story the president of the United States turns a parade around to please Jacob. The stories seem to be a funny mixture of reality and fantasy, and one can imagine that, in their frequent retellings, they have become embroidered and enlarged until they emerge as family tall tales or legends. The illustrations, by Harriet Pincus, depicting the family as funny looking, bordering on ugly, make the book all the more appealing.

Lucille Clifton's *Don't You Remember?* (1973) presents a black family seen from the viewpoint of its youngest child, vigorous, four-year-old Mary Tate. Mary Tate remembers everything except her own birthday, but her family remembers, and they make it a special day by fulfilling the catalogue of requests they have been putting off with that phrase so often heard by children, "Next time." Evaline Ness's exuberant pictures do much to create the character of the persistent Mary Tate.

Just as in *Don't You Remember?* the family does not always have time to fulfill Mary Tate's requests immediately, so in *Sam* (1967),

by Ann Herbert Scott, the family, middle-class and black, does not always have time to play with Sam, the youngest child. Mother is working in the kitchen, Sam's big brother is studying for school, his sister does not want her paper dolls meddled with, and his father gets angry when his son presses one of his typewriter keys. Being brushed aside by his family hurts, and when Sam sits down and cries, the family stops to notice. It is then that they find just the right job for him—making a raspberry tart in the kitchen with mother. Symeon Shimin's illustrations of Sam are poignant and warm, sensitively reflecting his changing moods.

Rosemary Wells's *Noisy Nora* (1973) also depicts a child in a family that is loving and affectionate, but the parents do not have quite enough time for all the children.

> Jack had dinner early,
> Father played with Kate,
> Jack needed burping,
> So Nora had to wait. . . .[8]

Nora is the middle child in a busy family and she goes to great lengths to get her parents to pay attention to her. Her characteristic banging windows, slamming doors, and knocking over lamps and chairs is simply background noise to which the family has become accustomed. However, when she temporarily runs away, she learns how important she is to her family. The verse and illustrations of the mouse family convey, with humor and understanding, how frustrating it is to be the child who always has to wait.

Rainey Bennett's *The Secret Hiding Place* (1960) reflects the need for a child to find some time and some space to be alone, slightly distant but still secure in awareness of family love. Little Hippo is the pet of the herd. Every morning the big hippos wait for him to wade so that they can take care of him. Little Hippo longs for a secret hiding place and finally he finds his own spot, secluded but still near the herd, a place where he can be alone, but not too alone.

Elizabeth Starr Hill's *Evan's Corner* (1967) also portrays a child's need to draw the boundaries of a special place, one that is uniquely his in the midst of bustling and affectionate family life. Eight people in a two-room apartment in Harlem do not leave Evan much room for privacy. So when his mother suggests that he choose a corner that will be his own, he is delighted. He decorates his corner, adding his own special touches, a turtle, orange crates, a plant carefully extricated from a nearby playground. However, when his corner is completed, Evan feels a little lonely, sorry that he has rejected the advances of his younger brother, Adam. The story concludes as Evan is helping Adam design his own special corner.

In Taro Yashima's *Umbrella* (1958), a three-year-old Japanese girl living in New York does not seek a place of her own, but she does make her first move toward independence, slightly

*The Little Island*

disengaging herself from the security of her family. On her third birthday Momo is delighted with the gift of red boots and an umbrella. She waits impatiently for rain, and when it finally comes, she walks down the street, listening to its tapping rhythm on her umbrella. For the first time in her life, she is holding neither her father's nor her mother's hand.

Striking out on an adventure against the secure backdrop of the family is also the theme of Marjorie Flack's *The Story About Ping* (1933). The setting of the story is China, where Ping, the duck, lives with his mother, father, sisters, brothers, aunts, uncles, and cousins on a wise-eyed boat on the Yangtse River. Every morning Ping and his family leave the boat, waddle down the ramp, and hunt for food on the shore. Every evening as they return to the boat, the duck who is last in line gets a small spank from the master of the boat. One evening Ping realizes that no matter how he may rush, he will end up last in line. So to avoid the spank, he hides in the rushes all night. The next morning he searches the river, but no wise-eyed boat and no family appear. His day alone is filled with adventures that culminate when he is almost cooked for a duck dinner. When he finally finds the wise-eyed boat, he rushes to reach the end of the line. The slap he receives seems insignificant compared to his contented sense of security as he rejoins his family.

Being separate and yet part of something larger, perhaps a family, even a part of the wide world, is the theme of Golden MacDonald's *The Little Island* (1946). Much happens to the little island in the ocean: wind and fog pass over and around it, and it becomes a home to spiders, insects, seals, and birds. A visiting kitten is curious at the island's apparent separateness, but it finally understands that the island is attached to the land under the sea. The book concludes as the island ex-

presses contentment in its simultaneous separateness and attachment.

And it was good to be a little Island.
A part of the world
and a world of its own
all surrounded by the bright blue sea.[9]

Leonard Weisgard portrays the island's landscape in rich yellows, blues, and greens. The
book won the 1947 Caldecott award.

*The Big World and the Little House* (1949),
by Ruth Krauss, depicts a warm, active family
making a desolate house into a home, one that
is integrally related to the rest of the world.
The little house is all alone on a big hill, without trees or flowers for company and without
doors or windows to keep out wind and rain.
A large family comes to this lonely house and
sets to work to make it into a home. They
paint and plant, put in furniture that can be
played on, and even reserve one wall for the
children to draw on. This picture book emphasizes the theme that a home is a special place
created with love, and for some people home
is the whole world.

Home is a way people feel about a place. These
people felt that way about the little house. Some
people feel that way about a room, which is just
part of a house. Some people feel that way about
a corner—which is just part of a room that is
part of a house. Some people feel that way about
the whole world.[10]

For the young child many picture books
present the family as a refuge of love and
security, one filled with warm intimacies and
small pleasures. Some picture books portray
parents and siblings as too busy to fulfill a
child's needs immediately, but this unrespon-
siveness is usually a temporary one and is
easily overcome. Another theme stresses the
need to establish a separate place for oneself
slightly distant from the family but within
easy reach of its affectionate reassurance.
Other books show that even in separateness

there is attachment to the immediate family,
and beyond that to the family of all men and
women.

## A disturbance in the family

Even in warm and loving families there can
be times when nothing seems right, as Judith
Viorst points out with rueful humor in *Alexander and the Terrible, Horrible, No Good,
Very Bad Day* (1972). Alexander, the youngest
of three brothers, knows from the moment
he gets up with gum in his hair that it is going
to be one of those days. His forebodings prove
justified as his day is filled with a series of
minor but very frustrating mishaps. His brothers find prizes in their cereal boxes but all he
gets is cereal. His teacher admires his friend's
picture of a sailboat more than his picture of
an invisible castle. He loses his ice cream cone,
his mother forgets to put dessert in his lunch
box, and the dentist finds cavities. He dreams
of escaping to Australia but his mother provides some small comfort: some days are just
awful, even in Australia. Ray Cruz's pictures

*Alexander and the Terrible Horrible
No Good Very Bad Day*

of a frustrated and disgruntled Alexander strike a chord of empathy in anyone who has experienced one of those terrible, horrible, no good, very bad days.

At times children's frustration and hostility are shown as more directly related to family relationships. For example, the established patterns of family life can be upset by the appearance of a new baby. In Ezra Jack Keats's *Peter's Chair* (1967) Peter is shown coping with the arrival of a baby sister. He watches as his baby furniture is taken away, painted pink, and given to his new sibling. He cannot accept the changes and runs away, although not very far, with the only momento of his baby days that is left, his little chair. When he discovers that he has grown too big to fit into his chair, he relinquishes it, and paints it pink.

In Russell Hoban's *A Baby Sister for Frances* (1964) a new baby is born into the family of badgers, and Frances, the older sister, feels unwanted and in the way. After dinner she runs away and hides under the dining room table. Her parents, aware of her presence, skillfully steer their conversation toward the topic of Frances, commenting on what a wonderful child she is and how much they miss her now that she is gone. Frances realizes that she still has her own special place in the family, so she "calls on the phone" and decides to come home.

Oliver's reaction to a new baby sister in Martha Alexander's *Nobody Asked Me If I Wanted a Baby Sister* (1971) is more overtly hostile. Oliver is sick and tired of hearing how cute and adorable his baby sister is. Instead of running away himself, he decides to give away his baby sister. He puts her in his wagon, wheels her off, and goes looking for potential new parents with whom he can leave her. He changes his mind when he finds that his baby sister refuse to go with anyone else because she likes him best of all.

In stories with brief texts and soft, charm-

ing pictures, Martha Alexander conveys some of the other frustrations that are part of childhood. Two of her books portray the brief anger that sometimes arises between young children and their mothers. In *We Never Get to Do Anything* (1970) the scene is a hot summer day and Adam's mother is too busy and tired to take him for the cooling swim he wants. He runs away, a naked figure searching for water in which to plunge, but his mother is vigilant and persistently brings him him back. Finally heat gives way to rain. Adam cleverly fills his sandbox with water from the spout and gets his swim at last.

Martha Alexander's *And My Mean Old Mother Will Be Sorry, Blackboard Bear* (1972) presents a child who, when his mother gets angry with him, seeks the comfort of an imaginary friend. While Anthony is playing with his teddy bear he spills honey on a freshly washed floor. His mother, thoroughly exasperated, scolds him. Anthony finds refuge in a fantasy of running away from home with his imaginary friend, Blackboard Bear. Far away in the woods with his friend there is freedom from small chores and there is adventure. He does not need his toothbrush and gets to sleep in a cave. However, there are discomforts too. The cave has bats and meals consist of fish that are still wiggling. Anthony decides to go home again because he misses the good food and because his mother is really a pretty good mom after all.

In these stories there is mild conflict, but parents are essentially warm and loving. Florence Parry Heide's *The Shrinking of Treehorn* (1971) offers one of the very few picture book portrayals of adult figures who are essentially indifferent and uncaring. In this book Treehorn is dismayed to find that he has begun shrinking. He tries to draw his mother's attention to his problem. "That's too bad dear," says his mother, looking into the oven. "I do hope this cake isn't going to fall. . . ." During dinner, when he again mentions that he is shrinking, his mother says, "If you want to pretend you're shrinking, that's all right . . . as long as you don't do it at the table." Adult response in school is also superficial and inappropriate. "Well, I'll let it go for today," says his teacher. "But see that it's taken care of before tomorrow. We don't shrink in this class." Treehorn manages to halt the shrinkage and returns to his normal size. But as the book ends he is confronted with a new problem: his skin is turning green. "I don't think I'll tell anyone," he thinks to himself. "If I don't say anything, they won't notice."[11]

## Parents without partners

Single parents, widowed, divorced, or unwed, are emerging as an important factor in American life. As of 1973, over 14 percent of children under eighteen were living with only one parent. The number of single-parent families has risen dramatically, increasing more than 31 percent between 1965 and 1973. This is a significant change in the reality of family life, one that children's picture books to a large extent do not adequately reflect. Jean Zwack, in her article "The Stereotypic Family in Children's Literature," comments:

Statistics indicate that one parent, no parent, communal, and common law families are increasing in numbers throughout the entire strata of society. The stereotype of the nuclear family as presented in most children's literature and reinforced by classroom teachers is becoming less relevant to the real life situation of many pupils in both rural and urban classrooms.[12]

In short, over 8½ million youngsters living in single-parent homes must search the library shelves if they are to find their particular family life-style portrayed and reflected in literature. These children must be forced to conclude that there is something wrong either with their family or with the books they read. Fortunately there is a recent trend toward depicting single-parent families in picture books.

In Eleanor Schick's *City in Winter* (1970), the usual pattern of family life is disrupted as a blizzard closes the city's schools. Despite the snow Jimmy's mother has to go to work, so Jimmy and his grandma spend the day together. The two work together tidying the house, and they play together, transforming a cardboard box into a barn, planting a sweet potato, and feeding the birds. Jimmy helps his grandmother make dinner and he welcomes his mother with a hug when she comes home. The father is not mentioned and no explanation for his absence is offered. *Joshua's Day* (1972), by Sandra Surowiecki, also presents a boy without a father. Joshua's mother enjoys her work as a photographer. In this case child care is provided not by a grandmother but by a local day-care center, where Joshua is shown experiencing the minor frustrations and joys of a typical day.

The two previous books offer no comment on a child's reactions to living without a father. In contrast, Charlotte Zolotow's *A Father Like That* (1971) lets a fatherless boy express his feelings and wishes. The story begins with a young boy talking to his mother, telling her how he wishes that he had a father. He goes on to draw a wistful portrait of the father he would like to have. The boy's mother is sewing very rapidly as her child talks. When he finishes she tells him that just in case such a father never comes, he can grow up to be a father like that someday. Paul Zindel's *I Love My Mother* (1975) is another portrayal of a single-parent family that depicts the deep love a boy holds for his mother as well as the way he misses his father.

These books depict a one-parent home with no explanation for the absence of the missing parent. Although the increase in one-parent families is due mainly to rising divorce rates, very few picture books portray or even mention divorce. Joan Lexau has written two of the picture books that portray a family in which divorce has occurred. *Emily and the Klunky Baby and the Next-Door Dog* (1972) portrays how life changes around the house when there is only one busy parent to cope with all the tasks that must be done. Since the divorce, Emily's mother always seems too busy to have any time for her. Instead of building a snowman, Emily's mother has to work on the taxes, and Emily is assigned the task of watching her baby brother. Her mother's preoccupation makes Emily feel unwanted. Tugging her brother on a sled and followed by the next-door dog, she trudges off to go and live with her father. As Emily and her companions turn the corner, the scenery begins to look frighteningly unfamiliar and she worries that they are lost. Emily finally

*Emily and the Klunky Baby and the Next-Door Dog*

finds her own house again and her reconciliation with her mother is a warm one.

*Me Day* (1971) presents Rafer, a black child who lives with his divorced mother. On his birthday Rafer expects to receive a letter from his father, but anticipation turns to disappointment when no letter arrives. However, the day ends happily with a surprise visit from his father.

"Daddy!" he screamed. "Daddy, Daddy, Daddy!"

His father swung him high. "You've grown taller than me," he said, "and heavy as a horse."

"Did you undivorce me?" Rafer asked.

Daddy said slowly, "Look, your mother and me are divorced. Not you kids. No way! You and me are tight, buddy. Together like glue, O.K.?"

"O.K., Daddy," Rafer said.[13]

The book is a sensitive portrayal of a young child's reactions and concerns as he struggles to understand the meaning of divorce.

In *Morris and His Brave Lion* (1975) Helen Spelman Rogers presents another young boy who must struggle to understand the meaning of divorce. When Morris is four his father goes away, leaving the boy a stuffed lion to remind him to be strong and brave. Loneliness and nightmares follow. On Morris' fifth birthday his father returns for a brief and joyful reunion. By that time Morris has come to understand that his parents will not live together again and that he, like his stuffed lion, must be strong.

With slight text and vivid pictures, *Lucky Wilma* (1973), by Wendy Kindred, presents a common problem in divorced families: What should the visiting father do on the one day a week he has with his child? On every Saturday, Wilma and her father go, rather sedately, to some museum in New York. One Saturday, plans to go to the Frick Museum are disrupted as father and daughter meet a sign announcing that children under ten are not allowed in the museum. The two are left with unstructured time to spend with each other rather than with

*Me Day*

objects in a museum. They spend their first mutually enjoyable Saturday, exuberantly running through the park and lying in the sun. Before her father leaves to go to his house, Wilma asks if they can do it again. Her father answers, "You bet, Punkin. We've got all the Saturdays in the world."[14]

Beth Goff's *Where Is Daddy?* (1969) presents an introspective child whose reactions to divorce are more painful. One morning when Janey wakes up, her daddy is not home, and she wonders if she has caused her father to become angry and leave. Janey and her mother go to live with grandmother, where Janey feels deserted as her mother leaves for work. When Janey's grandmother tells her that Mommy will not want to come home at all if Janey is bad or angry, the child becomes exceptionally quiet, afraid that if she talks, the angriness will break through. Finally it does break through, and then the adults in Janey's life become more understanding of her needs and concerns.

When children's picture books portray single-parent families, the parent who remains with the children is invariably the mother. A book that is quite unique in its portrayal of the single parent as a male is Margaret Eickler's *Martin's Father* (1971). This brief, simple book conveys the wonderful times Martin has with his father, who cooks for him, reads to him, and plays with him. Father and son appear to find contentment in one another's company. Although only 1 percent of American children live in families without a mother, it is necessary that the experience of this small minority be reflected in children's literature.

In picture books the safe world of the family—one with few problems and troubles—is presented. It is a world where children can find reassurance and security and where the less happy realities of family life rarely occur. Although the authors recognize the importance of providing young children with depictions of loving homes complete with both parents, we also applaud those books that sensitively depict single-parent homes and families coping with problems such as divorce.

## Portrayal of the family in books for children in the middle and the upper grades

Books about warm and close-knit families are among the most read and the most loved in children's literature. One of the best-known families of all is that depicted in Louisa May Alcott's *Little Women* (1868), a memorable portrayal of the March family, struggling with poverty and a variety of individual problems, but always loving and supportive of one another. The portrayal of the March family strongly and clearly reflects life in the Alcott household as Louisa was growing up. Louisa's father, Bronson Alcott, was a teacher and philosopher whose educational theories were far ahead of his time. Many of this educator's endeavors met with failure, and the Alcotts knew their share of poverty and hardship. Nevertheless, there were warm, creative times, private theatricals and traditional celebrations of old English customs. Louisa, independent and spirited, learned early that she would have to earn money to help support the family. In 1858 Louisa cared for her sister, Elizabeth, during a fatal illness, a tragic incident that is clearly reflected in *Little Women*. When Louisa finished writing *Little Women* she put her hopes for its success in its reality. "We really lived most of it, and if it succeeds, that will be the reason for it."[15]

Laura Ingalls Wilder is another author whose well-loved stories of a pioneering family settling the Midwest are based on her own childhood experiences. This chronicle of family life begins with *Little House in the Big Woods* (1932), popular with eight- or nine-year-olds, and ends with a book more appropriate for older children, *These Happy Golden Years* (1943), which describes the period when Laura Ingalls and Almonzo Wilder are married.

In *Little House in the Big Woods* (1932), Laura is a young girl growing up in a log cabin in the forests of Wisconsin. In the Ingalls household there is always a great deal of work to be done, but an underlying sense of warmth and security pervade both work and play. The house is also permeated by the smell of Ma's delicious cooking, meals created out of minimal resources. But for Laura, Pa is the special person who is her source of comfort and of fun. Pa, his hair standing on end, plays mad dog with Laura and her sisters. Crawling on his hands and knees, he chases the children about. He tickles their faces with his whiskers, and any fierceness is always belied by his laughing blue eyes. The family gathers about him in the evenings to listen to his stories and to hear him play his fiddle. The book concludes with

*Little House in the Big Woods*

Laura's awareness of the wonder of life in the special security of her family:

But Laura lay awake a little while, listening to Pa's fiddle softly playing and to the lonely sound of the wind in the big woods. She looked at Pa sitting on the bench by the hearth, the firelight gleaming on his brown hair and beard and glistening on the honey-brown fiddle. She looked at Ma gently rocking and knitting.

She thought to herself, "This is now." She was glad that the cozy house, and Pa and Ma and the firelight and the music were now. They could not be forgotten, she thought, because now is now. It can never be a long time ago.[16]

In other Little House books the settings change as the Ingalls family moves about, but the love and security of family life remain.

In *Little House on the Prairie* (1935) the Ingalls family has moved to unsettled Kansas country. *On the Banks of Plum Creek* (1937) describes the Ingalls' life in Minnesota, and in

*By the Shores of Silver Lake* (1939) the family has settled in the Dakota territory. *Farmer Boy* (1933) begins the story of the Wilder family of boys on their farm in New York. In *The Long Winter* (1940) the Ingalls family is living in town, and they and the community face starvation as a series of blizzards prevents the railroad from bringing supplies. The *Little Town on the Prairie* (1941) shows Laura gaining her teaching certificate and being courted by Almonzo Wilder. There is still the hard work and sacrifice, the family love, and the laughter of communal get-togethers, socials, sleigh rides, and spelling bees.

Hilda Van Stockum's stories also convey a sense of family life that is rich in love and understanding. In *The Cottage at Bantry Bay* (1938) the O'Sullivan family is introduced. *Francie on the Run* (1939) is a sequel, in which a successful operation is performed on Francie's club foot. And in *Pegeen* (1941) an orphan joins the warm circle of the O'Sullivan family.

One of the families most loved by children is portrayed by Eleanor Estes in *The Moffats* (1941), *The Middle Moffat* (1942), and *Rufus M* (1943). All three books are enhanced by the captivating illustrations of Louis Slobodkin. The Moffat family is comprised of four highly individualized children, appealing, ingenious, and always realistic. Their mother, good-humored and competent, manages to stretch a severely limited budget. Sylvia is the oldest and least visible of the Moffat children, busy with friends and school, immersed in music recitals and play rehearsals. Joey takes seriously his responsibility as the oldest boy in the family, but he still has time for fun and getting in and out of scrapes. Janey, at ten, has her own unique way of viewing the world. She finds it wonderful to look at life from between her legs, upside down; everything, even the shabby house across the street, looks cleaner and brighter that way. Five-and-one-half-year-

old Rufus is a cheerful, independent, tenacious youngster.

Janey is more fully characterized in *The Middle Moffat* where her circle has expanded beyond her family to include her best friends, Nancy Stokes, a neighbor of her own age, and ninety-nine-year-old Mr. Buckle, the town's oldest inhabitant. *Rufus M* shows the youngest Moffat as perhaps the funniest of them all. He diligently practices writing his name so that he can get a library card, but his large, sprawling letters allow only Rufus M to fit on the card, and that becomes his characteristic signature. His escapades are many. On his first day of school he leaves class with a friend he is supposed to take care of, and the two take a train ride to another community. His attempts at voice throwing almost get the amateur ventriloquist thrown out of school. Eleanor Estes won the Newbery Medal for *Ginger Pye* (1951), a story about another family in Cranbury Connecticut, one that loses a dog and then regains him through the help of three-year-old Uncle Benny.

Elizabeth Enright, in *The Saturdays* (1941), introduced the Melendy children, who pool their allowances so that each week one of the children has the whole amount to him or herself. These $1.60 Saturdays yield humorous and sometimes exciting results. The Melendys' adventures are continued in *The Four Story Mistake* (1942) and *Then There Were Five* (1944). All of the books are very popular with nine-, ten-, and eleven-year-olds.

Sydney Taylor's *All-of-a-Kind Family* (1951), *More All-of-a-Kind Family* (1954), and *All-of-a-Kind Family Uptown* (1958) are warmly nostalgic portrayals of Jewish family life in the early 1900s. The initial book introduces the five sisters—Ella, Henny, Sarah, Charlotte, and Gertie (hence the series name) —who stick together and help one another. When Sarah loses a library book the other girls contribute a penny a week, a significant portion of their allowance, to help her pay for it. The mother of the family is gentle, competent, and a natural child psychologist. When the girls rebel at the chore of dusting, she shrewdly retaliates by turning the task into a game and hiding buttons in the room to be dusted. The girls are proud of their mother and enjoy the opportunity of introducing her to their friends. Mama's competent household management and her faithful remembrance of the religious holidays provide a sense of security for her daughters.

At home, the kitchen was warm with the smell of fresh baked white bread. The room sparkled with cleanliness. . . . They were just in time to see Mama saying the prayer over the candles. . . . The children stood around the table watching her. A lovely feeling of peace and contentment seemed to flow out from Mama to them.[17]

Mama is also a source of strength in times of family stress. When four of Mama's five daughters get scarlet fever, she nurses them back to health and still finds time to make the exhausting preparations for the Passover holiday. The initial book in the series concludes with the birth of the family's first boy, Charles, much to Papa's delight. Now, although the children are no longer all of a kind in gender, they are still all of a kind in that they are all "close and loving and loyal."

Beverly Cleary's stories, tremendously popular with children in the intermediate grades, are permeated with the sense of small-town security and comfort in the 1950s. Her convincingly realistic children emerge from essentially happy homes where parents remain on the periphery but are always ready with help and understanding when the children's problems become more than they can handle alone.

*Henry Huggins* (1950), introduces an ordinary family living in a square white house on Klickitot Street. Henry Huggins, who is in the third grade, has hair that looks like a scrubbing brush, and, except for having his tonsils out when he was six and breaking his arm falling out of a cherry tree when he was seven, he has experienced no major mishaps. There is room outside Henry's house for playing football and inside his house for keeping his dog, Ribsy, and guppies that multiply with sufficient enthusiasm to fill every one of his family's canning jars. Henry's parents are loving, there are no major family squabbles, and the parents provide a secure backdrop for Henry's hilarious adventures with Ribsy. The book concludes as Ribsy's original owner comes back to claim him, and the problem of where Ribsy belongs is solved through a skillful bit of diplomacy.

There are many other books about Henry and the other children in his secure neighborhood. *Beezus and Ramona* (1935) is about Henry's friend, Beezus, and her nemesis, her incorrigible little sister, Ramona. Beatrice, or Beezus as she is called, does not know anyone who has a younger sister as exasperating as four-year-old Ramona. Ramona demands to read books only about steam shovels. She writes her name all over the library books taken out in Beezus' name, and she charges on her tricycle around the living room, leaving havoc in her wake. Beezus feels guilty because when Ramona is so exasperating, she feels that she does not love her younger sister. Finally she confesses this occasional absence of love to her mother and her Aunt Beatrice. She feels much better when they are not at all shocked but instead suggest that there are times when Ramona may not love Beezus either. They also tell her that when they were young, these two sisters did not always love each other either.

One of the funniest of Beverly Cleary's books is *Ramona the Pest* (1968). Ramona, irrepressible and enthusiastic, is still frustrating to her older sister, her parents, and now her teacher. Ramona adores her kindergarten teacher, Miss Binney, but she has trouble with the words she learns in school and with school norms. On the first day of kindergarten Miss Binney tells Ramona, "Sit here for the present." Ramona is devastated when she finally realizes that the teacher has not singled her out as the special recipient of a gift. When Miss Binney reads the story of *Mike Mulligan and His Steam Shovel* to the class, Ramona, persistently curious, wants to know when the characters have time to go to the bathroom. When Ramona quite honestly tells the teacher she will not be able to stop pulling a classmate's springy curls, she gets sent home. Ramona remains a kindergarten dropout until Miss Binney writes a note asking her to return.

Meindert DeJong's stories are of the joys and problems so often magnified when viewed through a child's eyes. He depicts children who are intensely responsive to the wonder in life and to warm relationship with adults, both parents and grandparents. *Shadrach* (1953) is the story of a young boy, Davie, and his joy in the miracle of owning his own rabbit, Shadrach. Davie is so anxious about the coming of Shadrach that a week before the rabbit is to arrive, he sneaks out, when he is supposed to be resting, to examine the hutch and gather clover. He is so excited that happy songs sing inside him. When the rabbit finally comes, Davie is dismayed and ashamed as his pet keeps losing weight. He feels great relief when he is able to talk over his problems with his father, a discussion that has an unpropitious start. He and his father are walking to church, his father moving so quickly that Davie is propelled into a headlong run to keep up. A stabbing pain in his side makes it impossible for him to keep pace, and he finally alerts his father to his discomfort. His father apologizes, saying that his mind was on some problems at work and that he had not realized how fast he was going. Davie is delighted.

"I was too, Dad," he said eagerly. "I was worrying out problems about Shadrach. I was worrying it out in my mind how Shadrach could have got

out." He laughed a little chummy laugh and shifted closer to his father. To think they'd both been worrying out problems.

"Tell me about it, Davie."

Now the ache was all gone. It was wonderful sitting there in the deep grass with just his father on this quiet Sunday morning.[18]

*Journey from Peppermint Street* (1968) won the National Book Award for Children's Literature. It tells of a sensitive boy's travels with his grandfather to visit an "inland aunt." The relationships between Siebran and his grandfather, and particularly his elderly aunt and his deaf uncle, are warm, and the boy takes great delight in their closeness. In 1962 Meindert DeJong won the Hans Christian Andersen International Award for his contribution to children's literature.

Jean Little is another author who depicts the warmth and support in family life. Born blind, she has unique perceptions of the child who is different, and she reflects them in *Mine for Keeps* (1962), a story about a child with cerebral palsy. The book begins as Sally Copeland is leaving the special school for handicapped children where she has spent the past five years. She is worried about fitting into active family life and into elementary school, where she will be different because she is crippled. The story emphasizes the adjustments Sally and her family have to make to one another. In *Home from Far* (1965), Jenny's twin brother, Michael, is killed in an accident. Jenny must adjust to the death and to two foster children, one of them named Mike, who are taken into her home.

The happy families that we have so far discussed live in rather traditional homes. Fathers work and mothers remain at home filling the kitchen with the fragrance of good cooking and the house with a sense of well-being and security. When mothers do work outside the home it is only out of dire necessity, usually because of the father's death.

As our society's strict conceptions of sex-typed male and female behavior deteriorate and are put aside, the roles assumed by mothers and fathers are becoming less rigidly delineated and are beginning to overlap in some of the more recent children's fiction. Mothers are beginning to be portrayed as working outside the home, and every rare now and then a book depicts a happy family in which the mother is the main breadwinner and the father works at home, cooking the meals and caring for the children. One such book is Marilyn Sachs's fine novel *The Truth About Mary Rose* (1973). Mary Rose's mother is a dentist who uses her maiden name at work. Her father is an artist who works at home, and, unlike his wife, he is a superb cook. Everyone pitches in with the housework, and the family environment is healthy and loving.

The return of women to work outside the home after years spent in child care and homemaking is an increasingly common occurrence in our society. This re-emergence, often accomplished with some trepidation and difficulty, is sensitively portrayed in M. E. Kerr's *Dinky Hocker Shoots Smack* (1972). In this book two families are portrayed. For Dinky Hocker, family life is unsatisfactory because her mother is so involved in community activities that she has no time for her daughter. In contrast, Dinky's friend, Tucker, is happy with his family and is particularly proud of his mother who, after spending fifteen years at home, returns to a demanding, although unfulfilling, job with a magazine during the day while she attends law school at night. The book succinctly captures her exhaustion, her occasional feeling of inadequacy, her commitment, and her new self-esteem and pride.

That spring, sometimes Tucker's mother would study until three or four in the morning and then report to *Stirring Romances* by nine thirty.
Once Tucker found her hunched over some work, crying, at the kitchen table just as dawn

was breaking. He had awakened to go to the bathroom, and at first he thought she was asleep sitting up. Then he saw her shoulders shaking. He went up behind her and looked down at the papers spread out in front of her. On one side were the page proofs of a manuscript called "I Married the Devil: He Wanted Me to Sleep in a Coffin." On the other were long yellow sheets marked with headings like "Ancillary jurisdiction of federal courts and the basis thereof," and "Implied judicial power."
"Mom?" he said, reaching out to touch her shoulder. "Are you okay?"
"It's hard, honey. It's so hard," she answered. Then she bawled in great wails, hanging on to him for a long time.
But there were days when he had never seen her so happy, and his father had this strange new way with her, almost as though he were courting her all over again. He would bring her flowers and breakfast in bed on Sunday mornings; Saturdays he and Tucker would clean the house from top to bottom, and the few times they had company, his father would turn into this bore, bragging about her to the guests. . . .
"She's really smart, though," Tucker did his own share of bragging about her to Natalia. "She's really going to make it."
"Aunt Helen says she's a credit to the community," Natalia answered.
"Who cares about the community?" Tucker said. "She's not doing it for the community. She's doing it for herself."[19]

This widening of roles and options allowed fathers and mothers is still the exception rather than the rule in most fiction for children. Bernard Lukenbill analyzed fifty randomly selected books with settings in the twentieth-century United States. He found that the father's role as head of the household and chief breadwinner is still emphasized. In 68 percent of the fictional families analyzed, fathers were heads of the household and in 71 percent of these cases fathers acted as the sole breadwinner. In fact, fathers were seldom depicted as involved in any activity other than that of earning money. Although Lukenbill did not specifically study the roles of wives and mothers, he notes that they were usually involved in child care and household management.[20] Thus, although the division of labor still prevails in children's literature, a small number of families are emerging quite happily to break out of the sex-typed norm.

In much of the fiction for children in the middle and upper grades, love and security permeate family life. When there are family problems, they are characterized by mild frustration rather than by harsh acrimony and volatile conflict. The family, often traditional, occasionally experimenting with new lifestyles, provides security and love, and it offers a supportive backdrop against which children cope with their probelms and venture out to seek new experiences.

## Growing apart

Most parents are very sad about getting a divorce because they know how much it will hurt their children. But they are often in so much pain themselves, because of the terrible problems of the marriage, that they feel they must get a divorce anyway. They do not want to hurt their children, but they must think of their own feelings as well.[21]

This quote is from Richard Gardner's *The Boys and Girls Book About Divorce* (1970), a book that attempts to explain divorce to children and help them understand its various aspects and their own reactions. This book is one sign of times that are characterized by rising divorce rates and increasing numbers of children who are struggling to understand why their parents are growing apart.

Children may meet divorce in their families with a myriad of complex reactions. Some may work persistently at bringing their parents together even when there are no signs that any reconciliation is possible. Other children feel guilt, certain that their bad behavior has formed the wedge that drove their parents apart. Still others may be fearful of complete abandonment, reasoning that if one parent can leave, then it is entirely possible for the other to go also. Yet other children may be filled with hostility and anger that is directed toward one or both parents or inside at themselves.

As we discussed in the previous section, there are many portrayals in children's literature of families growing together, in close, undisrupted units. There are also some portrayals, although not many, of parents who grow apart and whose divergent ways eventually result in divorce. In a few books divorce itself provides the main thrust of the story. In others divorce is part of the background situation. It either is a minor subplot never fully explored or is offered as motivating the main character's hostile or insecure behavior.

Constance Green's *The Unmaking of Rabbit* (1972) never fully explores divorce but presents it as one potential cause for at least some of the main character's behavior, in this case insecurity. Paul is ashamed that he cannot go to school on Monday and say to his classmates, "You see the game yesterday? My father took me. That was some game." Or, "Hey, my mother says you can sleep over Friday if you want."[22] Instead of being immersed in the average family situation that he longs for, Paul lives with his grandmother, an elderly woman for whom he has ambivalent feelings. Paul's mother has no time for him; even when she remarries there is just no room for him in her small city apartment. On one special occasion he travels into the city to visit his mother and stepfather, but they cannot spare even that one day. Although he asks to go to a movie or a museum, they take him to Paddy's, a bar, where they are soon involved in dialogue with their friends, and he is an outsider on the periphery of their conversation.

Paul is characterized as lonely and worried.

When he gets nervous he stutters, and many of his classmates taunt him with the nickname Rabbit. However, during the course of the story, Paul gains a good friend. He learns that his grandmother loves him and is proud of him; and he gains self-respect as he holds out against a gang's attempts to coerce him into joining their petty thievery.

Divorce is also a tangential element in Vera and Bill Cleaver's fine novel *Ellen Grae* (1969). Ellen Grae, whose divorced parents send her to stay with Mrs. McGruder, fascinates the small community with her rich imagination and her ability to spin fantastic tales. When Ira, a town curiosity who lives with his pet goat, shares with Ellen Grae a story of patricide, she is torn between conflicting responsibilities, that of protecting her friend and that of informing the police. When the burden of the secret changes Ellen Grae into a quiet, moping child, her divorced parents visit her. Ellen finally tells them Ira's story. Her reputation as an imaginative raconteur causes the secret to be met with friendly derision, and Ellen refrains from persistently shoving the truth at people. The relationship between the divorced parents is a dignified one, and they remain Ellen Grae's source of comfort when she is troubled.

In the preceding books divorce is a relatively minor factor in the plot development, although often a crucial variable in understanding the motivation for a particular character's behaviors and actions. In other children's fiction divorce is explored more fully. Often the reasons for divorce are presented, and the family's reactions, particularly the children's, are analyzed. The main thrust of these books is the study of the breaking up of a family.

One of the simplest and finest of these books is Marcia Neufield's *A Book for Jodan* (1975). Jodan had always felt her family was special, just as her name was special. There were the Sunday mornings when she and her father would bake pancakes and her mother would guess the special ingredients. There were sleigh rides, picnics, days at the beach. But then came the arguments, always about little things, like painting the ceiling or whose turn it was to do the laundry. When Jodan's parents finally separate, she goes to live with her mother in California, and her father stays in Massachusetts. She feels guilty, responsible for the divorce, and struggles to remember what her father looks like. Finally her father gives her a book filled with special memories, jokes, and advice, which helps her remember the good times and feel close to her father even when separated by great distance.

Another fine book dealing with divorce is Judy Blume's *It's Not the End of the World* (1972). Constant bickering has become an integral part of twelve-year-old Karen's home life. Incidental aggravations—dad's coming home a little late, cold rice, mocha frosting instead of chocolate, a glass of spilled milk—cause her mother and father to snap at one another and flare into arguments. Although the family's three children are well aware that life at home is far from smooth, news of a divorce is still devastating. Each child reacts differently. Amy, the youngest, creeps into bed with Karen, afraid to sleep, fearing that when she wakes up the whole family will be gone like Daddy.

Karen cannot understand why her parents are getting divorced. She asks if it is because her mother does not cook enough recipes or because her mother likes antiques and her father owns a modern furniture store. She cannot believe that her mother and father do not love one another any more, that they no longer enjoy each other's company. She tries desperately to bring them together again. She even sends them an anniversary card and passes out napkins inscribed with their names. When Karen's older brother, Jeff, disappears, her father comes over to help. The immediate bitter arguments between her parents make Karen finally realize the futility of reconciliation and the inevitability of divorce. The novel is rich with finely developed characterizations. The situation presented is poignant but relieved by some very funny moments.

Peggy Mann's *My Dad Lives in a Downtown Hotel* (1973) is a sadder book, one without Judy Blume's touches of humor to provide relief. Joey's mother and father have been bickering for a long time, usually quiet, hissing kinds of arguments. But one night the fighting is loud and Joey's father leaves. Joey, feeling guilty and responsible for his father's departure, takes the subway to his father's New York City office and presents him with a written pledge of new behaviors. Joey promises never to be fresh, play the television loud, or leave his toys around and always to do his homework and to go to bed on time. His declaration concludes, "From now on I'll try all the time to be the kind of boy you'd like to have around. So please dad give me another chance and come home. Love from your son Joey Grant."[23] Joey's father explains that the blame is not Joey's. "Sometimes it happens like that, Joey. I mean, the woman can be great. The man can be okay too. But they just don't—team up well, that's all."[24] Joey's initial disbelief finally turns to realization that his father will not be coming home. His hurt and anger are somewhat assuaged as he realizes that his predicament is not unique. He counts fifty-three children in his school and block who do not have fathers living at home.

Set in Sweden, Gunella Norris' *Lillan* (1968) is about a child who responds to divorce not with guilt but with the fear of being completely abandoned. Since Papa left, it seems to Lillan that everything is changing. Economic worries cast a large shadow over her life and her mother's. In order to make ends meet, their front rooms are rented, and purchases have to be totally practical, without room for frills and nonsense. But financial concerns are insignificant compared to Lillan's dread that her mother will stop loving her. As Lillan sees it, her father left because he stopped loving the family. If her father's love could terminate so abruptly, perhaps her mother's could too. A photograph in her mother's room symbolizes Lillan's anxiety of being cut out of her mother's life. The photograph is of Lillan and her father, but her mother has bent the father's head around, and the picture is deformed into one of Lillan smiling up at nobody. Lillan wonders if Mama could not just as easily bend Lillan out of the picture too. Lillan's mother, busy with her own readjustments, does not compre-

*My Dad Lives in a Downtown Hotel*

hend the full loneliness of her child. As she finds growing happiness in a new romantic attachment, Lillan feels painfully tangential and irrelevant to her mother's life. Finally Lillan is able to express her hurt and fear, and she finds comfort in her mother and the hope of beginning a new life.

Some children, such as Jeffrey in Rose Blue's *A Month of Sundays* (1972), are portrayed as reacting to divorce with anger. This book opens with a bitter argument:

Jeffrey covered his ears with his hands and turned toward the cork wall. He pressed his face against last year's Little League trophy as the voices grew louder.

"Where did you get that lawyer of yours?" his mother was shouting. "I might have known you wouldn't leave before you gave me a little more trouble."

"Oh turn it off," his father shot back. "If it wasn't for the kid I'd have gotten out long ago."[25]

Jeffrey is hurt by every aspect of his parent's divorce: the fighting; the removal of furniture followed by the departure of his father; the move to the city with his mother, where her energies are absorbed in her job and where he sees his father only on Sundays. When his mother, pleading exhaustion, refuses to make a cake for a block party, Jeff's anger reaches the surface. "I hate you," he screamed. "You made me move and you took away my Daddy. . . . You're not my mother anymore!"[26]

Jeff also has to work out a new relationship with his father. The precious Sunday visits seem harried as father and son hustle from one special event to another. What Jeff really longs for is simply some time to relax and talk with his father. The book ends on an optimistic note as both parents grow in understanding of their son's needs.

Norma Mazer's *I Trissy* (1971) presents an angry eleven-and-a-half-year-old heroine who pounds out on her typewriter her bitterness about her parents' divorce:

Trissy, Trissy, don't be late
Mom's in the kitchen till half past eight
Little brother Robert licked your spoon
Big brother Mitch hit him with a broom
And poor Daddy won't be home tonight
Cause he can't stand the way we fight.[27]

Most of Trissy's anger is vented at her mother, whom she views as the culprit who drove her father away. She types out nine practical suggestions by which her mother can win her father back, advice that ranges from putting an end to cigarette smoking to calling her former husband up on the telephone and apologizing. The bitter semi–stream of consciousness that emerges from Trissy's typewriter is laced with humor and reveals a girl who slowly grows in both perception and acceptance.

The books that have been discussed are representative of the limited but growing number of children's books that portray divorce. Considering the dramatic increase in divorce statistics, there is need for children's books to provide more accurate reflection of contemporary family life and to depict, with skill and sensitivity, not only those families that grow together but also those that grow apart.

## The country of themselves

No matter how you try to talk,
Screech, or squork, or scream, or squack,
Or melt, or burn, or boil, or smolder,
You just can't talk with people that are older.[28]

*Mike McCord, Grade 6*

Before we began our study of the portrayal of the family in children's literature, we asked several professionals involved in family counseling and therapy to describe how they supposed parents and adults were depicted in literature for children in the middle and upper grades. These professionals, familiar with children's literature only through memory of books they read when they were young, responded that parents were drawn as very positive figures, almost insipid and saccharine, so idealized and wholesome as to deny the total reality of human nature. The actual portrayal of adult characters in children's literature is often in ironic contrast to the common misconception demonstrated by these responses.

Alma Homze, through a content analysis procedure, examined 780 examples of realistic fiction published from 1920 to 1960. She compared books published between 1920 and 1940 to those published between 1945 and 1960 and found a marked difference in the way adult characters were portrayed. She notes that in the more recent books adults are less friendly, engage in fewer joint activities with children, and, in general, appear less concerned about child characters. In more recent children's literature adults are retreating from the child's world, there are fewer stories of happy family life, and children are more openly critical and less affectionate in their relationship with adult characters.[29]

During the fifteen years since 1960, the depiction of adults, particularly parents, has become, if anything, more negative. The portrait gallery of incompetent and ineffective adults has caused concern. Writing in the *Wilson Library Bulletin* in 1970, Betty Bacon notes:

During the past few years, in the name of "realism" there has been a steady stream of books with drunken mothers and no good fathers. The children are left defenseless and alone in a world which they do not understand and with which they cannot deal unaided. This is the great adult "cop-out." To be sure, there are drunken mothers and no good fathers, but the books wallow in guilt and lightly toss to children the responsibility for cleaning up the mess without tools. This is no more honest realism than the too-too wholesome books of a bygone era, in which adults were all-knowing and close to perfection and children learned to be good.[30]

Others, concerned about children and the books they read, have also noted that in novels with adolescent and preadolescent characters there is a ubiquitous stereotyping of adults as the enemy. In this section we examine some of these portrayals of adults who have either literally or symbolically deserted their children, and we shall also discuss some of the books in which parent and child collide with one another in harsh conflict.

One of the books that exemplifies the end of the perfect parent image in children's literature is Robert Burch's *Queenie Peavy* (1966). Queenie, living in rural Georgia during the Depression, idolizes her father, who is serving a jail term. When her classmates taunt her about her no-good father, she fights back with a veneer of toughness and with fierce loyalty. Queenie is ecstatic when her father returns home, but, embittered and irresponsible, he abruptly terminates his freedom by breaking his parole and carrying a gun. Queenie finally realizes that the reality of her father is far less than the image she has treasured. The book concludes with her awareness that her father cannot be counted on for help and that she will have to solve her own problems.

Queenie Peavy's father is representative of many other adult characters who also fail to measure up to standards. In this section we shall look at books in which adults, selfishly immersed in their own needs, betray their children by deserting them, by misunderstanding them, and by succumbing to phony, materialistic values. We shall also examine books in which there is a chasm of misunderstanding between parents and children, one that is occasionally so wide that children leave the home they find intolerable and establish a new life on their own.

## The adult cop-out

In several recent books, adults literally run away from their responsibilities and their children, who are left to fend for themselves. In

Eleanor Clymer's *My Brother Stevie* (1967) one of the last things Annie Jenner's mother says before she leaves her family is, "Take care of your brother." This is a heavy burden of responsibility for twelve-year-old Annie, for, at eight, Stevie is already on the outskirts of delinquency, breaking into candy machines and throwing rocks at trains. Their father dead and their mother gone, the children live in a project apartment with their grandmother, who whips Stevie when he gets into trouble, a response that seems only to feed his hostility. There is balance in the portrayal of adult characters, however, for it is through the intervention of a kind teacher that Stevie does begin to reject at least some of his hostile behaviors. Although no miracles transpire and the change in Stevie is moderate, the book does conclude on an optimistic note.

Another book dealing with adult desertion is Patricia Engebrecht's *Under the Haystack* (1973). Thirteen-year-old Sandi's mother and stepfather run off, leaving her to care for her younger sisters and keep the farm going as well. She hides the desertion from the authorities and remains financially solvent and emotionally under control. Again, adult portrayal is not totally negative, for a loving and capable mother, a neighbor, is presented. Moreover, some motivation is offered for the abandonment that in the end is only temporary, for Sandi's mother eventually does return.

A father's abandonment of his family is part of the background for Vera and Bill Cleaver's *Me Too* (1973). Lydia and Lornie Birdsong are twins. But there is one great difference between them: Lornie is retarded. She appears to live in her own world and at times speaks her own unique language. Their father wants his children to excel, to be winners. He tries desperately to teach Lornie, but his attempts are met with hostility and frustration. One day he goes away without saying good-bye and the twins are left with their mother. The desertion

is only a brief incident in the story that primarily concerns itself with one summer in which Lydia attempts to teach her retarded sister and learns a great deal about herself in the process. Lydia senses the hostility and the cruelty with which people surround mentally handicapped children, and she learns of her own lack of understanding. It is, however, a summer of growth and Lydia does what her father could not do—accepts Lornie on her own terms.

Adult desertion and weakness constitute a much stronger theme in Marilyn Sachs's unsettlingly pessimistic *The Bears' House* (1971). For Fran Ellen's father, on welfare and unable to hold a steady job, the birth of a new baby girl is just one more unwanted mouth to feed, and one night he does not come home. The mother, left with five children, is psychotically despondent, cries frequently, and leaves her bed only to get the mail. The children try to hide their absent father, sick mother, and unkempt house from outside interference. For Fran Ellen, this home situation would be unbearable except for her beautiful and happy baby sister Flora. School, too, is a dismal situation where Fran Ellen, who at ten still sucks her thumb, is the target of classmates' cruel pranks. There is only one bright spot, a doll house inhabited by tiny toy bears. Fran Ellen loves to sit before the doll house, fantasizing her life inside it, where, as a member of the bear's family, she is cared for and loved. The charade of family life is finally ended by Fran Ellen's teacher, Miss Thompson. Meddlesome and prone to platitudes, the teacher does at least confront a situation that has become intolerable. Finally Fran Ellen realizes that her lovely baby sister, frequently left untended, nourished on Kool Aid rather than milk, and unchecked by a doctor, is growing sickly and troubled. Then she accepts Miss Thompson's interference and realizes outside adult help is necessary.

## The tarnished adult

In the previous section we discussed books that present parental figures who, lacking the competence or responsibility to care for their children, abandon them to the good will of others or to their own instincts for survival. Other books present parents who remain with their children physically but are emotionally divorced from them, so estranged from their needs and concerns that disastrous consequences result.

Despite its title, M. E. Kerr's *Dinky Hocker Shoots Smack* (1972) is not about drugs. Rather it is about obese Dinky Hocker, a girl with a flip wit and a voracious appetite whose liberal mother is so involved in community problems and in running home encounter groups for drug addicts that she has no conception of her own daughter's problems. When Dinky, usually dateless, discovers P. John, a plump arch-conservative, Weight Watchers provides a bond, and the two chubby misfits find immediate rapport. Dinky is ecstatic until her parents, disturbed by P. John's reactionary philosophy, squash the burgeoning relationship. When Mrs. Hocker wins the community's Good Samaritan award, her daughter covers Brooklyn Heights in Day-Glo graffiti that blares "Dinky Hocker Shoots Smack." A recurrent theme in this funny and perceptive novel is that inside every fat person is a thin person waiting to get out. Despite parental insensitivities, Dinky and P. John do begin to emerge. Moreover, not all adults are criticized as insensitive to their children. One of Dinky's friends, Tucker, has parents who, even as they experiment with new roles and new life-styles, are aware of their son and his needs.

In another novel, *The Son of Someone Famous* (1974), M. E. Kerr also explores the relationship between parent and child. Adam is the son of an extremely famous father, one who by day plays a crucial role in American foreign policy and by night dates young, well-endowed Hollywood starlets. In contrast to his father, Adam sees himself as a zero who cannot even stay in school. As the novel opens, Adam has just been expelled from Choate for cheating on an English examination, and he has come to the small town of Storm, Vermont, where he takes his grandfather's name and determines to make it on his own.

Even in small-town isolation, Adam runs into problems. He has difficulties socially. His father has instructed him never to discuss manifest knowledge, the weather, or anything at all obvious. Given this range of restrictions, Adam is usually silent. Adam's only friends are his grandfather and Brenda Belle Blossom, who meets Adam when she slips into the drugstore to buy Hairgo, a depilatory she hopes will remove a small fringe of hair that is forming on her upper lip. Brenda Belle, a constant comic always ready with an absurd quip, has her own parental conflict. She does not meet her mother's standards of femininity: "Clowns aren't happy," her mother repeatedly warns. "Boys don't like clowns."[31]

Despite the subplot concerning Brenda Belle, the story is primarily of Adam and of the separate courses he and his father take, paths that seem to have no points of coincidence or of mutual communication. However, as the book closes, Adam has begun to accept his father as a very different and very extraordinary man. M. E. Kerr has a talent for humorous dialogue and characterization, but in this book she occasionally sacrifices depth of character development for a witty line or a funny episode.

The condemnation of adult characters is far more searing in John Neufeld's *Lisa, Bright and Dark* (1969). Lisa Shiller is a sixteen-year-old who pleads with her parents, trying to make them realize that she is going insane. When she announces her fear of insanity at the dinner table, her mother's only response is to ask if she would like a second helping. Even when she consciously pricks her veins with a needle, parental response is inadequate.

Since Lisa's parents will not help, her friends decide to try. They seek aid from the school guidance counselor, but Mr. Bernstein is afraid of getting involved and refuses to confront the Shillers: "I promise you, if I find a way to do something, I'll do it. But you must not depend on me."[32] After a series of disappointments with frightened and ineffectual adults, Lisa's friends finally conclude that they are the only ones willing to help her: "The trouble with reasonable adult human beings is that they collapse when they meet other reasonable adult human beings. We don't."[33] Indeed, it is only when a smiling and outwardly calm Lisa purposefully walks through a glass wall that adults finally respond to her plea for help.

Again, in Paul Zindel's *My Darling, My Hamburger* (1969) adult response to adolescent problems is at best absurdly ineffectual and at worst irrefutably harmful. It is the story of four teenagers, Sean and Liz, attractive and sophisticated, and Maggie and Dennis, socially awkward and bumbling. These teenagers make errors, but the blame can be traced to adults. Liz gets pregnant because her parents do not trust her, and Sean deserts her after a conversation with his crude and cynical father.

Parents persistently misinterpret their children's needs. When Dennis is preoccupied, hurt because Maggie has broken a date with him, his parents harass him about taking out the garbage. School personnel are also pathetically off target in meeting their students' needs. When a sex education teacher is questioned about what to do when a boy wants to go all the way, she suggests that the couple should go and get a hamburger. When Sean, after he has paid Liz off in abortion money, writes an English theme in which a young couple perform a ritualistic murder of their baby, the teacher gives the paper an A+ and the comment: "You have a remarkable imagination."[34]

## No meeting of the minds: conflict between parent and child

In many books with adolescent and pre-adolescent protagonists, parents and their children espouse different goals and values. They face one another warily, in baffled confusion. There is often little communication and much open conflict. In some books hostilities are resolved, but in others parent and child remain irreconcilable.

One of the gentler conflicts between a father and his son is portrayed in Joseph Krumgold's Newbery winner, *Onion John* (1959). Andy Rusch's father has the blueprints for his son's life already drawn. Mr. Rusch, the proprietor of a hardware store, regrets his own lost career as a radio engineer, and, with hopes to live again through Andy, he dreams of the boy's education at M.I.T. and his career in space technology. When Andy forms a friendship with the town hobo, Onion John, good-natured but eccentric and unconventional, Andy's father decides to change Onion John. Local clubs and civic organizations replace Onion John's ramshackle house with a new one, complete with all the modern conveniences. They also try to replace the hobo's belief in superstition and magic with a respect for the laws of science and logic. Onion John realizes that in order to preserve his identity, he must leave the town of do-gooders, and Andy's father realizes that people must not be shaped to meet the expectations of others. Reluctantly he gives Andy freedom to create his own life.

Emily Neville's Newbery winner, *It's Like This, Cat* (1963), depicts a boy, Davey, growing up in New York City, finding the first girl he feels comfortable with, and consistently running into arguments with his father. The story opens:

My father is always talking about how a dog can be very educational for a boy. This is one reason I got a cat.

My father talks a lot anyway. Maybe being a lawyer, he gets in the habit. Also, he's a small guy with very little gray curly hair, so maybe he thinks he's got to roar a lot to make up for not being a big hairy tough guy. Mom is thin and quiet, and when anything upsets her, she gets asthma. In the apartment—we live right in the middle of New York City—we don't have any heavy drapes or rugs, and Mom never fries any food because the doctors figure dust and smoke make her asthma worse. I don't think it's dust; I think it's Pop's roaring.

The big hassle that led me to getting Cat came when I earned some extra money baby-sitting for a little boy around the corner on Gramercy Park. I spent the money on a Belafonte record. This record has one piece about a father telling his son about the birds and the bees. I think it's funny. Pop blows his stack.[35]

When Davey sees his father through his friend's eyes he realizes that his father tries to boss him because he cares and that in many ways he and his father are very much alike.

Bernice Rabe's *Rass* (1973) portrays a love-hate relationship between a father and his son. Growing up on a Missouri farm during the Depression, Rass has always been told to honor his father. But Rass seems like a wild horse his father cannot tame. The two are continuously fighting, struggles that end with Rass's father beating him until the welts form and Rass is left harboring his resentment: "Dad don't care for the likes of me and I don't care for the likes of him. I'll hate him until I die."[36]

However, even though Rass hates and fears his father, he loves him too, and there is no one he would rather make proud. As Rass grows older, he realizes that the ignorance of his father's ways will limit him. His father insists that he work on the farm rather than go to high school, and the boy is astounded by the "power given to parents to trap a person." It is not until Rass catches the biggest catfish anyone has ever seen and his father takes credit for the accomplishment that Rass realizes he must leave his father's house. Given the perspective of distance, he makes his peace with his father.

Nat Hentoff, in *I'm Really Dragged but Nothing Gets Me Down* (1968), a novel set against the backdrop of the Vietnam war, offers one of the most perceptive delineations of misunderstanding between father and son, for both points of view are explored and made understandable. Jeremy is unsure of himself, in general, but he is most perturbed about the draft. He does not want to kill, and at the same time, he fears he lacks the courage to take any other action. Jeremy's father is also insecure in his success and his materialism, aware that somewhere along the way he has betrayed former, idealistic goals. Father and son go through painful arguments. However, although their values and life-styles differ, there are points of mutual respect.

Paula Fox's *Blowfish Live in the Sea* (1970) is a portrait of troubled, eighteen-year-old Ben as seen through the eyes of his twelve-year-old half-sister, Carrie. There is much about Ben that Carrie does not understand, but she loves him deeply. Carrie does not understand why Ben is obsessed with the sentence "Blowfish live in the sea," writing it on matchbook covers, supermarket paper bags, even on dust in the windows. She also does not fully understand the growing rift between Ben and his mother and stepfather.

Ben wears his hair long, tied back with a strip of rawhide, and he does not even want to think about his parents' plans for college. Eventually he drops out of school. When a letter arrives from his father, a man who has been an erratic correspondent, Ben decides to accept its invitation to meet his father in Boston. Carrie goes along for support.

At the last minute Ben's father tries to dodge their meeting, but Ben discovers him, drunk in his hotel room. He also discovers the web of false impressions his father has tried to create. He is not the successful entrepreneur who emerged in his infrequent letters, but rather the unsuccessful owner of the Happy Hunting Ground Family Motel. Ben is touched by his father's loneliness and tempted by the unconventional freedom of his life. He decides to stay with his father. After Carrie returns home alone she discovers the meaning of Ben's sentence. His father had once sent him a dried blowfish that, he wrote, he had found in the Amazon. After Ben discovered that blowfish live only in salt water, he continually recorded his statement of adult hypocrisy and betrayal. However, the novel does not end with condemnation of adult weakness, for Ben feels love and compassion for the man who had lied to and for him.

Barbara Wersba's *Run Softly, Go Fast* (1970) is a record of David Marks's attempt to make sense out of his tangled relationship with his father. As a young child David worshipped his father, Leo, but as he grew older the love twisted into loathing. As David thinks back on the growing rift, he sees it as the lack of understanding between a businessman obsessed with commercial success and an artist who loves to paint. When David was little he gave his father paintings for his birthday, but a bottle of shaving lotion would have been more appreciated. The father cannot understand his son's love for the theater, his poetry collection, the length of his hair, his manner of dress, or his friendship with Rick, a young conscientious objector who is also an artist. When Leo calls Rick a queer and throws him out of the house, David leaves too, moves to Greenwich Village, and becomes immersed in the drug culture. It is only when David learns his father is in the hospital suffering from cancer that he goes to him, making his first visit

in several years. Even at this point they fight over David's appearance and over his future. When Leo becomes critically ill, David finally cuts his hair and changes his clothes, but his father is too near death to recognize him. At the conclusion David draws his own sense out of the tortured relationship: "I ran from you only to see you everywhere, not knowing that you can't run from a thing when it's made you. I wanted a father in my image . . . and you wanted a son in yours . . . so we missed each other at every crossroad."[37] The novel is powerfully written, unfortunately slightly marred in that only one perspective is offered, that of youth.

In *The Dream Watcher* (1968), also by Barbara Wersba, the rift portrayed is between mother and son. Albert Scully grows to adolescence despising his mother's conventionality and her materialism:

"I have been saving for your college education from the day you were born, Albert. I've borrowed from the household money, taken part-time jobs, denied myself pleasures. Do you think I've done all that for myself? Do you?"
And then—Zap! Pow! Wham!—I saw it. The whole thing. She *had* been doing it for herself. All of it. The piano lessons, the clothes, everything. It was like I was a stock on Wall Street that she had invested in years ago, and now this stock wasn't paying off. This very expensive stock called Albert Scully was going bust—so she was furious.[38]

In conflict with his mother and out of step with his peers, Albert finds refuge in the dilapidated home of Mrs. Woodfin, an elderly, eccentric recluse. The novel concludes with her death and Albert's determination to listen to his own drummer and shape his own life.

Another condemnation of materialistic parents occurs in Judy Blume's *Then Again Maybe I Won't* (1971). When Tony's father sells his invention of electrical cartridges, the family leaves their modest home in Jersey City and moves to an impressive, expensive house in Rosemont, a wealthy Long Island suburb. Tony misses his paper route, his friends and their basketball games, but most of all he is puzzled by the airs his parents begin to assume. A snobbish neighbor's derogatory comment causes his father immediately to exchange the family pickup truck for a new Ford. His older brother, formerly committed to a career in teaching, sells out his idealism for a place in the family firm and a share of electrical cartridge money. When his mother, in deference to a presumptuous maid, forces his grandmother out of the kitchen, the old woman retreats to her bedroom, where she is lulled into senescence by a color television set. Tony internalizes his anger, develops a nervous stomach, and has to go to a psychiatrist. However, the condemnation of materialism is not nearly as searing as that portrayed in *The Dream Watcher*. Tony tries to understand his parents' reactions to sudden wealth, and his hostility is tempered as he accepts compromise and his parents as they are.

When female protagonists rebel against parental values, the conflict is often less harsh and volatile. Suzie Henderson, the protagonist in Hope Campbell's *Why Not Join the Giraffes?* (1968), does not rebel against conventionality and materialsm; instead she is frustrated by her nonconformist family, her author father, artistic mother, and a brother who is the lead guitarist in a rock band. When she meets Ralph, a boy from a stuffy, conventional family, she makes up a new identity and becomes further implicated in one lie after another. Finally she realizes that Ralph is unimpressed with his parents' false values and that he longs for the life-style her family embraces.

Suzie's father has always told her to listen to her own music and march to her own drums, a paraphrase of Thoreau's words in *Walden*.

Suzie finds this a beautiful idea that somehow never works when she tries to put it into practice. However, by the novel's conclusion, Suzie appreciates the honesty in her family's way of life and learns to value the freedom she is given and the work and challenges it involves.

Another book in which the daughter longs for greater conventionality in her family's way of life is Lila Perl's funny and perceptive *That Crazy April* (1974). Eleven-year-old Cress's mother is firmly committed to the women's movement, and her beliefs are reflected in the family's life-style. Cress and her parents rotate cooking responsibilities each week. Her parent's mail box, which once announced "Mr. and Mrs. Philip Richardson," is changed to read "Mary Dalton and Philip Richardson," Her mother travels around the country to various conventions on women's rights, and Cress and her father are frequently left alone together on weekends. Cress often mouths her mother's philosophies to her friends, but privately she rebels. To make matters more confusing, her two best friends are sex-typed to an extreme. David Peter Link, who comes from a long line of admirals and plans to make the line even longer, is a confirmed male chauvinist at ten. And Monique, slim and willowy, plans to follow her glamorous mother in a modeling career.

The rift between Cress and her mother grows wider when her lovely, intelligent cousin, Xandra, a sophomore majoring in biochemistry, announces plans to marry, drop out of college, and support her husband through medical school. Instead of joining Cress in applauding the good news, Cress's mother crisply interrogates Xandra, probing into the wisdom of her decision:

"Xandra, don't get me wrong, I respect your right to make this decision, even though I think you're confused. Just one question. Suppose *you* were the one who had gotten into medical school. Would

Bill give up college to take an ordinary unskilled job so he could support you and make a home for you while you studied for a medical degree for four or five years?"

Xandra looked stunned. "I honestly don't think so."

"Even if you were going to be a very good doctor? Even if you were going to be a much better doctor than Bill will ever be?

"But how could we know that?"

Mom sighed. "I guess we never will know that, Xandra. Not as long as women go on believing they are second-class people and keep on stepping aside to give men nearly all the chances to be doctors, engineers, presidents. . . ."

I kept wanting to say something. But what? Mom was getting me awfully confused. The idea of a man working, keeping house, cooking and cleaning and maybe even taking care of children while his wife went to medical school to become a doctor! It sounded crazy. Could it really work both ways?

Xandra grinned shyly. "Well, I *know* I wouldn't be any good as a doctor."

"But you're sure Bill will," Mom teased. "Now that's blind faith for you."[39]

When Cress is barred from her school's metal-working club because she is female and, when on an outing with a group of boys, she is expected to remain on shore preparing lunch while the males go boating and fishing, her resentments emerge and her consciousness is raised. Although staunchly refusing to be shaped into a replica of her mother, she comes to understand and admire her.

In Mary Rodgers' *Freaky Friday* (1972), a zany mixture of reality and fantasy, a teenage girl assumes her mother's role and with it greater understanding of its concomitant challenges and complexities. Annabelle Andrews is frustrated by her mother's strictness, her insistence on trimmed hair, a clean room, and a nourishing breakfast. In one of their biggest arguments Annabelle bemoans her own lack

of freedom and looks enviously at her mother's life: "You can tell yourself to go out to lunch with your friends, and watch television all day long, and eat marshmallows for breakfast and go to the movies at night. . . ."[40]

The next day Annabelle wakes up in her mother's body, and her mother has become Annabelle. In the madcap day that follows, Annabelle organizes the family budget and the schedules of family members as well. She copes with broken appliances, a last-minute dinner for visiting clients, a lost child, and a talk with the school guidance counselor. By the day's end, with respect for her mother renewed, Annabelle is relieved to return to herself.

Another girl seeking greater freedom is Wendy Allardyce in Lee Kingman's *The Peter Pan Bag* (1970). Wendy's loving family has provided her with an almost idyllic childhood —Monopoly games, a creek for swimming, apple trees and tree houses, dominoes before the fireplace. But now that she is seventeen Wendy finds that she is no longer understood. She sees the family's love as a net that confines her without offering her any clear spaces to step through and define herself. To her, "Do your own thing" is not a vague cliché but a very real statement of the times and of her needs. She drops out for a summer and joins the floating communes of young people who live on Boston's Beacon Hill and meet on the Commons. In the varied assortment of people she meets there, Wendy finds intense seriousness of purpose, involvement in drugs, and confusion of goals. The experience, touched by tragedy, gives her deeper insight into herself and greater understanding of her family.

Wendy's family is loving, and she remains on the periphery of drug abuse. In some books, however, escape from an unsatisfying family life leads to more serious teenage experimentation with drugs, as is demonstrated by Jeannette Eyerly's *Escape from Nowhere* (1969). Carla lives in a new, beautiful home, but it provides little happiness for her. Her sister is away at college, her father is gone frequently on business, and her mother is drinking more and more heavily. Carla seeks refuge with Dexter, a boy experimenting with a variety of drugs, who tells her, "Listen, baby, you don't have to pretend with me. I know all about it. Of all the things that happen to be wrong with the world, you can put home and parents right at the top of the list. If you've just found it out, welcome to the club."[41] Carla finds that initial drug experimentation leads to deeper involvement, and it ends in tragedy for Dexter and almost for herself.

Occasionally in children's literature, confrontation between parent and child reaches the point of physical brutality. Although child abuse is a frighteningly familiar occurrence in American life, one which resulted in 50,000 deaths and 300,000 permanently injured children in 1973, it is a phenomenon just beginning to be reflected in children's books. One book that portrays parental physical brutality is Bette Green's *Summer of My German Soldier* (1973). In this story a young Jewish girl not only suffers unhappiness because her materialistic and superficial parents do not understand or appreciate her, but she is also whipped so severely by a father unable to control his rage that a hiding German prisoner of war almost gives himself away in order to stop the beating.

Doris Buchanan Smith's *Tough Chauncey* (1974) offers a portrait of Chauncey Childs, a boy who has had to create an image of toughness in order to cope with parents who have deserted him and a grandfather who unleashes his rage by beating him with severe regularity. By the story's conclusion Chauncey realizes that Grandpa, without even realizing the consequences of his actions, "could kill a person the way he bangs them around." The book ends as Chauncey goes to an agency that he hopes will place him in a foster home. The situation is even worse for the protagonist in Gertrude Samuels' *Run, Shelley, Run!* (1974). Shelley keeps running from increasingly bad home situations until she ends up in prison in solitary confinement. The book is actually a journalistic piece with an intent to make readers aware of the lack of justice accorded young people who are not criminals but who are committed to state institutions along with far more serious offenders.

In June Jordan's *His Own Where* (1971) there is also adult brutality and violence. Sixteen-year-old Buddy, whose father is dying, is in love with Angela, who is fourteen. Angela's parents, afraid that she is wild, beat her, and her father comes dangerously close to causing serious injury.

His fist came down in her face, her cheek. She scream aloud. His knuckle slap her head around, and pound her punching through to ribs. Angela struggle her hand under the pillow where to protect herself she hide a kitchen knife not to be beaten like she is. Seize the handle, whip the knife into his view and tell him, "Leave me alone."

"You little prostitute."

He kick the cot over and she fall to the floor face down and lose the knife. He leap beside her beating her across her back.

"You get out of this house, get out of this house, get out."[42]

Angela's parents are charged with child abuse, and she is sent to a shelter in Manhattan and from there to a home for girls. Angela finds these institutions' hypocritical attempts at help corrupt and ineffective. When Angela gets a weekend pass she and Buddy leave the violence and the harshness of their world and go to a brick house near the cemetery where they love one another and start a new life together.

Much has been written about the generation gap. It is characterized as a wide chasm across which adolescents eye their parents with cold disaffection, and the adults respond with baffled, threatened anger. This certainly is the scenario portrayed in many children's books, but it may be a bit overdone. Research presents conflicting views as to exactly how widespread and intense the generation gap actually is. We are not ready to dismiss the concept of the generation gap, and it would be absurd to deny the existence of ineffective and even cruel parents. Yet the current, depressing portraits of unworthy parents in children's literature causes us to hope for greater balance in the portrayal of adult characters, particularly in fiction for adolescents.

Margaret Mead has said:

We must learn together with the young how to take the next steps. Out of their new knowledge— new to the world and new to us—must come the questions to those who are already equipped by education and experience to search for answers. The children, the young, must ask these questions that we would never think to ask but enough trust must be reestablished so that the elders will be permitted to work with them on the answers.[43]

We doubt that a steady reading diet of hypocritical, weak, and even cruel adults will help build this confidence. We also question whether reading only about perfect parents and idyllic families will establish this trust. Children, so sensitive to hypocrisy, demand candor and honesty in their books and in the portrayal of the spectrum of family relationships.

Nancy Larrick notes that many of the newer books deal honestly with many topics, family relationships included, and that children read these books eagerly. She tells of an eighth grader who brought an armload of books to her mother, an elementary school teacher. "Read these," she said. "They say what I want to say to you, but they say it much better than I could."[44] It is hoped that the honesty in such books will work toward re-establishing the trust for which Margaret Mead asks.

## NOTES

1. Betty Yorburg, "The Future of the American Family," *Intellect,* *101,* no. 2346 (January 1973), 253–260.
2. Ann Herbert Scott, *On Mother's Lap,* Glo Coalson, illus., New York, McGraw-Hill, 1972.
3. Margaret Wise Brown, *The Runaway Bunny,* Clement Hurd, illus. New York, Harper & Row, 1972.
4. Becky Reyher, *My Mother is the Most Beautiful Woman in the World,* Ruth Shephard, illus., Lothrop, 1945 (K–3).
5. Miriam Young, *Peas in a Pod,* pictures by Linda Neely, New York, Putnam, 1971.
6. Arnold Adoff, *Black Is Brown Is Tan,* Emily Arnold McCully, illus., New York, Harper & Row, 1973.
7. Charlotte Zolotow, *The Sky Was Blue,* New York, Harper & Row, 1963.
8. Rosemary Wells, *Noisy Nora,* New York, Dial Press, 1973.
9. Golden MacDonald, *The Little Island,* Leonard Weisgard, Garden City, N.Y., Doubleday, 1946. Caldecott Medal.
10. Ruth Krauss, *The Big World and the Little House,* Marc Simont, illus., New York, Harper & Row, 1949.
11. Florence Parrey Heide, *The Shrinking of Treehorn,* Edward Gorey, illus., New York, Holiday House, 1971.
12. Jean Zwack, "The Stereotypic Family in Children's Literature," *Reading Teacher,* 26, no. 4 (January 1973), 389–391.
13. Joan Lexau, *Me Day,* pictures by Robert Weaver, New York, Dial Press, 1971.
14. Wendy Kindred, *Lucky Wilma,* New York, Dial Press, 1973.
15. Quoted in Anne Thaxter Eaton, "The American Family," in Cornelia Meigs, Anne Thaxter Eaton, Elizabeth Wesbett, and Ruth Hill Viguers, *A Critical History of Children's Literature,* London, Macmillan, 1953; revised 1969.
16. Laura Ingalls Wilder, *Little House in the Big Woods,* Garth Williams, illus., New York, Harper & Row, 1953, p. 238.
17. Sydney Taylor, *All-of-a-Kind Family,* Helen John, illus., Chicago, Follett, 1951, pp. 77–78.
18. Meindert DeJong, *Shadrach,* Maurice Sendak, illus., New York, Harper & Row, 1953, p. 130.

19. M. E. Kerr, *Dinky Hocker Shoots Smack*, New York, Harper & Row, 1972, pp. 170–171.
20. W. Bernard Lukenbill, "Fathers in Adolescent Novels; Some Implications in Sex-Role Reinterpretations," *Library Journal*, *99*, no. 4 (February 1974), 536–540.
21. Richard Gardner, *The Boys and Girls Book About Divorce*, Alfred Lowenheim, illus., New York Science House, 1970, p. 132.
22. Constance Greene, *The Unmaking of Rabbit*, New York, Viking Press, 1972.
23. Peggy Mann, *My Dad Lives in a Downtown Hotel*, Richard Cuffari, illus., Garden City, N.Y. Doubleday, 1973, p. 29.
24. Ibid., p. 39.
25. Rose Blue, *A Month of Sundays*, Ted Lewin, illus., New York, Franklin Watts, 1972, p. 1.
26. Ibid., p. 44.
27. Norma Mazer, *I Trissy*, New York, Dell (Delacorte Press), 1971, pp. 8–9.
28. Mike McCord, "Advice to People, Generation Unknown," in Anne Power and Carole Rush, "Youth in the Seventies; Socially Conscious or Self-obsessed," *Social Education*, *38*, no. 4 (April 1974), 346.
29. Alma Homze, "Interpersonal Relations in Children's Literature, 1920–1960," *Elementary English*, *43*, no. 1 (January 1966), 26–27+.
30. Betty Bacon, "From Now to 1984," *Wilson Library Bulletin*, *45*, no. 2 (October 1970), 157.
31. M. E. Kerr, *The Son of Someone Famous*, New York, Harper & Row, 1974.
32. John Neufeld, *Lisa, Bright and Dark*, New York, New American Library (Signet), 1969.
33. Ibid., p. 82.
34. Paul Zindel, *My Darling, My Hamburger*, New York, Harper & Row, 1969, p. 111.
35. Emily Neville, *It's Like This, Cat*, Emil Weiss, illus., New York, Harper & Row, 1963, pp. 1–2.
36. Bernice Rabe, *Rass*, Nashville, Tenn., Thomas Nelson, 1973.
37. Barbara Wersba, *Run Softly, Go Fast*, New York, Atheneum, 1970, p. 157.
38. Barbara Wersba, *The Dream Watcher*, New York, Atheneum, 1968, p. 129.
39. Lila Perl, *That Crazy April*, New York, Seabury Press, 1974, pp. 37–38.
40. Mary Rodgers, *That Freaky Friday*, New York, Harper & Row, 1972, p. 6.
41. Jeannette Eyerly, *Escape From Nowhere*, Philadelphia, Lippincott, 1969, p. 57.
42. June Jordan, *His Own Where*, New York, Crowell, 1971, p. 33.
43. Margaret Mead, "Youth Revolt; The Future Is Now," *Social Education*, *38*, no. 4 (April 1974), 330.
44. Nancy Larrick, "Divorce, Drugs, Desertion, the Draft; Facing up to the Realities in Children's Literature," *Publishers' Weekly*, *201*, no. 8 (February 21, 1972), 91.

## BIBLIOGRAPHY

### Fiction for younger children

ADOFF, ARNOLD. *Black Is Brown Is Tan*, Emily Arnold McCully, illus., Harper & Row 1973 (preschool–3).

———. *Ma nDA LA*, Emily Arnold McCully, illus., Harper & Row, 1971 (4–7 yr).

ALEXANDER, MARTHA. *And My Mean Old Mother Will Be Sorry, Blackboard Bear*. Dial Press, 1972 (preschool–1).

———. *Nobody Asked Me If I Wanted a Baby Sister*. Dial Press, 1971 (preschool–1).

———. *We Never Get to Do Anything*. Dial Press, 1970 (preschool–1).

ARDIZONNE, EDWARD. *The Wrong Side of the Bed*. Doubleday, 1970 (3–6 yr).

BROWN, MARGARET WISE. *The Runaway Bunny*, Clement Hurd, illus., Harper & Row, 1972 (K–2).

CLIFTON, LUCILLE. *Don't You Remember?*, Evaline Ness, illus., Dutton, 1973 (K–2).

EICKLER, MARGARIT. *Martin's Father*, Bev Magennis, illus., Lollipop Power, 1971.

FISHER, MARGERY, and LEONARD FISHER. *But Not Our Daddy*, Dial Press, 1967 (K–3).

FLACK, MARJORIE. *The Story About Ping*, Kurt Wiese, illus., Viking Press, 1933 (preschool–3).

GOFF, BETH. *Where Is Daddy? The Story of a Divorce*, Susan Perl, illus., Beacon Press, 1969 (preschool–K).

GRAY, GENEVIEVE. *Send Wendell*, Symeon Shimin, illus., McGraw-Hill, 1974 (K–4).

HAZEN, BARBARA SHOOK. *Why Couldn't I Be an Only Kid Like You, Wigger*, Leigh Grant, illus., Atheneum, 1975 (preschool–2).

HEIDE, FLORENCE PARRY. *The Shrinking of Treehorn*, Edward Gorey, illus., Holiday, 1971 (K–3).

HILL, ELIZABETH STARR. *Evan's Corner*, Nancy Grossman, illus., Holt, Rinehart and Winston, 1967 (K–2).

HOBAN, RUSSELL. *A Baby Sister For Frances*, Lillian Hoban, illus., Harper & Row, 1964 (preschool–2).

KEATS, JACK EZRA. *Peter's Chair*. Harper & Row, 1967 (preschool–1).

KINDRED, WENDY. *Lucky Wilma*. Dial Press, 1973 (preschool–3).

KRAUS, ROBERT. *Whose Mouse Are You?*, Jose Aruego, illus., Macmillan, 1970 (2–5 yr).

KRAUSS, RUTH. *The Big World and the Little House*, Marc Simont, illus., Harper & Row, 1949 (K–3).

LEXAU, JOAN. *Emily and the Klunky Baby and the Next-Door Dog*, Martha Alexander, illus., Dial Press, 1972 (preschool–3).

———. *Me Day*, Robert Weaver, illus., Dial Press, 1971 (K–3).

MCCLOSKEY, ROBERT. *Make Way for Ducklings*. Viking Press, 1941, Caldecott Medal (K–3).

———. *One Morning in Maine*. Viking Press, 1952 (K–2).

———. *Time of Wonder*. Viking Press, 1957 (3–5).

MACDONALD, GOLDEN (pseud.) *The Little Island*. Doubleday, 1946, Caldecott Medal (4–8 yr).

RAINEY, BENNETT. *The Secret Hiding Place*, World, 1960.

REYHER, BECKY. *My Mother Is the Most Beautiful Woman in the World*, Ruth Gannett, illus., Lothrop, Lee & Shepard, 1945.

ROGERS, HELEN SPELMAN. *Morris and His Brave Lion*, Glo Coalson, illus., McGraw-Hill, 1975 (preschool–2).

SHARMAT, MARJORIE. *I Want Mama*, Emily Arnold McCully, illus., Harper & Row, 1974 (4–8).

SCHICK, ELEANOR. *City in the Winter*, Macmillan, 1970 (K–2).

SCOTT, HERBERT ANN. *On Mother's Lap*, Glo Coalson, illus., McGraw-Hill, 1972 (preschool–K).

———. *Sam*, Symeon Shimin, illus., McGraw-Hill, 1969 (preschool–1).

SEGAL, LORE. *Tell Me a Mitzi*, Harriet Pincus, illus., Farrar, Straus & Giroux, 1970 (K–2).

SHIEFMAN, VICKY. *Mindy*, Lisl Weil, illus., Macmillan, 1975 (1–3).

SKORPEN, LIESEL MOAK. *Kisses and Fishes*, Steven Kellogg, illus., Harper & Row, 1974 (4–8).

SONNEBORN, RUTH. *Friday Night Is Papa Night*, Emily Arnold McCully, illus., Viking Press, 1970 (K–2).

SUROWIECKI, SANDRA LUCAS. *Joshua's Day*. Lollipop Power, 1972.

TOBIAS, TOBI. *A Day Off*, Ray Cruz, illus., Putnam, 1973 (preschool–3).

UDRY, JANICE MAY. *What Mary Joe Shared*, Eleaner Mill, illus., Whitman, 1966 (K–3).

VIORST, JUDITH. *Alexander and the Terrible, Horrible, No Good, Very Bad Day*, Ray Cruz, illus., Atheneum, 1972 (K–3).

WELLS, ROSEMARY. *Noisy Nora*, Dial Press, 1973, (preschool–1).

YASHIMA, TARO. *Umbrella*, Viking Press, 1958 (preschool–1).

ZOLOTOW, CHARLOTTE. *A Father Like That*, Ben Shecter, illus., Harper & Row, 1971 (preschool–2).

———. *The Sky Was Blue*, Harper & Row, 1963 (preschool–2).

———. *The Summer Night*, Ben Shecter, illus., Harper & Row, 1974. Originally published under the title *The Night Mother Was Away*, 1958 (4–8).

———. *When I Have a Little Girl*, Hilary Knight, illus., Harper & Row, 1965 (K–3).

## Fiction for the middle and the upper grades

Anonymous. *Go Ask Alice*. Prentice-Hall, 1971.

ARUNDEL, HONOR. *A Family Failing*. Nelson, 1972 (6+).

BARNWELL, ROBINSON. *Shadow on the Water*. McKay, 1967 (6–8).

BAWDEN, NINA. *The Peppermint Pig*. Lippincott, 1975 (5–8).

———. *The Runaway Summer*. Lippincott, 1969 (4–7).

BLUME, JUDY. *Are You There God? It's Me, Margaret*, Bradbury Press, 1970 (5–7).

———. *Tales of a Fourth Grade Nothing*, Roy Doty, illus., Dutton, 1972 (4–7).

———. *It's Not the End of the World*, Bradbury Press, 1972 (5–7).

———. *Then Again, Maybe I Won't*, Bradbury Press, 1971 (5–7).

BLUE, ROSE. *A Month of Sundays*, Ted Lewin, illus., Watts, 1972 (3–5).

———. *Nikki 108*, Ted Lewin, illus., Watts, 1973 (4–8).

BRADBURY, BIANCA. *Those Travers Kids*, Marvin Friedman, illus., Houghton Mifflin, 1972 (5–7).

BROOKS, JEROME. *Uncle Mike's Boy*, Harper & Row, 1973 (5+).

BURCH, ROBERT. *Queenie Peavy*, Jerry Lazare, illus., Viking Press, 1966 (6–9).

———. *Simon and the Game of Chance*, Fermin Rocker, illus., Viking Press, 1970 (5–7).

BURTON, HESTER. *The Henchmans at Home*, Victor Ambrus, illus., Crowell, 1970 (6–10).

CAMERON, ELEANOR. *A Room Made of Windows*, Tina Schart Hyman, illus., Atlantic–Little, Brown, 1971 (5–8).

———. *To the Green Mountains*, Dutton, 1975 (6–10).

CAMPBELL, HOPE. *No More Trains to Tottenville*, Dell, 1971 (7+).

———. *Why Not Join the Giraffes?*, Norton, 1968 (6–9).

CARLSON, NATALIE SAVAGE. *The Half Sisters*, Thomas de Grazia, illus., Harper & Row, 1970 (4–6).

CARROLL, RUTH, and LATROBE CARROLL. *Beanie*, Walck, 1953 (3–5).

CAUDILL, REBECCA. *Somebody Go and Bang a Drum*, Dutton, 1974 (1–4).

CAVANAUGH, ARTHUR. *Leaving Home*, Fawcett, 1963.

CHILD STUDY ASSOCIATION (selected by). *Brothers and Sisters Are Like That: Stories to Read to Yourself*, Michael Hampshire, illus., Crowell, 1971 (1–6).

CHILDRESS, ALICE. *A Hero Ain't Nothin But a Sandwich*, Coward, McCann & Geoghegan, 1973 (5–9).

CLEARY, BEVERLY. *Beezus and Ramona*, Louis Darling, illus., Morrow, 1955 (3–5).

———. *Henry Huggins*, Louis Darling, illus., Morrow, 1950 (3–5).

———. *Ramona the Pest*, Louis Darling, illus., Morrow, 1968 (3–5).

CLEAVER, VERA, and BILL CLEAVER. *Ellen Grae*, Ellen Raskin, illus., Lippincott, 1967 (4–6.)

———, and ———. *Lady Ellen Grae*, Ellen Raskin, illus., Lippincott, 1968 (4–6).

———, and ———. *Me Too*, Lippincott, 1973 (5–7).

———, and ———. *Where the Lilies Bloom*, Jim Spanfeller, illus., Lippincott, 1969 (6–9).

———, and ———. *Dust of the Earth*, Lippincott, 1975 (7–9).

CLYMER, ELEANOR. *My Brother Stevie*, Holt, Rinehart and Winston, 1967 (4–6).

COLMAN, HILA. *Claudia, Where Are You?*, Morrow, 1969 (7–10).

CONE, MOLLY. *Annie Annie*, Marvin Friedman, illus., Houghton Mifflin, 1969 (6–9).

DEJONG, MEINDERT. *Journey from Peppermint Street*, Emily Arnold McCully, illus., Harper & Row, 1968 (4–6).

———. *Shadrach*, Maurice Sendak, illus., Harper & Row, 1953 (1–5).

DONOVAN, JOHN. *I'll Get There. It Better Be Worth the Trip*, Harper & Row, 1969 (6–9).

ENGEBRECHT, PATRICIA. *Under the Haystack*, Nelson, 1973 (6+).

ESTES, ELEANOR. *Ginger Pye*, Harcourt Brace Jovanovich, 1951. Newbery Medal (4–6).

———. *The Moffats*, Louis Slobodkin, illus., Harcourt Brace Jovanovich, 1941 (4–6).

———. *The Middle Moffat*, Louis Slobodkin, illus., Harcourt Brace Jovanovich, 1942 (4–6).

———. *Rufus M*, Louis Slobodkin, illus., Harcourt Brace Jovanovich, 1943 (4–6).

ETS, MARIE HALL. *Bad Boy, Good Boy*. Crowell, 1967 (K–3).

EWING, KATHRYN. *A Private Matter*, Joan Sanden, illus., Harcourt Brace Jovanovich, 1975 (2–5).

EYERLY, JEANNETTE. *Escape from Nowhere*, Lippincott, 1969 (7–10).

———. *The Phaedra Complex*, Lippincott, 1971 (6–10).

FITZHUGH, LOUISE. *Harriet the Spy*, Harper & Row, 1964 (5–7).

———. *Nobody's Family Is Going to Change*, Farrar, Straus & Giroux, 1974 (3–7).

FOX, PAULA. *Blowfish Live in the Sea*, Bradbury Press, 1973 (5–7).

FROLOV, VADIM. *What It's All About*, tr. by Joseph Baines. Doubleday, 1968 (8–10).

GARDNER, RICHARD. *The Boys and Girls Book About Divorce*, Alfred Lowenheim, illus., New York, Science House, 1970 (7+).

GREENE, BETTE. *Summer of My German Soldier*, Dial Press, 1973 (5–7).

GREENE, CONSTANCE. *The Unmaking of Rabbit*, Viking Press, 1972 (4–6).

HAMILTON, DOROTHY. *Mindy*, Edwin B. Wallace, illus., Herald, 1973 (7–12).

HAYWOOD, CAROLYN. *"B" Is for Betsy*, Harcourt Brace Jovanovich, 1939, 1968 (1–3).

———. *Little Eddie*, Morrow, 1947 (2–4).

HENTOFF, NAT. *I'm Really Dragged But Nothing Gets Me Down*, Simon & Schuster, 1968, (9–12).

HUNT, IRENE. *Up A Road Slowly*, Follett, 1966 (6–9).

JACKSON, JACQUELINE. *The Taste of Spruce Gum*, Lillian Obligado, illus., Little, Brown, 1966 (5–7).

JOHNSTON, NORMA. *Glory in the Flower*, Atheneum, 1974 (6–9).

———. *The Keeping Days*, Atheneum, 1973 (6+).

———. *Of Time and of Seasons*, Atheneum, 1975 (7+).

JONES, CORDELIA. *A Cat Called Camouflage*, Phillips, 1971 (7+).

JORDAN, JUNE. *His Own Where*, Crowell, 1971 (7–9).

KERR, M. E. *Dinky Hocker Shoots Smack*, Harper & Row, 1972 (7+).

———. *If I Love You, Am I Trapped Forever?*, Harper & Row, 1973 (7+).

———. *The Son of Someone Famous*, Harper & Row, 1974 (7+).

KINGMAN, LEE. *The Peter Pan Bag*, Houghton Mifflin, 1970 (8–11).

———. *The Year of the Raccoon*, Houghton Mifflin, 1966 (6–9).

KLEIN, NORMA. *Confessions of an Only Child*, Richard Cuffari, illus., Pantheon Books, 1974 (3–7).

———. *It's Not What You Expect*, Pantheon Books, 1972 (5+).

———. *Mom, The Wolf Man and Me*, Pantheon Books, 1972 (5+).

KREMENTZ, JILL. *Sweet Pea: A Black Girl Growing Up in the Rural South*, Harcourt Brace Jovanovich, 1969 (3–5).

KRUMGOLD, JOSEPH. *Henry 3*, Alvire Smith, illus., Atheneum, 1967 (6–9).

———. *Onion John*, Symeon Shimin, illus., Crowell, 1959, Newbery Medal (6–9).

LEE, MILDRED. *Fog*, Seabury Press, 1972 (7–10).

———. *Honor Sands*, Lothrop, 1966 (6–9).

———. *The Rock and the Willow*, Lothrop, Lee & Shepard, 1963 (9–11).

———. *The Skating Rink*, Seabury Press, 1969 (6–8).

LEE, VIRGINIA. *The Magic Moth*, Richard Cuffari, illus., Seabury Press, 1972 (4–6).

L'ENGLE, MADELEINE. *Meet the Austins*, Vanguard Press, 1960 (5–8).

LEXAU, JOAN. *Striped Ice Cream*, John Wilson, illus., Lippincott, 1968 (2–4).

LITTLE, JEAN. *Mine for Keeps*, Little, Brown, 1962 (3–7).

MANN, PEGGY. *My Dad Lives in a Downtown Hotel*, Richard Cuffari, illus., Doubleday, 1973 (5+).

MAYNE, WILLIAM. *A Game of Dark*, Dutton, 1971 (5–8).

———. *Ravensgill*, Dutton, 1970 (7–10).

MAZER, HARRY. *The Dollar Man*, Dell (Delacorte Press), 1974 (7+).

———. *Guy Lenny*, Dell (A Yearling Book), 1971 (4–7).

———. *I Trissy*, Dell (Delacorate Press), 1971 (4–7).

MILES, BETTY. *The Real Me*, Knopf, 1974 (3–7).

MOSKIN, MARIETTA. *Waiting for Mama*, Richard Lebenson, illus., Coward, McCann & Geoghegan, 1975 (3–7).

NEUFELD, JOHN. *Edgar Allen*, Phillips, 1968 (6–9).

———. *Lisa, Bright and Dark*, New American Library (Signet), 1969 (7+).

NEVILLE, EMILY. *It's Like This, Cat*, Emil Weiss, illus., Harper & Row, 1963, Newbery Medal (6–9).

NORRIS, GUNILLA. *Lillan*, Nancie Swanberg, illus., Atheneum, 1968 (3–7).

PERL, LILA. *That Crazy April*, Seabury Press, 1974 (4–8).

PEVSNER, STELLA. *A Smart Kid Like You*, Seabury Press, 1975 (4+).

RABE, BERNICE. *Rass*, Nelson, 1973 (6–8).

RODGERS, MARY. *Freaky Friday*, Harper & Row, 1972 (5+).

SACHS, MARILYN. *Amy and Laura*, Tracy Sugarman, illus., Doubleday, 1966 (4–6).

———. *The Bears' House*, Louis Glanzman, illus., Doubleday, 1971 (4–6).

———. *The Truth About Mary Rose*, Doubleday, 1973 (4–7).

———. *Veronica Ganz*, Louis Glanzman, illus., Doubleday, 1968 (5–7).

SAMUELS, GERTRUDE. *Run Shelley, Run*, Crowell, 1974.

SCHRAFF, ANN. *North Star*, Macrae Smith, 1972 (7+).

SMITH, DORIS BUCHANAN. *Kick a Stone Home,* Crowell, 1974 (5+).

———. *Tough Chauncey,* Morrow, 1974 (7–9).

SNYDER, ZELPHA KEATLEY. *The Witches of Worm,* Alton Raible, illus., Atheneum, 1973 (4–7).

STEWARD, A. C. *Dark Dove,* Phillips, 1974 (6–10).

STOLZ, MARY. *Leap Before You Look,* Harper & Row, 1972 (7+).

———. *By The Highway Home,* Harper & Row, 1971 (6–9).

TAYLOR, SYDNEY. *All-of-a-Kind Family,* Helen John, illus., Follett, 1951 (4–6).

———. *All-of-a-Kind Family Uptown,* Mary Stevens, illus., Follett, 1958 (4–6).

———. *More All-of-a-Kind Family,* Mary Stevens, illus., Follett, 1959 (4–6).

TERRIS, SUSAN. *The Drowning Boy,* Doubleday, 1972 (6–9).

THRASHER, CRYSTAL. *The Dark Didn't Catch Me,* Atheneum, 1975 (5–9).

WARWICK, DELORES. *Learning to Say Goodbye,* Farrar, Straus & Giroux, 1971 (7–9).

WERSBA, BARBARA. *The Dream Watcher,* Atheneum, 1968 (6–9).

———. *Run Softly, Go Fast,* Atheneum (Bantam), 1970 (8–10).

WILDER, LAURA INGALLS. *Little House in the Big Woods,* Garth Williams, illus., Harper & Row, 1951 (4–8). Other titles in the series are *Little House on the Prairie, On the Banks of Plum Creek, By the Shores of Silver Lake, Farmer Boy, The Long Winter, Little Town on the Prairie, These Happy Golden Years.*

WILLARD, BARBARA. *Happy Families,* Krustyna Turska, illus., Macmillan, 1974 (5+).

WINTHROP, ELIZABETH. *A Little Demonstration of Affection,* Harper & Row, 1975 (8+).

WOJCIECHOWSKA, MAIA. *Tuned Out,* Harper & Row, 1968 (9–11).

YATES, ELIZABETH. *A Place for Peter,* Nora Unwin, illus., Coward, McCann & Geoghegan, 1952 (7–9).

ZINDEL, PAUL. *The Pigman,* Harper, 1968 (7–9).

———. *My Darling, My Hamburger,* Harper & Row, 1969 (8+).

ZOLOTOW, CHARLOTTE. *An Overpraised Season: 10 Stories of Youth,* Harper & Row, 1973 (12+).

# 2
# Sex in Fact and Fiction

This is a time of increased sophistication and frankness about sexuality, when, despite raging controversy, sex education is increasingly common in schools. Nevertheless, the question "Where do babies come from?" still elicits some surprising responses from young children. Many children are still immersed in traditional myths and respond that they have been brought in doctors' bags, found in parking lots, bought in stores, or carried in with the laundry. Other children put together bits of information and arrive at more unique conclusions. One little girl, hearing that the birds and the bees were responsible for babies, worried that a bee sting would cause her to become pregnant. An eleven-year-old said that she had been baked like a cake in a stove and that when babies were left in the stove too long they became black. Many other young children think that whenever a baby is born, the doctor cuts open the mother's stomach, takes the baby out, and sews the stomach together. For such children the image of childbirth is one of a frightening and painful operation.[1]

Confusion and inaccuracies about sex are common not only among young children but among older ones as well. Lloyd Campbell, in his article "Sex Education: Let's Get On with It," notes that he has been asked the following questions by high-school students, queries that exhibit shocking gaps in sexual information:

If two people that have never had any trace of VD have intercourse, will they get VD?

Do you think people should be forced into marriage because of pregnancy?

When a guy and a girl do "go too far," why is it that the girl is always at fault and is shamed?

I heard that it is possible for a girl to get pregnant if she leaves her clothes on? Is this true?

Is it possible for a girl to get pregnant in a swimming pool? Could male sperms swimming about enter her body?

How long should the boy's penis be inserted for fertilization to occur?

If a girl gets pregnant and doesn't want to keep the baby, what can she do without having an abortion? Are quinine pills safe? Are there pills one can take for a miscarriage?

What is the most effective method of birth control?

Is it true peanut butter can make you sterile?

Does masturbation cause brain damage?[2]

Obviously not all children are confused and misinformed about sex. However, such comments make it clear there is need for more information and understanding about sex. One way for children to gain understanding is through their books, both fact and fiction. In this chapter we discuss sex information books for preschool and elementary school children. We analyze fiction for children in the middle and upper grades, books that depict characters who are becoming aware of ways their bodies are changing and developing sexually. We also examine recent books that depict former children's literature taboos such as premarital sexual relations and homosexual encounters.

## Answering the question "where do babies come from?"

"Where does a baby come from?" "How does it come out of the mother?" "How does it get into her?" According to *What Shall I Tell My Child* (1966), a book describing the Scandinavian system of sex education, these are the three questions young children ask most frequently about sex. There are now a growing number of children's books that attempt to answer these questions.[3]

One of the best of the sex education books for young children is Sidonie Matsner Gruenberg's *The Wonderful Story of How You Were Born* (1970). In a warm and personal style the author answers the three basic questions that children most frequently ask. She

explains that a baby begins as a tiny egg that was fertilized by a tiny sperm from the father's body. Gruenberg describes the baby's life inside the uterus and the baby's emergence from the mother's body through her vagina. She also explains how the sperm enters the mother's body, passing through the penis, which fits into the woman's vagina. Although the pertinent physiological information is here, the emphasis is on creating an attitude, a sense of wonder at the miracle of birth. Here, for example, is Gruenberg's discussion of intercourse:

When people are married, they feel very close to each other. A married man and woman feel this closeness with their hearts, and they also feel a special closeness with their bodies. They join their bodies together because they love each other. When they join their bodies, the man's penis enters the woman's vagina. That is how the sperm can fertilize the egg. Then the sperm and egg stop being two separate things and become one

*The Wonderful Story of How You Were Born*

new thing—which is the beginning of a baby. . . .

And all this is part of the same wonderful story —the most wonderful story in the world—the true story of how you were born.[4]

Highly detailed depiction of sexual reproduction is avoided in the pictures, which are delicate and for the most part emphasize interpersonal warmth and closeness.

Another good book that answers the three questions we raised in the introduction to this section is Andrew C. Andry's and Steven Schepps' *How Babies Are Made* (1968). Beginning with the reproductive process of plants, the book goes on to depict the mating of various animals, and it concludes by describing human reproduction. When the narrative describes intercourse, there is a corresponding picture showing a man and a woman lying down together, modestly covered by a blanket. Although the feelings experienced are not described in the text, the smile on the woman's face indicates that this union is a pleasurable one.

Although the suggested age for *How Babies Are Made* is between three and ten, repeated reading and explanation may be necessary for the younger child, particularly because of the comparison of plant and animal reproduction with human reproduction. When the authors first read the book to our four-year-old, we went through the descriptions of plant, then animal, then human reproduction. To get some idea of how much our daughter understood, we asked her, "When a sperm and an egg join together and the egg is fertilized, what will begin to grow?" "A little plant" was her initial prompt response. She liked the book and we read it a number of times during the next few weeks. Still she was not satisfied that she had been told all. "Well, we know where babies come from," she said. "But what about firemen? Where do they come from? Or policemen and doctors and teachers?"

Margaret Sheffield's *Where Do Babies Come From?* (1972) has been both praised as "blunt and beautiful" and condemned as too direct and explicit. With frank description and soft paintings, the book explains the terminology for the sexual organs, describes the growth of the baby within the uterus, and the process of delivery. Sheila Bewley's paintings make it clear that when a man and woman join together, there is love and pleasure involved. When intercourse is described in the text, a nude man and woman are shown holding one another and lying down together. There is an interesting difference between the narrative in the book and that in the abridged version that appeared in *Ms.* magazine. Consider how the book describes intercourse:

This is how babies are begun, with the man lying so close to the woman that his penis can enter her vagina.

If one of his sperms can get to one of her eggs, a baby will begin to grow.[5]

Here is the description of intercourse that appeared in *Ms.*:

This is how babies are begun, with the man laying so close to the woman that his penis, which becomes stiff, can enter her vagina.

If one of his sperms can join with one of her eggs, a baby will begin to grow.

If not, a man and a woman can still enjoy making love.[6]

It is curious that although the pictures show pleasure in sexual union, the narrative in the book is not allowed to convey the pleasure that is involved.

One of the most controversial of the sex education texts for children is Peter Mayle's *Where Did I Come From?* (1973). Nude cartoon characters and a humorous text purport to explain where babies come from to children as young as seven. The book notes that men and women are made differently and this becomes particularly apparent when they are in the bathtub together. The corresponding illus-

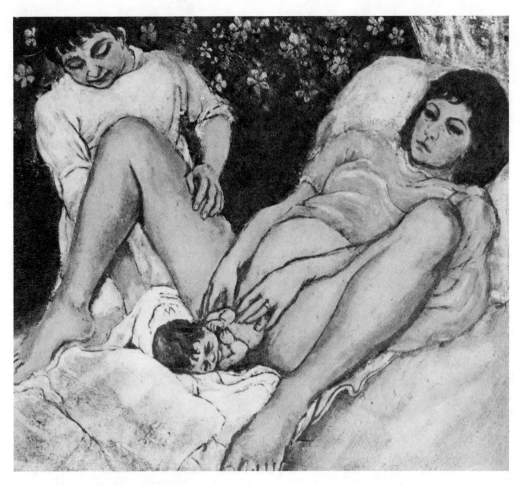

*Where Do Babies Come From*

tration displays a popeyed, pudgy man with an enormous penis and a popeyed, pudgy woman with erect nipples in the bath together. The book goes on to describe the different body parts and provides a unique pronunciation key. We are told that *penis* rhymes with *peanuts* without the *t* and that *vagina* rhymes with *Carolina*. The experience of making love is described with some baffling similes: "It's like scratching an itch but a lot nicer." Orgasm is compared to having a "tickle in your nose for a long time and then you have a really big sneeze."[7] At least some of the inaccuracies in description suggest a sexist view of sexuality. When a man and woman make love, the only position specified is that of the man lying on top of the woman. The narrative tells us that the parts that feel the best are the man's penis and the woman's vargina. Although the book explicitly deals with the pleasure of making love, there is no mention of the clitoris.

When this book was shown to several classes of college students, the reaction was mixed. Several pronounced the drawings repugnant, the narrative inaccurate, the book as a whole in bad taste, and one they would not choose to share with children. Others, however, although disapproving of occasional sexist overtones, found the book delightful. It was, these students noted, a great relief to find a book that discussed where babies came from with humor. These students said that they enjoyed reading the book themselves and they would also like to share the book with children.

By far the most controversial book dealing with sexuality for young children is *Show Me!* with photography and captions by Will McBride and explanatory text by Dr. Helga Fleischhauer-Hardt. This book is not so much a where-do-babies-come-from book as it is an expression of a very wide variety of feelings related to various aspects of sexuality.

The book is comprised of photographs of nude children and adults. There are, for example, pictures of nude children comparing genitals while a boy wonders whether his penis will be as big as his Dad's and a girl wonders what shape her breasts will be and whether they will be large or small. There are photographs of a male and of a female masturbating as well as photographs portraying two people making love. Toward the end of the book there are photographs showing a woman's intense pain during the process of childbirth and her great joy when her baby is finally born.

Almost universally students in our children's literature classes express shock and disbelief when they first see this book. Almost all agree that it is not one that they would use to discuss sexuality with children. We also find that this book is beyond our own comfort level. We are uneasy when showing it to students in college classes and baffled by the questions our own child asked about the photographs. There is nothing obscene or inaccurate in *Show Me!* However, our own backgrounds and even the current milieu will not allow us to feel comfortable with this book.

Some feel that Peter Mayles's *Where Did I Come From?* appears to be more appropriate as amusement for adults than as education for children, and outrage and controversy surround *Show Me!* In a review of sex education books for *Ms.*, Sheila Cole notes some of the other problems with sex education books for young children. For example, she has found books that supposedly tell children about their bodies but never mention the sex organs; books that purport to tell how babies are made, but never explain how the sperm gets into the woman's body so that it may reach the egg, and books that belabor the reproduction of plants and fish in such detail that the child is bored and frustrated long before the topic of human reproduction is introduced.[8]

Another difficulty with sex education books, particularly those for older children, is that not only is information conveyed, but values are expressed as well. At times these values are idiosyncratic and even inappropriate. For example, Frances Bruce Strain's *Being Born* (1954) provides the following questions and answers:

Do you have to have babies?
No, but most people want them. Marriage without children is not usually satisfying.[9]

Can you have a baby if you aren't married?
Yes, one may have a baby although one is not married. There may be no husband, but there must always be someone who takes the place of the husband and is the baby's father. There has to be a father to supply the sperm cells and fertilize the egg cell; otherwise there would be no baby. A baby needs a father after he is born too. He and his mother both need the father to love and care for them, and to provide for them and to give them security and I-belong-to-someone feeling in a home which bears his name. Mothers who do not have fathers for their babies lead a sorry life.[10]

In Eric Johnson's *Love and Sex in Plain Language* (1967) we also find values imparted, as, for example, the author's attitudes toward the birth of a child out of wedlock: "It is criminally selfish for an unmarried couple, or one unprepared for marriage, to risk having a baby—a young human being, yet unborn who has no say in the matter."[11]

In contrast, Wardell Pomeroy's *Girls and Sex* (1969) expresses a different value concerning premarital sex:

I believe, further, that the question of whether a girl should engage in any kind of sexual behavior depends on things like the attitudes of the people with whom she lives, especially those of her own age; the particular social level on which she lives; and whatever system of values, ethics or codes she has chosen to guide her, whether these are religious, or are something she has learned from her parents, or whether they rise from some deep inner conviction of her own.[12]

For a still more liberal attitude toward premarital sex, there is Siv Widerberg's *The Kids' Own XYZ of Love and Sex* (1971) in which a father explains to his daughter that

It's so nice to have sex together that lots of people don't want to wait until they are married or have found somebody to love.

And so they have sex with somebody just because they like it and, sometimes they may want to have a baby, sometimes not. They make up their own minds about it.[13]

In short, when an author describes sexuality to children, he or she is attempting to explain one of society's most value-laden areas. Consequently, both parents and children should be aware that what they are reading will in all likelihood be influenced by the author's values concerning such topics as premarital pregnancy, masturbation, homosexuality, and sex roles. Given the transmission of values in books that deal with sexuality, it is pertinent and beneficial that the clarification of values is becoming an integral part of many school curriculums.

Sex information books can be invaluable resources to be used within the context of a school's sex education program or a parent's discussion with a child. Often after reading such books, a child may have questions or may want to talk over what has been read with an adult. However, an adult who is unaccustomed to such discussions may find them difficult or embarrassing. Arlene Uslander, a teacher of sex education for eight years, offers some suggestions, particularly effective with younger children, to help adults answer children's questions about sex. Some of her more important guidelines are incorporated in the following discussion.

Uslander recommends answering a child's questions with short, simple answers because it is easier to add information than to take it away. Highly detailed and technical answers may bore and frustrate youngsters and diminish curiosity. She also suggests that before answering a child's questions about sex, one should be sure what the child is really asking. There is an old story about the child who asked a parent, "Where do I come from?" and then, after listening to a detailed explanation of the facts of life, bravely persevered with his original query, "I meant what city do I come from—was it Chicago or New York?"

One way to ascertain what the child really wants to know is to reflect his or her questions back, asking, "What do you think?" Uslander also notes that if the adult is unsure of the factual information or finds a question embarrassing or too personal, then the adult can simply express a lack of knowledge or discomfort and refuse to answer. Finally, Uslander points out that within a supervised discussion children can often answer one another's questions. She tells of a second grader who, after listening to the explanation of how babies were born, was still puzzled about how a baby could emerge through so small an opening. Another second grader explained with a simile that helped his peer understand:

You know how it is when you put on a turtleneck shirt? At first the opening is real small and you have to push very hard to get your head through it. But the opening gets wider—it stretches— and all of a sudden your head pops through. Well, that's the way it is when a baby is born. At first the opening is real small, but it stretches and gets wide enough for a baby to come through. Then it gets small again. The vagina is like a turtleneck shirt.[14]

Uslander tells of another experience in which a child was able to help a peer understand some information that was confusing. A fourth-grade girl said she understood the facts about sexual intercourse, but she could not picture it. Another student helped her with the explanation, "It's easy. . . . Men's and women's bodies are like puzzles—their parts were made to fit together."[15]

Answers to a child's first questions about sex may influence his or her developing attitudes. If responses are comprised of lies, evasions, and embarrassment, a child may learn that matters of sexuality are shameful and should not be discussed. There are now some fine books with sensitive text and illustrations that can help adults and children talk together with comfort, rapport, and honesty about one of society's most controversial and value-laden topics.

## Growing up female—growing up male

There are innumerable characters in children's literature who meet with confusions and problems as they grow to maturity. Some struggle for independence against parental confines that are drawn too tight. Yet others receive insufficient care and support from their parents and must learn early to fend for themselves. For some, maturity comes as they combat the forces of nature; for others, the struggle is an inner one, and they must combat some demon or obstacle within themselves. As characters in children's books mature, they seem to worry about everything from acne to obesity, from oversolicitous to absent parents, from friendless unpopularity to conformity and loss of identity. Children in books worry about their families, their friends, themselves, and a multitude of serious and not so serious issues.

The worries and concerns of children in books seem to reflect quite accurately those of their counterparts in real life. However, there is one major difference. Real children who are growing up are aware of and often concerned about changes that are taking place in their bodies. For book children, such changes seem to be nonexistent or worthy of only the most fleeting attention. There are some notable exceptions, and we will discuss a few of these. In order to convey a sense of how such topics as menstruation—for a long time a taboo area in children's literature—are described, we at times quote extensively from the very few children's books that portray characters who, as they grow to maturity, are aware of how their bodies are changing.

One such book is Louise Fitzhugh's *The Long Secret* (1965), the sequel to *Harriet the Spy,* in which the focus shifts from the individualistic Harriet to her shyer friend, Beth Ellen. The two girls become involved in solving a mystery, and Beth Ellen, who has been brought up by her grandmother, comes into conflict with her jet-set mother. The book also contains one brief chapter in which Beth Ellen, who is upset and depressed by her first period, meets with two of her friends, Harriet and Janie, and the three girls discuss the situation:

The next day was Saturday and Beth Ellen went to Harriet's house for the day. When she came into the bedroom, Harriet and Janie were discussing the situation.

"I've been working on a cure for this thing ever since it happened to me," Janie said, frowning and looking very serious, even though she was lying upside down on the bed in a bathing suit with her feet straight up against the wall. "What kind of cure?" asked Harriet, after she had said hello to Beth Ellen.

"I just want to end it, that's all," said Janie in a furious way.

"But . . . doesn't it have something to do with babies?" asked Harriet.

"How would you know, Harriet Welsch? You haven't even done it," snarled Janie, swinging her legs down to the floor and sitting up. "You wouldn't know a Fallopian tube if you fell over one."

Chagrined, Harriet pointed to Beth Ellen. "She's done it, yesterday. She told me."

Beth Ellen turned bright red, looked at the floor, and wanted to die. They both stared at her.

Janie finally spoke, and softly, "What's there to think about? It's a nuisance, that's all, and frankly, I think, should be done away with."

Beth Ellen kept looking at the floor.

"What's it feel like?" asked Harriet.

"Yuuuuuchk," said Janie. "It has absolutely nothing to recommend it." She looked at Beth Ellen as she continued. "You don't feel like working or playing or anything but just lying around and looking at the ceiling, right? Icky. Right, Mouse?"

Beth Ellen nodded but still couldn't look up for some reason.

Janie looked at her a minute, then said, "It happens to everybody, though, every woman in the world, even Madame Curie. It's very normal. And I guess, since it means you're grown up and can have babies, that it's a good thing. I, for one, just don't happen to want babies. I also have a sneaking suspicion that they're too many babies in the world already. So I'm working on this cure for people that don't want babies, so they won't have to do this."

Beth Ellen looked up at Janie and asked tentatively, "Do those rocks hurt you too?"

"Rocks?" Janie yelled.

"Those rocks inside that come down," said Beth Ellen timidly.

"WHAT?" screamed Harriet. "Oh, well, if they think I'm gonna do anything like that, they're crazy."

"There aren't any rocks. Who told you that?" Janie was so mad she stood up. "Who told you there were rocks? There aren't any rocks. I'll kill 'em. Who told you that about any rocks?"

Beth Ellen looked scared. "My grandmother," she said faintly. "Isn't that right? Aren't there little rocks that come down and make you bleed and hurt you?"

"Right? It couldn't be more wrong," Janie stood over her. "There aren't any rocks. You got that? There aren't any rocks at all!"

"wow!" said Harriet. "ROCKS!"

"Now, wait a minute," said Janie, holding up her hand like a lecturer, "let's get something straight here before you two get terrified."

They both looked up at her. Beth Ellen was frightened and confused. Harriet was angry and confused.

"Now, you must understand," said Janie, looking very earnest, "that the generation that Beth Ellen's grandmother is was very Victorian. They never talked about things like this, and her grandmother thought that telling her this was better than telling her the truth."

"What's the truth?" asked Harriet avidly.

Beth Ellen didn't care about the truth. The rocks were bad enough to think about. What could the truth be?

"That just goes to show you," said Janie, looking like a stuffy teacher, "that people should learn to live with fact! It's never as bad as the fantasies they make up."

"Oh, Janie, get on with it," said Harriet. "What is the truth?"

"Ah, what a question," said Janie.

"JANIE!" said Harriet in disgust. Janie could be very corny and exasperating when she turned philosophical.

"Okay, okay," said Janie as though they were too dumb to appreciate her, "it's very simple. I'll explain it." She sat down as though it would take a long time.

"Now, you know the baby grows inside a woman, in her womb, in the uterus?"

They nodded.

"Well. What do you think it lives on when it's growing?"

They both looked blank.

"The lining, dopes!" she yelled at them.

They blinked.

"So, it's very simple. If you have a baby started in there, the baby lives on the lining; but if you don't have a baby, like we don't, then the body very sensibly disposes of the lining that it's made for the baby. It just comes out."

"Falls right out of you?" screamed Harriet.

Oh, thought Beth Ellen, why me?

"No, no, no. You always exaggerate, Harriet. You would make a terrible scientist. You must be precise. It doesn't fall out like you say; it comes out a tiny bit at a time over a period of from, well, say four to six days, depending on the woman. It's very little at a time, and it doesn't hurt or anything. You just feel tired."

"I hurt," said Beth Ellen.

"Well . . ." said Janie, "sometimes there's a little pain, but it really isn't much. I just, frankly, don't care for it," she said, as though she'd been asked if she liked a certain book.

"Well," said Harriet.

"Another thing I don't like is people making up these silly stories about it, like those rocks. Why can't people just take life as it is?"

Beth Ellen thought of her grandmother taking life as it is. She couldn't imagine her grandmother talking to her about babies, linings, Fallopian tubes, and so forth. She felt a little sorry for her grandmother. She supposed that she had been trying to make it nicer for her, but it had been wrong because the rock story had scared her.

"The thing is," said Harriet, "does your grandmother really believe there are rocks? Maybe we should tell her."

"Of course she doesn't," said Beth Ellen, "and you won't tell her anything."

"That's silly," said Janie to Harriet. "You don't take into account how different each generation is."

"Well!" said Harriet, considerably miffed. "Instead of just lying there talking, why don't you make a cure?"

"I'm going to cure this one way or the other if it's the last thing I do." Janie looked determinedly out the window as though there were a cure sitting in the backyard.

"I just can't wait to not do this," said Harriet.

"Well," said Janie, "you might as well, since everyone else is. You'd feel pretty silly if you didn't. Besides, you get to skip gym when you have it."

"Yeah?" said Harriet and Beth Ellen in unison. They both hated gym.

"Yeah," said Janie with one of her fierce smiles.

"Well!" said Harriet.

That, thought Beth Ellen, is a decided advantage.[16]

College students in our children's literature classes express differing reactions to this discussion of menstruation. Almost all students agree that it is pertinent and appropriate that such a discussion appear in a children's book. Some female students say the characters' comments accurately reflect the feelings they had when they first menstruated. Yet other students feel the discussion is too negative. Harriet is bewildered, Beth Ellen frightened and confused, and Janie, who at least knows what's happening, sums up the experience as "Yuuuuuck." The discussion suggests that every girl who has her period feels lethargic or is in pain. There is perhaps need of a character with more positive feelings to give the discussion balance.

A more positive attitude toward menstruation is conveyed in Judy Blume's *Are You There God? It's Me, Margaret* (1970). Judy Blume has a realistic perception of the suburban upper elementary school child. With humor and understanding she draws a portrait of Margaret, the child of a mixed marriage, who, unable to choose between Judaism and Christianity, finds that she is best able to speak to God through her own private conversations. Margaret is in the sixth grade and belongs to a secret club whose members are concerned about boys and about their own sexual development. Each of the four members of the club waits impatiently to get her period. Margaret is so anxious she buys Teenage Softies and practices fitting her belt and pad for months before she actually gets her period. When she finally menstruates, she is overjoyed.

The girls in Margaret's club are anxious not only to menstruate, but also to get their first bras. There is a very funny scene in which Margaret shops for her first bra; she is informed by the saleslady that she is not quite ready for a double A and is fitted with a Gro-Bra instead. Margaret does exercises to increase her bust but the results are disappointing. She and her clubmates analyze the Playboy centerfolds, but those models seem too far advanced to emulate. Margaret, impatient for results, resorts to padding with cotton balls and to praying: "Are you there God? It's me Margaret. I just did an exercise to help me grow. Have you thought about it God? About my growing, I mean. I've got a bra now. It would be nice if I had something to put in it."[17]

Blume's *Deenie* (1973), a less successful book, is about an exceptionally pretty girl whose mother wants her to become a model. Deenie wants nothing to do with the modeling jobs and would rather go out for cheerleading, hang around with her girl friends, and go to the seventh-grade mixer. However, Deenie is turned down for the modeling jobs and even for cheerleading because of her awkward posture. A visit to the doctor discloses that Deenie has a curvature of the spine and will have to wear a Milwaukee brace for several years. Constant wearing of such an awkward contraption would be trying for most thirteen-year-olds, but for Deenie, whose mother has always emphasized beauty, it is particularly difficult. Deenie has another very different worry. Sometimes before she goes to bed at night she touches herself in a special place and gets a nice feeling. She does not know if there is a name for what she does, but she worries about whether it is right to touch herself.

There are discussions about sex in Deenie's gym class, and she drops an unsigned question into the box on the teacher's desk:

*Do normal people touch their bodies before they go to sleep and is it all right to do that?*

On Tuesday, when we walked into the gym, Mrs. Rappoport told us to sit in a circle so we could talk easily. The first questions she discussed were all about menstruation. But I already knew most everything from my booklet. After that she said, "Okay, now I think we can move on to another subject. Here's an interesting question." She read it to us. "Do normal people touch their bodies before they go to sleep and is it all right to do that?"

I almost died! I glanced around, then smiled a little, because some of the other girls did, and hoped the expression on my face looked like I was trying to figure out who had asked such a thing.

Mrs. Rappoport said, "Can anyone help us with an answer?"

Susan Minton raised her hand.

"Yes, Susan . . ." Mrs. Rappoport said.

"I wasn't the one who wrote the question but I've heard that boys who touch themselves too much can go blind or get very bad pimples or their bodies can even grow deformed."

"Has anyone else heard that?" Mrs. Rappoport asked.

Five other girls raised their hands.

Could it possibly be true? I wondered. And if it was true about boys maybe it was about girls too. Maybe that's why my spine started growing crooked! Please God . . . don't let it be true, I prayed. I felt my face get hot and I had to go to the bathroom in the worst way but I didn't move a muscle. I hoped nobody could tell what I was thinking.

"Well . . ." Mrs. Rappoport said, "I can see you've got a lot of misinformation. Does anyone here know the word for stimulating our genitals? Because that's what we're talking about, you know."

It got very quiet in the gym. Nobody said anything for a long time. Then one girl spoke. "I think it's called masturbation."

"That's right," Mrs. Rappoport told us. "And it's not a word you should be afraid of. Let's all say it."

"Masturbation," we said together.

"Okay," Mrs. Rappoport said. "Now that you've said it let me try to explain. First of all, it's normal and harmless to masturbate."

"You mean for boys . . ." Susan Minton said.

"No, I mean for anyone . . . male or female," Mrs. Rappoport told us. "The myths that some of you have heard aren't true. Masturbation can't make you insane or deformed or even give you acne."

I wanted to take a deep breath when she said that but I didn't. I just gulped and looked at the floor.

"Does everybody masturbate?" Barbara Curtis asked.

"Not necessarily," Mrs. Rappoport said. "But it's very common for girls as well as boys, beginning with adolescence."

Any minute I thought Mrs. Rappoport would ask us to raise our hands if we masturbate and I wasn't sure if I'd be able to tell the truth. I never knew there was a name for what I do. I just thought it was my own special good feeling. Now I wonder if all my friends do it too?

But Mrs. Rappoport didn't ask us to tell her if we did or we didn't masturbate and I was glad. It's a very private subject. I wouldn't want to talk about it in front of the class. She said the important thing to remember is that it is normal and that it can't hurt us.

"Nobody ever went crazy from masturbating but a lot of young people make themselves sick from worrying about it."

I couldn't help thinking about Buddy. Can he get that special feeling too? I'd like to find out how much Buddy really knows about girls. I hardly know anything about boys. I think we should have discussions every week. They're more important than modern dance![18]

In one of her finest books, *Then Again, Maybe I Won't* (1971), Judy Blume portrays a boy's problems in growing up and his confusions and worries about the way his body

works. When Tony and his family, newly rich from selling an invention involving electrical cartridges, arrive in a wealthy Long Island suburb, Tony is bothered by his family's burgeoning materialism. He is also bewildered by the changes going on inside his body. Next door lives Lisa, a beautiful sixteen-year-old cheerleader who does not close her blinds when she undresses at night. When Tony gets binoculars for his birthday (he tells his parents that he is interested in bird watching) he watches Lisa every night. When Tony watches Lisa or when he reads certain paperbacks, he feels himself getting hard. Sometimes this happens to him when he is not even thinking about anything sexy:

"It's getting so I don't have anything to say about what goes on. I think that part of me has a mind of its own.

Suppose it decides to go up in school and everybody notices? Or at a junior youth group meeting? What will I do to get it down? I think from now on I'm going to carry a raincoat with me every day. Then, if anything happens I'll have something to put over me in a hurry."[19]

In one funny scene in math class Tony is caught without his raincoat. He is at the front of the class and writing a math problem on the board:

Just as I finished writing the figure on the board I started to get hard. Mind over matter . . . mind over matter. I told myself. But still it went up. I kept my back to the class and prayed for it to go down.

Miss Tobin said, "That's an interesting way to solve the problem, Tony."

For a minute I thought she meant my real problem. But then I realized she was talking about the math problem.

"Could you explain your reasoning to the class, Tony?"

I started talking but I didn't turn around. I could just picture facing the class. Everybody would laugh and point to my pants. I wished I was wearing my raincoat.

"We'd hear better if you'd turn around," Miss Tobin said.

What could I do? Pretend to be sick and run out of the room? Maybe. Or just refuse to turn around? No. Ask to go to the bathroom? No. . . .

"Tony . . ." Miss Tobin said.

"Yes?"

"We're waiting for you to explain the problem."

"Oh, Okay Miss Tobin."

I was holding my math book in my left hand and a piece of chalk in my right. I turned sideways keeping my book in front of my pants. I explained my answer as fast as I could and Miss Tobin didn't ask me any questions. She said, "Thank you, Tony. You can sit down now."

I walked back to my seat still holding the math book close to me. But I didn't have to worry. By then it was down.

From now on I'm going to make sure I always have a stack of books with me. Books are a lot better than my old raincoat![20]

Tony is worried about another way his body seems to be working without the control of his mind. One night Tony dreams about Lisa, and when he wakes up his pajamas are sticky. He is worried that something is wrong with him, that he is really sick. Then he realizes he has had a wet dream. He throws the pajamas in the hamper and then dampens all the clothes so that no one will notice the unusual state of his pajamas. When he comes home from school, his maid has changed his sheet, and he feels that he can never look at her again, embarrassed at what she may know.

Judy Blume's characters, drawn with humor and unique understanding, are very normal, very human upper elementary school and junior high school children. They worry about sex and about how their bodies are changing —just as they worry about other aspects of growing up. In various ways, usually through discussions with other children or sessions in

school, these characters come to accept and understand the changes in their bodies.

Once in a while a character in children's literature does not emerge from adolescence in so healthy a fashion. For example, as David Marks in Barbara Wersba's *Run Softly, Go Fast* (1970), grows up, feelings of love and respect toward his father become partially twisted into contempt. David loathes his father's materialism and his inability to understand and appreciate art and poetry. David also hates his father for instilling in him feelings that sex is disgraceful and dirty. As an adolescent, David fantasizes about sex and masturbates in his room. His father catches him, and his furious reaction makes the boy feel unclean and abnormal. David's feelings concerning sex become more confused as he discovers that his father is making love to other women. When his father drives away his closest friend, Rick, with claims that the boy is a homosexual, David leaves home and immerses himself in the drug culture. When he meets Maggie, a gentle young woman who shows him that he can make love, some of the tangled pieces of David's life begin to fit.

Currently there are few books in which adolescent and preadolescent characters wonder about sex and the ways their bodies are changing and developing. Such books are important, for they reflect the concerns and curiosities of children reading these books. Unlike nonfiction books that give sexual information, fiction has the added dimension of not only relating facts but also conveying feelings and concerns about sexuality.

## New sexuality—old morality

Jane Howard, going steady for three years with comfortable Ken Sanderson, the boy next door, runs away when he tries to give her a first serious good night kiss. When Ken begins to date her younger sister, Jane, bitter and angry, struggles to accept the change and to achieve popularity with other boys.

*Betty Cavanna*, The Boy Next Door, 1956[21]

Jane Purdy is fifteen and has never had a date until she meets Stan, a good looking sixteen-year-old who earns spare money by delivering horse meat for the Doggie Diner. Jane and Stan date quite steadily; although the relationship has its share of confusions and misunderstandings, at the book's conclusion, Stan gives Jane his ID bracelet and they share a hurried first kiss.

*Beverly Cleary*, Fifteen, 1956[22]

Loretta Larkin, tops in athletics but a bumbler socially, wins a school essay contest with $100 worth of flying lessons as the prize. Rette finds flying exhilarating, and it also makes her something of a celebrity with her classmates. By the end of the book, she has gained poise and confidence, as well as Jeff Chandler, one of the most highly thought of and popular boys in the senior class. Although Loretta and Jeff have never touched, not even to hold hands, she has become one of his two best girl friends.

*Betty Cavanna*, A Girl Can Dream[23]

Vivacious, fun-loving Tobey Heydon is a high-school senior who enjoys life in a small town with her spirited family and her first boyfriend, Brose. Tobey and Brose have a relaxed, easy rapport with one another. Contented hand-holding sessions are usually as physical as they get. However, there are occasional kisses—at Christmas and at the book's conclusion when Brose gives Tobey his class ring.

*Rosamond du Jardin*, Practically Seventeen, 1943[24]

These are brief plot synopses of novels that were widely and eagerly read by teenage girls fifteen, twenty, and thirty years ago. To varying degrees they are still widely and eagerly read today—but usually not by teenagers. Their one-sided treatment of romance, a vision that almost totally excludes any physical dimension, today demands a much younger readership. As Ann Kalkhoff notes in her ar-

ticle "Innocent Children or Innocent Librarians," popular teenage romances by authors such as Betty Cavanna are no longer being read by the teenagers for whom they were intended but by fifth and sixth graders instead.[25] Others suggest that the children reading these books may be even younger.

Indeed there has been a marked change in the way sexual activities are described in novels for adolescents. For example, an analysis of twenty-three novels for adolescents reported in 1967 shows allusion to no sexual activity other than occasional kissing. Apparently times are changing. A 1974 analysis of thirty popular adolescent novels indicates that although there are no sex scenes equal to those appearing on television and in movies, in today's adolescent novels sexual activities are not merely alluded to but are directly reported.[26]

One such contemporary novel with direct reporting of adolescent sexual activities is Nora Stirling's *You Would If You Loved Me* (1969). Trudy Monroe is delighted when her boyfriend Tom invites her to the Bulldog dance, the most elite and prestigious social event on the high-school calendar. But she is confused as to how to react to Tom's persistent sexual advances. Her initial reaction is to respond, but when things become dangerous, an apparently built-in invisible alarm warns her to stop.

She didn't care. Suddenly nothing mattered but this.

But only for a moment. Tom's hand was sliding down her thigh, and she awoke from her daze. Sharply pulling her face aside she tore her mouth from his. "Tom! No!"

He paid no attention. Now wide awake, she caught his hand and pulled it away. "Tom, please. *Please*, Tom." With a tremendous effort she pushed herself out of his arms.[27]

Trudy must decide whether to sleep with Tom. She finally chooses chastity, and when the relationship breaks up, she is rewarded by the respect of her classmates.

A number of other contemporary adolescent books differ from this one in that the young couples opt for intercourse rather than abstinence. In most of these books the couples have been dating steadily for a while before they decide to sleep with one another. The emphasis is not on what goes on before or during the sexual act, but rather on what happens afterward —and what usually happens afterward in these books is a baby.

Patricia Dizenzo's *Phoebe* (1970) portrays the confusion and anguish of an unmarried sixteen-year-old girl who learns that she is pregnant. There is a brief depiction of Phoebe's relationship with her boyfriend, Paul, and a brief summer spent in lovemaking. However, most of the book details Phoebe's predicament when the summer ends. She does not feel she can confide in anyone—not in her parents, not in her family; not even, she is stunned to realize, in Paul. She suffers through morning sickness, is unable to concentrate on her studies, and searches the encyclopedia for the information she needs. The book ends as Paul and her parents finally find out, and there is no indication of how the problem will be resolved.

In Zoa Sherburne's *Too Bad About the Haines Girl* (1967) the problem is resolved, but with a sense of pessimism. Melinda is happy with her family, popular with her classmates, and going steady with Jeff, one of the nicest and best-looking boys in the senior class. Her sense of the idyllic is shattered when she learns that she is pregnant. When Jeff finds out, he too is stunned, but his immediate suggestion is marriage. Melinda is less certain and instead listens to the advice of an acquaintance who tells her where she can lose her worries for $200. However, when Melinda confronts the hard eyes of Dr. Granger (the Dr. stands for initials, not a medical degree) she

knows she cannot go through with the abortion. She and Jeff decide on marriage, and the book concludes with some hope that Melinda and Jeff, because they are good people, will create a workable marriage. However, there is also the terrible sense of youth that is lost and opportunities that will be missed.

Marriage is also the solution in Ann Head's *Mr. and Mrs. Bojo Jones* (1967), written for adults but coopted by adolescents. July is sixteen and Bojo is seventeen and they are both in the right crowd in high school. Both of their families have laid out good solid plans for their futures. Bojo, his family's hope for upward social mobility, has just won a football scholarship to the state university. July plans to follow in her mother's footsteps to a prestigious women's college in New England. However, when July gets pregnant, she and Bojo get married and everything changes. Upward mobility and the prestigious women's college vanish. The young couple moves into the Jones's home where they are shepherded into separate bedrooms and where Mrs. Jones gives July a crash course in ironing Bojo's shirts. The couple then move into a garage apartment and begin playing at husband and wife. He goes off to a montonous job; she restlessly wonders what she is supposed to do with herself during the day and serves a steady diet of hamburgers for dinner. There are misunderstandings, and bickering grows into full-fledged fights. There is also lovemaking in which sometimes July is "there" and "with it" and sometimes she is not. When their baby dies, the parents assume the marriage will too. But July and Bojo stay together. July misses the proms, the dates, the college she never went to—but she and Bojo will work things out. The novel ends with muted optimism and again a sense of some of life's richness lost.

In *Too Bad About the Haines Girl* Melinda considers an abortion and then rejects the idea as evil. In both Paul Zindel's *My Darling, My*

*Hamburger* (1969) and in Jeannette Eyerly's *Bonnie Jo, Go Home* (1972), a high-school girl gets pregnant, she does get an abortion, and the consequences are disastrous.

The focus in *My Darling, My Hamburger* alternates between two teenage couples, sophisticated Liz and Sean and awkward Maggie and Dennis. While Maggie and Dennis contemplate whether their date will end with a goodnight kiss, Liz tries to hold back Sean's insistence that they sleep together. Finally Sean's persistence, along with her parents' lack of trust, cause Liz to give in. Liz gets pregnant, Sean at first agrees to marry her, and then after a talk with his opportunistic father, brings her white roses and abortion money instead. Under the ruse of attending the prom, Liz, ironically dressed in white, goes to an abortionist. On the way home Liz begins hemorrhaging and her friend, Maggie, desperate, drives to Liz's home and rings the bell. The final scene of the book takes place at graduation with only three of the protagonists in cap and gown. The focus is shifted from Liz, and we are left baffled and pessimistic as to what will happen to her.

In *Bonnie Jo, Go Home*, the protagonist, Bonnie Jo, has been dating handsome and intelligent Mark Truro, the son of a well-to-do doctor. When he drops her, she reacts out of spite and goes out with Bill Lobos, an unsavory character who, on their first date, gets her so drunk that she is barely conscious during their first cold sexual encounter. The next time she has intercourse with him, it is in broad daylight in the back seat of his car. When Bonnie Jo learns she is going to have a baby, she rejects the thought of leaving high school pregnant and disgraced. She finally decides on an airplane trip that will take her from Omaha to New York, where she can get an abortion.

Bonnie Jo's stay in New York is prolonged, ghastly, and unnerving. The cabdriver, cognizant of why he is taking Bonnie Jo from the airport to the Women's Medical Arts Building, spits at her feet as she leaves the taxi. Bonnie Jo expects to get a vacuum aspiration, a process by which the contents of the womb will be emptied by a few minutes of carefully controlled suction. She learns, however, that she has been pregnant for longer than she had thought, and she will have to have a "salting out," an injection of salt solution into the uterus that can take place only in a hospital. This means the burden of increased cost and the necessity of staying in a rooming house until she can find a doctor to perform the operation and a hospital bed becomes available. She fears further barely endurable delays, the thinly hidden contempt of the nurses, and then finally the abortion. When Bonnie Jo prepares to return to Omaha, she is both psychologically and physically aged by her grisly experience.

. . . books, specifically for twelve and older in the years to come—and I would not be certain this category will long survive—are going to be much more complex, more shocking to librarians though not to the young, and much more openly and healthily erotic than "books for young readers" have ever been before.[28]

So wrote Nat Hentoff in *Horn Book Magazine* in 1966, and, in contrast to the romantic novels for adolescents of an earlier time, it is obvious that the books of the late 1960s and early 1970s are for the most part more complex and are certainly more shocking. We would seriously question, however, whether they have fulfilled Hentoff's prediction as more erotic. Indeed, as Lou Willett Stanek suggests in "The Maturation of the Junior Novel: From Gestation to the Pill," they may be as or more heavily moralistic than the books of the past that ignored any sexual activity other than the goodnight kiss. Considering their topics, the contemporary books do not attribute sexual desire to adolescents, particularly to girls; instead they moralize about the consequences of sexual activity. For the most part it is not youthful sex drive that causes these young women to become sexually involved, but rather liquor or hostility. In *Mr. and Mrs. Bojo Jones* and *Too Bad About the Haines Girl* the culprit is liquor in the forms of champagne and spiked punch. Anger and spite toward a third party are offered as the cause in *My Darling, My Hamburger* and *Bonnie Jo, Go Home.* Liz succumbs to Sean because she resents her parents' mistrust, and Bonnie Jo's anger at a former boyfriend causes her to get so drunk that she has intercourse with a boy whose name she hardly knows.

Ms. Stanek concludes her article, noting:

Written in the heat of a sexual revolution in our society, books of this nature, which ignore sexual desire, contraception (especially the pill and teen-agers confusion with it), and, in many cases, abortion, do not deal with reality. They simply exploit a time of change. A book dealing with premarital pregnancy can be as old fashioned as the cliche how-to-get-a-date-for-the-prom story. . . . These are old ideas against a new backdrop.[29]

Indeed it is hard to consider a book erotic when the narrator is mainly concerned with reporting a character's moral confusion and when characters are punished when they do become sexually involved by a catalogue of horrors and a hopeless future. Ironically, there is probably more eroticism and sensuality in some of the earlier love stories where a goodnight kiss is all. For example, consider Maureen Daly's classic *Seventeenth Summer* (1942), the story of Angie Morrow, a social outsider in the small town of Fond du Lac, Wisconsin, until she meets Jack Duluth, a high-school basketball star. With Jack she is introduced to a world of which she had been only dimly aware —beer parties, sailing, being part of the crowd at the drugstore, and those magical times when she is alone with Jack. It is at the country club dance on their third date that Angie and Jack first kiss:

In the loveliness of the next moment I think I grew up. I remember that behind him was the thin yellow paper arc of moon, turned over on its back, and I remember feeling my hands slowly relax on the rough lapels of his coat. Sitting on the cool grass in my new sprigged dimity with the little blue and white bachelor's buttons pinned in my hair, Jack kissed me—and his lips were as smooth and as baby soft as a new raspberry.[30]

The physical relationship between Angie and Jack is so intense that there is sensual pleasure when their hands accidentally touch. "Jack was sitting propped on his hands, with his head back looking at the sky and he moved his hand just a little so it barely touched mine. A tingling ran up my arm and I felt my face flush in the darkness."[31]

In the books of Mary Stolz, a fine writer of teenage novels, adolescent sexual feelings are expressed in only a kiss, but again it is a sensual and erotic moment. *The Sea Gulls Woke Me* (1951) tells of shy Jean, who at sixteen ventures away from her overprotective family and spends the summer with relatives who own an inn on an island in Maine. During that vacation, spent with a witty and vivacious group of college students, Jean grows up, gets invited to a Princeton weekend, and falls in love with an Amherst student, Mac, who, while teaching Jean to dance, gives her her first kiss.

She hesitated, put her hand in his, and their touching brought again the languid sweetness she had felt beside him on the dark porch. And their closeness, their gentle quickened breathing, their eyes searching changed the languor to a shy turbulence. So slow were all their motions that it was as if each had asked the other to keep as long as possible this delicate awareness of what they knew now would happen. Then Max pulled her hand down tight so that they moved together, and lingering a moment still, put his arms around her and held her close and they kissed. Then, with the charming dignity of the young, they drew apart, losing none of the magic but putting no words to it.[32]

Isabelle Holland in "Tilting at Taboos" captures the essence of the difference between older books such as those by Stolz and Daly and the more contemporary novels that portray sexuality:

The moment that used to occur a few pages before the end when the lovers have their first kiss was electric, not only for the participants but for the reader, and it had all the more impact for being filled with the yearnings of all the preceding pages. Again, speaking entirely from the literary point of view, I think the multiple orgasm is a poor substitute.[33]

Another aspect of the "new sexuality" is the lifting of the taboo against any mention of homosexuality. John Donovan's *I'll Get There. It Better Be Worth the Trip* (1969) is the story of thirteen-year-old Davey Ross, who goes to New York to live with his mother, divorced, temperamental, and quite frequently drunk. Davey is lonely and he forms a friendship with a boy from school, Douglas Altschuler. However, the friendship develops in an unexpected way. The two boys are horsing around on the living room floor when something funny happens. Davey feels unusual, and he and Altschuler look at each other strangely and then they kiss each other. The two boys are baffled at what has happened to them and plagued by doubts about themselves. The incident is brief; it is not repeated; and there is every indication that it is a minor "deviation" in otherwise "healthy" development.

Lyn Hall's *Sticks and Stones* (1972) is also about homosexuality and even more about the way vicious gossip in a small town can harm the individuals who live there. Tom Nayler and his divorced mother move from a suburb of Chicago to a small resort town of Birch Creek, Iowa. Tom is eager to get into the pattern of town life, but his presence generates envy among the local high-school students. Because of his friendship with Ward Alexander, a young man who, as town gossip puts it, is

"queer as a three dollar bill," rumors spread and Tom becomes "guilty" by association. At first Tom cannot comprehend the coldness and the outright contempt of his classmates. He is puzzled when, after a basketball game, he throws his arm around a fellow player's shoulders and the coach reacts sharply with "Nayler, watch your hands." Finally the word *homosexual* comes out into the open when the principal tells him that because of parental complaints, he will not be allowed to go to the state music fair. Tom succumbs to the gossip, turns away from Ward, and is filled with doubts. Perhaps, he feels, there may be an element of truth in the gossip. Many tormented months go by before Tom can confront the damage the gossip has done to him, to Ward, and to their friendship.

In Isabelle Holland's *The Man Without a Face* (1972) Charles Norstadt forms a close friendship with his tutor, Justin McLeod, whom the town calls the man without a face. Justin, burnt and disfigured in a car accident, has isolated himself from others until Charles comes to him seeking tutoring help so that he can get into a private school, St. Mathews. Eventually Charles turns to Justin for help not only as a teacher, but as a friend and as a replacement for the father whom he can barely remember. One night, when Charles learns that his real father was an alcoholic, he is so distraught that he interrupts Justin's sleep in order to talk to his friend. As Charles lies in bed next to Justin, his friend comforts him, and Charles is devastated by his own response: "I could feel his heart pounding, and then I realized it was mine. I couldn't stop shaking; in fact, I started to tremble violently. It was like everything—the water, the sun, the hours, the play, the work, the whole summer—came together. The golden cocoon had broken open and was spilling in a shower of gold."[34]

Charles feels bitter and accuses Justin of seducing him, although he knows he has initiated everything. Justin assures Charles that he is quite "normal," but it is months before Charles can sort out what happened. When he seeks Justin to reaffirm their friendship, he finds that the older man has died of a heart attack.

This is a time when concepts about homosexuality are changing, and as one manifestation of this change, homosexuality is beginning to be portrayed in children's literature. However, there are some interesting elements in the portrayal. Whenever a physical encounter between two people of the same sex (always male) is depicted, it is described so vaguely that it is difficult for the reader to understand what is taking place. Moreover, just as teenagers who participate in premarital relationships repent, so, too, those who might have become homosexuals go straight in the end. Indeed, in *The Man Without a Face* the adult character must die in payment for the role he has played. As Barbara Wersba suggests in the article "Sexuality in Books for Children," such books appear to be representative of the New Sex, but in their condemnation of unconventional sexual behavior, they actually conform to the Old Morality.

## New sexuality—new morality

In the books discussed in the previous section, we have seen characters defy the confines of conventional sexual behavior. Female characters momentarily sidestep the double standard to participate in premarital sexual relations. A few male characters become involved (or worry that they are involved) in homosexual encounters. In all these books, however, such controversial sexual behavior conforms in the end to previous traditions and former taboos. All unwed girls who make love get pregnant, are submitted to a catalogue of horrors, and heartily repent their wayward behavior. All male characters who tenuously move along the perimeter of a homosexual relationship, are assured, by the book's conclusion, that they are "normal," that their homosexual experience has been a fleeting phase of their development. In short, any rebellion against traditional sexual mores is punished, at times with draconian measures, and is, by the book's conclusion, thoroughly put down.

Only a few books describe unconventional sexual behavior in a nonjudgmental manner. Two such books, *It's Not What You Expect* (1973) and *Mom, the Wolf Man and Me* (1972), are by Norma Klein.

*Mom, the Wolf Man and Me* begins with a school Father's Day celebration at which Brett knows she will have to explain that her father is absent not because of a divorce but because her mother decided not to get married. Actually Brett feels very comfortable living with only one parent, and she loves her mother, a photographer, who takes Brett with her whenever she can. At a peace march on Washington, Brett's mother meets Theodore, whom Brett nicknames the Wolf Man because of his huge size, his bright red hair, and his Irish wolfhound. Brett worries that the relationship between Theodore and her mother will become serious and that her life-style will have to change.

One Sunday morning she wakes up to find the Wolf Man in his pajamas in the apartment, a meeting that leads Brett to ask her mother if she's having sexual relations with Theodore. There is a funny scene in which Brett explains to her grandmother that her mother has these sexual relations not because she wants a baby but because she enjoys them. Eventually Brett's mother and Theodore do get married, but not before Norma Klein has had time to offer a portrayal of an unwed mother quite happily and competently raising her child.

*It's Not What You Expect* is about the surprising summer of Car and Oliver, fourteen-year-old twins. The twins are immersed in their summer project of establishing and operating a French restaurant for which Oliver is the gourmet cook and Car the maître d'hôtel. During the summer the twins discover that their eighteen-year-old brother, Robert, and his girl friend, Sara Lee, are expecting a baby. Although the couple eventually plan to marry, now is just not the right time for a child. They both have plans for further schooling, and Sara Lee's goals involve becoming an architect. They consider an abortion as the best solution to their problem.

Car is troubled by the events of the summer and she finally confides in her mother, who, when she learns of Sara Lee's abortion, reacts with empathy and concern:

"I'm glad she's okay. . . . Poor thing, though. . . . You know, your generation is lucky, Car, really they are. Things are so much more open now. I remember when I had an abortion, the doctor was so nasty and cold. He made me feel so rotten, like I'd committed some heinous act. It was so humiliating. That was worse than the pain of it really."[35]

In these books the condemnation usually associated with premarital sexual relations, illegitimacy, and abortion are absent. However, the challenging of conventional morality is somewhat distant and removed. In both books it has taken place long before the story begins, and in both cases involves not the central character but her mother instead. Rosemary Wells's fine recent novel *None of the Above* (1974) offers a more immediate and a more dramatic challenge to traditional sexual mores.

*None of the Above* describes the gradual change in Marcia, an unambitious, submissive girl who, when her father remarries, finds herself in an alien environment—one that is, both intellectually and socially, far tenser and more demanding then any she has ever known. Used to reading movie magazines, watching the dating game on television, and giving a half-hearted effort to the general course in high school, she finds her new siblings busy with skiing, horseback riding, and intensive studying, their goals set on the most demanding and prestigious colleges. Marcia changes, succumbs to the driving nature of the household, and leaves the general course for the college track, where she achieves an outstanding record.

Although Marcia succumbs to the intellectual pressure, socially she defies the expectations of her new home. She begins dating Raymond Siroken, who looks like Robert Redford and is one of the high school's most popular and reputedly fastest boys. Raymond takes her to a party and then as a matter of course leads her to an upstairs bedroom. Afraid to say anything foolish, Marcia remains quiet while he lies on top of her and takes a foil package out of his pocket telling her that they are going to go all the way. She is completely unaroused, almost repelled, and Raymond, angry and frustrated, stops. Marcia continues to date Raymond and to submit to the rough violent bedroom sessions, although Raymond never again takes out the foil packet. As their relationship develops, Raymond and Marcia become more compassionate toward one another, and she understands the problem with their lovemaking:

"It's . . . me," he said, "I'm . . . it's my . . . fault. I can't."

"You . . . can't what?"

"Look . . . I'm not . . . I'm not a real man, I . . ." but he couldn't explain. . . .

"There's a word for . . . what I am. I know very well what it is. I can't say it. . . ."

"It'll get better, Raymie. I know it will." He said nothing.

"We'll work it out, you'll see," she said, looking questioningly at the cowlick in his hair. "And I won't leave," she added.[36]

Their lovemaking becomes more tender and sensual, and, as Marcia promises, they do work things out, Marcia using the pill to protect herself from becoming pregnant. By the novel's conclusion Marcia must choose between Sarah Lawrence or an early marriage to Raymond. Although one may question the wisdom of Marcia's choice, or indeed the appropriateness of either of her choices, one senses no condemnation of her behavoir. There is no premarital pregnancy, no ostracism, no forced early marriage. Quite simply Marcia chooses her own course of sexual behavior, and she uses a contemporary form of birth control to avoid pregnancy.

One book dealing with homosexuality also belongs in the category of "New Sexuality—New Morality." Sandra Scoppettone's *Trying Hard to Hear You* (1974) describes one summer in the life of Camilla Crawford when she develops a crush on a young college student, Phil Chrystie—until she is shocked to learn that Phil is in love with her best friend, Jeff. The two boys are discovered kissing in the bushes at a party, and the reaction of the other teenagers is disgust and fury. A pattern of discrimination begins. The boys are ostracized, and then there are the ugly jokes, culminating in a violent scene in which a gang of teenagers try to tar and feather the two young men. By the book's conclusion, Phil has died in a car crash, and whether the tragedy was by accident or intent remains unresolved.

The story is told from Camilla's point of view, a compassionate girl trying hard to understand something with which she has never before been confronted. Her initial ignorance and revulsion gradually changes as she grows to accept the legitimacy of the feelings Phil and Jeff have for one another. She concludes that the two boys were not doing any harm—that the only harm was done by others too biased and closed to accept their relationship.

This book differs from the others on homosexuality in that it does not leave the reader wondering. The style is dignified, tasteful, and

explicit, leaving no doubt that the boys are homosexuals. Moreover, Jeff is not killed and he does not change his behavior. Rather, he is left alone to survive and pursue his own lifestyle.

Currently there is something of a sexual revolution in children's literature. There are nonfiction books that explain to three-year-olds how babies are made. There are books that portray, at times judgmentally, at times without moralizing, premarital sexual relations and homosexuality. And there is confusion and controversy surrounding the appearance of such books and concern over their appropriateness for children.

It occurs to me that what we're talking about is political. We're talking about the control of one group of people by another group of people: namely, children by adults. We are not merely discussing what children should read about sex, but what they should do about sex—and the fascism implied by this is a bit mind-boggling. Yet somehow children tolerate us and go on doing the same things generation after generation: which is, reading those "forbidden" books, and indulging in sexual activity—and surviving.

*Barbara Wersba*[37]

I confess I am thinking in terms of shielding children from unnecessary, premature, unhealthy sexual stimulation, beyond their present maturity and capacity to manage. Just when and how that capacity arrives cannot be defined for all children. Their exposure to sexual behavior in the omnipresent media most certainly hastens their information and their sophistication. Whether it hastens their maturity is an unanswered question. So also is the question of the effect of these sexual exposures on their healthy growth in attitudes and perceptions. This applies to books, and other mass media.

*Josette Frank*[38]

These quotes, each written by a woman who works closely with children and books, reflect differing positions on the issue of sexuality in children's books and they give some indication of the controversy surrounding this whole topic. Donald Bissett, a reviewer of children's books for *Elementary English*, offers a comment, one of confusion and guarded optimism, that perhaps reflects the feelings of many teachers, librarians, and parents:

Where all this new freedom in children's books is leading is hard to predict. It's hard to read the books and respond calmly to them. It's hard to try them out with children in today's atmosphere of criticism of even the mention of sex in books for younger people. Let's hope the breaking down of taboos will pave the way for impressive books that will contribute to children's development of realistic, healthy adjustment to their sexuality.[39]

## NOTES

1. Arlene Uslander, "Everything You Always Wanted to Know About Sex Education," *Learning*, October 1974, 34–41.
2. Lloyd Campbell, "Sex Education: Let's Get on With It," *Phi Delta Kappa*, *55*, no. 4 (December 1973), 245.
3. *What Shall I Tell My Child?*, New York, Crown, 1966.
4. Sidonie Matsner Gruenberg, *The Wonderful Story of How You Were Born*, Symeon Shimin, illus., Garden City, N.Y., Doubleday, 1952.
5. Margaret Sheffield, *Where Do Babies Come From?*, Sheila Bewley, illus., New York, Knopf, 1972.
6. Margaret Sheffield, *Where Do Babies Come From?*, Sheila Bewley, illus., abridged in *Ms.*, *1*, no. 11 May 1973), 73–76.
7. Peter Mayle, *Where Did I Come From?*, Arthur Robins, illus., Secaucus, N.J., Lyle Stuart, 1973.
8. Sheila Cole, "What's Wrong with Sex Education Books for Kids," *Ms.*, *1*, no. 11 (May 1973), 70–72+.
9. Frances Bruce Strain, *Being Born*, rev. ed., New York, Appleton-Century-Crofts, 1954, p. 34.
10. Ibid.
11. Eric W. Johnson, *Love and Sex in Plain Language*, rev. ed. New York, Bantam (Pathfinder Edition), 1967, p. 77.
12. Wardell Pomeroy, *Girls and Sex*, New York, Dell (Delacorte Press), 1969, p. 27.
13. Siv Widerberg, *The Kids Own XYZ of Love and Sex*, trans. by Irene Morris, Michael Crimsdale, illus., New York, Stein and Day, 1973 (2–8).
14. Uslander, op. cit., p. 38.
15. Ibid.
16. Louise Fitzhugh, *The Long Secret*, New York, Harper & Row, 1965, pp. 92–97.
17. Judy Blume, *Are You There God? It's Me, Margaret*, Scarsdale, N.Y., Bradbury Press, 1970, p. 50.
18. Judy Blume, *Deenie*, Scarsdale, N.Y., Bradbury Press, 1973, pp. 90–93.
19. Judy Blume, *Then Again Maybe I Won't*, Scarsdale, N.Y. Bradbury Press, 1971, p. 50.
20. Ibid.
21. Betty Cavanna, *The Boy Next Door*, New York, Morrow, 1956.
22. Beverly Cleary, *Fifteen*, Joe and Beth Krush, illus., New York, Morrow, 1956.
23. Betty Cavanna, *A Girl Can Dream*, Harold A. Minton, illus., Philadelphia, Westminster Press, 1948.
24. Rosamond du Jardin, *Practically Seventeen*, Philadelphia, Lippincott, 1943.
25. Ann Kalkhoff, "Innocent Children or Innocent Librarians," *Library Journal*, *97*, no. 18 (October 1972), 3430–3434.
26. Al Muller, "Thirty Popular Adolescent Novels: A Content Analysis," *English Journal*, September 1974, pp. 97–99.
27. Nora Stirling, *You Would If You Loved Me*, New York, Evans, 1969, p. 25.
28. Nat Hentoff, "Getting Inside Jazz Country," *Horn Book Magazine*, October 1966, pp. 528–532.
29. Lou Willett Staneck, "The Maturation of the Junior Novel: From Gestation to the Pill," *Library Journal*, *97*, no. 22 (December 15, 1972), 4051.
30. Maureen Daly, *Seventeenth Summer*, Jay Robinson, illus. New York, Dodd, Mead, 1942, pp. 50–51.
31. Ibid., p. 134.
32. Mary Stolz, *The Sea Gulls Woke Me*, New York, Harper & Row, 1951, p. 153.
33. Isabelle Holland, "Tilting at Taboos," *Horn Book Magazine*, *49*, no. 3, (June 1973), 301–302.
34. Isabelle Holland, *The Man Without A Face*, Philadelphia, Lippincott, 1972, p. 142.
35. Norma Klein, *It's Not What You Expect*, New York, Pantheon Books, 1973, p. 115.
36. Rosemary Wells, *None of the Above*, New York, Dial Press, 1974, p. 152.
37. Barbara Wersba, "Sexuality in Books," *Library Journal*, *98* (February 15, 1973), 620.
38. Josette Frank, "Sexuality in Books," *Library Journal*, *98* (February 15, 1973), 623.
39. Donald Bissett, "Books in the Classroom," *Elementary English*, *51*, no. 5 (May 1974), 656.

# BIBLIOGRAPHY*

## For younger children

* Unlike most of the bibliographies in this book, the bibliography on sexuality contains nonfiction as well as fiction entries. The entries are meant to be representative rather than inclusive.

ANDRY, ANDREW, and STEVEN SCHEPP. *How Babies Are Made*, Blake Hampton, illus., Time-Life Books, 1968.

BENDICK, JEANNE. *What Made You You?*, McGraw-Hill, 1971 (3–5).

GORDON, SOL. *Girls Are Girls and Boys Are Boys*, Frank C. Smith, illus., John Day, 1974.

GRUENBERG, SIDONIE MATSNER. *The Wonderful Story of How You Were Born*, rev. ed., Symeon Shimin, illus., Doubleday, 1970 (3–5).

HOLLAND, VIKI. *We Are Having a Baby*, Scribner, 1972 (K–1).

KNUDSEN, PER HOLM. *The True Story of How Babies Are Made*, Children's Press, 1973.

MAYLE, PETER. *Where Did I Come From?*, Arthur Robins, illus., Lyle Stuart, 1973 (2–4).

MCBRIDE, WILL. *Show Me! A Picture Book of Sex for Parents and Children*, explanatory text by Dr. Helga Fleischhauer-Hardt, adapted by Hilary Davies. St. Martin's Press, 1975.

SHEFFIELD, MARGARET. *Where Do Babies Come From?*, Sheila Bewley, illus., Knopf, 1972 (preschool–2).

SHOWERS, PAUL, and KAY SPERRY SHOWERS. *Before You Were A Baby*, Ingrid Fetz., illus., Crowell, 1968 (K–3).

———. *A Baby Starts to Grow*, Crowell, 1969 (K–3).

STEPTOE, JOHN. *My Special Best Words*, Viking Press, 1974 (Preschool–2).

## For children in the middle and upper grades

BLUME, JUDY. *Are You There God? It's Me, Margaret*, Bradbury Press, 1970 (5–7).

———. *Deenie*, Bradbury Press, 1973 (5–7).

———. *Then Again, Maybe I Won't*, Bradbury Press, 1971 (5–7).

CLEAVER, VERA, and BILL CLEAVER. *I Would Rather Be a Turnip*, Lippincott, 1971 (5–7).

CLIFTON, LUCILLE. *The Times They Used to Be*, Susan Jeschler, illus., Holt, Rinehart & Winston, 1974 (5+).

CRAIG, MARGARET. *It Could Happen to Anyone*, Crowell, 1961 (6–9).

DAY, BETH, and MARGARET LILEY. *The Secret World of the Baby*, photos by Lennart Wilsson, Susan Szasz, and others. Random House, 1968 (5+).

DIZENZO, PATRICIA. *Phoebe*, McGraw-Hill, 1970 (9+).

DONOVAN, JOHN. *I'll Get There. It Better Be Worth the Trip*, Harper & Row, 1969 (6–9).

EYERLY, JEANNETTE. *Bonnie Jo, Go Home*, Lippincott, 1972 (7+).

FELSEN, HENRY GREGOR. *Two and the Town*, Morrow, 1967.

FITZHUGH, LOUISE. *The Long Secret*, Harper & Row, 1965 (6–8).

GORDON, SOL. *Facts About Sex: A Basic Guide*, Vivien Cohen, illus., Day, 1973 (7+).

———. *Facts About VD*, Day, 1973 (7+).

GRUENBERG, BENJAMIN, and SIDONIE M. GRUENBERG. *The Wonderful Story of You*, Lee J. James, illus., Garden City Books, 1960.

HALL, LYN. *Sticks and Stones*, Follett, 1972 (7–10).

HEAD, ANN. *Mr. and Mrs. BoJo Jones*, Putnam, 1967 (9+).

HOLLAND, ISABELLE. *The Man Without a Face*, Lippincott, 1972 (6–9).

JOHNSON, ERIC. *Love and Sex in Plain Language*, rev. ed., Edward Smith, illus., Lippincott, 1974 (7–12).

———, and CORINNE JOHNSON. *Love and Sex and Growing Up*, Viser-Direction Studio, illus., Lippincott, 1970 (5–7).

———. *Sex: Telling It Straight*, Lippincott, 1970 (7+).

———. *V.D.*, Lippincott, 1973 (7+).

JORDAN, JUNE. *His Own Where*, Crowell, 1971 (7–9).

KLEIN, NORMA. *It's Not What You Expect*, Pantheon Books, 1973 (7+).

———. *Mom, the Wolf Man and Me*, Pantheon Books, 1972 (4–8).

LOEBEL, SUZANNE. *Conception, Contraception: A New Look*, McGraw-Hill, 1974 (9+).

MADISON, WINIFRED. *Growing Up in a Hurry*, Little, Brown, 1973 (7+).

NEUFELD, JOHN. *Freddy's Book.* Random House, 1973 (4–7).

POMEROY, WARDELL. *Boys and Sex,* Dell (Delacorte Press), 1968 (6–8).

———. *Girls and Sex,* Dell (Delacorte Press), 1969 (8+).

PORTAL, COLETTE. *The Beauty of Birth,* adapted by Guy Daniels. Knopf, 1971 (4+).

SCOPPETTONE, SANDRA. *Trying Hard to Hear You,* Harper & Row, 1974 (7–12).

SHERBURNE, ZOA. *Too Bad About the Haines Girl,* Morrow, 1967 (8–12).

STIRLING, NORA. *You Would If You Loved Me,* Evans, 1969 (6+).

TERRIS, SUSAN. *Plague of Frogs,* Doubleday, 1973 (6–10).

TOWNSEND, JOHN ROWE. *Good Night, Prof, Dear,* Lippincott, 1970 (7–9).

———. *The Summer People,* Lippincott, 1972 (9+).

WERSBA, BARBARA. *Run Softly, Go Fast,* Atheneum, 1970 (8–10).

WELLS, ROSEMARY. *None of the Above,* Dial Press, 1974 (8+).

WIDERBERG, SIV. *The Kids' Own XYZ of Love and Sex,* trans. by Irene Morris, Michael Grimsdale, illus., Neville Spearman, 1971 (2–8).

WINTHROP, ELIZABETH. *A Little Demonstration of Affection,* Harper & Row, 1975 (7+).

ZINDEL, PAUL. *My Darling, My Hamburger,* Harper & Row, 1969 (8+).

Hands lie heavy on my lap—vein ridged, spotted. Once they were like white birds in graceful flight over keys of a piano, stirring savory pots of food, gentling a crying child. Agile, useful, they were never still. Now they too are done with reaching out. They are folded, inward. . . .

"I know; I know," they say. "There are problems with being old." But they do not know. Everyone has been a child. All can understand through muffled memory how childhood was. But none has been old except those who are that now.

Who can speak for the old? And who speaks to us? . . . No one looks at me—at me, into my eyes, into the core of me. It is as if I am like all who have lived too long, a being to be tolerated or bypassed or humored.

*"An Old Woman Speaks"*[1]

# 3
# Growing Old in the Literature of the Young

These words, written by an old woman, are her statement of what it means to age and her plea that younger members of society take time to speak to the elderly, to empathize with them, and to accept the realization that growing old is part of the total life experience.

Despite such entreaties, the younger generations often do not have time or do not want to have time to listen to the elderly. Too often the young and the middle-aged, immersed in the business of living, raising families, moving ahead in careers and shouldering various responsibilities, listen casually to pleas such as this old woman's, but are essentially deaf to their meaning. And too often the young and the middle-aged perpetrate a variety of ploys and maneuvers that deny the process of aging and help them hide from its reality. Simone de Beauvoir notes that, "Society looks upon old age as a shameful secret that it is unseemly to mention."[2] She tells of a comic strip artist who was ordered to redraw an entire series because he included a pair of grandparents among his characters. And she tells of peoples' reactions when they learned that she was writing a book about old age, reactions that grew monotonously similar: "What an extraordinary notion! But you aren't old! . . . What a dismal subject."[3]

Young people and adults find it immensely difficult to grasp the reality, in anything more than a purely intellectual fashion, that they will one day grow old. When young people are asked about their futures, most set the upper limits of their life span at sixty years. They cannot fathom they may become older than that; they assume that they will die first.[4] Thus the experience of growing old is one very often denied. "It will not happen to me, or at any rate, I will not think about its happening to me" is a common response. So the aging and elderly are forgotten, pushed aside, and when those not yet old do take time to consider the elderly, their reactions are often negative and stereotyped. Studies show that society views the aged as physically infirm, mentally deteriorated, sexually inactive, unhappy, isolated, and useless.[5] Although much evidence indicates that these stereotypes have little or no basis in fact and that they apply to only a minority of persons now over sixty-five in the United States, the elderly themselves have come to believe the stereotypes. They too cite old age as the most undesirable time of life; they too share in society's worship of the young.

Contemporary society's denial of aging, its refusal to see and understand the difficulties and problems of those who grow old results in abysmal care afforded the elderly in the United States, too many of whom are condemned to poverty, to ill health, to loneliness, and to a callous stripping away of dignity. In our society of planned obsolesence, we exchange old models of cars, houses, television sets, and appliances for newer, more up-to-date versions. Getting rid of things that are old (unless they have become so unusually old that we call them antiques) is part of the pattern of our times. And so, albeit with some attempt at humaneness and subtlety, we also discard old

people. Frequently the elderly are forced into mandatory retirement at age sixty-five or age sixty-eight, and, because of our small living units that have room to house only the nuclear family, they are denied comfortable inclusion in the extended-family pattern of earlier times.

However, as population characteristics shift, the assumed blindness that refuses to see the elderly becomes a state more and more difficult to maintain. Because of medical advances, the elderly have been growing in numbers at a rate much faster than other segments of the population. Since 1870 the total population has become five times as large, the middle-aged population has become nine times as large, and the older population has become seventeen times as large. In 1973 approximately one in ten Americans was sixty-five or older, a percentage that promises to increase until by the year 2000 the elderly in the United States will number at least 28 million.[6]

As numbers increase, so do problems. In our society growing old means becoming detached from two primary institutions that give form and meaning to adult life—the nuclear family and the occupational system. The elderly often are involved in the emotional turmoil of two major adjustments, widowhood and retirement. They may also be required to cope with loneliness, physical infirmity, and limited financial means. Of the 7.2 million families with heads of sixty-five or over in 1970, half had incomes of less than $5053. Of the 5.8 million elderly living alone or with nonrelatives, half had incomes of less than $1951. Despite such indications of poverty, society's lack of concern is evident. In 1970 the United States spent more than $5 billion on cosmetics and hair dyes and only $1.86 billion on assistance for the elderly.[7] Although in 1970 only 5 percent of the elderly lived in nursing homes, the care provided by such institutions ranged from excellent to appallingly inadequate.

Thus growing old too often involves a gradual loss of dignity and of much that gives meaning to life—job, family, friends, health, sense of esteem and well-being. The profound devastation of such loss is reflected in the fact that the suicide rate in our population is highest among the elderly. The gap between scientific advance that enables people to live longer and the level of societal concern and compassion that gives quality to extended life appears to be appallingly great.

There is a story about Buddha, when he was still Prince Siddartha, that tells of his escape from the fine palace where his father kept him. During the prince's travels through the countryside, he met an old man so infirm as to be capable only of hobbling forward slowly with the aid of his cane. Prince Siddartha was amazed at this sight, and the charioteer explained to him what it meant to become old. "It is the world's pity," cried Siddartha, "that weak and ignorant beings, drunk with the vanity of youth, do not behold old age!" The prince hurried back to the palace, struck with the realization that his body too would one day be so transformed by age.[8]

Siddartha, unlike many too busy to take note of the elderly, stopped to consider the profound reality of aging and to accept, both emotionally and intellectually, old age as part of life's totality. This is an acceptance that Simone de Beauvoir says we all must achieve: "Let us recognize ourselves in this old man or in that old woman. . . . And when it is done, we will no longer acquiesce in the misery of the last age; we will no longer be indifferent, because we shall feel concerned, as indeed we are."[9]

In our analysis of children's books we examine the frequency with which elderly characters are depicted and the nature of the various portrayals. We also attempt to judge whether current literature provides children with some awareness that old age is part of life's totality and that there must be care and

concern about the quality of life experienced by the nation's elderly. We first examine folk literature, then proceed to picture books, and finally to realistic fiction for children in the middle and upper grades.

## The elderly in folktales

The basic purpose of folktales, carried from country to country, transmitted from generation to generation, is to entertain. Nevertheless, folktales also present themes and often express the values of the different cultures from which they emerged. Characters in folktales are often drawn as having but one dimension—as being completely good or completely evil. Beautiful young girls are usually sweet, obedient, kind, and loving; heroes are handsome, brave, strong, and kind; stepmothers are ugly, cross, and sometimes dangerously evil. Elderly characters who emerge in folktales also fit into clearly categorized patterns. In order to identify these patterns we analyzed Virginia Haviland's fairy tale collections from different countries. The elderly character types that we discuss in the following pages are based on the patterns that appeared in Haviland's collections supplemented on occasion by folktales from other sources.

### Elderly parents

Some folktales present childless elderly parents who long for a boy or girl even of the most unusual nature, to bring happiness to their old age. "One Inch Fellow" in Haviland's *Favorite Fairy Tales Told in Japan* (1967) is representative of this pattern. It tells of a good-hearted elderly couple who pray for a child, even one as small as a thumb, and one day a cloud brings them a tiny boy just that size. The elderly couple call their son One Inch Fellow. When One Inch Fellow grows to young manhood, he leaves his parents to make a name for himself, a quest he achieves by saving a great lord's daughter from a huge monster called an Oni. The small fellow's brave deeds win him fame and fortune, and his elderly parents are happy sharing in his wealth and honor.

A similar tale, again from *Favorite Fairy Tales Told in Japan*, is "Momotaro or the Story of the Son of a Peach." Again an elderly couple sorrows because they have no child. Their lamentation is heard, and they are given a beautiful child who steps out of a large peach. He eventually goes off to seek his fortune, and conquers a land of devils. His elderly mother and father are well provided for and take great joy in their son's accomplishments.

## Wise old helpers

Frequently in folktales old men and old women make brief appearances as helpful beings, sometimes possessing magic powers, who provide direction for a troubled hero or heroine. One such elderly helper emerges in "The Flying Ship" found in *Favorite Fairy Tales Told in Russia* (1961). Three sons, upon hearing that the tsar will give his daughter in marriage to anyone who can build a flying ship, leave home to try their luck. The youngest son is the most foolish of the three and it appears most unlikely that he will be able to win the princess. When he agrees to share his dry bread and water with an old man he meets during his travels, he is amazed to find that his meager lunch has become white rolls and savory meats. The old man gives him instructions for obtaining the magical flying ship. When the ship appears, the youngest son flies away in it, gathers a company of men with unusual skills, and with the help of his uniquely competent followers, the lad wins the tsar's daughter.

In many other folktales from different countries, old people help confused heroes and heroines reach seemingly unattainable goals. In "Constantes and the Dragon," in *Favorite Fairy Tales Told in Greece* (1970), Constantes relies on the advice of an old woman to outwit a formidable dragon, to steal the creature's diamond coverlet, his horse and bell, and finally to capture the dragon himself. "Perifool," in *Favorite Fairy Tales Told in Scotland* (1963), presents an intrepid youngest daughter who, with the aid of an old woman, discovers that the name of the fairy lad who has turned her wool into cloth is "Perifool." Through this discovery the young princess outwits a cruel giant and saves her two older sisters.

## Competence in age

In a few folktales the problems of aging are touched upon, and the cleverness and bravery of the elderly in meeting these problems are stressed. "The Bremen Town Musicians," in *Favorite Fairy Tales Told in Germany* (1959) tells of a group of animals, a donkey, a dog, a cat, and a rooster, about to be killed by their owners because they have grown old. The animals decide to run away and travel together to Bremen where they plan to become musicians. Along the way they prove themselves clever enough to outwit a band of robbers and to win for themselves a fine feast and a comfortable home.

Kuaku Ananse, the "spider man," an elderly figure in African folk literature, demonstrates skill and cunning. Gail Haley's *A Story, a Story*, the 1971 Caldecott winner, shows Ananse using his wits to buy the Sky God's stories. The Sky God tells Ananse that the price of his stories is Osebo, the leopard of-the-terrible-teeth; Mnboro, the hornet-who-stings-like-fire; and Mnoatia, the fairy-whom-men-never-see. When Ananse says he will gladly pay the price, the Sky God chuckles, "How can a weak old man like you, so small, so small, so small, pay my price?"[10] Not by

brute strength and force, but rather by using his wits, Ananse quite easily manages to capture the leopard, the hornet, and the fairy. As his reward, Ananse takes the Sky God's stories, now called "Spider Stories," back to earth, where they are scattered to the edges of the world.

Margaret Hodges' *The Wave* (1964), illustrated with dramatic vividness by Blair Lent, is an adaptation of an ancient Japanese tale. It emphasizes the wisdom and courage of Ojiisan, the wealthy elder of the village, who burns his rice fields to warn the villagers of an impending tidal wave and to call them to refuge in his home, safe on the mountain. His foresight and his sacrifice save 400 lives, and

in return a temple is built that is said to still be standing in honor of the brave old farmer.

## The old fool

In contrast to the folktales showing competence in age, there is also folk literature about elderly sillies or numbskulls, characters who are ridiculously absurd in their approach to solving life's probelms. It is interesting that many of these silly characters are old women. Often they seek roundabout solutions to simple problems. In the cumulative folktale "The Old Woman and Her Pig" an old woman is confronted with an obstinate pig who will not go over the stile. Rather than carry the pig over, she seeks the aid of various passersby. Finally the pig does get over the stile, but not until a ludicrous sequence of events has been put into motion.

As soon as the cat had lapped up the milk, the cat began to kill the rat; the rat began to gnaw the rope; the rope began to hang the butcher; the butcher began to kill the ox; the ox began to drink the water; the water began to quench the fire; the fire began to burn the stick; the stick began to beat the dog; the dog began to bite the pig; the little pig in fright jumped over the stile; and so the old woman got home that night.[11]

A stingy, foolishly gullible old woman appears in "The Old Woman and the Tramp," found in *Favorite Fairy Tales Told in Sweden* (1966). A clever tramp comes to the home of a miserly old woman and begs for food and shelter. Grudgingly, she lets him in to sleep on the floor. After assessing the old woman's wealth, he cunningly tells her that he plans to make soup from a nail. As he cooks the nail in a pot of water, he gradually persuades her to drop in some meal, some salted beef, po-

tatoes, barley, and milk. Eventually a savory broth is bubbling on the hearth, and the old woman is so delighted that she brings out meat and wine and bread to complete the meal. The next morning, as she bids the tramp good-bye, the old woman pays him for teaching her the secret of making nail soup.

In "The Old Woman and the Fish," also from *Favorite Fairy Tales Told in Sweden*, an old woman's foolishness turns a splendid opportunity into a disastrous occurrence. An old woman promises to let a fish go free in return for three wishes. Without much forethought she wishes that her pails would go by themselves to the well. Thinking of her dull ax, she wishes that whatever she strikes will break right off, and, remembering that the material she is weaving is not long enough, she wishes that whatever she pulls will become

Favorite Fairy Tales Told in Sweden

long. When her pails begin to climb up the hill by themselves, she is so pleased that she slaps herself across the knees, and, in accordance with her second wish, her legs fall off. She begins to cry at her terrible predicament, and as she blows her nose, her third wish comes true and her nose grows strangely long. The story concludes as the incapacitated old woman sits immobilized on the lid of the well.

## The mean old witch

In several fairy tales elderly women emerge as evil crones, hags, and witches, eager to perpetrate some villainy on the hero or heroine. One of the most well-known old women in folk literature is the witch of the gingerbread house in "Hansel and Gretel," found in Haviland's *Favorite Fairy Tales Told in Germany*. When the two children, Hansel and Gretel, are abandoned by their parents, they wander lost in a wood until they come upon a house made of gingerbread. An old, old woman, leaning on a crutch, hobbles out of the house and comforts the children, promising to take care of them. Actually she plans to eat them, but she is outwitted when Gretel shoves her in the oven, and the two children escape with her treasure.

In these folktales not only the wickedness but also the hideous appearance of witches, hags, and crones is stressed. For example, C. S. Evans in *Sleeping Beauty* emphasizes the grotesque physical appearance of the old fairy who comes to the christening to put a curse on the newborn princess:

There came an old woman bent almost double with age, her gray head with matted hair hung deep between her shoulders. Her face was white and twisted with anger, and her green eyes flashed spitefully. . . . The old crone muttered and mouthed over her food, now and again smiling to herself as though she were cherishing some secret and evil triumph.[12]

It is pertinent that the one to soften the old crone's curse so that the princess does not die but instead sleeps for one hundred years is the *youngest* fairy of all those assembled.

One might conclude that, given the stereotyped nature of many characters in fairy stories, the portrayal of the elderly is a relatively varied one: they are drawn as childless parents; helpful interveners; competent characters using cunning and wit to achieve their ends; numbskulls and sillies; and witches, hags, and crones with evil powers and evil intentions. However, it seems that one role old people assume in folk literature has been far more powerful than the others in capturing the imagination of young readers. When we asked students in an elementary school and students in a children's literature course to mention roles that elderly people played in fairy stories, the responses were surprisingly similar: "They are witches," said the students at both age levels unhesitatingly, noting such stories as "Snow White," "Sleeping Beauty," and "Hansel and Gretel." The image of the old woman as a witch is dynamic, pervasive, and apparently obscures other roles the elderly assume in folk literature.

## The elderly in picture books

### Bridge across generations

It has often been said that there exists a special bond, a unique alliance between the very old and the very young. Unlike the middle generations, immersed in employement and raising families, the oldest and the youngest in society have more time to spend as they wish, and more time to share with one another. This feeling of closeness between children and the elderly is one of the most common themes occurring in picture books that include elderly characters.

Many picture books present grandparents as

invariably wise, comforting, and understanding; even more so than parents. One such book is Charlotte Zolotow's *William's Doll* (1972). Young William wants a doll, a desire that gives rise to worry and consternation among family and friends. "Don't be a creep!" William's brother tells him. "Sissy, sissy, sissy!" taunts the boy next door. William's father gets him a basketball and electric trains, toys that William loves—but he still wants a doll. Finally, grandmother comes to visit, and she is someone who understands. She immediately goes out and buys William a doll, explaining to his father that William needs a doll to love and to cuddle and to take care of so that he will know how to be a father one day.

There are a number of other close relationships depicted between grandmother and grandchild. In Martha Alexander's brief picture book *The Story Grandmother Told* (1969), Lisa asks grandmother to tell her a story. However, Lisa is so excited about the story that grandmother ends up listening while Lisa tells it herself. The pictures present a very warm relationship between a black child and her grandmother. Another warm relationship is portrayed in Helen Buckley's *Grandmother and I* (1961). In this book a little girl feels totally peaceful and comforted as she rocks on grandmother's lap.

Grandfathers also are shown enjoying a warm rapport with their grandchildren. *Grandfather and I* (1959) is about a slow, relaxed walk a young boy takes with his grandfather. The old man and the boy take time to stop and look at things, to examine a snail, to pat horses, and to watch a squirrel climb a tree. Everything about them is in a hurry—cars, buses, trains. Mothers and fathers hurry, and so do sisters and brothers, but this grandfather and grandson always take their time.

> Grandfather and I
> never hurry.
> We walk along
> and walk along
> And stop . . .
> And look . . .
> Just as long
> as we like.[13]

Barbara Borack's *Grandpa* (1967) describes some treasured rituals that a little girl and her grandfather share. Every morning, grandpa hides in the same place, and the girl always finds him. He snips off her nose and hides it between his fingers; she sits on his leg and they play horse. When the little girl goes away, grandma and grandpa stand on either side of her and give her a sandwich kiss. The sense of enjoyment and affection that characterize the relationship of grandfather and granddaughter is conveyed with warmth and humor.

Grandpa

## Problems

In a few picture books the close relationship between grandparents and grandchildren is disrupted by illness or death. Joan Lexau's *Benjie on His Own* (1964) vividly describes a young black child's feelings of worry, helplessness, and fear when he finds that his grandmother is sick. When Benjie's grandmother does not come to pick him up at school as she usually does, he fearfully makes his way home alone, managing to escape the hassling of some of the bigger boys. Benjie finds his grandmother sick in their apartment, and he calls for an ambulance. The frightened child does not know whether to stay outside and wait for the ambulance or to run back upstairs and help Granny. He finds the dilemma so disturbing he begins to pray, and then he just opens his mouth and yells, "Help! Please somebody HELP!" A woman goes upstairs to wait with Granny until the ambulance finally comes. Benjie watches as Granny is carried away. "Don't you worry about this old lady. We'll take good care of her," one of the ambulance men assures Benjie. "Who you calling an old lady?"[14] Granny responds crossly, trying to cheer Benjie up. Benjie's feelings of worry and frustration about his grandmother's illness are movingly conveyed.

Three other books that describe a grandchild's attempts to cope with the illness of a grandparent are Janice Mae Udry's *Mary Jo's Grandmother* (1970), Ruth Sonneborn's *I Love Gram* (1971), and Lynn Schoettle's *Grandpa's Long Red Underwear* (1972).

Some researchers describe the unique closeness between the old and the young, and others note that children harbor many negative associations concerning old age. In one study children characterized the aged as "scary," "mean," and "crabby," and they grouped old age with infancy as the worst pos-

sible times of life.[15] One story that recognizes this fear and hostility young children may feel for the elderly is Carol Carrick's *Old Mother Witch* (1975). David and his friends regard their neighbor, Mrs. Oliver, as a crank and call her "Old Mother Witch." They decide to play a Halloween trick on her, but when David approaches the house he finds her lying on the front porch. With David's help, Mrs. Oliver is rushed to the hospital. As a result of the experience, David regrets his former pranks and feels greater empathy and understanding for his elderly neighbor.

Findings from many other studies show that children harbor negative reactions toward the elderly not because of any characteristics of old age per se, but rather because old age is closely associated with dying. There are some fine picture books that may help children understand and accept the relationship between death and old age.

Charlotte Zolotow's *My Grandson Lew* (1974) takes the form of a nighttime conversation between a young boy and his mother. Lewis calls his mother in the middle of the night to tell her that he misses his grandfather and is waiting for him to visit again. Lewis tells his mother everything that he can remember about his grandfather—his scratchy beard, his blue eyes, the smells of powder and tobacco, and the warm feel of grandfather's pipe on his hands. Lewis' mother is very surprised. Unaware that her young son held these memories, she had not told him of his grandfather's death. Then the mother shares her memories of grandfather. She tells of his joy when Lewis was born, his skill in caring for the new baby, and his enjoyment in taking Lewis to museums with him. Sharing memories makes mother and son feel less lonely, for they realize that now they can remember grandfather together.

Sickness and death are touched upon at the picture book level, but other problems associated with old age are rarely mentioned. One of the few picture books that suggests that older people sometimes have to cope with loneliness is Mildred Kantrowitz' *Maxie* (1970). Maxie is an old woman who lives in three small rooms on the top floor of an old brownstone. She has lived there a long time, and her schedule, from raising her shades to collecting her milk bottles, is as regular as clockwork. One day, however, Maxie becomes despondent, certain that no one needs her and no one cares about her. The old woman is so sad she goes to bed and stays there all the next day. Soon her living room is filled with neighbors telling Maxie how important she is and how they all set their schedules by her various movements. This makes Maxie happy. She gets up, makes tea, and thinks about how many people are touched by her activities and her sounds. Although the book does bring out Maxie's loneliness, one might question whether its conclusion, Maxie's knowledge that she serves as a neighborhood clock, comprises a satisfying mode of contact between Maxie and the outside world.

*Matt's Grandfather* (1970) by Max Lundgren attempts to portray senility to young readers. Matt and his parents visit grandfather at a rest home on his eighty-fifth birthday. Matt is warned by his parents that grandfather sometimes forgets things and at times is almost like a baby again, unable to go out alone because he might get lost. Grandfather does not seem to understand who has come to visit him. When he learns that one of the visitors is his son, he is amazed. "I can't believe that. . . . He looks twice as old as I do. He even wears glasses. . . . Besides, he talks to me as if he were *my father*."[16] Matt is confused, for despite grandfather's lapses of memory, the elderly man seems contented and happy. The book ends leaving Matt and perhaps the book's readers confused as to the nature of senility.

## The best is yet to be

Although a few picture books attempt to portray the problems of the elderly, others stress the competence and wisdom that age brings. Elsa Beskow's *Pelle's New Suit* (1929) is a realistic picture book that portrays the skills of the elderly and stresses cooperation between the old and the young. Pelle is a Swedish boy who needs a new coat. He shears his lamb and gives the wool to his grandmother to card for him. In return, she asks that he pull the weeds in her garden. Then Pelle asks his other grandmother to spin the wool into yarn, and she agrees if he will tend her cows. The book pictures various other adults whose skills Pelle uses, and he provides them with labor in return. In the end, Pelle is outfitted in a fine new suit, one made by old and young working together.

In Liesel Moak Skorpen's *Old Arthur* (1972) both the difficulty and the worth of age are demonstrated, this time with an animal as the main character. Old Arthur is supposed to bring the cows home, hunt for rabbits, and guard hens, but the dog is tired, walks slowly, and often falls asleep, so he cannot carry out these tasks very effectively, any more. "What a dumb old dog," is the farmer's judgment, and he decides to shoot the animal. Arthur, aware of the farmer's plans, runs away. He tries to befriend a group of children, but he cannot run fast enough for their games, and they consider him worthless. He is picked up by the dog catcher and brought to the animal shelter where people pass him by as they look for puppies. Finally, one boy, William, decides he wants Old Arthur for his own. The dog catcher tries to dissuade him, "That dog is awful old. . . . He's not good to anyone any more."[17] William, however, is adamant, and it turns out that Old Arthur is the perfect dog for this particular boy. Old Arthur is good at waiting for William to come home from school, and at going for slow walks with him, and at lying on his back while William rubs his tummy. He is also good at wagging his tail for everybody in the family, especially for William.

There is little doubt that when age is presented in picture books, the image presented is essentially a positive one, perhaps one that is even idealized. In the pages of picture books, loving grandparents emerge, and the competence and worth of age is stressed. Although most of the difficulties associated with age are omitted, a small number of picture books show the elderly facing impending death as young grandchildren struggle to understand and accept this ultimate finality.

We have discussed books that include elderly characters. However, in most realistic picture books old age is totally omitted, evidently considered as a phase of life far removed from and unimportant to childhood. One group of researchers discovered that in elementary school texts, people over sixty-five rarely appear.[18] An analysis of Caldecott winners indicates an absence of elderly characters in those books that do not retell an old folktale, song, or ballad.[19]

The invisibility of the elderly in books for young children has, at this point, been most definitively illustrated by Edward Ansello's content analysis of 549 children's books in circulation at the library system of Montgomery County, Maryland.[20] He found that only 16 percent of these books portrayed older characters in any significant fashion, *significant* meaning that the character spoke a line of one word or more or was clearly identified as being related to the story. After analyzing 18,000 pictures, excluding crowd scenes, Ansello found that only 4.5 percent of the illustrations included older characters.

Besides this pervasive invisibility, Ansello also found stereotyped portrayals of those elderly characters who were depicted. Older characters were rarely shown as caring for themselves or as solving problems. Instead they were most often involved in routine repetitive tasks or in telling other people to do things.

This study also revealed sex bias in the depiction of the elderly in children's books. Over one-half of all older characters were male, although a reverse depiction would have been more appropriate, for in real life there are approximately three females to every two males over age sixty-five. Moreover, elderly males are shown as directing and physically exertive whereas females are subservient and helping.

The problem is not so much that age is portrayed in a negative manner in books for young children as that the depiction is so constricting and limited. Buckley's *Grandfather and I* is a case in point. The relationship between young and old is warm and loving. However, grandfather's most positive characteristic is that he has plenty of time and, as he stands passively with his grandchild, he clasps his hands behind his back as though physically restraining himself from becoming more active and involved.

Thus in books for young readers we find an essentially positive, but a limited and one-dimensional portrait of age. In the next section we look at images of age that are more multi-faceted and complex.

## Books for the middle and the upper grades

Roald Dahl's *Charlie and the Chocolate Factory* (1969) is an epicurean rags-to-riches tale in which a boy leaves poverty and starvation to become the owner of the world's most marvelous chocolate factory. Young Charlie Bucket lives with his mother and father and four grandparents who are so old they never get out of bed. The family is poor and hungry, but fortunes change when Charlie is one of the five lucky contest winners whose prize is a visit to Willy Wonka's secret and incredible chocolate factory. The other four children who hold winning tickets are so obnoxious that they disqualify themselves, and Willy Wonka tells Charlie that he will become the fabulous chocolate factory's new owner.

*Charlie and the Chocolate Factory* is enormously popular among elementary school children. Indeed, Eleanor Cameron notes that it is one of the most widely read books in elementary schools across the country. She also notes that it is one of the worst.[21] Recently the book has come under fire because of its racist overtones. Were there greater sensitivity to mistreatment and misrepresentation of the elderly, it would have received criticism as an "ageist" book as well. At the book's conclusion Charlie arrives home in triumph in a glass elevator piloted by Willie Wonka himself. When the bedridden grandparents learn that they are to live out the rest of their days in the chocolate factory, they refuse to go and scream that they would rather die in their beds. Willie Wonka and Charlie, taking no notice whatsoever of their protests and screams, simply push the old people, beds and all, into the glass elevator. The message with which we close the book is that the needs and desires and opinions of old people are totally irrelevant and inconsequential.

*Charlie and the Great Glass Elevator* (1972) picks up the elevator and ageism where *Charlie and the Chocolate Factory* put them down. Because of an error in timing, the elevator does not return to the chocolate factory but instead orbits Willy Wonka, Charlie, and his parents and grandparents into space. There follows a variety of space adventures as well as a potpourri of demeaning comments about being old. When astronauts spot the unique flying vehicle, they comment on its elderly inhabitants: "There's these three old birds in nightshirts floating around in this crazy glass box."[22] The elevator's cantankerous elderly crew throw insults at one another in which the word *old* seems to be the main derogatory comment: "You miserable old mackerel." "My dear old dotty dumpling." "Be quiet you balmy old bat."[23]

When the elevator returns to the chocolate factory, Mr. Wonka offers the old ones a pill, Wonka-Vite, that will make them become young again. The Oompa Loompas, the factory's black servants, advertise the miracle drug to the old ones:

> If you are old and have the shakes,
> If all your bones are full of aches,
> If you can hardly walk at all,
> If living drives you up the wall,
> If you're a grump and full of spite,
> If you're a human parasite,
> Then what you need is Wonka-Vite!
> Your eyes will shine, your hair will grow,
> Your face and skin will start to glow.
> Your rotten teeth will all drop out
> And in their place new teeth will sprout.
> Those rolls of fat around your hips
> Will vanish, and your wrinkled lips
> Will get so soft and rosy pink
> That all the boys will smile and wink
> And whisper secretly that this
> Is just the girl they wish to kiss.[24]

This portrayal of old age as grotesque, cantankerous, and irrational fortunately does not characterize most of children's literature. In contrast, the image of old age, when presented, is overwhelmingly positive and at times perhaps idealized. In the next sections we look at books that depict the elderly as a source of special wisdom and as participants in a unique and intimate bond with the young. We conclude by discussing some of the recent books that attempt to describe realistically the problems that old people in our society must confront, the pain this confrontation causes them, and the pain it causes the children who love them.

## Older and wiser

One common conception of the elderly is that they are a source of accumulated wisdom, of knowledge that has accrued over time and has been honed by experience. The image of the elderly as wise teachers is one that pervades many children's books and can be seen in two books by James Houston, *Akavak* (1968) and *The White Archer* (1967).

*Akavak* is the story of the hazardous journey made by an Eskimo boy and his grandfather, who, realizing that he soon will die, wishes to travel to see his brother once more. Before Akavak leaves, his father talks to him about his grandfather.

Remember that he is strong and determined and almost always wise. . . . Listen to the words he says to you and learn from him, for that is the way in which all knowledge has come to this family. . . .

But sometimes now he does not hear the words that are spoken to him, and his eyes stare, and his spirit seems to go away from him and wander to some distant place, for he is very old. If he does not seem to hear you and his spirit seems to leave him, you must then be careful and decide everything for him.[25]

Akavak and his grandfather begin the long, dangerous trip, one that does indeed test all the old man's wisdom and all the boy's strength. Although, as his father had warned, Akavak sometimes has to take care of his grandfather, he gains much in knowledge and wisdom from the aged man.

Houston's *The White Archer: An Eskimo Legend* traces the actions of Kungo, a young boy filled with an overriding desire to take revenge upon a raiding band of Indians who have killed his parents and carried off his sister. Kungo goes to live with Ittok, an old man

almost blind but still a great archer, and with his wife, an old woman renowned for her ability to sew animal skins. Kungo finds not only skill and wisdom in this elderly couple, but physical beauty as well, and the old woman's wrinkles are not ugly disfigurements but rather "like the fine grain in an ancient piece of driftwood."[26] From the old man, Kungo learns not only great skill in archery but also the profoundly more difficult art of tempering hatred with forgiveness.

Moses Howard's *The Ostrich Chase* (1974) is a story about the Bushmen who live in the Kalahari Desert and about Khuana, a young girl who loves her grandmother and learns much from her. When the Bushmen prepare to leave their parched water hole, Old Gaushe is not well enough to travel, so she is left behind in the desert. Khuana is determined to stay with her grandmother, and the two strike out across the desert with the desperate hope that Khuana's strength and Old Gaushe's wisdom will enable them to reach a water hole. Progress is excruciatingly slow, and the two, suffering from hunger and thirst and the intense desert heat, feel that they can continue no longer, when Old Gaushe senses that water is near. At the water hole there is nourishment and medicinal herbs for Old Gaushe's leg, and there, also, Khuana fulfills her dream of hunting and killing an ostrich. Restored, they catch up with the Bushmen, who are amazed that a young girl and an old woman have together conquered the desert. T. Degen's *Transport 7-41-R* (1974) is another fine novel of young and old who go on a difficult journey together, in this case, one across war-torn Germany.

Rachel Field's *Calico Bush* (1931) portrays the courageous and loyal Marguerite Ledoux, a girl of well-to-do upbringing in prerevolutionary France, who, through a series of misfortunes, becomes the bound-out girl of a struggling English family. Pledged to serve the Sargent family for six years, Maggie, as they call her, becomes busily immersed in caring for the Sargent's brood of children. When the family settles in the wilderness of Maine, hardships are many: there is hunger, constant labor, loneliness, and fear of Indians. However, Marguerite is fortunate in her closest neighbor, Hepsa Jordan, an old woman "as grotesque as a crooked apple tree decked out in print calico . . . with bright black eyes in nests of crisscross wrinkles."[27] Alert and spry, Hepsa arrived on the unsettled Maine coast when she was seventy-three, and she has not been sick a day since. Marguerite finds the old woman's home a source of enduring comfort, and from Hepsa the twelve-year-old girl learns skill in healing, in needlecraft, and in singing old ballads. When Marguerite, with ingenuity and bravery, turns aside an Indian raid, Hepsa says that one day people may be singing ballads about her.

Another elderly character who emerges as surprisingly helpful is Paul's grandmother in Constance Greene's *The Unmaking of Rabbit* (1972). Paul, nicknamed Rabbit by his classmates, is troubled by a nervous stutter and by his mother's remarriage. He feels ambivalent toward his grandmother; he loves her but is embarrassed at how she must appear to the other kids, especially when she gets dressed up and puts on her "face," "two bright circles of rouge and the crooked mouth she drew on with lipstick."[28] However, it is with his grandmother's love and support that Paul grows toward greater self-knowledge and self-respect.

In *Trouble River* (1969) by Betsy Byars, there is another grandparent who first appears to be a burden but turns out to be a character of unique competence and determination. His parents away in Hunter City, Dewey is left with his grandmother in their cabin surrounded by prairie. Learning of a planned Indian attack, the boy and the old women have no place to hide and no place to go for help. In desperation, they board a raft the boy has made in his

spare time, and they warily head out onto the unknown waters of Trouble River. Although Dewey loves his Grandma, he initially finds her very trying. Perched on her rocking chair, she querulously complains about the way he handles the raft, and her advice is mingled with dire warnings and discomforting superstitions. On occasion Dewey is freshly impressed with her frailty: "Her voice was helpless and old, and her hands clutched the arms of her rocker like vines on pale sand."[29] However, by the book's conclusion Dewey is struck more by his Grandma's unexpected competence and bravery than by her frailty. She survives a close bout with wolves, the knowledge that friends with whom she hoped to seek shelter have been killed in the raid, and an exhausting trip without adequate food or rest. And when the sluggish river unexpectedly becomes a rapids, she survives that too. "Dewey looked at his Grandma's back, so straight and proud, and at the white lace-edged bonnet which hung over the back of the chair. Removing her bonnet had been the only concession to the difficulties of the trip."[30]

## Old and young together

As with picture books, many stories for children, particularly those for the middle elementary grades, emphasize a special rapport between young and old. On occasion the close tie is with a grandparent, but in other cases it is with an elderly friend.

One fine statement of close affection between young and old occurs in Meindert DeJong's *Journey from Peppermint Street*, winner of the 1969 National Book Award. Set in Holland during the early 1900s, it tells of young Siebren's journey with his grandfather to visit a great-aunt. With his elderly great-aunt Hinka, Siebren develops a totally loving relationship. She is full of fun and comfort, and she is honest with him. Siebren finds it easy to talk to Aunt Hinka about all his worries and fears.

Oh, it had never been so easy to talk to anybody. Maybe it was because Aunt Hinka was as small as he. He didn't have to look up to talk to her. You had to talk to other grown-ups that way, and then you felt small and helpless, and without enough words—sometimes so helpless it made you shake.[31]

Not only does Aunt Hinka understand Siebren, but she helps him understand himself.

The relationship between Jane and ninety-nine-year-old Mr. Buckle, Cranbury's oldest inhabitant, as recorded in Eleanor Estes' *The Middle Moffat* (1942) is one of the warmest and funniest portrayed in children's literature. As their friendship grows, Jane begins to feel responsible for the continued good health of the oldest inhabitant. She kicks branches out of the street on the chance that he might pass by and trip, and she takes to carrying an old umbrella around in case she should ever meet Mr. Buckle caught in the rain. When a thick fog rolls into Cranbury, she is so worried about the elderly gentleman that she pays him a visit, and the two get involved in Janey's favorite game, double solitaire. Janey solicitously resolves to let Mr. Buckle win, but she has a thing or two to learn about the oldest inhabitant's skill in solitaire. He shuffles with dazzling finesse; he flips cards in the air between plays; and he trounces his young opponent easily. Janey leaves with her head spinning and her admiration of the oldest inhabitant soaring. *The Middle Moffat* concludes with a big celebration honoring Mr. Buckle's one hundredth birthday. Amidst all the hoopla, Mr. Buckle has time to appreciate Janey's gift, a clump of one hundred bluets, and to give her a ride home in his automobile, flanked by cheering crowds.

The elderly's reminiscence of times long ago is a strong theme in Carol Lee Lorenzo's *Mama's Ghosts* (1974). What Ellie likes more than anything is spending time with her grandmother, whom she calls Mama. Mama walks slowly, her weight shifting from side to side. She keeps near furniture and the sides of walls for she has fallen before. And Mama shares her "ghosts" with Ellie, the memories of when she was a young girl, a bride, and then a wife and mother; and she shows Ellie the souvenirs of her life that she keeps safely hidden in the black pocketbook that never leaves her side. Illness temporarily interrupts the close relationship between Ellie and her grandmother, but Ellie realizes that when it is finally time to let Mama go, she will have "ghosts" of her own.

Closeness to the past, however, is not always portrayed as a desirable characteristic. In contrast, in some stories an elderly character's ties to the past are shown as so binding that they mar a relationship with a young friend or grandchild. Two books that emphasize this adherence to past ways are Robert Abrahams' *The Bonus of Redonda* (1969) and Louise Shotwell's *Magdalena* (1971). However, both books also indicate that tight bonds can be loosened and the elderly can learn new ways.

Set in a fishing village in the West Indies, *The Bonus of Redonda* is about a young boy, Bonus, and his gran'pa Simms, leader of all the fishermen in the village. To Bonus, gran'pa Simms is the biggest man in the whole world —or at least on the island. However, when gran'pa rejects the new warden's plan to modernize the island's fishing techniques, his status becomes severely diminished. To stop the encroachment of the new ways, King Simms enlists the aid of a self-proclaimed witch, and the result of the unhappy conspiracy, so gran'pa believes, is a fire that destroys many fishing boats. Fearful of punishment and censure, King Simms, along with Bonus, flees the island. When they return they learn that there is but minimal damage and minimal blame. King Simms decides to try the modern techniques declaring, "I am not so old I cannot see new wonders. . . ."[32] and the fishing expert learns that a mountain cannot be moved all at once, but only by inches.

In *Magdalena* there is a conflict between grandchild and grandmother over the new American ways versus the older Puerto Rican customs. Magdalena loves and respects her grandmother, but nevertheless she is an obstacle for "her ideas were set solid like mountains." When Magdalena, taunted by nicknames like Miss Two-Ropes, tells Nani that she hates her braids, her grandmother is shocked and responds, "God go with you, Magdalena. May he protect you from the American influence."[33] Despite Nani's blessing, Magdalena still hates her braids. With the persuasion of a classmate and an eccentric elderly woman, Miss Lilley, who wears an enormous orange hat and black lace gloves that expose orange fingernails, Magdalena is persuaded, and the braids come off. Nani is horrified, certain that Miss Lilley has bewitched her granddaughter.

Miss Lilley goes with Magdalena to open up Nani's eyes to today's world. In the confrontation between the two elderly women, Miss Lilley collapses from hunger and is taken to the hospital. During the crisis the eccentric Miss Lilley becomes friendly with the traditional grandmother, and Nani does indeed change, announcing an important principle: "It is always in season for the old ones to learn."[34] Then she gives Magdalena money for a second hair cut. Not only does *Magdalena* present an image of an old woman as bound to the traditions of her culture and past ways, but also through Miss Lilley it touches upon the loneliness and poverty that many of the elderly experience.

Books for older children often deal with the potential for betrayal inherent in the close relationship between old and young, a betrayal that at times ends in death. Two books that portray a betrayal of friendship are Paul Zindel's *The Pigman* (1968) and Barbara Wersba's *The Dream Watcher* (1968).

In *The Pigman* two high-school students, Lorraine and John, form a friendship with a lonely, generous, and possibly senile old man, Mr. Pignati. When the Pigman, as they call him, suffers a heart attack and is taken to the hospital, he offers the teenagers use of his home. Mr. Pignati returns from the hospital to find a wild party in process, one in which his most important possessions, those treasured for their memories, are destroyed. Shocked by the betrayal of trust, the Pigman succumbs to a stroke, and John and Lorraine are left with the realization that "there was no one else to blame anymore" and that they must take responsibility for the death of their elderly friend.

In *The Dream Watcher* an old woman betrays a young friend. Albert Scully, a misfit in conflict with his parents and at odds with his peers, finds his source of refuge in the home of Mrs. Woodfin, an elderly, somewhat eccentric recluse. Mrs. Woodfin, dressed in shabby velvet and living in a dilapidated house covered with cobwebs and filled with books, tells Albert marvelous stories of her life as a young actress. She is also a compendium of quotes and proverbs, and from her Albert learns that his may be a different drummer and that he must step to his own music. When Mrs. Woodfin dies, Albert realizes that she had been not an actress but an unmarried school teacher, and an alcoholic on welfare. Albert's anger and hurt dissipate as he understands that, in spite of the lies, Mrs. Woodfin was as special as he had always believed; her life was sad, but still she made poetry out of it—and she was able to help Albert accept himself.

## Not going gentle into that good night

Do not cast me off in the time of old age; forsake me not when my strength is spent.

For my enemies speak concerning me, those who watch for my life consult together, and say "God has forsaken him; pursue and seize him, for there is none to deliver him."

*Psalm 71, Verses 9–11*

Most of the books we have discussed so far emphasize the positive aspects of aging. They portray great age as a time of accumulated wisdom, and even apparent frailty is only a deceptive veneer for underlying competence and determination. Age is also drawn as a time of unique rapport with the young, although the friendship is occasionally marred by misunderstanding and by betrayal. Until recently, however, the very real and the very serious problems that the elderly may experience were almost totally neglected in children's literature. For example, researchers who analyzed fifty-three Newbery Medal winners found an extreme lack of development of elderly characters and their absence from the crucial mainstream of the story. Moreover, they were seldom shown as senile, ill, disabled, or, in fact, struggling with any of the problems that actually do confront the elderly in contemporary America.[35]

One of the interesting developments in realistic fiction has been the emergence of some fine new books for children that take a hard and poignant look at the process and the problems of growing old. For example, some current realistic fiction touches upon the loneliness of the elderly who live by themselves in shabby apartments and decaying houses. Set in London, Janet McNeil's *Goodbye, Dove Square* (1969) tells of deserted Dove Square, which residents have been forced to vacate because of renewal. Only one inhabitant remains, elderly Shakey Frick, who, with his two dogs,

lives in a deserted building in fear of being discovered by the authorities.

Betsy Byars' *After the Goat Man* (1974), and Sharon Bell Mathis' *The Hundred Penny Box* (1975) also present elderly characters fighting to hold on to a place of their own. There are several sensitively drawn characters in *After the Goat Man*, particularly Harold V. Coleman, the chubby adolescent who was assigned the role of the extra hippopotamus in the school play and who all his life has avoided looking at hurt people. But the book's prevailing image is that of the Goat Man, the hurt and fiercely independent old man who refuses to let plans for a new superhighway drive him from the home he loves on the side of a hill.

The need for an older person to have a place of his or her own is also reflected in Mathis' *The Hundred Penny Box* illustrated with great sensitivity by Leo and Diane Dillon. This fine book is a poignant exploration of what it means to be very old, and it is also a perceptive study of shifting family relationships when great-great-aunt Dewbet Thomas, one hundred years old, moves in with Michael and his parents. Michael's mother wants to throw out Aunt Dew's hundred-penny box so that the old woman will look forward instead of backward into the past. But Aunt Dew insists that "Anybody takes my hundred penny box takes me!"[36] Michael tries to protect his great-great-aunt, but there is no resolution of the conflict. In its expression of love and great empathy between young and old, *The Hundred Penny Box* offers one of the most finely developed portrayals of an elderly character available in children's literature for middle-grade readers.

Many of the stories that portray old people who live alone depict women who are held in contempt by their neighbors. Eleanor Clymer's *We Lived in the Almont* (1970) is about the Martin family and other tenants who live in the apartment building called the Almont. Many of the tenants are old, but one elderly woman stands out in Linda Martin's mind—Miss Clark, the plant lady. Miss Clark is always dressed in a worn gray sweater and sneakers, and her gray hair hangs down her back in a braid. Her apartment is filled with plants, cats that are never allowed outside, and a devastating odor. All the neighboring children, Linda among them, mimic the plant lady and poke fun at her, but it is from this old woman that Linda learns a lesson in charity. When Linda steals Miss Clark's guitar and her mother discovers it in her daughter's room, Linda is marched to the old woman's apartment for explanations. As Linda stammers her thanks for the "loan," the eccentric plant lady generously responds, "you misunderstood me. I didn't lend it to you. I gave it to you."[37] When the Almont is sold and the tenants forced to leave, Miss Clark, penniless and without friends, goes to a home where she must give up her cats and plants. Whenever Linda plays her guitar, she thinks of Miss Clark and wonders where she is.

Often old women living alone are not only mimicked and made fun of but are actually imagined to be witches by the neighborhood children. Zelpha Keatly Snyder's *The Witches of Worm* (1972) portrays a lonely and bitter girl, Jessica, who becomes so emotionally disturbed that she attributes her selfish and cruel impulses to her cat, Worm, whom she decides is a witch's cat. One of Jessica's few friends is elderly Mrs. Fortune, but then Jessica decides that Mrs. Fortune is a witch and must be punished. "She's ugly and horrible with her stinking old cats, and she knows all sorts of things that she has no right to know. She knows everything because she's a witch. She's an ugly old witch, and she knows too much."[38] Fortunately Jessica is prevented from putting her vague plan of punishment into effect.

Thus some children's books indicate not only that age is a time of wisdom and rapport with the young, but that it can also be a time of loneliness, eccentricity, and rejection. Other books such as Eleanor Clymer's *Me and the Eggman* (1972) and Jean Robinson's *The Secret Life of T. K. Dearing* (1973) emphasize another problem of aging—that of making others aware that old age is not synonymous with incompetence and that the elderly are worthy of dignity and respect.

Eleanor Clymer says that the main point of *Me and the Eggman* "is actually conservation of people as well as places. People, young and old, have strength and want to be needed; . . . it's wrong to just throw them away."[39] The book is about a boy, Donald, and an old man who delivers eggs and vegetables to his house every Wednesday. Donald pictures the eggman's farm as one with flowers and horses and a red barn. He wants to go there so badly that one Wednesday he hides in the eggman's truck. After spending a week on the farm, Donald learns that it's not at all as he had imagined. There is no flower garden, but just bare earth and mud, and the work proves to be exhausting and dirty. Donald learns a great deal—not only about running a farm but also about growing old and how it feels to have others lose confidence in a person's ability to take care of himself competently. When the eggman hurts his back, he is elaborately careful that others do not find out, for he fears being sent to the county home by those who wish to obtain his property. Donald's new awareness makes him angry at the inequitable treatment the elderly receive: "It's not fair. A thing doesn't have to be thrown out on the junk pile just because it's old. You can put in a new part. A person doesn't have to be thrown away either. I suddenly remembered Aunt Lizzie telling Mom, 'Sarah, just because I'm old doesn't mean I'm ready for the junk pile.' I could see what she meant."[40]

In a more humorous vein, Jean Robinson's

*The Secret Life of T. K. Dearing* also depicts people's refusal to attribute competence to the elderly. When Teke Dearing and his parents learn that Grandpa Kindermann is coming to live with them, their plans include a balanced, bland diet and enrollment in the Soaring Sixties Club. However, Grandpa Kindermann at seventy-eight has plans of his own. He likes corned beef sandwiches, pizzas, donuts, and black coffee. He does not take naps. He refused to wear the soft bedroom slippers and the cardigan sweater his daughter has bought for him. He despises the Soaring Sixties and firmly states that old-age clubs "make a person feel plain . . . segregated!"[41] The story illustrates the struggle of the elderly to preserve dignity and independence in the face of limiting stereotypes.

A young protagonist's adjustment to the death of a beloved grandparent or an elderly friend is another theme portrayed in recent literature for children. Often in these books we are told little or nothing about the elderly person's attitudes toward death, but rather feelings and reactions are described from the point of view of the confused and sorrowing child. In many stories death comes immediately or after a brief stay in the hospital. Any physical or emotional suffering the old person experiences is minimized as the emphasis remains on the child's feelings.

Doris Orgel's *The Mulberry Music* (1971) is one fine novel that follows this pattern. Libby loves her Grandma Liza better than anyone else in the world, even her parents. They share many wonderful times together: swimming, cards on Friday nights, and playing the piano, especially Libby's favorite piece, the opening of Mozart's Jupiter Symphony, which Libby calls "the mulberry music." Libby thinks everything about Grandma Liza is beautiful, even her wrinkles that are "like trails through pleasant, familiar countryside. . . ."[42] When Libby learns her grandmother has been taken to the hospital, she is deeply troubled, for she views the hospital as a place where people go to be born or to die. Libby takes a taxi to the hospital and manages to enter her grandmother's room, but she is appalled at the sight of an inert gray figure with liquid dripping through a tube into her arm. The rasping, unseeing woman on the bed is no one Libby knows; she feels it cannot be her beloved Grandma Liza, and she flees the hospital and goes to her grandmother's house, looking for her Grandma Liza there. When word comes soon after that Grandma Liza has died, Libby plans the funeral. It is a home service at which her mother plays the mulberry music of Mozart's Jupiter Symphony, music that will stay with Libby all of her life.

In *The Mulberry Music* we never know what Grandma Liza is thinking and feeling. In fact, we never actually meet her. Barbara Cohen's *Thank You, Jackie Robinson* (1974), Constance Greene's *A Girl Called Al* (1969), and Eleanor Cameron's *A Room Made of Windows* (1971) are some other fine books that portray an elderly person's death as seen from the point of view of a child.

In a few other books the experience of aging is vividly presented as an awareness that one's body has lost strength and agility and one's mind has lost sharpness and clarity. Although most of Alice Childress' *A Hero Ain't Nothin' But a Sandwich* (1973) is a composite portrayal of Benjie, a thirteen-year-old black boy in danger of being hooked on heroin, in a brief aside, Benjie's grandmother makes her statement of what it means to grow old:

Bein old is strange to me, cause I'm not yet used to it. I have sat in the narrowness of this room, my hands folded in my lap, broken at the knuckles and veins of my fingers; they seem larger, knotty-lookin, my mind tells me that's old. But if old was only looks, then old could be better dealt with. Old is also *ailin*, you get a sudden jab or pain in your shoulder or knee joint, and that pain be so perfectly sharp it's like somebody stabbed a long, hot ice pick right down to the bone. . . . But old is also more than pain, I guess. Maybe old is in your mind goin one way whilst you go another. . . . There's a part of being old that's got nothin to do with aches and pains, you get sudden thoughts that flash in from no place. Thoughts will not hang together long enough for me to sort a matter through. . . .[43]

This statement of the betrayal of a failing body and a failing mind is a brief note in a book primarily concerned with matters other than aging. In three fine recent books—Rose Blue's *Grandma Didn't Wave Back* (1972), Gil Rabin's *Changes* (1973), and Norma Fox

Grandma Didn't Wave Back

Mazer's *A Figure of Speech* (1973)—depiction of the physical and the emotional pain that may accompany aging comprises the key thrust.

*Grandma Didn't Wave Back* is a poignant and moving description of senility. It is the most optimistic of these three final books to be discussed. For Debbie, Grandma is the most special person in the world, the first to hear about a funny thing that happened in school, or a high mark, or something that is worrying Debbie. Debbie also loves Grandma's *tstozkes*, her old things from Europe, the hand-crocheted shawl, the china figurines, and the old clock.

But then Debbie is puzzled as Grandma begins behaving strangely. She becomes confused and calls Debbie by her mother's name, Helen. She walks around the apartment in her nightgown with her hair uncombed, and she talks as though she was a young woman not yet married. Once she set an extra place at the table for her cousin George who had been dead for twenty years. Debbie is baffled by her grandmother's behavior, but her failures of memory last for only short periods and Debbie hopes they will soon go away, much like a cold. The doctor explains to Debbie what senility means, but the intellectual definition does not really help her understand the changes in her grandmother. When Debbie overhears her parents talking about sending Grandma to a nursing home she furiously accuses them: "You're killing Grandma!" However, one night when a neighbor finds Grandma dressed in her nightgown walking dazed in the street, the parents are certain that for her own safety, Grandma must go to a home.

As soon as possible, Debbie, still not fully accepting what has happened, goes to visit Grandma. Debbie is dismayed at what she finds in the nursing home and thinks that it is better to die in the night as Grandpa had than to have to live alone like this, away from everyone you love. As though reading her granddaughter's mind, the old woman asks Debbie to draw the blinds to her window that overlooks the ocean, and she explains:

"Look, Debbie. Look at the sun shining on the ocean. Look at the first birds flying home from the South. Soon the sunshine will grow warmer and there is time for me to see the spring." She touched Debbie's cheek. "And there is time to see my grandchildren get bigger. Time to see my Debbie grow. Time to watch you make me more and more proud. . . . Do you understand what I am saying to you now?"[44]

The book ends on a positive note as Debbie tells her grandmother that she does understand.

In *Changes*, physical illness, senility, and life in a nursing home are also depicted, but the portrait that emerges is far more pessimistic. In this book an elderly grandparent is so sick and depressed that death appears preferable to existence in a nursing home that is called a "living graveyard." Chris, busy making friends in a new neighborhood and in love for the first time, tries to cope with his grandpa's failing health and to understand the changes in the old man. Ever since Chris's father died, Grandpa has been a help and a source of strength for Chris and his mother. However, when he suffers a heart attack, he is so physically weak that he must be taken to a nursing home.

When Chris visits the home, he is overwhelmed by the smell of decay and stunned by his grandfather's lapses in memory. Grandpa is crowded into a room with three other elderly men. He sleeps almost constantly, has no interest in eating, and seems to understand less and less of what is happening around him. He sits in his chair all day long with his head hanging, no one paying attention to him other than to bring him his unappetizing soft-diet meals. At first Chris does his homework in the nursing home beside his grandfather. Then one day the stench and the insane game of not knowing who has died in the night become so devastating that Chris knows he cannot go inside the home again. He becomes angry, furious at his mother for leaving his grandfather in such a place, even though he knows she must work and cannot provide the care grandfather needs. He even becomes irrationally angry at the grandfather for getting sick. When Chris gets a telephone call in school that Grandpa is dying he makes no effort to hurry, and Grandpa is dead when he arrives at the nursing home. For Chris, Grandpa had died several weeks ago—when he didn't know who people were: "He had died when his memories had died."[45]

Norma Fox Mazer's *A Figure of Speech* is the most powerful statement of the hypocrisy and the lack of decency that too often characterize treatment of the elderly. Written for older children, *A Figure of Speech* has some themes in common with the two previously discussed books, but its tone is angrier and harsher. In this book there is again the close bond between grandparent and grandchild and again the grandchild's censure of parents for not taking adequate care of the grandparents. In this case, however, there are no excuses made for the adults in the Pennoyer family: through their selfish behavior they are held responsible for grandfather Pennoyer's death.

Carl Pennoyer comes to live with his son the same year that Jenny is born. Both grandfather and granddaughter share a bond in common, for neither was planned for and neither was really wanted. So Carl takes Jenny out of her mother's busy hands and wheels her for hours in the stroller. As the years pass, a deep and close affection grows between Jenny and her grandfather, so much so that now, at thirteen, Jenny wakes up early in the morning to run down to her grandfather's basement room and visit with him before she goes to school. Carl wakes up at six even though he has nowhere to go and no work to do. He feels that he has nothing to live for, and then he remembers Jenny; she is his reason. Grandfather leaves his basement room to eat meals upstairs, and his presence seems to cause countless minor aggravations in the Pennoyer family. His stories are repetitious and irrelevant, and he often fumbles, breaking glasses and spilling water. When Jenny pleads with her mother to think more about Grandpa's feelings, she responds,

"Let me tell you something, Jenny, it's no picnic living with that man. . . . He's not the cleanest old man in the world. Sometimes he doesn't change his underwear for a week. . . . And the same stories over and over—when he gets going he doesn't give anyone a chance to get a word in edgewise."[46]

Into these family tensions Jenny's older brother, Vince, returns from college, without a diploma and with a wife. Taut emotions snap into bickering as the young couple eye grandfather's room as a potential basement apartment of their own. The conflict between mother and grandfather becomes intensified, as does the theme of hypocrisy that runs throughout the book. At one point Mother says to Grandpa: "Everyone passes away. My parents, God rest them, passed away. When people get to be senior citizens, their time is coming closer every day. . . ."[47] Late that night a note is pinned to the bulletin board. It is grandfather's angry attempt to rip through the euphemisms and the hypocrisy and to state things as they are.

I ain't going to "pass away." I'm going to die.
   My time ain't going "to come." I'll be dead.
   I ain't a "senior citizen." I'm an old codger of eighty-three.[48]

*A FIGURE OF SPEECH*

*a novel by*
*Norma Fox Mazer*

Grandpa begins to show signs of aging. When he starts a fire in his basement room, he is taken upstairs, and his apartment is confiscated by Vince and Vicki. Upstairs, out of place and in the way, Carl Pennoyer thinks of himself as a clumsy old man, a useless creature, a nuisance. Jenny learns that her parents are planning to send Grandpa to a home for senior citizens, Castle Haven, where there are health and personality files on all the patients, number codes on all special diets, and even numbers on the living room chairs to make the old people feel more secure and to cut down on bickering. To escape from Castle Haven, Grandpa and Jenny run away to his old farm with a dream of finding freedom there. It is dilapidated and in ruin, and they realize that their dream cannot become reality. When Jenny wakes up the following morning, she finds that Grandpa is not in bed; and when she goes outside into the chilly morning air, she finds him dead under a maple tree. She knows that rather than go to a rest home, he has gone outside to die. After the funeral Jenny listens to the adults talking—about what a clean old man grandfather had been, how he had lived to a ripe old age and died with his boots on, and Jenny goes outside and runs to get away from the hypocrisy.

## Profiles in age

There is a need for picture books that draw a more complex profile of what it means to age, a profile that should not only present the positive aspects of aging but that should touch upon problems the elderly may confront as well. For children in the middle and upper grades, there must be more books such as *A Figure of Speech*, books that will help a young person better understand aging and better cope with feelings of hurt and bewilderment that may arise as changes in a beloved grandparent or an elderly friend occur.

There is an old Hindu folktale, one with different versions in different countries, about a little boy who meets his father carrying a large wicker basket. The father explains to his son what he plans to do with the basket: "Since grandfather is so old that he can no longer work in the garden or even take care of himself, I plan to put him in the basket and lower him into the river. Then he will no longer be a burden on us." The little boy eyes the basket thoughtfully and then says, "Be sure and bring back the basket, father. I may need it some day for you."

From their literature children can learn about the different ways people grow old, the varying profiles in age. From books that present old age with reality, complexity, and compassion, children can come to realize the terrible injustice involved in mistreatment of the elderly. It is hoped that they can also come to a more

personal awareness that old age lies in the future of those who are now young, and that all generations must be involved in preserving the dignity of the old.

## NOTES

1. "An Old Woman Speaks," in Bert Kruger Smith, *Aging in America*, Boston, Beacon Press, 1973, p. 2.
2. Simone de Beauvoir, "Frank Talk on a Forbidden Subject," in *Annual Editions, Readings in Human Development '73–'74*, Guilford, Conn., Dushkin, 1973, p. 251. From *The New York Times Magazine*, March 26, 1971.
3. Ibid.
4. Ibid.
5. Erdman Palmore, "Attitudes Toward Aging as Shown by Humor," *The Gerontologist*, 2, no. 3, 181–186.
6. Smith, op. cit.
7. Ibid.
8. Simone de Beauvoir, *The Coming of Age*, trans. by Patrick O'Brien, New York, Putnam, 1972, p. 1.
9. de Beauvoir, "Frank Talk on a Forbidden Subject," op. cit., p. 253.
10. Gail Haley, *A Story, A Story*, New York, Atheneum, 1970.
11. Paul Galdone, ill., *The Old Woman and Her Pig*, New York, McGraw-Hill, 1960.
12. C. S. Evans, *Sleeping Beauty*. Dover, 1920.
13. Helen E. Buckley, *Grandfather and I*, pictures by Paul Galdone, New York, Lothrop, Lee and Shepard, 1959.
14. Joan Lexau, *Benjie on His Own*, Don Bolognese, illus., New York Dial Press, 1964.
15. Boaz Kahana, "Old Age Seen Negatively by Old as Well as Young," *Geriatric Focus*, 9. no. 10 (November–December 1970), 1+.
16. Max Lundgren, *Matt's Grandfather*, trans. by Ann Pyk, Fibben Hald, illus., New York, Putnam, 1970.
17. Liesel Moak Skorpen, *Old Arthur*, pictures by Wallace Tripp, New York, Harper & Row, 1972.
18. Lenore Weitzman, Presentation at Center for Sex Role Stereotypes, National Education Association, Washington, D.C., April 1974.
19. Analysis conducted by authors.
20. Edward Ansello, "The Depiction of Age in Children's Literature," *The Gerontologist* (in press).
21. Eleanor Cameron, "McLuhan, Youth, and Literature," *The Horn Book*, 48, no. 5 (October 1972), 433–440.

22. Roald Dahl, *Charlie and the Great Glass Elevator,* Joseph Schindelman, illus., New York, Knopf, 1972, p. 16.
23. Ibid., pp. 25, 48, 22.
24. Ibid., p. 101.
25. James Houston, *Akavak: An Eskimo Journey,* New York, Harcourt Brace Jovanovich, 1968, p. 12.
26. James Houston, *The White Archer: An Eskimo Legend,* New York, Harcourt Brace Jovanovich, 1967, p. 29.
27. Rachel Field, *Calico Bush,* engravings by Allen Lewis, New York, Macmillan, 1931, p. 47.
28. Constance Greene, *The Unmaking of Rabbit,* New York, Viking Press, 1972, p. 21.
29. Betsy Byars, *Trouble River,* Rocco Negri, illus., New York, Viking Press, 1969, p. 117.
30. Ibid., p. 129.
31. Meindert Dejong, *Journey From Peppermint Street,* Emily Arnold McCully, illus., New York, Harper & Row, 1968, pp. 196–197.
32. Robert Abrahams, *The Bonus of Redonda,* Peter Bramley, illus., New York, Macmillan, 1969.
33. Louisa Shotwell, *Magdalena,* Lilian Obligado, illus., New York, Viking Press, 1971, p. 21.
34. Ibid., p. 121.
35. David Peterson and Elizabeth Karnes, "Older People in Adolescent Literature," presented at the Gerontological Society, Louisville, Ky. 1975.
36. Sharon Bell Mathis, *The Hundred Penny Box,* Leo and Diane Dillon, illus., New York, Viking Press, 1975, p. 20.
37. Eleanor Clymer, *We Lived in the Almont,* David K. Stone, illus., New York, Dutton, 1970, p. 95.
38. Zelpha Keatley Snyder, *The Witches of Worm,* Alton Raible, illus., New York, Atheneum, 1972, pp. 148–149.
39. Eleanor Clymer, *Me and the Eggman,* David K. Stone, illus., New York, Dutton, 1972, book jacket.
40. Ibid., p. 48.
41. Jean Robinson, *The Secret Life of T. K. Dearing,* drawings by Charles Robinson, New York, Seabury Press, 1973, p. 34.
42. Doris Orgel, *The Mulberry Music,* pictures by Dale Payson, New York, Harper & Row, 1971, p. 11.
43. Alice Childress, *A Hero Ain't Nothin' But a Sandwich,* New York, Coward, McCann & Geoghegan, 1973, p. 53.
44. Rose Blue, *Grandma Didn't Wave Back,* Ted Lewin, illus., New York, Watts, 1972, p. 59.
45. Gil Rabin, *Changes,* New York, Harper & Row, 1973, p. 147.
46. Norma Fox Mazer, *A Figure of Speech,* New York, Dell (Delacorte Press), 1973, pp. 43–44.
47. Ibid., p. 87.
48. Ibid.

# BIBLIOGRAPHY

### Fiction for younger readers

ABBOTT, SARAH. *The Old Dog,* George Mocniak, illus., Coward, McCann & Geoghegan, 1972 (3–5).

ALEXANDER, MARTHA. *The Story Grandmother Told,* Dial Press, 1969 (preschool–1).

BARTOLI, JENNIFER. *Nonna,* Joan Drescher, illus., Harvey House, 1975 (K–3).

BORACK, BARBARA. *Grandpa,* Ben Shecter, illus., Harper & Row, 1967 (K–3).

BRIGGS, RAYMOND. *Jim and the Beanstalk,* Coward, McCann & Geoghegan, 1970 (4–7).

BUCK, PEARL. *The Beech Tree,* K. Werth, illus., Day, 1955 (2–6).

BUCKLEY, HELEN. *Grandfather and I,* Paul Galdone, illus., Lothrop, Lee & Shepard, 1959.

———. *Grandmother and I,* Paul Galdone, illus., Lothrop, Lee & Shepard, 1961.

BURTON, VIRGINIA LEE. *The Little House,* Houghton Mifflin, 1942, Caldecott Medal (K–3).

———. *Maybelle, the Cablecar,* Houghton Mifflin, 1952 (K–3).

———. *Mike Mulligan and His Steam Shovel,* Houghton Mifflin, 1939 (1–3).

CARRICK, CAROL. *Old Mother Witch,* Donald Carrick, illus., Seabury Press, 1975 (K–4).

DE PAOLA, TOMIE. *Nana Upstairs and Nana Downstairs,* Putnam, 1973 (preschool–3).

ETS, MARIE HALL. *Mister Penny,* Viking Press, 1935 (1–3).

———. *Mister Penny's Race Horse,* Viking Press, 1956 (1–3).

GALDONE, PAUL. *Old Mother Hubbard and Her Dog,* McGraw-Hill, 1960 (preschool–3).

———. *The Old Woman and Her Pig,* McGraw-Hill, 1960 (preschool–2).

GAUCH, PATRICIA LEE. *Grandpa and Me,* Symeon Shimin, illus., Coward, McCann & Geoghegan, 1972.

GOFFSTEIN, M. B. *Two Piano Tuners,* Farrar, Straus & Giroux, 1970 (3–4).

HALEY, GAIL (adapted). *A Story A Story: An African Tale,* Atheneum, 1970, Caldecott Medal (K–2).

HODGES, MARGARET. *The Wave*, Blair Lent, illus., (Adapted from Lafcadio Hearn's *Gleanings in Buddha-Fields*), Houghton Mifflin, 1964.

KANTROWITZ, MILDRED. *Maxie*, Emily Arnold McCully, illus., Parents' Magazine Press, 1970 (K–3).

LEXAU, JOAN. *Benjie*, Don Bolognese, illus., Dial Press, 1964 (K–2).

———. *Benjie on His Own*, Don Bolognese, illus., Dial Press, 1964 (K–3).

LUNDGREN, MAX. *Matt's Grandfather*, Fibben Hald, illus., trans. by Ann Pyk. Putnam, 1972 (preschool–3).

RYAN, CHELI DURAN. *Hildid's Night*, Arnold Lobel, illus., Macmillan, 1971 (K–3).

SCHICK, ELEANOR. *City in the Winter*, Macmillan, 1970 (K–2).

———. *Peter and Mr. Brandon*, Donald Carrick, illus., Macmillan, 1973 (preschool–2).

SCHOETTLE, LYNN. *Grandpa's Long Red Underwear*, Emily Arnold McCully, illus., Lothrop, Lee & Shepard, 1972 (preschool–2).

SEGAL, LORE. *Tell Me A Mitzi*, Harriet Pincus, illus., Farrar, Straus & Giroux, 1970 (K–2).

SHECTER, BEN. *Across the Meadow*, Doubleday, 1973 (1–3).

SKORPEN, LIESEL MOAK. *Mandy's Grandmother*, Martha Alexander, illus., Dial Press, 1975 (4–8).

———. *Old Arthur*, Wallace Tripp, illus., Harper & Row, 1972 (preschool–3).

SMALL, ERNEST. *Baba Yaga*, Blair Lent, illus., Houghton Mifflin, 1966 (K–3).

SONNEBORN, RUTH. *I Love Gram*, Leo Carty, illus., Viking Press, 1971 (K–3).

ULDRY, JANICE MAY. *Mary Jo's Grandmother*, Eleanor Mill, illus., Whitman, 1970 (K–3).

WAHL, JAN. *Grandmother Told Me*, Mercer Mayer, illus., Little, Brown, 1972 (K–3).

WILLIAMS, BARBARA. *Kevin's Grandma*, Kay Chorao, illus., Dutton, 1975 (preschool–1).

ZOLOTOW, CHARLOTTE. *My Grandson Lew*, William Pene DuBois, illus., Harper & Row, 1974 (4–8).

———. *The Sky Was Blue*, Garth Williams, illus., Harper & Row, 1963 (K–3).

———. *William's Doll*, William Pene DuBois, illus., Harper & Row, 1972 (preschool–3).

## Fiction for the middle and upper grades

ABRAHAMS, ROBERT. *The Bonus of Redonda*, Peter Bramley, illus., Macmillan, 1969 (5–7).

AITMATOV, CHINGIZ. *The White Ship*, trans. by Mirra Ginsburg. Crown, 1972 (7+).

ANDERSON, MARY. *Just the Two of Them*. Atheneum, 1974 (4–6).

BARNWELL, ROBINSON. *Shadow on the Water*, McKay, 1967 (6–8).

BAWDEN, NINA. *A Handful of Thieves*, Lippincott, 1967 (5–7).

BENARY-ISBERT, MARGOT. *The Ark*, trans. by Clara and Richard Winston. Harcourt Brace Jovanovich, 1953 (7+).

BLUE, ROSE. *Grandma Didn't Wave Back*, Ted Lewin, illus., Watts, 1972 (3–5).

BOSTON, LUCY M. *The Children of Green Knowe*, Peter Boston, illus., Harcourt Brace Jovanovich, 1955 (4–6). Other Green Knowe stories include: *An Enemy at Green Knowe, The River at Green Knowe, A Stranger at Green Knowe.*

BRADBURY, BIANCA. *Andy's Mountain*, Robert MacLean, illus., Houghton Mifflin, 1969 (5–7).

BUCK, PEARL. *The Big Wave*, Hiroshige and Hokusai, illus., Day, 1948 (4–8).

BURTON, HESTER. *In Spite of All Terror*, Victor G. Ambros, illus., World, 1969 (6–9).

BYARS, BETSY. *After the Goat Man*, Ronald Himler, illus., Viking Press, 1974 (5–9).

———. *The House of Wings*, Daniel Schwartz, illus., Viking Press, 1972 (4–6).

———. *Trouble River*, Rocco Negri, illus., Viking Press, 1969 (3–7).

CAMERON, ELEANOR. *A Room Made of Windows*, Trina Schart Hyman, illus., Little, Brown, 1971 (5–8).

———. *To the Green Mountains*, Dutton, 1975 (6–10).

CARLSON, NATALIE SAVAGE. *The Family Under the Bridge*, Garth Williams, illus., Harper & Row, 1958 (4–6).

CHILDRESS, ALICE. *A Hero Ain't Nothin' But a Sandwich*, Coward, McCann & Geoghegan, 1973 (5–9).

CHRISTOPHER, JOHN. *The White Mountains*, Macmillan, 1967 (6–9).

———. *The City of Gold and Lead*, Macmillan, 1967 (6–9).

CLYMER, ELEANOR. *Me and the Eggman*, David K. Stone, illus., Dutton, 1972 (3–6).

———. *My Brother Stevie*, Holt, Rinehart and Winston, 1967 (4–6).

———. *The Spider, the Cave and the Pottery Bowl*, Ingrid Fetz, illus., Atheneum, 1971 (3–5).

———. *We Lived in the Almont*, David K. Stone, illus., Dutton, 1970 (4–6).

COHEN, BARBARA. *Thank You, Jackie Robinson*, Richard Cuffari, illus., Lothrop, Lee & Shepard, 1974 (5–6).

CORCORAN, BARBARA. *This Is a Recording*, Atheneum, 1971 (5–8).

DAHL, ROALD. *Charlie and the Chocolate Factory*, Joseph Schindelman, illus., Knopf, 1964 (5–6).

———. *Charlie and the Great Glass Elevator*, Joseph Schindelman, illus., Knopf, 1972 (5–7).

DEJONG, MEINDERT. *Journey From Peppermint Street*, Emily Arnold McCully, illus., Harper & Row, 1968, National Book Award (4–6).

DONOVAN, JOHN. *Good Old James*, James Stevenson, illus., Harper & Row, 1975 (all ages).

ENRIGHT, ELIZABETH. *Gone-Away Lake*, Beth and Joe Krush, illus., Harcourt Brace Jovanovich, 1957 (3–5).

ESTES, ELEANOR. *The Middle Moffat*, Louis Slobodkin, illus., Harcourt Brace Jovanovich, 1942 (4–6).

FIELD, RACHEL. *Calico Bush*, engravings by Allen Lewis. Macmillan, 1931 (5–9).

FOX, PAULA. *A Likely Place*, Edward Andizzone, illus., Macmillan, 1967 (4–6).

GREENE, CONSTANCE. *A Girl Called Al*, Byron Barton, illus., Viking Press, 1969 (4–6).

———. *The Unmaking of Rabbit*, Viking Press, 1972 (7+).

HAVILAND, VIRGINIA, adapted. *Favorite Fairy Tales Told in Czechoslovakia*, Trina S. Hyman, illus., Little, Brown, 1966 (3–5).

———, adapted. *Favorite Fairy Tales Told in Denmark*, Margot Zemach, illus., Little, Brown, 1971 (4–6).

———. *Favorite Fairy Tales Told in England*, Bettina, illus., Little, Brown, 1959 (3–4).

———. *Favorite Fairy Tales Told in France*, Roger Duvoisin, illus., Little, Brown, 1959 (3–5).

———. *Favorite Fairy Tales Told in Germany*, Susanne Suba, illus., Little, Brown, 1959 (K–3).

———. *Favorite Fairy Tales Told in Greece*, Nonny Hogrogian, illus., Little, Brown, 1970 (3–6).

———. *Favorite Fairy Tales Told in India*, Blair Lent, illus., Little, Brown, 1973 (K–3).

———. *Favorite Fairy Tales Told in Ireland*, Artur Maro Kvia, illus., Little, Brown, 1961 (2–6).

———, adapted. *Favorite Fairy Tales Told in Italy*, Evaline Ness, illus., Little, Brown, 1965 (3–5).

———, adapted. *Favorite Fairy Tales Told in Japan*, George Suyeoka, illus., Little, Brown, 1967 (3–5).

———, adapted. *Favorite Fairy Tales Told in Norway*, Leonard Weisgard, illus., Little, Brown, 1961 (3–6).

———, adapted. *Favorite Fairy Tales Told in Poland*, Felix Hoffman, illus., Little, Brown, 1963 (3–5).

———, adapted. *Favorite Fairy Tales Told in Russia*, Herbert Danska, illus., Little, Brown, 1961 (3–6).

———, adapted. *Favorite Fairy Tales Told in Scotland*, Adrienne Adams, illus., Little, Brown, 1963 (3–5).

———, adapted. *Favorite Fairy Tales Told in Spain*, Barbara Cooney, illus., Little, Brown, 1963 (3–5).

———. *Favorite Fairy Tales Told in Sweden*, Ronni Solbert, illus., Little, Brown, 1966 (2–6).

HELLBERG, HANS ERIC. *Grandpa's Maria*, trans. by Patricia Crampton, Joan Sandin, illus., Morrow, 1974 (2–5).

HOUSTON, JAMES. *Akavak: An Eskimo Journey*, Harcourt Brace Jovanovich, 1968 (4–6).

———. *The White Archer: An Eskimo Legend*, Harcourt Brace Jovanovich, 1967 (5–7).

HOWARD, MOSES. *The Ostrich Chase*, Barbara Seuling, illus., Holt, Rinehart and Winston, 1974 (5–9).

JONES, WEYMAN. *Edge of Two Worlds*, J. C. Kocsis, illus., Dial Press, 1968 (5–8).

KERR, M. E. *The Son of Someone Famous*, Harper & Row, 1974 (7+).

KLIBERGER, OMA. *Grandmother Oma*, Wallace Tripp, illus., Atheneum, 1967 (2–5).

KONIGSBERG, ELAINE. *From the Mixed-Up Files of Mrs. Basil E. Frankweiler*, Atheneum, 1967, Newbery Medal (5–7).

LOBE, MIRA. *The Grandma in the Apple Tree*, trans. by Doris Orgel, Judith Gwyn Brown, illus., McGraw-Hill, 1970 (3–4).

LORENZO, CAROL LEE. *Mama's Ghosts*, Eros Keith, illus., Harper & Row, 1974 (4–7).

MATHIS, SHARON BELL. *The Hundred Penny Box*, Leo and Diane Dillon, illus., Vilang, 1975 (3–6).

MAZER, NORMA FOX. *A Figure of Speech*, Dell (Delacorte Press), 1973 (7+).

MCNEIL, JANET. *Goodbye Dove Square*, Mary Russon, illus., Little, Brown, 1969 (5–8).

MILES, MISKA. *Annie and the Old One*, Peter Parnall, illus., Little, Brown, 1971 (1–3).

MIRSKY, REBA PAEFF. *Seven Grandmothers*, W. T. Mars, illus., Follett, 1955 (4–6).

MONJO, F. N. *Grand Papa and Ellen Aroon*, Richard Cuffari, illus., Holt, Rinehart and Winston, 1974 (1–5).

———. *Poor Richard in France*, Brinton Turkle, illus., Holt, Rinehart and Winston, 1973 (K–4).

MORGAN, ALISON. *Ruth Crane*, Harper & Row, 1974 (4–7).

ORGEL, DORIS. *The Mulberry Music*, Dale Payson, illus., Harper & Row, 1971 (4–6).

PEARCE, PHILIPPA. *Tom's Midnight Garden*, Susan Einzig, illus., Lippincott, 1958, Carnegie Medal (3–7).

RABE, BERNICE. *Rass*, Nelson, 1973 (5–9).

RABIN, GIL. *Changes*, Harper & Row, 1973 (5+).

ROBINSON, JEAN. *The Secret Life of T. K. Dearing*, Charles Robinson, illus., Seabury Press, 1973 (3–6).

SAWYER, RUTH. *Roller Skates*, Valenti Angelo, illus., Viking Press, 1936, Newbery Medal (7–8).

SCHAEFER, JACK. *Old Ramon*, Houghton Mifflin, 1960 (6–10).

SHOTWELL, LOUISA. *Magdalena*, Lilian Obligado, illus., Viking Press, 1971 (5–7).

SPYRI, JOHANNA. *Heidi*, Greta Elgaard, illus., Macmillan, 1962 (first published in 1884) (4–6).

STEELE, MARY Q. *Journey Outside*, Rocco Negri, illus., Viking Press, 1969 (5–7).

STOLZ, MARY. *The Dragons of the Queen*, Edward Frascino, illus., Harper & Row, 1969 (5–7).

———. *By the Highway Home*, Harper & Row, 1971 (6–9).

WERSBA, BARBARA. *The Dream Watcher*, Atheneum, 1968 (6–9).

WIER, ESTER. *The Barrel*, decorations by Carl Kidwell. McKay, 1966 (5–7).

WILKINSON, BRENDA. *Ludell*, Harper & Row, 1973 (6–8).

ZINDEL, PAUL. *Let Me Hear You Whisper*, Stephen Gammell, illus., Harper & Row, 1974.

———. *The Pigman*, Harper & Row, 1968 (7–9).

# 4
# Facing the Reality of Death in Children's Literature

Man alone among the things that live knows that death will come. And man, knowing that he has to die, fears death, the great unknown as a child fears the dark. "We fear to be we know not what, we know not where," said John Dryden. But what man dreads more is the dying, the relentless process in which he passes into extinction, alone and helpless and despairing. So he puts death and dying out of his mind, denying that they exist, refusing to discuss them openly, trying desperately to control them.

*John Langone*, Death Is a Noun[1]

In our contemporary society death is hidden and camouflaged. Many writers have noted that, as sex was an unmentionable aspect of life for the Victorians, for us the process has become reversed, and the end of life rather than its inception has become our great taboo.[2] Our devices for avoiding death, for hiding from its reality are many. We replace the word with a myriad of euphemisms: we speak of "the deceased," of one's "passing on," "meeting his or her maker," "going to an eternal rest." It is symptomatic that only quite recently did the *Christian Science Monitor* permit mention of the word *death* in its pages.[3] We rely on embalmers, applying their cosmetics, to affect a strange paradox, that of making the dead appear as lifelike as possible. We remove our elderly to homes for the aged. When they become ill, we transfer them to hospitals, hygienic and distant, where children are forbidden to visit the terminally ill, even when the dying are their parents.[4]

It was not always possible to expel death from our immediate reality in these ways. In an earlier, predominantly rural America, death was an integral part of the common experience. People were born at home, and it was there that they died. Mothers and infants frequently perished during childbirth in the family bedroom. Without the aid of recent medical sophistication, childhood disease was rampant and

## Death of a Young Poet*

Michele Murray is not listed in the highest ranks of American letters—her rise was prevented by many forces—but for a group of her followers she was unique as a human being and as an artist. She died last Thursday, at 40, tormented by cancer, death coming in her home with her husband offering final mercies and thoughts. The last hours of her life, amid her family and the books of her home library where she studied and wrote, were a stirring resistance against the tyranny of death. Perhaps if she had died the conventional American death—stuck in a hospital room, ministered to by strangers and kept from knowing the end was coming—many of those who knew her would not now be thinking that her life and ideas also had special meaning. The beauty of her death called out for reflections on the beauty of her life and writing. . . .

The evening before she died, Mrs. Murray, lying on a small couch in her library, had a conversation with each of her four children, the oldest 18 and the youngest seven. She explained as she did before several times that she was dying but this time she felt her body was finally giving out. She had been to hospitals several times in recent months for treatment, but there was little use in going again. She spoke in tender whispers with her children, one mind seeking communion with another, a communion not to end when a physicality ended but to endure in the longevity of feelings, backed by the human will, that no darkness can ever put out. She said good night to each of the children, and spent the hours until morning in cancerous agony that no drug could ease.

By 10 a.m., she began losing consciousness. Her husband Jim read the Psalms to her—the joyful psalms which Mrs. Murray had learned to recite in her Jewish childhood—and tried to slip water past her lips. Alone with his dying wife—the children in school—he could do nothing now except acknowledge that an awesome mystery was occurring, the power of fatality forcing themselves in another freedomless confrontation. Between one and two in the afternoon, she died. Mrs. Murray had declined the help of doctors in her last hours; keeping her alive was their business now past, but dying was hers.

At three in the afternoon, the two oldest children came home from school, and the father took them in to see the body of their mother. One son, with skills in drawing, closed the door and sketched a picture. Americans have been conditioned to avoid even thinking about death, much less looking at it, but for months this one family had been gently coached by its dying member not to hide from death when it came.

Washington Post, *March 19, 1974*

*Michele Murray is a highly regarded author of children's fiction including *Nellie Cameron* and *The Crystal Nights*.

inexorable. Given such conditions it was impossible to protect or shield children; knowledge of death was part of their informal education.

This earlier realism and directness in confronting death has no place in our contemporary way of life and in our current patterns of child rearing. Yet we must question the wisdom of hiding from death, a denial that permeates life in our families, our schools, indeed almost all of our agents of socialization.

As long as death remains one of our society's pervasive taboos, we remain uneducated regarding its complexity and unprepared to cope with this basic reality of life. So often we react inadequately in any situation involving death. We are unable to talk to a dying person, uncomfortable in his or her presence; we are at a loss for words when trying to comfort those who grieve. We are often incredibly ignorant of the sheer medical cost of dying and of expenses that may leave unaware survivors in financial need. Fiefel has noted that "evasion and avoidance have a place in man's psychic health, but an excessive ignoring of death is not healthy. A consistent recognition of the reality of death, a socialization process beginning with the youngest of children, will generally create the kind of individuals who are best prepared for their own death and that of others."[5]

There is growing evidence that many aspects of our present "death system" and its concomitant taboos and devices of camouflage can and should be changed. The books children read may be one entering wedge to help affect such change. In the remainder of this chapter we discuss the conceptions that children, at various stages of chronological development, hold of death and their reactions and their fears. We analyze the ways death has been avoided and treated in children's literature, and we review selected children's books for their portrayal of death.

## The universal fear

Where am I going,
And what is my purpose in life?

Who are my friends?
And who are my enemies?

Will they drop the atomic bomb?
Is God dead?

No man is an island,
But are all men brothers?

"Hush, now, and go to sleep!"

*Thirteen-year-old-boy*[6]

Conceptions of death develop and change as children mature. Maria Nagy studied 378 children between the ages of three and ten to determine their feelings concerning death. She found that what death means to the child can be categorized into three major developmental stages, although these are far from watertight compartments.[7] Children between three and five, at the first stage of conceptual development concerning death, may deny death as a final process. They do not recognize its irreversibility; rather, for them death is only a temporary state. It is like sleep; one dies for a while and then wakes up again. Or it is like a journey; one goes away for a while, but then comes back. This conception of death is exemplified by the young John Kennedy's reaction to the death of his father, the late President Kennedy. Returning to the White House some time after his father's death, he saw his father's secretary. "When is my Daddy coming back?" he asked.[8]

Between the ages of five and nine, children appear to realize the permanence of death, but they do not accept its universality, particularly as it applies to themselves. It is also during this stage that children personify death, as can be seen in the following discussion between an interviewer and a child.

"What is he [death] like?"

"White as snow. Death is white everywhere."

"It's wicked; it doesn't like children. . . . Once I talked about it and at night the real death came. . . . It came and messed about everywhere. It came over to the bed and began to pull away the covers. I covered myself up well. It couldn't take them off. Afterwards it went away."[9]

Beginning at approximately age nine, the child recognizes death's universality and its inevitability. He or she comes to realize that death is something that will happen, that no one is privileged or exempt. Nagy's research also demonstrated that there are three main areas in which the child has questions: What is death? What makes people die? What happens to people when they die, where do they go?

Many researchers have documented the fears children have concerning death. Fears reported at varying ages seem to parallel developmental changes in children's conceptions of death. Children between five and seven anthropomorphize death as a monster, whereas children between seven and ten associate death with separation and bodily mutilation.[10] Earl Grollman, who has written extensively concerning children's reactions to death, says that all children are frightened by death. He notes that some children have even wished they would not have to grow up, "because if you grow up you get old and die."[11]

Flora Arnstein, an author who has taught creative writing for over thirty years, finds that children express their fears and concerns about death in their poetry. For example, a ten-year-old wrote:

I met death one clumsy day,
And soon after I died.
I died coldly,
And I died mysteriously,
But I faintly remember life,
Warm life, fragrant life,

And then I left it forever,
And life left me forever.[12]

She receives poems that reflect cynicism and anger in the face of death:

Life is so lovable.
God made a world to be liked.
How friendly God is
To make a nice and amiable world!
How deceitful is God,
To fool us with a lovable world.
For he can also cause death,
And he used love as an excuse.[13]

Montaigne has remarked that "only the man who no longer fears death has ceased to be a slave."[14] Children, so many of whom have fears about death, must have an opportunity in their families and their schools to express these fears and to discuss them with others. And for those children who face death, there is need for freedom to express their grief in whatever ways are their own. For some this expression may be in the form of tears, for others in noisy or rambunctious play. Above all, children should have opportunity to discuss death, their conceptions of it, their worries, their confusions. They should feel free to discuss one who has died and to express not only positive feelings but negative ones that they may harbor as well.

Adults who work with children should be aware of the many complex ways in which youngsters react to death. For example, a child, feeling abandoned, may become hostile toward the dead person whom he views as having deserted him. Or hostility may be turned toward others, perhaps toward hospital staff for being so unskilled as to lose the life that was entrusted to their expertise. Another common reaction is for children to feel that some wrongdoing or bad deed that they committed is the cause for another's death. Thus they may be troubled and burdened by a sense of guilt.

Bereaved children may become depressed and anxious, unable to lose themselves in play, uninterested and despondent about school work and activities. Sometimes a child's grief reactions to the death of a family member or a very close friend are so well resolved at home that there are few apparent complications at school. In many cases, however, school behavior and performance are noticeably affected. In one study of forty-nine bereaved elementary school children, nearly all showed a decline in grades, and they became more passive and withdrawn in general. During the first year of bereavement, teachers were usually very kind and gave these children higher grades than they had earned. However, these teachers had trouble understanding that even two or three years after a death, a child could remain uninterested in school, still failing to work up to his or her capacity.[15]

Adults, fearful of death themselves, often reluctant even to mention the word, may be at a total loss in handling a discussion about death. Earl Grollman, in his excellent book *Explaining Death to Children*, suggests ways to approach the topic of death with them.[16] Grollman notes that an initial discussion about death should not be about the death of a child's parents. Rather, the discussion might be focused on how flowers die or on the death of a pet. He makes quite clear several unhealthy approaches that should not be taken when talking about death. For example, one should not suggest to a child that one who has died has gone on a journey, for the child may feel abandoned without even a good-bye, or the child may wait in continual hope for the one who has died to return from the long trip. Explaining death as sleep is also a comparison that is not beneficial, for children may develop a fear of bedtime, worried that when they go to sleep they may never wake up again.

The views that children hold concerning death and the emotions that the topic triggers are many and are complex. Adults whose responsibility is the emotional and intellectual growth of children must confront their own feelings about death. Moreover, opportunity should be provided for children to learn about death, for it is a process in which all will be involved.

There is a need for guidance and knowledge about dying, grief, and bereavement, but accent needs to be given to the death education of children and youth, for that has been relatively ignored. Ideally, death education should be that process whereby each person is helped to develop from childhood through maturity, and to senescence with an acceptance of death as a fact of life.[17]

Death, our universal taboo, is our children's universal concern; they have a right and a need to learn about it.

## What books have told children about death

### Unmagnificent obsession

During the 1600s a young child would have seen only one illustration in his New England Primer, a picture of Mr. John Rogers being burned at the stake as a Christian martyr. In all likelihood the child would have been encouraged by his elders to examine the picture, to note the martyr's devotion to God, and to learn from it how to die.[18]

Two centuries later a child in the 1800s might have opened the New England Primer to read:

> I in the burying place may see
> Graves shorter there than I
> From death's arrest no age is free
> Young children too must die.
> My God may such an awful sight,
> Awakening be to me!
> Oh! that by early grace I might
> For death prepared be.[19]

In *For Infant Minds* this child might have also read a very graphic depiction of decay and worms:

> You are not so healthy and gay
> So young, so active and bright,
> That death cannot snatch you away,
> Or some dread accident smite.
>
> Here lie both the young and the old,
> Confined in the coffin so small
> The earth covers over them cold,
> The grave worms devour them all.[20]

For the Puritans death was not a topic to be avoided. On the contrary, it was frequently discussed in sermons and in books. The portrayal of death in literature for children was designed to instruct young readers in the Puritan view "that the life of man on earth is a sinful one and he must be saved, but he *must* pass through death in order to reach salvation. Therefore, death should be welcomed, provided that it does not catch him while in disfavor with God, for then he shall be damned."[21] These books also used the powerful threat of death to frighten children into good behavior.

This preoccupation with death, engendered by the Puritans, remained widely prevalent in literature for children during the seventeenth, eighteenth, and nineteenth centuries. Reading through such literature for children, one has a sense of the macabre, the perverted. However, this seemingly morbid preoccupation lasting for centuries does become more understandable when viewed in the perspective of high death rates and the resultant constant awareness of dying that characterized life in these times.

Among these macabre and frightening depictions of death, a notable exception emerges, and that is Louisa May Alcott's *Little Women* (1955, first published 1868–1869). Beth's death and its effect on the close-knit March family may have been somewhat sentimentally portrayed. Nevertheless, in this book death is presented as a peaceful occurrence among loving relatives, depicted without threat or horror and without morbid concern over salvation.

## Death is dead

During much of the 1900s the treatment of death in children's literature has been in diametric contrast to that of the three preceding centuries. Instead of preoccupation and obsession with death, we find its pervasive invisibility. Evelyn Swenson in her article "The Treatment of Death in Children's Literature" states, "for almost all of the twentieth century, or for the past fifty years, death has been a taboo subject in children's books."[22] She has found that the word *death* is omitted in many of the subject indexes to the standard bibliographies in children's literature, and although some others list it as a subject heading, only a few book titles are listed under this category.

Others have also noted the current inadequate treatment of death in children's books. Marshall and Marshall, writing in 1971, note that they could find no comprehensive bibliography of children's literature concerning death. These authors also found that books concerning death for children from preschool to age seven are the most inadequate, and this inadequacy is particularly unfortunate when one considers that it is during this critical period that children's conceptions of death are being formed.[23] Judith Moss, in her article, "Death in Children's Literature," also mourns the absence of death in books for children. She describes searching the library shelves for books to read with children who were facing the loss of a dearly loved relative. She enlisted the aid of librarians who wanted to be helpful but were able to offer only a few suggestions. Disappointed, she left the library with but a handful of books to help the children cope with the death that was soon to affect their lives.[24]

In our review of children's literature we too have become aware that mention of death apparently has been systematically avoided in books for young children. We studied Caldecott award–winning picture books between 1953 and 1973. In these twenty-one award-winning books there were only two allusions made to death, one in Evaline Ness's *Sam Bangs and Moonshine* (1966), where the main character's mother is dead, and the other in Lynd Ward's *The Biggest Bear* (1952), where Johnny is requested to shoot his lovable pet bear who has grown so big that he is rapidly diminishing the family's food supplies. However, neither book actually portrays death. Sam's mother died when the girl was younger, before the story begins. Johnny does not shoot his bear, but rather his huge pet ends up ensconced in a zoo. We are forced to conclude that a young child, witness to the fading and wilting of plants and flowers, the observer of 18,000 murders on television by the time he or she is fourteen, perhaps the mourner of his or her own pet, or possible a dearly loved friend or relative, is denied the reality of death in picture books. Indeed, it would be quite probable, at least in some libraries, that a young child read through every picture book on the shelves and find only an occasional, vague allusion to a process that it will be impossible for him or her to avoid.

Fortunately, books for children today do not include the morbid, frightening portrayals of death that so often characterized children's literature in the past. Unfortunately, books for children today too rarely provide any portrayal of death at all. Despite this neglect we must emphasize that there is some mention of and some education about death in books that our children are reading. In many of the nursery rhymes, and in the folktales, the hero tales, and myths that have been passed on for centuries, death does occur. Moreover, some very recent books for children, most of them written during the late 1960s and the 1970s, are beginning to deal with the issue of death and are doing so in a wise and understanding manner.

## Portrayals of death: from Mother Goose to Hans Christian Andersen

For a child of today a first encounter with death in literature might very well be in the nursery jingles of his favorite Mother Goose edition. Of the 550 English nursery rhymes Iona and Peter Opie collected in the *Oxford Dictionary of Nursery Rhymes*, approximately 11 percent deal with death.[25] Many of the sixty rhymes that mention death portray the rather violent killing of animals, and the verse's playful rhyming is at strange odds with the images conveyed.

> There was a little man, and he had
>          a little gun;
> And his bullets were made of
>          lead, lead, lead;
> He went to the brook, and saw a
>          little duck,
> And shot it right through the
>          head, head, head.[26]

In "The Death and Burial of Poor Cock Robin," the manner of Cock Robin's death is established, and a long list of funeral assignments are made for the burial of the dead bird.

> Who killed Cock Robin?
> "I," said the sparrow,
> "With my little bow and arrow,
> I killed Cock Robin."
>
> Who saw him die?
> "I," said the fly,
> "With my little eye,
> I saw him die."
>
> Who caught his blood?
> "I," said the fish,
> "With my little dish,
> I caught his blood."[27]

The beetle volunteers to make the shroud, the linnet will carry the torch, the lark will be the clerk, the owl will dig his grave, the rook will be the parson and the dove the chief mourner, the thrush will sing a psalm, the kite will carry the coffin, and the bull will toll the bell.

> All the birds of the air
> Fell sighing and sobbing
> When they heard the bell toll
> For poor Cock Robin.

The brief mention of death, almost lost in the catalogue of Old Mother Hubbard's trials, is uniquely in tune with the preschool child's conception of death.

> Old Mother Hubbard
> Went to the cupboard,
>   To give her poor dog a bone;
> But when she got there
> The cupboard was bare,
> And so the poor dog had none.
>
> She went to the baker's
>   To buy him some bread;
> When she came back
>   The dog was dead.
>
> She went to the undertaker's
>   To buy him a coffin;
> When she got back
>   The dog was laughing.[28]

The dog denies the permanence of death by laughing as he is resurrected.

Human death is less often present in the standard collections of Mother Goose rhymes easily available to children. However, on occasion it does occur, and in "Solomon Grundy" the complete life and demise of this fellow are succinctly captured in a brief verse. The short, staccato lines emphasize the abrupt end of Solomon Grundy's neatly packaged life.

> Solomon Grundy,
> Born on a Monday,
> Christened on Tuesday,
> Married on Wednesday,
> Took ill on Thursday,
> Worse on Friday,
> Died on Saturday,
> Buried on Sunday,
> This is the end
> of Solomon Grundy.[29]

Myths, the attempts of primitive people to put in some order the painful realities of existence, also portray death. In Greek myths, for example, a child would see death, although rarely presented in a realistic manner. Instead, mythical characters underwent metamorphosis into flowers, animals, constellations, and natural earth formations. For example, Arachne the skillful weaver who sets herself above the gods is transformed into a spider. And Narcissus, the beautiful youth in love with himself, becomes a flower.

In tales of legendary heroes such as Beowulf, Havelock, The Cid, Roland, and King Arthur, children meet men of phenomenal strength and enormous courage who live with the possibility of ever-present death, but they seem to be without fear. In the death of King Arthur, a phenomenon occurs that is prevalent in many hero tales. "The dying hero is mysteriously spirited away to return when his people have need of him."[30] As with King Arthur, Finn McCool, one of Ireland's legendary heroes, does not die but instead sleeps, awaiting the time when Ireland will again have need of him.

In folk and fairy tales the child also meets death, frequently depicted as a wicked character's just retribution. For example, in "Snow White," the wicked queen dances out her life in red-hot iron shoes. The giant in "Jack and the Beanstalk" careens to his death as the beanstalk is hacked down. The evil troll is destroyed by the biggest billy goat in "Three Billy Goats Gruff." In "Hansel and Gretel" Gretel shoves the wicked witch into the oven just as the cannibal is about to devour her brother. In these tales poetic justice through death is quickly accomplished, and then just as quickly forgotten.

Hans Christian Andersen's imaginative fairy tales, written during the 1800s, reflect the author's religious faith in their portrayal of death, but they are never morbid or a threat to children. "The Steadfast Tin Soldier," about the death of two toys, is one such story. The tin soldier, one of twenty-five in a boy's nursery, is in love with a paper dancing lady who wears a blue ribbon adorned by a glittering spangle. The tin soldier falls out a window and after many adventures in the wide world, finally returns to his original home. For no apparent reason a boy throws the tin soldier into the stove and a draft blows the paper dancing lady into the flames to join the soldier. In the morning when a servant cleans out the ashes, all that is left is a little tin heart and a spangle black as coal.

"The Little Mermaid" deals not with the death of toys but rather with that of a mythical creature. The little mermaid is the youngest of five sisters who live in the lowest depths of the sea. She falls in love with a human prince, longs to win his love in return and also to gain an immortal soul. After drinking a potion prepared by the hideous sea witch, she is given a human form. But she has paid severe penalties. Whenever she walks the pain is as if she were treading on a sharp-edged knife, and she cannot speak for her beautiful voice has been relinquished to the sea witch. Moreover, the mermaid is warned that if the prince marries someone else, she will become nothing more than transient, unsubstantial foam on the sea. Although the little mermaid, unable to win the prince's love, must look on as he marries a human princess, she does not become foam, but instead one of the daughters of the air. The daughters of the air bring cool breezes to people and the fragrance of flowers and solace and healing, and through good deeds they can gain immortal souls.

Perhaps the story that best exemplifies Andersen's conception of death, a vision firmly rooted in the Christian ethic, is "The Little Match Girl." Intolerably poor, the match girl wanders the city streets on Christmas Eve and tries to sell her matches. She has no shoes and although her feet are red and blue with cold, she dares not return home, for fear of being beaten. She strikes her last matches to keep herself warm, and with each blaze a different vision appears—a warm fire, a sumptuous dinner, a magnificent Christmas tree. Finally she sees her Granny who, when alive, had always been kind and loving to her. The old Granny takes the girl in her arms and carries her up to God. In the dawn the little match girl is found frozen to death. "She was evidently trying to warm herself, people said. But no one knew what beautiful visions she had seen, and in what a blaze of glory she had entered with her dear old Granny into the heavenly joy and gladness of a new year."[31] Children often find these stories that deal with death very sad, but they evidently "speak" to children for they are among the best loved of Andersen's stories.

A number of recent books for children depict death as a reality of life. The approach these books take is a secular one, emphasizing children's reactions to death and the importance of expressing grief. As the characters in these books confront the deaths of people who are dear to them, the child who reads about them, experiencing their emotions vicariously, may grow in understanding and in acceptance of the meaning of death.

Elizabeth Kubler Ross has said, "It would be helpful if we could rear our children with the awareness of death and of their own finiteness."[32] There are a small number of fine picture books that can aid young children in gaining this awareness. The following books are, for the most part, written with sensitivity and understanding, and the themes they emphasize are important ones for children to understand.

Alvin Tresselt's *The Dead Tree* (1972) is a brief ecological study in which the death of a tree is portrayed as a dignified natural process. The oak tree has given happiness to others during its life, has provided shade and shelter for birds and animals, but even as it grows it is dying. Carpenter ants and termites tunnel through it, and a fungus grows around it causing the beginning of rot. During a hurricane the weakened tree crashes to the ground where it lies decaying. But it still continues to provide shelter for small animals and food for insects. Finally, as the years pass the disintegration of the tree becomes complete. But even in death the tree leaves its richness behind for the benefit of the living. ". . . As new trees grew in strength from acorns that had fallen long ago, the great oak returned to the earth. On the ground there remained only a brown ghost of richer loam where the proud tree had come to rest."[33]

A large percentage of the picture books that deal with death are concerned with the death of an animal, often a child's pet. *The Tenth Good Thing About Barney* (1971), by Judith Viorst, portrays a boy's hurt and confusion when his cat, Barney, dies. It also attempts to grapple with a question very much on the minds of many young children: when someone dies, where does he or she go? When his cat dies, the boy is very sad. He does not want to eat or watch television; all he wants to do is go to bed and cry. The family makes plans for a funeral for the cat and, as part of the ceremony, the boy is supposed to say ten good things about Barney. He thinks and thinks but can only come up with nine: Barney was brave, smart, funny, clean, cuddly, handsome, and only once ate one bird; he made the boy happy when he purred in his ear and when he slept on the boy's belly, he kept it warm.

After the funeral the father plants some seeds and tells the boy that the ground will give them food and a place to live while they are growing into flowers. The boy realizes that Barney is part of the ground that is helping the flowers grow, and he is finally able to tell his mother the tenth good thing about Barney.

> Barney is in the ground and he's
> helping grow flowers.
> You know, I said, that's
> a pretty nice job for a cat.[34]

Like the dead tree, Barney returns to the earth where he helps new life grow.

Sandol Warburg's *Growing Time* (1969) also shows a boy, Jamie, facing the death of a pet, his dog, King. King had been with Jamie since the boy was very young. They had played together for years, but now that King was old he spent most of his time sleeping and dreaming. One morning Jamie's mother tells him that King is dead. Jamie speaks to various members of his family seeking explanations and understanding. His Uncle John tells him that death is not a going away, but rather a return to the earth, and now that King is in the ground he is helping new life grow. Jamie still feels sad and angry at King for having deserted him when he still needs him so much. Jamie's Granny comforts him by telling him that King's spirit is not in the ground, for the spirit of someone he really loves does not die but will always live within him. Jamie's parents bring home a new puppy. At first he rejects the dog, but when he realizes the awkward, bumbling puppy needs him, Jamie decides that he will help the dog grow.

Another book dealing with the death of an animal is Ben Shecter's *Across the Meadow* (1973). Alfred the cat is getting old. He does not seem to be able to put up with the noise of the children, the liver patties are getting too tough, and his old injury is acting up. Alfred knows that it is time for a vacation, a long one from which he will not be coming back. He takes a trip across the meadow, and on his way he says good-bye to his old animal friends and takes time out to rescue a young cat whom he directs toward his own house. As Alfred journeys across the meadow, he is very aware of the pleasures of old friendships and the beauty of his surroundings; he feels regret for some past minor transgressions such as chasing the birds that now give him so much pleasure. The story concludes as Alfred finds a rusting car hidden by cornflowers and a tangle of vines. The car's cushions are soft and Alfred decides that here is a good place for his vacation. As he curls up and goes to sleep, at the white house with green shutters the young cat whom he had rescued is drinking milk out of Alfred's dish. *Across the Meadow* handles many pertinent themes well: the intensified pleasure in life that impending death brings, the sense of continuity as the young cat takes Alfred's place. However, this book is marred by the unfortunate metaphor of death as a vacation. Unless appropriate discussion takes place as the book is read to a young child, it is not hard to imagine his or her confusion and worry about family trips and vacations. Also, there is an unsatisfying, distasteful sense

Nana Upstairs, Nana Downstairs

conveyed by Alfred's burial ground, a junked and rusting old car.

A simple but effective picture book dealing with death is Margaret Wise Brown's *The Dead Bird* (1958). A group of children find a dead bird. Its heart is not beating and it is stiff. The children bury the bird in the woods, hold a funeral service, and inscribe a tombstone. Every day the children put fresh flowers on the grave and sing to the bird—until they forget. The children in this brief picture book recognize death and find relief from their sorrow in the funeral rituals they provide. In its final words, the book also suggests that life must continue for the living and preoccupation with death must not last.

There are only a few picture books that present dying in human terms. Two of these are concerned with a child's coping with the death of a grandmother. Tomie de Paola's *Nana Upstairs and Nana Downstairs* (1973) is about Tommy, his grandmother, and his great-grandmother. When Tommy visits every Sunday afternoon, his grandmother is always standing by the big black stove in the kitchen downstairs, and his great-grandmother, who is ninety-four years old, is always in bed upstairs. So Tommy calls them Nana Upstairs and Nana Downstairs. One morning Tommy's mother tells him that Nana Upstairs has died. His mother explains that death "means that Nana Upstairs won't be here any more." Tommy asks if Nana Upstairs will ever come back and his mother answers, "No dear. . . . Except in your memory whenever you think about her."[35] From then on he calls Nana Downstairs just plain Nana. Once he sees a shooting star from his window and his mother suggests that this might have been a kiss from Nana Upstairs. When Tommy grows older, Nana Downstairs dies, and then he thinks of them both as Nana Upstairs. The slight text and the pictures combine to create a moving story. Death's permanence is stressed as well as life's continuity through memory of the dead. The falling star as a kiss from Nana Upstairs adds a touch of fantasy to the story's realism.

One of the finest picture books dealing with death is Miska Miles's *Annie and the Old One* (1971). Annie loves everything about her Navaho world, but most of all she loves the evenings when her grandmother tells her stories of long ago. Annie's mother is weaving a rug, and the Old One tells Annie that when the rug is taken from the loom, her grandmother must go to Mother Earth. In the days that follow, Annie tries many different schemes to keep her mother from weaving. When these fail, Annie gets up during the night and pulls out the work her mother has accomplished during the day. Then the Old One takes a walk with Annie through the cornfields and explains that time cannot be held back, that she is ready to die, and that all things come from the earth and to the earth they must return. Annie understands that her beloved grandmother is ready to die.

The sun rose but it also set. The cactus did not bloom forever. Petals dried and fell to earth. She knew that she was part of the earth and the things on it. She would always be a part of the earth, just as her grandmother had always been, just as her grandmother would always be, always and forever. And Annie was breathless with the wonder of it.[36]

When Annie returns to the hogan, she picks up the weaving stick her grandmother had given her and begins to weave "as her mother had done, as her grandmother had done." The book portrays a touching and warm relationship between granddaughter and grandmother and the lyrical text conveys life's transiency, the inevitability of death. Yet there is a sense of permanence as the Old One's work is continued by her daughter and granddaughter.

There is nothing threatening or macabre about death as presented in these picture books, nothing, with the possible exception of *Across the Meadow*, to confuse or trouble the young child. Death is dignified, it is a natural process. Human closeness with nature and the earth is stressed as is the ability of the dead to keep on giving—whether they make flowers grow or provide a memory—to those who continue to live. There is also a suggestion of permanence even in death, for one's work can be continued by those who live after.

There is cause for optimism in the recency of these books for it suggests that we will be finding more fine picture books that deal with death. With the exception of *The Dead Bird*, the books discussed were published during the 1970s. Written with compassion and wisdom, they can help children begin to face the reality of death and begin the difficult process of accepting their own finiteness.

## Fiction for children in the middle and the upper grades

Just as there are recent picture books that deal honestly and openly with the reality of death, so also for older children there is an increasing number of books concerned with death. Some characters in these books must face the death of a close friend; others cope with a death in their families; and yet others, suffering from terminal illness, are forced to confront their own impending deaths. There is also a trend toward portraying senseless and violent death, and some characters must look within themselves to deal with the realization that they may have been responsible for the death of another human being. Reactions to death, as portrayed in these books, are complex and varied: there is intense suffering; there is rage, guilt, resentment, calm acceptance, and an intensified appreciation of the beauty in life.

## The death of a friend

Doris Buchanan Smith's *A Taste of Blackberries* (1973) presents a boy stunned by the sudden, unexpected death of his closest friend, Jamie. One day Jamie is playing with the boy and other friends, teasing a bees' nest with a long stick. In a matter of minutes Jamie is on the ground, dead from an allergic reaction to a bee's sting. The boy cannot believe that death can come from nowhere like this, taking its toll with such incredible swiftness. When the boy sees Jamie fall, he assumes, with some impatience and resentment, that his friend is clowning around again. Tired of Jamie's jokes, he does not bother to help his friend get up, and he even considers the arrival of the ambulance a tribute to Jamie's expert ability as an attention getter. Thus the boy must cope not only with sorrow but also with guilt. Finally the boy works his way through the tangle of emotions that facing death has created, and he is able to cry, to face Jamie's mother, and to go berry picking, a special activity that he and Jamie had always loved to share.

Many young characters are somewhat out of place among their peers, seeking the friendship and understanding of older people. In Constance Greene's *A Girl Called Al* (1969) two girls form a special relationship with elderly Mr. Richards, their apartment building superintendent. There is much that is both intriguing and comforting about Mr. Richards.

He serves the girls carrot sticks and shooters of coke, waxes his floor by gliding over it with skates made of cloth, and, perhaps most important of all, he is a very understanding listener. One night Mr. Richards dies of a heart attack in his sleep. The girls listen to explanations that this is a good way to die, that Mr. Richards has had a happy death. They puzzle over the paradoxical notion of a happy death and are not sure whether they like the idea. One thing they are sure of, however, is the happiness that knowing Mr. Richards has brought them. "There is one thing about knowing a person like Mr. Richards. You never forget. When I feel depressed I remember all the laughs we had and all the carrot sticks and all the shooters of coke, and I feel better."[37]

The death of another elderly man is the central theme of Barbara Cohen's *Thank You, Jackie Robinson* (1974). Sam Greene is a fatherless, lonely boy who loves the Brooklyn Dodgers with a unique intensity. He has memorized the strategies of every Dodger's

Annie and the Old One

game, and he yearns for someone with whom he can share the Brooklyn Dodgers. He finds a soul mate in Davy, the elderly black man who cooks for the boarders in his mother's rooming house. Together the boy and the old man re-hash old plays, analyze the sports pages of the *Daily News,* listen with rapt attention to games on the radio, and on special occasions go down to Ebbets Field to cheer in person. When Davy, suffering from a heart attack, is taken to the hospital, Sam wants to offer him a special present, something so wonderful that its magic will make Davy well again. Drawing on *chutzpah* he did not know he had, Sam manages to get a very special ball, one on which autographs of all the team members surround the words *For Davy. Get Well Soon. Jackie Robinson.* Since children are not allowed to visit the intensive care ward, Sam sneaks up to present the magic ball to Davy. Davy looks so small and so tired that merely opening his eyes seems to take great effort. The old man is delighted with the ball, but Sam realizes that there is no magic in it, that it will not make Davy well. A week later Davy dies. The boy is reluctant to go to his friend's funeral, and viewing the body bothers him. For him, the body lying in the coffin is not Davy, but rather a meaningless shell of what Davy was. Sam's mother tries to comfort him, explaining that as long as you remember people, they are not really dead. However, memories are of little comfort to Sam, and his hurt is so great that he wishes he had never known Davy at all.

If I'd never known him, I wouldn't have had this funny feeling in my stomach right then. . . . If I hadn't known him, if I hadn't loved him, Davy could have died and it wouldn't have made any difference to me at all. . . . I thought the emptiness I felt where I was supposed to have a heart was never going to go away.[38]

Sam leaves the funeral and with a dull anger he repeatedly throws a ball against the ceiling.

After a while he turns on the ball game on the radio for Davy might just be somewhere listening.

This book emphasizes the intense, terrible hurt of losing someone close. It raises many questions that children ask: Where does a dead person, not his shell but the essence of the person, go? Where does one turn to find comfort and strength when facing death? As Sam reaches over to turn on the ball game, the book closes with the theme that intense, overwhelming involvement with death is not healthy, that the activities of the living must go on.

## "A death in the family"

There are some memorable portrayals of children who face the death of a family member. For some of these children death leaves their lives so drastically changed that they have no time to express grief and sorrow as they struggle for sheer survival. Two characters, so involved in staying alive themselves that they barely have time to grieve for their dead, are Minty Lou in Olivia Coolidge's *Come by Here* (1970) and Mary Call in Vera and Bill Cleaver's *Where the Lilies Bloom* (1969).

Minty Lou is a child who had been loved and cared for, provided with starched new pinafores and plenty of food to eat. Her mother, Big Lou, intelligent and forceful, works as a supervisor in a hospital, a job of unusual status and remuneration for a black woman living in the early 1900s. Life changes suddenly and drastically for Minty Lou when her parents are killed in an accident. Gone is the love, comfort, and attention Minty Lou has always known. Now she is passed along from relative to relative. At first she is tolerated. Then hidden jealousies of Big Lou surface, and these, combined with Minty Lou's bewilderment and suspicion, cause tolerance to turn to cruelty and even physical brutality. Based on an actual life story, *Come by Here* portrays Minty Lou, given no time to grieve and no one with whom she can share her sorrow, growing defensive and hardened, struggling to regain the place of her own that death has taken away.

In *Where the Lilies Bloom* (1969) Roy Luther, the father of an Appalachian family, dies. The orphaned children, headed by the oldest girl, Mary Call, must fend for themselves. To begin with they must hide their father's death to avoid outside interference. The father has an unforgettable burial as, in the dead of night against the stark background of the Appalachian Mountains, the courageous Mary Call and her brother lower Roy Luther into the ground.

For other characters the concern is not one of survival, but of coping with the grief that loss of a parent brings. Mildred Lee's *Fog* (1972) describes the painful process of growing up. Seventeen-year-old Luke Sawyer feels lucky; he has nice parents, a clubhouse gang, and he adores his girl friend, Milo. Then in one summer his luck comes crashing down around him, as his clubhouse burns down, he loses his girl friend, and his father unexpectedly dies of a heart attack. The father, mild, quiet, and unpretentious, was in his own way heroic. The intense sorrow that pervades the Sawyer household as well as the guilt that consumes Luke for being too busy with his own affairs to spend time with his father is skillfully and compassionately conveyed.

The beautifully written *Up a Road Slowly* (1966), by Irene Hunt, begins as the Trelling family must face the death of their mother. Seven-year-old Julia reacts hysterically, and she spends her first morning in the home of her Aunt Cordelia barricaded in a closet screaming. Finally Julia finds refuge in her aunt's arms, and they both cry until there are no more tears left. The story goes on to describe Julia's life from the death of her mother

until her graduation from high school ten years later. It portrays Julia's growing love for her severe but sincerely loving and honest Aunt Cordelia. The story also handles the problems of Julia's first love, her father's remarriage, and alcoholism and emotional disturbance in adult characters.

*By the Highway Home* (1971), by Mary Stolz, shows the Reed family trying to face the terrible loss of a son, Beau, killed in Vietnam. Thirteen-year-old Catty cannot bear to watch the changes that death has wrought in her family. Her mother too often stares into space, not hearing when Catty speaks to her. Her father does not laugh any more or call himself Handsome Daddy. Her parents, who never used to fight, now argue with one another in quiet, hard voices. Worst of all, although Catty wants desperately to talk about Beau, no one else in the family seems able to mention him. A key theme stressed in this book is the need to be able to talk about someone who has died and to be able to express grief openly rather than keeping it controlled and hidden inside.

The need to express grief, to cry aloud, is also one of the themes of *Grover* (1970), by Vera and Bill Cleaver. Grover's mother is dying of cancer and, unable to bear her family's watching her slow decline and death, she commits suicide. The remaining family, Grover and his father, flounder desperately before they learn to cope with her death. Father and son each have a different way of handling their sorrow and neither can understand the other. Grover's father is distraught with grief. For him life has to stop for a while as he mourns long and intensively. He cannot bear to have any item in his wife's room touched. When Grover asks if he can go fishing, his father's reaction is one of cold fury that the son could think of any form of pleasure in this period of intense grief. In contrast to his father's emotional outbursts, Grover appears almost cooly stoical. Above all, he is determined not to let his terrible sorrow show.

I'm tough, that's because I've got more Cornett in me than Ezell. My mother was a Cornett before she married my father. Us Cornetts don't howl about things. There's no sense in howling; it doesn't do a bit of good. When something bad happens to you, like your mother dying, you've got to go it alone the way I've got it figured out.[39]

Father and son grope to answer questions about death and to cope with their sorrow. Their struggle to accept the inevitable is sensitively portrayed.

*The High Pasture* (1964), by Ruth Harnden, relates Tim McCleod's adventures on a Colorado ranch. It is also a superb study of this boy's reactions to the death of his mother; his emotional turmoil encompasses grief, anger, guilt, and finally acceptance of her death.

Tim is sent to live with his Aunt Kate on her ranch in Colorado while his mother is sick in the hospital. Although worry about his mother is a constant fear on the edge of Tim's mind, he does manage to get involved in the activities of the ranch and in trying to win the affection of a dog whose former owner has been killed. There is a foreshadowing of the death of Tim's mother early in the book. On Tim's return from the high pasture, he sees Aunt Kate's dog, Old Mac, limping down the road, slowly and stiffly as though he can hardly move. Tim whistles to call the dog back, and when old Mac turns, he collapses to the ground and dies. Tim's immediate reaction is one of guilt; he feels that if he had not whistled, if he had stayed at the ranch instead of going to the high pasture, perhaps old Mac would still be alive. Aunt Kate smiles grimly as Tim unburdens his feelings. "Do you think you can stop death?" she asks.

When Tim learns that his mother has died, he feels a pain in his chest so tight that he can hardly get his breath around it and he fights desperately to keep back tears.

"Go ahead and cry!" she [Aunt Kate] said. "Or go out and cry if you've got to. But you listen to me!" she said then, and she sounded almost angry. "Real men have got real feelings and it's no disgrace to them."[40]

The news of death leaves Tim to grapple with many conflicting emotions. He feels angry that no one had told him that his mother's illness was to be fatal. He feels hostility toward his mother for dying, a futile, betrayed feeling that somehow she could have gotten well if she had really tried. He is furious with the doctors who were supposed to make people well, but who had not been able to cure his mother.

When Tim's father arrives at the ranch, Tim confronts him, and the boy and the man discuss death. They share their feelings and try to cope with questions that have no answers. Tim expresses his hostility, telling how angry he is that he had not been allowed to stay with his mother, had not been included as the family coped with death. Tim's father explains that sending Tim away was the hardest action he and Tim's mother had ever taken and that even now he is not sure that their decision to send Tim away was the wisest one. Because Tim was so close to his mother, so dependent on her, they had wanted him to get some space and to develop self-reliance.

Tim questions the unfairness of death, the inequity of his mother's having so much less time than Aunt Kate, the injustice of some dying as babies and others enduring into old age. The father admits that he too is terribly baffled, and he tells his son his way of living with death's injustice:

"Guess all I can say," he told Tim a minute later, "is what I've been saying to myself over and over—in anything and everything, it isn't the quantity that counts. It's the quality. The quality of your mother was something beautiful—and if she lived to be a hundred years old it couldn't have been any greater." He sighed a deep sigh.

"We have to remember that, Tim," he said. "We have to remember her. We have to talk about her as time goes by and remember all the fine, lovely things she was."[41]

The father and son are able to share their feelings with one another, and to struggle from hostility toward an acceptance of death.

In some children's books a closely knit family is shown as providing the security, the patient understanding, and the love that help a child face death. One such book is Madeleine L'Engle's *Meet the Austins* (1960). The warm, happy family life of the Austins is touched by the death of a close friend whom the family calls Uncle Hal. Orphaned Maggy Hamilton, whose father perished in the plane crash along with Uncle Hal, comes to live with the Austins. Troubled and spoiled, she disrupts the smooth pattern of family life until she learns to accept and to love the Austins—and they her. The Austin children express anger at death and the inability to understand it. Their mother responds, saying that perhaps no one can really understand death, but that awareness of its inevitability can help people realize that "being alive is a gift, the most wonderful and exciting gift in the world."[42]

Virginia Lee says that she wrote *The Magic Moth* (1972) to express her belief that "there is enough genuine mystery surrounding death without further hiding it behind the false mystery of secrecy."[43] Maryanne, the middle child of the five children in the Foss family, has been sick for a long time. Lying in her bedroom, she sleeps frequently and seems to be getting consistently weaker. One evening the father tells the children that Maryanne's heart is not big enough to keep pumping for her, and that she must die. Mark-O, the youngest child in the family, is very worried about what will happen to Maryanne when she dies. He knows that his dead guinea pig had been buried in the ground, and he is disturbed at the thought of Maryanne's having to stay in the cold, wet earth. His mother explains that Maryanne will not feel anything after she dies and that the most important part of her, the part that does the dreaming, will be somewhere else. Hearing this makes Mark-O feel better.

This book contains a moving scene in which Maryanne dies, not separate and removed from her family in a hospital but in her own bedroom. One night the father tells the children that it is time to say good-bye to Maryanne. It is so quiet in her room that Mark-O can hear her soft breathing—and then it stops. At the moment of Maryanne's death a white moth flies out of the window, and it seems to Mark-O as if the dreaming part of Maryanne is going away. Then the family leaves Maryanne's room and sits down together around the kitchen table to drink hot cocoa. The closeness and the warmth help ease the terrible loneliness in Mark-O. When Mark-O questions why Maryanne has to die, his mother says that she does not know, that perhaps some people are not meant to live very long but that, "We all learned many things from Maryanne . . . mostly I guess, how much we appreciate our family."[44]

*The Magic Moth* is a straightforward and yet delicate story, emphasizing the importance of talking about death within the comfort and warmth of the family. It also illustrates how death can help people appreciate with greater intensity the love and beauty that is part of life.

Robert Newton Peck's *A Day No Pigs Would Die* (1972) tells of life in the Peck family, plain people living on a farm in Vermont without "frills," in the Shaker way. It also tells of how twelve-year-old Robert must accept the death of Haven Peck, the father whom he idolizes. Haven works hard, and although he smells from killing pigs, Robert understands that this is work that has to be done, that his father does it very well, and to

Robert the smell of butchered pigs is a proud one. Even when his father kills the only thing that Robert has ever owned, his pig Pinky, because she is barren and there is no money to support an animal that does not give in some way to the farm, Robert understands that his father has done what must be done.

When Robert faces the death of his father, he grows to manhood. Haven Peck feels that he is going to die soon, and he asks his son to be ready. The father's dying is treated without sentimentality; the funeral is plain, as Haven's life has been plain, and Robert accepts his father's death as a return to the earth that he loved: "I got to the fresh grave all neatly mounded and pounded. Somewhere down under all that Vermont clay was my father, Haven Peck. Buried deep in the land he sweated so hard on and longed so much to own. And now it owned him."[45] The theme that pervades this book is that of accepting death with fortitude and dignity because it is something that has to be done.

The need to accept death as part of life is also reflected in Pearl Buck's *The Big Wave* (1947). Kino lives in Japan on a mountain farm high above the sea. His closest friend, Jiya, lives on the beach, for his father is a fisherman. The two boys learn that although land and sea seem friendly, both hold the potential for doing great harm. It is the latent danger of the sea that becomes unleashed as a tremendous wave threatens to sweep over the beach. The children of the families on the beach are sent up the mountain. Jiya reaches Kino's house, and as he turns to look back, he sees the great wave cover the fishing village and return to the sea, sucking away everyone and everything that had been on the shore. Kino's family resolves to take Jiya in as their own son, but Jiya is so overcome with grief that he has little comprehension of what is going on around him. Kino's father says that Jiya will cry for a long time, but the family

must allow him his sorrow and Jiya will one day be happy again "for life is always stronger than death." Jiya does recover from his sorrow, and when he grows older he marries Kino's sister, Setsu. The young couple choose to once again live close to the sea and they, and others like them, restore life to the devastated beach. Their decision to live at the scene of the former tragedy exemplifies the theme of the book. As Kino's father says:

To live in the presence of death makes us brave and strong . . . that is why our people never fear death. We see it too often and we do not fear it. To die a little later or a little sooner does not matter. But to live bravely, to love life, to see how beautiful the trees are and the mountains, yes, and even the sea, to enjoy work because it produces food for life—in these things the Japanese are a fortunate people. We love life because we live in danger. We do not fear death because we understand that life and death are necessary to each other.[46]

The central metaphor of the book is that of a great gateway through which we must pass to be born and to die. Just as we were afraid to be born so we are afraid to die, because we do not know what awaits us on the other side of the gateway.

Acceptance of death as an integral part of life characterizes the two previous books. In contrast, John Gunther's moving *Death Be Not Proud* (1949) is filled with rage and despair, and its impact is all the more powerful because the desperate struggle for life that it chronicles actually took place.

Johnny Gunther was an exceptionally intelligent student with a passionate love for knowledge and for life. Throughout his fight for life, the series of painful operations, the innumerable treatments, the failing vision, the loss of control over the left side of his body, his uppermost concern appears to be for the feelings of those around him, particularly for his parents. The Gunthers watch, with agonizing hope and despair, the desperate struggle and the gradual deterioration as Johnny finally succumbs to a brain tumor. His father expresses the struggle his only child must endure as

a primitive to-the-death struggle of reason against violence, reason against disruption, reason against brute unthinking force—this was what went on in Johnny's head. What he was fighting against was the ruthless assault of chaos. What he was fighting for was, as it were, the life of the human mind.[47]

After his son's death the father, John Gunther, is able to make a modicum of peace with death, and to see it, however unjust as it may seem, as an inherent part of the process of life.

But to anybody who ever knew him he is still alive. I do not mean merely that he lives in both of us or in the trees at Deerfield or in anything he touched truly, but that the influence, the impact of a heroic personality continues to exert itself long after mortal bonds are snapped. Johnny transmits permanently something of what he was, since the fabric of the universe is continuous and eternal.[48]

This book raises many crucial questions: What is the meaning of death? How is it to be faced —with fear, loathing, resignation, acceptance? How do those who survive a loved one find comfort and courage? What is the justification for death? Why should this brilliant child filled with exceptional promise have been stolen by death at so early an age?

One of the most haunting and well-written novels that deals with a child's struggle to accept death is Mollie Hunter's *A Sound of Chariots* (1972). Growing up in Scotland after World War I, Bridie has a special place in the sun as her father's favorite of the five children in the McShane family. Her father's death ravages the whole family and provides Bridie with an experience so intensely painful that she

emerges sensitive and precocious far beyond her years. She watches her mother, formerly so quiet and gentle, react violently to the loss of her husband, and she experiences vicariously her mother's terrible sorrow. All she sees, she senses vicariously, and she is tortured as she passes in the street men with stumps of legs and arms, reminders of the devastation of the past war. Above all, she realizes with stunning clarity that if death could happen to her father, it could also happen to her, and she becomes obsessed with the passage of time. She feels that she must experience each moment of her life fully, for soon it will be past, out of her grasp, never again to be called back. As the novel closes Bridie is leaving home, and she is aware that she has the talent, as a poet, to express her awareness of "each passing moment as a fragment of the totality of life itself."

## The "I" of death

In the previous sections we have discussed the portrayal of survivors who must face the death of a friend or relative. In a few books the main characters must travel to the eye of death, where they are forced to confront their own impending demise.

*In Hang Tough, Paul Mather* (1973 by Alfred Slote, a young boy is suffering from leukemia. The story takes Paul from a vibrant athlete with the seeds of his disease already hampering his physical ability, to a hospital bed, praying for time and a medical miracle. Despite frustration, pain, and anguish, Paul hangs toughly and tenaciously onto life.

Also suffering from leukemia is nineteen-year-old Annika Hallen in Gunnel Beckman's *Admission to the Feast* (1972). Annika accidentally learns from a substitute doctor that she is dying. Distraught and appalled, she seeks solitude at her family's summer cottage, where she pounds out on the typewriter her intense mourning for all of the richness of life that she must learn to relinquish.

I want to have the earth and the sun and the flowers which wither away in the autumn and people who live and squabble and work and play and sing, and children who are born, and new things that are discovered, and love. . . . I try, indeed I do, to think of all the children who die of starvation every day, of all the people who are killed every day all over the place, young people like me, who have only been allowed to take a sniff at life. . . . but it is other people's deaths. It is not mine.[49]

Annika contemplates suicide but rejects the idea because of the burden of guilt it would leave on those who survive her, and because of the desperate hope that a miracle might be discovered. She finally works her way through the emotional upheaval and begins to face her remaining time with courage and dignity. Paige Dixon's *May I Cross Your Golden River?* (1975) presents Jordan, who learns that he has Lou Gehrig's disease, that he must cope with the knowledge of impending death.

E. B. White's *Charlotte's Web* (1952) is a superb fantasy in which the heroine, the brilliant and loyal spider, Charlotte A. Cavatica, meets death without sentimentality and with complete courage at the peak of her talents. The Zuckerman barn is a good, warm place, close to the essence of life, the cyclical changes of nature, and birth and death. "It was the kind of barn that swallows like to build their nests in. It was the kind of barn that children like to play in,"[50] and it was here that Wilbur the pig lived, along with Templeton the rat, the goose who is sitting on her eggs, and Charlotte A. Cavatica, the spider who becomes Wilbur's lifelong friend. When the animals learn that Wilbur is being well fed and fattened only to be butchered eventually, it is Charlotte who devises and implements a scheme that saves Wilbur's life. She spins a web and within it she writes "Some Pig." This is followed by a series of webs in praise of Wilbur. People come from miles around to see the miracle of the spider webs and of the pig who inspired their creation. When Wilbur wins a special prize at the state fair, Charlotte knows that Mr. Zuckerman will never part with him and his life is assured. It is then that Charlotte creates her magnum opus, the laying of her egg sac, knowing even as she works that spiders always die after they have hatched their eggs. In contrast to Wilbur's hysterics at the thought of dying, Charlotte faces death without as much as a momentary shudder. There is no scheme around this death, and Charlotte accepts what she knows is inevitable with perfect dignity.

When Charlotte's eggs hatch, Wilbur is delighted with her children, and although most of them leave the Zuckerman barn, three spiders stay because they like the barn and they like Wilbur. Wilbur is never without friends, for Charlotte's children and her grandchildren and her great-grandchildren live in the doorway of the barn.

Life in the barn was very good—night and day, winter and summer, spring and fall, dull days and bright days. It was the best place to be, thought Wilbur, this warm delicious cellar, with the garrulous geese, the changing seasons, the heat of the sun, the passage of swallows, the nearness of rats, the sameness of sheep, the love of spiders, the smell of manure, and the glory of everything.[51]

Charlotte knows that life into death, like the changing of the seasons and the turning of day into night, is part of the way of things, an unavoidable given in the process of nature. She lives on in her children and her children's children, and in Wilbur's memory, and in the memories of all children who read *Charlotte's Web*.

## Violent death and an immune society

In this section we discuss a representative sample of books that portray death with harsh realism. Sometimes these books present a main character who dies, leaving few people who care enough to mourn. Other books portray violent death in a violent culture of gangs, drugs, or war. In yet other stories, the main characters must face the terrible awareness of bearing some responsibility for the death of another human being.

John Donovan's *Wild in the World* (1971) is a chronicle of the deaths of the last members of a large New Hampshire mountain family, the Gridleys. Of seven brothers and four sisters, only three brothers are left alive as the story opens. In the initial two-and-one-half pages the book documents how eight of the children and the parents had died. By page 6, two of the remaining brothers are dead, one killed by a cow, the other from an infection caused by a fishhook. John Gridley buries his brothers and begins to live alone. The Gridleys have never paid taxes, are not on anybody's records, and no one knows that John is the only member of his family left. John's one friend is a wild dog, or possibly a wolf. John handles all the chores of the farm, does haying for summer people, and takes pleasure in the camaraderie of his dog, Son. John is very casual about death, believing that "God takes as easily as he gives." Finally John is taken, dying of pneumonia. Eventually John's body is discovered on the steps of his house, and people, nervous about the total demise of the Gridley family, begin to stay away from Rattlesnake Mountain. Only Son returns to the Gridley farmhouse from time to time, to pay his respects. This story of a boy who meets death alone with only his dog has a keen dramatic intensity.

*The Loner* (1963), by Ester Wier, is about a boy without a name or a family who has been picking crops for as long as he can remember. He has learned early that he must take care of himself, for he has always been met by indifference and hostility. The one exception had been Raedy, with whom he traveled for a while picking beans and potatoes. Raedy had started to teach him to write, and promised to find a name that was just right for him. But their friendship is a brief one. The two friends are picking behind a digging machine and Raedy is about to tell him the name she had picked for him when her yellow hair gets caught in the moving parts of the machine. "Powerless to help, he stood and watched in cold horror while the machine ripped and tore."[52]

Death is again treated with stark realism in Jean Renvoize's *A Wild Thing* (1970). Morag had run away from a series of foster homes to find her own space in the mountains, one she had pictured and dreamed of for years. Alone in the wilderness, she learns to fulfill her physical needs of food and shelter and she grows in independence. However, many emotional needs go unsatisfied. Lonely and disturbed, she worships a decaying skeleton, the "Mossman," and she becomes preoccupied with the dream of a baby of her own to bring warmth and companionship to her life. When she does become pregnant and the baby grows within her, Morag realizes she must seek help. She goes for aid into the civilized world of the village, but to the villagers she is a crazed wild thing haunting the mountains, and they try to shoot her on sight. She runs back to the wilderness where she collapses in pain and exhaustion.

When the baby came she hardly felt it slipping away from her. . . . When she opened her eyes some time later, night had fallen. . . . Again the stags roared to each other and she was glad of their sound.

It seemed to her now that she could see them, leaping near her, crossing the stream, flying like birds almost, just as they had in the picture she had so carefully guarded all those years. Satisfied at last now that she had recognized where she was, she lay back smiling. The picture was opening up for her. With total love and familiarity she unclenched her hands and entered her own land.[53]

Morag's death goes unnoticed and unmourned. It is a long time before another human comes to the spot where she had died, and by then her bones are white sand. The harshness of Morag's death is softened by the beauty and the comfort that death holds for her. Morag's death does not come in the image of the "grim reaper," but rather as a "gentle night" bringing solace and release from struggle.

In books that deal with drugs and with war, death often occurs violently and senselessly. In Rose Blue's heavily didactic *Nikki 108*, Nikki lives with her mother and her older brother, Don, whom she had always depended on. But at nineteen Don is hooked, everything about him is changed. Nikki eventually faces the shattering experience of finding him outside, dead beside the lamppost, an eyedropper still in his arm. His death and the bitter, unsatisfied lives of his friends make Nikki realize that she must work for something better for herself, and she joins her school's honors science class to work toward becoming a nurse or doctor.

Sharon Bell Mathis' *Teacup Full of Roses* (1972), a fine novel with intense dramatic impact, also portrays the drug culture and the tragedy it causes in a black family, the deterioration of a gifted artist, and the violent death of a brilliant boy. Paul, the family's oldest son is on drugs, wasting his talent as an artist, existing only for his next fix. His mother loves him intensely, almost to the neglect of her other two children, and with unrealistic expectations, convinces herself of his potential miraculous change. The middle son, Joe, realizes this reformation will never come, and he

puts his money, literally, on his younger brother, Davey, a student of exceptional promise. When Paul steals the war bonds Joe had planned to give Davey, there is a violent struggle to get the money back, and Davey is killed. Davey's death and Joe's vision of the heaven where his brother will go conclude the book: "The people are together and trouble never comes. . . . It is a love place, a real black love place. . . . Joe tried to smile and couldn't. 'I wouldn't kid you, Davey. Only the smart ones get to go—people like you! The good ones.' "[54] With Davey's death Joe knows that if anyone's going to "make it," it will have to be him; and he will try for himself and for Davey.

Death is also portrayed as a companion to the brutal insanity of war. In Gail Graham's *Crossfire* (1972), Harry, a soldier in Vietnam lost from his platoon, comes upon a family of enemy children, the only survivors of a village raid. The oldest one is a twelve-year-old girl, Mi; the youngest is a baby. The children take Harry to a burnt-out clearing and the realization comes to him like a blow to the stomach that it had once been a village. "Those bits of charred wood, tipped and skewed had been houses. The bloated piles of charred matter had been people." As the novel progresses, this grotesque scene of mass death is intensified by the individual deaths of all of the central characters.

Harry and the children view one another with suspicion and hostility, but they unite in an effort for survival. Understanding and tolerance begin to grow as Harry saves one of the children from drowning and mourns with them over the sudden death of the little baby. This bourgeoning friendship is cut short as Harry is wounded in a B-52 raid and never regains consciousness. Mi stays with him until she is certain that he is dead. As she is about to leave him, new planes emerge, and instead of bombs, men in parachutes bail out. They machine-gun Mi's brother, and the book con-cludes with Mi's own brutal death.

"Murderers! Killers! They were only children.
. . . Children!"

The tall soldier slapped her so hard that she stumbled and fell. . . . He flung her to the ground. Crouching there, she saw the fire leap from the muzzle of his gun.

The universe itself seemed to open beneath her in a flaming burst of sound and crimson that was beyond pain, beyond everything. . . . and then there was nothing and she knew no more.[55]

Gang warfare, too, yields violent death. Susan Hinton's powerful *The Outsiders* (1967) portrays the conflict between two gangs, one, the Greasers, lower class and filled with resent-ment at being outside the American dream of affluence; the other, the Socs, wealthy and filled with contempt for the Greasers in their blue jeans, T shirts, and leather jackets. Ponyboy, orphaned and living with his two older broth-ers, is a member of the Greasers. The hatred that simmers between the two gangs frequently erupts in violence, and in one deadly fight, Ponyboy's friend kills one of the Socs. The two boys flee, but eventually decide to give themselves up. They stop to rescue some small children from a fire, and Ponyboy's friend dies from injuries and burns. Through his encounter with death, Ponyboy grows in compassion and learns that, although no advantages have been handed to him, he can help himself.

In *The Outsiders* a boy from one gang kills a boy from another. In other books for older children, adolescents are shown as bearing some responsibility, by actions that are cir-cuitous rather than direct, for the deaths of others. In Paul Zindel's *The Pigman* Lorraine and John, two high-school sophomores, be-friend Mr. Pignati, a lonely old man, eccentric but generous and loving. Mr. Pignati, who has spent years collecting china pigs, is nick-named the Pigman by his youthful friends,

and he brings them the sympathy and under-standing that they cannot find in their own homes. "Would you like a glass of wine?" he asks them, instead of telling them to eat their peas. The two fifteen-year-olds give to the Pigman a sense of returned youth, a feeling of joy and abandon he has not had since the death of his wife. When the Pigman suffers a heart attack, he offers John and Lorraine the use of his house while he is in the hospital. On an impulse, the teenagers throw a wild party. The Pigman returns to a scene of mayhem and finds his house desecrated and his friendship betrayed. When the Pigman also finds that Bobo, the baboon he faithfully visits every day at the zoo, has died, the old man can cope with no more betrayal or loneliness and succumbs to a stroke. Lorraine and John are left with their sorrow and their guilt. "There was no one to blame anymore. . . . And there was no place to hide. . . . Our life would be what we made of it—nothing more, nothing less."[56]

Richard Peck's *Dreamland Lake* (1973) de-picts two boys whose thoughtless actions yield consequences far more dramatic and ultimate than they had ever envisioned. Flip and Brian are exploring the old, deserted amusement park called Dreamland Lake when they find a dead body, already deteriorating. With this discov-ery the boys become overnight school celebri-ties, and Flip, who has a penchant for the macabre, seems determined to build the dis-covery into a full-scale murder mystery. In contrast, Brian is haunted by his memories of the dead body and plagued by nightmares.

The two boys find that a classmate, Elvan Helligrew, has begun to follow them. He is a strange, overweight boy, without friends, ob-sessed with his collection of Nazi mementos. Elvan is a natural victim, and when the two boys chase him through Dreamland Lake, he attempts to run across a dilapidated bridge that cannot hold his weight, and he is killed. The boys, like John and Lorraine in *The Pig-*

*man*, must face the reality that actions have consequences, sometimes so tragic and ultimate that death is the result. " 'Goddamn us,' I [Brian] said, looking across at Flip. 'Oh Goddamn us.' "

June Jordan's *His Own Where* (1971), a lyrical book written in black dialect, portrays new life emerging out of death and out of violence. It is the story of two lovers, Buddy, sixteen, and Angela, fourteen, who meet in the hospital where Buddy's father lies dying, struck down in an automobile accident. Angela's parents mistreat her, sometimes with words, sometimes with physical brutality, and she runs to Buddy for help. Angela is sent to a shelter in Manhattan, a hypocritical place that offers no shelter, and when she gets a weekend pass, she and Buddy seek refuge in an empty brick house near the reservoir and the cemetery. It is there that they share their love and their hopes for a new life together.

Morning and they do not move. Arms around and head and cheek the skin and temperature of touch. Buddy hold his Angela but closer now and near enough to hear her breathing regular. Here is how they feel a happiness. Angela awaken looking to his open eyes.

"I hope I'm pregnant Buddy."

"Hey, Angela. We make that sure enough. And soon."

And so begins a new day of the new life in the cemetery.[57]

John Donovan says in his forward to Anne Moody's *Mr. Death; Four Stories* (1975):

Read beyond the deaths. Read these stories slowly. Inside each of them—whatever their surfaces may suggest—the attempt Anne Moody makes is to help us understand the nature of love. . . . Consciously or otherwise, Anne Moody is calling on us to experience a kind of catharsis in reading her four stories. They will frighten and horrify you; they will make your life richer than it was.[58]

The age level on the book jacket suggests that *Mr. Death* is appropriate for children as young as age ten. It is our feeling that many children would have to be older than this to experience anything other than horror and fright in reaction to these four stories.

The first short story, a chilling psychological study, is presented as the nightmare of Rodney Witherspoon, tape-recorded just before he commits suicide four years after his mother's death. The nightmare, ghastly and elaborate, involves Rodney and his father on a macabre limousine ride chauffered by Mr. Death. The trip culminates in an ornate room where several doctors and nurses are operating on an inert figure who is revealed as Rodney's mother. The doctors bring in a tray of freshly extracted human organs removed from the body of the son while the father, realizing that these are the elements needed to restore the woman to life, is driven into a state of distraction and grief.

The second story, "The Cow," presents a young black couple trapped by poverty and their own bitter frustration, and their portrayal culminates as their five-year-old child is killed by a car. In "Bobo" a girl is devoured alive by a mad dog, and "All Burnt Up" deals with the death of an elderly couple and the ways people contrive to avoid facing the deaths of those close to them.

Although it is important to face the reality of death and its potential impact on their own lives, we feel that some reservations must be offered concerning the compelling and often finely written stories in *Mr. Death*. As Reynolds Price noted in his review in the *New York Times*, these stories "lack an undergirding vision of safety—or even sheltered harbor —which would allow a child to fill his appetite for horror and still acquire the consolation that the basic condition of human life is not one in which the innocent and vulnerable are invariably sent into a world that lacks all protection or the visible concern to protect."[59]

## Living with death

There is an Indian story about a woman who had long been childless, and after many years finally gave birth to a son. As the child was playing one day among the bullrushes, he was bitten by a poisonous snake and died. The distraught woman came to the Buddha and begged him to restore her son. The Buddha told her to bring him some mustard seeds from the home of people who were not mourning a death. The mother wandered from one town to another, seeking such a home, but after many years of searching she returned, her task unfulfilled. The Buddha told her, "When you departed, you thought that you, and you alone were the only one who had ever suffered a loss through death. Now that you have returned . . . you know that the law of death governs us all."[60]

Death touches everyone from the elderly to the very young. It is crucial that we do not deny its existence, but rather that we live with an awareness and an acceptance of death. For a long time death was portrayed in children's books in a macabre, frightening manner, or it was ignored. Today many of the newer books for children treat death and the issues and emotions that surround it with compassion and sensitivity. These books can help children accept death's inevitability and gain a richer, more intense appreciation of the value and the wonder of being alive.

## NOTES

1. John Langone, *Death Is a Noun*, Boston, Little, Brown, 1972, pp. 3–4.
2. Herman Feifel, "Attitudes Toward Death in Some Normal and Mentally Ill Populations," in Herman Feifel, ed., *The Meaning of Death*, New York, McGraw-Hill, 1959.
3. Ibid.
4. Elizabeth Kubler Ross, "Facing Up to Death," in *Readings in Human Development*, Guilford, Conn., Dushkin, 1973, pp. 258–260.
5. Herman Feifel, quoted in Donald P. Irish, "Death Education: Preparation for Living," in Betty R. Green and Donald P. Irish, eds., *Death Education: Preparation for Living*, Cambridge, Mass., Schenkman, 1971.
6. Quoted in Flora J. Arnstein, "I Met Death One Clumsy Day," *English Journal*, 61, no. 6 (September 1972), 853–858.
7. Maria H. Nagy, "The Child's View of Death," in *The Meaning of Death*, op. cit.
8. Earl Grollman, "Prologue," in Earl Grollman, ed., *Explaining Death to Children*, Boston, Beacon Press, 1967, pp. 3–27.
9. Nagy, op. cit., p. 88.
10. Donald H. Bauer, "Children's Fears: Reflections on Research," *Educational Leadership*, 31, no. 6 (March 1974), 555–560,
11. Grollman, op. cit.
12. Arnstein, op. cit., p. 854.
13. Ibid.
14. Montaigne quoted in Feifel, "Attitudes Toward Some Normal and Mentally Ill Populations," op. cit.
15. Hella Moller, "Death: Handling the Subject and Affected Students in the Schools," *Explaining Death to Children*, op. cit.
16. Grollman, op. cit.
17. Irish, op. cit., p. 53.
18. Robin L. Carr, "Death as Presented in Children's Books," *Elementary English*, 50, no. 5 (May 1973), 701–705.
19. *The New England Primer* (Hartford, Conn., 1834), quoted in Evelyn J. Swenson, "The Treatment of Death in Children's Literature," *Elementary English*, 49, no. 3 (March 1972), 401–404.
20. A. Taylor and J. Taylor, *Original Poems for Infant Minds*, quoted in Thomas J. Schur, "What Man Has Told Children About Death," *Omega*, 2 (1971), 87.
21. Ibid., p. 86.
22. Swenson, op. cit., p. 401.
23. Joanne Marshall and Victor Marshall, "The Treatment of Death in Children's Books," *Omega*, 2 (1971), 36–45.
24. Judith Moss, "Death in Children's Literature," *Elementary English*, 49, no. 4 (April 1972), 530–532.
25. John P. Brantner, "Death and the Self," in *Death Education: Preparation for Living*, op. cit.
26. "A Little Man," *The Real Mother Goose*, Blanche Fisher Wright, illus., Skokie, Ill., Rand McNally, 1916, p. 36.
27. "The Death and Burial of Poor Cock Robin," ibid., pp. 124–125.
28. "Old Mother Hubbard," ibid., p. 43.

29. "Solomon Grundy," ibid., p. 24.
30. Eulalie Steinmetz Ross, "Children's Books Relating Death: A Discussion," in *Explaining Death to Children*, op. cit., pp. 249–271.
31. Hans Christian Andersen, "The Little Match Girl," in *It's Perfectly True and Other Tales*, trans. by Paul Leyssac, ill. by Richard Bennett, New York, Harcourt Brace Jovanovich, 1938, p. 112.
32. Ross, op. cit.
33. Alvin Tresselt, *The Dead Tree*, Charles Robinson, illus., New York, Parents' Magazine Press, 1972.
34. Judith Viorst, *The Tenth Good Thing About Barney*, Erik Blegvad, illus., New York, Atheneum, 1971, p. 24.
35. Tomie de Paola, *Nana Upstairs and Nana Downstairs*, New York, Putnam, 1973.
36. Miska Miles, *Annie and the Old One*, Peter Parnall, illus., Boston, Little, Brown, 1971, p. 42.
37. Constance Greene, *A Girl Called Al*, Byron Barton, illus., New York, Viking Press, 1969, p. 127.
38. Barbara Cohen, *Thank You, Jackie Robinson*, drawings by Richard Cuffari, New York, Lothrop, Lee and Shepard, 1974, p. 117.
39. Vera and Bill Cleaver, *Grover*, Frederic Marvin, illus., Philadelphia, Lippincott, 1970, p. 102.
40. Ruth Harnden, *The High Pasture*, Vee Guthrie, illus., Boston, Houghton Mifflin, 1969, p. 125.
41. Ibid., p. 184.
42. Madeleine L'Engle, *Meet the Austins*, New York, Vanguard Press, 1960, p. 40.
43. Virginia Lee, *The Magic Moth*, drawings by Richard Cuffari, New York, Seabury Press, 1972, book jacket.
44. Ibid., p. 56.
45. Robert Newton Peck, *A Day No Pigs Would Die*, New York, Knopf, 1972, p. 150.
46. Pearl S. Buck, *The Big Wave*, Hiroshige and Hokusai illus., New York, John Day, 1947, p. 36.
47. John Gunther, *Death Be Not Proud*, New York, Harper & Row (Perennial Library), 1949, p. 66.
48. Ibid., p. 112.
49. Gunnel Beckman, *Admission to the Feast*, trans. by Joan Tate, New York, Holt, Rinehart and Winston, 1972.
50. E. B. White, *Charlotte's Web*, Garth Williams, illus., New York, Harper & Row, 1952; New York, Dell (Yearling Book), 1973, p. 14.
51. Ibid., pp. 183–184.
52. Ester Wier, *The Loner*, Christine Price, illus., New York, David McKay, 1963, p. 13.
53. Jean Renvoize, *A Wild Thing*, Boston, Little, Brown, 1970, pp. 246–247.
54. Sharon Bell Mathis, *Teacup Full of Roses*, New York, Viking Press, 1972, p. 125.
55. Gail Graham, *Crossfire*, New York, Pantheon, 1972, p. 135.
56. Paul Zindel, *The Pigman*, New York, Dell, 1969, **p. 159.**
57. June Jordan, *His Own Where*, New York, Dell, 1971, p. 93.
58. John Donovan in the Foreword to Anne Moody, *Mr. Death; Four Stories*, Harper & Row, 1975, pp. vi–vii.
59. Reynolds Price, *Mr. Death*, a review in *The New York Times Book Review*, 1975, p. 32.
60. Martin Disken and Hans Guggenheim, "The Child and Death as Seen in Different Cultures," in Grollman, op. cit., p. 123.

# BIBLIOGRAPHY

## Fiction for younger readers

ABBOTT, SARAH. *The Old Dog*, George Mocniak, illus., 1972.

BORACK, BARBARA. *Someone Small*, Anita Lobel, illus., Harper & Row, 1972 (preschool–3).

BROWN, MARGARET WISE. *The Dead Bird*, Young Scott Books, 1958 (K–2).

BUCK, PEARL. *The Beech Tree*, K. Werth, illus., Day, 1955 (2–6).

COUTANT, HELEN. *First Snow*, Vo-Denh, illus., Knopf, 1974 (1–3).

CUNNINGHAM, JULIA. *Wings of the Morning*, photos by Katy Peake. Golden Gate Junior Books, 1971 (1+).

DE PAOLA, TOMIE. *Nana Upstairs and Nana Downstairs*, Putnam, 1973 (preschool–3).

HARRIS, AUDREY JANE. *Why Did He Die?*, Susan Sallade Dalke, illus., Lerner, 1965 (K–5).

LIBERMAN, JUDITH. *The Bird's Last Song*, Addison-Wesley, 1976 (K+).

MILES, MISKA. *Annie and the Old One*, Peter Parnall, illus., Little, Brown, 1971 (1–3).

SHECTER, BEN. *Across the Meadow*, Doubleday, 1973 (1–3).

TRESSELT, ALVIN. *The Dead Tree*, Charles Robinson, illus., Parents' Magazine Press, 1972 (K–2).

VIORST, JUDITH. *The Tenth Good Thing About Barney*, Erik Blegvad, illus., Atheneum, 1971 (K–4).

WARBURG, SANDOL. *Growing Time*, Leonard Weisbard, illus., Houghton Mifflin, 1969 (K–3).

ZOLOTOW, CHARLOTTE. *My Grandson Lew*, pictures by William Pene DuBois, Harper & Row, 1974 (preschool–3).

## Fiction for the middle and the upper grades

AGEE, JAMES. *A Death in the Family*, McDowell, Obolensky, 1956 (11–12).

ALCOTT, LOUISA MAY. *Little Women*, Barbara Cooney, illus., Crowell, 1955 (5–8) (first pub. in 1868–69).

ALEXANDER, ANNE. *Trouble on Treat Street*, John Jones, illus., Atheneum, 1974 (3–6).

ANDERSEN, HANS CHRISTIAN. *It's Perfectly True and Other Stories*, Richard Bennett, illus., trans. by Paul Leyssac. Harcourt Brace Jovanovich, 1938 (6–9).

ANONYMOUS. *Go Ask Alice*, Prentice-Hall, 1971 (7+).

ARMSTRONG, WILLIAM HOWARD. *Sounder*, James Barkley, illus., Harper & Row, 1969 (7–10).

BECHMANN, GUNNEL. *Admission to the Feast*, trans. by Joan Tate. Holt, Rinehart and Winston, 1972 (7+).

BEHN, HARRY. *The Faraway Lurs*, World, 1963 (7–10).

BLUE, ROSE. *Nikki 108*, Ted Lewis, illus., Watts, 1973 (4–8).

BOSTON, LUCY M. *A Stranger at Green Knowe*, Peter Boston, illus., Harcourt Brace Jovanovich, 1961 (4–6).

BROOKS, JEROME. *Uncle Mike's Boy*, Harper & Row, 1973 (5+).

BUCK, PEARL. *The Big Wave*, Hiroshige and Hokusai, illus., Day, 1948 (4–8).

BURCH, ROBERT. *Simon and the Game of Chance*, Fermen Rocker, illus., Viking, 1970 (5–7).

CLEAVER, VERA, and BILL CLEAVER. *Grover*, Frederic Marvin, illus., Lippincott, 1970 (4–6).

——. *Where the Lilies Bloom*, Jim Spanfeller, illus., Lippincott, 1969 (6–9).

COBURN, JOHN. *Anne and the Sand Dobbies: Story About Death for Children and Their Parents*, Seabury Press, 1964 (6+).

COHEN, BARBARA. *Thank You, Jackie Robinson*, Richard Cuffari, illus., Lothrop, Lee & Shepard, 1974 (5–6).

COOLIDGE, OLIVIA. *Come by Here*, Milton Johnson, illus., Houghton Mifflin, 1970 (5+).

COOPER, SUSAN. *Dawn of Fear*, Margery Gill, illus., Harcourt Brace Jovanovich, 1970 (5–6).

DIXON, PAIGE. *May I Cross Your Golden River?*, Atheneum, 1975 (7+).

DONOVAN, JOHN. *Wild in the World*, Harper & Row, 1971 (6–9).

EWING, KATHRYN. *A Private Matter*, Joan Sanden, illus., Harcourt Brace Jovanovich, 1975 (2–5).

FAST, HOWARD. *The Hessian*, Morrow, 1972 (9+).

FRANK, ANNE. *The Diary of a Young Girl*, Doubleday, 1967.

FRENCH, HARRY. *The Lance of Karana*, Lothrop, Lee & Shepard, 1932.

GARDAM, JANE. *The Summer After the Funeral*, Macmillan, 1973 (7+).

GRAHAM, GAIL. *Crossfire*, Pantheon Books, 1972 (7+).

GREEN, BETTE. *The Summer of My German Soldier*, Dial Press, 1973 (7+).

GREENE, CONSTANCE. *A Girl Called Al*, Byron Barton, illus., Viking Press, 1969 (4–6).

GUY, ROSA. *The Friends*, Holt, Rinehart and Winston, 1973 (7–9).

GUNTHER, JOHN. *Death Be Not Proud*, Harper & Row, 1949 (9+).

HARNDEN, RUTH. *The High Pasture*, Vee Guthrie, illus., Houghton Mifflin, 1964.

HINTON, S. E. *The Outsiders*, Viking Press, 1967 (9+).

HOUSTON, JAMES. *Akavak: An Eskimo Journey*, Harcourt Brace Jovanovich, 1968 (4–6).

HOLLAND, ISABELLE. *Of Love and Death and Other Journeys*, Lippincott, 1975 (7+).

HUNT, IRENE. *Across Five Aprils*, Follett, 1964 (7+).

——. *Up a Road Slowly*, Follett, 1966 (6–9).

HUNTER, MOLLIE. *A Sound of Chariots*, Harper & Row, 1972 (7–10).

ISH-KISHOR, SULAMITH. *Our Eddie*, Pantheon Books, 1969 (6–9).

JORDAN, JUNE. *His Own Where*, Crowell, 1971 (7–9).

KELLY, ERIC. *The Trumpeter of Krakow*, Macmillan, 1966 (7+).

LEE, MILDRED. *Fog*, Seabury Press, 1972 (7–10).

——. *The Skating Rink*, Seabury Press, 1969 (6–8).

LEE, VIRGINIA. *The Magic Moth*, Richard Cuffari, illus., Seabury Press, 1972 (4–6).

L'ENGLE, MADELEINE. *Meet the Austins*, Vanguard Press, 1960 (5–8).

LINDGREN, ASTRID. *The Brothers Lionheart*, trans. by Joan Tage, J. K. Lambert, illus., Viking Press, 1975.

LITTLE, JEAN. *Home from Far*, Jerry Lazare, illus., Little, Brown, 1965 (5+).

LUND, DORIS. *Eric*, Lippincott, 1974.

MATHIS, SHARON BELL. *Listen for the Fig Tree*, Viking Press, 1974 (7+).

———. *Teacup Full of Roses*, Viking Press, 1972 (2–4).

MAZER, NORMA FOX. *A Figure of Speech*, Dell (Delacorte Press), 1973 (7+).

MIKOLAYCAK, CHARLES, and CAROLE KISMARIC. *The Boy Who Tried to Cheat Death*, Charles Mikolaycack, illus., Doubleday, 1971.

MOHR, NICHOLASA. *Nilda*, Harper & Row, 1973 (5+).

MOODY, ANNE. *Mr. Death: Four Stories*, Harper & Row, 1975 (5+).

MORGAN, ALISON. *Ruth Crane*, Harper & Row, 1974 (3–7).

MORRIS, JEANNIE. *Brian Picolo: A Short Season*, Dell (Delacorte Press), 1971.

ORGEL, DORIS. *The Mulberry Music*, Dale Payson, illus., Harper & Row, 1971 (4–6).

PECK, RICHARD. *Dreamland Lake*, Holt, Rinehart and Winston, 1973 (4–7).

PECK, ROBERT NEWTON. *A Day No Pigs Would Die*, Knopf, 1972 (7+).

RABIN, GIL. *Changes*, Harper & Row, 1973 (5+).

RAWLINGS, MARJORIE KINNAN, *The Yearling*, N. C. Wyeth, illus., Scribner, 1939, 1962 (7+).

RENVOIZE, JEAN. *A Wild Thing*, Atlantic–Little, Brown, 1970 (7+).

SALTEN, FELIX. *Bambi*, Simon and Schuster, 1929 (5–8).

SCOPPETTONE, SANDRA. *Trying Hard to Hear You*, Harper & Row, 1974 (7+).

SLOTE, ALFRED. *Hang Tough, Paul Mather*, Lippincott, 1973 (7+).

SMITH, DORIS BUCHANAN. *A Taste of Blackberries*, Crowell, 1973 (2–5).

SMITH, GENE. *The Hayburners*, Ted Lewin, illus., Dell (Delacorte Press), 1974 (5–9).

STOLZ, MARY. *By the Highway Home*, Harper & Row, 1971 (6–9).

———. *The Edge of Next Year*, Harper & Row, 1974 (6–11).

TAYLOR, THEODORE. *The Cay*, Doubleday, 1969 (6–10).

———. *Teetoncey*, Richard Cuffari, illus., Doubleday, 1974 (6–11).

TER HAAR, JAAP. *Boris*, trans. by Martha Mearns, Rien Poortvliet, illus., Dell (Delacorte Press), 1970 (5–7).

THRASHER, CRYSTAL. *The Dark Didn't Catch Me*, Atheneum, 1975 (5–9).

TUNIS, JOHN. *His Enemy, His Friend*, Morrow, 1967 (7–10).

WERSBA, BARBARA. *Run Softly, Go Fast*, Atheneum, 1970 (8–10).

———. *The Dream Watcher*, Atheneum, 1968 (6–9).

WHITE, E. B. *Charlotte's Web*, Garth Williams, illus., Harper & Row, 1952 (5+).

WIER, ESTER. *The Loner*, Christine Price, illus., McKay, 1963 (6–9).

WILDE, OSCAR. *The Selfish Giant*, Gertrude and Walter Reiner, illus., Harvey, 1968 (4–6).

WINDSOR, PATRICIA. *The Summer Before*, Harper & Row, 1973 (7+).

ZEI, ALKI. *Petros' War*, trans. by Edward Fenton. Holt, Rinehart and Winston, 1968 (5–7).

ZINDEL, PAUL. *The Pigman*, Harper & Row, 1968 (7–9).

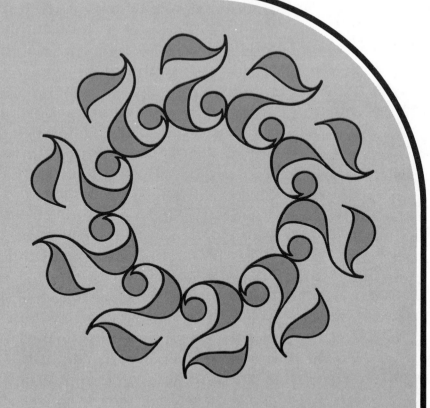

# The
# American
# mosaic

## The invisible people

I am an invisible man. No, I am not a spook like those who haunted Edgar Allan Poe; nor am I one of your Hollywood-movie extoplasms. I am a man of substance, of flesh and bone, fiber and liquids—and I might even be said to possess a mind. I am invisible, understand, simply because people refuse to see me.[1]

Ralph Ellison wrote those words in *Invisible Man* over twenty years ago, but for far longer, for centuries the books we gave our children to read refused to see black America. For decades black characters were presented as shuffling, lazy, shiftless, singing subhumans. Without mind, purpose, or aspiration, blacks danced across the pages of children's books fostering prejudice and ignorance in the minds of countless young readers. The only saving grace, and it was not much of a saving grace, was that for many years, in the vast majority of children's books, black characters simply never existed.

As recently as the early 1960s, Nancy Larrick was forced to characterize the situation as "The All White World of Children's Books."[2] Over 93 percent of children's books published between 1962 and 1964 did not include a single black character. In books where a black was included, he or she was removed from our contemporary society, placed in the past or in another country. Fewer than 1 percent of the children's books published in this three-year period contained a contemporary black character in the United States. And at times, when blacks were depicted, the illustrations were such that it was often difficult to determine if a character were black or sun-tanned white.

In her study, Julie Ann Carlsen found that Negro characters were more often found in children's books published between 1927 and 1938 than during the years from 1959 to 1968. Although the treatment of the Negro was less stereotyped in these latter years, it is stagger-

# 5 The Black Experience in Children's Literature

ing that in the shadow of a national civil rights movement, children's books were failing to reflect the black experience in America.[3]

The noted black leader Whitney Young has written, "There is no better way to reach the black child than through his books. He must see himself in books, as he is, as he can be. . . . Omission of these crucial images in books . . . tells the black child . . . you have no image today and no future tomorrow."[4]

Through omission and negative stereotyping, the positive literary black image that Whitney Young spoke of has been historically denied to young children. In fact, it has only been in the last few years that we have witnessed the publication of a growing number of fine books concerning the lives of blacks.

The obvious question is why has it taken so long for positive and realistic images of black characters to appear in children's books? There are many reasons for this, not the least being the social, political, and economic discrimination that has so long been a part of America. But another reason that should not be overlooked concerns the composition of the publishing world. *Time* magazine reported in 1970 that there were only four top-level black editors in New York trade publishing, and probably fewer than thirty in the whole book publishing world.[5] Bradford Chambers, writing in *Publishers' Weekly* in 1971, noted that none of the major publishers of children's books included a single black editor, or indeed an editor of any minority group, on their staffs.[6]

Moreover, this trend continues in the world of authors as well. The dearth of black writers has been the subject of much concern. Some white writers have tried to fill the void, with mixed success and mixed appreciation. Their attempts have raised a pertinent question: Is it possible for a white author to understand and to reflect sensitively and accurately the lives of black people? Julius Lester, a noted black writer of children's books, does not

think so. "Whites can only give a white interpretation of blacks which tells us a lot about whites, but nothing about blacks. . . . Could you take seriously a history of Jews written by an Arab? The idea is so ridiculous as to be insulting."[7]

George Woods, *New York Times* children's book editor, states the position that many white authors of black stories adhere to "I try not to look at kids as white or black. . . . I don't want to break kids down into all different kinds."[8] Julius Lester's retort is a stinging one: "Ultimately, it is to no one's benefit to be color blind. Even in the best of all possible worlds I want to be looked upon as black. . . . Where are the books for children that deal with whites and their racism? They don't exist, because it is easier to be paternalistic than honest."[9]

A more sympathetic view of white authors who write about the black experience is offered by Darwin Turner, Chairman of Afro-American Studies at the University of Iowa.

There certainly can be white writers who capture it [the black experience] effectively. The tendency of some contemporary white writers, is to view the black as an individual to be admired for a kind of recklessness or to be pitied. . . . White writers aren't the only ones who have difficulty presenting members of another group. It often happens with a black author trying to present a white character, with a male trying to present a female. . . .[10]

The debate is a thought-provoking one and, even as it continues we have reason to be hopeful that the cloak of invisibility and misrepresentation that has distorted and hidden the experience of black Americans will be lifted.

Recently a number of talented authors, many of them black, have emerged to reflect with realism and with sensitivity the black experience in children's books. They are beginning to fill the gap. We review many of these positive portrayals later in this chapter. But first come with us to the past, to the treatment of blacks in children's books. In the next section we turn to Nancy Drew and Mary Poppins, among others, to see offensive treatment awarded blacks in some of our best-known books for children, and we analyze the way blacks were depicted in their pages.

## Watermelon heaven: the treatment of Negroes in children's books before 1945.

[The Negro] is light hearted, irresponsible, careless; he lives in the present, like a child or a beast; he does not aim high or persist; he is fond of big words and of gay colors; he wants to strut, to display himself, rather than to be; and therefore seen against the background (or the foreground, if you will) of a civilization which he apes with fantastic imitation, he is a subject for comedy, not tragedy. . . . The tragic hero has been through the ages a person of exalted qualities and usually of world eminence.[11]

Written in 1916, this quote was George Greever's attempt to explain why the Negro had never been the subject of great writing. His comments reflected the tenor of the times. Black characters that appeared in books written before 1945 were distorted into some of the most crude stereotypes imaginable, and these derogatory portrayals were drawn in many well-known children's books, several of which are still popular today.

Annie Vaugh Weaver's *Frawg* (1930) sported a cover depicting a black boy holding a watermelon, and the final pages of this book portrayed the black path to heaven, one lined with watermelons. This presentation reflected the perception that many whites held of blacks. Indeed the *Library Journal*, in its 1930 review of *Frawg*, noted, "Characteristic illustrations enhanced its charm."[12] Offensive illustrations of Negroes often received favorable comments. The *New York Times* review of

*Nicodemus*, another book published in the 1930s, concluded that "there is humor in the presentation of both pigs and pickaninnies."[13]

Jane Bingham analyzed realistic fiction written between 1930 and 1968 that contained illustrations of Negroes and that had been cited in popular book lists. These books were generally picture books designed for children eight years of age or younger. She discovered that in approximately forty years, only forty-nine of the books on these lists contained any illustration of blacks. The invisibility of the black American in children's books was once again reaffirmed. In addition, she also found that during the period before 1945, blacks were pictured in the stereotyped image of the time. They smiled with thick lips and flexed exaggerated muscles.[14]

The demeaning pictures of black characters drawn by illustrators affect young readers in several ways. Pictures are examined with intense interest and illustrations provide a powerful force in molding the opinions and attitudes of young readers. Even before children learn to read the printed word, they are "reading" pictures. Illustrations bring children enjoyment, understanding, and heightened awareness of themselves and others. But denigrating and inaccurate illustrations, such as those of black characters before 1945, can be powerful instruments of misinformation, a lowered self-concept for black children, and a decreased appreciation of the black experience for white readers.[15]

> I believe that image is a great instrument of instruction; what a child gets out of any subject is simply the image he himself forms with regard to it.
>
> *John Dewey*

We began our discussion of the early illustration of Negroes with the watermelon emphasis in *Frawg*. We continue the watermelon theme in the following passage:

> A watermelon, large and fine,
> Was in the kitchen shed;
> The bullet drilled a hole through it
> As on its way it sped.
> "Who plugged dat melon?" Mammy cried,
> As through the door she came;
> "I'd spank de chile dat done dat trick,
> Ef I could learn his name."[16]

Black dialect, written and interpreted by white authors, often served as another technique for portraying the Negro as a subservient being, destined to fill his life with the menial tasks and the childish fun one might expect from someone with limited intelligence. Dialect by itself need not be demeaning. When dialect reflects speech accurately it adds realism. But when dialect is exaggerated, it can be used as a tool to portray ignorance. When all black characters speak with the same heavy dialect, the book does not reflect reality; instead it denies it. Unfortunately, authors of some of our most famous children's books have managed to combine negative character traits, menial roles, and tortured dialects into powerfully unflattering stereotypes.

The Nancy Drew series was introduced in 1930 and its continued enormous success is reflected in sales figures, indicating that over 30 million copies have been sold. Until 1957, Negro characters in this series uttered such comments as "You po'h chile." "She speaks de troof." "Scuze me, sah, but de bank am closin."[17] This dialect, put into the mouths of black characters, complemented the menial roles to which they were assigned. In the first seventeen Nancy Drew mysteries there are a total of seventeen Negro characters. Only four of the seventeen affect the plot development in any way, and only four are given names. The majority of these Negro characters are faceless menials. They include five maids, four porters, two cooks, one caretaker, one butler, one elevator "starter," one out-of-work servant, and two professional criminals. These characters do a considerable amount of lying, a dubious talent surpassed only by their even more considerable amount of drinking. And although some Negroes are portrayed as courteous and industrious, no black in any of the Nancy Drew books is ever shown as exerting a significantly good influence.

> Eva Knox Evans was reading her own book, *Araminta's Goat*, to a kindergarten class of black children in 1941. The children soon began to protest that the black characters in the book were not speaking in dialect. When Ms. Evans pointed out that they were not speaking in dialect either, the children responded that black children in books were supposed to speak that way.[18]

Negroes smiled, waddled, and shuffled through the pages of other famous children's series as well. Books featuring the Hardy Boys, Tom Swift and the Bobbsey Twins have been read by generations of young Americans, and in them blacks have been treated as ignorant and somewhat lazy, although generally good-natured. Although blacks live in the white world of these books, they are clearly not an integral part of it.

Sam and Dinah are two black characters in *The Bobbsey Twins* (1904). Sam is a chauffeur and a general handyman; Dinah is the family maid. Yet they do not quite fit in, as even young white Flossie can tell. In describing her five dolls, Flossie explains that the fifth doll was Jujube. Jujube is a colored boy doll, dressed in flashy colors, who has lost his popularity with Flossie.

"He doesn't really belong to the family, you know," Flossie would explain to her friends. "But

I have to keep him, for mamma says there is no colored orphan asylum for dolls. Besides, I don't think Sam and Dinah would like to see their doll child in an asylum. . . ." Flossie always took pains to separate Jujube from the rest by placing the cover of a pasteboard box between them.[19]

In these books tortured speech patterns are again used to portray inferior status. In 1919 Dinah and Sam were inflicted with a severe case of dialect.

DINAH: What's aa dish yeah I heah Nan say?
SAM: I'll put back de hay fo' yo' all. Taint much. . . .

Recent editions of such famous series as that of the Bobbsey Twins have eliminated the more blatant forms of stereotyping. *Nigger* no longer appears as a commonly used noun. Fat black women no longer waddle in and out of story lines. By 1953 Sam had undergone a complete language change.

SAM: Well, I don't know. . . . Folks say that if a horseshoe is thrown so that it lands with two ends pointing toward you, that means good luck![20]

But generations of Americans have already read the older versions, and some libraries still retain these racist editions. Moreover, the newer editions of these series do not completely rectify this racist picture. Although blatant stereotypes have been omitted, more subtle forms still remain. Inferior status is still observed, and although Sam and Dinah have lost their dialects, they have retained their stations in life. Both are still servants.

One of our much-read literary classics is Mark Twain's *The Adventures of Huckleberry Finn*. In this work Twain presented the social context of small-town America almost one hundred years ago. After the publication of *The Adventures of Tom Sawyer*, readers were fascinated with Tom's friend, Huck Finn, a boy from the wrong side of town and the son of the town drunkard. Twain's sensitive portrayal of Huck interested readers, and their fascination resulted in a new book centered on Huckleberry Finn's adventures. A major character of this book is Nigger Jim. Nigger Jim is superstitious, consistently fetching witches and casting spells. He communicates through a thick dialect: "You's gwyne to marry do po' fust en de rich one by en by."[21] Nigger Jim is cast as ignorant in a variety of fields. His business acumen is summed up neatly in his speculation in the "stock market" (i.e., livestock.) "I put ten dollars in a cow. But I ain gwyne to resk no mo' money in stock. De cow up'n died. . . ."[22] And in the ways of the world, Nigger Jim is equally ignorant. It proves impossible for Huck Finn to explain why Frenchmen speak French. Huck finally gives up, "I see it ain't no use wasting words—you can't learn a nigger to argue."[23]

But Twain does attempt to illustrate some of the social pressures weighing on Huck Finn to form his racist attitude. In one passage Jim confesses to Huck that he is a runaway slave. Huck promises to keep his word and not turn Jim in, even though, "People would call me a low down Abolitionist and despise me for keeping mum. . . ."[24] And again, after playing a practical joke on Nigger Jim, Huck apologizes. "It was fifteen minutes before I could work myself up to go and humble myself to a nigger; but I done it, and I wain't even sorry for it afterward neither."[25] Huck, under Tom Sawyer's guidance, participates in an attempt to free Nigger Jim from jail. During the escape Jim demonstrates his compassion and self-sacrifice, but all this earns for him is a better lot as a slave. And Huck agrees that it is better for Jim to be a slave, "As long as he got to be a slave."[26]

Mark Twain offers us a black character with many of the stereotypic elements common in other works of this period. But there are some redeeming qualities. It is significant that whites in this book also speak in dialect. Moreover, Nigger Jim is a major, not an incidental character, one clearly capable of humane and good acts. Although filled with derogatory passages, Mark Twain's *The Adventures of Huckleberry Finn* presents complex characters and a Negro who begins to break out of the stereotype.

Another book published some time ago but still popular today is *Little Black Sambo* (1900). The object of the censor's attention in many areas (see Chapter 13), this famous story of a black boy outwitting the hungry status-seeking tigers, all of whom wanted to be the "grandest" in the jungle, has been cited as racist in two areas. One point criticized is the boy's name, for *Sambo* had acquired negative connotations from the days when simpleton Negroes, often call Sambos, rattled their tambourines in minstrel shows. The colored clothes that are given to Sambo as a present and that he in turn is forced to give to the tigers, have also been cited as an example of stereotyping.

This picture book, however, is different from the insulting graphic portrayals noted in the other books we have discussed. To most of today's children for whom minstrel shows are a bit of lost Americana, *Sambo* has no negative meaning. The illustrations of flashily colored clothing is a stereotyped detail of such subtlety that one may question whether it is even noticed. And in reading this book to children, we could not help noticing how all children, white and black, identify with the trials and successes of Sambo. He is a success figure, one who uses his courage and his wits. Although the book is undoubtedly offensive to some, it does not have the heavy-handed, one-dimensional treatment found in many works.

Unfortunately, racist portrayals are apparent in some well-known children's books that have been rejuvenated by Walt Disney studios. If Mary Poppins and Dr. Dolittle were charged with racism, they would be wise to plead "no

contest." *Mary Poppins* (1934), by P. L. Travers, was reissued in 1962 with a cover that included the inviting phrase "the famous characters on which the Walt Disney film is based."[27] But the racism, although not advertised, was nonetheless very much present.

Mary Poppins, the fast, crisp character, magically blown by an East wind, is the nurse for the Banks's children. She is also their guide to many imaginative adventures. On a trip around the world, Mary Poppins and her two charges, Jane and Michael, mistakenly arrive in the southern United States instead of the South Pole. They see a man and a woman "quite black all over with very few clothes on." But they are wearing quite a few beads. Some of the beads were worn as necklaces, "some in their ears, one or two in their noses."[28] The narrative continues, describing their black baby as a naked pickaninny. The pronoun used to refer to the baby is neither *he* nor *she*, but *it*. Finally, the black woman speaks: "Ah bin 'specting you a long time, Mar' Poppins," she said, smiling. "You bring dem chillum dere into ma li'l house for a slice of watermelon right now. My, but dem's very white babies. You wan't use a li'l bit black boot polish on dem. Come 'long, now. You'se mightly welcome."[29] Mary Poppins explains that they are in a hurry and must pass up the invitation for watermelon. She and her two charges leave as the black man, smiling, rubs the end of a club along his cheek. And the woman continues laughing, "as though the whole of life were one big joke. . . ."[30]

The Dr. Dolittle books, by Hugh Lofting, one of which (*Voyages of Dr. Dolittle*) won the 1923 Newbery Medal, have delighted many children with their role reversals, in which animals guide and care for helpless human beings. Unfortunately, these books must have also affected children with their racist character portrayals, incidents, and epithets. In the books *Dr. Dolittle*, *Voyages of Dr. Dolittle*, and *Dr.*

*Dolittle's Zoo*, Hugh Lofting introduces Prince Bumbo, perhaps the most outrageously drawn of all African characters. Dr. Dolittle and his animal friends are arrested in a mythical African kingdom after unknowingly breaking the law. King and Queen Jollizinki are the stupid and pompous black rulers of this kingdom. Their son, Prince Bumbo, "The Black Prince," is portrayed as a very fat and very ignorant man, complete with loin cloth. Prince Bumbo's current concern revolves around a fair-skinned princess whom he wishes to marry. But, alas, she will not have him because he is black. Dr. Dolittle agrees to turn Prince Bumbo white if he will help him escape. Dr. Dolittle covers the prince with a white ointment, easily outwits him, and escapes.[31]

The adventures of the Black Prince are continued in other Dolittle books. At one point Prince Bumbo appeals to Dr. Dolittle to permit him to join his expedition to Spider Monkey Island. Lofting meticulously describes the Prince's ludicrous attire, as well as his fractured attempt at the king's English. The prince explains that he can leave Oxford at this time, for he plans to take a three-month "abscension." He will not be neglecting his "edification" because Dr. Dolittle is so "studiosity." Dr. Dolittle relents and Prince Bumbo becomes the expedition's cook. Even the animals in the Dolittle books look down on the Africans as "These bloomin' heathen."[32]

The Dolittle books continue to enjoy good sales. Although some words have been altered in later editions (*native* has replaced *nigger*), the racist character portrayals and plots continue. And as children still read, Dr. Dolittle one cannot help but wonder to what degree they are influenced by the pages of bigotry.

What can we do about such books? Some advocate censoring these works to stop racist learning. Although the issue of censorship is explored in another chapter, let us state here that we do not support such an approach.

Rather, we would treat these books for what they are, works that reflect the social milieu of their time. In addition, they suggest the need for children to look at the publication date, and become sensitive to our changing social consciousness .

Augusta Baker writes of the difficulties she encountered in the 1930s as she attempted to find appropriate books for black children. Working on a Harlem-based committee, she helped to identify three important criteria:

1. *Illustrations* were reviewed to find illustrations of black characters that were of interest to children.
2. *Language* was examined to avoid derogatory terms and inappropriate dialects.
3. *Themes and attitudes* were analyzed in terms of positive treatment of black characters.

Even these simple criteria were too demanding for most of the books of that time. Augusta Baker feels certain that none of the books written in the 1930s would be accepted by the standards of the 1970s.[33]

These famous children's books written before 1945 reflect the prejudice of previous years. *Dr. Dolittle*, *Nancy Drew*, and other books offer us an insight into how far we as a nation have come in recognizing overt racism. As a mirror of the past, they provide educators with a potential learning experience. Moreover, such books offer a unique opportunity to share with children the progress we have made. And in the difficult years we have yet to face in improving race relations, they offer us hope that change, growth, and greater racial sensitivity are indeed possible.

## Black and white together

Natalie Savage Carlson, a noted children's author, has suggested four ways that blacks have been portrayed in children's literature in recent years. Two of those portrayals, as caricatures and as stereotypes, have been demonstrated in the previous section. The remaining two types of portrayals are blacks as individuals with race problems and blacks as individuals with universal problems. An example of black characters with race problems would be a book theme concerned, for example, with the desegregation of schools. Universal problems concern issues that all children face: sibling relationships, friendships, family crises, and the like.[34]

In this section we focus on children's books concerned with a racial theme, specifically black characters attempting to integrate into white society. Several books were written on this theme soon after World War II, and the number increased markedly after the 1954 Supreme Court decision to desegregate schools.

*Call Me Charley* (1945), by Jesse Jackson, tells the story of a black family moving into the white suburbs. Twelve-year-old Charley has difficulty being understood by his white classmates and teachers, but he does manage to win over Tom as his first real friend. Tom and Charley join forces to build a model of a swimming pool for a school project. After winning first prize, a free pass to the local swimming club, both boys are tremendously elated. Their joy is soon shattered when Charley's prize is taken from him and replaced with cash because the pool does not allow "coloreds."

This is one of the several hardships Charley faces. He is harassed by George, the book's young bigot. He is placed in the last seat in the class, until his grades can be "checked." Charley must even overcome his own father's skepticism about schooling. "Like I said—it's all a lot of foolishness. Charley ought to be thinking about a job instead of keeping his head in a book all the time."[35] But when a teacher blatantly refuses to give Charley a part in the school play, white parents unite in

support of Charley and he eventually is allowed to participate in the school play.

In this book Jackson attempts to offer readers a glimpse of the discrimination facing black children, a bigotry personified in the character of George. George is destined to fail, however, because a basic message of the book is that right and justice will prevail. Charley's mother is one vehicle for this hopeful message. She urges him to do well in school, and advises him on the virtues of good manners and patience. " 'As long as you work hard and try to do right,' his mother went on, 'you will always find some good people like Doc Cunningham or Tom and his folks marching along with you in the right path. And fellows like George may come along too, sooner or later.' "[36] *Anchor Man* (1947) continues the trials of Charley in a white society. In this book Jackson takes Charley through high school, and his encounters with athletic and personal crises.

The story about the integration of a parochial school in Louisiana is told in *The Empty Schoolhouse* (1965), by Natalie Savage Carlson. Lullah Royall is a ten-year-old black girl who helps mother take care of a motel. She is especially excited about attending St. Joseph's because her best friend goes there. But when Lullah integrates St. Joseph's, whites stop sending their children. Even her best friend deserts her. The situation is brought to a head when two professional haters, outsiders to the community, go beyond jeering and shoot Lullah. That shot, heard around the community, galvanizes the white citizenry. The opposition to integration is ended. Luckily Lullah receives only a superficial wound, the conflict subsides, and the story concludes on an optimistic note.

Several similarities between *The Empty Schoolhouse* and *Call Me Charley* should be noted. In both books education is seen as a vehicle of change. Attending good schools is

The Empty Schoolhouse

plexion of "coffee and cream," with long, wavy hair. The advantage of being light and the desirability of fitting into white society's cultural value system are introduced, if not fully explored.[37]

In a series of three books published between 1958 and 1969, Lorenz Graham traces the plight of the Williams family as they try to enter America's mainstream. The first of the series, *South Town* (1958), reflects the overt forms of racism inflicted upon the Williams family: low pay, separate churches and schools, verbal and physical abuse meted out by white citizens as well as white police officials. David Williams cannot understand how the American Dream is being denied them, nor can David's father, who recalls the sacrifices blacks and whites made together during the war. "By God, if we fight together and die together, we'd ought to be able to live together."[38]

The violence and abuse of *South Town* prove to be too much for the Williams family, and they move to North Town. *North Town* (1965) confronts the family with the problems of an integrated society. At school David is officially treated courteously, but he is not fully accepted. He survives a run-in with the police and acquires a white friend, who teaches him to play football. Just when things seem to be working out, Mr. Williams is hospitalized, and David is forced to go to work to support the family. Because of the talents of a sympathetic Jewish surgeon, Mr. Williams is nursed back to health. By the book's end the American Dream seems within grasp. David is a football star with plans to be a doctor, his father is back at work, and his family is living in their new house. All the hopeful expectations for the Williams family and the nation at large seem to be summed up by David as he is playing football. He looks up from the football field and he can see in symbols the success of an integrated society: "but the late afternoon sun

important for future success. Like Charley, Lullah has one best friend, who happens to be white. Both Charley and Lullah are transplants into a white world. Both have adopted its values.

An interesting issue confronted in *The Empty Schoolhouse* is the awareness blacks have of color variance within their own race. Historically, many Negroes believed that brown is more desirable than black. Although Lullah's sister is dark black, Lullah has a com-

had broken through the clouds lighting a row of American flags silhouetted against the sky. David knew that his father was there, and Jeanette. . . . He could not pick out faces, white or black or brown, but he knew they were all there. This, he thought, was like America."[39]

But in the last book of the three, *Whose Town?* (1969), we see that many questions have not been answered. Racial strife once again occurs. As in *South Town*, there is trouble with the police, and the simple integration theme of *North Town* is questioned as David searches for his role as a black man in a white society. *Whose Town?* has more a black identity theme than an integration theme, and it is discussed more fully later in the chapter.

The relatively peaceful integration of David Williams into his nothern school is in contrast to Dorothy Sterling's *Mary Jane*, a book written during and about the school desegregation turmoil in the South. The book's two main characters, Mary Jane and Fred Jackson, represent the hardships and strife faced by black children throughout the South. Mary Jane and Fred are the first Negroes to attend Wilson High School. The anguish of those early days of integration is seen through Mary Jane's eyes as she walks to her first day at Wilson. She is assailed by the jeers of an angry white mob.

"Go back to Africa!"

Mary Jane turned her head trying to see who it was. What did he mean?

A woman, high pitched—could it have been a woman? "Pull her black curls out!"

Mary Jane's scalp tingled as if someone were tugging at it. Automatically her hand jerked up toward her forehead, toward the little fluff she'd combed so carefully at her dressing table that morning. Then Daddy caught her hand squeezing it in his own.

Heads up. Eyes front. Eyes on the broad blue backs of the policemen.[40]

Fred's quicker acceptance in the school, because of his basketball abilities, does not ease Mary Jane's problems. She is turned down as a cheerleader because her color does not "match" the others. She is invited to join the choir, because her "people" are so good at that sort of thing. Pressures exerted by white parents create continual problems for Mary Jane, and her only white friend. Sally, is forced to limit their friendship to the school grounds. Through Mary Jane's confrontations with bigotry, her friend Sally, and, it is hoped, the children who read this book, gain an understanding of the nature of prejudice.

The books discussed in this section have integration as their theme, and they share several common characteristics. As a given, the black characters want to become part of white America. Black identity is submerged as these characters try to create and join an integrated society. In most of these books the obstacle to integration is represented by a small minority of whites. In some books it is a single individual, like George in *Call Me Charley*, or two grisly outsiders, as in *The Empty Schoolhouse*. Most of white society is portrayed as passively in favor of integration. But it takes a crucial event or a hundred pages of patience to win their active support.

Education is often presented as a critical tool for success, as can be seen in David Williams' desire to become a doctor in *North Town* or Lullah's desire not to become a scrubwoman in *The Empty Schoolhouse*. Even at the cost of violence and hostility, attending a good school is worth all the trauma and danger involved.

These books provide children with an elementary awareness of racial bigotry. Conflict, sacrifice, and courage are clear elements in most of these works. Yet the books, seen from the perspective of the 1970s, ignore the full complexity of the racial situation they endeavor to present. Prejudice is a limited disease, one that can be remedied by relatively superficial attention. Obstacles and bigots are present but not ubiquitous, and they are optimistically viewed as surmountable in the end. The support of the white community is viewed as an essential ingredient to the success of integration, so much so that the fate of the pure and good black characters seems to some extent at the mercy of white whim and white control. To many readers the notion of black destiny in the hands of a white community is itself repugnant.

These traditional treatments of school integration can be contrasted with a more recent approach found in Ann Waldron's *The Integration of Mary-Larkin Thornhill* (1975). In this case a white author reflects the impact of court-ordered integration on the life of a white child. As one of the few white students in a predominantly black school, seventh grader Mary-Larkin faces both hostility and friendship from her new black classmates. Called "honky" and hustled out of her lunch money in the cafeteria, Mary-Larkin nevertheless enjoys new friendships, experiences new triumphs, and gains a greater awareness of herself and the people around her. Unlike the traditional integration stories of the past, Waldron offers neither a supercourageous character, a picture of racism as a limited disease suffered by only a few, nor integration as a simple solution to racism. Through the eyes of a very human character, we are presented a picture of the problems and promise of integration, as well as the scope of racism. And the book acquires special significance because the issue is explored by a white author who views integration through the eyes of a white character.

These books, written about blacks and whites and concerned with racial issues, can be contrasted with the next group of books to be discussed. In the following section we discuss books that include black characters but usually avoid racial issues. They are often based on universal human themes, sometimes touching upon a racial concern but more often not. Mary Jane's friend, Sally, described the approach fairly well: "I always thought that all Negroes looked alike and were different somehow from whites. But now I know—I mean, they're just people like anybody else."[41]

## Universal problems

The books about black characters discussed in this section do not deal primarily with racial issues, but with universal problems, which confront children of all races. In some of these books there may be an incidental reference to race; in other books the single clue to the race of a particular character is through the book's illustrations. The first group of books that we consider is designed for young children and depends primarily on illustrations to depict blacks confronting universal problems.

One of the earlier books in this category is Lorraine and Jerrold Beim's *Two Is a Team* (1945), a Dick and Jane type of story, with a black boy replacing Jane in the story line.

A Letter to Amy

Written for the primary elementary school years, it describes two young boys who play together. Building scooters leads to a race, and property damage, but by the story's end the damage is paid for and the boys' friendship is still intact. In spite of the sterile plot, the illustrations of a white and a black boy playing together are noteworthy for a 1945 children's book. At the time of its publication, a number of communities violently objected to the illustrations of black and white characters playing together.

A more recent book, *The Two Friends* (1968), by Grete Mannheim, uses a more realistic pictorial treatment to present an integrated society. Photographs show the friendship between a black girl, Jenny, and her white friend, Nancy. The photographs include Jenny's parents, brothers, and sisters. The book is a simple story of daily events, including visits to the ice-cream parlor and the library.

A story with more drama is Joan Lexau's *Benjie* (1970). Benjie is a small black boy who lives with his grandmother, and his characteristic shyness is exceeded only by his love for her. When she loses an earring of sentimental value, Benjie goes out on his own to find it. In his quest he overcomes his shyness and finds the earring. The warm story is complemented by appealing black-and-white illustrations.

An author famous for his warm stories and beautiful and vibrant illustrations is Ezra Jack Keats. In a well-written series of books, the main character, a black boy named Peter, encounters the trials and joys of childhood. In *The Snowy Day* (1962) Peter romps through the snow, makes snow angels, and makes an intriguing variety of tracks in the snow. To savor his memory, he tucks a snowball into his pocket. Peter's disappointment at the snowball's disappearance is alleviated the following day when it is again snowing, and he goes off once more to play in the snow. *The Snowy*

*Day* was awarded the Caldecott Medal for the best picture book of 1963.

In *Whistle for Willie* (1964) a simple problem is presented, that of Peter's attempts to learn how to whistle to call his dog. After much frustration and failure he finally emits a whistle and Willie comes running. Another problem faced by children is dealt with in *Peter's Chair* (1967). Peter's parents are preparing to give Peter's old furniture to his younger sister. At first enraged, especially at losing his chair, Peter is eventually won over, and the situation is happily resolved as Peter participates in painting his former chair for his younger sister. In *A Letter to Amy* (1968) Peter runs into difficulty when he wants to invite his friend Amy to his birthday party. A misunderstanding causes Peter to be uncertain of Amy's accepting his invitation; this problem, happily, is resolved. *Goggles* (a 1970 Caldecott Honor Book), *Hi Cat!* (1970), *Apt. 3* (1971), and *Pet Show!* (1972) are four of Keats's more recent books about Peter.

In most of the books in this series, Peter encounters problems and delights common to children of all colors. The fact that Peter is black seems to be a chance occurrence and does not affect the story. To at least one critic, however, Peter represents a symbolic insight into black-white relations. Ray Anthony Shepard believes that Keats's works reflect the changing attitudes and perceptions of the book-buying public.[42] He supports his claim by drawing analogies between Keats's various books about Peter and the sociopolitical climate of America at the times of their publication. *The Snowy Day* (1962) was produced during the high point of the civil rights movement. It received the Caldecott Medal in the same year that Dr. Martin Luther King, Jr., was leading his march on Washington. In this book Shepard believes that Peter reflects this strong integrationist tide. The illustrations show Peter engulfed in the whiteness of snow.

His enjoyment of snow is seen as the "warm sunshine" of the integration movement. *Whistle for Willie* (1964) and *Peter's Chair* (1967) continue this theme. Peter's parents are seen partaking of middle-class values, in dress and in action. The illustration of a black and a white girl jumping rope together adds emphasis to a single, integrated society.

Published in 1968, *A Letter to Amy* suggests more troubled times. Dr. King is dead. Black rage is high. Peter's neighborhood looks more like a ghetto than a middle-class environment. Threatening clouds in the book indicate the approaching storm of black protest in America, and the absence of Peter's father reflects the sense of loss America felt in 1968. *Goggles* (1969) represents the end of the integration dream. Peter and another character, Archie, are involved in a fight with older boys. Peter's mother is now omitted from the story, and the illustrations are of the ghetto. Peter views the world through the windows of a locked car.

Shepard's analysis of the subtle symbolism in Keats's books is intriguing, but most readers see Peter in simpler terms. The story about Peter deals with a boy who happens to be black, not with a black boy. Peter is a very popular character with the white reading public, a black character they can identify with and feel compassin for. For many whites Peter is a bridge between the black and white worlds.

Another picture book series that serves as a similar bridge was written by Janice May Udry and illustrated by Eleanor Mill. In *What Mary Jo Wanted* (1969) Mary Jo, a young black girl, wants a dog. When she gets one she experiences the difficulties that emerge along with the new puppy. The sleepless nights, caused by the dog's loneliness and whining, dampen Mary Jo's enthusiasm. She solves the problem by moving her cot into the kitchen to sleep with the puppy, and thus puts an end to the sleepless nights. *What Mary Jo*

*Shared* (1966) relates the story of Mary Jo's anxious search to find something exciting to share with her classmates. She solves the problem by bringing her father to school. His talk with the class represents an exciting solution to Mary Jo's quandary. In *Mary Jo's Grandmother* (1970) Mary Jo visits her grandmother, who lives alone in a small house in rural America. When the elderly woman falls and hurts her ankle, Mary Jo must walk through a heavy snowfall to find help. Like Peter, Mary Jo is a middle-class child facing problems that are universal to childhood rather than related to race.

Phyllis Hoffman's *Steffie and Me* (1970) masterfully captures the nuances of childhood. Two girls, one white and one black, are friends who confront life's smaller problems with cunning ingenuity. That terrible feeling of a sock that has slipped totally into one's shoe, one of childhood's more frustrating, if not overly serious, problems, is conquered through the use of a strategically placed rubber band. Meeting parental needs for a child to consume a full glass of milk presents still another small problem. A little milk swished around the inside of a glass leaves a milky coating that satisfies both parents and children. *Steffie and Me* is an enjoyable picture book for children and will jog some pleasant memories of childhood for adults.

Ann Herbert Scott's *Sam* (1967) presents a middle-class black family. Sam is a young boy looking for ways to spend his time. His sister does not want him playing with her paper doll, and his father keeps him away from the typewriter. His mother and brother also discourage him from their respective domains. The entire family eventually becomes aware of Sam's dilemma and sadness. "For a minute everyone was quiet. The rocking chair creaked back and forth as Sam curled in his mother's arms."[43] Sam's problem is resolved when he becomes involved in his own activity, making a rasp-

> ## Blacks in Award-Winning Picture Books[44]
>
> The Caldecott Medal is one of the most prestigious awards a child's picture book can win; it was established in 1938. The following picture books won the award and included black representation. Note the development from noninclusion, to stereotypic inclusion, to white authors of the black experience, and finally to black authors of the black experience.
>
> *1938 to 1962.* No award made to any picture book that included a black child as a major character.
>
> *1944.* A Caldecott Honor Book, *Small Rain: Verses from the Bible* included one illustration depicting blacks.
>
> *1946.* The Caldecott award for this year went to *The Rooster Crows.* The book had one illustration of black children. The illustration was so stereotypic and offensive that it was removed from later reprints in spite of the fact that it had been among the illustrations recognized as the best of the year by winning the Caldecott Medal.
>
> *1963. The Snowy Day* won the award this year. It is a story of a black boy. The book has been praised for its illustrations, as well as condemned for being a white story with a black cast.
>
> *1971. A Story—A Story,* an African folktale retold by a white author; it won the Caldecott Medal for 1971.
>
> *1972. Moja Means One* was the first Caldecott Honor Book written and illustrated by blacks (Muriel and Tom Feelings). This is a Swahili counting book about Africa for black children in the Western Hemisphere.

berry tart. *Sam* is enhanced by the warm and dignified illustrations of Symeon Shimin.

For children in the intermediate grades there are several books with a racially mixed group of characters who confront universal issues. Zelpha Keatly Snyder's *The Egypt Game* (1967) is the story of April, a white girl forced to live with her grandmother, and Melanie, a black girl who is her new neighbor and friend. Both girls are avid readers with vivid imaginations. Their fascination with Egypt leads to their creation of an ancient temple complete with artifacts. Their play centers around this temple as they immerse themselves in appropriate roles and fantasies. This Egyptian fantasy attracts other children as well, and eventually includes Asian Americans as well as blacks, boys as well as girls. The game becomes more serious when elements of murder and mystery are introduced into the plot. It is an engrossing story.

Another well-written story is E. L. Konigsburg's *Jennifer, Hecate, Macbeth, William McKinley and Me, Elizabeth* (1967). Two girls, one black and one white, each a misfit in her own way, form an unusual relationship, one girl claiming to be a witch and the other girl becoming her apprentice. Their unique status as witch and apprentice is replaced by friendship at the story's conclusion. In both books it is only through the illustrations that the reader can tell that the characters are multiracial.

Most of the characters in the books in this

Sam

flicting points of view into focus and that may help you form your own opinion on the value of the universal approach.

After all, none of us can be completely described by an ethnic label. Most of us are composites of many cultures. . . . We grow rich by sharing, and we must continue to share an ever-widening circle. For we are all earthlings, sharing a spaceship that grows smaller each decade.[45]

A generation ago white children were taught to look directly at black people and pretend they didn't realize that they were black. Viewing such behavior today, with our experience of the civil rights movement behind us, it appears to be the most unsophisticated and racist behavior imaginable. But *at the time* it was a sincere effort by an ignorant white populace who were truly concerned about equality to express equality by pretending that difference did not exist.[46]

## The struggle and the dream

Where does it stop if a guy doesn't fight back? He gets beat until he's ready to salute every time they pass him.[47]

Poverty, violence, and racism are elements in children's literature that relate the hardship of being black in America. Sometimes black characters respond to these obstacles with direct action; at other times their response takes the form of hopes and dreams that are sometimes fulfilled and that in other instances remain unrealized. These books portraying black struggle, frustration, and hope offer the reader some insight and feeling for the black experience in America.

A brief and effective story for young children that incorporates the themes of struggle and hope is Sharon Bell Mathis's *Sidewalk Story* (1971). Lilly Etta, a young black girl, shares the torment of eviction that faces her friend Tanya. Tanya's mother has attempted to work and take care of a large family, but the obstacles are too great, and she is unable to

section are from middle-class backgrounds. The poverty and racism of the ghetto are replaced by secure homes with caring families. These books focus on one aspect of a black child's life: those common and universal issues that all children face. Yet this approach is not without its critics.

Authors differ on the validity and value of such a presentation. Some say it is a romanticized and unrealistic presentation, devoid of issues and ignoring racial differences. They believe it is a misrepresentation of Black Americans—what they are and what they hope to be. These two points of view have created a controversy among authors and critics of children's books. We conclude this section with two quotes that bring these con-

meet the rent payments. The eviction of Tanya's family is accepted as inevitable by everyone except Lilly Etta. Lilly Etta, hopeful that the eviction can be stopped, calls a local newspaper in an attempt to gain public sympathy. A reporter dampens her optimism, telling her evictions are fairly common and not particularly newsworthy. Despondent, Lilly Etta returns home to hear a forecast of rain. With Tanya's furniture already piled up on the sidewalk, Lilly Etta rushes outside to cover the household belongings with a pile of sheets. Holding down the sheets until late into the night, she eventually falls asleep atop the furniture. She wakes up to find that newspaper photographers and reporters are recording the small drama. Public sympathy is raised, and Tanya and her family get a new apartment. Through her hope and courage Lilly Etta saves her friend from becoming homeless.

*Evan's Corner* (1967), by Elizabeth Starr Hill, is the story of a black boy whose dream for a place of his own is fulfilled. This picture book relates the story of a boy who lives in a crowded apartment and needs a private place just for himself. His mother provides the solution by assigning a corner of the apartment to Evan. He then takes command, bringing in a plant, a picture, and his own furniture. Evan shares his happiness by fixing up another corner of the house for his younger brother. *Sidewalk Story* and *Evan's Corner* present young black characters who successfully confront ghetto housing problems, the same kinds of problems faced by many urban blacks today.

Louisa Shotwell's *Roosevelt Grady* (1963) portrays the Gradys, a family with more than its share of hardships but rich in dreams for a better life. The difficulties of the life of migrant workers range from dilapidated housing to inadequate medical care. What seems to be most annoying to Roosevelt, the oldest Grady boy, is irregular school attendance. The Gradys dream of a permanent place to live, work, and go to school. Roosevelt and his friend devise a plan to establish a permanent life-style. Their plan succeeds and a converted bus becomes the new Grady home. The struggles of their transient existence are overcome as they realize the fulfillment of their dream.

In *The Nitty Gritty* (1968), by Frank Bonham, Charlie Mathews, young and black, learns that the transformation of a wish into reality requires planning and effort. Charlie dreams of escaping Dogtown, the black ghetto, but instead of depending on his own resources, Charlie pins his hopes on his idol, Uncle Baron. Charlie abandons school to collect junk and even sells his own blood in order to raise money for Uncle Baron's "big deal." The big deal turns out to be a fighting cock who is fatally wounded in his first and last fight. The disappointment Charlie feels is compounded when Uncle Baron runs off, leaving Charlie to confront a police raid alone. Charlie learns the hard way that to escape Dogtown he must rely on his own efforts. His easy dream denied, he returns to school to start the difficult task of creating his own future and turning his own hopes into reality.

James Douglas, in *How Many Miles to Babylon?* (1967), by Paula Fox, finds refuge from his ghetto environment through dreams and fantasy. James lives in a single room with his three aunts because his mother is hospitalized and his father has abandoned them some time ago. He vaguely remembers his father's departure, for when he asked where his father was, his mother had said, "Gone, gone, gone . . . just like that, three times."[48] He replaces his lost family with a fantasy. He dreams that his mother is not in a hospital, but instead is a queen in Africa. This fantasy helps to sustain James as he suffers through an ordeal as a kidnap victim. When he escapes his young captors and returns home, he finds his mother there waiting for him. He quickly abandons the fantasy, which has served its purpose.

A more recent book is *The Slave Dancer* (1973), by Paula Fox, which vividly re-creates the horrors of the American slave trade of over a century ago. The story is told through the eyes of thirteen-year-old Jessie Bollier, who is kidnapped and taken on board a slave ship. Jessie's usefulness is that he can play the fife and provide music for the human cargo, the premise being that a dancing slave is a healthy slave, and a healthy slave provides a good profit. The power of the book is provided by the graphic descriptions of the intolerable conditions of the slaves on the ship, a story of beatings, cruelty, sickness, and death. The rationalizations and depravity of the crew are also presented, a point of view usually omitted in children's books.

Although *The Slave Dancer* recently received the Newbery Medal, it has not been immune from some critical attack. Several critics have questioned the historical accuracy of the book, and other critics have decried the dehumanized portrayal of blacks. The slaves are depicted as dirty, ignorant savages, scurrying about the ship like rats and all too willing to sell each other into bondage. Although these faults do detract from the book, *Slave Dancer* still provides a poignant insight into the human degradation, both white and black, of the slave trade. It is a moving account of an unhappy chapter of American history, and most readers will find it an intriguing and harrowing story.

The struggle and the dream are two strong elements in the very popular *Soul Brothers and Sister Lou* (1968), by Kristin Hunter. Fourteen-year-old Lou, enmeshed in the world of violence and gangs, attempts to find a better way of life for herself and her friends. But in her efforts she continually encounters white hostility, and the ensuing struggle helps to form her black consciousness.

The institutional inequities of the welfare system constitutes one facet of Lou's struggle. Lou's mother explains to her why her father left home.

. . . they told him a family with a father at home couldn't get on welfare. A married woman with children could get welfare money, all right, but only if her husband wasn't with her. So we talked it over, and I begged and pleaded with him—but there still wasn't any money. So he left.[49]

Another element of her struggle is represented by the street gang society and the peer pressure toward violence. Lou's older brother, William, avoided this experience because of a severe illness when he was younger.

It never occurred to Momma to give William credit because he was so hard working and ambitious instead of being a bum or a jailbird like most of the southside fellows of his age. If anything, Momma gave herself the credit because she had nursed him for five years while he was recovering from polio which kept him in the house so he couldn't get into trouble like all the other boys. William himself often said that polio was the best thing that ever happened to him.[50]

Lou and her brother attempt to respond to the needs of the gang members by organizing a dance and using the proceeds for purchasing musical instruments. These instruments would provide a positive direction for Lou's friends and, it is hoped, replace the violent milieu of the gang society. But police brutality brings the dance to an early and disastrous conclusion.

Police brutality, or at least the brutality of some policemen, is a constant undercurrent in the book and provides another facet of the black struggle. In one episode Lou protests after a policeman strikes a pregnant black girl. The police officer, "showing his uneven, yellowish teeth," responds, "Well, fine. That'll be one less to deal with when he grows up. . . .

But that's not likely. You colored gals are tough. You're no different from animals."[51]

Through her confrontations with such institutional violence, the inequities of the welfare system and the brutality of the streets, Lou emerges with a greater sense of black identity. Eventually her dream is realized, as she and her friends become famous and successful as members of a singing group. This Hollywood-type ending has been criticized as phony and unrealistic. The treatment of black militants has also been cited as shallow, for they are portrayed as lacking well-thought-out motivations and even a minimal degree of compassion. Although these criticisms have validity, *Soul Brothers and Sister Lou* should be recognized for the number and variety of issues explored and the insight it offers into the black experience.

The Jazz Man

Lorenz Graham's *South Town* (1958), *North Town* (1965), and *Whose Town?* (1969) comprise a trilogy depicting the struggle of a black family confronting prejudice. Although the struggle against racism is a theme in all three books, David's dream does undergo modifications in the last book of the series, *Whose Town?* Graham's *South Town* and *North Town* contrast the living conditions of the Negroes in the North and South. These two books, discussed in the previous section, deal with a strong integrationist theme. In *Whose Town?* black frustration is apparent, and the integrationist theme is questioned. In this volume David Williams is no longer gazing into the football stands, seeing neither black nor white, but only Americans.

In his last year of high school David is beaten up by some white youths, and the police falsely charge David with assault. As a result of this fight, David's friend, Lonnie, is shot by a white man. The anger building up in David is fueled when his father and many other Negroes are laid off at the local foundry. Such events lead David to a heightened awareness of black pride, and he considers the more militant goal of separatism. But like Lou in the previous book, David finally chooses a moderate position.

*Daddy Was a Numbers Runner* (1970), by Louise Merriwether, is an account of a black family living in Harlem during the Depression. Told through twelve-year-old Francie's eyes, in graphic language, we are introduced to the difficulties and depravation of a black family whose major source of income is from illegal book making. The world of the ghetto, the pervasive poverty, and the dehumanization of going on welfare are all elements of the story. Although the period is forty years ago, the struggle of ghetto life is strikingly similar to that of today.

Another story told through the diary of a young child is found in Eloise Greenfield's

*Sister* (1974). Doretha began her diary when she was nine; now, at thirteen, she reads the pages of triumph and sorrow: the day she watched her father die (and as he fell his "face *plopped* in the dirt"); her hardworking mother; her troubled sister, and the stories of her proud ancestor, Grandpa Jack, who never found his freedom but never lost his pride. Doretha's dreams are also included in her diary, such as the pride she finds in "Nduga Na Ndada," a club dedicated to the brothers and the sisters and black freedom. Doretha's diary reveals not only the hard times but the "good times that rainbow their way through."

A particularly sensitive insight into the lives of blacks in the South in the 1950s is found in the recently published *Ludell* (1975), by Brenda Wilkinson. The horizons in Waycross, Georgia are severely limited for a young black girl like Ludell. The segregated school, washing other people's clothes for a meager living, and the pervasive poverty that engulfs the black community do not prevent Ludell from discovering her writing talents and yearning for a brighter future, beyond the confines of her small Southern community.

The final book that we consider in this section relates the ordeal of a black boy named Zeke. In *The Jazz Man* (1966), by Mary Hays Weik, we are introduced to Zeke, who lives in a five-story walk-up in Harlem. Zeke shuns the active world because of his crippled leg. His days are spent at his window, watching people who live across the alley. Most of his attention focuses on the window of a jazz pianist, but his interest is soon diverted as his hardworking mother stops coming home and his father becomes an irregular visitor.

Zeke slowly eats all the food remaining in the house. With the jazz pianist no longer playing and all his food gone, Zeke takes to his bed and his fantasies. He dreams of walking downstairs and seeing the jazzman playing on a gold piano. When he pinches himself, he wakes up to see his parents back home, and the jazz pianist playing across the street. "It was real, Zeke knew. He was not afraid any more, the hurt in his chest was gone. They were all together now."[52]

This sad and engrossing story is enhanced by beautiful woodcuts done by the author's daughter, Ann Grifalconi. The ending of the book can be taken by the reader literally or it can be interpreted as suggesting Zeke's death.

Some of the books in the next section also contain the themes of black struggle and aspiration. They are widely read and widely acclaimed; we discuss them and also analyze some of the attacks that have been made upon them.

## From *Chocolate Factory* to *Sounder*: recent racism

Many of the books to be discussed here can be found in most school and public libraries, for they are popular among children and highly respected by teachers. In several instances schools have adopted them as required reading. Although they are widely read and widely acclaimed, they have been criticized for their negative portrayals of black characters. Some of these criticisms are of blatant racism; others point to more subtle negative stereotyping. Becoming aware of these criticisms helps one gain not only a greater appreciation of the books but also a deeper insight into the nature of racism in literature. You may not agree with every criticism, but you are likely to find the reviewers' comments useful in sharpening your perception of how racism can occur in books.

Several imaginative and popular books have been written by Roald Dahl. In *Charlie and the Chocolate Factory* (1964), Mr. Willie Wonka is the strange owner of the mysterious chocolate factory. Mr. Wonka opens the doors of the factory to five young contest winners and shares his chocolate-making secrets with them. The contest winners include greedy, fat Augustus Gloop; spoiled, rich Veruca Salt; television addict Mike Teevee; champion gum chewer Violet Beauregarde; and the hero, brave but poor, honest but starving Charlie Bucket. This morality tale has the four obnoxious children involved in appropriately obnoxious accidents while virtuous Charlie and his family are rewarded as Charlie is promised future ownership of the factory.

The lively dialogue and creative plot have led to critical applause and critical scorn. Some critics cite *Charlie and the Chocolate Factory* as racist, basing their criticisms on the characters Dahl calls the Oompa-Loompas.

On a visit to Africa Mr. Wonka crosses paths with a tribe of pygmies who live in trees, eat horrible green caterpillars, and manage to keep just one step ahead of starvation. Mr. Wonka strikes a deal with the chief of the tribe and promises to provide the tribe with chocolate in return for all 3000 of them agreeing to work in his chocolate factory. "They are wonderful workers. They all speak English now. They love dancing and music . . . I must warn you, though, that they are rather mischievous. They like jokes. . . ."[53] But Mr. Wonka accepts the humor and dancing of the Oompa-Loompas because they provide cheap labor, as well as ready subjects for the testing room. The testing room is the scene of Mr. Wonka's experimentation with new candies. One experiment attempts to create candy that will grow hair on bald boys and girls. Unfortunately, the candy is not yet perfected, as any of the now bearded Oompa-Loompas can attest. Another experiment involves gum that is supposed to taste like an entire meal, but it too has gone awry, turning twenty Oompa-Loompas into blueberries, much to Mr. Wonka's annoyance.

This devastating portrayal is continued in Dahl's later book *Charlie and the Great Glass Elevator* (1972). Charlie, his parents, grandparents, and Mr. Wonka are sent into an earth orbit in a glass elevator. The trip has beneficial results for the earth as well as Charlie's elderly relatives (see Chaper 3). But in this tale also, the Oompa-Loompas act like a ludicrous Greek chorus. One of their songs tells the story of an unfortunate individual who eats her grandmother's chocolate-covered laxative. The resultant chromosome change has dire consequences.

> For seven hours every day
> Within the everlasting gloom
> Of what we call the Ladies Room
> And there she sits and dreams of glory
> Alone inside the lavatory.[54]

Devising such lyrics, dancing, making chocolate candies, and being used as subjects of experimentation comprise the major activities of the brown Oompa-Loompas in Dahl's books.

The negative portrayal of the Oompa-Loompas has been criticized in several reviews as stereotyping Negro characters as ignorant and musical. In addition, the Oompa-Loompas work for low wages in Mr. Wonka's factory, and this has been cited as a form of colonialism in miniature. Mr. Wonka's factory represents the industrialized societies, and the cheap labor of the Oompa-Loompas symbolizes the exploitation of the developing and usually nonwhite countries of the world. In addition to the exploitation symbolism, a new degree of injustice is introduced in the form of experimentation on the Oompa-Loompas. In bringing the Oompa-Loompas from Africa, Willie Wonka has used and abused them for his own ends.

Roald Dahl has defended his Oompa-Loompas in particular and his books in general because of their appeal to children. He asserts that the Oompa-Loompas are caricatures, not meant to be used as carrying deep significance. One need not question Mr. Dahl's intention to assume that some children may also derive negative images of blacks from Mr. Dahl's presentations.

---

### Negro, Black, Colored, and Afro-Americans[55]

Language can be used for a variety of purposes other than communication. The terms used to refer to blacks have often had the effects of lowering blacks' self-images and increasing racist attitudes of whites. *Nigger* and *boy* applied to a sixty-five-year-old man are two terms that reflect and reinforce racism. Negative connotations are often associated with phrases that include the word *black:*

| | |
|---|---|
| *blacken* | to speak evil of; to defame |
| *black eye* | a mark of shame; dishonor |
| *blackguard* | a low, contemptible person; a scoundrel |
| *black-hearted* | disposed to doing or wishing evil; malevolent; malicious |
| *blacklist* | an indication of failure or censure |
| *black market* | a market operating in violations of the law |
| *black sheep* | a person who causes shame or embarrassment because of his deviation from the accepted standards of his group |
| *black Friday* | any of the various Fridays on which disastrous events occurred |
| *black hand* | secret society for blackmail violence |
| *black hole* | military cell |

To emphasize self-pride, black Americans now use the word *black* to stand for pride and dignity. They have redefined it to represent a new awareness and esteem in their blackness.

---

Although today's illustrations have come a long way from the hideous, stereotypic pictures of the past, many readers and critics still find some illustrations offensive. For example, Polly Greenberg's *Oh Lord, I Wish I Was a Buzzard* (1968), a story set in the Mississippi Delta, depicts a family of smiling cotton pickers. Some readers object to the neatly pressed clothes and happy faces as incongruent with the real life of cotton pickers and suggest that these romanticized illustrations distort reality.

The illustrations in Jacob Lawrence's *Harriet and the Promised Land* (1968) have also been criticized. This strong story of the effects of slavery is depicted through stylized illustrations of bony figures, disproportionate bodies, and skull-like heads. When reading this book to children, black and white children, we frequently receive negative reactions to the illustrations. Obviously, expressionistic art is not always understood or appreciated by young (or adult!) readers.

This is not to say that the works by Greenberg or Lawrence are of poor quality or should be avoided. Rather, the point is that in these and other stylized or expressionistic illustrations, care must be taken in explaining the purpose of this approach and exploring personal reactions to the illustrations. Realism alone simply does not speak to all readers and cannot touch the same responsive chords as expressionistic art.

*Amos Fortune, Free Man* (1950), by Elizabeth Yates, is a popular book in many school and public libraries. Published in 1950 and winner of the 1951 Newbery Medal, it is the story of At-Mun, a young prince from the Gold Coast, who is captured and brought to eighteenth-century America. As a slave, he is owned by several families. Later, when he is a free man, he travels through New England. His name is quickly Americanized to Amos Fortune. The biography concerns his life as a slave and as a free man.

The story is based on historical records and is written for children in upper elementary and junior high school. Some areas worth critical attention can be found in Amos's character traits. For example, Amos possesses tolerance and patience that would challenge a saint. When his owners, a very "Christian" family, must pay off a debt, they are forced to sell all their possessions, including Amos. In spite of the warm feelings between Amos and this family, they abandon Amos, who nonetheless remains optimistic: "But there were debts to be paid and Amos had comforted them with his assurance of a right outcome for them all. He had not dwelt half of his lifetime in a Christian household without absorbing trust and confidence."[56]

During the auction Amos even bids on himself. His good humor and his long period of contentment as a slave have been criticized as portraying slavery as an acceptable and necessary prerequisite to freedom. Amos's own characteristics of tolerance, humanity, strength, and ability seem to contradict the long period of slavery and dependence that even he accepts as necessary. As one of his owners, speaking of giving Amos his freedom, points out, "in his untamed state it would not be well to give it to him too soon."[57]

Comparisons made between America and Africa, although reflecting historically accurate opinions of Americans in the eighteenth century, may require special attention by today's readers. Africa is portrayed as an uncivilized land, its people lacking in even the most fundamental human qualities. Even among whites sympathetic to Amos, ignorance and derision of Africa emerge. Children should be made aware that the image of "darkest Africa" reflects the degree of white knowledge of the continent and not the stage of development of various African tribes. Amos's love for and memory of Africa, however, are included in the story.

Another stereotype of colonial Americans presented in *Amos Fortune, Free Man,* and one that many still believe, is that of the Negro as a musical superstar. As Mrs. Richardson in *Amos Fortune, Free Man* notes, "If you had a slave for no other reason than their singing, I often think it would be worth it."[58]

Attention to these criticisms can add to this book's power, for it is an otherwise well-written biography. Since the story occurs some time ago and is set in New England, it is an important addition to the literature on slavery. The presentation of Amos is generally warm and positive, indicating his hard-won position as a skilled and respected free man.

Another book that has stirred some controversy is *The Cay* (1969), by Theodore Taylor. During World War II Phillip and his mother are aboard a ship attempting to avoid German submarines. When their boat is torpedoed, Phillip is knocked unconscious and awakens to find himself on a raft with a man called Timothy. As Phillip tells it:

I saw a huge, very old Negro sitting on a raft near me. He was ugly. His nose was flat and his face was broad; his head was a mass of wiry gray hair. . . . His face couldn't have been blacker, or his teeth whiter. They made an alabaster trench in his mouth, and his pink-purple lips peeled back over them like the meat of a conch shell. . . .[59]

Phillip's bigotry is at least in part derived from his mother, whose Southern background has led to a very low image of blacks. But living on the cay (island), where Phillip and Timothy eventually land, brings about changes in Phillip's attitudes. Timothy is responsible for Phillip's survival, especially after Phillip goes blind as a delayed result of the shipwreck. The black man teaches Phillip how to fend for himself. In their conversations Phillip learns about the nature of prejudice, and his love and respect for Timothy grow. During a severe storm Timothy shields Phillip with his own body, protecting him from the ravages of the storm, at the cost of his own life. Phillip is eventually rescued from the island, reunited with his parents, and his sight is restored, but his life has forever been changed. His relationship with Timothy has brought racial tolerance and compassion to Phillip.

A review in the *New York Times* praised *The Cay*.[60] The reviewer interpreted the book as promoting racial tolerance by showing the superficiality of racial differences. When Phillip is blind he is also color blind, and his relationship with Timothy is then based on grounds other than an awareness of race. This treatment suggests that racial differences are only a product of color and that different racial experiences and psychology are nonexistent.

Other critics refute the notion that *The Cay* promotes racial understanding. These critics point to the fact that Timothy, although kind, is incredibly ignorant, as is evidenced in his dialect and his lack of awareness of even the existence of a place called Africa. As a character, Timothy lacks both a past and a future,

and he seems to exist only to serve Phillip. His subservient relationship is emphasized as Timothy refers to Phillip as "young bahs." Moreover, Timothy's goodness is presented as a product of his humanity, with racial identity intentionally minimized. Timothy even notes that beneath the skin color people are similar. His humanity is explicitly separated from his blackness. Even at the book's end, Phillip is portrayed as a white who enjoys talking and listening to black people, because he "liked the sound of their voices" and he "felt close to them." Critics see in this another indication of a patronizing and condescending attitude, one that may indicate more a lack of racial awareness than a sensitivity to racial issues. Although Phillip may "feel close" to black people, his understanding is still at a low stage of development.[61]

It is interesting that a book as popular and noted as *The Cay* can be applauded for its message of racial understanding and at the same time derided for its message of racial inferiority. To some young readers at a certain level of understanding, *The Cay* will provide an emotional experience and help establish positive attitudes toward blacks. At a deeper level, for children of more penetrating insight, the racist portrayal of Timothy and the superficial nature of the tolerance that Phillip has gained will serve to cripple the book's message. The effect of *The Cay* depends on the reader's level of awareness.

Another noted book, which won the Newbery Medal and was made into a popular film, *Sounder* (1969), by William Armstrong, has also received plaudits and criticisms for its racial messages. *Sounder* is written by a white author and is based on a story told to him as a child by a black man. It is the story of a black sharecropper family living in the depths of poverty. The father steals food for his family and is arrested and taken to a work camp.

During the arrest, Sounder, their coon dog, is shot and badly wounded. The boy in the story decides to search for his father and wanders throughout the state, visiting prison camps and chain gangs in a fruitless search. He does, however, meet a teacher who teaches him to read, and the boy gains strength from reading the stories of David and Joseph in the Bible.

Years later his father finally returns, and for the first time since the night of the arrest, Sounder barks. But his father, injured in a dynamite accident, is only a shadow of the man who left, and in a few months he is dead. Also broken by the experience is Sounder, who soon dies as well.

The moving story paints a graphic picture of white bigotry, black poverty, and the kind of endurance that ensures survival of a family even in the most difficult circumstances. The drama and the harsh realism of the plot add to the power of the book, and some have likened the story to a Greek tragedy. As both a book and a movie, *Sounder* has been very popular among children.

As with *The Cay*, positive reviews of *Sounder* relate to its racial message and the insight it offers children concerning the desperation and dignity of a poor black sharecropper's family. But several critics cite its portrayal of blacks as racist, and they point out a variety of instances to support their charge. The first point questioned is the validity of the story itself: Can a white author really understand the plight of an oppressed black family? Even though the story is reported to have been told to the author by a black man, one might question the degree of openness a black storyteller might have. The oppressed may be less than candid when speaking to a member of the oppressor race, and the result may be a white interpretation of a black experience.[62]

Other reviewers have complained about the shallow treatment of the impact of such devastating events on a black family. In relating the passive endurance of the family, the author neglects the economic and psychological damage such an existence may cause. Instead we are treated to continued optimism, even in the light of outrageous injustice. Hostility and rage have been omitted from the portrayal of the black family; resignation seems to be their overwhelming characteristic. The closest we get to outrage is when Sounder is shot. The harm to the dog receives more active concern by the children than the jailing of their father. Moreover, the black characters in the book are nameless. The only character awarded a name is the dog. In several ways Sounder's attributes afford him more human qualities than the book's black characters.

To many who have read *Sounder*, as well as *The Cay*, these criticisms may open entirely new avenues of thought. Having enjoyed the stories, readers often miss the nuances of stereotyping. But it is wise for us and our students to consider such criticism, and to become aware of what some critics describe as racist portrayals.

The books in the following section have also won acclaim and have received fewer negative criticisms. Many of these books have been written by black authors and all of them are about the black experience, black consciousness, and black pride. In terms of both literary style and black portrayal, they are highly recommended.

## Black is beautiful

I play it cool and dig all jive
That's the reason I stay alive.
My motto, as I live and learn,
Is dig, and be dug in return.

     *Langston Hughes,*
     **Montage of a Dream Deferred**

In several ways the books in this final section bring us full circle from our initial discussion. We have noted that black characters traditionally had been omitted from or outrageously stereotyped in the vast majority of children's books. The relatively recent publication of the books in this section indicate that sensitive books by and about blacks are gaining currency. Books included in this final section are highly recommended, and when grouped with books favorably reviewed in previous sections, they provide teachers with a wide variety of children's books sensitive to racial issues. These books will help nonblack children to understand the black experience, as well as enhance the self-image and pride of black children.

We have discussed the earlier presentation of Negroes that lasted into the 1940s and 1950s. The stereotypes and caricatures that dominated those books are in sharp contrast to the realistic character development of the books in this section. It is interesting that in some of these books the characters themselves directly confront stereotypes in an attempt to debunk myths and misconceptions about black Americans.

In addition to realistic character development, language and dialogue are used to provide accurate presentations. We have seen how some books used apostrophes and contractions to present Negro dialect, a device that promoted the image of the Negro as ignorant. Other authors resorted to identical dialects and language patterns for white and black characters. A common fault of both approaches was to suggest a uniform speech pattern for blacks. A more contemporary approach is to present black characters as speaking with a variety of speech patterns, including black English.

Black English reflects the speech pattern often used by many black Americans. It is more than the use of certain idioms and phrases not generally used in standard English, for black English affects the very construction of sentences, and it varies from the rules of standard English. The following example from *Listen for the Fig Tree* suggests some of the construction and flavor of black English:

"Marvina doing okay. Marvina doing better than you. Marvina got a boy come here every day to see if she okay and keeps a funny-looking, broken-down car to take her to school every morning. Don't you worry about Marvina. Marvina doing a hell of a lot better than you!"[63]

Some believe that such language should not be accepted and that schools should teach all children to speak according to the same rules. They suggest that to permit blacks to speak English differently is to suggest that they are unable to learn standard English and is equivalent to treating them differently from all other ethnic groups. Moreover, black English has the effect of separating blacks from whites in such areas as advanced schooling, job interviews, and training in the professions. They argue that black English is inferior English, a vestige of an inferior state. Most school systems and teachers labor under this premise and attempt to replace black English with standard English.

A cogent, if less voiced, argument in favor of maintaining black English is made by June Jordan, author, poet, and teacher. She submits that language is power and that demanding a single acceptable form of the language leads to "a homogenized, complacent, barbarous society where standard means *right*, where *right* means *white*. Therefore, *non*standard means *sub*standard, and means *wrong*, and means *dangerous*, and will be punished, even unto death of the spirit."[64]

Jordan maintains that language can be and has been corrupted to support psychological and political beliefs. For example, the Vietnam war produced a litany of corrupted words and phrases: "pacification" through war, "protective reaction," "carpet bombing"; and of course we had to "destroy the village to save it." One can see language used for this purpose in the recent Watergate scandal. The term *national security* was used where *political espionage* would have been more appropriate; there was "humanitarian" hush money; and a statement was labeled "inoperative" rather than as a lie. Therefore Jordan believes that to condemn black English is to deny its psychological and political meaning, for black English represents the struggle for freedom of blacks; its development is Afro-American and carries the black survivor consciousness.

Practically no one has ever suggested that black English cannot be understood. It is grammatically similar to Russian and Arabic in that it does not use the copulative verb be-

tween predicate and subject. Whether black language should be used in schools and accepted by society is still an open question. But as a literary technique used to reflect the reality of black America it is appropriate and powerful.

John Steptoe, in his picture books for young children, combines black English with bold and striking illustrations. When he illustrated and wrote *Stevie* (1969), Steptoe was still a teenager. *Stevie* was an auspicious beginning. It is the story of an older boy, Robert, whose life is disrupted when young Stevie comes to his house to stay. Robert is forced to take Stevie with him when he meets his friends, who jeer at Robert because he tags along. Stevie plays with Robert's toys and annoys him in an assortment of ways. But when little Stevie leaves, Robert discovers that he misses him. He misses teaching him how to write his name; he misses playing with him. "Aw, no! I let my cornflakes get soggy thinkin' about him. He was a nice little guy. He was kinda like a little brother. Little Stevie.[65]

*Stevie* deals with a universal situation, a younger child's intrusion into an older child's life. But the book relates this universal situation in a ghetto context through the use of language, environment, and illustrations. The ghetto context is also used in *Uptown* (1970), the story of two black boys as they reminisce about their past and daydream about their future. Their discussions include experiences with junkies, black power, karate experts, and hippies. One boy even considers becoming a policeman but is dissuaded by his friend: "nobody digs cops, you wouldn't have no friends." Finally, they agree. "Guess we'll just hang out together for a while and just dig on everythin' that's goin' on."[66]

*Birthday* (1972) continues the bold illustrations that have marked Steptoe's work, and it relates a strong black theme. Javaka Shatu lives in Yoruba, a small American town, and he is celebrating his eighth birthday. It is a future place, in a distant time, where black pride and brotherhood are all-pervasive. Perhaps the brotherhood theme of *Birthday* may be Steptoe's dream for America.

Another strong black theme is presented in *All Us Come Cross the Water* (1970), written by Lucille Clifton and illustrated by John Steptoe. Ujamaa (Unity) is a young black boy who is unable to answer his teacher's question about where he is from. When the teacher supplies the answer "Africa," he is still unsatisfied. From his grandmother he learns that his ancestors were from Whydah, Dahomey and Ghana. His friend at a black book store tells him that all his black brothers and sisters are here as a result of forced passage; they are as one, from the same slavery experience. The next day in class Ujamaa stands up and says that "my name is Ujamaa and that means Unity and that's where I'm from."[67] And his black classmates stand up with him.

The search for identity and the formation of black pride is a thread that can be found also in Tom Feelings's *Black Pilgrimage* (1972), a collection of paintings and drawing that recount the author's experiences in the Bedford-Stuyvesant ghetto in New York, in the Southern United States, and in Africa. The illustrations portray the difficult life of the ghetto, the warmth of the Southern black children, and the spirit and pride of blacks in Africa. Feelings has written *Black Pilgrimage* to aid in the development of a strong self-image.

Pride in African heritage is a strong element in many books with black characters, including Sharon Bell Mathis's *Listen for the Fig Tree* (1974). Muffin Johnson is blind and living with her mother after her father was brutally murdered. She confronts serious hardships living in the ghetto and providing support for her mother, who never adjusted to her father's death. In celebrating the ancient African festival of Kwanza, Muffin gains a greater understanding of her black brothers and sisters, and of her own strength.

To be Black was to be strong, to have courage, to survive. And it wasn't an alone thing. It was family. It was her father automatically trusting two Black men. It was a crumbling old man coming out of his safe place into a danger place. It was a man who knew everything and had everything, giving it to her, letting her butt into his life whenever she wanted. It was a preacher saying God was Black and you are God. It was a lady finding her life in other families, helping them. It was a boy being a man all the time. It was her mother.[68]

*Jazz Country* (1965), by Nat Hentoff, looks at the black experience through the eyes of a white adolescent, Tom Curtis. Tom must decide whether to go to college or follow a career in jazz. His decision is complicated by the fact that the best jazz musicians are black. He is told by some black musicians that his life has been too easy for him to "feel" jazz, and Tom responds by attempting to get closer to the black experience. His attempts are often awkward, as when he asks a young black musician named Tim to join his band. Tim turns out to be a musician without talent. " 'Some of us,' said Tim, 'are even lousy dancers.' "[69] But the more time Tom spends with blacks, the closer he gets to understanding black life in America.

*Jazz Country* does not offer the same degree of realism and perceptive analysis of black America that the other books in this section do. It is a valuable book because it speaks to young white readers about the difficulty of touching and understanding black America. The book relates the failures and successes of Tom as he tries to appreciate the meaning of blackness. Easy stereotypes and glib generalizations are denied Tom. Tom is not readily able to grasp the feelings and lives of blacks, but Tom's attempts at understanding do result in an initial success, and a beginning to communication.

Julius Lester's books, *To Be a Slave* (1964) and *Long Journey Home: Stories from Black History* (1972), use historical narrative as a technique in presenting black American history. *To Be a Slave* is a well-edited series of eyewitness accounts of the horror of slavery. The accounts cover the treacherous crossing from Africa; the deplorable living conditions on plantations, such as the one owned by George Washington; and finally, the granting of freedom. *To Be a Slave* is forceful because each account reflects firsthand experience with suffering. For example, Ida Hutchinson, a former black slave, described how black mothers put their babies in a long trough to take out to the fields with them. In this way they would lose little of their work time when they nursed their infants. One day there was a sudden downpour; the mothers, scattered throughout the fields, ran back to the trough filled with black infants, only to find that the "trough was filled with water and every baby in it was floating round in the water, drowned. They never got nary a lick of labor and nary a red penny for any of them babies."[70] In *Long Journey Home* Lester relates six stories, based on interviews, about slaves and freed men. The diverse stories are dramatic and effective. As in *To Be a Slave*, Lester presents history through the eyes of the men and women who lived it.

A well-written story, one filled with hardships and written for adolescent readers, is Rosa Guy's *The Friends* (1973). Phyllisia Cathy has just arrived in Harlem from the West Indies. Her West Indian accent and success in her school work soon lead to friction and fights with other children. Phyllisia is befriended by Edith, a girl from a poor and broken family, and although Phyllisia looks down on Edith, she relies on her for protec-

tion on Harlem's streets. As a result of a variety of tragedies and deaths suffered by both Phyllisia and Edith, their friendship is strengthened. This is a tough story of the deprivations and conflicts of ghetto life, including physical dangers ranging from malnutrition to street violence. This graphic and poignant book also includes elements of a Jewish-black antagonism, one that we explore more fully in the section on books with a Jewish theme.

Another superb book about the need for human relationship is June Jordan's *His Own Where* (1971). Jordan provides us earlier in this section with a rationale for the use of black English. *His Own Where*, written in lyrical black English, might provide an even more eloquent argument. The flow of language and style of the book provide feeling and power in a story of a black boy and girl growing into adulthood. Buddy, sixteen years old, spends most of his nights in the hospital by his dying father's bedside. Since his mother left, Buddy and his father have had a good life together. In the hospital Buddy meets Angela, fourteen, whose mother works there. Angela is the victim of beatings by her parents, and after a particularly brutal beating, she is sent to a shelter by court order. On a weekend pass Angela goes to meet Buddy, and they find refuge in an empty house near a cemetery. There they set up a household and begin to live their lives together. Their mutual love binds and gives purpose to their lives.

Another powerful book that makes its impact through style as well as content is Alice Childress' *A Hero Ain't Nothin' But a Sandwich* (1973). The story provides a picture of a young boy, Benjie Johnson, through the eyes of a variety of people. Each chapter is written in a first-person account, using the perceptions as well as language of individuals who know Benjie: his friends, family, school teachers, and pusher.

Benjie is black and hooked. Benjie himself

does not believe he is hooked. He thinks he can give it up any time; he just does not want to. We see Benjie through the eyes of his parents, who have problems communicating with him, and his teachers, who disagree on the most effective approach for teaching him. There is also a section written from the point of view of Benjie's pusher, who sees himself as a salesman performing a needed service to addicts who do not heed his warnings. The failure of these individuals to reach Benjie results in a suicide attempt that is foiled by his stepfather. Growing understanding between Benjie and his stepfather suggests a more hopeful future.

*A Hero Ain't Nothin' But a Sandwich* touches upon a variety of issues, from narcotics to schooling. We see the forces affecting the perception of whites and blacks, and we view these pressures through their eyes and in their words. Black English and standard English are both used to paint a multidimensional picture of Benjie, one that adults and children will find intriguing.

The final books to be discussed in this chapter were written by Virginia Hamilton and are exciting in terms of black issues and literary quality. In *Zeely* (1967) two black children, Elizabeth and her brother John, are spending the summer on their uncle's farm. Elizabeth's creative imagination and curiosity keep her involved with farm chores; that is, until she sees Zeely. Zeely is over 6½ feet tall, dark, slim, and graceful. Elizabeth, now calling herself Zender, sees a picture of a Watusi queen who looks like Zeely, and she proceeds to tell all her friends that Zeely is an African Queen. She even takes to imitating Zeely, until the two have a talk. Zeely tells her of the importance of accepting oneself. As a result, Elizabeth does less fantasizing, and concentrates more on her own personality and interests.

*Zeely* picks up several elements that we have previously discussed. The book deals directly with the dreaming theme, and by describing both the function of dreams as well as the need to confront reality, *Zeely* places a value and a limit on dreaming. The African Queen imagery suggests the identity search present in many black books. In telling Elizabeth to concentrate on reality and on her own growth, Zeely demonstrates confidence in the competencies and self-esteem of a young black girl. In *Zeely* we see the African identity and dreams for the future confirmed, but most of all we see a commitment to the present.

A story of unusual sensitivity is the engrossing *The Planet of Junior Brown* (1971). Junior and Buddy are eighth graders who go to school, but not to class. Along with Mr. Pool, teacher turned school janitor, they retreat to their secret place behind a false wall in the school basement. There they talk and enjoy the mechanized solar system Mr. Pool has constructed hanging from the ceiling.

Junior Brown is a 300-pound musical prodigy who lives with a neurotic and overprotective mother. His friend Buddy is a loner who watches out for Junior. Junior's music teacher is insane, and she manages to give Junior piano lessons without letting Junior touch her piano. When she enlists Junior's support in carrying an imaginary dead body from the piano, Buddy is faced with the task of bringing Junior back to reality.

In a tenement basement Buddy has built a place for a family of his own: black boys who are alone and in need of trust and confidence. Here he hopes to be able to retrieve Junior from his fantasy world. In this new hideaway Buddy explains the rules for staying, his new name (a hope for the future), and the new name for the hideaway:

"We are together . . . because we have to learn to live for each other. . . . If you stay here, you each have a voice in what you will do here. But the highest law for us is to live for one another. . . . I'll help you just as long as you need me to.

I am Tomorrow Billy." His instinct told him what to do as it always did. Buddy's face glowed with new light ". . . and . . . this is the planet of Junior Brown."[71]

*The Planet of Junior Brown* is an engrossing story that both deals with and goes beyond survival in the streets. It reflects the failure of societal institutions, the family, and the school. The book demonstrates Buddy's ability to replace the failures of these institutions with a new institution, his own family, a unique response to the hardships of the ghetto.

Children who find these two books exciting may be directed to other works by Virginia Hamilton. *The House of Dies Drier* (1968) is a fascinating story about a Negro family involved in a mystery because their new house, a former stop on the underground railroad, had been the scene of a set of murders. *The Time-Ago Tales of Jahdu* (1969), appropriate for elementary students, is a story within a story, about Jahdu's adventures, his strength, his pride, and his cunning. This, like the other books by Virginia Hamilton, is a combination of strong black theme and literary strength.

One of Hamilton's more recent works, *M. C. Higgins, the Great* (1974), has received the Newbery Medal. M. C. (Mayo Cornelius) Higgins is a young boy living on Sarah's mountain and enjoying the view from atop a 40-foot pole. Two outsiders—a young, independent girl named Lurnetta and a "dude" with a tape recorder—offer a way out of M. C.'s backwoods mountain home to a new and more promising future. M. C. finds that he has the ability to make choices, and, at the book's conclusion, he and his father rebuild a wall to prevent a spoil heap from destroying their home. In *M. C. Higgins, the Great*, Virginia Hamilton has written an unusual and intriguing story of a young boy's growth toward maturity in a setting of poverty and tradition.

All the selections discussed here provide teachers with fine books for children. These books are well written and well illustrated; they portray the black experience poignantly and effectively and give a strong answer to the stereotyped treatment traditionally afforded Negroes. These books provide ample evidence of the trend toward quality children's books concerned with black issues.

## NOTES

1. Ralph Ellison, *Invisible Man*, New York, Random House (Modern Library), 1963 (original 1952).
2. Nancy Larrick, "The All White World of Children's Books," *Saturday Review, 48* (September 11, 1969), 63–65, 84–85.
3. Julie Ann Carlsen, "A Comparison of the Treatment of the Negro in Children's Literature in the periods 1929–1938 and 1959–1968," Storrs, University of Connecticut, 1969 (unpublished doctoral dissertation), *DA* A30:3452–A.
4. Whitney Young quoted in the *Evening News*, Newark, N.J., October 1965, pp. 23–24.
5. *Time*, April 6, 1970, p. 100.
6. Bradford Chambers, "Book Publishing: A Racist Club," *Publishers' Weekly, 199* (February 1, 1971), 94.
7. "Black and White: An Exchange," George Woods and Julius Lester in *The Black American in Books for Children*, Donnarae MacCann and Gloria Woodard, ed., Metuchen, N.J., Scarecrow Press, 1972, p. 29.
8. Ibid., pp. 30–31.
9. Ibid., p. 34.
10. Tony Manna and Jan Yoder, "Focus on Black Literature, Conversations with Darwin Turner," *English Journal, 64*, no. 9 (December 1975), 79.
11. George Greever, "Communications," *Dial* (June 8, 1916).
12. Annie Vaugh Weaver, *Frawg*, New York, Stokes, 1930; *Library Journal, LV* (November 15, 1930), 925.
13. *New York Times*, July 29, 1934, p. 9.
14. Jane Bingham, "The Pictorial Treatment of Afro-Americans in Books for Young Children 1930–1968," *Elementary English, XLVIII* (November 1971), 880–885.
15. See Patricia Jean Cianciolo, "What Can the Illustrations Offer?" in *Reading Ladders for Human*

*Relations*, 5th ed., Virginia Reid, ed., Washington, D.C., American Council on Education, 1972.

16. Peter Newell, *The Hole Book*, New York, Harper & Row, 1908.

17. James P. Jones, "Negro Stereotypes in Children's Literature: The Case of Nancy Drew," *Journal of Negro Education*, 40, no. 1 (Winter 1971), 122.

18. Eva Knox Evans, "The Negro in Children's Fiction," *Publishers' Weekly*, XL (October 18, 1941), p. 650.

19. Laura Lee Hope, *The Bobbsey Twins*, New York, Grosset & Dunlap, 1904, p. 56.

20. Paul C. Deane, "The Persistence of Uncle Tom: An Examination of the Image of the Negro in Children's Fiction Series," *Journal of Negro Education*, 37, no. 2 (Spring 1968), 140–145.

21. Mark Twain, *The Adventures of Huckleberry Finn*, New York, Harper & Row, 1931 (original 1884), p. 25.

22. Ibid., p. 64.

23. Ibid., p. 109.

24. Ibid., p. 60.

25. Ibid., p. 120.

26. Ibid., p. 294.

27. P. L. Travers, *Mary Poppins*, New York, Harcourt Brace Jovanovich, 1962 (original 1934).

28. Ibid., p. 92.

29. Ibid.

30. Ibid., p. 93.

31. Dewey Chambers, "How Now, Dr. Dolittle?" *Elementary English*, 45, no. 4 (April 1968), 437–439, 445.

32. Isabelle Suhl, "The 'Real' Doctor Dolittle," *International Books for Children*, II, nos. 1 and 2 (1969).

33. Augusta Baker, "Guidelines for Black Books: An Open Letter to Juvenile Editors," *Publishers' Weekly*, July 14, 1969; reprinted in *The Black American in Books for Children*, Donnarae MacCann and Gloria Woodard, eds., Metuchen, N.J., Scarecrow Press, 1972, 50–56.

34. Natalie Savage Carlsen quoted in Jane Granstrom and Anita Silvey, "A Call for Help: Exploring the Black Experience in Children's Books," *Horn Book Magazine*, August 1972, pp. 395–404.

35. Jesse Jackson, *Call Me Charley*, New York, Harper & Row, 1945, p. 76.

36. Ibid., p. 156.

37. See also Betty Baum, *Patricia Crosses Town*, New York, Knopf, 1965, for another treatment of brown and black coloration.

38. Lorenz Graham, *South Town*, Chicago, Follett, 1958, p. 104.

39. ———, *North Town*, New York, Crowell, 1965, p. 213.

40. Dorothy Sterling, *Mary Jane*, Garden City, N.Y., Doubleday, 1959, p. 51.

41. Ibid., p. 152.

42. Ray Anthony Shepard, "Adventures in Blackland with Keats and Steptoe," *Interracial Books for Children*, 3, no. 4 (Autumn 1971).

43. Ann Herbert Scott, *Sam*, New York, McGraw-Hill, 1967.

44. Adapted from *Interracial Book for Children*, IX, nos. 3 and 4 (Winter 1972–1973), p. 14.

45. Arlene Harris Kurtis "Who Speaks for a Culture?" in Harold Tanyzers and Jean Karl, *Reading, Children's Books and Our Pluralistic Society*, Newark, Del., International Reading Association, 1972.

46. Vine Deloria, Jr., *We Talk, You Listen*, New York, Macmillan, 1970, p. 26.

47. Frank Bonham, *Durango Street*, New York, Dutton, 1965, p. 113.

48. Paula Fox, *How Many Miles to Babylon?*, New York, David White, 1967, p. 24.

49. Kristin Hunter, *Soul Brothers and Sister Lou*, New York, Avon Books, 1968, p. 40.

50. Ibid.

51. Ibid., p. 78.

52. Mary Hays Weik, *The Jazz Man*, New York, Atheneum, 1968, p. 42.

53. Roald Dahl, *Charlie and the Chocolate Factory*, New York, Knopf, 1964, p. 76.

54. ———, *Charlie and the Great Glass Elevator*, New York, Knopf, 1972.

55. Adapted from Mavis Wormley Davis, "Black Images in Children's Literature," *Library Journal*, January 1972.

56. Elizabeth Yates, *Amos Fortune, Free Man*, New York, Dell, 1950, pp. 49–50.

57. Ibid., p. 35.

58. Ibid., p. 55.

59. Theodore Taylor, *The Cay*, New York, Avon Books, 1969, pp. 31–32.

60. Charles Dorsey, *New York Times Book Review*, June 29, 1969, p. 26.

61. Albert Schwartz, "The Cay: Racism Still Rewarded," *Interracial Books for Children*, Autumn 1971.

62. ———, "Sounder: A Black or a White Tale?", *Interracial Books for Children*, Autumn 1970.

63. Sharon Bell Mathis, *Listen for the Fig Tree*, New York, Viking Press, 1974, p. 13.

64. June Jordan, "Black English the Politics of Translation," *Library Journal*, 98, no. 10 (May 15, 1973), 1631.

65. John Steptoe, *Stevie*, New York, Harper & Row, 1969.

66. ———, *Uptown*, New York, Harper & Row, 1970.

67. Lucille Clifton, *All Us Come Cross the Water*, New York, Holt, Rinehart and Winston, 1973.

68. Mathis, op. cit., p. 170.

69. Nat Hentoff, *Jazz Country*, New York, Harper & Row, 1965, p. 16.

70. Julius Lester, *To Be a Slave*, New York, Dell, 1968, p. 38.

71. Virginia Hamilton, *The Planet of Junior Brown,* New York, Macmillan, 1971, p. 210.

# BIBLIOGRAPHY

## Picture books

ADELMAN, BOB, and SUSAN HALL. *On and Off the Street,* Viking Press, 1970 (K–2).

ADOFF, ARNOLD. *Black Is Brown Is Tan,* Emily Arnold McCully, illus., Harper & Row, 1973 (preschool–2).

———. *MA n DA LA,* pictures by Emily McCully. Harper & Row, 1971 (4–7).

ALEXANDER, MARTHA. *Sabrina,* Dial Press, 1971 (3–5).

———. *The Story Grandmother Told,* Dial Press, 1969 (3–6).

BANNERMAN, HELEN. *The Story of Little Black Sambo,* Lippincott, 1923 (orig. 1900) (preschool–3).

BEIM, LORRAINE, and JERROLD BEIM. *Two Is a Team,* Ernest Crichlow, illus., Harcourt Brace Jovanovich, 1945 (K–3).

BROWN, MARGERY. *Animals Made by Me,* Putnam, 1970 (K–2).

CAINES, JEANETTE FRANKLIN. *Abby,* Steven Kellogg, illus., Harper & Row, 1973 (K–2).

CLIFTON, LUCILLE. *All Us Come Cross the Water,* John Steptoe, illus., Holt, Rinehart and Winston, 1973 (K–4).

———. *The Boy Who Didn't Believe in Spring,* Brinton Turkle, illus., Dutton, 1973 (K–3).

———. *Don't You Remember,* Dutton, 1973 (K–2).

———. *Everett Anderson's Year,* Ann Grifalconi, illus., Holt, Rinehart and Winston, 1974 (K–2).

———. *My Brother With Me,* Moneta Barnett, illus., Holt, Rinehart and Winston, 1975 (K–3).

FREEMAN, DON. *Corduroy,* Don Freeman, illus., Viking Press, 1968 (K–3).

GRAY, GENVIEVE. *Send Wendell,* Symeon Shimin, illus., McGraw-Hill, 1974 (K–4).

GREENBERG, POLLY. *Oh Lord, I Wish I Was a Buzzard,* Aliki, illus., Macmillan, 1968 (K–2).

GREENFIELD, ELOISE. *She Come Bringing Me That Little Baby Girl,* John Steptoe, illus., Lippincott, 1974 (K–2).

GRIFALCONI, ANN. *City Rhythms,* Bobbs-Merrill, 1965 (K–4).

HILL, ELIZABETH. *Evan's Corner,* Nancy Grossman, illus., Holt, Rinehart and Winston, 1967 (K–2).

HOFFMAN, PHYLLIS. *Steffie and Me,* Emily Arnold McCully, illus., Harper & Row, 1970 (1–4).

KEATS, EZRA JACK. *A Letter to Amy,* Harper & Row, 1968 (4–8).

———. *Goggles!,* Macmillan, 1969 (K–2).

———. *Hi, Cat!,* Macmillan, 1970 (K–2).

———. *Peter's Chair,* Harper & Row, 1967 (4–8).

———. *Pet Show!,* Macmillan, 1972 (K–2).

———. *The Snowy Day,* Viking Press, 1962 (5–7).

———. *Whistle for Willie,* Viking Press, 1964 (3–6).

KING, HELEN. *Willy,* Carole Byard, illus., Doubleday, 1971 (5).

LEXAU, JOAN. *Benjie,* Don Bolognese, illus., Dial Press, 1970 (K–3).

———. *Benjie on His Own,* Don Bolognese, illus., Dial Press, 1970 (K–3).

———. *I Should Have Stayed in Bed,* Syd Hoff, illus., Harper & Row, 1965 (K–3).

———. *Me Day,* Robert Weaver, illus., Dial Press, 1971 (K–3).

MANNHEIM, GRETE. *The Two Friends,* Knopf, 1964 (K–3).

MCGOVERN, ANN. *Black Is Beautiful,* photos by Hope Wurmfeld. Four Winds Press, 1969 (K–3).

PRATHER, RAY. *New Neighbors,* McGraw-Hill, 1975 (K–3).

SCOTT, ANN HERBERT. *Sam,* Symeon Shimin, illus., McGraw-Hill, 1967 (3–6).

STEPTOE, JOHN. *Birthday,* Holt, Rinehart and Winston, 1972 (preschool–3).

———. *My Special Best Words,* Viking Press, 1974 (K–3).

———. *Uptown,* Harper & Row, 1970 (preschool–3).

———. *Stevie,* Harper & Row, 1969 (preschool–3).

THOMAS, DAWN. *Downtown Is,* Colleen Browning, illus., McGraw-Hill, 1972 (2–6).

THOMAS, IANTHE. *Lordy, Aunt Hattie,* Thomas di Grazia, illus., Harper & Row, 1973 (K–2).

UDRY, JANICE MAY. *Mary Jo's Grandmother*, Eleanor Mill, illus., Whitman, 1970 (K–2).

———. *What Mary Jo Wanted*, Eleanor Mill, illus., Whitman, 1968 (K–2).

———. *What Mary Jo Shared*, Eleanor Mill, illus., Whitman, 1966 (K–2).

WELBER, ROBERT. *The Train*, Deborah Ray, illus., Pantheon Books, 1972 (K–3).

## Fiction for middle and upper grades

ARMSTRONG, WILLIAM. *Sounder*, James Barkley, illus., Harper & Row, 1969 (7–10).

BACON, MARGARET HOPE. *Rebellion at Christiana*. Crown, 1975 (7–12).

BACON, MARTHA. *Sophia Scrooby Preserved*, David Omar White, illus., Atlantic–Little, Brown, 1968 (7–9).

BAUM, BETTY. *Patricia Crosses Town*, Knopf, 1965 (4–8).

BONHAM, FRANK. *Durango Street*, Dutton, 1965 (9+).

———. *Hey, Big Spender!*, Dutton, 1972 (8+).

———. *The Nitty Gritty*, Alvin Smith, illus., Dutton, 1968 (6–9).

BROOKS, GWENDOLYN. *Bronzeville Boys and Girls*, Ronni Solbert, illus., Harper & Row, 1956 (1–4).

BURCH, ROBERT. *Queenie Peavy*, Jerry Lazare, illus., Viking Press, 1966 (6–9).

CARLSON, NATALIE SAVAGE. *The Empty Schoolhouse*, John Kaufman, illus., Harper & Row, 1965 (4–6).

CAUDILL, REBECCA. *A Certain Small Shepherd*, William Pene du Bois, illus., Holt, Rinehart and Winston, 1965 (3–5).

CHILDRESS, ALICE. *A Hero Ain't Nothin' But a Sandwich*, Coward, McCann & Geoghegan, 1973 (5–9).

CHISHOLM, SHIRLEY. *Unbought and Unbossed*, Houghton Mifflin, 1970 (7+).

CLYMER, ELEANOR. *The House on the Mountain*, Leo Carty, illus., Dutton, 1971 (3–4).

COLEMAN, HILA. *End of the Game*, photos by Milton Charles. World, 1971 (4–6).

COLES, ROBERT. *Dead End School*, Norman Rockwell, illus., Little, Brown, 1968 (4–6).

CONE, MOLLY. *The Other Side of the Fence*, John Gretzer, illus., Houghton Mifflin, 1967 (3–5).

DAHL, ROALD. *Charlie and the Chocolate Factory*, Joseph Schendelman, illus., Knopf, 1964 (3–5).

———. *Charlie and the Great Glass Elevator*, Joseph Schendelman, illus., Knopf, 1972 (3–5).

DE ANGELI, MARGUERITE. *Bright April*, Doubleday, 1946 (3–5).

DOUTY, ESTHER M. *Forten the Sailmaker: Pioneer Champion of Negro Rights*, Rand McNally, 1968 (7–10).

DUCKETT, ALFRED. *Changing of the Guard: The New Breed of Black Politicians*, Coward, McCann & Geoghegan, 1972 (5–7).

DURHAM, JOHN. *Me and Arch and the Pest*, Ingrid Fetz, illus., Four Winds Press, 1970 (3–5).

ERWIN, BETTY. *Behind the Magic Line*, Julia Iltis, illus., Little, Brown, 1969 (4–6).

FEELINGS, TOM. *Black Pilgrimage*, Lothrop, Lee & Shepard, 1972 (7–10).

FOX, PAULA. *How Many Miles to Babylon?*, Paul Giovanopoulos, illus., White, 1967 (4–5).

———. *The Slave Dancer*, Eros Keith, illus., Bradbury Press, 1973 (6+).

GRAHAM, LORENZ. *North Town*, Crowell, 1965 (7–10).

———. *South Town*, Follett, 1958 (7–10).

———. *Whose Town?*, Crowell, 1969 (7–10).

GREENE, BETTE. *Philip Hall Likes Me. I Reckon Maybe*, Dial Press, 1974 (3–6).

GREENFIELD, ELOISE. *She Come Bringing Me That Little Baby Girl*, John Steptoe, illus., Lippincott, 1974 (K–3).

———. *Sister*, Moneta Barnett, illus., Crowell, 1974 (5–8).

GUY, ROSA. *The Friends*, Holt, Rinehart and Winston, 1973 (7+).

HAMILTON, VIRGINIA. *The House of Dies Drier*, Eros Keith, illus., Macmillan, 1968 (6–9).

———. *M. C. Higgins, the Great*, Macmillan, 1974 (7+).

———. *The Planet of Junior Brown*, Macmillan, 1971 (7+).

———. *The Time-Ago Tales of Jahdu*, Nonny Hogrogian, illus., Macmillan, 1969 (3–5).

———. *Zeely*, Symeon Shimin, illus., Macmillan, 1967 (4–7).

HENTOFF, NAT. *Jazz Country*, Harper & Row, 1965 (8+).

HONIG, DONALD. *Johnny Lee,* McCall, 1971 (5–9).

HUNTER, KRISTIN. *Guests in the Promised Land,* Scribner, 1973 (5+).

————. *The Soul Brothers and Sister Lou,* Avon Books, 1968 (7–10).

JACKSON, JESSE. *Call Me Charley,* Doris Spiegel, illus., Harper & Row, 1945 (5–8).

————. *Charley Starts from Scratch,* Harper & Row, 1958 (8+).

————. *The Fourteenth Cadillac,* Doubleday, 1972 (8–12).

————. *Tessie,* Harold James, illus., Harper & Row, 1968 (6–9).

JORDAN, JUNE. *His Own Where,* Crowell, 1971 (7–9).

KAUFMAN, MICHAEL. *Rooftops and Alleys: Adventures with a City Kid,* Lee Romero and Michael Edwards, illus., Knopf, 1973 (3+).

KONIGSBURG, E. L. *Altogether, One at a Time,* Gail E. Haley, et al., illus., Atheneum, 1971 (4–6).

————. *Jennifer, Hecate, Macbeth, William McKinley, and Me, Elizabeth,* Atheneum, 1967 (4–6).

KREMENTZ, JILL. *Sweet Pea, A Black Girl Growing Up in the Rural South,* Harcourt Brace Jovanovich, 1969 (3–5).

LARRICK, NANCY (ed.). *On City Streets,* Evans, 1969 (7+).

LAWRENCE, JACOB. *Harriet and the Promised Land,* Simon & Schuster, 1968 (1–5).

LESTER, JULIUS. *To Be a Slave,* Tom Feelings, illus., Dell (Delacorte Press), 1968 (6+).

————. *Long Journey Home.* Dell (Delacorte Press), 1975 (4–7).

LEXAU, JOAN. *Striped Ice Cream,* John Wilson, illus., Lippincott, 1968 (2–4).

LIPSYTE, ROBERT. *The Contender,* Harper & Row, 1967 (9+).

LOFTING, HUGH. *The Story of Dr. Doolittle,* Lippincott, 1948 (orig. 1922) (4–6).

MATHIS, SHARON BELL. *The Hundred Penny Box,* Leo and Diane Dillon, illus., Viking Press, 1975 (3–6).

————. *Listen for the Fig Tree,* Viking Press, 1974 (7+).

MEANS, FLORENCE CRANNELL. *Shuttered Windows,* Armstrong Sperry, illus., Houghton Mifflin, 1938 (6–9).

————. *Us Maltbys,* Houghton Mifflin, 1966 (6–9).

MERRIAM, EVE. *The Inner-City Mother Goose,* Lawrence Ratzkin, illus., Simon & Schuster (1969) (7+).

MERRIWETHER, LOUISE. *Daddy Was a Numbers Runner,* Pyramid, 1970 (7+).

MYERS, WALTER DEAN. *Fast Sam, Cool Clyde, and Stuff,* Viking Press, 1975 (7+).

NEUFELD, JOHN. *Edgar Allan,* Phillips, 1968 (6–9).

NEWELL, HOPE. *A Cap for Mary Ellis,* Harper & Row, 1965 (6–9).

NORTON, ANDRE. *Lavender-Green Magic,* Judith Gwyn Brown, illus., Crowell, 1974 (3–6).

QUAMMEN, DAVID. *To Walk the Line,* Knopf, 1970 (6+).

RINKOFF, BARBARA. *Member of the Gang,* Harold James, illus., Crown, 1968 (5–7).

ROSE, KAREN. *A Single Trail,* Follett, 1969 (5–6).

SHEARER, JOHN. *I Wish I Had an Afro,* Cowles, 1970 (4–6).

SHOTWELL, LOUISA R. *Adam Bookout,* W. T. Mars, illus., Viking Press, 1967 (4–6).

SNYDER, ZELPHA KEATLY. *The Egypt Game,* Alton Raible, illus., Atheneum, 1967 (4–7).

STERLING, DOROTHY. *Mary Jane,* Ernest Crichlow, illus., Doubleday, 1959 (5–8).

STOLZ, MARY. *A Wonderful, Terrible Time,* Louise S. Glanzman, illus., Harper & Row, 1967 (3–5).

TAYLOR, MILDRED. *Song of the Trees,* Dial Press, 1975 (3–6).

TAYLOR, THEODORE. *The Cay,* Doubleday, 1969 (7–10).

TWAIN, MARK. *The Adventures of Huckleberry Finn,* Harper & Row, 1931 (orig. 1884) (5+).

UNDERWOOD, BETTY. *The Tamarack Tree,* Bea Holmes, illus., Houghton Mifflin, 1971 (6–9).

WALDRON, ANN. *The Integration of Mary Larkin Thornhill,* Dutton, 1975 (5–7) .

WEIK, MARY HAYS. *The Jazz Man,* woodcuts by Ann Grifalconi. Atheneum, 1966 (4–5).

WEINER, SANDRA. *It's Wings That Make Birds Fly: The Story of a Boy,* Pantheon Books, 1968 (5+).

WILKINSON, BRENDA. *Ludell,* Harper & Row, 1975 (5+).

YATES, ELIZABETH. *Amos Fortune, Free Man,* Nora S. Unwin, illus., Dell (Delacorte Press), 1950 (3–7).

They told us they only wanted a little land, as
much as a wagon would take between the wheels.
You can see now what it was they wanted.

*Black Elk Speaks*

# 6 Native Americans in Children's Literature

It happened in 1996, but after years of activity
and demonstrations it still seemed shocking—
unbelievable. World pressure, student protest, the
conscience of millions of Americans, and finally
violence led to the creation of a state within a state,
or more precisely, many states within a state.
From the Canyon de Chelly in the Southwest, to
the coast of Maine, a string of small but independent nations were reestablished. Each state was
a link in an archipelago of Indian tribes called the
United Tribes of America. The UTA would be
closely linked with the economy of the USA, but
politically aligned with the third world. Language,
laws, government and culture were Navaho or
Hopi or Apache or Cheyenne, depending on the
tribal state one was in. Ancient cultures were
recreated as the native American tribes begin to
live again the ways of the past, ways so brutally
interrupted by the arrival of the Europeans.

This future fantasy may present an unbelievable picture to many readers, but to Finis
Smith, leader of the Five County Cherokee
Movement, the idea of establishing an independent Indian nation represents the best hope
for developing dignity and direction for American Indians.[1] And Finis Smith is not alone in
his beliefs, for many native Americans have
abandoned the hope of ever being able to live
successfully within the culture of contemporary
America. The following statistics explain part
of the reason for that despair. If one were to
review the status of the American Indian, and
present those statistics in a format that is quite
familiar to educators—the report card—that
report card might look something like this:[2]

1. Educational Potential
   The Indian adolescent dropout rate from
   high school is 50 percent.

2. Employment Potential

The unemployment rate is 40 percent, approaching ten times that of the national average.

3. Income Potential

The average annual income is $1500 a year, 75 percent less than the national average and about $1000 below the income of an average black family.

4. Quality of Life

Fifty thousand Indian families live in grossly substandard housing, in many cases without running water or electricity.

5. Life Expectancy

The average Indian life expectancy is 63.9 years; on a reservation the life expectancy is only 43 years.

An Indian baby is three times as likely to die as a non-Indian American baby.

The teenage suicide rate among Indians is one hundred times greater than that of white teenagers.

These conditions have been dramatically summarized by John Wooden Legs, president of the Cheyenne tribe: "White men die of heart disease and cancer, we still die of pneumonia, tuberculosis, and diphtheria. When we, too, will live long enough to die of heart disease and cancer, we'll know we have made it at last."[3]

The physical deprivation, as severe as it is, represents only part of the problems facing native Americans. Tribal integrity and the self-concept of the American Indian have been dealt severe blows by Anglo (white) Americans. Forced to leave their lands, massacred time and again, reduced to a mere 240,000 by the turn of the century, and finally herded into reservations, many tribes have ceased to function, and some have ceased to exist. Living in the restricted environments established by the federal government, the surviving tribes were unable to live as they had or to merge significantly into the mainstream of American society. Treated as defeated nations, Indian reservations took on the appearance of undeveloped countries in the midst of a technically advanced society.

Reservations are managed by the federal government in a way not unlike colonies. Missionary activity has been directed at converting Indians, sometimes by force, to Christianity. Schools organized under the Bureau of Indian Affairs have generally tried to "educate" Indians to the ways of white American society, and the success of such education has been measured in terms of Indian assimilation of white values and life-styles. For example, when the late Senator Robert F. Kennedy was visiting a school with an 80 percent Shoshone student population, he asked the principal if the heritage and history of the Indian children was part of the curriculum. The principal's curt response was that the Shoshone had no history.

Frequently the entire life of a reservation is heavily influenced by the activities of the Bureau of Indian Affairs, which holds responsibility for a great many functions besides education. Since reservations often lack capital and tribal councils lack power and resources, the BIA serves as banker, social worker, employment service, utility, land developer, patron of the arts, police, housing authority, Chamber of Commerce, and provider of vocational training.[4] The Indian struggle for physical survival still continues, as does the struggle to maintain cultural identity, pride, and purpose. What the United States Cavalry did not take from the Indian people by force, missionaries, educators, movie producers, and authors have appropriated in more subtle but no less effective ways.

## Two distorted views of the native American

From colonial times the Indian has provided a popular character for authors. In the vast majority of instances the Indian character is distorted and serves to popularize the misconceptions that non-Indian writers hold of Indians. Unlike most ethnic groups in our society, the Indian population has not been victimized by too few books, but rather by too many. Too many books, especially children's books, as well as television shows and movies feature the savage Indian, engaged in howling dances, covered by a ferocious combination of paint and feathers, scalping helpless white women and children only to be thwarted finally by the U.S. Cavalry. The Indians are portrayed as lacking reason for their activity, motivated only by a senseless thirst for violence.

Another common stereotype is that of the Indian as drawn bigger than life, with greater endurance to injustices than other humans and a closeness to nature so intense that it approaches the spiritual, if not the mystical. In this romanticized version the Indian is presented as a noble rather than a bloodthirsty savage, as a pure human being untainted by the corruption of white civilization. But both stereotypes, although very different, share some important similarities. Native Americans in either case are grouped together as a single type, without regard to tribal or individual differences. Tribal customs and individual personalities are submerged in illustrations and text that deny a realistic presentation of native Americans and instead reflect the popular stereotypes of non-Indian authors.

Indian stories were in the beginning the focus of adventure books, and the Indians were often romantically idealized. Early examples of this idealization are James Fenimore Cooper's

*The Last of the Mohicans* (1826), originally written for adults but also read by older children, and Longfellow's *Hiawatha*. In these books the Indian is presented as pure and good and living in ideal harmony with nature. This portrayal of the Indian as a Noble Red Man dates back to the early explorations of America. In describing the beauty of the New World, the early explorers told tales of the natives, uncorrupted by civilization and living in peace and tranquility. The American Indian became a romanticized character in children's books, as well as in the works of Emerson, Thoreau, and even Faulkner. But to the pioneers settling the West, the Noble Red Man was not as useful an image as it was to writers in the East. For westerners in quest of Indian lands, a different image was needed, and a new stereotype was formed.

For western settlers interested in gaining land, the most useful image of the Indian was that of an ignoble savage, a bloodthirsty, treacherous heathen lacking even the most fundamental human qualities. Picturing Indians as subhumans helped white settlers rationalize taking Indian land and lives. An example of this portrayal occurs in Walter Edmonds's *Drums Along the Mohawk* (1936). In this book the Iroquois Indians are aligned with the English against the colonists. They are depicted as dirty, foul-smelling, savage, and easily recognized by the bloody scalps hanging from their belts. In Edmonds's *The Matchlock Gun* (1941), an ALA distinguished contribution to children's literature, the Indians are presented as treacherous and murderous but sufficiently unintelligent to be easily outwitted.

Although some books, often written by Indian authors, do provide a more accurate, sensitive, and coherent view of the life and the conflicts of various Indian tribes, most of the books in circulation provide a distorted treatment of native Americans. In a comprehensive four-year study of well over 600 children's books, the Association on American Indian Affairs rejected outright approximately two out of every three books about Indians because the content or illustrations were conspicuously offensive. The remaining 200 books still included subtle stereotypes, misconceptions, and clichés. As a result, the association approved only books written by Indian authors, for these most accurately reflected the Indian experience. From the original list of over 600, the Association on American Indian Affairs recommended only sixty-three.[5] In 1972 Blanche[6] found that native Americans were still being misrepresented in children's literature, and in 1973 Falkenhagen, Johnson, and Balasa[7] mantained that stereotyping was still commonplace. These results suggest that although the representation of Indians has been historically distorted, a recent publication date by no means ensures that a book offers a fair and nonstereotyped presentation. Although not all native Americans accept the thinking of the AAIA, the association does reflect a growing concern with Indian stereotyping.

So the two stereotypes, that of noble Indian and that of savage Indian, continue to be common even in today's literature for children. However, we must note the attempts to avoid these distorted extremes and to present a more accurate picture of the various Indian tribes that have been taking place since the 1930s. *Waterless Mountain* (1932 Newbery winner) is distinguished for its early realistic treatment of the life of a Navaho boy. The mystical and ancient beliefs of the Navaho religion are reported within a twentieth-century context. Indian life is also sensitively portrayed in Therest O. Demings' *Little Eagle* (1931) and *Indians in Winter Camp* (1931). These books, although few in number, are significant because they introduced a realistic treatment of native Americans and demonstrated to pub-

lishers that exaggerated stereotypes were not a crucial ingredient in attracting readers.

By the 1960s exciting books, both fiction and nonfiction, were being written that not only accurately portrayed Indian life of the past, but also focused on contemporary concerns of native Americans. In *Custer Died for Your Sins* (1970), Vine Deloria, a talented Sioux author, offers a personal statement of American Indians. His account includes the history of Indian-white relations, the perception Indians hold of white society, and an insight into the concerns of contemporary Indians. Another Sioux author, Frank LaPoude, also writes of the life of contemporary Indians, in this case relating the pressures facing a Sioux family living on a reservation in *The Sioux Today* (1972). These books are representative of a growing number of authentic books about and by native Americans.

The force of these books, however, must be placed in perspective, for most of the works currently available to children are still replete with stereotypes and distortions. Before reviewing the realistic presentations of tribal life and of the contemporary Indian experience in children's books, we shall analyze in greater depth some of the more common distortions and inaccuracies children are likely to read. The more informed and aware teachers and librarians are about stereotypes of Indians, the more likely it is that such stereotypes will be analyzed and neutralized in classrooms and libraries.

## Tonto and other Indian stereotypes

Great Spirit
grant that I
may not criticize
my neighbor
until I have
walked a mile
in his moccasins.

Unfortunately, most of the authors of children's books about Indians are non-Indians who do not heed the message in this ancient Indian prayer. As a result, children's books often reflect an image of native Americans that differs from reality. In "The Image of American Indians Projected by Non-Indian Writers" Mary Gloyne Byler reviews some of the common portrayals of Indians available to children. She notes that one common image is that of the unidentifiable savage devoid of any humane characteristics. This image is supported by attributing to an Indian character acts of wanton cruelty, which are reinforced by denying the Indian any personal identity. The Indian is presented as a being without a motive, a tribe, a family, or even a name.[8]

Nameless Indians are found in Peggy Parrish's *Good Hunting Little Indian* (1962), where they are simply referred to as Little Indian, Mama Indian, and Papa Indian, in a manner reminiscent of the Three Bears. In Parrish's *Granny and the Indian* (1972) the Indians lose even this meager identity and are simply called Indians. Such anonymity robs the reader of the ability to identify with them or to acquire even a minimum understanding of Indian behavior.[9]

This depersonalized portrayal is frequently buttressed by illustrations that show all Indians dressed alike and looking alike. Ignoring the great differences in dress among various tribes, many white authors show all Indians with feathers and paint, carrying tomahawks and stealthily moving in and out of the shadows. Legrand Henderson's *Cats for Kansas* (1948) illustrates a war party of eleven braves and four Indians wearing the war bonnets of chiefs. Each chief is shown wearing enough feathers to indicate status and triumphs that few Indians achieve (perhaps equivalent to the rank of a four-star general in the army). Yet the braves and the chiefs are all engaged in manual labor, and the incongruity of four chiefs commanding only eleven braves is obviously not as important as providing an illustration with a generous measure of Indians and feathers.[10]

> Where do I look?
> What book,
> On what shelf
> Tells why I am?
>
> *The Whispering Wind: Poetry*
> *by Young American Indians*

Another technique that distorts reality and depersonalizes and defames Indians is the portrayal of native Americans as commonly engaged in scalping white men, women, and children. By emphasizing and exaggerating Indian cruelty and atrocities, the reader is led to view Indians not as individuals but as bands of inhumane or subhuman creatures. For example, in *Indian Summer* (1968) one of the white characters observes, "They could have scalped you a long way from the cabin. That's an old Indian trick." In Ruth and Latrobe Carroll's *Tough Enough Indians* (1960) one of the characters explains that the Indians were busy "huntin' and fishin' and beatin' drums and scalpin' other Injuns and white folks, cuttin' their skin and hair right off, somethin' terrible, and burnin' 'em up at stakes." In *Pontiac, King of the Great Lakes* (1968), Clide Hollmann writes, "A warrior had only to drop his canoe into water and he was on his way to a council, a feast, or some scalp-taking expedition of his own."[11]

The use of emotion-laden words and generalizations also adds to the picture of the inhumane Indian. *Savage, buck, squaw,* and *papoose* trigger emotions quite different from *man, boy, woman,* or *baby.* Unsupportable generalizations are also frequent, as can be seen in *The Indians of the Plains* (1960), by Rachlis and Evers, in which we are told that, "War was the Indian's career and hobby, his work and play,"[12] in spite of the fact that some tribes totally avoided war and others endured great hardships before finally being pressed to fight.

These distorted accounts, words, and generalizations present the Indian as a ruthless and senseless murderer. Such books not only degrade the Indian but overlook Indian motivation and the cruelties whites inflicted on Indians. For instance, there is a great deal of evidence that scalping was initiated and practiced by the early European settlers. In 1637 the Puritans offered rewards for Indian scalps, with ears attached. Such rewards were not uncommon in the colonies, but any reference to non-Indians scalping Indians is rarely mentioned in children's books. An exception is Richard Erdoes' *The Sun Dance People* (1972), which recounts the history and contemporary life of the Plains Indians through both text and photographs. One account describes the exploits of Colonel John M. Chivington, a former clergyman, who led a raid against a village of the Plains Indians with the cry:

> Kill and scalp all,
> big and small,
> nits make lice![13]

But the historical truth of such white atrocities against Indian people is generally omitted from the pages of children's books.

The Indian character is also depersonalized by authors who exaggerate Indian stoicism. Stoicism is a characteristic frequently generalized to all Indians, and serves to "de-emotionalize" the Indian personality, to make Indians somehow different from the rest of humanity. In Flora Hood's *Pink Puppy* (1966), for example, the author attempts to describe a Cherokee wake. Eight-year-old Cindy Stand-ingdeer's mother has died, and Cindy's grandmother advises Cindy to hide her sadness: "Cherokees don't cry. You'll have to learn the old Indian way—it's a good way."[14] The author does not seem to realize that Cherokees do cry and that a funeral for one's mother might in fact cause a child to cry.

An interesting antidote for this stoic stereotype is found in Vine Deloria's *Custer Died for Your Sins* (1969), which contains a chapter devoted totally to Indian humor. The author, a Sioux, emphasizes the importance of humor to Indians, offering many examples of jokes Indians tell about various tribes, non-Indian culture, and the Bureau of Indian Affairs. For example, the famous Indian Clyde Warrior was once talking to a group, trying to encourage them to return to and revitalize Indian life. Several in the crowd remained skeptical about the possibility of rebuilding Indian communities. But Clyde Warrior resorted to statistics, explaining, "when the United States was founded, it was only five percent urban and ninety-five percent rural and now it is seventy percent urban and thirty percent rural." The crowd agreed with these statistics, but did not understand what his point was. "Don't you realize what this means?" he continued. "It means we are pushing them into the cities. Soon we will have the country back again."[15]

Stories that demonstrate the human emotions that Indians feel permit the reader to identify with Indian characters. Indians have experienced more than their share of joy and sorrow, and to depict them as consistently stoic serves to rob them of their humanity, and the reader of reality.

Not only has the Indian been depersonalized, but he has been pictured as an innocent and ignorant individual who could easily be outwitted by a white man or woman. Pioneering men, such as Daniel Boone in Bakeless' *Fighting Frontiersman* (1948), were always able "to know exactly what they [the Indians] were going to do next."[16] In Monjo's *Indian Summer* (1968) a frontier woman in Kentucky outwits the attacking Indians, as does the pioneer wife in *The Matchlock Gun* (1942 Newbery winner), by Walter Edmonds. In the latter book the mother and young children, armed only with an antique gun, manage to defeat a small war party.

In all these books the Indian is shown invading a white settlement, and it is easy to get the impression that it was the Indian who intruded on the land owned by the whites rather than the reverse. Although white women and children are present, the Indians in these books tend to be warriors without families. It is easier for readers to identify with the white settlers, their home life, aspirations, and at the same time to gain negative impressions of the homeless and simpleminded Indian.

Another popular misconception is that Indians lack any concept of land ownership. In *Small Wolf* (1972), by Nathaniel Benchley, Small Wolf's father says that the Indians "had no right to sell the land. The land and the sky and the sea are all Mother Earth for everyone to use."[17] Such dialogue does not recognize that tribes did in fact claim specific areas for hunting or farming. Perhaps the lack of paper deeds is one reason that settlers assumed that the Indians did not "own" the land. More likely, however, this myth of nonownership gained widespread currency because it was a convenient myth: one cannot take land from tribes that do not own land. Encroachment on Indian lands, therefore, could be rationalized as settling unclaimed, unowned, untitled land that Indians just happened to be living on.

Some authors have gone beyond distorting history, Indian personality characteristics, and Indian beliefs, and they confuse, misrepresent, and casually interchange the culture and customs of various tribes. In *The Indian Knew*

(1957), by Tillie S. Pine, the noted illustrator Ezra Jack Keats presents some striking illustrations, which are unfortunately compromised, as he confuses the hair styles of the eastern tribes with the teepees of the West, and the ceramics of the southwestern tribes with the travois, a transport device of the north.[18] The result is a book with illustrations that represent what Indian life was not. Margaret Friskey's *Indian Two Feet and His Eagle Feather* (1967) does an effective job of reducing the courage and honor associated with earning an Eagle Feather to a cute child's game. Peggy Parrish's *Little Indian* (1968) does an equally adept job of portraying the name-giving practices of some tribes as an amusing but meaningless event.

For most non-Indian readers, confusing the culture and customs of Indian tribes would generally go undetected. Yet these distortions do have a telling impact, for they confuse and blur the great diversity among Indian tribes and suggest that tribal differences are of little value. In some cases tribal customs and beliefs are replaced, and the reader is introduced to an Indian whose customs and practices reflect a remarkable resemblance to non-Indian customs and practices.

Sigrid Henck's *Buffalo Man and Golden Eagle* (1970) relates the story of Golden Eagle, who would hunt six days a week and then relax on the seventh day, in spite of the fact that the six-day workweek was not an ancient Indian concept but a non-Indian practice. On the seventh day Golden Eagle would put on a "beautiful headdress, put his peace pipe in his mouth and stroll into the hills." But the headdress and the peace pipe were actually intended for specific occasions and ceremonies, and not designed for casual strolls. Golden Eagle is drawn to conform with a non-Indian's perceptions, and the outcome is more congruent with the Bible and the Sunday sabbath than with

Indian culture. This is not particularly surprising when one considers that the author was born, educated, and lives in Germany.[19]

By presenting the Indian with negative characteristics, and in an inaccurate cultural and historical setting, native Americans and the heritage they represent are portrayed as inferior to non-Indians and their civilization. The cultural superiority of non-Indians is stated in the dialogue contained in *Trading Post Girl* (1968), by Lynne Gressner.

". . . You wait and see, some day they'll (Indians) be real fine American citizens."

"Oh, Daddy, not those savages."

"They've got a lot of things to learn, too, honey. Give them time. They've got lots of good in them."[20]

Cultural bias is also obvious in the descriptions provided by some authors. In *Something for the Medicine Man* (1962) by Flora M. Hood, an older Cherokee woman is described as having a face that is "dried up like a persimmon," a Cherokee baby has eyes "like a baby fox," and the entire family eats "like hungry dogs." The non-Indian teacher, on the other hand, is "tall as the trees" with eyes "like blue flags."[21] In *My Name Is Lion* (1970), by Margaret Embrey, the non-Indian teacher is young and smells "like too many flowers." The old Navaho man is drunk, dirty, and "whining in Navajo about money."[22]

The patronizing attitude in these books with a cultural bias theme is brought to a clear focus in the still popular *Voyages of Dr. Dolittle* (winner of the 1923 Newbery Medal), by Hugh Lofting. The victimized Indian character, in this instance an Indian from South America, is a renowned naturalist named Long Arrow. Long Arrow and the other "red Indians" quickly assume a subservient and childlike relationship to the famous white doctor who introduces them to everything from sewers to schools. Crowned King Jong, Dr. Dolittle works tirelessly for his subjects, much to the chagrin of his parrot, Polynesia, who had grown very tired of the Indians: "The very idea . . . of the famous John Dolittle spending his valuable life waiting on these greasy natives! —Why, it's preposterous!" When Dr. Dolittle finally returns to England, he fears that the Indians will go back to "Their old habits and customs: wars, superstitions, devil worship. . . ."[23]

A popular example of cultural superiority over Indians is apparent in the Lone Ranger stories. In comics strips, in films, and on television children are treated to the tale of a strong, pure, and clever white man who rides the powerful, white horse Silver. The minor partner in the Lone Ranger's exploits is his "faithful" companion Tonto, mounted on a more modest horse named Scout. Tonto follows the Lone Ranger on numerous adventures, and on each adventure Tonto demonstrates about as much personality as a glass of water. He speaks in grunts and broken English and is clearly inferior to the Lone Ranger. Tonto has abandoned his Indian culture to enter the white world, but his subservient role is reminiscent of that of the black slave. It is not surprising that Tonto's name means "silly" or "foolish."[24]

The treatment of Indians by the vast majority of non-Indian authors has ranged from disappointing to degrading. Although some non-Indian authors have written some fine books, the great number of children's books about Indians present distorted and stereotypic presentations. Teachers and librarians who are aware of some of these more common misrepresentations will be better able to neutralize their effects on children. Before we review some of the more sensitive books about the native American experience it might be helpful to summarize briefly some common distorted representations of Indians in children's literature.

1. Although early works about Indians tended to portray them as superhuman, noble savages, later books tended to downgrade Indians with negative stereotyping.
2. One common stereotype was and is to portray the Indian as a bloodthirsty savage, both subhuman and inhuman. Many of these books deprive the Indian of a personal or tribal identity, and text and illustrations tend to depersonalize the native American characters.
3. Many books have distorted and depersonalized Indian character traits, customs, and history. Scalping has been attributed solely to Indians, who are also often described as stoic. Other misconceptions concern the practices and beliefs of various tribes, which are often presented inaccurately and unrealistically.
4. A natural outcome of the negative portrayal of Indians has been the development of themes expressing the cultural superiority of non-Indian civilizations. In story development as well as physical descriptions, Indians have been presented as less important and desirable than non-Indians.

## Between two cultures

An Indian who takes on white man's ways is like an oak tree struck by lightning. . . . As lightning splits the oak's trunk in two, so the white man's touch splits the red man. He is no longer one good tree, but two worthless ones, part white, part Indian, no good to either tribe.[25]

A recurrent theme of many children's books centers on the cultural differences and values between Indian and white civilizations. The theme is generally presented in one of two ways. In one approach a white child, usually a boy, is captured by an Indian tribe and brought up as a member of the tribe. These books frequently offer a sympathetic picture of tribal life, and usually the main character must choose between returning to white society and remaining with the tribe that adopted him.

In the second approach an Indian child, again usually a boy, becomes involved in white society. Sometimes he is adopted by whites, and sometimes he is attracted to white education, technology, or medicine in an attempt to integrate Indian and non-Indian cultures. It is interesting that the Indian's desire to explore white culture is frequently voluntary, whereas the white child's introduction to Indian culture is usually by force, perhaps symbolizing the power (not to be confused with the superiority) of the dominant white American culture. The books in this section present characters caught between two cultures, characters who do not always resolve the culture conflict.

There are several books the depict the life of the white child growing up in an Indian culture. Jim Heath, in *Moccasin Trail* (1952) by Eloise McGraw, is rescued from a grisly bear by the Crow Indians, who raise him as one of their own. Comfortable among the Crows, Jim is shocked into a desire to rejoin his family when Crow warriors return to camp with a blond scalp, the same color as Jim's mother's hair. He leaves the tribe and eventually rejoins his white brothers and sister. His mother and father have died, but Jim is determined to help the younger children establish a home. Jim's Indian braids, feathers, and trapping are offensive to his sister, Sally, and his brother, Jonnie. Jim clings to his Indian ways, causing family friction, and he eventually decides to leave. His younger brother, Daniel, follows him but is captured by the Umpqua Indians. Jim rescues him and decides to abandon his desire to return to the Crows. Although Indian culture is perceived as logical and sensible by Jim, the portrayal of the Crow Indians has its share of stereotypes.

A popular book with a related theme is Conrad Richter's *The Light in the Forest*

(1963). True Son is a white captive of the Delaware Indians for eleven years, but is forced to return to white society by the terms of a new treaty. Because of his Indian values and customs, True Son has difficulty adjusting to white society, and he returns to his Indian village and to the life he misses. But True Son's memories of his younger brother, Gordie, prevent him from participating in an ambush of white settlers. Banished from his tribe because of his warnings to the white settlers, True Son finds himself unable to return to the Delawares and unable to adjust to the whites. He is caught between two cultures.

In *A Country of Strangers* (1966), a sequel to *The Light in the Forest*, Richter writes the story of Stone Girl, a white girl who is captured by the Indians. The novel is set in the late 1700s and focuses on the conflict Stone Girl faces when, after her husband's death, she returns to her white family. Her rejection by white society is made somewhat more bearable through the help of True Son, who, like her, is caught between two cultures.

Some other books that focus on the white captive theme and depict the lives of white children in various Indian tribal cultures are Stephen Meader's *River of the Wolves* (1948), Elizabeth Coatsworth's *Sword of the Wilderness* (1936), Lois Lenski's *Indian Captive: The Story of Mary Jemison* (1941), and *Calico Captive* (1957), by Elizabeth Speare. A more unusual story of a white captive, *Little Big Man* (1969), by Thomas Berger, gained widespread popularity when it was made into a movie. Dustin Hoffman played the 111-year-old Jack Crabb, who is adopted and raised by the Cheyenne Indians. The book has elements of both humor and tragedy and presents a number of famous characters: Buffalo Bill, Wild Bill Hickok, Wyatt Earp, Calamity Jane, Chief Old Lodge Skins, and General Custer. The book provides a moving documentary of the injustices and cruelty inflicted on Indians

by whites, and it is all the more powerful because it is told through the eyes of a white who lived with and cherished Indian culture.

These stories share the common plot of white children who are forced to live with their Indian captors. Sometimes, but not always, the white children learn to appreciate and even prefer Indian culture. When the reverse situation occurs—that is, when an Indian child is introduced to white civilization—there are usually several significant differences in the story. Indians are introduced to white culture not as a result of captivity but as an outcome of the pervasive influence of the dominant white culture. The material rewards and advanced technology of white society attract the Indian character, who attempts to bring white accomplishments, such as medical advances, to his Indian tribe. The central question of these books often concerns whether tribal identity, "the old ways," can survive the intended cultural transplants. The constant struggle of Indians to maintain their culture is pitted against the external pressures to adapt, modify, or abandon Indian ways. This conflict comprises a common focus of the following group of children's books.

Betty Baker's *Killer-of-Death* (1963) is an exciting story of the world of the Apaches during the time when the Mexicans, and later the Americans, began settlement of the Southwest. Killer-of-Death is the son of an Apache chief, and he is anxious to pass the trials necessary to become a warrior, and to fight those who are trying to take tribal lands. Life in the Apache village comes to a tragic end as the Mexican settlers deceive, ambush, and massacre most of the tribe. The survivors, led by powerful Mangos, seek revenge on Mexican soldiers and settlers. When Mangos is wounded and dying, Killer-of-Death recalls the medicine of the Mexicans, and removes the bullet. Mangos recovers and the dream that led to the naming of Killer-of-Death comes true; he has earned his name. As the futility of continued hostility to Mexican and American encroachment becomes obvious, Killer-of-Death begins to consider a new way to save his people. He feels that different times require new responses if the Apache is to survive, and he hopes that his son can use the white man's education to find a new way to save the Apaches.

Schooling as a means of survival for the Indian is a discovery also made by Billie Tommie in Phyllis Reynolds Naylor's *To Walk the Sky Path* (1973). Billie Tommie, a contemporary Seminole boy, attempts to balance his home life, where he learns of the old Seminole ways, with his schooling, which seems to contradict Seminole culture. The personification of the old ways is his grandfather Abraham, who teaches Billie ancient songs, skills, and lore. He explains that a bright, starry night signifies that a good person has died and that the heavens are lighting a clear path to the city in the sky. A cloudy, starless night signifies the death of an evil person, who will not be able to find and walk the sky path. Tommie loves hearing the ancient tales and songs, but is also attracted to some potential careers available through schooling, such as becoming a forest ranger or working with animals. The conflict is heightened when the family is forced to leave their isolated but inundated island and live closer to the highway. When Billie's teacher stresses that with work he can be better than other Indians, Billie's reaction is, "Be better than them all? Nobody ever walked the sky path for that . . . what kind of pride did white people have that they had to top somebody else to be important?"[26] On another occasion Billie is scolded by the teacher for fishing and hunting for frogs legs rather than doing his homework. To Tommie Indian ways such as fishing and hunting are an important part of his education. To the teacher, however, Indian practices and lore detract from school work, which is Tommie's "real" education.

A number of overused Indian characteristics are included in *To Walk the Sky Path*. For example, Tommie's grandfather extols the virtues of stoicism, and Tommie's uncle remains polite and smiling while being abused by tourists, but then drinks "himself into a stupor." In spite of such stereotypic characteristics, *To Walk the Sky Path* does focus on the conflict between Indian civilization and white schooling, between the old and the new Indian. Before grandfather Abraham dies, before he walks the sky path, he tries to bridge these two worlds. "New Indian, old Indian—all the same. . . . The true Indian is a man who remembers the ways of his forefathers, even in the white man's world, who does not step on his brother to get more for himself."[27]

Ann Nolan Clark, author of many fine books about Indians, presents a similar old-Indian–new-Indian conflict as faced by a female character in *Medicine Man's Daughter* (1963). From birth Tall Girl, daughter of the medicine man, seems to possess the magic and will to become a great medicine woman. The spiritualism and ceremonies of the Navaho provide an intriguing part of the story, but Navaho medicine is not capable of curing the burns on a small infant. When Tall Girl's cousin takes the child to the white man's hospital, she is warned by Tall Girl that the baby will not recover. The child does recover and Tall Girl takes this as a sign that she must learn this medicine and make the difficult journey to the alien world of the white school and hospital. While at the school Tall Girl is discouraged from pursuing medicine, and she leaves the school only to become lost in a storm. Her father senses the problem and goes out to find her, only to falter and collapse himself. They are both rescued and the white doctor, who understands Tall Girl's talents and status among the Navaho people, agrees to teach her the medical knowledge she seeks. Her disdain for white society and the distrust of whites felt by her father are submerged as Tall Girl learns of the white man's medicine. The prophetic last words of her dying mother now become meaningful: "You will be a great Medicine Woman. But first something must be taken from you; something must be given to you. This will not happen in the carigons or on the plateaus. You must find it elsewhere."[28]

White contribution to Indian civilization is also evident in several books about the famous Sequoyah. *In Talking Leaves; The Story of Sequoyah* (1969) Bernice Kohn, with a relatively brief text and a series of boldly colored pictures, presents the story of Sequoyah, including his participation in both the white and Indian civilizations. Living in the white society

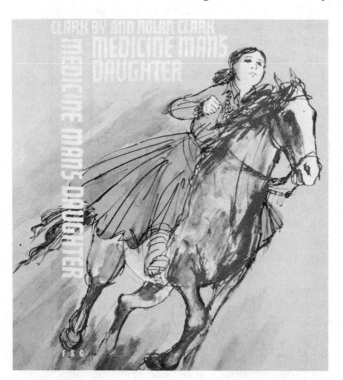

Medicine Man's Daughter

taught Sequoyah many things, but nothing caught his imagination more than the written word. He spent many difficult years attempting to develop a written language for the Cherokees. In spite of ostracism by the Cherokees, Sequoyah persevered and finally developed a written Cherokee language that could be learned in a short time. His effort was recognized by whites and Indians, including the U.S. president, who awarded him a yearly stipend of $500 for his accomplishment.

Another story about Sequoyah, which is more fictional in approach and written for an older child, is Weyman Jones's *Edge of Two Worlds* (1968). Calvin Harper survives a Comanche raid of a wagon train and finds an old Indian living in a cave. Initial hatred of and prejudice toward the Indian dissipates with Calvin's realization that he cannot survive alone. As he learns how to survive without white civilization, Calvin also learns of the life of this seventy-year-old Indian, who is named Sequoyah. Sequoyah had participated in a treaty that forced the Cherokees to leave their home on the Tennessee River and move west. Although he believed the pressure of the whites would make such a move inevitable, he now hopes to find evidence that would support his belief that the Cherokees once lived in these western lands. Such a discovery would reduce the difficulties of the relocation of his people. Calvin is impressed with Sequoyah's dignity, his simple and honest approach to life, and his reverence for nature. This well-written book relates the story of an old Cherokee whose wisdom and courage help a dependent boy grow to manhood.

As Sequoyah's contribution to the Cherokee language illustrates, contact with white society may lead to an improved situation for Indians. But this is not always the case. Contact with white civilization has also led to frustration and disappointment. Sarah, in Florence Crannel Means's *Our Cup Is Broken* (1969), lives with white families for nine years. Never really part of her adopted white family or community, Sarah's first real joy comes with a part in the school play as Pocahontas, and the love she feels for the leading man, Kirk. When Kirk's parents break up the romance and Sarah's adopted white parents pressure Sarah into attending college, she rejects her white world and returns to her Hopi culture. Her experience in the white world makes her unhappy with her Hopi community, and she struggles to adjust to the simple life, pervasive poverty, and a series of tribulations, including being raped and bearing a blind child. In spite of these hardships she continues her struggle to recapture her Hopi world.

A candid account of Indian alienation and frustration in the white world is the Pulitzer Prize novel by Oliver LaForge, *Laughing Boy* (1959). Although written for adults, *Laughing Boy* is enjoyed by older children as well. It relates the conflict between an urban environment and the ways of the Navaho as experienced by Slim Girl, whose alienation in the white world leads to prostitution. Because of the candid nature of the text and Slim Girl's prostitution, the book should probably be recommended only for young adults. *Laughing Boy*, however, is a powerful and honest account of the alcoholism, alienation, and devastation that sometimes result from the Indian's contact with white America.

White culture touches the lives of the characters in Eleanor Clymer's *The Spider, the Cave and the Pottery Bowl* (1971). One Who Dips Water, called Kate in school, spends her summers with her brother and her grandmother in a simple house on the mesa. The opportunity to earn money and succeed seems to exist only in the white man's city, where both her parents work. The advantages of white civilization seem to be confirmed for Kate as she comes in contact with rich and well-dressed white tourists. But she learns to love the an-

cient Indian legends and traditions that she hears about from her grandmother. When she and her brother find clay of good quality in a cave, her grandmother's pottery making, which they all love, can once again resume. Kate's pride in her Indian ways seems to be confirmed when she meets a young, well-dressed white girl who admits her admiration for the Indian way of life and the simple Indian village. "It's so old. It's as if this place has been here forever. You'd always know where you belonged."[29] In *The Spider, the Cave, and the Pottery Bowl* the initial frustration felt because of contact with white society gives way to a deeper appreciation of Indian culture.

The conflict between white and Indian cultures is a particularly harsh reality in bicultural families. In Eth Clifford's *The Year of the Three-Legged Deer* (1972) the divisive nature of culture conflict is felt by white Jesse Benton; his Indian wife, Mekinges; their son, Takawsu; and their daughter, Chilili. Set on the Indiana frontier in 1819, a semblance of peace between the white and Indian communities exists, but there are some, both Indian and white, who harbor intense hatred. When an Indian attacks Takawsu because he has white blood, his life is saved by Sakkaape, a black slave. A series of actions and reactions between a few vengeful whites and Indians results in tragedy for the Benton family as young Chilili is killed. The tragedy destroys the family unity, and Mekinges, Takawsu, and Sakkaape choose to live with the Lenni Lenape Indians. Jesse Benton, alone, returns to white society and eventually marries a white woman. Years later, a reunion between Jesse and his son, Takawsu, brings back memories of those years when their family was one and cultural differences were not as divisive as their love was binding.

A very different story concerning the child of a bicultural marriage is presented in *Half Breed* (1967), by Evelyn Sibley Lampman. Pale Eyes takes the name of Hardy Hollingshead and leaves his life with the Crows and his mother to search for his father, who is living somewhere in the Northwest. Hardy faces prejudice as well as culture shock in the white world. His meeting with his father, who is more adept at avoiding responsibility than supporting a family, is a great disappointment to Hardy. But strong Aunt Rhody helps provide Hardy with the support he needs and he eventually develops empathy for his father and chooses to stay in the white society with his Aunt Rhody.

Robert Newton Peck has recently written an engrossing historical novel about a child of a bicultural marriage. *Fawn* (1975) describes the son of a captured French Jesuit and a lame Mohawk woman. Although Fawn was raised by his Mohawk grandfather in the ways of his tribe, he matures to appreciate his father's Christian and European views. In this way Fawn is a unique and strong character who is not so much caught between two cultures as he is nourished by them. Although only seventeen, Fawn is already developing wisdom from both cultures, identifying the weaknesses and strengths of Mohawk and European philosophy, and exploring new communities to increase his personal growth.

*Fawn* is also a powerful story because it is set against the vivid panorama of the French and English struggle for Fort Ticonderoga. The courage and sacrifice of the combatants are graphically depicted. This historical novel is a fast-moving account of a unique teenager living in an important period in American history.

The books in this section feature characters who bridge two cultures. Some of these characters are able to adjust to Indian or white civilization, and others are at home in neither society. In some cases one society offers some improvements or insights for the other society, but more frequently the contact between the two societies results in friction and conflict.

The warfare between Indian and white societies is one of the subjects included in the next section.

## Searching for the past

> In the beginning God gave to every people a cup of clay, and from this cup they drank their life. They all dipped in the water, but their cups were different. Our cup is broken now. It has passed away.
>
> *Proverb, "Digger Indians"*

For the American Indian to recapture the past presents certain problems unlike those faced by any other minority group. In books, on television, and in movies Indians and non-Indians are treated to a distorted and frequently negative portrayal of Indian history. Unlike the lack of recognition of the history of many other ethnic groups, Indians suffer from too much treatment replete with many distortions. A variety of books, for both younger and older children, present a more accurate historical perspective of the native American.

The search for the past is a theme in a beautiful picture book entitled *When Clay Sings* (1972), by Byrd Baylor and illustrated by Tom Balti. This book pieces together pottery fragments to recapture the spirit of the past, and the life and songs of an ancient people are re-created. The story is illustrated with a flowing black and brown Indian motif, itself derived from prehistoric pottery of the Indians of America's Southwest. The ancient pottery tells the story of times past:

Indians who find this pottery today say that everything has its own spirit—even a broken pot. They say the clay remembers the hands that made it. Does it remember the cornfields too? And the summer rains? And the ceremonies that held life together?[30]

The life of an ancient Indian tribe is also the subject of Mary and Conrad Buff's *Hah-Nee of the Cliff Dwellers* (1956). This book, enhanced by attractive charcoal illustrations, is set in the western United States about 700 years ago, when Hah-Nee, a Ute, is adopted as a baby. When a drought endangers the food supply and the very existence of the cliff dwellers, Hah-Nee becomes one of the targets of hostility, as superstition and fear divide the members of the tribe. Hah-Nee and his family leave the cliffs to find a new home and a new food source in the Rio Grande area.

*Walk the World's Rim* (1965) by Betty Baker also provides an insight into the challenge of survival for an ancient Indian civilization. Written for children in the upper elementary and junior high school grades, *Walk the World's Rim* is an intimate story of Esteban, a black slave, and of Chakoh, a young Avavare Indian, and their experiences with the early Spanish settlers of Mexico. The book is based on the survival of four men who journeyed to the new world from Spain. After escaping a sea disaster, starvation, and warfare, which claimed the lives of 600 of their comrades, the four survivors must make their way from Florida to Mexico. The strength and bravery of Esteban is critical as the group negotiates its way through a variety of ancient Indian civilizations. During their stay with one of the Indian tribes, Chakoh, son of the chief, joins the four on their trek to Mexico. Chakoh's mission is to learn from the Spaniards the techniques of survival and to save his people from starvation. Esteban and Chakoh become comrades, but Chakoh does not heed Esteban's warnings of Spanish duplicity. Once in Mexico, Chakoh falls prey to the comforts of Spanish civilization, the zeal of Spanish missionaries, and a newly acquired full stomach. Chakoh eventu-

ally comes to see the greed and insincerity of the Spaniards, but not before Esteban loses his life.

*Raven's Cry* (1966) is another book about the white man's arrival on Indian land in which the ominous forebodings of *Walk the World's Rim* prove justified. Written by Christie Harris and awarded the Canadian Library Association's award as the best children's book of the year in English, *Raven's Cry* records the dissolution of the Haida people, beginning with the arrival of the white man in 1775. Liquor, guns, disease, and greed create havoc when introduced into the traditional Haida civilization. White medicine and religion deny the significance of the totem pole and the potlatch,

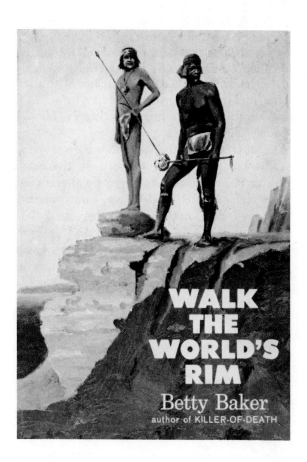

and this dramatic narrative records the decline of the Haida. The book is enhanced by black and white line drawings by a descendant of the last Haida chief.

The devastation of many Indian civilizations that followed the arrival of European settlers is hinted at in Nathaniel Benchley's *Small Wolf* (1972). In this picture book Small Wolf, a young Indian boy, goes hunting on Manhattan Island and is surprised to discover a colony of white settlers. An irate Dutchman sees Small Wolf and chases him and his father away. As the settlements increase, Small Wolf and his father are repeatedly forced to move on. Although generally it gives a sympathetic portrayal of the Indian situation, *Small Wolf* does contain several misconceptions. The plight of Small Wolf and his family is portrayed as especially hopeless because they lack any resistance to the encroachment of whites on their land. They are characterized as being defenseless, being without attachment to their land, and gradually ceasing to exist.[31]

The struggle to survive is keenly felt by young Ishi in *Ishi: Last of His Tribe* (1964), by Alfred Kroeber. In the late 1800s the surviving Yahis hid from the white settlers, the hated Saldu. Their villages destroyed by the whites, they clung to their ancient ways until one by one they died and only Ishi remained. Ishi wandered away from the ruins and encountered the feared Saldu. To his surprise he was not killed but taken to a museum, where he served as a consultant on the practices of the Yahi. Through the efforts of the museum people and Ishi the ways of the Yahi were not lost. Alfred Kroeber was curator of the Museum of Anthropology and Ethnology at the University of California when Ishi was brought there. The book reflects the understanding and insight of an author who is able to combine his personal and professional knowledge. It is written from Ishi's point of view and in the cadence of the Yahi, a prose that approaches poetry.

Several children's books relate the clash between Indian and white civilization as seen through the eyes of a white youngster. Frequently the child has a greater insight than the older generation, more set in their ways and values, and develops an independent and usually sympathetic view of Indians. *The Courage of Sarah Noble* (1954), by Alice Dalgliesh, is the story of an eight-year-old girl whose courage and compassion overcome the bigotry of most of the adults presented in the story. The difficulties of establishing a new home on the frontier are overcome through Sarah's courage and the help of a local Indian family. Sarah and her father ignore the warnings of white settlers in the wilds of Connecticut that the "heathen savages" will skin them alive. The trust that Sarah and her father place in the Indians is returned in this story, which is based on a true incident.

Don Schelle's *Me, Cholay and Co: Apache Warriors* (1973) is another story featuring a young white character who views Indian civilization with compassion. Like *The Courage of Sarah Noble*, this book is based on a historical incident, in which young Joshua Thane becomes friends with Cholay, an Apache boy. Together they undertake an exciting and dangerous mission to save Apache children, survivors of a white and Papago massacre. In spite of the difficulties involved in their relationship, Joshua and Cholay remain friends in the face of Indian and white hostility.

The nature of the warfare between white and Indian societies is an important aspect of the history of the American Indian. The popular image of an encircled wagon train being attacked by savage Indians, only to be rescued by the cavalry at the last moment, provides a cruel distortion of historical reality. The encroachment on Indian lands, the broken treaties, and the difficulties of forced relocation of the Indian people is one of the darker chapters in American history. A number of children's books present a realistic account of this chapter of history.

Scott O'Dell's *Sing Down the Moon* (1970) is based on the forced resettlement of the Navahos from the Canyon de Chelly to Fort Sumter in 1863. The events are made vivid through the eyes of Bright Morning, a courageous Indian woman. The resettlement of the Navahos led to poverty and a smallpox epidemic, but most devastating of all, the resettlement robs the Navahos of their way of life and of their spirit. Bright Morning convinces her husband to escape to the caves of the Canyon de Chelly, where he recovers from the injustices and spiritual deprivation of Fort Sumter, and together they pick up the pieces of their lives.

"Only the earth and sky last forever" is an ancient Indian war prayer chanted to gain confidence before a battle. Nathaniel Benchley uses this prayer as the title of a book written for the junior high school student. *Only the Earth and Sky Last Forever* (1972) is the story of Dark Elk, born Cheyenne but orphaned when both parents were killed by soldiers. His stepparents live on agency handouts, and his stepfather is portrayed as useless, starving, and alcoholic. The plight of Indians living empty lives as agency "loafers" is repulsive to Dark Elk, who joins Crazy Horse to fight the whites. The futility and courage of the Indian resistance is contrasted with the broken treaties and atrocities of the whites. Crazy Horse describes his view of whites by quoting his father, "one does not go to a hill top for water, or to a white man for the truth." Although Dark Elk participates in the battle of Little Big Horn, the victory is placed in a historical and personal context. Lashuka, whom Dark Elk wished to marry, is killed, as is the great leader, Crazy Horse. The inevitability of the

Indian defeat is clear. After the death of Crazy Horse, Dark Elk stops "trying for freedom, because it didn't seem to mean much. It means whatever the winner wants it to mean and nothing more."

Young Elk, in Mari Sandoz's *The Horsecatcher* (1957), also rejects the path of the warrior. *The Horsecatcher* is the story of a young Cheyenne who pursues his great desire to catch and tame wild horses. Young Elk encounters difficulties, danger, and shame as he avoids the respected role of a warrior and attempts to prove himself a great horsecatcher. He also manages to be instrumental in bringing peace between the Cheyenne and the Kiowa. For his efforts his tribe gives him the name of Horsecatcher.

The famous battle at the Little Big Horn, the popularized "Custer's Last Stand," has been the subject of many books and films. Too often, however, the significance of the battle, the personality of Custer, even the motivations of the conflict have been distorted. Several children's books attempt to remedy this situation by reconstructing the battle from the accounts and records of the Indian warriors who participated. *Wooden Leg: A Warrior Who Fought Custer* (1962), retold to Thomas B. Marquis and originally published in 1931, is one of several books that relate the Little Big Horn battle from the Indian point of view. Wooden Leg was a Cheyenne warrior who fought against Custer, and his account also includes observations on Cheyenne life and customs. *Red Hawk's Account of Custer's Last Battle* (1970), by Paul and Dorothy Goble, is an account of the battle against Custer told by Red Hawk, a fictional character. The events surrounding the Little Big Horn battle are recorded with close attention to historical detail, and the authors indicate the significance of the battle in the context of the continuous warfare waged against the Indians. *Red Hawk's Account of Custer's Last Battle* is appropriate for upper elementary and junior high school students, as is another book on the same topic, Evelyn Lampman's *Once Upon the Little Big Horn* (1971).

Another of Lampman's books for this age group, the popular *Cayuse Courage* (1970), is the story of the Whitman Massacre as told from the viewpoint of a young Indian boy. Dr. Marcus Whitman and Narcissa Whitman were missionaries living with the Cayuse Indians of the Northwest. When a young Cayuse, Samuel, catches his hand in a white man's trap, the Cayuse medicine man is unable to save him. Dr. Whitman saves Samuel, but not without amputating his hand. When the white man's disease, measles, attacks the tribe and Samuel's friend, Amos, dies, the tribe blames the white man and his medicine and the Whitman Massacre is the result. *Cayuse Courage* was published almost thirty years after *Narcissa Whitman: Pioneer of Oregon* (1941), by Jeanette Eaton, an account of the Whitman Massacre from a strictly white point of view.

Relating the events of the Whitman Massacre or the Battle of the Little Big Horn from the Indian point of view as well as the white point of view brings the search for the past into clearer focus. Many of the books reviewed in this section will help to dissipate myths and misconceptions children might hold about the role of the American Indian in our nation's history. The books discussed in the next section will help children gain a keener appreciation of the life-styles and beliefs of various Indian tribes.

## Walking in his moccasins: touching the Indian experience

At last he understood the pain of beauty that he had felt on top of the western mountain. He remembered how he had wondered if there were anyone in the world who felt as he felt.

Now he knew that all of his people felt as he felt. Had not the little pottery drums been telling the secret in the moonlight for thousands of years? . . . Younger Brother greeted the east with a consciousness rising within him.[32]

The preceding quote is from Laura Armer's *Waterless Mountain* (1931), one of the first children's books that attempted to provide a realistic insight into the life and beliefs of the American Indian. In *Waterless Mountain* a Navaho boy, Younger Brother, reveals some of the beliefs and practices of the Navaho people. Younger Brother's growing awareness of and pride in his Indian heritage is maintained in spite of the dominant white civilization. *Waterless Mountain* was a forerunner of the type of books included in this section, books that realistically portray Indian life and thought.

No author represents this movement of presenting an accurate portrayal of Indian life more than Ann Nolan Clark. A prolific and talented author, Clark first became interested in children's books as a teacher who was unable to locate quality reading materials about Indians for her Indian students. She responded by writing a number of children's books that demonstrated her knowledge of and involvement with Indian cultures. Her first book, *In My Mother's House* (1941), is the story of a typical day on a Pueblo reservation as seen by a young Tewa Indian child. *In My Mother's House* is representative of the kind of story Clark writes, relating the everyday events in Indian society rather than focusing on the unusual and the more adventurous stories. Clark's literary style demonstrates a sensitivity to detail, a strong sense of rhythm, and an emphasis on the use of simile and metaphor. The following excerpt from *In My Mother's House* is representative of Clark's literary style and indicative of her manner of conveying the various elements that comprise daily Indian life.

The pueblo
The people
And fire,
And fields
And water,
And land,
And animals—
I string them together
Like beads.
They make a chain,
A strong chain,
To hold me close
To home,
Where I live
In my Mother's house.[33]

The ceremonies and daily activities of the Navaho are presented in Clark's *Little Navajo Bluebird* (1943). The close relationship between Navaho and nature is stressed, and white civilization is seen as a competitive force that offers definite advantages to the Navaho. *Secret of the Andes* (1952), a Newbery Medal winner, although not about an Indian in the United States, is an effective story of a Peruvian Indian boy who grows to understand his heritage and his responsibilities as the last in a royal line. The activities and ceremonies of the Papago Indians are recounted in *The Desert People* (1962), another realistic book for elementary children.

Ann Nolan Clark, noted for her many fine books for younger children, has also written several insightful books appropriate for older children. *Journey to the People* (1969) consists of ten essays that reflect the author's experiences of over fifty years of working among the Zuni, Navaho, Pueblo, Sioux, and Guatemala Indians. Clark refutes some common misconceptions about Indian beliefs by discussing Indian concepts of land, work, time, and spiritual life. In *Circle of Seasons* (1970) Clark provides a description of the rites and practices of the Pueblo year and a sense of reverence for and appreciation of the closeness of the Pueblo to nature.

A theme that runs through several books about Indians concerns the right of passage. In most cases this is reflected in the efforts of a young child to prove himself and to win the privileges and responsibilities of adulthood. For example, *The Mighty Hunter* (1943), by Bertha and Elmer Hader, relates the tale of a brave Indian boy who wishes to prove himself as a hunter, but the right of passage is thwarted by the boy's confrontation with a large, hungry bear. In *Salt Boy* (1968), by Mary Perrine, a young boy manages to achieve his right of passage by roping and saving a sheep trapped in a storm. This act shows both his courage and his skill and demonstrates to his father that he is mature enough to learn the tasks of adults.

For the Indian of the North, the Eskimo, right of passage is translated into the daily struggle against a difficult environment. Pipaluk Freuchen, a native American, writes of the struggle of the Eskimo with insight and realism in *Eskimo Boy* (1951), a book that relates the relentless fight for survival of young Ivik, who assumes responsibility for providing for his family after his father is killed in a hunting accident. When all the food is exhausted and even the dogs are eaten, Ivik starts out for the mainland to get help. On this arduous journey Ivik encounters a polar bear and manages to kill the bear and ensure the survival of his family.

The theme of survival in a difficult environment is dealt with in a less dramatic way by Lorraine and Jerrold Beim in *The Little Igloo* (1941). Young Tipou is so pleased when his parents give him Kiva, a sled dog, that he builds a small igloo for him. Although others laugh at the small igloo, the idea of building a tiny shelter later saves Tipou and Kiva from the ravages of a storm. *Eskimo Boy* and *The Little Igloo* are interesting stories about Eskimo survival and can be complemented by *Indian and Eskimo Children* (1966), published by the

U.S. Bureau of Indian Affairs. *Indian and Eskimo Children*, also written for the early elementary years, provides a nonfiction account with brief text and photographs of Eskimo life, work, school, and play in today's world. Benjamin Brewster's *The First Book of Eskimos* (1952) also attempts to illustrate house building, ice fishing, hunting, and the games of the Eskimos, but it has been criticized for the stereotypic portrayal of happy, carefree Eskimos.

Naturally some of the best insights into Indian life are provided by Indian authors. Some of these books have been translated into English and are appropriate for children. Abeita's *I Am a Pueblo Indian Girl* (1939) includes descriptions of preparing food, hunting, and the nature of clothing worn by the Pueblo. Life on a Navaho reservation is the subject in Kay Bennett's *Kaibah: Recollections of a Navajo Girlhood* (1964). A candid and authentic account of the hardships of an Indian woman is found in *Mountain Wolf Woman: Sister of Crashing Thunder* (1961), edited by Nancy O. Lurie. Other books about Indian life by Indian authors include *Cheyenne Memories* (1967), by John Stands in Timber; *Zuni Pueblo* (1972), by the Zuni People and translated by Alvina Quam; and *Here Are the News* (1966), by Edith Josie.

Another primary source of information about Indian thought and culture is found in Indian myths, folktales, and legends. An extensive and accurate collection of the ancient Indian myths, legends, and folktales has survived, and many of these works are appropriate for children.

A beautiful picture book about a Paiute folktable is *The Firebringer* (1972), retold by Margaret Hodges. When an Indian boy, who lived long ago when humans and animals could communicate with one another, becomes worried about the difficulty of keeping warm in the winter, the coyote explains that fire can en-

sure the tribe's safety. The fire spirits live on Burning Mountain, a journey of one hundred days. Though a difficult task, the coyote, the boy, and members of the tribe manage to take some fire from the fire spirits, and the boy wins the name of Firebringer.

And this is the sign that the tale is true. All along the coyote's thin sides the fur is singed yellow to this very day, as it was by the flames that blew backward from the brand when he brought it down from Burning Mountain.[34]

*Firebringer* is representative of a type of folktale called a *pourquoi*, or why story, explaining the reason for certain animal traits, or characteristics or customs of certain peoples. These stories are found in numerous societies around the world, and like *Firebringer*, frequently end with a summarizing statement of the reason for the characteristic that is developed in the story. Toineeta, a Crow author, has included such folktales and various tribes in *Indian Tales of the Northern Plains* (1972) and *Indian Tales of the Northern Rockies* (1972), both appropriate for the early primary grades.

The oneness of Indians and nature, and the dependence of Indians on nature, is reflected in legends that, like *Firebringer*, relate humans and animals as friends who communicate and live in the world as equals. In Arthur Parker's *Skunny Wundy: Seneca Indian Tales* (1970) the animal characters assume various traits: the bear is strong but stupid, the rabbit is gullible, the fox is clever, and the wolf is a villain.

Flights of fantasy add an exciting element to the Indian legends. In *The Angry Moon* (1970), retold by William Sleator and boldly illustrated by Blair Lent, Lupan and Lapowinsa are close friends who become separated when Lapowinsa insults the moon. A shadow and a rainbow fetch her, but Lupan goes to her rescue, a journey that includes magical flowers and pebbles, a helpful old woman, and a wild, exciting escape back to earth.

Legends frequently serve to reinforce moral values and the norms of various tribal societies. Such is the case in Roessel and Dillon's *Coyote Stories of the Navaho People* (1968), a collection of the oral stories transmitted from one generation to the next, which point to the pitfalls of human nature. "Trotting Coyote," for example, illustrates the disasters that are a product of behavior that does not benefit the existence of the tribe. These exciting stories serve to affirm and sanction tribal practices and norms by endowing them with the prestige of antiquity. George Mitchell's illustrations en-

hance these stories, which appeal even to very young children. Also appropriate for young children is *The Long Tailed Bear and Other Indian Legends* (1961), by Natalie M. Belting. The folktales of eighteen different tribes are enhanced by a brief description of each tribe.

Eskimo folktales often reveal the humor, endurance, and courage of the Eskimo as they confront the grim environment around them. *Tikta Liktak: An Eskimo Legend* (1965), by James Houston, is the story of a legendary Eskimo hunter who was isolated when an ice pack broke. Hungry and depressed, Tikta Liktak builds a coffin and climbs into it to die. But as he dreams of the past he is encouraged

The Angry Moon

to live, and through skill and bravery he triumphs over nature. The courage of Tikta Liktak is seen again in the collected Eskimo stories of Ramona Maher's *The Blind Boy and the Loon and Other Eskimo Myths* (1969).

The books in this section help children touch the Indian experience. They share a common approach of authentically representing tribal life-styles, beliefs, and folktales. The realism of these books in recounting the traditional aspects of Indian life is complemented by the books in the final section, stories that emphasize the contemporary pressures and problems confronting native Americans.

## Old Indian, new Indian: a contemporary search

> As Indians we will never have the efficient organization that gains great concessions from society in the market place. We will never have a powerful lobby or be a smashing political force. But we will have the intangible unity which has carried us through four centuries of persecution. We are a people unified by our humanity—not a pressure group unified for conquest. And from our greater strength we shall wear down the white man and finally outlast him . . . We Shall Endure.
>
> *Vine Deloria*

In this final section we turn our attention to books that concern the difficulties facing native Americans in a contemporary and predominantly white America. These books reflect the psychological and economic pressures confronting Indians as they attempt to adjust to the demands of a complex, technological, and urban society. One of the best statements of the status, aspirations, and problems of the

American Indian is found in Vine Deloria's *Custer Died for Your Sins: An Indian Manifesto* (1970). With wit and force Deloria relates the contemporary Indian's perception of America, including the work of missionaries and the ineffective and unwieldy Bureau of Indian Affairs. Deloria provides the older child with a view of the contradictions and barriers that Indians see in contemporary America.

The economic difficulty facing a contemporary Sioux family living on a plains reservation is the subject of Virginia Driving Hawk Sneve's *High Elk's Treasure* (1972). William High Elk and his family are trying to re-establish the once great herd of their ancestors, but their hopes are dealt a severe blow when young Joe loses their only filly during a storm. Taking refuge in a cave, Joe discovers an old parchment that reveals the Battle of the Little Big Horn as well as the brave who killed Custer. The filly is eventually retrieved, and selling the parchment provides the money needed to re-establish the herd.

No such romantic solution to economic hardships on the reservation is found in Clyde Robert Bulla's *Indian Hill* (1963). Looking for a more promising livelihood, a Navaho family moves to the city. Although the father is pleased with his job as a carpenter and with the urban environment, his wife and child find the adjustment more difficult. *Indian Hill* presents an interesting account of the difficulties involved in leaving the familiar surroundings of the reservation for the more harried and alien urban world.

The role of the Indian in contemporary America is the central theme of *Chief* (1971), by Frank Bonham. Although Henry Crowfoot was too young to be treated as a leader, he was hereditary chief of the Santa Rosa Indians and was called Chief. Chief becomes excited when a down-and-out lawyer tells him that some old documents show that valuable property actually belongs to the Santa Rosa tribe.

The story focuses on an exciting courtroom battle as the Indians, with the help of their medicine man and their has-been attorney, attempt to force the white establishment to maintain their treaty commitment.

Recourse in the law is probably the last thing in the mind of Charles Hobuhet in Frank Herbert's *Soul Catcher* (1972). Abandoning his scholastic accomplishments and white name, Charles Hobuhet becomes Katsuk, the center, the core from which all perception radiates. In this mystical role Katsuk comes to understand a message that for all the innocent Indians who have died at the hands of the white man, an innocent white must be taken and sacrificed. The victim is thirteen-year-old David Marshall, son of the undersecretary of state. David is unable to comprehend the significance of his kidnapping or the reason for this act of vengeance. As they talk, Katsuk tries to explain to David the deceit and errors in the ways of white civilization. Katsuk explains that doctors, lawyers, and the police are dependent on illness, injustice, and crime for their very existence. This transactional, dependent relationship causes them to ensure the existence of those very things they are supposed to eliminate. Katsuk speaks of the havoc whites have inflicted on nature, of the starving in the midst of plenty and of the deceit even within the language of the whites. To Katsuk white civilization is so barren and insensitive that only an outrageous act, the killing of an innocent, can make the whites hear and feel the message: "An innocent for all our innocents." In the last pages Katsuk sacrifices David in the traditional manner: "He heard the *whang* of the walrus gut. The sound flew straight across the clearing with the arrow. Straight it went into the boy's chest."[35]

*Soul Catcher* is for the mature adolescent reader, as is *Zach* (1972), by John Craig. Zach Kennebec searches for information about, or survivors of, the Agawa Indians, for as far as he knows, he may be the last of the Agawa. Zach searches the Great Lakes region and the Plains states for information about his people, and himself. On his quest he befriends Willie, a young black, and D. J., a white, middle-class girl who rejects college and middle-class values. The three alienated travelers find comfort in each other and in their shared quests for direction. This is a sensitive novel that will be appealing to many young adults.

Elizabeth Witheridge's *Just One Indian Boy* (1974) is the story of a young Indian named Andy, who is also searching for direction to his life. After running away from high school Andy works in a lumber camp. Andy's experiences in the camp convince him that education is necessary for him to achieve his goals, and he returns to school. This book is particularly

pertinent because it is based on a compilation of true stories.

In Elliott Arnold's *The Spirit of Cochise* (1972) Joe Murdock acquires his direction from his experiences on the battlefields of Vietnam. After serving as a sergeant in the war, the injustices of life on the reservation become all the more unbearable. The exorbitant prices at the company store, the paternalism of the Indian agent and, perhaps most of all, the accepting nature of his fellow Apaches become intolerable. Hardships and even jail do not deter Joe from establishing a rival store with competitive prices and making inroads on the tribal governance. Following the advice of the once great leader, Cochise, Joe learns from the white man ways to help the contemporary Apache survive in the white man's world.

With this last group of books, we have traced the treatment of native Americans in children's books from romantic and savage stereotypes to the concerns and actions of contemporary American Indians. On any school or library shelf, a wide range of treatments of the American Indian exist. Teachers who are aware of the best of children's literature concerning native Americans can avoid the demeaning and stereotypic characterizations that are all too common. As Rey Mickinock points out: "There are apparently three kinds of people in this hemisphere: those who believe Lief Erickson discovered America, those who think Cristoforo Colombo stumbled upon it, and those who know American was never really lost."[36]

It is our hope that teachers can help children understand the Indian civilizations that flourished on this continent long before the arrival of the white settlers. An effective reading program can help children to reach this goal, and to appreciate the American Indians, their sacrifices, contributions, and visions for a more humane and just America.

A voice
I will send
Hear me
The land
All over
A voice
I am sending
Hear me
I will live

*The Trees Stand Shining—Poetry of the North American Indians*

# NOTES

1. Midge Abel, "American Indian Life as Portrayed in Children's Literature," *Elementary English*, 50, no. 2 (February 1973), 202–208.
2. Donald R. Thomas, *The Schools Next Time*, New York, McGraw-Hill, 1973, pp. 72–76.
3. John Wooden Legs quoted in Richard Erdoes' *The Sun Dance People; The Plains Indians, Their Past and Present*, New York, Knopf, 1972, p. 188.
4. Richard Erdoes, *The Sun Dance People; The Plains Indians, Their Past and Present*, New York, Knopf, 1972.
5. Mary Gloyne Byler (compiler), *American Indian Authors for Young Readers; A Selected Bibliography*, New York, Association on American Indian Affairs, 1973..
6. J. Blanche, "Ignoring It Won't Make It Go Away," *Journal of American Indian Education*, 12 (October 1972), 2.
7. Maria Falkenhagen, Carole Johnson, and Michael A. Balasa, "The Treatment of Americans in Recent Children's Literature," *Integrated Education*, 11 (July 1973), 58–59.
8. Mary Gloyne Byler, "The Image of American Indians Projected by Non-Indian Writers," *Library Journal*, 99, no. 4 (February 15, 1974), 546–549.
9. Ibid., p. 546.
10. Rey Mickinock, "The Plight of the Native American," *Library Journal*, September 1971, p. 2848.
11. Byler, op. cit., p. 548.
12. Byler, op. cit., p. 549.
13. Erdoes, op. cit.
14. Byler, op. cit., p. 547.
15. Vine Deloria, Jr., *Custer Died for Your Sins*, New York, Avon Books, 1969, pp. 167–168.
16. Mickinock, op. cit., p. 2849.
17. Byler, op. cit., p. 547.

18. Mickinock, op. cit., p. 2848.
19. Byler, op. cit., p. 547.
20. Ibid.
21. Ibid., p. 549.
22. Ibid.
23. Isabelle Suhl, "The 'Real' Doctor Dolittle," *Interracial Books for Children*, Spring-Summer 1968.
24. Anna Lee Stensland, *Literature By and About the American Indian*, Urbana, Ill., National Council of Teachers of English, 1973, p. 15.
25. William Steele, *Wayah of the Real People*, Isa Barnett, illus., New York, Holt, Rinehart and Winston, 1964, p. 6.
26. Phyllis Reynolds Naylor, *To Walk the Sky Path*, Chicago, Follett, 1973, p. 24.
27. Ibid., p. 137.
28. Ann Nolan Clark, *Medicine Man's Daughter*, Don Bolognese, illus., New York, Farrar, Straus & Giroux, 1963.
29. Eleanor Clymer, *The Spider, the Cave and the Pottery Bowl*, Ingrid Fetz, illus., New York, Atheneum, 1971, p. 66.
30. Byrd Baylor, *When Clay Sings*, Tom Balti, illus., New York, Scribner, 1972.
31. Byler, op. cit., pp. 548–549.
32. Laura Adams Armer, *Waterless Mountain*, Sidney Armer and Laura Adams Armer, illus., New York, McKay, 1931, p. 211.
33. Ann Nolan Clark, *In My Mother's House*, Peter Parnall, illus., New York, Viking Press, 1941, n.p.
34. Margaret Hodges, *The Firebringer; a Paiute Indian Legend*, Peter Parnall, illus., Boston, Little, Brown, 1972, p. 31.
35. Frank Herbert, *Soul Catcher*, New York, Bantam Books, 1972, p. 215.
36. Rey Mickinock, "The Plight of the Native American," *Library Journal*, September 15, 1971, p. 2848.

# BIBLIOGRAPHY

* Indicates books recommended by the Association on American Indian Affairs.

## Fiction for younger children

BAKER, BETTY. *Little Runner of the Longhouse*, Arnold Lobel, illus., Harper & Row, 1962 (K–3).

BEIM, LORRAINE, and JERROLD BEIM. *The Little Igloo*, Howard Simon, illus., Harcourt Brace Jovanovich, 1941 (K–3).

BELTING, NATALIA. *Tailed Bear and Other Legends*, Bobbs-Merrill, 1961 (K–3).

BENCHLEY, NATHANIEL. *Red Fox and His Canoe*, Harper & Row, 1964 (K–1).

*BLUE EAGLE, ACEE. *Echogee, the Little Blue Deer*, Palmco, 1971 (K–3).

BUFF, MARY, and CONRAD BUFF. *Hah-Nee of the Cliff Dwellers*, Houghton Mifflin, 1956 (K–4).

DEMING, THERESE. *Little Eagle*, Lardlow, 1931 (K–3).

*EASTMAN, CHARLES ALEXANDER. *Wigwam Evenings: Sioux Folktales Retold*, Little, Brown, 1909 (K+).

HADER, BERT, and ELMER HADER. *The Mighty Hunter*, Macmillan, 1943 (K–1).

HEUCK, SIGRID. *Buffalo Man and Golden Eagle*, Dutton, 1970 (K–3).

HOFF, SYD. *Little Chief*, Harper & Row, 1961 (K–3).

JONES, WEYMAN. *The Talking Leaf*, Dial Press, 1965 (2–5).

*LYONS, OREN. *Dog Story*, Holiday, 1973 (K–1).

MAHER, RAMONA. *The Blind Boy and the Loon and Other Eskimo Myths*, Day, 1969 (1–6).

MONJO, F. N. *Indian Summer*, Harper & Row, 1968 (K–3).

PARISH, PEGGY. *Good Hunting Little Indian*, Addisonian Press, 1962 (pre-school–2).

———. *Granny and the Indians*, Brinton Turkle, illus., Macmillan, 1969 (1–4).

———. *Little Indian*, Simon & Schuster, 1968 (K–3).

PERRINE, MARY. *Salt Boy*, Leonard Weisgard, illus., Houghton Mifflin, 1968 (K–3).

PINE, TILLIE S. *The Indians Knew*, Ezra Jack Keats, illus., McGraw-Hill, 1957 (1–4).

ROESSEL, ROBERT, and DILLON PLATEVO (eds.). *Coyote Stories of the Navajo People*, Navajo Curriculum Center, 1968 (K–6).

SLEATOR, WILLIAM. *The Angry Moon*, Blair Lent, illus., Little, Brown, 1970 (K–3).

*TOINEETA, JOY YELLOWTAIL. *Indian Tales of the Northern Plains with Sally Old Coyote*, Montana Reading Publications, 1972 (2–4).

*———. *Indian Tales of the Northern Rockies with Sally Old Coyote*, Montana Reading Publications, 1972 (1–4).

U.S. BUREAU OF INDIAN AFFAIRS. *Indian and Eskimo Children*, U.S. Government Printing Office, 1966.

## Books for the intermediate and upper grades

*ABEITA, LOUISE. *I Am a Pueblo Girl*. Morrow, 1939 (2–5).

ALLEN, TERRY (compiler). *The Whispering Wind: Poetry by Young American Indians.* Doubleday, 1972 (5+).

*ANANTA. *Children of the Blizzard,* with Helniz Chandler Washburne, Dobson, 1960 (5+).

*———. *Wild Like the Foxes: The True Story of an Eskimo Girl,* Daly, 1956 (5+).

ARMER, LAURA ADAMS. *Waterless Mountain,* Sidney and Laura Armer, illus., McKay, 1931 (5–8).

ARNOLD, ELLIOT. *Broken Arrow,* Frank Nicholas, illus., Duell, 1947 (6+).

———. *The Spirit of Cochise,* Scribner, 1972 (7–12).

BAKELESS, JOHN. *Fighting Frontiersman,* Morrow, 1948 (5+).

BAKER, BETTY. *Do Not Annoy the Indians,* Harold Goodwin, illus., Macmillan, 1968 (4–6).

———. *Killer-of-Death,* John Kaufman, illus., Harper & Row, 1963 (5+).

———. *The Shaman's Last Raid,* Leonard Shortall, illus., Harper & Row, 1963 (4–6).

———. *Walk the World's Rim,* Harper & Row, 1965 (5+).

BAYLOR, BYRD. *When Clay Sings,* Tom Balsti, illus., Scribner, 1972 (1–5).

BEHN, HARRY. *The Painted Cave,* Harcourt Brace Jovanovich, 1957 (1+).

BENCHLEY, NATHANIEL. *Only Earth and Sky Last Forever,* Harper & Row, 1972 (7+).

*BENNET, KAY. *Kaibah: Recollections of a Navajo Girlhood,* Western Lore, 1964 (8+).

BERGER, THOMAS. *Little Big Man,* Fawcett, 1969 (6+).

*BLACK ELK. *Black Elk Speaks: Being the Life Story of a Holy Man of the Oglala Sioux,* as told to John Neihardt, Standing Bear, illus., University of Nebraska Press, 1961 (10+).

*BLACK HAWK. *Black Hawk: An Autobiography,* edited by Donald Jackson. University of Illinois Press, 1955 (10+).

BONHAM, FRANK. *Chief,* Dutton, 1971 (6+).

BORLAND, HAL. *When the Legends Die,* Lippincott, 1963 (10+).

BROWN, DEE. *Bury My Heart at Wounded Knee: An Indian History of the American West,* Bantam, 1971 (7+).

BUFF, MARY, and CONRAD BUFF. *Dancing Cloud: The Navaho Boy,* Viking Press, 1937 (3–5).

———. *Magic Maize,* Houghton Mifflin, 1953 (4–7).

BULLA, CLYDE ROBERT. *Eagle Feather,* Tom Two Arrows, illus., Crowell, 1953 (3–5).

———. *Indian Hill,* James J. Spanfeller, illus., Crowell, 1963 (3–5).

CARROLL, RUTH, and LATROBE CARROLL. *Tough Enough Indians,* Walck, 1960 (4–7).

*CHIEF JOSEPH. *Chief Joseph's Own Story,* Montana Reading Publications, 1972 (6+).

CLARK, ANN NOLAN. *Circle of Seasons,* Farrar, Straus & Giroux, 1970 (3–6).

———. *The Desert People,* Alan Houser, illus., Viking Press, 1962 (3–7).

———. *In My Mother's House,* Velmo Herrara, illus., Viking Press, 1941 (3–7).

———. *Journey to the People,* Viking Press, 1969 (2–4).

———. *Little Navajo Bluebird,* Paul Lantz, illus., Viking Press, 1943 (3–7).

———. *Medicine Man's Daughter,* Don Bolognese, illus., Farrar, Straus & Giroux, 1963 (5–8).

CLIFFORD, ETH. *The Year of the Three-Legged Deer,* Richard Cuffari, illus., Dell, 1972 (4–5).

*CLUTESI, GEORGE. *Son of Raven, Son of Deer,* Gray, 1967 (5+).

CLYMER, ELEANOR. *The Spider, the Cave and the Pottery Bowl,* Ingrid Fetz, illus., Atheneum, 1971 (4–8).

COATSWORTH, ELIZABETH. *Sword of the Wilderness,* Harve Stein, illus., Macmillan, 1936 (7+).

*COHOE, WILLIAM. *A Cheyenne Sketchbook,* University of Oklahoma Press, 1964 (4+).

COOPER, JAMES FENIMORE. *The Last of the Mohicans: A Narrative of 1757,* New American Library (Signet), 1962 (7–12).

CRAIG, JOHN. *Zach,* Coward, McCann & Geoghegan, 1972 (7+).

DALGLIESH, ALICE. *The Courage of Sarah Noble,* Leonard Weisgard, illus., Scribner, 1954 (4–6).

DELORIA, VINE, JR. *Custer Died for Your Sins.* Avon Books, 1969 (7+).

———. *We Talk, You Listen: New Tribes, New Turf,* Dell, 1970 (7+).

EATON, JEANETTE. *Narcissa Whitman: Pioneer of Oregon,* Woodi Ishmael, illus., Harcourt Brace Jovanovich, 1941 (7+).

EDMONDS, WALKER D. *The Matchlock Gun*, Paul Lantz, illus., Dodd, Mead, 1941 (5–7).

EMBRY, MARGARET. *My Name Is Lion*, Holiday, 1970 (4–6).

ERDOES, RICHARD. *The Sun Dance People: The Plains Indians, Their Past and Present*, Knopf, 1972 (5–8).

*FREUCHEN, PIPALUK. *Eskimo Boy*, Ingrid Vang Hyman, illus., Lothrop, Lee & Shepard, 1951 (3–7).

GOBLE, PAUL, and DOROTHY GOBLE. *Brave Eagle's Account of the Fetterman Fight, 21 December 1866*, Pantheon Books, 1972 (4+).

———. *Red Hawk's Account of Custer's Last Battle: The Battle of The Little Bighorn, June 1876*, Pantheon Books, 1969 (5+).

GRESSNER, LYNNE. *Trading Post Girl*, Fell, 1968 (6+).

HARRIS, CHRISTIE. *Raven's Cry*, Bill Reid, illus., Atheneum, 1966 (5–7).

HENDERSON, LEGRAND. *Cats for Kansas*, Abingdon, 1948 (5+).

HERBERT, FRANK. *Soul Catcher*, Bantam, 1972 (7+).

HOLLMAN, CLIDE. *Eagle Feather*, Hastings House, 1963 (4–6).

———. *Pontiac, King of the Great Lakes*, Hastings House, 1968 (6–9).

HOOD, FLORA M. *Pink Puppy*, Putnam, 1966 (2–4).

———. *Something for the Medicine Man*, Melmont, 1962 (2–6).

JONES, HETTIE (compiler). *The Trees Stand Shining: Poetry of the North American Indians*, Robert Andrew, illus., Parker, 1971 (4+).

LAFARGE, OLIVER. *Laughing Boy*, Pocket Books, 1959 (9–12).

LAMPMAN, EVELYN SIBLEY .*Cayuse Courage*, Harcourt Brace Jovanovich, 1970 (6–9).

———. *Half-Breed*, Ann Grifalconi, illus., Doubleday, 1967 (10+).

———. *Navaho Sister*, Paul Lantz, illus., Doubleday, 1956 (5–8).

———. *Once upon the Little Big Horn*, Crowell, 1971 (5–7).

———. *Treasure Mountain*, Richard Bennett, illus., Doubleday, 1949 (7–9).

*LAPOINTE, FRANK. *The Sioux Today*, Macmillan, 1972 (7+).

LENSKI, LOIS. *Indian Captive: The Story of Mary Jemison*, Lippincott, 1941 (7–9).

LORENZO, CAROL LEE. *Heart of Snowbird*, Harper & Row, 1975 (7+).

*MARKOOSIE. *Harpoon of the Hunter*, Germaine Arnaktauyok, illus., McGill–Queen's University, 1970 (7+).

MCGRAW, ELOISE JARVIS. *Moccasin Trail*, Coward, McCann & Geoghegan, 1952 (5–8) .

*MCNICKLE, D'ARCY. *Runner in the Sun: A Story of Indian Maize*, Allan Houser, illus., Holt, Rinehart and Winston, 1954 (7+).

MEANS, FLORENCE CRANNEL. *Our Cup Is Broken*, Houghton Mifflin, 1969 (6+).

MOMADAY, N. SCOTT. *House Made of Dawn*, New American Library (Signet), 1969 (7+).

*NABOKOV, PETER (ed.). *Two Leggings: The Making of a Crow Warrior*, Crowell, 1967 (10+).

NAYLOR, PHYLLIS REYNOLDS. *To Walk the Sky Path*, Follett, 1973 (6+).

*NULIGAK. *I, Nuligak*, trans. by Maurice Metayer. Pocket Books, 1968 (7+).

O'DELL, SCOTT. *Island of the Blue Dolphins*, Dell, 1960 (7+).

———. *Sing Down the Moon*, Houghton Mifflin, 1970 (5+).

*PARKER, ARTHUR. *Skunny Wundy: Seneca Indian Tales*, Whitman, 1970 (5+).

PECK, ROBERT NEWTON. *Fawn*, Little, Brown, 1975 (6+).

RACHLIS, EUGENE, and JOHN C. EWERS. *The Indians of the Plains*, Harper & Row, 1960 (5+).

RICHTER, CONRAD. *The Light in the Forest*, Bantam Books, 1953 (9+).

———. *A Country of Strangers*, Knopf, 1966 (9+).

RUSH, WILLIAM MARSHALL. *Red Fox of the Kinapoo*, Charles Banks Wilson, illus., McKay, 1949 (5+).

SANDOZ, MARI. *The Horsecatcher*, Westminster Press, 1957 (8+).

———. *The Story Catcher*, Elsie J. McCorkell, illus., Westminster Press, 1963 (6–9).

SCHELLIE, DON. *Me, Cholay and Co.: Apache Warriors*, Four Winds Press, 1973 (5–9).

SMUCKER, BARBARA. *Wigwam in the City*, Gil Miret, illus., Dutton, 1966 (5–7).

SNEVE, VIRGINIA DRIVING HAWK. *Betrayed*, Holiday, 1974 (4–7).

————. *The Chichi Hoohoo Bogeyman,* Nadema Agard, illus., Holiday, 1975 (3–7).

————. *High Elk's Treasure,* Oren Lyons, illus., Holiday, 1972 (3–6).

————. *Jimmy Yellow Hawk,* Oren Lyons, illus., Holiday, 1972 (3–6).

————. *When Thunders Spoke,* Oren Lyons, illus., Holiday, 1974 (4–7).

SPEARE, ELIZABETH GEORGE. *Calico Captive,* W. T. Mars, illus., Houghton Mifflin, 1957 (6–10).

*STANDS IN TIMBER, JOHN. *Cheyenne Memories,* Yale University Press, 1967 (11+).

STEELE, WILLIAM O. *Waydah of the Real People,* Isa Barnett, illus., Holt, Rinehart and Winston, 1964 (6–8).

*TALL BULL, HENRY. *Grandfather and the Popping Machine,* Montana Reading Publications, 1970 (4–8).

WALTRIP, LELA, and RUFUS WALTRIP. *Indian Women: Thirteen Who Played a Part in the History of America from the Earliest Days to Now,* McKay, 1964 (5–9).

WARREN, MARY PHRANER. *Walk in My Moccasins,* Victor Mays, illus., Hale, 1966 (4–6).

*WELCH, JAMES. *Riding the Earthboy 40,* World, 1971 (9+).

WEST, JESSAMYN. *The Massacre at Fall Creek,* Harcourt Brace Jovanovich, 1975 (7+).

WILLIAMS, BARBARA. *The Secret Name,* Harcourt Brace Jovanovich, 1972 (3–7).

WITHERIDGE, ELIZABETH. *Just One Indian Boy,* Atheneum, 1974 (5–9).

WOOD, NANCY. *Hollering Sun,* photos by Myron Wood, Simon & Schuster, 1972 (4–12).

*WOODEN LEG. *Wooden Leg: A Warrior Who Fought Custer,* as told to Thomas B. Marquis, University of Nebraska Press, 1962 (10+).

## Jews in America

In the long history of the Jewish people the growth of the American nation is a relatively recent event. Yet Jews have had a significant impact on America, and America has had a profound impact on the Jews.

Jews first reached the Western Hemisphere with Columbus, although significant Jewish immigration occurred only in the last one hundred years. Jewish migration to America was initiated by the same forces that have caused Jews to emigrate for thousands of years: religious persecution and the hope of economic opportunity. Discrimination throughout Europe, specifically in Germany in the 1800s and later in Russia and eastern Europe, accounted for the heaviest waves of Jewish refugees. The number of Jewish immigrants, however, was never high in proportion to our total population. By the early 1900s Jews comprised only 2 percent of the American population. Today they comprise barely 3 percent.

The contribution to America made by Jews has been far out of proportion to their numbers. Jewish impact on American life has been so great as to afford Judaism national recognition. At national events we often hear religious prayers from a priest, a minister, and a rabbi. In fact, we refer to ourselves as a nation of Protestants, Catholics, and Jews, although Jews form only a small percentage of the population.

In American literary history Horatio Alger's name has become associated with the idea that equality of opportunity alone can enable industrious and conscientious citizens to achieve success. If Horatio Alger's unbounding faith and optimism in the potential of the individual has been confirmed for any group, that group has been the Jewish Americans. Entering as poor, laboring immigrants, Jewish Americans have managed to achieve extraordinary success in America. Their traditional emphasis on education and socioeconomic advancement has proved to be a successful combination. A report published in 1900 stated that "Jewish

# 7
# Jewish Americans in Children's Books

children are the delight of their teachers for cleverness at their books, obedience, and general good conduct."[1]

The pressure for education from Jewish homes found release in America's free public education system. Even before the twentieth century, New York City, with a large Jewish population, offered free education through college. The results were striking. Studies in several American cities in the 1960s revealed that between 22 and 32 percent of Jewish males were in the professions; 25 and 39 percent were proprietors and managers, respectively; and only 10 to 20 percent were manual workers.[2] Similarly, Jewish contributions to the arts, sciences, education, law, and medicine have been far greater than would be expected from a group that numbers only 3 percent of the U.S. population.

The success of Jewish Americans has altered the nature of Judaism in America. Orthodox Jewish religious practices, including dietary restrictions, frequently have been modified or abandoned. Traditional cultural expressions, including Jewish theater, newspapers, books, and even the Yiddish language, are rapidly becoming cultural vestiges.

The emerging American Jew represents a departure from some traditions of the past, and is in the process of redefining what it means to be a Jew in contemporary America. But this process is not completely new. There has, in fact, been a long-standing debate, even among Jews, as to whether they are a religious, cultural, or national group. In America the balance between ethnic identity or cultural pluralism, on the one hand, and assimilation, on the other, represents a significant area of concern for Jews. And the Jewish American community demonstrates an incredible variety of responses to this issue, ranging from distinct orthodox Jewish communities with special dress, diets, and strict religious practices to Jewish Americans who have abandoned all

connection with Judaism. Most Jewish Americans fall between these two extremes, observing the more salient Jewish religious traditions, participating in Jewish cultural activities, and strongly affirming their role as both Jews and Americans.

Although the Jewish experience in America has been explored by noted authors in books for adults, few children's books portray the Jewish American experience with depth, sensitivity, sophistication, or even seriousness. Young readers must look to other times and other lands to find significant books about Jews. The particularly rich and significant experience of Jews in America is often treated superficially, if at all.

Several reasons have been advanced to explain the dearth of fine children's books about the Jewish American experience. Some point out that the small percentage of Jews in the total population may result in a limited market for such books and deters their publication. Others suggest that Jewish success in America has reduced the need for potential authors to explore the issue and, consequently, their interest in doing so. Although we are not certain of the actual reason, neither of these explanations seems adequate.

Another, more plausible, explanation concerns the desire of Jews to maintain a low profile in a non-Jewish nation. Some individuals maintain that the traditional response of a Jewish community living, even flourishing, in the midst of a Christian population is to play down its Jewishness, that which makes it "different" from the rest of the population. Therefore Jewish Americans choose to avoid indepth discussions of their Jewishness, especially with their children or in children's books. It is hypothetical whether the desire to maintain a low profile is the reason for the limited number of significant children's books. But it does point out an important aspect of the Jewish American experience. Even though Jewish

Americans have earned both respect and status in America, even though America has provided Jews with a much valued refuge in a generally hostile world, the shadow of anti-Semitism has not been dispelled in America. The fear of widespread, if below-the-surface, anti-Semitism persists and is buttressed by a history replete with Christian and Moslem persecution of the Jews. The fear of anti-Semitism is increased as American Jews view the treatment afforded Soviet Jews or watch in horror as the United Nations singles out Jewish nationalism (Zionism) as a form of racism. The existence of anti-Semitism in America is confirmed not only in individual anti-Semitic slurs that American Jews experience but also in anti-Semitic statements made by government leaders, including a military chief of staff and a recent president of the United States.[3]

Whatever the reason might be, the evidence of the limited treatment of the American Jew in children's reading materials is clear. Most bibliographies concerned with ethnic understanding list few, if any, books about American Jews. *Red, White and Black: Minorities in America*, published by the Combined Paperback Exhibit, for example, lists less than a dozen Jewish entries from over 600 books cited. Even the children's bibliography published by the American Jewish Committee contains more non-Jewish than Jewish books. Moreover, most library reference systems do not even contain a listing directly concerned with contemporary Jewish life.[4]

Jewish youth may provide the hungriest readership today for a satisfying ego image, an objective exposure to their own life style; such fiction might play checkers with the generation gap, replacing some of the missing cultural heritage which the youth's parents could not pass down to him from the last generation of grandparents.[5]

In discussing the treatment of Jews in children's books, we focus on four areas. We ana-lyze major Jewish characters and themes in America, traditional Jewish folklore, and the portrayal of Jews in children's books primarily concerned with black Americans. Finally, we shall look at children's literature in terms of its treatment of the two major Jewish events in modern times: the Holocaust and the re-establishment of Israel.

## The superficial treatment of the American Jew in children's books

The conflict Jews confront in maintaining their Jewish identity while participating in a Christian-oriented America has resulted in several modifications of Jewish identity and behavior. Many Jewish Americans have adapted their religious practices and cultural traditions to the American scene. The result is less orthodoxy in religious practices and new cultural expressions in such areas as literature and theater. These changes are not unexpected outcomes; in fact, they are anticipated results of living in the new American environment.

In some children's books, however, these changes have been exaggerated and perverted. The result is that the American Jew is portrayed as a superficial Jew, and these religious and cultural changes are presented as empty gestures to Jewish identity. In these books no significant discussion of the Jewish American experience is presented. In fact, Jews are portrayed as Americans practicing inexplicable, if humorous, religious and cultural customs. The following passage is a composite picture of the typical Jewish American character that emerges in children's books:

The typical major character is a twelve-year-old boy who is basically American, and incidentally Jewish. In the immediate future there is a bar mitzvah, which is a confirmation into the religion. But he knows little if anything about the ceremony, and generally dislikes the rather repulsive rabbi. Most of the time is spent playing with his non-

Jewish friends. An anti-Semitic incident is likely to pop up, but will be minor in nature and quickly shrugged off. A personal problem of a universal nature will provide the book's major focus.

The child's home environment consists of a humorous and protective mother, and most likely sibling rivalry of one sort or another. Being Jewish generally entails lighting Chanukah candles, demonstrating a good sense of humor, and eating corned beef sandwiches. It is indeed a rare occurrence for such a character to identify the meaning of being a Jew or to dwell upon Jewish issues. He is too busy learning how to play second base.

Although this picture may seem to be exaggerated, all these elements were taken from children's books about Jews. Moreover, they represent patterns that run through such books.

E. L. Konigsburg's *About the B'nai Bagels* (1969) contains many of these elements. The B'nai Bagels is a Little League baseball team, and Mark Setzer is a member. Although not a particularly good player, Mark's problems really start when his mother becomes the team's coach. By practicing in the local housing projects he improves his baseball skills and at the same time avoids his religious training. Besides his desire to become a good baseball player, Mark also faces the potential loss of his best friend and the trauma of his bar mitzvah.

Mark's family must be recognized for its extraordinary sense of humor. When Mark habitually manages to drop food on the floor, his father asks, "Mark, why don't you try eating on the floor and see if you can drop things up to the table."[6] When practicing his singing for his bar mitzvah, the rabbi asks Mark where he practices, and Mark responds that he sings his bar mitzvah prayers in the shower. When the rabbi asks why, Mark explains, "Because, sir, Niagara Falls is not available."[7]

Konigsburg's light touch and humor are both strengths and weaknesses. The humor adds to the enjoyment of the book, but it also detracts from the development of complete characters. Mark's mother, for example, uses an array of Jewish idioms and speaks to God in the form of a light fixture. She is funny to read about, but a bit too funny to be believed. She is a Jewish caricature, although not very knowledgeable in Jewish religion, culture, or history. Continually rationalizing into insignificance various religious practices, such as dietary restrictions, she avoids any inconveniences such rules might cause. Her total emergence into the world of the Little League, even at the expense of her family obligations, is more funny than believable. Nevertheless, *About the B'nai Bagels* is a book many children will enjoy reading for its wit and style.

A more complete, if not more complimentary, portrait of a Jewish mother is created by Marilyn Sachs in *Peter and Veronica* (1969), set in New York City in the 1940s. Veronica was introduced in *Veronica Ganz* (1968) as the class bully who met her match in Peter, the smallest boy in the class. In *Peter and Veronica* the two are close friends despite parental opposition because of religious differences. After Peter struggles to have his mother agree to invite Veronica to his bar mitzvah, Veronica infuriates him by not coming. Peter and Veronica eventually re-establish their friendship based on a greater understanding of themselves and the bigotry that exists in their households.

Peter's mother, Mrs. Wedemeyer, represents an all too typical presentation of Jewish mothers in children's and adult literature. As such, it is a revealing example of an unfortunate, stereotypic, and superficial Jewish portrait. To understand the potential negative influence of this stereotype we first describe and then briefly analyze its components. In many books Jewish mothers are

*Stereotype 1.* Overprotective.
When twelve-year-old Peter is invited to a party, his mother insists that his father accompany him. The party is only a block

Peter and Veronica

away, and Peter manages to win the dispute and to go to the party without parental supervision, "but it wasn't easy, and he certainly wished she'd stop treating him like a five-year-old."[8]

*Stereotype 2.* Chief decision maker for the family.

"Don't bother your father," his mother said. "Let him rest."[9]

A Jewish mother serves as the family traffic cop, judge, and the crucial factor in any family decision. There is no need to wake the father; go straight to the top.

*Stereotype 3.* Public relations officer.

A Jewish mother is the chief advocate of the talent and success of family members, especially the children. Peter's mother and Mrs. Rappaport are involved in a public relations war to determine whose children have been more successful. The issues range from who is taller to who has achieved the honor role in school. But when Peter arrives in the midst of the debate to reveal that he has been skating (he's too old for that) with Veronica (a non-Jewish girl), it is clear that Peter's mother has lost the battle of one-upmanship.

*Stereotype 4.* Prejudiced against non-Jews.

When Mrs. Wedemeyer objects to Peter's non-Jewish girl friend, Peter accuses her of being prejudiced. " 'Prejudiced! I'm prejudiced!' shouted Mrs. Wedemeyer. 'That I should live to see the day that my own son stands there to my face and calls me prejudiced! And for what? For an ignorant, stupid, ugly stranger.' "[10]

*Stereotype 5.* Pro-food.

In many books, including *Peter and Veronica*, Jewish mothers emphasize the importance of consuming large amounts of food, and the caricature of a Jewish mother praising the curative powers of chicken soup is well known.

*Stereotype 6.* Projector of guilt.

Keep that up and "you'll drive me to an early grave."[11]

The Jewish mother has been portrayed as a master of the martyr syndrome. She is unexcelled at building up debts of guilt in family members, so that every action and joy must be measured against the potential injury or hurt it may cause her.

This caricature of a Jewish American is offensive on several counts. First, being Jewish is presented as form without substance. It is represented by a concern for some Jewish traditions, such as a bar mitzvah, but no substantive exploration of what it means to be a Jew. The prejudice against non-Jews is also an unfortunate aspect of this portrayal. The result is a character with a shallow Jewishness, yet holding a prejudice against non-Jews.

In more universal terms, the mother is domineering to the point of being a danger to the development of all the lives she touches. Her husband is presented as an uninfluential and insignificant family member, relegated to an easy chair in some far corner of the house. The children seem to be in constant danger of having their psyches swallowed up whole by the mother. There is nothing gentically Jewish about these offensive traits. Jewish mothers may or may not have some of these characteristics. The same holds true for non-Jewish mothers. Yet these traits persist in many books with Jewish characters, perhaps partially because they provide humor. Although we stand solidly behind humor, the continuous use of such stereotypic characteristics is offensive, and the humor involved has become a thin excuse for ignoring significant Jewish issues and the development of realistic characters. Such caricatures are not appropriate vehicles for establishing an understanding of Jews by non-Jews, in providing literary models for Jewish children, or in accurately relating the Jewish experience in America.

In a book in a series by Marilyn Sachs, *Laura's Luck* (1956), Amy and Laura are friends in the Bronx in the 1930s. Although the characters are Jewish, the book is generally concerned with family and interpersonal problems. Although the series is very well written, the characters are only incidentally Jewish and little understanding of Jewish issues is offered. The Amy and Laura series represents an approach to Jewish stories for children in which the treatment of Jewish issues is so superficial that it is sometimes difficult to discern even the presence of Jewish characters. Although the Amy and Laura series does provide a view of the universal side of American Jews, it does not explore Jewish issues directly and sheds no light on issues particularly relevant to American Jews.

Sidney Taylor's *All-of-a-Kind Family* (1951), *More All-of-a-Kind Family* (1954), and *All-of-a-Kind Family Uptown* (1958) are stories of an immigrant Jewish family from the Lower East Side of New York at the turn of the century. The All-of-a-Kind title is derived from the family's five daughters and their identical clothes. These stories relate the joys and sorrows of a poor immigrant family. The family crises range from a lost child at Coney Island to a bout with scarlet fever. A somewhat romanticized version of a poor but close immigrant family, the All-of-a-Kind series touches upon some Jewish history and holidays but generally focuses on more universal issues. Compared to some of the recently published children's books, this series offers a slower-paced style.

Another book that takes the "holiday and history" road to Judaism is Judith Ish-Kishor's *Joel Is the Youngest* (1967). Although this is the story of a Jewish boy, it focuses on the problems of a youngest child. This major theme is broken from time to time with interludes of the history behind various Jewish holidays. The Jewish issue is purely incidental.

Several books attempt to confront some of the issues of Jewish identity in America. *Berries Goodman* (1965), by Emily Cheney Neville, is concerned with bigotry and housing restrictions as practiced in suburbia. The Goodmans have moved to the suburbs, and there they discover the unspoken agreement among local realtors that has divided the town into Jewish and Gentile sections. The Good-

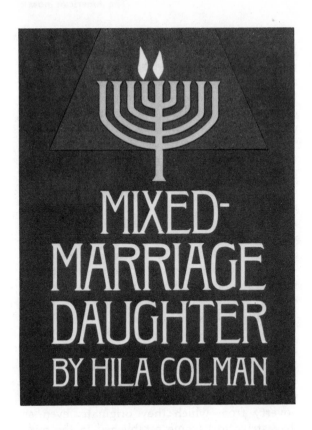

mans are not Jewish, but Berries' best friend, Sidney Fine, is. Sidney is taunted by Sandra, Berries' anti-Semitic next-door neighbor, and is eventually led into a nearly fatal accident. Although Berries' mother and older brother have accepted the anti-Semitic status quo, Berries is disturbed by the slurs and housing restriction.

The confrontation with anti-Semitism is rather simplistic and falls flat in several places. No reasons or rationales are offered for such prejudice, and Sidney Fine is so uncontroversial that it is difficult to imagine why he is the object of such intense hatred. *Berries Goodman* shows that anti-Semitism exists, but it does not suggest the causes of anti-Semitism. Moreover, Sidney Fine is Jewish in name, but

it is difficult to discern what, if anything, there is to being Jewish. Jewish identity is not explored.

Several children's books do capture a part of the significance of being a Jew in Christian America. In *Mixed-Marriage Daughter* (1968), by Hila Colman, Sophie, the child of a Jewish mother and a Gentile father, is in search of identifying her Jewishness. Although the answers she finds are based more on tradition than reason, the book does present a search for meaning.

In *Our Eddie* (1969), by Ish-Kishor, the Raphaels, a family of poor English Jews, migrate to America. The head of the family, Mr. Raphael, is passionately committed to Jewish education and issues but insensitive to the poverty and concerns of his own family. His inability to relate to his family is brought to a moving climax with the death of his oldest son, Eddie. The death brings about a metamorphosis in Mr. Raphael's personality, and his stern demeanor is modified. Beyond the powerful story, *Our Eddie* touches upon a fundamental conflict confronting Jews. The strict adherence to a Jewish life-style is accomplished at the sacrifice of material rewards. Although the story does not treat both sides of this conflict in an even-handed manner, it does present the material advantages offered Jews by a Western, industrialized, and Gentile society— advantages to be gained by sacrificing traditional Jewish practices.

Children's literature offers a limited insight into the meaning of being a Jew in America. Children's books generally reflect either stereotyped characters or superficial treatment of Jewish issues. Although a few books do touch upon the issue of defining Jewish identity, even these offer a narrow view of a complex issue. Realistic children's books on the Jewish American experience are difficult to find, and children must look to other times and other countries to help them understand the meaning of being a Jew. One way Jewish children can learn about themselves is through the eyes of others.

## Portrayal of Jews in books about black characters

Jews and blacks in America have shared a unique relationship. As the victims of centuries of discrimination in foreign lands, Jews have rallied to the cause of civil rights for blacks in America. Joining with black leaders like Martin Luther King, Jews marched in demonstrations, became involved in voter registration drives, and rode freedom buses into Southern states. When, in the 1960s, three civil rights workers were killed in Mississippi, one was black and two were Jews. Jewish money and legal services helped to oil the civil rights machinery. But by the late 1960s the Jewish-black relationship showed signs of strain.

A number of factors contributed to deteriorating relations. With the death of Martin Luther King and the growing influence of more militant black leadership, whites in general and Jews in particular were not welcomed in leadership positions of the civil rights movement. Moreover, militant black leadership supported the Arab's position in the Arab-Israeli conflict. In urban areas, as blacks moved into formerly Jewish neighborhoods, Jewish store owners became a major target of black anger and frustration, and the image of the Jew as an economic parasite was once again raised. In the late 1960s the New York City teachers' strike further divided the groups, as predominantly Jewish teachers struck over the issue of community control of the schools. Much of this controversy occurred in black neighborhoods, where black parents were frustrated with the performance of the schools.

The history of Jewish-black relations is reflected in children's literature about black people in America, and most of the books discussed here are more fully explored in Chapter 5. In this section we focus on the treatment of Jews in these books about the black experience.

Several of these books emphasize similarities between blacks and Jews. *Sounder* (1969), by William Armstrong, is the story of Southern poverty and bigotry endured by a black family. The boy in the story learns how to read and finds continual encouragement by reading the Old Testament. He finds the story of David and Goliath particularly inspiring. Thus, in *Sounder*, parallels are made between the persecution of Jews and the persecution of blacks.

These parallels are also noted in *North Town* (1965), by Lorenz Graham. David Williams and his family undergo various problems as they attempt to achieve security and a degree of success in North Town. David's father emphasizes the importance of not forgetting the poverty from which they originate, even as they strive to become established in the middle class. To make this point he quotes a Jewish saying about a man who succeeds and forgets his people: "He forgets the ghetto."[12] When David's father is gravely ill, a Jewish surgeon, Dr. Meyers, is called in to operate, and he volunteers his philosophy that blacks, like Jews, have an exceptional survival instinct. When Mr. Williams does survive, Dr. Meyers is delighted that "this case once again supported his theory about the power of certain people to survive."[13]

Other books about the black experience relate some of the difficulties and points of conflict between Jews and blacks. Conflicts with Jewish store owners emerge in *The Contender* (1967), by Robert Lipsyte, and in *Daddy Was a Numbers Runner* (1970), by Louise Merriwether. In *The Contender* Alfred performs menial work for a Jewish store owner. Although he is unhappy with his job, he refuses to join his friends in a robbery of "them Jews,"[14] and eventually Alfred's relationship with his Jewish employers improves. Francie, in *Daddy Was a Numbers Runner*, offers a mixed picture of Jewish store owners in Harlem during the Depression. The Jewish characters vary from sexual perverts to generous and kind friends. Nevertheless, Francie's family is always in debt to the Jewish store owners.

The difficulties encountered by Jewish teachers and black students is touched upon in several books. *The Friends* (1973), by Rosa Guy, concerns the poverty and difficulties of two black girls growing up in Harlem. In a candid scene, underlying antiblack and anti-Semitic hostility comes roaring to the surface. Miss Lass, the Jewish teacher, begins the encounter:

"The way most of you come to school I wouldn't think that any of you had mothers. You come to school like pigs! Greasy, oily, filthy pigs! The filth in your streets shows what kind of people you are!"

. . . "She ain't nothing but a Jew!" Someone else put it into a song, "Miss Lass is a Jew-a!"

. . . Her face darkened to the color of a beet, veins strained out of her neck like ropes and foam bubbled at the corners of her mouth.[15]

Bernard Cohen, in Alice Childress' *A Hero Ain't Nothin' But a Sandwich* (1973), is a Jewish teacher who hangs pictures of Malcolm X and Martin Luther King in his classroom but is still frustrated by the challenges of teaching black children.

I'm whitey, I'll be the goat, okay? You have no idea how things go down when you're whitey in a Black set up. I go out to work every morning, like a lamb to the slaughter. . . . Was *I* ever a slave master? Did *I* bring slaves over here? Did *I* ever lynch a Black? Am *I* the one?[16]

Bernard Cohen, in spite of his frustration, is a diligent and successful teacher, and his black students achieve in spite of his anger.

The mixed picture of Jewish Americans that emerges from the pages of books about black characters offers some insight into the secular dimension of American Jews. We see Jews functioning as successful middle-class Americans, and in many books Jews demonstrate both social concern and social commitment. These books also reflect the reality of Jewish-black relations as a common history of persecution binds black and Jewish Americans, and contemporary social and economic pressures weaken those bonds.

## Jewish folklore

When I want to know more about the Jewish experience, I read I. B. Singer. There is as yet no black writer who has done for the black experience what Singer has done for the Jewish experience, but he has the advantage of being able to look back, of not having to be involved in a day-to-day battle.[17]

As the noted black author Julius Lester has indicated, no contemporary writer has captured the folklore of European Jewry with more precision or feeling than Isaac Bashevis Singer. In *A Day of Pleasure* (1969) Singer recounts his experiences as a boy growing up in Warsaw. The book is a collection of stories written for children in upper elementary and secondary school. Singer describes his childhood as the son of a prominent rabbi and a wise mother, in a hurried yet intimate Jewish community. Singer has retrieved from his youth those tales told to him, and he has translated them from Yiddish. They have become charming children's books that can be enjoyed by preschool as well as elementary school children and, perhaps most frequently, by adults.

These folktales are often concerned with the

superstition and spiritualism of Jews in the ghetto. *Mazel and Shlimazel or the Milk of a Lioness* (1967) is the tale of a contest between Mazel (the spirit of good luck) and Shlimazel (the spirit of bad luck). They select Tam, the poorest peasant in town, as the subject of their experiment. For the first year Mazel is able to have his way, and Tam becomes invaluable to the king and beloved by the princess. But as the year runs out, Shlimazel is able to create havoc, and only by cunning is Tam spared execution.

The spirit world is found once again in Singer's *The Fearsome Inn* (1967). The inn is owned by Doboshova, a witch with an interesting marital history. Her first husband had been a thief, and her present husband is half man, half devil. The witch and her husband cast a spell on the road to the inn so that it leads nowhere, and in this way they cut off escape for the three maidens they hold captive. Naturally, three young men come by, and they match magic with the innkeepers. The innkeepers are outwitted and banished to a mountain that is neither day nor night, but exists in a perpetual twilight zone. The three young

Mazel
and Schlimazel

men match in numbers and interests the three young maidens. They pair, marry, and become wealthy and respected.

The spiritual element is picked up in Singer's *When Shlemiel Went to Warsaw and Other Stories* (1968). This collection of eight brief stories re-creates the Jewish ghetto of a hundred years ago. In one story in this collection, "Rabbi Leib and the Witch Cunegunde," we are once again treated to a battle between the good spirit of the rabbi and the evil spirit of the witch.

Another character of Yiddish folklore, and one also found in Singer's work, is the fool. Through the magic of literature many of these simpleton characters are brought to new levels of idiocy. In Singer's *When Shlemiel Went to Warsaw* (1968) the title story is about Shlemiel's ill-fated attempt to walk to Warsaw. When without his knowledge he is turned around, he walks back into his home town of Chelm. Naturally, Shlemiel assumes this to be another town, and he is amazed at the similarity. He convinces the townspeople that he is not the Shlemiel they know, and he eventually is paid by the town to fill the role of the identical Shlemiel who left for Warsaw but never returned.

The people of Chelm prove their foolishness in other tales as well. In *Zlateh the Goat* (1966), by Singer, another collection of Jewish folktales, the elders of Chelm decide to collect the pearls and diamonds of the snow. But to ensure that the people of Chelm do not ruin their endeavor, a messenger is sent out to tell them to stay indoors. Just in time, the elders realize that the messenger would have to walk on the snow. They solve this difficult problem in typical Chelm fashion, by having four men carry the messenger on a table, to ensure that he does not ruin the jewels in the snow.

It appears that the longer people live in Chelm, the more foolish they become, and the elders are the most foolish. As we see in an-

other story in this collection when Lemel, a new father in Chelm, is asked by an elder if the baby is a girl. Lemel says no. The elder then asks if the child was a boy. " 'How did you guess?' " Lemel asks. The elder responds, " 'For the wise men of Chelm there are no secrets.' "[18]

Singer's translations and stories based on Jewish tradition capture much of the humor and sense of community of European Jews. His books are enhanced by illustrations drawn by Maurice Sendak and Margot Zemach, among others. They represent unique Jewish folklore presented in an appealing manner.

Another delightful story in Singer's *When Shlemiel Went to Warsaw* is "Shrewd Todie and Lyzer the Miser," which presents a common character in Jewish folktales—the miser. Shrewd Todie asks Lyzer the Miser if he can borrow a silver soup spoon for a special occasion. The next day he returns not only the soup spoon but a silver teaspoon as well. Lyzer the Miser is overwhelmed by his good fortune, as he is told that the soup spoon gave birth to the teaspoon. A week later, as Lyzer was sitting "in his underdrawers, to save his pants," Todie again has a request, this time for silver candlesticks. Remembering his previous fortune, Lyzer is quick to respond to this latest request. But the silver candlesticks are never returned, for as Todie explains, they had died. An enraged Lyzer the Miser calls upon the rabbi to adjudicate the dispute. The rabbi dismisses the case: " 'Did you expect the candlesticks to give birth to other candlesticks? the rabbi said admonishingly. 'If you accept nonsense when it brings you profit, you must also accept nonsense when it brings you loss.' "[19]

*Simon Boom Gives a Wedding* (1973), by Yuri Suhl, is the story of a man who is overly concerned with having the best, regardless of cost. Simon would buy the best suit he can find, even if it does not fit him. His determination to buy the best for his daughter's wedding results in his serving the guests barrels of water, which he is convinced is the best of all possible refreshments.

Simon Boom's exaggerated extravagance can be an anticipated characterization, spawned from the profound poverty of the European ghetto. A beautiful story relating the poverty that Jews faced is *The Magician* (1973), by Uri Shulevitz. A magician invites himself to a Passover Seder and provides food and wine that the poor Jewish family is unable to provide for themselves. Taken back by such a feat, the family goes to ask the rabbi if the magician represents a good or an evil spirit. The rabbi advises them that if the provisions are edible, the spirit is a good one. When they return home the magician has departed. They find the food and the wine to be indeed edible. "Only then did they know it was not a magician but the prophet Elijah himself who had visited them."[20]

*The Magician* is a sensitive portrayal of ghetto poverty. But to many young eyes some of the other folktales we have reviewed, especially some of those recounted in Singer's books, present Jewish characters with negative or stereotyped characteristics. Stories of miserly or superstitious Jews, for example, fit many popular stereotypes. It is important that children be made aware of the conditions that spawned such tales. These tales represent the stories told by a people living in a tremendously hostile society. European nations, such as Poland and Russia, which provide the settings for many of these stories, imposed very heavy restrictions upon Jews. Jews were forbidden training in the professions, denied entry into many trades and clerical fields, restricted to living in certain geographic areas, allowed only a certain number of marriages a year, and made constantly fearful of physical attack. These conditions should be explained to children so that they can better understand the psychological escape valves such folktales have provided. Foolish characters, superstitions, and the quest for material wealth in these stories served as insulation against a hostile environment. Without a realization of these deprivations, children may attempt to stereotype Jews through these stories.

One method of providing this information to children is through literature that depicts the nature of Jewish life in the ghetto. For example, the difficult life of the Jews in the Middle Ages is the story told in *Boy of Old Prague* (1963), by Sulamith Ish-Kishor. Tomas is a peasant boy who accepts the attitudes and practices of the feudal system in which he lives. When his mother becomes ill he steals food for her, is caught, and is sentenced to be a servant to an old Jew living in the ghetto. Tomas is horrified, for he believes the prevailing attitudes about the "evil" Jews, but when he lives with a kind and understanding Jewish family, his attitudes change. After a devastating pogrom he searches for his Jewish family, not knowing if they have survived. The story reveals not only the hardships of the Jewish ghetto but the growth of a boy away from intolerance and toward love and compassion.

Life in the Jewish ghettos of Europe provides the setting for several fine children's books: Ethel Vineberg's *Grandmother Came from Dworitz* (set in Russia), Sidney Taylor's *A Papa Like Everybody Else* (Czechoslovakia), and Florence Slobodkin's *Sarah Somebody* (Poland). The harsh life of the Jewish peasant, presented in these books, provided a foundation for the unparalleled terror that was to follow: the Holocaust.

## The Holocaust and the re-creation of Israel

The attempt of the Nazis to destroy the Jewish people was an atrocity of such proportion that a generation later we are still unable to grasp its dimensions. Jews in countries dominated by Germany during World War II were first harassed, later persecuted, and finally executed. The attempt to eliminate all Jews succeeded in destroying 6 million Jewish men, women, and children.

Many of those who survived the Holocaust as children have recently published books of their experiences. These children of the war have come of age. Their books view the Holocaust through children's eyes, and recreate the experience for young readers.

*The Diary of a Young Girl* (1952), by Anne Frank, is not a recent book, but it is a well-known, widely read view of the Holocaust as witnessed by a teenage girl. The book is the actual diary of a Dutch Jewish girl who, along with her family, hid from the Germans in cramped and difficult quarters. Anne's diary records her maturation, her love, and her perception of her shattered world.

Although 6 million Jewish deaths are difficult to comprehend, the agonizing existence of a single girl is an experience many children can relate to. Anne Frank went into hiding when she was thirteen; her family was discovered and arrested eighteen months later. Anne Frank was executed just before her sixteenth birthday.

*The Upstairs Room* (1972), by Johanna Reiss, relates the struggle of another Dutch Jewish family during World War II. In this autobiography Reiss describes how the members of her family were forced to split up and go into hiding in different homes. The story is told in a direct style, and we see the longings of young children for friendship and the outside world. There are squabbles and illnesses, surprise Nazi searches, and constant danger, but they all manage to avoid capture and to survive. Moreover, the *Upstairs Room* is one of several books that relate the sacrifice and risk taken by non-Jews in hiding Jewish citizens from the Nazis. The brave actions of many Christians, especially, but far from ex-

clusively, in countries like the Netherlands and Denmark, are featured in several books about the Holocaust and underscore once again basic human qualities.

In Judith Kerr's *When Hitler Stole Pink Rabbit* (1972) Anna is nine and much more concerned with her friends and her school than with the fact that she is Jewish. Her father, a noted German writer, is anxious over Hitler's rise to power. Before the election that witnessed Hitler's assumption of leadership, Anna's father wisely sends his family out of Germany and then joins them. All their possessions, including Anna's pink rabbit, are confiscated by Hitler. Their foresight has saved their lives, but ahead of them lie the difficult years of new schools, new languages, and new beginnings as refugees.

The story realistically portrays incidents of anti-Semitism and the plight of those who lost their hard-won careers and were forced to start life again as refugees. The task of seeking acceptance in a new society is described by Anna's father: " 'We have to be more hard-working than other people,' said Papa, 'to prove that we're not lazy, more generous to prove that we are not mean, more polite to prove that we're not rude.' "[21]

*Miriam* (1963), by Aimee Sommerfelt, relates the experiences of young Miriam, a teenage Jewish girl living in Norway during the war. Although Miriam escapes to Sweden, most of her family perish. The pervasiveness of anti-Semitism and the development of a lasting friendship with a non-Jewish girl, Hanne, are sensitively presented. Miriam's attempt to win acceptance for herself and her people and her desire to pick up the pieces of her life demonstrate the perseverance of European Jews.

A very direct, hard-hitting story of the Holocaust is Hans Peter Richter's *Friedrich* (1970). This book, by a non-Jewish author, paints a graphic picture of the growing repression in

Germany. The Schneiders and their only son, Friedrich, are Jewish neighbors to a Christian family. Friedrich and the Christian boy become friends, but their relationship is always in jeopardy because of the growing anti-Jewish sentiment in Germany. When they go together to join the *Jungvolk* (German Youth Organization) Friedrich is ostracized and forced to say, "The Jews are our affliction."

Anti-Semitic myths, only touched upon in some of the other books, are presented in detail in *Friedrich:* Jews as the killers of Christ; as crafty, sly, and avaricious people; and as economic parasites. Graphically explained is the myth of the kosher laws by which cruel Jews watch "the animal slowly bleeding to its pitiful death."[22] Laws are passed to buttress this hatred as Jews are barred from movie theaters and swimming pools, forced to wear the star of David on their clothing, restricted from park benches, evicted from apartments, fired from jobs, and expelled from schools. After Friedrich is expelled from his school, he sees his former classmates marching down the street singing:

> Crooked Jews are marching along,
> they're marching through the Red Sea
> The waves close over them,
> and the world is at peace![23]

Friedrich's father views the current terror campaign as one of many that Jews have suffered over the past 2000 years. He feels that he is a German as well as a Jew, and he is determined to stay in Germany. This error costs his family dearly, as Friedrich's mother is killed and Mr. Schneider is taken to a concentration camp. Left to himself, Friedrich strives to survive. During an Allied bombing, Friedrich is refused entry to an air raid shelter, and on the steps in front of his former home, Friedrich is killed by Allied bombs.

The Holocaust was one of two major events affecting Jews in modern times. The world's reaction to its horrors gave new political momentum to the re-establishment of the state of Israel. After 2000 years Jews once again had a homeland.

Like the Holocaust, the re-creation of Israel has profoundly affected American Jews. For the first years of Israel's existence, 1948–1967, American Jewry had positive feelings about the new state but was little affected by it. A series of events, commencing in 1967, created among American Jews an intense commitment to Israel. The 1967 Arab-Israeli conflict endangered the very existence of Israel, and in a few days 6 million American Jews donated $432 million to the Israeli cause. An ever-increasing number of American Jews migrated to Israel and became Israeli citizens.

Another factor resulting in a heightened sense of American Jewish commitment to Israel was the Soviet backing of the Arab cause. Arab armies, many times the size of the Israeli army, were now equipped with sophisticated Soviet military equipment. Moreover, Soviet policies of harassing Soviet Jews, restricting their schooling and employment, and preventing them from leaving the Soviet Union had a frighteningly familiar ring. American Jews realized that the last two significant Jewish populations still remaining outside the United States, those of the Soviet Union and Israel, were in jeopardy. American Jews would not silently stand by and watch another Holocaust.

These conditions caused an increased awareness of and commitment to the Jewish nation for a large number of American Jews. Moreover, this commitment is felt most strongly in the younger generations. Wearing Jewish jewelry, donating money to Israel, attending Jewish instruction, visiting and even migrating to Israel are some of the forms that this commitment has taken. Yet the field of children's literature has been slow to connect with this rising concern of American Jews. Although there have been many books published about Israel, especially easily obtainable paperbacks, they have been aimed at adult readers. Much yet needs to be written for children about the struggle and significance of Israel for Jewish children in America.

One book that responds to this need is *My Enemy, My Brother* (1969), by James Forman, which traces the steps of an early Israeli settler. Dan is sixteen when he starts the dangerous journey to the coast. He has survived the Warsaw ghetto and a concentration camp and is now on the way to a new life in Israel. Although a friend dies on the trip and Dan is arrested by the British as an illegal infiltree, he manages to escape and complete the hazardous journey to an Israeli kibbutz. There he longs for peace, to forget the atrocities of the war, to preserve human life. But his dreams are shattered as Arab and Jewish hostility erupts into war. His friendship with an Arab, Said, is destroyed, and he is once again entangled in killing. Forman shows both the struggle to create Israel and the difficult moral questions facing the nation. The Arab and Jewish viewpoints are presented, and no easy answers to the current conflict are provided.

*Flight to the Promised Land* (1957), by Laszlo Hamori, is the story of the migration of Jews from Yemen to Israel. The story is told through a young boy who makes the trek; it is based on the actual experiences of an immigrant. The dark-skinned Jews of Yemen lived in conditions unchanged for hundreds of years. They waited for the fulfillment of the prophecy that they would return to their homeland on the "wings of eagles." Their return to their ancient homeland by jeep and plane is amazing and, at the same time, threatening to these ancient people. A trip on the silver wings of the first airplane they had ever seen seems close enough to fulfilling their ancient prophecy.

The difficulty of assimilating Jews from all corners of the globe was one of many problems faced by the new country. Many of these difficult issues confronting a young Israel are found in *My Cousin, the Arab* (1965), by Thelma Nurenberg. The common heritage felt by Jews from different nations does not remove cultural discrimination or antireligious feelings. The political and social problems of a young Israel are presented through the lives of realistic characters who give an insight into the problem of re-establishing a country's united spirit.

The pioneering effort of Israel is depicted in a trilogy by Sally Watson. In the first book, *To Build a Land* (1957), Israeli pioneers labor to reclaim the land and establish a state. The children in *To Build a Land* appear as adults in *Other Sandals* (1966), which is set in three Israeli environments: the kibbutz, the modern city of Tel Aviv, and an Arab village. The different cultural settings, and the cultural prejudice, offer a multidimensional view of Israel. The final book, *Mikhtar's Children* (1968), returns to the 1948 War of Independence to portray the perceptions of Arabs and their leaders as they view the Israelis, who they both envy and hate.

These books, and others, paint a picture of Israel that children, especially Jewish children, find informative and moving. But the story of Israel in children's fiction is still incomplete. It is a subject in need of more coverage, for it is fascinating, complex, and unique, and Jewish children are turning to such topics for information and inspiration.

We conclude this section with a book about Israel 2000 years before the Holocaust. *The Rider and His Horse* (1968), by Erik Christian Haugard, is the story of the Masada. When the Romans defeated the Jews of ancient Israel, they created a wandering people without a nation (the Diaspora). But the Roman victory was not complete. On a high plateau, the Masada, a thousand Jews under the leadership of Eleasar ben Ya'ir, fought a long battle against the Roman legions. When defeat became inevitable, the Jewish defenders chose suicide rather than submit to Roman bondage.

The Masada is a cherished event in Jewish history, but it is more than that. To Israel the Masada is a living psychology. After the Holocaust many Jews feel that Israel is their Masada. Surrounded by hostile and overwhelming armies and facing the active hostility of the Soviet Union, Israelis hope for a better future but prepare for the worst.

With an increasing awareness of the Holocaust and the significance of Israel, American Jews are experiencing a heightened sense of their Jewish identity. For Jewish children there are too few books that would help them in acquiring a sense of their Jewish heritage. Although the Holocaust is receiving more attention by writers of children's books, Israel remains an infrequent topic. Moreover, as children turn to books about American Jews, they encounter many superficial treatments of the meaning of being a Jew in America.

As we have seen, humor is a common element in the current children's books about American Jews. Humor contributes to the enjoyment of these books, but often at the expense of honestly dealing with Jewish identity. Yet even in this superficial treatment, where being Jewish consists of having a bar mitzvah and eating bagels, we see that being Jewish does require behavior different from that of non-Jews. There are only a limited number of noteworthy books that help children grapple with the real issues of Jewish American identity. Teachers of young children will find some excellent stories in picture books about Jewish folklore (such as Singer's books) and biblical stories (see bibliography). For older children, books about the holocaust often provide valuable insights into Jewish identity. The heightened awareness of Jewish identity felt by Jewish American children suggests the need for more penetrating and meaningful books of the Jewish experience in America.

## NOTES*

1. "Report of the U.S. Industrial Commission" XV (Washington, 1901), 325–327.
2. American Jewish Year Book, 1968, quoted in Nathan Glazer American Judaism, 2nd ed., Chicago, University of Chicago Press, 1972, p. 167.
3. U.S. Air Force General Brown was tape recorded at a college campus lecture stating that Jews have too much power in America, particularly in the banking area. This is an old stereotype which is readily refuted by the fact that less than one-half percent of banking officers and owners are Jewish. General Brown was reprimanded, but retained his position. Former President Nixon in the infamous Watergate tapes, made several anti-Semitic remarks which were not widely publicized because of the public's concern with impeachment and possible criminal charges. In one such statement, President Nixon did not permit his daughter Tricia to move to Boston for fear she might marry a "communist or a Jew."
4. Leona Daniels, "The 34th Man: How Well Is Jewish Minority Culture Represented in Children's Fiction?" in Lillian Gerhardt, ed., Issues in Children's Book Selection, New York, Bowker, 1973, 90–101.
5. Ibid., p. 91.
6. E. L. Konigsburg, About the B'nai Bagels, New York, Atheneum, 1969, p. 36.
7. Ibid., p. 78.
8. Marilyn Sachs, Peter and Veronica, Garden City, N.Y., Doubleday, 1969, p. 72.
9. Ibid., p. 45.
10. Ibid., p. 47.
11. Ben Shecter, Someplace Else, New York, Harper & Row, 1971, p. 137.
12. Lorenz Graham, North Town, New York, Crowell, 1965, p. 95.
13. Ibid., p. 196.
14. Robert Lipsyte, The Contender, New York, Harper & Row, 1967, p. 2.
15. Rosa Guy, Two Friends, New York, Holt, Rinehart and Winston, 1973, p. 46.
16. Alice Childress, A Hero Ain't Nothin' But a Sandwich, New York, Coward, McCann & Geoghegan, 1973, 34–35.
17. Julius Lester, "Black and White: An Exchange Between George A. Woods and Julius Lester," New York Times Book Review, May 24, 1970.

18. Isaac Bashevis Singer, *Zlateh the Goat and Other Stories*, Maurice Sendak, illus., trans. by the author and Elizabeth Shub, New York, Harper & Row, 1966, p. 50.
19. Isaac Bashevis Singer, *When Shlemiel Went to Warsaw and Other Stories*, pictures by Margot Zemach, trans. by the author and Elizabeth Shub, New York, Farrar, Straus & Giroux (an Ariel Book), 1968, p. 12.
20. Uri Shulevitz, *The Magician*, adapted from the Yiddish of I. L. Peretz. New York, Macmillan, 1973, p. 32.
21. Judith Kerr, *When Hitler Stole Pink Rabbit*, New York, Coward, McCann & Geoghegan, 1972, p. 86.
22. Hans Peter Richter, *Friedrich*, trans. by Edite Kroll, New York, Dell, 1970, p. 44.
23. Ibid., p. 96.

# BIBLIOGRAPHY

## Picture books

COHEN, BARBARA. *The Carp in the Bathtub*, Joan Halpern, illus., Lothrop, Lee & Shepard, 1972 (1–5).

DELESSERT, ETIENNE, and ELEANORE SCHMID. *The Endless Party*, Harlin Quist Books, 1970 (K–2).

ELKIN, BENJAMIN. *The Wisest Man in the World*, Anita Lobel, illus., Parents' Magazine Press, 1968 (K–3).

KIPPER, MORRIS, and LENORE KIPPER. *Debbie and Joey in God's World*, A. Komrad, illus., Shengold, 1968 (4–9).

PETERSHAM, MAUD, and MISKA PETERSHAM. *David*, Macmillan, 1967 (K–3).

SERWER, BLANCHE. *Let's Steal the Moon*, Trina Schart Hyman, illus., Little, Brown, 1970 (1–5).

SHIEFMAN, VICKY. *Mindy*, Lisl Weil, illus., Macmillan, 1974 (K–3).

SHULEVITZ, URI. *The Magician*, Macmillan, 1973 (K–3).

SINGER, ISAAC BASHEVIS. *The Fearsome Inn*, Nonny Hogrogian, illus., trans. by the author and Elizabeth Shub, Scribner, 1967 (K–2).

———. *Joseph and Koza, or the Sacrifice of the Vistula*, Symeon Shimin, illus., trans. by the author and Elizabeth Shub, Farrar, Straus & Giroux, 1970 (2–7).

SUHL, YURI. *Simon Boom Gives a Wedding*, Margot Zemach, illus., Four Winds Press, 1973 (K–3).

## Fiction for the middle and upper grades

Because of the limited number of children's books about the Jewish-American experience which is produced by the major publishing houses, the following list of publishers may be useful. Behrman House, New York; Hebrew Publishing Co., New York; The Union of American Hebrew Congregations, New York; the Jewish Publication Society, Philadelphia; Ktar Publishing, New York; Block Publishing, New York, are several of the not widely known publishing companies producing biographies, histories, and other works concerned with Jews in America.

ARNOLD, ELLIOT. *A Kind of Secret Weapon*, Scribner, 1969 (4–7).

AZIMOV, ISAAC. *The Land of Canaan*, Houghton Mifflin, 1971 (7+).

BEIM, LORRAINE. *Carol's Side of the Street*, Harcourt Brace Jovanovich, 1951 (4–6).

BERG, LEILA. *A Box for Benny*, Bobbs-Merrill, 1961 (3–5).

BIDERMAN, SOL. *Bring Me to the Banqueting House*, Viking Press, 1969.

BISHOP, CLAIRE HUCHET. *Ten and Twenty*, Viking Press, 1954 (4–6).

BLOCK, IRVIN. *Neighbor to the World: The Story of Lillian Wald*, Crowell, 1969 (5–8).

BLUE, ROSE. *Grandma Didn't Wave Back*, Ted Lewin, illus., Watts, 1974 (5–7).

BRENNER, BARBARA. *A Year in the Life of Rosie Bernard*, Joan Sandin, illus., Harper & Row, 1971 (4–6).

COHEN, FLORENCE CHANOCK. *Portrait of Deborah*, Messner, 1961 (6–8).

COLMAN, HILA. *Mixed-Marriage Daughter*, Morrow, 1968 (7+).

CONE, MOLLY. *A Promise Is a Promise*, Houghton Mifflin, 1964 (6–8).

ELLIS, HARRY B. *Israel: One Land, Two Peoples*, Crowell, 1972 (7–10).

EMERY, ANNE. *Dinny Gorden, Junior*, Macrae Smith, 1964 (6–8).

FAST, HOWARD. *Haym Salomon: Son of Liberty,* Eric Simon, illus., Messner, 1941 (4–9).

FITZGERALD, JOHN. *The Great Brain,* Mercer Mayer, illus., Dial Press, 1967 (5–7).

FEDER-TAL, KARESH. *Stone of Peace,* trans. by H. R. Kousbroek, Abelard-Schuman, 1961 (6–8).

FORMAN, JAMES. *My Enemy, My Brother,* Meredith, 1969 (7–12).

———. *The Traitors,* Farrar, Straus & Giroux, 1968 (8+).

FRANK, ANNE. *The Diary of a Young Girl,* Pocket Books, 1952 (9+).

HAMMRI, LASLO. *Flight to the Promised Land,* Harcourt Brace Jovanovich, 1963 (6–8).

HAUTZIG, ESTHER. *The Endless Steppe: Growing Up in Siberia,* Crowell, 1968 (6–10).

HAUGARD, ERIK CHRISTIAN. *The Rider and His Horse,* Leo and Diane Dillon, illus., Houghton Mifflin, 1968 (7–12).

HIRSCH, MARILYN. *The Pink Suit,* Crown, 1970 (3–6).

HOBART, LOIS. *Strangers Among Us,* Funk & Wagnalls, 1957 (6–8).

HOFF, SYD. *Irving and Me,* Dell, 1967 (5–8).

ISH-KISHOR, JUDITH. *Joel Is the Youngest,* Jules Gotlieb, illus., Pocket Books, 1967 (4–6).

ISH-KISHOR, SULAMITH. *Boy of Old Prague,* Ben Spahn, illus., Pantheon Books, 1963 (4–9).

———. *The Carpet of Solomon,* Uri Shulevitz, illus., Pantheon Books, 1966 (4+).

———. *Our Eddie,* Pantheon Books, 1969 (6–9).

———. *The Master of Miracle: A New Novel of the Golem,* Arnold Lobel, illus., Harper & Row, 1971 (5+).

KERR, JUDITH. *The Other Way Round,* Coward, McCann & Geoghegan, 1975 (5–12).

———. *When Hitler Stole Pink Rabbit,* Coward, McCann & Geoghegan, 1971 (4–7).

KEIR, LEOTA HARRIS. *Freckle-Face Frankel,* Coward, McCann & Geoghegan, 1959 (4–6).

KONIGSBURG, E. L. *About the B'nai Bagels,* Atheneum, 1969 (3–7).

KRENTZEL, MILDRED. *I See Four,* William Lent, illus., Loizeaux Brothers, 1959 (4–6).

KUPER, JACK. *Child of the Holocaust,* Doubleday, 1968 (8+).

LEVIN, JANE WHITBREAD. *Star of Danger,* Harcourt Brace Jovanovich, 1966 (7–10).

LEVITIN, SONIA. *Journey to America,* Charles Robinson, illus., Atheneum, 1970 (5–7).

LITTLE, JEAN. *Kate,* Harper, 1971 (5–8).

MERRIAM, EVE. *The Voice of Liberty: The Story of Emma Lazarus,* Charles Walker, illus., Jewish Publishing Society, 1959 (5–8).

MUDRA, MARIE. *Look Beyond Tomorrow,* Dutton, 1957 (8+).

MURRAY, MICHELE. *The Crystal Nights,* Seabury Press, 1973 (6–8).

NATHAN, DOROTHY. *The Shy One,* Carolyn Cather, illus., Random House, 1966 (4–6).

NEVILLE, EMILY CHENEY. *Berries Goodman,* Harper & Row, 1965 (7+).

NOSTLINGER, CHRISTINE. *Fly Away Home,* trans. by Anthea Bell, Watts, 1975 (6–10).

NURENBERG, THELMA. *My Cousin, the Arab,* Abelard-Schuman, 1965 (6–8).

OMER, DEVORAH. *Path Beneath the Sea,* trans. by Israel I. Taslitt, Sabra (Funk & Wagnalls), 1969 (5–9).

PEARLMAN, MOSHE. *The Zealots of Masada; Story of a Dig,* Scribner, 1967 (8+).

POTOK, CHAIM. *My Name Is Asher Lev,* Knopf, 1972 (7+).

———. *The Chosen,* Fawcett, 1967 (7+).

RABIN, GIL. *False Start,* Harper & Row, 1969 (6+).

REISS, JOHANNA. *The Upstairs Room,* Crowell, 1972 (4–7).

RICHTER, HANS PETER. *Friedrich,* trans. by Edite Kroll, Dell, 1970 (6–9).

SACHS, MARILYN. *Amy and Laura,* Tracy Sugarman, illus., Doubleday, 1966 (4–6).

———. *Peter and Veronica,* Doubleday, 1969 (5–7).

———. *Veronica Ganz,* Louis Glanzman, illus., Doubleday, 1968 (5–7).

SANTALO, LOIS. *Wind Dies at Sunrise,* Bobbs-Merrill, 1965 (8+).

SHECTER, BEN. *Someplace Else,* Harper & Row, 1971 (4–6).

SIMON, NORAH. *Ruthie,* Meredith, 1968.

SINGER, ISAAC BASHEVIS. *Zlateh the Goat,* Maurice Sendak, illus., trans. by the author and Elizabeth Shub, Harper & Row, 1966 (5–7).

————. *When Shlemiel Went to Warsaw and Other Stories*, Margot Zemach, illus., trans. by the author and Elizabeth Shub, Farrar, Straus & Giroux, 1968 (5+).

————. *Mazel and Shlimazel or the Milk of the Lioness*, Margot Zemach, illus., trans. by the author and Elizabeth Shub, Farrar, Straus & Giroux, 1967 (3–5).

————. *A Day of Pleasure: Stories of a Boy Growing Up in Warsaw*, photos by Roman Vishniac, Farrar, Straus & Giroux, 1969 (6+).

————. *Elijah the Slave*, Ezra J. Keats, illus., Farrar, Straus & Giroux, 1970 (4–8).

————. *Enemies, A Love Story*, Farrar, Straus & Giroux, 1972 (7+).

SLOBODKIN, FLORENCE. *Sarah Somebody*, Louis Slobodkin, illus., Vanguard Press, 1970 (3–5).

SOMMERFELT, AIMEE. *Miriam*, trans. by Pat Shaw Iversen, Criterion Books, 1973 (7+).

SUHL, YURI. *The Merrymaker*, Thomas di Grazia, illus., Four Winds Press, 1975 (3–6).

————. *Uncle Misha's Partisans*, Four Winds Press, 1973 (5–10).

TAYLOR, SIDNEY. *All-of-a-Kind Family*, Helen John, illus., Follet, 1951 (4–6).

————. *A Papa Like Everyone Else*, George Porter, illus., Follett, 1966 (4–6).

VINEBERG, ETHEL. *Grandmother Came from Dworitz: A Jewish Story*, Rita Briansby, illus., Tundva, 1969 (4–7).

WATSON, SALLY. *Mukhtar's Children*, Holt, Rinehart and Winston, 1968 (5–8).

————. *Other Sandals*, Holt, Rinehart and Winston, 1966 (6+).

————. *To Build a Land*, Holt, Rinehart and Winston, 1957 (6+).

WEILERSTEIN, SADIE ROSE. *The Adventures of K'tonton, a Little Jewish Tom Thumb*, National Women's League of the United Synagogue of America, 1964 (4–8).

WUORIO, EVA LIS. *To Fight in Silence*, Holt, Rinehart and Winston, 1973 (5–9).

ZIEMAN, JOSEPH. *The Cigarette Sellers of Three Crosses Square*, Lerner, 1975 (7+).

# Other Selected Minority Groups as Portrayed in Children's Literature

## The Spanish-American experience

On New York subways, in stores in El Paso, in Los Angeles schools, and on the streets of Miami, Spanish is frequently spoken. Public signs, the labels on canned goods, and the language used on radio and television programs and in many classrooms also reflect the influence of the Spanish heritage in America. Although Americans from Mexico, Puerto Rico, Latin America, and Spain comprise our country's second largest minority group, it is difficult to determine their exact number. Estimates of their size range from 9.2 million to 15 million, with 10 million a commonly accepted figure. Although Spanish-Americans share a common language and religion, their racial and ethnic backgrounds are from Indian, European, and African cultures. Yet the significant number of Spanish-Americans and their diverse and unique cultural heritage have not been reflected in American literature. As Walt Whitman pointed out many years ago, "I have an idea that there is much . . . of importance about the Latin race's contribution to American nationality . . . that will never be put with sympathetic understanding and tact on the record."[1]

In the following sections we examine some selected children's books to understand better how Hispanic Americans from two specific regions, Puerto Rico and Mexico, have been depicted in children's literature.

## A minority nobody knows

Helen Rowan, in an article in *The Atlantic*, explains some of the reasons behind the frequently inaccurate conception of Mexican-Americans. Mexicans entering the United States did not come in large numbers; no war was ever fought over them, although military and legal maneuvers combined to confiscate most of their land holdings; discrimination against them is spotty; and they have not wielded significant political power.[2] The common picture of a poor, immigrant Mexican-American farm worker is only partially correct, in that more than 80 percent of all Mexican-Americans live and work in cities. Prejudice against the approximately 6 million Mexican-Americans is still all too prevalent, especially in the Southwest. But under the leadership of such Mexican-Americans as Cesar Chavez, the Chicano is slowly gaining increased political visibility and making economic advances.

The picture of Mexican-Americans that emerges from children's books has been both praised and denounced by various critics. Some critics have pointed to the overused Mexican-American character, the typical portrayal of a dark-skinned Mexican in a rural setting, uninterested in education, poor, and Catholic.[3] Others note that although this image is overused, the Mexican characters are still portrayed as individuals who possess such positive traits as bravery, enthusiasm, industry, and perseverance.[4] The differing interpretations of the image of Mexican-Americans in children's literature suggests the need for particular care and scrutiny on the part of teachers and children when reading books about Mexicans and Mexican-Americans.

## The Mexican in books for young children

Books for young children about the Mexican experience focus on both universal concerns and themes that emphasize Mexican customs, holidays, and heritage. Those emphasizing Mexican customs and heritage attempt to introduce children to some of the ceremonies and traditions of Mexicans and Mexican-Americans, as well as to simple Spanish vocabulary and songs. One such book is Marie Hall Ets and Labistida Aurora's *Nine Days to Christmas* (1959), a 1960 Caldecott Medal winner. In this warm and gentle story set in Mexico, five-year-old Ceci is introduced to the Christmas holiday customs, is allowed to stay up late and enjoy a Christmas *posada* (party), and is even allowed to choose her own piñata.

The activities and traditions of the Mexican-Americans living on famous Olvera Street in Los Angeles are portrayed in several picture books by Leo Politi. *Pedro the Angel of Olvera Street* (1946) is about the Christmas procession and festivities on Olvera Street. Pedro, the young boy with the voice of an angel, is asked to lead the Christmas procession. Another warm picture book about the festivities on Olvera Street, in this case the parade to receive the "Blessing of the Animals," is Politi's *Juanita* (1948). Mexican crafts and music and even some Spanish vocabulary are woven into this simple story about a loving Mexican-American family.

Song of the Swallows

In contrast to books depicting specific customs and holidays, other books for young children emphasize universal themes, those common to all children as they grow to maturity. One story of a universal nature is Marie Hall Ets's *Gilberto and the Wind* (1963). The simple, attractive drawings and text in this picture book tell the story of young Gilberto and his playmate, the wind. Gilberto chases, races, and uses the wind in a story that might have been set either in the United States or in Mexico.

Another story with a universal theme is Leo Politi's Caldecott winner, *Song of the Swallows* (1949). This brief and colorful picture book tells the story of Juan, a young boy who lives near the mission of Capistrano, Juan tells of the coming of spring and anxiously awaits for the annual return of the swallows.

Several of the stories that portray universal concerns and problems also stress a love and appreciation of artistic expression. For example, Eugene Fern's *Pepito's Story* (1960) is the story of a boy who is ostracized by his peers because, rather than swim or fish, he prefers to dance. When Estrellita, the daughter of the Lord Mayor, becomes ill, the children bring her gifts to cheer her up. Poor Pepito can only bring her the gift of his dancing, but it is Pepito's gift that cheers her and saves the day.

Another colorful picture book that demonstrates the resourcefulness of the major character as well as an appreciation of art is Barbara Ritchie's *Ramon Makes a Trade* (1959). Although young Ramon has made a beautiful jar, it is not as desirable as his father's wares, and he encounters difficulty during market day as he attempts to trade it for a parakeet. Through a combination of hard work and a series of clever trades, Ramon

Pepito's Story

manages to overcome his shortage of resources and acquire his parakeet.

A more difficult situation confronts the main character in *Benito* (1961), by Clyde Bulla. With his mother dead and his father away, Benito is sent to live with relatives. His Uncle Pedro is harsh and cruel to Benito, forcing him to work long hours on the farm and to sleep in the barn, and worst of all, he denies Benito the tools necessary to pursue his love of art. Encouraged by the artist Manuel Vargas, Benito creates a small wood carving of a girl. His work receives recognition and becomes part of an art collection that is sent around to schools to be enjoyed by children. Benito, with his self-confidence reestablished, asserts his right to pursue his interest in art and his studies.

Another difficulty that frequently appears in children's books about Mexicans and Mexican-Americans is poverty. It is poverty that forces Francisco Flores, the mayor of Topo-El-Bampo, to sell his prize possessions, his two burros, Leandro and Tiger, in Scott O'Dell's *The Treasure of Topo-El-Bampo* (1972). This story, set in ancient Mexico, is about the exploitation of the people of Topo-El-Bampo in the nearby silver mines, where the metal they mine is carried by burros to the coast and then shipped to Spain. When the two burros Leandro and Tiger wander away from one of the caravans and stray back to their village, the silver bars on their backs help to feed the poor villagers. The story is enhanced by striking illustrations by Lynn Ward.

Another story about Mexican poverty is *The Fence* (1969), by Jan Balet. Two families, separated by a fence, are also separated by a disparity in income. The rich family is upset with their poor neighbors, who, they believe, are stealing the goodness from their food by standing by the fence and enjoying the aroma. Through a clever trick in the courtroom the poor father manages to free himself and his family of the charge of stealing the goodness from the food.

Poverty and social obstacles are very much a part of the contemporary scene in Marie Hall Ets's *Bad Boy, Good Boy* (1967). Roberto's move from Mexico to the United States causes difficulties. His behavior is not socially accepted in his new environment, and his dependence on the Spanish language complicates his problems. In addition, Roberto faces crowded living quarters, a teacher who sometimes loses her temper, and parents who quarrel. This is a candid and blunt account of some contemporary problems confronting Mexican-American children, and the presentation of these issues makes *Bad Boy, Good Boy* an important book for young children.

Difficult issues constitute the central theme of many books about Mexican-Americans written for older children. In the next section we discuss some of these books that concern "the difficult road north."

## The difficult road north

The barriers confronting Chicanos as they strive for full participation in American society constitute the subject of a number of books for children in the middle and upper grades. Chicanos face prejudice in Anglo America, and they are the victims of economic exploitation. Although much of this prejudice and exploitation occurs in urban centers, many of the books written for children deal with these problems as they affect migratory farm workers.

The plight of the migrant worker is the subject of Evelyn Sibley Lampman's *Go Up the Road* (1972). Yolanda Ruiz and her family live in New Mexico but spend much of their time on the road, following the harvest. The dilapidated condition of the migrants' camps and the exploitation of their labor is graphically presented. When a newborn baby almost dies, the Chicanos organize a peaceful march to protest the lack of adequate medical facilities. Yolanda joins the peaceful protest and hears taunts from the onlookers: "Go home, if you don't like it here!" "Dirty Mex."[5] Yolanda's experiences do not deter her from her dream of acquiring an education. Because of her constant movement from camp to camp, twelve-year-old Yolanda is once again repeating the fourth grade. The help of a sympathetic Anglo teacher and the encouragement of her Aunt Connie fortify Yolanda's resolve to force her community in New Mexico to provide Mexican-Americans with education beyond the sixth grade.

"Today we live in an Anglo world," explained Aunt Connie. "But it will not always be that way. Someday the brown, the black, the red man will have equal voices, but only if the words they speak are worth listening to. They cannot be words of hate and anger. They must be calm and filled with wisdom. Learning comes from education. . . ."[6]

Another story of exploitation is Theodore Taylor's *Maldonado Miracle* (1973). Twelve-year-old Joseph Maldonado is an illegal Mexican immigrant who, after his arrival in the United States, is not able to locate his father. As Joseph works in the fields, he is befriended by a black American, who encourages Joseph's interest in art, an interest Joseph's father could never understand. After a run-in with another American, Joseph hides out and eventually decides to return to Mexico. Joseph looks to art and his native land for sustenance as he rejects the life of a migrant worker in the United States.

Other books that deal with the plight of the "wetback" and the migrant workers include Marian Garthwaite's *Marco: A Mexican Boy's Adventure* (1960) and Joe Molnar's *Graciela: A Mexican American Child Tells Her Story* (1972).

The inability of a child to communicate or relate to a parent is another problem often faced by Mexican and Mexican-American characters. Aimee Sommerfelt's *My Name Is Pablo* (1965) is the story of Pablo, a poor shoeshine boy in Mexico who struggles to help his family out of their economic difficulties. But Pablo shines shoes without the appropriate permit and daily risks arrest. His mother implores his father to purchase the permit for Pablo:

"All the same, shouldn't we pay for Pablo's permit? He brings in quite a few pesos each month with his shoe shining. We would feel it if he were taken away. Think of that, Roberto."
"Mule first!" he said.[7]

Pablo is finally arrested, and although he is eventually set free, it is not before he undergoes an ordeal in a gruesome reformatory. Although Pablo and his family are the victims of circumstances, Pablo's predicament is at least partially due to his father's authoritarian and rigid position.

The traditional and strict role of the father appears again in Joseph Krumgold's . . . *And Now Miguel* (1953). Although this is the story of an American family originally from Spain, many of the same traditions as those of Mexican-American families are reflected. In this Newbery award book, twelve-year-old Miguel has difficulty relating to his father and proving himself to be a mature and competent shepherd. His older brother, Gabriel, seems to have gained most of the love and respect of the family. After several disappointments, Miguel finally achieves some success in winning his father's approval. . . . *And Now Miguel* presents several of the prevalent Spanish traditions commonly attributed to Mexican-American families: pride in one's work, the strong influence of religion, the impact of tradition, and the importance of gaining approval from one's elders.

These strong traditions sometimes create

special difficulties in the context of contemporary America. The clash of the Mexican heritage and the norms and mores of the United States can lead to special problems and conflicts for young Chicanos as they attempt to construct a new path that includes both Mexican and American cultures. In this process Chicanos frequently must face prejudice and discrimination.

Betty Ochoa, in Bob and Jan Young's *Across the Tracks* (1969), attempts to build a new path but runs into hostility from both the Anglo and Mexican-American students. Although a popular senior at Bellamar High, Betty feels hurt when she loses the election for president of the Girls's League. A Mexican boy accuses Betty of turning away from her Mexican identity because of her Anglo friends and because she lives in the better part of town. Betty's attempt to increase understanding and friendship between Anglo and Chicano students is aided with her nomination as activities commissioner for the high school. Although a vandal scrawls *spic* across her election poster, Anglos and Chicanos rally behind her, and a bridge between the two communities is built.

Donna Martinez is less successful in Hila Coleman's *Chicano Girl* (1973). Fed up with her life of boredom and poverty in her Arizona village, Donna seeks to enjoy all the pleasures she has seen on television. She sets off for Tucson to attend a beauty school, but a date with a prejudiced boy and the discrimination she discovers when she goes job hunting quickly bring her back to harsh realities and the difficult road ahead.

Young Kiki also faces prejudice in *Chicano, Amigo* (1972), by Maurine Gee. Kiki is a young Chicano boy whose efforts to join the Cub Scouts are made particularly difficult by his knack for making mistakes. Although Kiki works hard to earn the money for his uniform, his real challenge is winning acceptance by his peers. Marc, an Anglo, assumes primary responsibility for Kiki. The only other Chicano in the group, Gonny, is unfriendly to Kiki and "treats him like dirt." Gonny explains, "You don't know what a struggle my mother and my father had to get where they are . . . we're the only Mexican-Americans in our neighborhood. How long would we be welcome if we had Kiki and his kind hanging around?"[8] In spite of Gonny's insecurity, Kiki eventually is accepted by the other Cub Scouts, and he is rescued from the ruins of an earthquake by his new friends.

The problems facing Keeny Duran's acceptance by, and of, American society are told in Frank Bonham's *Viva Chicano* (1970). Keeny Duran is a Chicano who has been in trouble since he was seven. When his younger brother accidentally falls from a window while Keeny is supposed to be watching him, everyone assumes that Keeny pushed him. Keeny runs away and takes refuge in an abandoned police station. His gang, the Aztecs, helps him to stay in hiding. Keeny and his friends steal a cardboard cutout of Emiliano Zapata from the front of a movie theater. The cutout talks to the Aztecs, through Keeny, advising them to avoid gang warfare, to take pride in their Mexican heritage. Keeny is eventually brought to trial because of his brother's accident and gets a new chance. His new pride in himself and his Mexican heritage suggests an optimistic conclusion.

It should also be noted that *Viva Chicano* in particular and Bonham's works in general have not been received with complete acceptance by the Chicano community. Some readers are concerned with the image of Mexican-Americans painted by Bonham and find negative stereotypic characteristics that still persist even in the primary characters of the story.

The books in this section suggest some of the problems that confront Mexican-Americans on "the difficult road north." Most of the books suggest that these problems can be overcome, that individual and cultural pride can be achieved in the context of contemporary America. The difficult path of Puerto Ricans who come to live on the mainland is the subject of the next section.

## The Puerto Rican flight to the mainland

Puerto Rico has a unique relationship with the United States. Acquired as a result of the Spanish-American War (1898), Puerto Rico became neither a state nor an independent nation, although movements toward each of these goals are still active. As a commonwealth, Puerto Rico shares a limited role in relation to national elections and taxation, and its present status as neither totally within nor outside the United States is frequently questioned.

As citizens of a commonwealth, Puerto Ricans enjoy unrestricted rights to migrate to the mainland. Although in 1945 the migration to the mainland amounted to only 13,500, for 1953 the number of new arrivals from the island peaked at 69,000. A recent survey reveals that about 250,000 have left the island and generally have settled in New York City. Puerto Ricans have been attracted to the United States by the promise of better economic conditions and increased social services, including the tuition-free and open-admission policies of the New York City university system. Frequently Puerto Rican newcomers have settled in El Barrio, a poverty-stricken ghetto neighborhood in New York City. The problems of resettling in a new and difficult environment and of severing ties with island life comprise the major theme of children's books about Puerto Ricans.

The memory of life in Puerto Rico weighs heavily on Santiago, a new arrival to New York City in Pura Belpre's picture book

> I have tried to give a voice to people who are rarely heard, and to provide the reader with an inside view of a style of life which is common to the deprived and marginal groups in our society but which is largely unknown, ignored, or inaccessible to most middle-class readers.
>
> *Oscar Lewis*, La Vida, *National Book Award winner about the lives of Puerto Ricans*

*Santiago* (1969). Symeon Shimin illustrates this story of a young Puerto Rican boy whose love for his native island is symbolized by his longing for Salina, his pet hen. On his way to school Santiago sees a hen, but has difficulty convincing his classmates that a hen is actually running about in the middle of New York. The class and teacher investigate and not only discover the hen but visit Santiago's home to view a picture of Salina through a stereoscope. Ernie, a previously skeptical black classmate, is now convinced of the existence of Salina, and he and Santiago become friends.

The story of another young new arrival to New York is found in Sandra Weiner's *They Call Me Jack* (1973). After the death of his mother, Jacinto Barreras, his father, two brothers, and sister leave Puerto Rico for New York City. Cold weather, cramped living conditions, drugs, and violence add to Jacinto's adjustment problems. Although the warmth and wildflowers of Puerto Rico are missed, Jack learns to appreciate the variety of things to do in New York, as well as his new friendships. This honest narrative of the problems and experiences of a new arrival to New York is augmented by a collection of candid photographs of El Barrio.

A number of other books for young children concern the problems confronting Puerto Rican children who are immigrants to the urban centers of the mainland. The difficulty of communicating in a new language is presented in Edna Barth's *The Day Luis Was Lost* (1971), Bouchard's *The Boy Who Wouldn't Talk* (1969), and Norma Simon's *What Do I Say?* (1967). Other problems range from getting around in a new environment, as in Barbara Brenner's *Barto Takes the Subway* (1962), to acquiring a library card, in Sue Felt's *Rosa-Too-Little* (1950).

Puerto Ricans are frequently portrayed as immigrants struggling on the edge of poverty. Young Jose, in Joan Lexau's *Jose's Christmas Secret* (1963), must assume some of the responsibilities for supporting his family after his father's death. By diligently and secretly working after school selling Christmas trees, Jose manages to earn enough money to buy his mother a blanket for Christmas. Jose's hard work contrasts with the prejudiced comments he hears about Puerto Ricans who come to New York in order to go on welfare.

Hard work rather than welfare is emphasized in the difficult life of Papa in Ruth Sonneborn's *Friday Night Is Papa Night* (1970). Away working at two jobs all week, Friday becomes the special night when Papa returns home. But one Friday night Papa does not return home. Although the rest of the family eventually goes to bed, Pedro waits up and is the first to see his Papa arrive laden with gifts. Papa explains that he is late because he was helping a sick friend. As in *Jose's Christmas Secret*, the Puerto Rican family, although short of money, is portrayed as happy, warm, loving, and kind.

For older readers, a harsher and more comprehensive account of growing up Puerto Rican in New York is presented in the controversial Piri Thomas' *Down These Mean Streets* (1967). This is the autobiography of a young Puerto Rican growing up in Spanish Harlem and experiencing the violence and prejudice of the city. As the only "Negrito," or dark-skinned child, in his family, Piri feels that he does not belong. He becomes involved in gangs, drugs, and ultimately armed robbery, for which he received a six-year prison sentence. The brutal language and issues included in this book have made this realistic account an object of censorship in some school districts. But *Down These Mean Streets* remains an honest insight into the barriers that faced at least one Puerto Rican child in America.

*Down These Mean Streets* is an exception to the typical presentation of Puerto Rican life in children's books. To summarize, the typical story reads something like this:

Living on a farm in Puerto Rico, a loving family decides to move to New York City. They settle into a badly overcrowded apartment. Hard work, with little to show for it, is combined with a continual longing for Puerto Rico, former friends and a tropical climate. There may be a minor run-in with police or social workers, and a minimum contact with racism. As the characters assume more and more of the language and customs of the United States, at the expense of their Puerto Rican heritage, life becomes easier. Generally, problems are resolved when a) English is mastered b) friends are acquired c) a pet or plant is acquired and cared for d) the family moves into a new apartment, or e) the child's first view of snow is taken as a good omen.

For older children, these simplistic plots are replaced by stories of teen-agers in trouble, gang warfare, drugs and crime.[9]

The frequency of this plot, the inaccurate portrayal of Puerto Rican names and customs, and the emphasis on the adoption of American values at the expense of Puerto Rican heritage are some of the faults with many children's books that portray Puerto Rican characters. The Council on Interracial Books for Children reviewed one hundred children's books, published between 1932 and 1972, concerning Puerto Rican characters. Only six were written by Puerto Rican authors, and many contained misconceptions and inaccuracies.[10] The council also found consistent evidence of sexism, a finding explored in the next section.

## The girl from Puerto Rico

Although there are not many books about Puerto Rican females, some of those that are available have become fairly popular. According to the Council on Interracial Books for Children, many of these books teach lessons in sexism and relegate female characters to secondary roles.

A well-known book, *Candita's Choice* (1959), by Mina Lewiton, contains the typical theme of adjusting to New York and also has elements of paternalism and sexism. Eleven-year-old Candita refuses to speak English until she masters it completely. Secretly she studies English, eventually speaks the language perfectly, and wins honors in school. Candita's white girl friend is crucial to her happiness, and the white girl friend's father gets Candita's sculptor father a job in a museum, sweeping floors. This paternalism is matched by sexism, which is reflected in Candita's dream of being with her father, "to live in his house and learn his work, and then to cook and sew for him."[11]

Another "adapt to New York" book that emphasizes sex role stereotyping is the popular *Maria* (1964), by Joan Lexau. Young Maria receives a special gift through the mail, a China doll with a beautiful mantilla. Sent by her grandmother, this ancient family heirloom is too precious and fragile for Maria to play with, and it serves only to frustrate her. With her grandmother's permission Maria's mother sells the doll and buys a chicken, a pair of shoes, and a doll Maria can play with. The accuracy of the portrayal of Hispanic culture in this book has been questioned. It is doubtful that Spanish parents would so readily sell a cher-

ished family heirloom that belonged to a great-grandmother and had been carefully passed from generation to generation. Selling this heirloom for such a small return emphasizes the overwhelming desire to assimilate, even at the cost of one's cultural heritage. From a feminist point of view Maria's brother is a strong character who makes decisions and protects Maria. Maria, on the other hand, strives only to acquire the dominant object in her life, a doll.[12]

A particularly unrealistic book with elements of sexism is Yetta Speevac's *The Spider Plant* (1965). The problem of adjusting to New York City is reduced to an earnest attempt to acquire friends. The poverty of the ghetto, school difficulties, and prejudice do not exist in this book. Twelve-year-old Carmen eventually proves herself by giving cuttings of her spider plant to her classmates. At home Carmen washes dishes while her brother begins his homework, and she joins the Girl Scouts, where she will learn homemaking and gardening. *The Spider Plant* promotes sex role stereotyping while avoiding Puerto Rican problems, concerns, and reality.[13]

Fifteen-year-old Felicidad encounters both racism and sexism in Hila Coleman's *The Girl from Puerto Rico* (1961). After the death of her father, Felicidad and her family migrate to New York. Her brother has problems with the police, her mother has difficulty adjusting, and Felicidad must work hard to help support the family. On her first date with a "real New Yorker," Felicidad encounters racist and sexist attitudes. Her date explains, "I did think you girls were different . . . you're the ones who are supposed to be so passionate."[14] Felicidad becomes so discouraged with her attempt to become an "American" that she abandons the effort and returns to Puerto Rico—one of the few characters in children's literature to do so. *The Girl from Puerto Rico* also touches upon the conflict between black and Puerto Rican, another issue infrequently found in children's books.

One of the better books in this section is the well-written *Magdalena* (1971), by Louisa Shotwell and effectively illustrated by Lilian Obligado (see Chapter 3). Rather than focusing on strictly Puerto Rican issues, Magdalena is concerned with growing up and identifying her role in society. Although Magdalena wishes to cut off her braids, her traditionally oriented grandmother insists she keep them. The story is peopled with some fascinating characters, black and white, male and female, old and young. *Magdalena* is both witty and exciting, an adventure story with touches of fantasy and a unique cast of interesting female characters.

One of the finest books about the Puerto Rican experience is *Nilda* (1973), a poignant story of ten-year-old Nilda Ramirez, living in Spanish Harlem during the 1940s. Nicholasa Mohr has written a powerful story of the hardships of being Puerto Rican and of the barriers facing women. For example, at a Catholic summer camp, Nilda is given equal doses of discipline, anti-Semitism, and laxatives (to purify her when she greets God). The welfare system also comes under attack. The visit of a welfare worker becomes a degrading experience as she pries into the private life of Nilda's family. Finally, directing her hostility at Nilda, she demands, "Let me see your hands! Wake up young lady. Let me see your hands. . . . You have filthy nails. Look at that Mrs. Ramirez. She's how old? Ten years old? Filthy. . . . How often do you bathe?"[15] Nilda's socialist stepfather has little tolerance for capitalism or Catholicism. "The Catholic Church helped Franco as well, with that kind of shit that your mama believes. . . . Garbage to enslave the masses."[16] As he lies dying in a hospital bed, he finds enough energy to attack a priest praying by his bedside. Vivid accounts

of police prejudice against Puerto Ricans, Puerto Rican prejudice against blacks, spiritualism, and superstition are also presented in *Nilda*. The story is enhanced by a series of powerful and surrealistic illustrations. The illustrations, language, and strong antiestablishment themes combine to make *Nilda* a moving statement about the Puerto Rican experience in America.

Nilda is made aware by her mother of the crushing effect of sex role stereotyping. Re-

Nilda

flecting on her life as a woman whose total involvement was in raising children, her mother's
last words to Nilda suggest the loss she has
felt:

Do you have that feeling, honey? That you have
something all yours . . . you must . . . like
when I see you drawing sometimes, I know you
have something all yours. Keep it . . . hold on,
guard it. Never give it to nobody . . . not to
your lover, not to your kids. . . . We are all born
alone . . . and we all die alone. And when I
die, Nilda, I know I take nothing with me that
is only mine.[17]

Although the treatment of females in the
literature of young people is the focus of another chapter, sexism also can be analyzed as
it appears in the literature of specific minority
groups. The limitations of space prevent us
from reviewing the role of females of minority
groups in children's literature, but this section
suggests how sexist and nonsexist approaches
are reflected in several of the more popular
children's books with Puerto Rican characters.
Although many of these books do contain sexist portrayals, *Magdalena* and *Nilda* are noteworthy exceptions. Nonsexist books about
native Americans (Scott O'Dell) or black Americans (Virginia Hamilton) do exist, but sexism
pervades many of these books as well. In
books with Jewish American characters, sexism
appears in the form of the insensitive and
humorous Jewish mother, although there are
a number of nonsexist books about the Jewish
experience during the Holocaust. The traditional and authoritarian role of the father in
books about Mexican-Americans and Puerto
Ricans frequently relegates females to a secondary and uninfluential role. The emphasis
on tradition and strict adherence to sex role
stereotyping are elements that also appear in
children's books with Chinese-American and
Japanese-American characters, and some of
these books are discussed in the concluding
sections.

## Chinese-Americans in children's literature

Drawn to the nineteenth-century United
States by tales of gold and riches, Chinese
immigrants became exploited workers in mines
and on the transcontinental railroad. Without
legal rights, denied the ownership of land, and
prohibited from joining unions, the Chinese
became the object of official and unofficial
prejudice. Classified as neither black nor white,
Chinese-Americans were denied citizenship,
and the Chinese Exclusion Act of 1882 also
isolated the Chinese in America by halting further Chinese immigration. Strong family ties, a
common language and dress, widespread prejudice, and the need for mutual protection caused
the Chinese to live in close-knit neighborhoods
called Chinatowns.

The continued existence of Chinatowns in
various American cities has had several effects.
Chinatowns have insulated several generations
of Chinese-Americans from the mainstream of
the American experience, as well as from such
social problems as juvenile delinquency. The
stereotype of the clannish Chinese is another
result of the existence of Chinatowns. Because
the Chinese often live together in highly visible
communities in the midst of urban areas, their
population is usually estimated as significantly
larger than the actual figure, which is less than
1 percent of the total U.S. population.[18]

Many contemporary Chinese, often third-
generation, no longer accept the traditional
life. They question the absolute authority of
parents and a life-style apart from the rest of
America. For example, the number of Chinese
professionals has increased from 3 percent of
the Chinese population in 1940 to 18 percent
in 1960, one sign of the changing status of
Chinese-Americans.[19]

Despite a complex reality, most children's
books, whether set in China or the United
States, present a uniform and one-dimensional

image of the Chinese people. Typically, the Chinese are portrayed as close-knit, even clannish, adhering to ancient customs and revering the older generation. Although not altogether negative or inaccurate, this sterotype does blur and even eliminate individual differences. One reason for this persistent stereotype is that many of the children's books about the Chinese are set in prerevolutionary China, and they reflect rigid class segregation and strict adherence to sex roles, as well as other traditional cultural patterns.

One such book is the 1939 Caldecott award winner *Mei Li* (1938), by Thomas Handforth. Although girls usually must stay at home, Mei Li manages to go to the New Year's Fair and watch circus performers, the trick bear, and even the fortuneteller. When she returns home she meets the Kitchen God, who reveals that the fortuneteller's prophecy that she is a princess is true. Her house is her kingdom.

The historical economic exploitation and poverty of the lower social classes in China serve as background to several children's books by Eleanor Francis Lattimore. Family life, customs, and economic deprivation appear in Lattimore's *Three Little Chinese Girls* (1948), *Little Pear* (1931), *Little Pear and His Friends* (1934), and *The Little Tumbler* (1936), a collection of simply written and illustrated stories of Chinese life during the earlier part of the twentieth century. Lattimore has also written the story of a young Chinese girl as she learns of American society in *The Chinese Daughter* (1960). Ai-Li is a young Chinese girl who is adopted by Dr. and Mrs. Randall, American missionaries living in China. Ai-Li is uncomfortable in the school with American children, and she does not feel at ease when she meets her Chinese parents. The romanticized solution to Ai-Li's identity problem includes a decision to go to America, become a nurse, and return to China as a missionary.

These books about the Chinese in their native land portray the traditional life of pre-Communist China. Many of these books were published during the 1930s and 1940s, and there is little in contemporary children's literature to reflect the changing picture of China during the past twenty-five years.

When portraying the experiences of the Chinese in America, many of the children's books available inadequately consider the problems and prejudices of the past and the conflicts and questions currently facing Chinese-Americans. With only a few exceptions, children's books focus on a single aspect of the Chinese-American experience, the customs and holidays that mark life in Chinatown.

## Chinatown, my Chinatown

The life, sounds, activities, and holidays central to Chinatown comprise the focus for many, if not most, of the childern's books with Chinese characters. For example, there is Leo Politi's *Moy Moy* (1960), a picture book about a young girl anxiously awaiting the New Year celebration. Moy Moy, a preschooler, is the youngest sister, who participates in New Year's activities on Chan King Street, in the Chinese section of Los Angeles. Another book of this type, one for middle-grade readers, is Lois Lenski's *San Francisco Boy* (1955), the story of a Chinese youth whose homesickness for a small western town is overcome by the activities and strong family structure found in a new home in San Francisco's Chinatown. A typical day in the life of a young Chinese girl is told in text and photographs in Seymour Reit's *Rice Cakes and Paper Dragons* (1973). Marie Chan lives in a large, modern apartment building in New York's Chinatown, and she is looking forward to the celebration of the Chinese New Year. Marie Chan attends both the public school system and the Chinese schools, and she learns about her American and Chinese heritage. Although briefly ill,

Marie recovers in time to enjoy the dragon parade and other celebrations of the New Year.

In other books set in Chinatown the concern is with the resolution of universal problems. *Mr. Charley's Chopsticks* (1972), by Doris Portwood Evans, is the story of a Chinese family living in an apartment above their shop in Chinatown. Mr. Wu carves and sells chopsticks made of wood and ivory. A minor catastrophe occurs when Mr. Wu's present for Mr. Charley, his best customer, disappears. One of the beautifully carved chopsticks has been hidden by Ping, the family dog, but young Wu Lin retrieves it and saves the day.

San Francisco's Chinatown is the scene for Patricia Miles Martin's *The Rice Bowl Pet* (1962), illustrated by Ezra Jack Keats. Young Ah Jim "spoke English without an accent" but his "thoughts were in Cantonese." Although

Mr. Charley's Chapsticks

he loves animals his mother objects to his owning a pet because of their crowded apartment. Finally she relents if Ah Jim can find a pet that can fit into a rice bowl. Searching San Francisco for just the right pet, Ah Jim finally selects a tiny dog that fits into the bowl. Keats's illustrations capture both the Chinese influence and the San Francisco environment.

Reflecting problems that are somewhat more serious than a lost chopstick or a search for a pet is Clara Ingram Judson's *The Green Jar: A Chinatown Mystery* (1949), set in Chicago's Chinatown in the 1930s. Twelve-year-old Ai-me is anxious to adopt American ways, but such important family decisions are made by Lao-po-po, the wise, strict, old-fashioned grandmother. The pride of the family is fourteen-year-old Lu-ping, the son who wants to become a doctor. For Lu-ping's education, grandmother has secretly hidden a ruby at the bottom of the old green ginger jar, a jar that Ai-me has foolishly given away to a young American girl. The search for and finally the recovery of the valuable jar provides the plot for *The Green Jar*. A number of Chinese values and commonly held stereotypes are also found in the book. The influence and status of age; the desire for education, honor, and loyalty to the family; and the greater importance of the son over the daughter are traditional Chinese values found in *The Green Jar*. The "inscrutable oriental" stereotype emerges when Keller, a newspaper reporter, explains, "You never can tell what a Chinese is thinking."[20] Polite and mannerly behavior is presented as a force so powerful that it becomes debilitating. When Ai-me finally finds the valuable green jar, she refrains from asking for its return for fear it would be a rude thing to do. *The Green Jar* contains a curious mix of commonly held stereotypes: positive characteristics, such as a respect for elders and education, are mixed with the inscrutable and clannish traits frequently attributed to the Chinese. Yet non-

Chinese frequently do hold both positive and negative perceptions of the Chinese, and *The Green Jar* reflects this.

The variety of children's books about Chinatown provides young readers with an insight into one facet of Chinese-American life. Unfortunately, other important areas are omitted. Prejudice against Chinese, problems concerned with assimilation, the contemporary relationship between Chinese-Americans and the People's Republic of China, and the early history of the Chinese in America are issues infrequently found or superficially treated in children's literature.

Two significant exceptions to the generally dismal and limited portrayal of Chinese-Americans are found in Kay Haugaard's *China Boy* (1971) and Laurence Yep's *Dragonwings* (1975). Both books deal with the enormous difficulties faced by Chinese immigrants on the West Coast. Haugaard's *China Boy* is set in California in 1851 and relates the experiences of Lee Sung Cheong. Flood, famine, persecution, and the loss of his parents spark Lee's voyage to America. Verbal and physical abuse await Lee in California, where prejudice against the Chinese is epidemic. But Lee perseveres, his hard work is rewarded, and in a somewhat improbable ending, Lee is at long last reunited with his sister. In spite of the romanticized conclusion *China Boy* does manage to convey some of the bigotry and difficulty that confronted these new immigrants.

Yep's *Dragonwings* is a historical fantasy that offers a poignant insight into the deprivations facing Chinese immigrants at the turn of the century. In 1903, six-year-old Moon Shadow sailed from China to join his father in San Francisco. During this time Chinese husbands and sons journeyed to America alone, working for years and sending money to their families in China before returning home or attempting the difficult task of bringing their loved ones to America. But Moon Shadow's father had another dream as well, a dream to fly. The painstaking effort of building a flying machine, of proving that he was in fact a great and honored dragon in a previous life, makes for an engrossing story. Based on an actual account of a Chinese immigrant who constructed a flying machine in 1909, *Dragonwings* provides a moving insight into the dreams and suffering of these early Chinese immigrants.

The emergence of books like *China Boy* and *Dragonwings* is a welcome addition to the generally inadequate collection of children's books about Chinese-Americans. Although there are some fine books about the folk literature of the Chinese (see Wolfram Eberhardt, *Folktales of China*), much remains to be written about the Chinese experience in America. The differences between contemporary Chinese-Americans and the traditional image that still pervades the literature need to be explored. And the new society of the People's Republic of China, which affects so many millions of people, can no longer be omitted from children's books. The sporadic and superficial treatment of Chinese-Americans represents a serious omission in children's literature; it is hoped that authors will remedy this shortcoming.

## Japanese-Americans in children's books

Japanese-Americans have historically shared some of the same problems and prejudices faced by Chinese-Americans. The victims of persecution, restrictive immigration policies, and discriminatory domestic laws, Japanese-Americans nevertheless worked long and hard to overcome those obstacles and achieve a significant level of economic prosperity in America. Unlike the Chinese, the history of the Japanese in America contains an additional and more recent chapter of discrimination: forced internment in camps during World War II. The World War II experience of Japanese-Americans is now being reflected in children's books. We review some of these recently published books later in this section, but first we discuss some of the beautifully illustrated picture books written for young children.

Many of the picture books about the Japanese, which frequently are illustrated in an exciting, imaginative manner, are really about problems common to all people. One of the most talented authors and illustrators of these picture books is Taro Yashima (who has also published under the name of Iwamatsu). The main character in several of Yashima's books is a young Japanese girl named Momo. In *Umbrella* (1958) Momo anxiously waits for rain in order to use her two new presents, an umbrella and a pair of boots. One day Momo finally awakes to rain and she happily walks the streets of New York in her new boots and with her new umbrella, "like a grown-up lady." In *Momo's Kitten* (1971) Momo's family moves from New York to Los Angeles, where Momo finds a *Nyan-Nyan* (Japanese for *kitten*). When Momo's cat has a litter, Momo must face the difficult task of giving away the five new kittens. Beautiful pictures also supplement the simple text in *Youngest One* (1962), the story of Momo's new friendship with a shy two-year-old boy named Bobby.

Yashima's *Crow Boy* (1955), set in Japan, was a Caldecott Honor Book. Crow Boy is a small, quiet child who walks to school alone, sits by himself, does not talk to the other children, and sometimes takes refuge in his own dreams. The children make fun of him and taunt him by calling him Chibi (tiny one). Years pass before Crow Boy wins their respect and his name by his perfect imitation of crow calls and his extensive knowledge of nature. Mr. Isobe, Crow Boy's understanding teacher, explains to the other children that Crow Boy has learned the crow calls on his trips to and from school, a long daily journey on which he leaves for school at dawn and does not return home until after sunset. After understanding more about Crow Boy, the other children regret their callous behavior.

The story of Crow Boy is one of several of Yashima's books about life in Japan. *Plenty to Watch* (1954) relates the daily routine of a Japanese village, including school activities, crafts and manufacturing, and home life. *The Village Tree* (1953) describes the meeting place by the river where Japanese children learn lessons about nature and enjoy summer activities. Yashima's universal themes, simple text, and exquisite illustrations provide young readers with a collection of fine and beautiful books concerning Japanese characters.

The barriers facing Japanese assimilation into American society should provide yet another theme for books portraying the Japanese experience. Unfortunately problems inherent to assimilation—prejudice, loss of cultural identity, compromise, and sacrifice—are too often treated superficially or not at all. Instead, assimilation is portrayed as a quest for friends or romance.

Sam Suzuki, a visitor from Japan, is a central character in Christopher's *Shortstop from Tokyo* (1970). Sam creates a budding rivalry when he outplays a local American for shortstop. Sam Suzuki's assimilation problem seems to be that he is too American, more proficient at being American than the Americans. Another superficial treatment of assimilation is presented in *Myeko's Gift* (1966), by Kay Haugaard. Unable to look like other American children, young Myeko relies on her skills in art, her talent for kite making, and her friendliness to overcome hostility and to become accepted by her new American friends. Myeko is able to maintain her Japanese skills and identity while avoiding any real problems concerned with assimilation.

For older children the assimilation issue is

sometimes placed in the context of a romantic encounter between a Japanese and an American teenager. Two such books are Betty Cavanna's *Jenny Kimura* (1964) and Winifred Madison's *Growing Up in a Hurry* (1973). These books concern romance, and in the latter case, sexual experience, pregnancy, and abortion. In each book the American girl has an artificial, romanticized notion of what it means to be Japanese, and although there are brief allusions to prejudice, the complexity of what it means to be Japanese in America is not reflected in these books.

At the beginning of my sixteenth year I fell in love with everything Japanese. Why, I don't know. It happened. I suddenly discovered that there were Japanese people and that they had a kind of beauty and quick intelligence that other people did not have. Even when I could see that not all Japanese people were exactly beautiful and that some of the Japanese students in my classes were no brighter than anyone else, still I found in all of them a quality I could not quite define, a quality that made me want to be one of them.[21]

Not all books romanticize or gloss over the difficulties involved in being Japanese in America. Yoshiko Uchida's *Samurai of Gold Hill* (1972) is a true account of a group of early Japanese settlers who, as an aftermath of internal fighting in nineteenth-century Japan, come to California to establish a silk and tea farm. In California the Japanese settlers are the objects of curiosity and hostility by some, and of friendship by others. The courage of the Samurai and the hard work of the settlers are not sufficient to overcome the natural and man-made obstacles to the success of their venture. The Japanese settlers go on to other ventures, and the new colony at Gold Hill withers.

Based on fact, *Samurai of Gold Hill* offers a fascinating insight into the experiences of the early Japanese settlers and presents a realistic view of the Japanese experience in America. Too few books are available to children that provide realistic accounts of the Japanese-American. One chapter of the Japanese-American experience, however, is being written about with candor and force: the internment of Japanese-Americans as ordered by President Franklin D. Roosevelt in Executive Order 9066.

## Executive Order 9066

Executive Order 9066 directed that Japanese-Americans be evacuated from the West Coast and relocated in camps scattered throughout the deserts and mountains of Utah, Arizona, Idaho, Colorado, Arkansas, and Wyoming. It was a precautionary step. After all, the United States was at war with Japan, an invasion of Hawaii or even the West Coast was possible, and Japanese-Americans might provide aid and comfort to the enemy. It seemed only prudent to take such a precautionary measure.

At the time little attention was paid to those who protested the internment. The fact that the United States was also at war with Germany and Italy, and German- and Italian-Americans were not confined did not seem important. The fact that so many of those arrested had never seen Japan and were second- and third-generation Americans also seemed unimportant. The loss of Japanese-owned land, homes, and businesses as a result of the internment was only a minor problem to the government. And the cruel irony of Japanese-American soldiers fighting and dying for the United States while their families lived under guard in tar paper shacks was an irony lost on most Americans.

The depressing life of those Japanese-Americans who suffered through this ordeal is now coming to light in several powerful books written for children. *Executive Order 9066: The Internment of 110,000 Japanese Americans* (1972), by Maisie and Richard Conrat, is a photographic history of this ordeal, supplemented by a brief text of the injustices suffered by the Japanese in America. The physical deprivation and mental anguish are recorded in poignant photographs.

The deprivations of an internment camp in Canada as seen through a child's eyes is presented in Schizuye Katashima's *A Child in Prison Camp* (1974). The text is presented in diary format and enhanced by the author's striking water colors. Recalling her years spent as a child in New Denver, the author writes of the despair and of the small victories that marked life in an internment camp. These accomplishments included the acquisition of a coal lamp to replace candles, the creation of highschool classes, the establishment of running water, and the attempt of the Japanese through gardening, carpentry, concerts, and plays to make life in the camp more bearable. This autobiography of a noted Canadian artist also recounts the difficulty of relocating and starting over again after the war.

Yoshiko Uchida's *Journey to Topaz* (1971) describes the disrupted life of eleven-year-old Yuki, who, with her family, is subjected to forced relocation. Yuki's father is sent to a camp in Montana; the rest of the family is given quarters in a stable at a racetrack. Eventually moved to a tar paper house in a camp at Topaz, Utah, the family survives in spite of extreme hardships. Ken, Yuki's older brother, is forced to abandon his university career. A friend of the family is accidentally shot and killed by a guard. Yuki's family must eventually start over again after their release from camp, but their experiences in the camp have permanently altered their lives and have forced them to reconsider their status in American society: "Mr. Kurihara shrugged, 'When this war ends, I may just go back to Japan,' he murmured. 'At least I won't be an enemy alien there.' "[22]

The ordeal and sacrifices of the Japanese who suffered in these camps is a vital, albeit

Journey to Topaz

little-appreciated, chapter in American history. The appearance of children's books about this experience is a welcome and useful addition to the literature about the American experience, and increased awareness of this chapter of American history may help to prevent its repetition in the future.

## NOTES

1. Walt Whitman quoted in Alberta Eiseman's *Manana Is Now; The Spanish Speaking in the United States*, New York, Atheneum, 1973, pp. 170–171.
2. Helen Rowan, "A Minority Nobody Knows," *The Atlantic*, 219 (June 1967), 47–52.
3. David K. Gast, quoted in Gloria T. Blatt's, "The Mexican-American in Children's Literature," *Elementary English*, 45, no. 4 (April 1968), 449.

4. Gloria T. Blatt, "The Mexican-American in Children's Literature," *Elementary English*, 45, no. 4 (April 1968), 446–451.
5. Evelyn Sibley Lampman, *Go Up the Road*, Charles Robinson, illus., New York, Atheneum, 1972, p. 111.
6. Ibid., p. 171.
7. Aimee Sommerfelt, *My Name Is Pablo*, Hans Normann Dahl, illus., New York, Criterion Books, 1965, p. 24.
8. Maurine H. Gee, *Chicano, Amigo*, Ted Lewin, illus., New York, Morrow, 1972, p. 15.
9. "One Hundred Books About Puerto Ricans: A Study in Racism, Sexism and Colonialism," *Interracial Books for Children*, 4, nos. 1 and 2 (Spring 1972), 1, 14–16.
10. Ibid.
11. "Feminists Look at the 100 Books: The Portrayal of Women in Children's Books on Puerto Rican Themes," *Interracial Books for Children*, 4, nos. 1 and 2 (Spring 1972), 9.
12. Ibid., p. 8.
13. Ibid., p. 9.
14. Hila Coleman, *The Girl from Puerto Rico*, New York, Morrow, 1961, pp. 148–149.
15. Nicholasa Mohr, *Nilda*, New York, Harper & Row, 1973, p. 68.
16. Ibid., p. 78.
17. Ibid., p. 277.
18. Betty Lee Sung, *The Chinese in America*, New York, Macmillan, 1972.
19. Ibid.
20. Clara Ingram Judson, *The Green Jar; A Chinatown Mystery*, Paul Brown, illus., Boston, Houghton Mifflin, 1949, p. 191.
21. Winifred Madison, *Growing Up in a Hurry*, Boston, Little, Brown, 1973, p. 3.
22. Yoshiko Uchida, *Journey to Topaz*, Donald Carrick, illus., New York, Scribner, 1971, p. 72.

# BIBLIOGRAPHY

## Books about Chinese-Americans for young children

ANDERSON, JUANITA. *Charley Yee's New Year*, Dave Bhang, illus., Follett, 1970.

BEHRENS, JUNE. *Soo Ling Finds a Way*, Golden Gate, 1965 (K–3).

BISHOP, CLAIRE, and KURT WIESE. *The Five Chinese Brothers*, Coward, McCann & Geoghegan, 1938 (K–2).

BULLA, CLYDE ROBERT. *Johnny Hong of Chinatown*, Doug Kingman, illus., Crowell, 1952 (2–5).

EVANS, DORIS PORTWOOD. *Mr. Charley's Chopsticks*, Richard Cuffari, illus., Coward, McCann & Geoghegan, 1972 (1–3).

FLACK, MARJORIE. *The Story About Ping*, Viking Press, 1933 (K–2).

HANDFORTH, THOMAS. *Mei Li*, Doubleday, 1938 (K–3).

HURD, EDITH THATCHER. *The White Horse*, Tony Chen, illus., Harper & Row, 1970 (K–3).

KEATING, NORMA. *Mr. Chu*, Bernarda Bryson, illus., Macmillan, 1965 (K–3).

LATTIMORE, ELEANOR FRANCIS, *The Little Tumbler*, Morrow, 1963 (2–4).

————. *Little Pear and His Friends*, Harcourt Brace Jovanovich (orig. pub. 1934), 1962 (2–4).

————. *Little Pear: The Story of a Little Chinese Boy*, Harcourt Brace Jovanovich, 1931 (2–3).

LENSKI, LOIS. *San Francisco Boy*, Lippincott, 1955 (4–6).

MARTIN, PATRICIA. *The Pointed Brush*, Lothrop, Lee & Shepard, 1959.

————. *The Rice Bowl Pet*, Ezra Jack Keats, illus., Crowell, 1962 (K–2).

MOLNAR, JOE. *Sherman: A Chinese-American Child Tells His Own Story*, Watts, 1973 (4–7).

POLITI, LEO. *Moy Moy*, Scribner, 1960 (K–2).

## Books about Chinese-Americans for the intermediate and upper grades

HAUGAARD, KAY. *China Boy*, Abelard-Schuman, 1971 (7+).

JUDSON, CLARA INGRAM. *The Green Ginger Jar: A Chinatown Mystery*, Paul Brown, illus., Houghton Mifflin, 1949 (4–6).

LATTIMORE, ELEANOR FRANCIS. *The Chinese Daughter*, Morrow, 1960 (2–5).

NORTON, ANDRE. *Dragon Magic*, Robin Jacques, illus., Crowell, 1972 (5–8).

REIT, SEYMOUR. *Rice Cakes and Dragons*, photos by Paul Conklin, Dodd, Mead, 1973 (2–5).

WONG, JADE SNOW. *Fifth Chinese Daughter*, Katherine Uhl, illus., Harper & Row, 1950 (9+).

YEP, LAURENCE. *Dragonwings*, Harper & Row, 1975 (6–9).

## Books about Japanese-Americans for young children

COPELAND, HELEN. *Meet Miki Takino*, Lothrop, Lee & Shepard, 1963 (K–1).

ISHII, MOMOKO. *Issun Boshi the Inchling: An Old Tale of Japan*, trans. by Yone Mizuta, Fuku Akino, illus., Walker, 1967.

MATSUNO, MASAKA. *A Pair of Red Clogs*, World, 1960 (K–3).

MCDERMOTT, GERALD. *The Stone-Cutter: A Japanese Folk Tale*, Viking Press, 1975 (K–2).

MOSEL, ARLENE. *The Funny Little Woman*, Blair Lent, illus., Dutton, 1972 (K–3).

POLITI, LEO. *Mieko*, Golden Gate, 1969 (1–3).

TAYLOR, MARK. *A Time for Flowers*, Golden Gate, 1967 (K–3).

YASHIMA, TARO. *Crow Boy*, Viking Press, 1955 (K–3).

YASHIMA, MITSU, and TARO YASHIMA. *Momo's Kitten*, Viking Press, 1961 (K–2).

YASHIMA, MITSU, and TARO HASHIMA. *Plenty to Watch*, Viking Press, 1954 (K–3).

YASHIMA, TARO. *Umbrella*, Viking Press, 1958 (K–2).

———. *The Village Tree*, Viking Press, 1953 (K–1).

———. *Youngest One*, Viking Press, 1962 (K–1).

YOSHIKO, SAMUEL (ad.). *Twelve Years, Twelve Animals: A Japanese Folk Tale*, Margo Locke, illus., Abingdon, 1972 (K–3).

## Books about Japanese-Americans for the intermediate and upper grades

BEHN, HARRY (trans.). *Cricket Songs: Japanese Haiku*, Harcourt Brace Jovanovich, 1964 (K–12).

CAVANNA, BETTY. *Jenny Kimura*, Morrow, 1964 (6+).

CHRISTOPHER, MATT. *Shortstop from Tokyo*, Harvey Kiddex, illus., Little, Brown, 1970 (3–6).

CONRAT, MAISIE, and RICHARD CONRAT. *Executive Order 9066: The Internment of 110,000 Japanese Americans*, California Historical Society, 1972 (6+).

HAUGAARD, KAY. *Myeko's Gift*, Dora Terner, illus., Abelard-Schuman, 1966 (7+).

MADISON, WINIFRED. *Growing Up in a Hurry*, Little, Brown, 1973 (7+).

TAKASHIMA, SHIZUYE. *A Child in Prison Camp*, Morrow, 1974 (7–9).

UCHIDA, YOSHIKO. *Journey to Topaz*, Donald Carrick, illus., Scribner, 1971 (5–7).

———. *Samurai of Gold Hill*, Ati Forberg, illus., Scribner, 1972 (4–7).

YOSHIDA, JIM. *The Two Worlds of Jim Yoshida*, with Bill Hosokawa, Morrow, 1972 (8+).

## Books about Mexican-Americans for young children

BALET, JAN. *The Fence*, Dell, 1969 (K–3).

BEIM, LORRAINE, and JERROLD BEIM. *The Burro That Had a Name*, Hale, 1965 (K–2).

BULLA, CLYDE ROBERT. *Benito*, Valenti Angelo, illus., Crowell, 1961 (2–5).

ETS, MARIE HALL. *Bad Boy, Good Boy*, Crowell, 1967 (K–3).

———. *Gilberto and the Wind*, Viking Press, 1963 (K–2).

———, and AURORA LABISTIDA. *Nine Days to Christmas*, Viking Press, 1959 (preschool–2).

FERN, EUGENE. *Pepito's Story*, Farrar, Straus & Giroux, 1960 (preschool–4).

FRANCHERE, RUTH. *Cesar Chavez*, Earl Thollander, illus., Crowell, 1970 (2–4).

GARRETT, HELEN. *Angelo the Naughty One*, Leo Politi, illus., Viking Press (orig. pub. 1944), 1966 (K–3).

GRIFALCONI, ANN. *The Toy Trumpet*, Bobbs-Merrill, 1969 (K–3).

LEXAU, JOAN M. *Maria*, Ernest Crichlow, illus., Dial Press, 1964 (K–3).

O'DELL, SCOTT. *The Treasure of Topo-El-Bampo*, Lynn Ward, illus., Houghton Mifflin, 1972 (K–4).

POLITI, LEO. *Juanita*, Scribner, 1948 (preschool–3).

———. *Song of the Swallows*, Scribner, 1949 (K–2).

RITCHIE, BARBARA. *Ramon Makes a Trade*, Earl Thollander, illus., Parnassus, 1959 (1–3).

TODD, BARBARA K. *Juan Patricio*, Gloria Kamen, illus., Putnam, 1972 (2–3).

## Books about Mexican-Americans for the intermediate and upper grades

ALEXANDER, ANNE. *Trouble on Treat Street,* John Jones, illus., Atheneum, 1974 (3–6).

BONHAM, FRANK. *Viva Chicano,* Dell, 1970 (7+).

CLYMER, ELEANOR. *Santiago's Silver Mine,* Ingrid Fetz, illus., Atheneum, 1973 (3–5).

COLEMAN, HILA. *Chicano Girl,* Morrow, 1973 (7+).

GEE, MAURINE. *Chicano, Amigo,* Ted Lewin, illus., Morrow, 1972 (4–8).

KRUMGOLD, JOSEPH. *And Now Miguel,* Jean Charlot, illus., Crowell, 1953 (8–12).

LAMPMAN, EVELYN SIBLEY. *Go Up the Road,* Charles Robinson, illus., Atheneum, 1972 (5–7).

MOLNAR, JOE. *Graciela: A Mexican-American Child Tells Her Story,* Watts, 1972 (4–6).

NEWTON, CLARKE. *Famous Mexican-Americans,* Dodd, Mead, 1972 (6–9).

O'DELL, SCOTT. *The Black Pearl,* Milton Johnson, illus., Houghton Mifflin, 1967 (7+).

———. *Child of Fire,* Houghton Mifflin, 1974 (7+).

SMITH, NANCY COVERT. *Josie's Handful of Quietness,* Ati Forberg, illus., Abingdon Press, 1975 (3–7).

SOMMERFELT, AIMEE. *My Name Is Pablo,* Hans Normann Dahl, illus., Criterion, 1965 (6–9).

STOLZ, MARY. *Juan,* Harper & Row, 1970 (3–7).

TAYLOR, THEODORE. *The Maldonado Miracle,* Doubleday, 1973 (6–8).

VAN DER VEER, JUDY. *Long Trail for Francisco,* Children's Press, 1974 (3–7).

WEINER, SANDRA. *Small Hands, Big Hands: Seven Profiles of Chicano Migrant Workers and Their Families,* Pantheon Books, 1970 (5+).

YOUNG, BOB, and JAN YOUNG. *Across the Tracks,* Messner, 1958 (7+).

## Books about Puerto Ricans for young children

ALGERIA, RICARDO (ed). *The Three Wishes: A Collection of Puerto Rican Folktales,* Harcourt Brace Jovanovich, 1969 (K–3).

ALLYN, PAUL. *The Picture Life of Herman Badillo,* Watts, 1972 (2–4).

BARTH, EDNA. *The Day Luis Was Lost,* Lilian Obligado, illus., Little, Brown, 1971 (3–5).

BELPRE, PURA. *Santiago,* Symeon Shimin, illus., Warne, 1969 (K–2).

BINZEN, BILL. *Miguel's Mountain,* Coward, McCann & Geoghegan, 1968 (K–3) .

BOUCHARD, L. *The Boy Who Wouldn't Talk,* Hawthorn Books, 1969 (1–3).

BRENNER, BARBARA. *Barto Takes the Subway,* Knopf, 1962 (1–3).

FELT, SUE. *Rosa-Too-Little,* Doubleday, 1950 (K–1).

LEXAU, JOAN M. *Jose's Christmas Secret,* Don Bolognese, illus., Dial Press, 1963 (3–6).

———. *Maria,* Ernest Crichlow, illus., Hale, 1967 (K–3).

ORMSBY, VIRGINIA. *What's Wrong with Julio?,* Lippincott, 1965 (K–3).

REIT, SEYMOUR. *Dear Uncle Carlos,* photos by Sheldon Brody, McGraw-Hill, 1969 (K–3).

SIMON, NORMA. *What Do I Say?,* Joe Lasker, illus., Whitman, 1967 (K–1).

SONNEBORN, RUTH A. *Friday Night Is Papa Night,* Emily A. McCully, illus., Viking Press, 1970 (K–2).

———. *The Lollipop Party,* Viking Press, 1967 (K–1).

———. *Seven in a Bed,* Don Freeman, illus., Viking Press, 1968 (K–2).

THOMAS, DAWN C. *Mira! Mira!,* Harold L. James, illus., Lippincott, 1970 (K–2).

## Books about Puerto Ricans for the intermediate and upper grades

COLEMAN, HILA. *The Girl from Puerto Rico,* Morrow, 1961 (6–9).

JACKSON, JESSE. *Room for Randy,* 1950 (2–6).

LEWITON, MINA. *Candida's Choice,* Howard Simon, illus., Harper & Row, 1959 (4–6).

MOHR, NICHOLASA. *El Bronx Remembered,* Harper & Row, 1975 (7+).

———. *Nilda,* Harper & Row, 1973 (5+).

SHOTWELL, LOUISA. *Magdalena,* Lilian Obligado, illus., Viking Press, 1971 (5–7).

SPEEVAC, YETTA. *The Spider Plant,* Wendy Watson, illus., Atheneum, 1965 (3–7).

TALBOT, CHARLENE JOY. *Tomas Takes Charge,* Reisie Lonette, illus., Lothrop, Lee & Shepard, 1966 (4–7).

THOMAS, PIRI. *Down These Mean Streets*, Knopf, 1967 (7+).

———. *Savior, Savior Hold My Hand*, Doubleday, 1972 (7+).

WEINER, SANDRA. *They Call Me Jack: The Story of a Boy from Puerto Rico*, Pantheon Books, 1973 (3–7).

Dear God,

Are boys really better than girls? I know you are one but please try to be fair.

Love,
*Sylvia*[1]

This letter, written by an elementary school girl, appeared in a book, *Children's Letters to God*. It is an expression of loss of potential and self-esteem that has occurred at an early age. A growing body of research also attests to loss of female potential as girls go through school, and many writers have analyzed the way sex stereotyping occurs in classrooms across the country—from sexist teaching patterns to segregated activities.[2]

One key way that girls learn to undervalue themselves is through the books they read. When children open elementary school texts, they read most often about the activities and adventures of boys. For example, one group of feminists, the Women on Words and Images, studied 134 elementary school readers from sixteen different publishers and found the ratio of boy-centered stories to girl-centered stories to be 5 to 2.[3] Moreover, when girls are present they are frequently stereotyped as passive and ineffectual. Boys do many things in these readers: play baseball, put on magic shows, have daring adventures. In contrast, girls play with dolls, help mother, and do nothing but sit and watch their brothers.

Adults in these readers are also characterized by stereotyped behavior, particularly in terms of their occupations. The Women on Words and Images tabulated 147 different occupations for males in elementary readers and only 25 for females. Among the 25 they found were fat lady in the circus, witch, and queen.[4] In an analysis of a series of social studies books produced by ten publishing houses, De-Crow found no women portrayed as working outside the home except as teachers or nurses. Moreover, all teachers and nurses were called "Miss," suggesting that only unmarried women work.[5]

# 9
# Breaking Out of the Pumpkin Shell: The Image of Women in Children's Literature

Graebner tried to determine whether the portrayal of women in elementary school texts had changed from the early 1960s to the early 1970s. She concluded that little change had occurred in the portrayal of women and that texts "have not kept pace with a changing society."[6] However, one of the major changes she did find between old and new versions was that 42 percent of mothers wore aprons and carried dish towels in the old versions and in the newer texts only 28 percent were perpetually garbed in this kitchen costume.

Children's literature has also been analyzed recently; the result has been many charges that children's books teach sexist lessons. The issue of sex stereotyping in children's literature is a complex one. In the following pages we explore in more detail how sexism occurs in children's literature. We try to determine what is a sexist and what is a nonsexist book, and we discuss some of the finer nonsexist portrayals of girls and women in children's literature. Although the emphasis is on the depiction of women, for it is here that bias has had the more devastating impact, sexism is a two-edged sword, limiting the potential of boys as well as girls. Consequently, we also discuss sexist and nonsexist portrayals of male characters in children's literature.

## Analyzing sexism in children's literature: some standards for evaluation

Following is a summary of criteria that may be helpful in indicating the presence of sex bias in children's books.

### Denigrating quotes

Obviously it would be offensive and harmful for a book to contain quotes explicitly stating that blacks are stupid, Mexicans are shiftless, or Jews are money-hungry. These are almost absurd examples, for it would be rare to find prejudice about minority groups in such obvious form in children's books today. However, blatant quotes denigrating one sex, usually women, are relatively common in children's books, and it is not at all difficult to find

From *The Tall Book of Mother Goose*

statements that girls are dumb, silly, unable to keep secrets, and generally incompetent.

If reading material for children contains quotes that group all males or all females together and makes insulting, disparaging remarks about either sex as a whole, the reading material may be sexist. When analyzing material for sexism it is important that quotes be considered within the context of the total book rather than in isolation. For example, a character may express contempt for males or females at one stage of his or her development and later grow toward realization of the prejudice inherent in such an attitude. If a sexist comment is later repudiated as a character matures and changes, the material is not necessarily sexist.

## Numerical disparities

Reading material that numerically underrepresents either sex in text or pictures may be considered sexist. Currently girls and women are not included in children's books in numbers that indicate their presence in the general population. However, one must be careful not to term a single book sexist if it does not include equitable numbers of girls and boys or even if it totally omits one sex. Obviously there are stories that, for a variety of legitimate reasons, exclude either sex. However, if an illustrator is depicting a street scene and 85 percent of the people drawn are males and are in the foreground of the picture, this is an example of sex bias. And if there is a pattern in books in a library and/or reading center, where in page after page one sex is portrayed more frequently than another, the general collection must be considered sexist.

## Stereotyped behavior patterns and characteristics

Another criteria for evaluating sexism in literature is that of stereotyped character por-

trayal. When female characters are depicted by one constellation of behaviors—typically, passivity, dependency, and helplessness—and male characters are depicted by a polar grouping—typically, aggressiveness, independence, and forcefulness—the material probably is sexist. Of course, when an author creates his or her characters, a female character may emerge as timid and gentle, a male character as brave and strong. In our society there are passive, gentle girls and brave, independent boys. These people should be represented in children's reading, and if a book portrays such characters as individuals and offers adequate and believable motivation for their unique behavior, it must not be dismissed as sexist. However, brave, independent girls and gentle,

From *The Real Mother Goose*

timid boys also exist in our society, and these people also must be represented in what children read. If a pattern emerges in a book or in a collection of books where unique individuality is betrayed as characters conform to stereotypes, the book or collection of books must be considered sexist.

## Stereotyped occupations

A pattern of sex-stereotyped occupational roles is another criterion for identifying a book or collection of books as sexist. Contemporary society is characterized by greater flexibility of roles and occupations available to women, and women are entering the labor force in increasing numbers and in a widening variety of jobs. Children's books that depict contemporary times must offer more than the limited occupational profile in which adult females are consistently shown primarily as homemakers, teachers, nurses, and secretaries and men are depicted as holding all the other jobs in the labor force and never doing anything in the kitchen other than consume foods.

In our society there are wives and mothers who exhibit no wish or need for work outside their homes and husbands and fathers who exhibit no wish or need for work inside their homes, and these people should be represented in children's literature. However, our society is also comprised of women who seek fulfillment and/or money through work outside their homes; it is also comprised of men who need and/or want to be involved in the care of their children and homes; and these people also must be represented in the books children read.

Author John Rowe Townsend has remarked "We would wish every child to experience to his or her full capacity the enjoyment and the broadening of horizons, which can be derived from literature."[7] Sexist literature does not broaden horizons but, either subtly or bla-

tantly, suggests to children that they are limited, solely on the basis of gender, as to how they must behave and to what they can become.

In the following sections we analyze the way sex bias emerges in Mother Goose rhymes, folktales, and fiction for children from preschool through the adolescent years. We then discuss examples of some of the finer nonsexist portrayals in children's literature.

## Of pumpkin shells and shoes

Some of the most famous characters in literature are still alive and well in the pages of Mother Goose. Children savor the humor, the nonsense, and the inherent music of these nursery jingles, as well as the swiftly developed plot action and characterization. In spite of the way their childhoods may have differed in terms of economic circumstance, ethnic background, or religious belief, youngsters share a common literary culture peopled by an unforgettable cast of Mother Goose characters.

Unfortunately, even a cursory glance through a collection of the Mother Goose rhymes discloses denigrating comments and stereotyped behavior patterns. In Blanche Fisher Wright's extensive collection *The Real Mother Goose*, there are 69 rhymes that refer to women and/or femininity and 90 that refer to men or to masculine themes.[8] Moreover, there are recurrent stereotyped themes that surface in these jingles. For every state of woman's chronological development, from early childhood to old age, a nursery rhyme put-down can be found. For the young girl, some rhymes are training manuals in appropriate behavior. Girls should be sweet:

What are little girls made of, made of?
What are little girls made of?
"Sugar and spice, and all that's nice;
And that's what little girls are made of."[9]

Girls should be neat:

> Little Polly Flinders
> Sat among the cinders
>   Warming her pretty little toes;
> Her mother came and caught her,
> Whipped her little daughter
>   For spoiling her nice new clothes.[10]

Girls are also timid, at times cowardly:

> Little Miss Muffet
> Sat on a tuffet,
> Eating of curds and whey;
> There came a big spider,
> And sat down beside her,
> And frightened Miss Muffet away.[11]

Young women are portrayed as sitting passively at home dreaming of faraway, adventuring lovers:

> Bobby Shaftoe's gone to sea,
> With silver buckles on his knee:
> He'll come back and marry me,
> Pretty Bobby Shaftoe![12]

When dreams are fulfilled by wedding bells, the marital behavior of these young women is condemned:

> Needles and pins, needles and pins,
> When a man marries his trouble begins.[13]

> Peter, Peter, Pumpkin-eater,
> Had a wife and couldn't keep her;
> He put her in a pumpkin shell,
> And there he kept her very well.[14]

When the babies arrive, motherhood is a frustrating experience, handled incompetently:

> There was an old woman who lived in a shoe
> She had so many children she didn't know what
>   to do.
> She gave them some broth without any bread.
> She whipped them all soundly and put them to
>   bed.[15]

Woman's reward in old age is to be characterized as eccentric and ridiculous:

> Old Mother Hubbard
> Went to the cupboard,
> To get her poor dog a bone;
> But when she came there
> The cupboard was bare,
> And so the poor dog had none.

> She went to the baker's
> To buy him some bread;
> When she came back
> The dog was dead.

> She went to the undertaker's
> To buy him a coffin;
> When she got back
> The dog was laughing.[16]

The old woman is outwitted by her dog at every step. Finally, at the rhyme's end, she succumbs totally as she bows before him and proclaims herself his servant.

Of course, Mother Goose is a treasury of humor and nonsense, and when looking for sex stereotypes, there is the danger of taking oneself too seriously. Nevertheless, from the confines of a code of conformity and neatness, to the pumpkin shell, to the shoe, to her old age, the female in Mother Goose is imprisoned by sex stereotyping.

## Sleeping beauties

Folktales, sometimes called the mirror of a people, have been loved by generation after generation of children. Unfortunately, the most popular and well-known folktales, those that appear in Walt Disney movies and Little Golden Books, offer a catalogue of sex-stereotyped heroines. Marcia Lieberman analyzed the stories in *The Blue Fairy Book*, compiled by Andrew Lang, as a very influential collection containing some of the most famous stories. She finds that *The Blue Fairy Book* is a catalogue of passive and submissive female stereotypes. After Cinderella loses her slipper at the ball, she meekly sits at home and waits for the prince to ferret out the smallest foot in the kingdom. Sleeping Beauty does not even remain awake to wait for her prince to come, but sleeps throughout a major part of her story; she would have to be literally dead to become any more passive. The Princess on the Glass Hill sits on a mountain of glass waiting to be claimed as a prize by any suitor who can make it to the top. Lieberman says, "So many of the heroines of fairy stories, including the well-known Rapunzel, are locked up in towers, locked into a magic sleep, imprisoned by giants or otherwise enslaved and waiting to be rescued by a passing prince, that the helpless, imprisoned maiden is the quintessential heroine of the fairy tale."[17]

In contrast to these good and beautiful and powerless heroines, there are older women who do have power and are able to influence the action of the story of their own accord. These women, who are strong-willed and ambitious, who take action, who have power or are trying to get it, are portrayed as ugly, repulsive, and evil. For example, Cinderella's aggressive, ugly stepmother is a foil for Cinderella's beauty and passivity. Older women who are powerful and good are not human but are usually fairies, and even among the fairies powerful older women are more often evil than good. The independence and aggressiveness that is praised in males is condemned in women. The counterpart of the energetic, aspiring boy is the scheming, ambitious woman. Dan Donlan, in his article "The Negative Image of Women in Children's Literature," notes that women in folktales are either incompetent, powerless women whom men must dominate or powerful, competent monsters whom men must destroy.[18]

Fairy and folktales were written long ago when brute strength was a necessity for most activities. In order to triumph, characters who were not strong physically had to use cleverness and perseverance. Such characters were often female. It should be of prime concern to make these stories readily available for children to counterbalance the tales that are already very familiar.

## Pretty as a picture

Picture books provide an important source through which young children learn about appropriate sex role behavior. These books are read again and again before other socialization agents, such as the school and peers, have a direct impact on the young child.

Many picture books have great charm. Children delight in them and carefully examine pictures for a faithful representation of the brief text; they enthusiastically respond to the humor, the action, and themes of love, reassurance, and achievement that are often portrayed. Unfortunately, children also respond to the sex bias that too frequently is found in these books.

Lenore Weitzman and her colleagues analyzed the depiction of sex roles in those picture books that have won the Caldecott Medal given by the Children's Service Committee of the American Library Association for the most distinguished picture book of the year. The books analyzed were the Caldecott winners and runners-up between 1953 and 1971.[19]

Since women comprise 51 percent of the population, an equitable representation would suggest that girls or women should be drawn in approximately half of the pictures in these books. The researchers, however, found a situation that was far from an equitable representation. There were 261 pictures of males and only twenty-three pictures of females, a ratio of 11 to 1 in these Caldecott winners. The ratio of male to female animals was a staggering 95 to 1. In close to one-third of the sample of recent Caldecott winners, there were no women at all. Moreover, when women did appear in these Caldecott winners, they were minor, background figures.

In the Caldecott winners studied, boys were active and aggressive; the epitome of activity is Mickey in Maurice Sendak's *In the Night Kitchen* (1970). Mickey sails past his parents' bedroom into the fantastic world of the night kitchen. He punches his way through bread dough, dives into a giant milk bottle, makes an airplane, and flies into the night. In other picture books males take responsible roles. Emberly's *Drummer Hoff* (1967) has the responsibility for firing a cannon. In Sleator's *Angry Moon* (1970) the Indian boy, Lupin, rescues Lapowinsa, a girl his own age, from the moon god.

In contrast, girls are passive. They are more frequently found indoors, where they watch from windows and perform service activities for male characters. When girls are involved in danger, they are rarely able to rescue themselves, but rely on boys to save them.

Another important difference in the way males and females are portrayed is that boys are shown as friends with other boys. Male camaraderie is a theme emphasized in these books, as can be seen in Ransome's *The Fool of the World and the Flying Ship* (1968), Lionni's *Frederick* (1967), and Lobel's *Frog and Toad Are Friends* (1970). In contrast, women are defined primarily as they interact with male characters rather than as they relate to one another.

Working women, particularly those in the professions, have been almost totally omitted from picture books. Stewig and Higgs analyzed 154 randomly selected picture books.[20] Eighty-three percent of the books that portrayed women showed them only in homemaking roles. Only 17 percent of the books showed women in professional roles outside the home, and these work roles revealed some interest-

ing stereotypes. The most common occupation was that of teacher, involving 30 percent of the working women. The second most prevalent work role for women was that of maid. Fifteen percent of women who worked were cleaning; 12 percent of the working women were nuns. Although the remaining jobs did involve some variety, women were noticeably absent from such professional roles as doctors, lawyers, concert musicians, and scientists.

In the Weitzman study of the eighteen Caldecott winners, women were almost totally involved in homemaking activities. They emerged in only three other roles: one was a fairy, another a fairy godmother, the third an underwater maiden. Not one woman in this Caldecott sample had a job or profession.[21] When over 40 percent of women are working, when 90 percent of women in this country will work at some time in their lives, when motherhood is for many women a part-time ten-year commitment with years of professional work ahead, when millions of mothers with young children are working, their absence in children's books is troubling and baffling.

There are some books for children whose central purpose is to prescribe appropriate vocations and behaviors for boys and girls. In these books the sex typing is so blatant that aware children, even in the earliest grades, comment on the falsity of the reading material presented to them. One of the worst offenders is a little picture book called *I'm Glad I'm a Boy! I'm Glad I'm a Girl!* This book presents large cartoon figures of a male on one page and a female on the corresponding page. The captions beneath the figures announce the appropriate roles for each sex. For example: "Boys are doctors, girls are nurses." "Boys are pilots, girls are stewardesses." "Boys are presidents, girls are first ladies." "Boys invent things, girls use what boys invent."[22] This shocking allocation of one role to males and another of lesser prestige and remuneration to females was published as recently as 1970.

A student teacher in a children's literature class of one of the authors asked a first-grade class whether *I'm Glad I'm a Boy! I'm Glad I'm a Girl!* would be a good book to read to younger children. The awareness with which they viewed this stereotyped book is promising.

Not true. Girls can be president too. And other stuff.

No. It's too dumb and telling what boys and girls should do is wrong.

I think that it is not a good book because it doesn't have very many words and also because it doesn't tell the truth.

## "Girls—ugh"

We have been analyzing picture books and noting their lack of women and their stereotyped behaviors, roles, and occupations attributed to male and female characters. These same patterns apply, although perhaps not so severely, to many books for children in the middle and upper grades. In 1971 the Feminists on Children's Literature examined past Newbery award winners and books recommended by the American Library Association.[23] Of the forty-nine Newbery award winners that had been published at that point, they found that books about boys outnumbered books about girls by a margin of 3 to 1, and in the American Library Association lists of notable books, the ratio was 2 to 1.

In books for children in the middle and older grades there are often the stereotyped behaviors and comments and character portrayals that express contempt for the experience of being a girl or a woman. Following are but a very few of the sample quotes that denigrate women that we found as we reviewed children's books.

"I guess you'll go right and tell." he said. "Just like a girl, can't keep anything to herself."

> *Virginia Sorensen*, Miracles on Maple Hill, *New York, Harcourt Brace Jovanovich, 1956, p.73; Newbery Winner, 1957*

"Aw, you're just a dumb girl," sneered Scooter. "Yes, a dumb girl," echoed Robert.

> *Beverly Cleary*, Henry Huggins, *New York, Morrow, 1950, pp. 42–43*

"I don't know anything about him," snapped Mary.

"I know you don't," Basil answered. "You don't know anything. Girls never do. . . ."

> *Frances Hodgson Burnett*, The Secret Garden, *Philadelphia, Lippincott, 1938, p. 11*

At times Rass felt a little sorry for Sally having to be a girl and not being able to do anything about it.

> *Bernice Rabe*, Rass, *Nashville, Thomas Nelson, 1973, p. 65*

As these quotes suggest, girls are viewed as dishonorable, dumb, cowardly, and, quite simply, inferior.

In books that are about girls, feminist critics have noted the prevalence of what they have termed the "cop-out" book. These books often begin with a courageous, competent, and intriguing heroine who, by the story's end, grows up, succumbs to the demands of womanhood, and relinquishes at least some of her wild, spunky, imaginative ways. In this process of maturation she becomes quieter, more passive, more demure, and less interesting. This metamorphosis usually comes toward the end of the book, sometimes happening so rapidly and demanding such inconsistency on the part of the heroine that the integrity of the character portrayal is violated.

One such "cop-out" book is *Veronica Ganz* (1968), by Marilyn Sachs. No one in the sixth grade fooled with Veronica Ganz. She was the biggest kid in the class and had early squelched all challenges to her authority. Considered the class bully, Veronica is a highly realized character, whose anger and aggressiveness are made understandable. The child of divorced parents, living in somewhat strained conditions, she remembers a time when life was happier, when her mother's face was younger and smiling. The memories and the contrast between past and present make her feel like lashing out and hitting.

A new boy, small, clever Peter Wedemeyer, joins the sixth grade. He teases Veronica and outfoxes her at all her own tricks. Peter's schemes climax when he forms a vigilante committee. A group of boys, each of whom Veronica had bested alone, join forces and beat her up. When Peter is terribly ashamed and embarrassed at what he has done, Veronica realizes that she has both lost and won. She discovers that her secret weapon is that she is a girl. In an apparently instantaneous transformation, it appears that Veronica will exchange her aggressiveness and hostility for the subtle power that comes with being female. The final note does not ring true.

In *A Girl Called Al* (1969), by Constance Greene, Al (short for Alexandria), goes through a sudden metamorphosis for which the reader is totally unprepared. Al is chubby, wears glasses, has very straight pigtails, and is a self-avowed nonconformist. She wants to take shop to make a bookcase, but the school will not allow it. She is furious, so Mr. Richards, her apartment building superintendent, offers to teach her and her friend how to make a bookcase. Much of the book centers on the close friendship of these three and the girls' reactions to Mr. Richards' death. Suddenly, within the last few pages of the book, some remarkable changes occur in Al. She becomes thin and pretty, exchanges her pigtails for a more feminine style, and is on her way to popularity. Al's friend notes wistfully that she misses Al's pigtails. We miss them too, and the nonconformity and individuality that they represent.

In the Newbery award winner *Caddie Woodlawn* (1935) the main character is not angry or a nonconformist; instead she is spontaneous, spunky, mischievous, and courageous. And it is these characteristics that she must shed, at least in part, in order to emerge as a woman. The book opens: "In 1864 Caddie Woodlawn was eleven, and as wild a little tomboy as ever ran the woods of Western Wisconsin."[24] Instead of learning to cook and sew and be mannerly, Caddie romps with her brothers, Tom and Warren. She is a fair-minded girl and a courageous one. When Obidiah, one of the roughest, most obstreperous older boys in her class, bullies the younger pupils, she does not hesitate to take him on. When fear of a rumored Indian attack creates suspicion, distrust, and potential war, it is Caddie who achieves a truce, albeit an uneasy one. Finally Caddie's father, whom she loves and respects, talks to her about growing up and offers the following advice:

It's a strange thing, but somehow we expect more of girls than of boys. It is the sisters and wives and mothers, you know, Caddie, who keep the world sweet and beautiful. What a rough world it would be if there were only men and boys in it, doing things in their rough way! A woman's task is to teach them gentleness and courtesy and love and kindness. It's a big task, too, Caddie —harder than cutting trees or building mills or damming rivers. It takes nerve and courage and patience, but good women have those things. They have them just as much as the men who build bridges and cane woods through the wilderness. A woman's work is something fine and noble to grow up to, and it is just as important as a man's. But no man could ever do it so well. . . . Do you think you would like to be growing up into that woman now? How about it, Caddie, have you run with the colts long enough?[25]

The man offering this philosophy is honest and well intentioned; the advice sounds noble, and Caddie decides that "her own wild past has ended." In the role outlined for Caddie there is room for courage, but it must be of a quieter, gentler kind. In short, as Caddie grows up, her vitality must be subdued and her unique spark put out.

In *The Witch of Blackbird Pond,* a 1959 Newbery winner written by Elizabeth George Speare, romance brings a change in the heroine, an immediate lessening of her independence and self reliance. After Kit's beloved grandfather dies, Kit finds herself without a guardian or money. She bravely sets forth by herself from Barbados to the home of her aunt and uncle in Wethersfield, Connecticut.

Kit's spontaneity and high spirits are out of tune with the solemn puritanism that pervades Wethersfield in 1687. During her journey to Wethersfield she gets a taste of the disapproval that will follow her about there. When a young child's doll falls overboard, Kit leaps into the icy water to save it for the girl. The passengers and sailors are aghast that she stays above water. One of the tests for witchcraft, she learns, is the ability to float.

Kit finds life in her relatives' household difficult. She is unused to physical labor, to the long, sober religious ceremonies, to the bigotry that surfaces in the accusation of Hannah Tupper, an elderly Quaker, as a witch.

When sickness sweeps through Wethersfield, many of the townspeople need a scapegoat, and they seize upon Hannah. In a dramatic climax, Kit rescues Hannah, but finds that she herself is then accused of witchcraft. The rescuer becomes the rescuee, as Kit is saved by Nat Eaton, with whom a romance has been developing throughout the book. At the book's conclusion Kit realizes that she loves Nat, that the plans she has been making for her future are irrelevant, that it would not matter where she went, to Barbados or up and down the river, so long as she were with him. Nat is made of hard New England stock, and she can

lean on him. This new dependency and relinquishing of her own goals comes as a disappointment in a young woman who, to this point, has been a passionately independent thinker following no drummer but her own.

These four books are very well written and, although each is slightly marred by a betrayal of the main characters' inner reality, they are included in the listing of nonsexist books at the chapter's end. Another book, not as well written as these and far more disturbing in its character portrayal, is *The Boyhood of Grace Jones* (1972) by Jane Langton. This story takes place during the late 1930s and chronicles Grace Jones's first year at Winslow S. DeForest Junior High School. Grace has a unique style of her own: she has short brown hair, wears her father's blue serge navy middy, strides rather than walks, and on her first day of school manages to beat one of the strongest boys in school in a wrestling match. Grace practices push-ups in her spare time and dreams of becoming a sailor. Another aspect of Grace's unique style is her contempt for girls; she merges all girls into a detestable mass of incompetence:

It was just that girls (ugh!) were so stupid. They were so silly. All they cared about was stupid silly things like clothes and movie stars and chasing boys, or even painting themselves all over with stupid silly powder and lipstick, like Dot. And they never did anything more exciting than maybe taking stupid piano lessons. Grace herself took piano lessons, but she hated it. Boys were the ones who did all the really interesting things. And they didn't care about silly stupid things like how they looked. They were too busy collecting rocks, like her father, or making radios like Will, or inventing light bulbs like Thomas Edison, or flying the Atlantic Ocean like Lindbergh.[26]

The last quarter of the book documents the transformation of Grace Jones. For her birthday Grace's father fulfills his daughter's dream by taking her sailing. Grace's stomach and the water do not agree, and she is thoroughly sick. After her sailing fiasco, Grace begins to curl her hair and to wear an angora sweater and a gold locket. As the book closes, Grace is busily at work on a movie star scrap book. Grace stereotypes males and females and feels contempt for girls. Gradually she sheds her "tomboyish" behavior and, retaining nothing of her former spunk, conforms totally to the image she has previously despised.

## Snips and snails and puppy-dogs' tails

In *The Rooftop Mystery* (1968), by Joan Lexau, two boys, Sam and Albert, are helping Sam's family move. They are asked to carry a doll to the family's new apartment. The thought of carrying a big doll through the city is so abhorrent to the boys that they run to a rooftop, leave the doll there, and go in search of a girl to carry the doll for them so that they will not have to be seen with it.

> Girls demand books that demonstrate maternal feelings in action. Their sympathy is won by heroines who are kind to the afflicted, charitable to the poor, devoted to the sick; by those who take up bravely the daily tasks of the household so as to provide for the loved ones not only the security of affection, but well-being, material comfort, a happy life. Boys demand books of valor, where cowards make a poor showing, where liars are unmasked and punished, and the vainglorious are derided; stories of generous rivalries, where the best man wins; adventure and vicissitude which exalt the human and increase his strength.
>
> *Paul Hazard*, Books, Children and Men, *Boston, Horn Book, 1944, p. 168*

This brief story is a devastating comment on sex roles. It is obviously an expression of male contempt for girls' doll play. It also illustrates a code of behavior that denies boys a full range of activities and emotions.

Another book that illustrates, in greater detail and complexity, the strict code of behavior that the young male must follow is *Miracles on Maple Hill*, the 1957 Newbery winner by Virginia Sorensen. Ever since Marly's father returned from a prisoner of war camp, he has seemed bitter and angry. The family moves to the country to the mother's childhood home, beautiful Maple Hill, in the hope that a miracle will be worked and that father will become himself again.

There is an intense rivalry between Marly and her older brother, twelve-year old Joe. The brother and sister continually compete with one another to win parental approval. However, whenever Marly beats Joe at something, she lets Joe win their next competition because, "Boys were queer. They seemed afraid they'd stop being boys altogether if they couldn't be first at everything."[27] Marly sums up the difference between herself and Joe in the following comment:

For the millionth time, she was glad she wasn't a boy. It was all right for girls to be scared or silly or even ask dumb questions. Everybody just laughed and thought it was funny. But if anybody caught Joe asking a dumb question or even thought he was the littlest bit scared, he went red and purple and white. Daddy was even something like that, as old as he was.[28]

This book outlines a code of behavior that is less demanding for girls than for boys. Girls can be scared, silly, incompetent. They can cry; they can afford to lose. Boys, on the other hand, must always be intelligent and brave. They must be perennial winners. Boys never cry, even when sickness or death threatens and tears may provide a healthy release for sorrow. A whole range of emotions is denied male characters. One can imagine Joe having a heart attack before he reaches fifty-five.

These books also demand extraordinary behavior in terms of the occupations to which males must aspire. They must aim high and attempt to become astronauts or even president of the nation. Boys are rarely shown performing household tasks or service functions. Male characters in children's books are not preparing boys to live life as it really is in the 1970s. As one male columnist notes:

I discovered at a relatively early age, that I was not a prince. It is nice for boys to know that it is possible to be a sea captain, a shepherd, or a sheriff, but what is he to think when he takes an office or a factory job, rents an apartment and enters battle with urban dirt and cockroaches. . . . Pity the poor little boy who grows up into a world his reading books never prepared him for.[29]

### Nonsexist children's books

If women are to be treated as full human beings, we must confront sexist bias in the same way we have begun to confront racist and religious bias: recognize its existence, look for its causes, and then, step by step and little by little, work toward elimination of the causes and the bias. Change can't be made by fiat or legislation. It can't be made by committees or by handwringing. But it can be made if all concerned individuals, women and men alike, become personally accountable for seeing that it happens.

Every teacher knows that what we read, both on the printed line and between the lines, affects what and how we think. It is especially important, then, that all publications—periodicals, newsletters, book lists, announcements, programs—

treat women fairly. We are not asking publications to become propaganda organs for women's rights: we are only asking them not to be, consciously or unconsciously, advocates for current negative conditions and attitudes.[30]

This quote, from the "Guidelines for Publications" by the NCTE Committee on the Role and Image of Women in the Council and the Profession, is indicative of the growing concern about the stereotyped portrayal of male and female in all written material. It is hopeful, yet even within such burgeoning awareness, new difficulties and issues emerge.

"Would you tell me, please, which way I ought to go from here?" asked Alice in Wonderland of the Cheshire Cat.
"That depends a good deal on where you want to get to," said the Cat.
"I don't much care where—" said Alice.
"Then it doesn't matter which way you go," said the Cat.[31]

We who are concerned about nonsexist portrayals in books that children read could well take some time to ponder the Cheshire Cat's advice. What exactly is a nonsexist children's book? Is a nonsexist book simply one about a female character? Is a nonsexist book one in which female characters show that they can emulate males and display their own share of independence, daring, and aggression? Where do we really want to get to? There are now numerous lists of nonsexist books available, many from public libraries and school systems. When one begins analyzing books on these lists, there is much agreement to be found, but also disparities and confusions. Occasionally books that are considered sexist by one group can be found on another group's nonsexist list.

Out of this mild chaos some sensible definitions of nonsexist books have begun to emerge. The Feminists on Children's Media note, "a nonsexist portrayal would offer the girl reader a positive image of woman's physical, emotional, and intellectual potential . . . free of traditionally imposed limitations."[32] One member of the staff of the Feminist Press held a community workshop on children's books, and from this workshop, the following definition emerged. A nonsexist children's book is one "that conveys the concept of personhood . . . it recognizes and respects the human qualities of people not demeaned or distorted by sex, race, ethnic, or economic background."[33]

It would be hard to argue with such definitions, although when one begins to apply them to books, the need for greater specificity quickly becomes apparent. Nevertheless, they do provide a basic semantic framework on which our discussions will be based. In the following pages, themes that emerge in nonsexist children's books will be identified, and selected books that demonstrate these themes will be discussed.

## Nonsexist portrayals in picture books

There are several elements that comprise nonsexist picture books about female characters. One is the inclusion of a nonstereotyped heroine who is confident and independent, who masters a challenge with competence and courage, or who shows spirit and inventiveness in her daily encounters with her own immediate world. For example, Astrid Lindgren's *Of Course Polly Can Ride a Bike* (1971) stresses competence and bravery as its four-year-old heroine learns to ride a two-wheeler. *Christina Katerina and the Box* (1971), by Patricia Lee Gauch, is a tribute to a girl's imagination, resourcefulness, and perseverance. When Christina's mother gets a new refrigerator, Christina takes the discarded cardboard box, and in her play it becomes a castle, a clubhouse, a racing car, and a summer mansion. Another girl with an exuberant, tenacious approach to life is portrayed in *Don't You Re-*

*member?* (1973), by Lucille Clifton. Desire Mary Tate remembers everything. She is black, is four years old, and likes to be called Tate; when she grows up she plans to work at the plant just like her daddy. Her father promises to take her to the plant "next time," but he never seems to remember. Her mother, who works in a bakery, promises to bring home a black cake with *Tate* written in pink letters, but her mother never seems to remember. Her brothers promise that she can drink coffee, but they never seem to remember either. However, when Tate forgets her own birthday, her family does remember. Evaline Ness's illustrations add warmth and vitality to the story of this young black girl.

Other nonsexist picture books depict girls in occupations traditionally reserved for males. Sometimes the aspirations occur only in the girl's fantasy world, and there is no suggestion that they will become a reality. In *Hurray for Captain Jane* (1971), by Sam Reavin, Jane soaks in her bathtub and daydreams. She imagines that she is the captain of an ocean liner, and she saves her ship from crashing into a giant iceberg. Jane's vision of herself as an intrepid ship captain vanishes as the bathtub water goes down the drain.

In other books aspirations do not take the form of private fantasy. Instead they are very real and the female main character must struggle or prove herself before she is allowed to pursue a certain job or career. However, these books typically portray the heroines as so dedicated and competent that success in their chosen occupations seems assured.

In M. B. Goffstein's *Two Piano Tuners* (1970) Debbie wants to become a piano tuner, like her grandfather, Reuben Weinstock, reputed to be one of the world's best piano tuners. Reuben cannot accept Debbie's ambitions; instead he wants to see her become a concert pianist or at least a piano teacher. Debbie follows her grandfather and observes closely as he tunes pianos and without his knowledge tries to tune a neighbor's piano herself. Reuben then realizes that Debbie must not be made into something she does not want to be simply because it meets his expectations. Finally, he begins to teach her to become a piano tuner.

*Firegirl* (1972), by Gibson Rich, shows the female main character encountering more widespread opposition. When Brenda's father tells her that only boys can become firemen, she is momentarily crushed. However, she simply cannot take such a ridiculous pronouncement seriously. When she rescues a forgotten pet rabbit from a burning building, she earns a place as the fire department's volunteer firegirl.

In some picture books that depict females aspiring to roles and occupations that have been stereotyped as male, hostility and antagonism between male and female characters become quite explicit. In *I Can Be Anything You Can Be* (1973), by Joel Rothman, boys announce to girls a catalogue of jobs that boys can do but girls cannot. For example, one boy states, "I can be a trombone player, but I've never seen a girl play trombone." Girls, pictured on the corresponding pages, answer the challenges, retorting that girls not only can do these jobs but often can do them better. This book has sparked differing reactions among feminist critics. Some feel that its stress on boy-girl rivalry only stimulates an unhealthy competitiveness. Others assert that this competitiveness is real and should be dealt with rather than ignored.

In Norma Klein's *Girls Can Be Anything* (1973) potential animosity between male and female is resolved more amicably. A young boy and girl play many games together, but the roles are always stereotyped: Adam is the doctor and Marina is his nurse; he is a pilot, she a stewardess; he is president, she his wife. Marina does not like the roles she is assigned and asks her parents if she must accept them. Her parents explain that women can be doctors, pilots, and although there has never been a woman president in the United States, Golda Meir and Indira Ghandi have been leaders in their respective countries. Marina, in turn, explains this to Adam, and their play becomes more equal.

Other picture books present the adult world with women functioning in a wide range of nonstereotyped professions. *My Doctor* (1973), by Harlow Rockwell, presents a little boy's visit to his female doctor. The visit is handled matter-of-factly, with no surprise or worry expressed because the doctor is a woman. Eve Merriam's *Mommies at Work* (1961) shows women in dual roles. They are mommies who find missing mittens, kiss hurt places, and tuck in favorite toys. These mommies are also employed in jobs that run a gamut ranging from teachers to bridge builders. The book concludes as these working mothers do what they like to do best, return home to their waiting children.

Joe Lasker's *Mothers Can Do Anything* (1972) shows women in a variety of ages, colors, shapes, and sizes doing jobs that are usually reserved for men. There is a woman digging ditches with a satisfied look on her face and a grandmother who is building big houses. There is a woman dentist with a male assistant, and there are a woman principal and a woman judge, both of whom are black. Books such as *Mommies at Work* and *Mothers Can Do Anything* are one-sided, for they offer no portrayal of what fathers do. However, they do serve to balance the preponderance of books showing mothers waving good-bye from windows and doorsteps as fathers go forth to their various jobs.

## Wonder women: the female in fantasy

The special uniqueness of fantasy is that it tells of characters and creatures who do not exist and of events that could not possibly occur. There has been such prolific development of modern fanciful stories that it is impossible to consider all those in which women play prominent roles. In this section we review some of the recent imaginative stories that cleverly twist traditional fairy tale plots out of sexist knots. We also discuss the intrepid, self-assured girls who enter fantastic worlds, and the remarkable female characters who emerge in our real world. In addition, we briefly analyze the role women and girls have played in science fiction for children.

Feminists have criticized fairy and folktales for their stereotyped characters, beautiful passive damsels in distress, imprisoned on glass hills, in towers, in seemingly interminable sleep, waiting for their princes to come. Currently there are some fanciful picture books in which the female main characters are breaking out of the enchanted prisons and out of the stereotypes.

Jane Yolen's *The Girl Who Loved the Wind* (1972) is an example of the imprisoned girl who liberates herself. The story tells of Danina, whose father so loves her that he wants to protect her from all harm and unpleasantness. He brings her to a great house surrounded by walls and water where she grows up knowing nothing of the world. Although the father tries to keep everyone from Danina, the wind, who cannot be kept away, tells her of a world that is not always kind and not always pleasant. The wind's world is sometimes sad, sometimes happy, but different every day. Danina listens to the wind and comes to understand that her magnificent palace is a magnificent prison. She lets the wind fill her cape, and she sails off to the ever-changing world.

Jay Williams, with Friso Henstra as the illustrator, has written a number of picture books that cleverly break heroines out of stereotyped characterizations. In *The Practical Princess* (1969), Princess Bedelia is given the gifts of beauty, charm, and common sense. Although there is nothing wrong with beauty and charm, it is her common sense that serves her best. When a dragon demands Bedelia as his prize, there is no time to advertise for a prince to rescue her, so, through her common sense, she rescues herself. When she is imprisoned in a tower by an undesirable suitor, Lord Garp, she again uses her common sense to save not only herself but an enchanted prince as well.

*Petronella* (1971) is another princess who breaks with fairy tale tradition. When Petronella comes of age, she is determined to seek her fortune and perhaps rescue a prince if she has to, although everyone tells her that it is impossible for a girl to do such things. Petronella does find an enchanted prince, but he is so lazy and complacent that he neither wants nor deserves rescuing. The story concludes as Petronella brings home an enchanter, who has turned out to be far more to her liking than the prince, and she is wondering how to explain such an unconventional suitor to her parents.

In *The Silver Whistle* (1971) Prudence, the heroine, is cheerful, wise, and homely. She rejects the opportunity to become beautiful, noting, "I don't think I want to be beautiful. . . . I might be different outside but I'd be the same inside, and I'm used to me the way I am."[34] She eventually does win herself a prince, not because she is the most beautiful but because she suits him best.

In *Fairy Tales for Today's Children* (1974), Richard Gardner, a child psychiatrist, has rewritten fairy tales to "make use of the psychological insights available in the twentieth century and retain the themes and drama of tales created in the past."[35] His rewritten stories often change the passive nature of the female characters, who, in his stories, rely on themselves rather than on princes or fairy godmothers. In his story "Cinderelma," for example, the abused stepdaughter longs to attend the ball and wishes for a fairy godmother to help her. But no matter how hard she wishes, no fairy godmother appears. Consequently, Cinderelma must rely upon herself; she borrows beautiful clothes from her stepsisters and, since she has no carriage, walks to the palace. When she arrives, the prince dances with her all night. The prince and Cinderelma plan to marry, and Cinderelma moves to the castle while preparations are made for the royal wedding. Cinderelma finds that she is bored by castle life and that after a while she and the prince really have very little to talk about. They decide not to marry after all. Cinderelma has learned to become a skillful seamstress while in the palace, and she eventually earns enough money to open her own dress shop. As time passes she becomes well known for the fine quality of her gowns. She marries the printer who has a shop next door and with whom she has much in common and a lot to talk about.

Several of the modern fantasy stories are developed around the concept of the imaginary world or kingdom, and often it is a girl who crosses from our world into the unreal one. Hans Christian Andersen has been called the originator of the modern fairy tale, and in "The Snow Queen," often considered his masterpiece, he portrays a girl who, through her courage and her love, invades the Snow Queen's ice palace. Kay and Gerda are two real children, the closest of friends. A piece of glass, a sliver from a mirror that makes people see only the ugliness and worthlessness around them, lodges in Kay's eye. Everything that he had once found beautiful now appears horrid

to him. He leaves his friend, Gerda, and is carried off to the Snow Queen's palace, where he finds that the cold iciness suits him and where he plays "the ice puzzle of reason."

Gerda loves her friend and is determined to find him. As she journeys, she comes under the spell of a witch, meets a prince and princess, and is captured by a robber band. She is befriended by a wild robber maiden, a marvelous character, independent and uncontrollable, who first threatens Gerda's life and then, won over by the girl's kindness and her story, gives her a reindeer to transport her to the Snow Queen's palace. Gerda is also helped along her way by the Lapp woman and by the Finn woman, who decide against endowing Gerda with the strength of twelve men because such brute strength is worthless when compared to Gerda's innocence and her love. Gerda enters the Snow Queen's palace and her warmth and love melt the lump of ice that has become Kay's heart. In this superb adventure story underlined by subtle symbolism, we find a female protagonist and a female villain and the thrust of the action is carried forward by a series of dynamic, unique female characters.

L. Frank Baum, in *The Wizard of Oz* (1900), presents another well-known heroine, Dorothy, who enters the enchanted land of Oz when her house is swept away in a storm. Although Dorothy is a courageous heroine who carries out the two feats that liberate Oz, the killing of the wicked witches, both acts are accomplished accidentally. One wicked witch is killed when Dorothy's house accidentally lands on her and the other when Dorothy, unaware that contact with water is the witch's Achilles' heel, douses her and causes her to melt.

With a good deal more aplomb, the intrepid Alice handles her adventures in the far more complex and elaborate Wonderland. *Alice's Adventures in Wonderland*, by Lewis Carroll, opens with a restless, bored Alice ready for something unusual to happen. The White Rabbit appears, and immediately Alice follows him down the rabbit hole. Despite a dizzying barrage of size changes, from 10 inches high to towering over all about her, Alice manages to keep her head (regardless of its size) and her wits about her. True, the madness of Wonderland has Alice quite confused: " 'Who are you?' asked the Caterpillar. This was not an encouraging opening for a conversation. Alice replied, rather shyly, 'I—I hardly know, sir, just at present—at least I know who I *was* when I got up this morning, but I think I must have been changed several times since then.' "[36] Nevertheless, through a series of madcap interviews with an array of incredible characters from the Caterpillar, to the Duchess, whose baby turns into a pig; to the Cheshire Cat, who leaves his smile behind; to the Queen of Hearts, the "embodiment of ungovernable passion—a blind and aimless fury,"[37] Alice manages to stay remarkably in control of the chaos about her.

*Adventures in Wonderland* and *Through the Looking Glass* contain some of the most-quoted lines in literature and some of the most famous nonsense verse. Sir John Tenniel's illustrations of the remarkable Alice are superb, the somber face framed by long, bedraggled hair; it is regrettable that for most children the Alice who comes to mind is probably the sweeter, tidier girl of the Disney movie.

We have been discussing some of the realistic heroines who enter imaginary worlds. There are also some very well-known magical heroines who dazzle and baffle their friends and neighbors in the everyday world of reality. *Pippi Longstockings* (1950), by Astrid Lindgren, presents one of these fantastic females living in the real world. Pippi is a superchild, a nine-year-old who lives without supervision and handles every situation she encounters with unruffled competence. No one tells Pippi what to do or when to do it, and she is the envy of the neighborhood children.

It is an east wind that blows the remarkable *Mary Poppins* (1934), by P. L. Travers, into the real world of the Banks nursery. The Banks children soon learn that their new nurse

Alice's Adventures in Wonderland

is someone out of the ordinary, a character with nothing saccharine or insipid about her. Tart, vinegary, sometimes cross and snappish, but with a soft spot for Bert the chimney sweep, Mary Poppins introduces her charges to magical people and marvelous places. Jane and Michael Banks adore Mary Poppins and love the adventures she takes them on. Lightened by laughing gas, they attend a tea party suspended in midair. They find a compass and journey about the world, an adventure unfortunately marred by racial stereotyping. They watch the stars being spread across the sky. When the wind changes, Mary Poppins leaves, lifted into the air as the wind catches her umbrella.

The eight-year-old in Roald Dahl's *The Magic Finger* (1966) is a normal girl except for one magical power. When she puts the magic finger on someone, there is no telling what will happen. She finds hunting abhorrent and cannot bear the thought of animals being killed for pleasure. When she sees the Gregg family returning from a hunting expedition, she is infuriated and turns the magic finger on them. As Mr. Gregg awakens the next morning, he tries to check his watch and pulls out a wing instead of an arm. Every member of the family has turned into a tiny winged creature, and four enormous ducks with arms that hold guns threaten to kill them. After the Greggs promise never to hunt again, they are returned to their former size and shape. The girl, satisfied with their reformation, goes off in search of someone else who may need the magic finger.

Another form of modern fantasy revolves around the device of a talking inanimate object, most frequently a vehicle or a toy. There are few portrayals of female vehicles and, indeed, feminists have commented that although our language refers to cars, boats, and trains as "she," in children's literature they all turn into

The Magic Finger

males. However, in the picture book *Katy and the Big Show* (1943), by Virginia Lee Burton, we have the story of a competent, persevering female steam shovel who plows out an entire city by herself.

Female dolls who come alive are more common. Carolyn Sherwin Baily's *Miss Hickory*, winner of the 1947 Newbery Medal, is a twig doll with a hickory nut head who has been left behind by the children. Businesslike and thoroughly able to take care of herself, with a little help from Crow, she faces the adversity of abandonment with courage.

*Impunity Jane* (1954), by Rumer Godden, is a finger-sized doll who is eager for a taste of life's adventures. After being left untouched in the dollhouse for generations, she finally finds the perfect home for herself in the pocket of a seven-year-old boy.

A number of modern fantasies are about talking animals, but very few of these animals are females. Remember the ratio of male to female animals in one sample of Caldecotts studied was 95 to 1. However, perhaps quality helps make up for quantity, and in E. B. White's *Charlotte's Web* (1952) we have the remarkable Charlotte A. Cavatica, one of the best-known and most-cried-over characters in children's literature. Charlotte is a spider, shrewd, persevering, and loyal, who saves her dear friend, Wilbur, from becoming ham and bacon by spinning the words "Some Pig" in

Charlotte's Web

her web. She follows this by advertising Wilbur as "terrific," "radiant," and "humble."

When Wilbur asks Charlotte, "Why did you do all this for me? . . . I don't deserve it. I've never done anything for you," Charlotte responds:

You have been my friend. . . . That in itself is a tremendous thing. I wove my web for you because I liked you. After all, what's a life anyway? We're born, we live a little while, we die. A spider's life can't help being something of a mess, with all this trapping and eating flies. By helping you, perhaps I was trying to lift up my life a trifle; Heaven knows anyone's life can stand a little of that.[38]

Janice Tate, in her article "Sexual Bias in Science Fiction for Children," notes that science fiction has traditionally been considered "boys' literature."[39] The characters in this genre have been mainly white, middle-class males. For example, in science fiction by Robert Heinlein, females are either not present or are left working and worrying in the kitchen. The exciting books by John Christopher are also antifeminine. His trilogy, including *The White Mountains, The City of Gold and Lead*, and *The Pool of Fire*, deals with humanity's struggle to win back freedom in a world controlled by invaders from space, and it is noteworthy that no girl or woman joins the colony of the free. Even worse, the invaders keep the most attractive girls in coffins as objects of beauty.

Tate's study is optimistic, for she finds that as science fiction develops, it is written more with girls in mind and more frequently includes significant female characters. One of the finest nonsexist science fiction books is Madeleine L'Engle's *A Wrinkle in Time*, winner of the 1963 Newbery Medal. On a stormy night when no one should have been out, Meg, her precocious five-year-old brother, Charles Wallace, and their mother, Mrs. Murray, a scientist with doctor's degrees in biology and bacteriology, are getting warm drinking cocoa. A strange old woman, Mrs. Whatsit, joins the family group, and as she leaves she counsels them, "There is no such thing as a tesseract." Mrs. Who, Mrs. Whatsit, and Mrs. Which guide Meg, Charles, and a friend, Calvin O'Keefe, on a strange interplanetary journey in search of Meg's and Charles's father, a brilliant scientist who has disappeared. They travel by means of a tesseract, a wrinkle in space and time. The children learn from their three guides that, in the process of finding their father, they will be involved in a classic struggle of good against evil.

The children begin their struggle in earnest on the planet of Camazotz, where the inhabitants seem to be automatons, behaving as though they had no will of their own. The planet is controlled by It, who urges the three children to come to him, for he is peace, utter rest, and freedom from all responsibility. Charles Wallace confronts It and is unable to resist Its power. Meg and Calvin find Mr. Murray, and, in danger of becoming submerged within It themselves, they tesser away from the planet of Camazotz, leaving Charles Wallace behind. It is Meg who has to go back again, to the center of evil, to rescue her brother. She has nothing to fight It with—except love. Like Gerda in "The Snow Queen," Meg journeys to the heart of her enemy and is able to conquer, her only weapon being the ability to love.

Other modern fantasies involve intrepid girls in strange manipulations of time. In Penelope Farmer's *Charlotte Sometimes* (1969) Charlotte finds herself existing in two worlds. Sometimes she wakes into the everyday world of her boarding school and at other times she wakes as Clare back in the days of World War I; during her time as Clare a double functions in her place and time.

Eleanor Cameron's *The Court of the Stone Children*, winner of the 1974 National Book Award, is about Nina, a contemporary girl fascinated by museums, who meets Dominique, who lived during the time of Napoleon. At first Nina is stunned by the notion of ghosts, but gradually she redefines her conception of time. The two girls, one from the past, the other from the present, manage to clear Dominique's father of a murder for which he was unjustly convicted.

The powerful and moving 1958 Carnegie Medal winner, *Tom's Midnight Garden*, by Philippa Pearce, is about Tom, a resentful visitor to his relative's flat until he discovers a strange and wonderful garden, one that appears only at night. In the garden Tom finds the friend he has been longing for, Hattie, a girl who loves to play with bows and arrows, climb trees, and go skating. Tom learns that when he enters the garden, he goes into the past, to the late 1800s, and that there no one except Hattie can see him. On the final night of his visit, Tom is distressed to discover that Hattie and the garden have vanished. Only then does he learn that the elderly landlady of the house has been dreaming of her childhood in the garden and her dreams have been the key to Tom's entry into the past.

## Realistic fiction for children in the middle and upper grades

### Keeping the home fires burning

If a man does not keep pace with his companions, perhaps it is because he hears a different drummer. Let him step to the music which he hears, however measured or far away.

*Henry David Thoreau*, Walden

After a few twists in our sexist language, this quote from Thoreau captures the essence of many of the nonsexist heroines in realistic children's fiction. Each of these heroines is a girl seeking her own unique personhood in her own unique way.

One researcher studied heroines in notable children's fiction published between 1960 and 1970. She found that the new female protagonist does not conform to the stereotyped version of femininity. She is not beautiful, passive, dependent, or gentle. Her life does not revolve around attracting boys. She is not an outstanding success in her social life, in scholarship, or in athletic activities. "She is, for the most part, an uneasy, independent, critical, nonconformist; she behaves as she feels and does not try to fit into the conventional life patterns around her."[40] In the following pages we discuss a small selection of books with heroines who barter away no measure of their own independence and uniqueness.

The prototype of the independent heroine emerged not in the 1960s but in the 1800s. Elizabeth Janeway says of Jo March, the protagonist in *Little Women:*

Jo is a unique creation; the one young woman in nineteenth century fiction who maintains her individual independence, who gives up no part of her autonomy as payment for being born a woman—and who gets away with it. Jo is the tomboy dream come true, the dream of growing up into full humanity with all its potentialities instead of into limited femininity: of looking after oneself and paying one's way and doing effective work in the real world instead of learning how to please a man who will look after you, as Meg and Amy do with pious pleasure. . . . It's no secret that Jo's story is the heart of *Little Women.*[41]

Although Jo may be responsible for the lasting response to *Little Women,* it is not Jo's story alone, but a story about a family as well. And many of the most interesting female characters in children's books fight their struggles for independence and autonomy against the background of home and family.

For some female protagonists the fight is one of sheer survival, of keeping families intact against the impingement of outside forces. *Where the Lilies Bloom* (1969), by Vera and Bill Cleaver, is the story of an Appalachian family's courageous attempt to stay together and take care of themselves after the death of their father, Roy Wither. Above all, it is the story of Mary Call, the fourteen-year-old who, since both parents are dead, becomes the head of the family and struggles desperately for their survival. She, with the help of her younger brother, buries her father at night and then hides his death for fear the county people will come and divide the family. She must also earn enough money to buy food and clothing, and this she manages to do, barely, by learning wildcrafting, the gathering and selling of medicinal herbs that grow on the mountain slopes. Mary Call copes with death, poverty, hunger, and the constant fear of losing her family—but she survives with fierce independence and dignity.

Another, more recent story of a young girl's holding a family together is *Under the Haystack* (1973), by Patricia Engelbrecht. When thirteen-year-old Sandy finds her parents have deserted the children, she keeps the farm going, cares for her younger sisters, and hides the desertion for fear that local authorities will break the family up. Although Sandy lacks the dimension and shrewd, fierce resourcefulness of Mary Call, *Under the Haystack* is a warm story of a self-reliant girl who struggles admirably with a lonely and difficult situation. In Norma Johnston's *Of Time and of Seasons* (1975), Bridget is also a young woman who helps keep her family together. Although her parents are close and loving, each member of her family is so individualistic and creative that Bridget's interpersonal sensitivity and empathy is necessary for family harmony.

For other heroines the burden is not one of

family survival but of learning to perceive a certain member of the family with greater realism and honesty. One such story is *Queenie Peavy* (1966), by Robert Burch. Growing up in Georgia during the Depression, Queenie Peavy has a chip on her shoulder so heavy it threatens to weigh her down. Her mother works long hours at the plant: her father, whom she idolizes, is serving a jail term, and her classmates taunt her about it. Queenie handles her situation with strength and a veneer of toughness. She is the only girl in Cotton Junction who can chew tobacco and spit it with deadly accuracy. She is in constant trouble with the principal and lives on the edge of expulsion. Competent, clever, and tough, Queenie finally understands that her father comes nowhere near to measuring up to the man she has envisioned him to be; eventually this realization helps her grow in wisdom and compassion.

*The Truth About Mary Rose* (1973), by Marilyn Sachs, is also a story about a girl who must reassess her idolatry of a family member. Everything seems to be going right for Mary Rose Ramirez. She has a loving family and each of her parents is successful in his or her own right; her mother is a dentist and her painter father, who has always done the family's cooking, is just beginning to be appreciated by critics and buyers. Mary Rose is also happy that she is named after a family heroine who died in a fire after saving her brother and other families in their apartment house. When Mary Rose finds a box left by her namesake, she finds its contents disconcerting: some tawdry jewelry, several paper cigar rings, and a buxom woman in a low-cut dress with the word *Me* printed next to it. Mary Rose eavesdrops on a conversation and learns that her idolized heroine had been a bully and that someone else had actually saved the other families in the apartment house. She feels stunned and betrayed. With the help and understanding of her family she learns to cope with "the truth about Mary Rose" and grows more sensitive to the complexities of human relationships. She realizes that the living hold many different perceptions of the dead girl and there is, in fact, no one truth about Mary Rose.

In *No More Trains to Tottenville* (1971), by Hazel Campbell, Jane's idolatry is not shattered; rather, she comes to terms with the frustrations her mother has been forced to live with, a realization that comes with strongly feminist overtones. In the Andrews family the two children and even the father seem to be constantly dropping out and running away, leaving the mother to function as the central core, trying to keep some semblance of organized family life. Finally the mother notifies the family that she has "had it," and, financed by her American Express card, unexpectedly, without any promise that she will return, leaves for an ashram in India. When Jane assumes the role her mother had always played, she gets a stunning insight into what it means to be a mother, a woman who apparently exists for everyone but herself.

Another heroine who must learn that her mother is not simply an appendage whose sole purpose is service for children is Julia in Eleanor Cameron's *A Room Made of Windows* (1971). More than anything else, Julia wants to be a writer. She loves her many-windowed room, where she works on her stories, and she loves her elderly neighbors, Daddy Chandler and Mrs. Rhiannon Moore, the mother of a renowned pianist. Uncle Phil, the man her mother hopes to marry, is one person that Julia does not like, and she presents a major stumbling block to their plans. Mrs. Moore admonishes Julia, "I think you're wrong, Julia. I think you're wrong. Have you ever thought about your mother when you and Greg go your own ways? Have you ever thought about her as someone separate from yourself? Or is she simply an attachment, living for your own private use and benefit?"[42]

Julia comes to accept her mother's right to her own life, and she also comes to realize that if she is to fulfill her dream of becoming a writer, she must keep a piece of her own life to herself: "I'm never going to hand on my ambition to *anyone*—to a bunch of *kids*. I'm going to keep it and work on it and make it grow." Mrs. Moore responds, "Then maybe you can manage better than I have done. Maybe you can have it all, your work and everything else besides."[43]

Another nonsexist heroine emerges in Eleanor Cameron's *To the Green Mountains* (1975). This is a richly textured novel in which the protagonist, thirteen-year-old Kath Rule, longs to escape from the hotel her mother runs in small-town Ohio and return to her grandmother's home in Vermont. During one summer Kath matures as she comes into contact with the complexities and ambiguities of life and realizes that there are seldom clear-cut delineations of good and evil. For example, when her independent mother finally extricates herself from an unsatisfactory marriage, the girl's relief is marred by a sense of her father's devastation. And her mother's attempt to help the intelligent black headwaiter, Grant, results in the destruction of his marriage.

*Harriet the Spy* (1964), by Louise Fitzhugh, portrays a heroine who wants to become a writer. Harriet, perhaps the most fiercely individualistic of all these heroines, also realizes that she must have a piece of her life that is private, hers alone. Harriet's parents have too active a social life to pay much attention to their only child, and Harriet confides in her nurse, Ole Golly, and in her secret notebook,

in which she jots down totally honest observations about her parents, classmates, and friends. When classmates read her secret notebook, Harriet's life changes dramatically. There is something negative about everyone in the notebook, and everyone turns against her. Her classmates write insulting notes; they throw spitballs, they form a Spycatcher's Club. Harriet begins to feel the whole world hates her and writes in her notebook, "When I wake up in the morning, I wish I were dead."[44] Following advice from Ole Golly, Harriet realizes that she will have to apologize and to say what she had written wasn't true because some lies are necessary to spare people's feelings. The story's resolution is a compromise, but a compassionate one, and Harriet's essential integrity and individuality remain intact.

Claudia in E. L. Konigsburg's *From the Mixed-Up Files of Mrs. Basil E. Frankweiler*, winner of the 1968 Newbery Medal, also needs something special that will make her different, help her establish her own uniqueness, and she runs away from home to find it. She also runs away because of injustice. She is the oldest child and the only girl, and she has both to empty the dishwasher and to set the table, whereas her brothers do not have to do anything. A lover of comfort and beauty, Claudia spurns more traditional runaway haunts and decides to run away to the Metropolitan Museum of Art in New York City; she takes along her brother, Jamie, because he is a miser and his horde of money will be necessary.

The sister and brother eat at the automat, wash their clothes in the laundromat, sleep in a heavily draperied bed in the museum's hall of the English Renaissance, and bathe in the museum fountain. They also become involved in the mystery of trying to establish whether a statue said to be by Michelangelo was really his work. Claudia and Jamie seek the answer from wealthy Mrs. Basil Frankweiler, who donated the statue to the museum. This elderly lady gives Claudia the secret that will make her different for a lifetime.

It is being different that bothers Sara Jane in Doris Buchanan Smith's *Kick a Stone Home* (1974). Since her parents' divorce, Sara has built walls around herself, barriers that hide her awkwardness and her feelings of inadequacy. However, as Sara Jane matures, she learns her own secret for breaking through her protective barriers and feeling comfortable with herself and her unique interests and goals.

The heroine whose struggle for self-determination is most openly tied to the issue of sexism is Barbara Fisher in Betty Miles's *The Real Me* (1974). Barbara Fisher wants to take tennis instead of the class in slimnastics, but she learns that her school does not offer tennis for girls. She takes over her brother's newspaper route and then finds that girls are not allowed to deliver newspapers. She protests and is amazed to find that she is called a nut. However, her efforts finally prove successful, and she becomes the city's first newspaper girl. Moreover, she finds that she has become a role model for younger children.

I felt really proud when Lorraine and Laverne used me for an example and realized that no matter what the books said . . . I, Barbara Fisher, had stood up for my true feelings and now people were changing their minds. And even little kids could see that the times were changing.

Some day, when Lorraine and Laverne and other girls about six or so grow up to be free and be themselves and take classes they want in PE, and become paper deliverers or mechanics or newspaper reporters or doctors or astronauts, partly it will be because of people like me who helped to change the times.

I am *not* a nut. I am a pioneer.[45]

Although each of these independent, resourceful characters discussed in this section struggles for selfhood in different ways and in different circumstances, there is a common bond. They all have the need and the drive to find and preserve their own life space, their special elbow room for self-definition.

## Women and the call of the wild

Researchers who have analyzed children's books have found that women are frequently found indoors. They watch from the safety of their homes as men leave on journeys, and they observe from their windows the activity of the outside world. There are, however, some extremely fine books that portray female characters immersed in the world of nature.

Frances Hodgson Burnett's *The Secret Garden* (1938) shows the salutary effects that life on the English moors has on a sour, petulant girl. Mary lived in India where her parents had little time for her, and she was waited upon by servants. When cholera swept through the area, Mary was left an orphan and was sent to England to live with relatives. In the huge estate where she is sent to live, Mary is left alone to explore. With the help of the warmhearted Yorkshire maid, Martha, and her brother, Dickon, who is more a woodland spirit than a boy, Mary discovers the revitalizing force of the moors. Her new excitement with life, particularly with making a forgotten garden bloom again, is transmitted to her cousin, Colin, a sickly, pampered boy. Mary, along with the restorative powers of nature, helps Colin regain his strength and his excitement for life.

Mary gains strength and happiness in the outdoors, but her natural world is essentially a civilized, well-manicured one. In contrast,

Sarah, in *The Courage of Sarah Noble* (1954), by Alice Dalgliesh, ventures into the wilderness. This book is based on the true story of eight-year-old Sarah Noble who, in 1707, came to keep her father company and cook for him while he built the first house in New Milford, Connecticut. Sarah travels with her father through the wilderness, is threatened by wolves in the forest, lives in a cave while her father builds their house, and waits with a kindly Indian family while her father goes to bring the rest of the family to their new home. Whenever fear seems to be getting the best of her, she bolsters her courage with her mother's words, "Keep up your courage, Sarah Noble." At one point in this story, John Noble says, "It was a blessing the Lord gave me daughters as well as sons."[46] This attitude is a refreshing contrast to the usual parental delight and pride in male offspring.

Scott O'Dell's *The Island of the Blue Dolphins*, winner of the 1961 Newbery Award, portrays the courage and resourcefulness of a twelve-year-old Indian girl who lived alone for eighteen years making a home of a deserted island. Karana's tribe, weakened by war, sails away from the island. Just as the ship leaves, Karana realizes that her younger brother, Ramo, has been left behind. She jumps from the ship and swims to the island to care for him. Shortly afterward, Ramo is killed by wild dogs, and Karana is left with her grief and the realization that she must survive alone on the Island of the Blue Dolphins. Although she has not been taught to hunt, for tribal laws had forbidden women to make weapons, she teaches herself to construct weapons and to use them skillfully. She obtains food, makes a shelter, and explores the nearby waters by canoe. Some of the tasks she sets herself are truly formidable. She tames the leader of the wild dogs left roaming the island; she has in-

credible battles with a bull sea elephant and a devilfish. Karana not only learns to confront and fight natural surroundings that at times appear hostile, but she also becomes part of the natural cycle of the island. When she finally leaves the Island of the Blue Dolphins, her memories are happy ones.

*Julie of the Wolves*, by Jean Craighead George, winner of the 1973 Newbery Medal, presents another courageous girl who not only survives alone with nature but also learns to live in tune with her natural surroundings. Mijax, an Eskimo girl whose English name is Julie, has run away from an intolerable early marriage, and she attempts to reach San Francisco. On her way she gets lost on the North Slope of Alaska, where she becomes dependent on a pack of wolves for her food and her very survival. Mijax had been taught by her father that wolves do not eat people, that they are gentle brothers. The Eskimo girl exhibits skill and remarkable courage as she learns to communicate with the wolves and becomes accepted by them. She also becomes deeply involved in the Eskimo way of life, and through months of living on the tundra without contact with other people, she is immersed in the natural cycles of life.

"A skua!" She was closer to the ocean than she had thought, for the skua is a bird of the coastal waters of the Arctic. As her eyes followed it, they came to rest on an oil drum, the signpost of American civilization in the North. How excited she would have been to see this a month ago. Now she was not so sure. She had her igloo and needles, her sled and her tent, and the world of her ancestors. And she liked the simplicity of that world. It was easy to understand. Out here she understood how she fit into the scheme of the moon and stars and the constant rise and fall of life on earth. Even the snow was part of her, she melted it and drank it.[47]

*Julie of the Wolves* portrays a girl's courage and her eventual realization of the duality with which she must learn to live. Her life must combine the old Eskimo ways with the newer, changing ones.

### "It's all right to cry": nonsexist portrayals of males in children's literature

The inexpressive male is a frequent image in children's literature. These are men and boys who are coolly competent, fearless, in charge or determined to be in charge of every situation. These males no not allow themselves to show fear or tenderness; for them tears are anathema. They often express contempt for girls, and the worst embarrassment they can imagine is being caught holding a doll or a baby.

Fortunately, there are many fine children's books with male characters who do not conform to this uncommunicative, insensitive stereotype. For younger children there are picture books that show boys loving and caring for dolls or stuffed animals.

In *William's Doll* (1972), by Charlotte Zolotow, William wants a doll because he has a great deal of love and tenderness that he wants to express. William's request for a doll is greeted with ridicule and scorn. "Don't be a creep!" says his brother. "Sissy, sissy, sissy!" says the boy next door. His father is worried and buys William a basketball. William becomes a fine basketball player, but he still wants a doll. His father gets him electric trains, and William loves to play with them, but he still wants a doll. William's grandmother is wise and understanding and, when William explains his request, she immediately buys him the doll that he so persistently wants. She translates the boy's request to his father:

> He needs it, she said,
> to hug
> and to cradle
> and to take to the park
> so that
> when he's a father
> like you,
> he'll know how to
> take care of his baby
> and feed him
> and love him
> and bring him
> the things he wants,
> like a doll

William's Doll

so that he can
practice being a father.[48]

The text is poetic and William Pene du Bois's illustrations sensitively express the rightness of William's need. However, some feminists find fault with the grandmother's explanation. They suggest that, considering changing family patterns and life-styles, it is possible that William may never be a father and his potential fatherhood is irrelevant anyway. He is obviously a child who needs a doll, and for that reason alone he should have one.

*William's Doll* asks "Should boys play with dolls?" and answers the question with an emphatic yes. However, there are frequently mixed reactions among elementary school children who read *William's Doll*, and it is interesting to look at their responses. A student from a children's literature class of one of the authors asked a fourth-grade class to respond to the following letter:

Dear Abby,
My four-year-old son wants me to buy him a doll. I am troubled over his request. Should I get him the doll? Please answer!

*Concerned*

Overwhelmingly, members of the class, both males and females, answered *Concerned's* letter, advising that the boy not be given a doll. "Get him a ball and bat or a gun" was a common response. "Get his mind off the doll." The student teacher began reading *William's Doll*. At first, giggles and snickers erupted from the class, and then a contingent of boys expressed active hostility by booing and hissing. It was only with frequent reprimands to keep the noise down that the teacher was able to finish. She then asked the class to look again at the letters they had written, and to reconsider the advice they had given, making any changes that they might wish. A few did. "Get him a doll," they said. "But make sure it's a G.I.

Joe." *William's Doll* may not be the answer to breaking the stereotype of the machismo male, but it puts a few cracks in the armor.

*Ira Sleeps Over* (1972), by Bernard Waber, presents Ira, whose problem centers around his beloved teddy bear, TaTa. Ira, invited to sleep overnight at his friend's house, is very excited, for he has never slept away from home before. However, his sister asks a troublesome question, "Are you taking your teddy bear along?" Ira is worried. If he does not take his teddy bear, he may not be able to sleep; if he does, Reggie may laugh at him. Ira's parents guarantee that Reggie will not laugh. "He'll laugh," taunts his diabolical sister. Ira decides not to take TaTa.

Ira and Reggie have a wonderful evening looking through Reggie's junk, playing office with his rubber stamp, and telling ghost stories. When they finally settle into bed, Ira realizes that his parents were right. Reggie will not laugh, because he has a teddy bear of his own. Through warmly humorous pictures and text, *Ira Sleeps Over* shows that boys can be fearful, and they have a right to a teddy bear's comfort and security.

Margery Williams' *The Velveteen Rabbit* (1926), a book for all ages and seasons, is a sensitive and gentle expression of the very special love between a boy and his stuffed animal, a velveteen rabbit. The Velveteen Rabbit is given to the boy for Christmas, and for a long time he lies forgotten on the nursery shelf, snubbed by the sophisticated, mechanical toys, comforted only by his long talks with the old Skin Horse.

"What is REAL?" asked the Rabbit one day. . . .
"Does it mean having things that buzz inside you and a stick-out handle?"
  "Real isn't how you are made," said the Skin Horse. "It's a thing that happens to you. When a child loves you for a long, long time, not just to play with, but REALLY loves you, then you become Real."

"Does it hurt?" asked the Rabbit.

"Sometimes," said the Skin Horse, for he was always truthful. "When you are Real, you don't mind being hurt."

"Does it happen all at once, like being wound up," he asked, "or bit by bit?"

"It doesn't happen all at once," said the Skin Horse. "You become. It takes a long time. That's why it doesn't often happen to people who break easily, or have sharp edges, or who have to be carefully kept. Generally, by the time you are Real, most of your hair has been loved off, and your eyes drop out and you get loose in the joints and very shabby. But these things don't matter at all, because once you are Real you can't be ugly, except to people who don't understand."[49]

The boy finally discovers the Rabbit and loves him, holds him tightly in bed, takes him everywhere. The boy becomes very sick and the Rabbit stays with him constantly and faithfully until he recovers. When the Rabbit, filled with scarlet fever germs, is discarded on a rubbish heap to be burnt, the fairy of nursery magic, who turns all playthings that children have loved into Real, gives the Velveteen Rabbit life.

A fine picture book that presents a boy who, with competence and affection, takes care of a baby is *Go and Hush the Baby* (1971), by Betsy Byars. Will is on his way to play a game of baseball when his mother asks him to take care of the baby while she is painting. To hush the baby Will performs a series of antics and offers a cookie. He then tells a story that so involves him that he is surprised when he loses the baby's attention to a bottle the mother brings in. Only momentarily crushed, Will announces, "Well, I have to play this game of baseball anyway." Though only briefly sketched, Will is a likable, good-natured character and his relationship with the baby is an affectionate one.

Warm fathers who do household chores and who love and care for their children are also portrayed in some picture books. A boy's need for this kind of father is shown in Charlotte Zolotow's *A Father Like That* (1972). "I wish I had a father. But my father went away before I was born," says a little boy to his mother. And then he tells his mother what his father would be like if he were around. He'd hug the boy and the mother, he'd help take care of the boy if he got sick, and he'd comfort the boy at night when he had nightmares. Zolotow's *Summer Evening* also presents a nonstereotyped father who spends a gentle summer evening with his daughter. In the picture book *Martin's Father* (1971), by Margarit Eickler, a loving, comforting father reads to his son, plays lion with him and hide-and-go-seek. The father and son do the laundry together and feed the pigeons. The book presents a simple but very satisfying depiction of a one-parent family.

There are also some fine portrayals of older boys who do not fit the pattern of the competent "superior" male, in tight control of every situation and of every emotion as well. Artie Granick in *Irving and Me* (1967), by Syd Hoff, is a marvelous portrait of a nonstereotyped male. Thirteen-year-old Artie is uprooted from his neighborhood in Brooklyn when his family moves to Florida. There are many situations that Artie does not handle too well. When it comes to playing baseball, he's an asset to the opposing team. When it comes to swimming, he's buoyant, but his body isn't. Out of four fights he has had in his lifetime, three were losses and one was a draw. He has problems with girls, bullies, and a friend, Irving, who has a knack for getting into trouble. He also has a strong sense of fair play. Even when his own safety is jeopardized, he will defend seagulls, orphans, and anyone or anything that is weak and being abused. Whenever he is in danger of taking himself or his troubles too seriously, his ability to laugh at himself takes over. His story is told with a light sophisticated humor, and the reader will laugh along with Artie, a very likable boy not at all in the machismo mold.

In Barbara Wersba's *The Dream Watcher*, Albert Scully reaches adolescence as a misfit. Sensitive and introspective, he is out of step and out of tune with his surroundings. He has little sense of competitiveness, does not want to go to college, despises the materialism his mother worships, and can find no group, in school or out, to which he belongs. It is only through his visits to Mrs. Woodfin, an eccentric, elderly woman, that Albert is able to talk about himself and to clarify what he wants out of life.

Another sensitive boy, an artist, is Auguste, in *Burnish Me Bright* (1970), by Julia Cunningham. Auguste is a mute boy who has experienced little besides harsh treatment and contempt. The delight of his life is his friendship with Monsieur Hilaire, a once famous mime who is now elderly and close to death. The mime recognizes the sensitivity in Auguste and trains him in his craft. *Burnish Me Bright* is a strange book, dramatizing the ugly conflict between a town and the gentle, artistic, mute boy whom it neither appreciates nor understands.

*Josh* (1971), by Ivan Southill, presents a complex individual, reacting to encounters with sensitivity and emotion, highly critical of himself and others, certain only of one thing—his desire to become a poet. The book centers on one episode in Josh's life, his visit to Ryan Creek, the country town that was settled by his great grandfather and where his Aunt Clara is a legend in her own time. Ryan Creek is very different from Melbourne, where Josh has lived, and Josh does not understand its rules nor the boisterous, at times coarse, manner of its people. He hopes for a soul mate in Aunt Clara, but neither can really understand the other. Josh tries to explain himself to her:

You see, Aunt Clara, I'm going to be a poet. A fellow came to school once. He wasn't like the fellows who usually come to speak. Not a footballer or a cricketer, or a policeman or a parson with his collar back-to-front. A fellow all bent, leaning on a stick. You've got to get hurt, he said, if you want to write books. When you cry, you cry for someone else. When you laugh, you laugh at yourself. When you're cruel it's your own life you tear to bits. There he was, Aunt Clara, all stooped and bent, poking fun at himself. He had us in fits. When I grow up I'd like to be like that.[50]

The book climaxes in a violent conflict between Josh and members of the town.

Artie Granick is not cut out of the stereotyped pattern but he handles his lack of fit with humor. Albert, Auguste, and Josh are utterly at odds with their surroundings, outsiders, keenly aware of their lonely uniqueness. On the record "Free to Be You and Me," a collection of nonsexist songs, Rosie Greer sings a lyric telling boys that it's alright to cry and to feel things. There are several boys in children's literature who do.

## Jam today

Since sexist attitudes are interwoven throughout the whole fabric of our society, it would be foolhardy to suggest that if we simply make a wide array of nonsexist books available to children, we can expect to see a new generation of unbiased, nonstereotyped adults emerge. Yet it is undeniable that children's books reach individuals who are young, whose value systems are not yet rigid, who are still flexible and open to change. Already there is some limited research indicating that nonsexist literature can be effective in changing children's stereotyped attitudes.[51] More research is needed, and the potential impact of nonsexist books for children is not yet known.

It is obvious that there is a great need for nonsexist children's books. However, it is of primary importance that literary quality not be sacrificed on the altar of that need. Many critics have argued that at least some of the recent nonsexist books constitute literature of mediocre quality, or that, indeed, some of them are merely propaganda and not literature at all. Some books deserve this criticism and to these books, no matter what their message, children will not respond. We have seen them brush aside books heavily laced with propaganda but inadequate in style, character, or plot development. For example, we have seen children react in such a manner to the picture book *Exactly Like Me* (1972), by Lynn Phillips. In this book a young girl makes it very clear that stereotyped feminine characteristics do not apply to her at all.

> They say, "Girls are sweet."
> They say, "Girls are neat."
> They say, "Girls just don't like
> to get mud on their feet."
> They say, "Girls are soft."
> But I'm tough as a wall.
> They say, "Girls are dainty."
> But I'm not at all!
> I'm more like the horses
> Who won't stay in pens
> Or the wolves in the forest
> Who stick up for their friends.[52]

This tough heroine rejects such traditionally feminine occupations as nurse, teacher, or stewardess. Instead she considers becoming an aquanaut or a chemist; she thinks of playing football or repairing automobiles. She says that she can become a farmer or fly an airplane, and when she grows up she will show what women can do. Large pictures and few words suggest this to be a book for young children. However, adults with feminist concerns respond far more enthusiastically to this propaganda piece than most children we have seen react to it.

There are now many, and there must be more, nonsexist books of high literary quality, yet when there is a need, even a propaganda piece has its place. When we were reading *Exactly Like Me* to a group of children, one five-year-old girl interrupted and insisted we stop reading. "I don't want to hear about that girl because I'm sweet, not tough," she said. We asked her to name some people she knew who were sweet. She mentioned her mother, several aunts, and a catalogue of female friends. When asked to name people who were tough, she mentioned only males. We asked her if it would be possible for a girl to be sweet and tough. "No, only sweet," she responded emphatically. Her responses engendered some heated discussion and debate among the young children, and the little girl left with her pigeonholed definitions of male and female not quite so firmly entrenched.

In *Through the Looking Glass* the White Queen informs Alice, "The rule is, jam tomorrow and jam yesterday—but never jam today."[53] It is true that there is need for more and better nonsexist children's books, but still the White Queen's rule does not apply. There are many fine, nonstereotyped portrayals of girls and women, of boys and men, but unlike the White Queen's elusive jam, they are here today.

## NOTES

1. Eric Marshall and Stuart Hample, compilers, *Children's Letters to God*, New York, Simon and Schuster (Pocket Books), 1966.
2. Nancy Frazier and Myra Sadker, *Sexism in School and Society*, New York, Harper & Row, 1973.
3. Women on Words and Images, *Dick and Jane as Victims*, P.O. Box 2163, Princeton, N.J., 1972.
4. Ibid.
5. K. DeCrow, "Look, Jane, Look! See Dick Run and Jump! Admire Him!" in S. Anderson, ed., *Sex Dif-*

*ferences and Discrimination in Education*, Worthington, Ohio, Charles A. Jones, 1972.

6. Diane Bennett Graebner, "A Decade of Sexism in Readers," *Reading Teacher*, 26, no. 1 (October 1972), 52–58.
7. John Rowe Townsend, May Hill Arbuthnot Honor Lecture, April 1971.
8. Ardell Nadesan, "Mother Goose; Sexist?" *Elementary English*, 51, no. 3 (March 1974), 375–378.
9. In Blanche Fisher Wright, *The Real Mother Goose*, Skokie, Ill., Rand McNally, 1916, p. 108.
10. Ibid., p. 26.
11. Ibid., p. 38.
12. Ibid., p. 127.
13. Ibid., p. 92.
14. Ibid., p. 98.
15. Ibid., p. 116.
16. Ibid., p. 43.
17. Marcia Lieberman, "Some Day My Prince Will Come; Female Acculturation Through the Fairy Tale," *College English*, 34, no. 3 (December 1972), 383–395.
18. Dan Donlan, "The Negative Image of Women in Children's Literature," *Elementary English*, 49, no. 4 (April 1972), 604–611.
19. Lenore Weitzman et al., "Sex Role Socialization in Picture Books for Preschool Children," *American Journal of Sociology*, 77, no. 6 (May 1972), 1125–1150.
20. John Stewig and Margaret Higgs, "Girls Grow Up to be Mommies; A Study of Sexism in Children's Literature," *Library Journal*, 98, no. 2 (January 15, 1973), 236–244.
21. Weitzman, op. cit.
22. Whitney Darrow, *I'm Glad I'm a Boy! I'm Glad I'm a Girl!*, New York, Simon & Schuster (Windmill), 1970.
23. The Feminists on Children's Literature, "A Feminist Look at Children's Books," *School Library Journal*, 17, no. 5 (January 1971), 19–24.
24. Carol Ryrie Brink, *Caddie Woodlawn*, Kate Seredy, illus., New York, Macmillan, 1935, p. 1.
25. Ibid., pp. 239–240.
26. Jane Langton, *The Boyhood of Grace Jones*, pictures by Emily Arnold McCully, New York, Harper & Row, 1972, p. 30.
27. Virginia Sorensen, *Miracles on Maple Hill*, Beth and Joe Krush, illus., New York, Harcourt Brace Jovanovich, 1956, p. 21.
28. Ibid., p. 99.
29. Quoted in Graebner, op. cit.
30. "Guidelines for Publications" by the NCTE Committee on the Role and Image of Women in the Council and the Profession, quoted in *Elementary English*, 50, no. 7 (October 1973), 1019.
31. Lewis Carroll, *Alice's Adventures in Wonderland*, John Tenniel illus., in *The Annotated Alice*, introduction and notes by Martin Gardner, Cleveland, World (Meridian), 1963, p. 88.
32. Quoted in Verne Moberg and Merle Froschl, "The Dilemma of Dick and Jane: Nonsexist Books to the Rescue," *Colloquy*, 6, no. 9 (November 1973), 12–15.
33. *Ibid.*
34. Jay Williams, *The Silver Whistle*, Friso Henstra, illus., New York, Parents' Magazine Press, 1971.
35. Richard Gardner, *Fairy Tales for Today's Children*, Alfred Lowenheim, illus., Englewood Cliffs, N.J., Prentice-Hall, 1974.
36. Ibid., p. 25.
37. Ibid., p. 109.
38. E. B. White, *Charlotte's Web*, Garth Williams, illus., New York, Harper & Row, 1952.
39. Janice M. Tate, "Sexual Bias in Science Fiction for Children," *Elementary English*, 50, no. 7 (October 1973), 1061–1064.
40. Selma R. Siege, "Heroines in Recent Children's Fiction—An Analysis," *Elementary English*, 50, no. 7 (October 1973), 1039.
41. Elizabeth Janeway, "Meg, Jo, Beth, Amy, and Louisa," in *Only Connect: Readings on Children's Literature*, Sheila Egoff et al., eds., Oxford University Press, 1969, p. 288.
42. Eleanor Cameron, *A Room Made of Windows*, Trina Schart Hyman, illus., New York, Dell (A Yearling Book), 1971, p. 231.
43. Ibid., p. 123.
44. Louise Fitzhugh, *Harriet the Spy*, New York, Harper & Row, 1964.
45. Betty Miles, *The Real Me*, New York, Knopf, 1974, p. 118.
46. Alice Dalgliesh, *The Courage of Sarah Noble*, Leonard Weisgard, illus., New York, Scribner, 1954, p. 4.
47. Jean Craighead George, *Julie of the Wolves*, New York, Harper & Row, 1972, p. 130.
48. Charlotte Zolotow, *William's Doll*, pictures by William Pene du Bois, New York, Harper & Row, 1972, pp. 31–32.
49. Margery Williams, *The Velveteen Rabbit*, William Nicholson, illus., Garden City, N.Y., Doubleday, pp. 16–17.
50. Ivan Southall, *Josh*, New York, Macmillan, 1971, p. 62.
51. Lisa Barclay, "The Emergence of Vocational Expectations in Preschool Children," paper presented at the American Educational Research Association, 1973.
52. Lynn Phillips, *Exactly Like Me*, Chapel Hill, North Carolina, Lollipop Power, 1972.
53. Lewis Carroll, *Through the Looking Glass*, John Tenniel, illus., in *The Annotated Alice*, introduction and notes by Martin Gardner, Potter, 1963, p. 247.

# BIBLIOGRAPHY

## Fiction for younger children

BABBITT, NATALIE. *Phoebe's Revolt*, Farrar, Straus & Giroux, 1968 (3–4).

BEMELMANS, LUDWIG. *Madeline's Rescue*, Viking Press, 1953 (K–3).

BIANCO, MARGERY. *The Velveteen Rabbit*, William Nicholson, illus., Doubleday, 1926 (1–4).

BONSALL, CROSBY. *And I Mean It, Stanley*, Harper & Row, 1974 (K–3).

BURTON, VIRGINIA LEE. *Katy and the Big Snow*, Houghton Mifflin, 1943 (preschool–4).

BYARS, BETSY. *Go and Hush the Baby*, Emily Arnold McCully, illus., Viking Press, 1971 (preschool–K).

CLIFTON, LUCILLE. *Don't You Remember?*, Evaline Ness, illus., Dutton, 1973 (preschool–2).

DANISH, BARBARA. *The Dragon and the Doctor*, Feminist Press, 1971 (preschool–3).

DRAGONWAGON, CRESCENT. *When Light Turns into Night*, Robert Andrew Parker, illus., Harper & Row, 1974 (K–3).

EICKLER, MARGARIT. *Martin's Father*, Bev Maginnis, illus., Lollipop Power, 1971 (preschool–K).

ETS, MARIE HALL. *Play with Me*, Viking Press, 1955 (preschool–1).

GAUCH, PATRICIA LEE. *Christina Katerina and the Box*, Doris Burn, illus., Coward, McCann & Geoghegan, 1971 (K–3).

GOFFSTEIN, M. B. *Two Piano Tuners*, Farrar, Straus & Giroux, 1970 (3–4).

HOCHSCHILD, ARLIE RUSSELL. *Colleen the Question Girl*, Gail Ashby, illus., Feminist Press, 1974 (K–5).

HOFFMAN, PHYLLIS. *Steffie and Me*, Emily Arnold McCully, illus., Harper & Row, 1970 (1–4).

JEFFERS, SUSAN. *All the Pretty Horses*, Macmillan, 1974 (K–3).

KATZ, BOBI. *Nothing But a Dog*, Esther Gilman, illus., Feminist Press, 1972 (preschool–1).

KLEIN, NORMA. *Girls Can Be Anything*, Ray Doty, illus., Dutton, 1973 (preschool–3).

LASKER, JOE. *Mothers Can Do Anything*, Whitman, 1972 (K–3).

LINDGREN, ASTRID. *Of Course Polly Can Ride a Bike*, Don Wikland, illus., Follett, 1972 (K–3).

MCCLOSKEY, ROBERT. *Blueberries for Sal*, Viking Press, 1948 (preschool–1).

MERRIAM, EVE. *Boys and Girls, Girls and Boys*, Harriet Sherman, illus., Holt, Rinehart & Winston, 1972 (preschool–3).

———. *Mommies at Work*, Beni Montresor, illus., Knopf, 1961 (K–2).

NESS, EVALINE. *Do You Have the Time, Lydia?*, Dutton, 1971 (K–3).

PHILLIPS, LYNN. *Exactly Like Me*, Lollipop Power, 1972 (preschool–3).

REAVEN, SAM. *Hurray for Captain Jane*, Emily Arnold McCully, illus., Parents' Magazine Press, 1971 (K–2).

RICH, GIBSON. *Firegirl*, Charlotte Purington Farley, illus., Feminist Press, 1972 (K–3).

RIZZO, ANN. *The Strange Hocket Family*, Feminist Press, 1974 (1–5).

ROCKWELL, HARLOW. *My Doctor*, Macmillan, 1973 (preschool–2).

ROTHMAN, JOEL. *I Can Be Anything You Can Be*, Susan Perl, illus., Scroll Press, 1973 (K–4).

SCHICK, ELEANOR. *City in the Winter*, Macmillan, 1970 (K–2).

SCHLEIN, MIRIAM. *The Girl Who Would Rather Climb Trees*, Judith Gwyn Brown, illus., Harcourt Brace Jovanovich, 1975 (K–2).

SKORPEN, LIESEL MOAK. *Kisses and Fishes*, Steven Kellogg, illus., Harper & Row, 1974 (K–3).

———. *Mandy's Grandmother*, Martha Alexander, illus., Dial Press, 1975 (preschool–3).

SUROWIECKI, SANDRA LUCAS. *Joshua's Day*, Lollipop Power, 1972 (preschool–1).

UDRY, JANICE MAY. *Mary Jo's Grandmother*, Eleanor Mill, illus., Whitman, 1970 (K–2).

———. *The Moon Jumpers*, Maurice Sendak, illus., Harper & Row, 1959 (K–3).

VIORST, JUDITH. *Rosie and Michael*, Lorna Tomei, illus., Atheneum, 1974 (preschool–2).

WABER, BERNARD. *Ira Sleeps Over*, Houghton Mifflin, 1972 (K–3).

WILLIAMS, JAY. *Petronella*, Friso Henstra, illus., Parents' Magazine Press, 1971 (K–3).

———. *The Practical Princess*, Friso Henstra, illus., Parents' Magazine Press, 1969 (K–3).

———. *The Silver Whistle*, Friso Henstra, illus., Parents' Magazine Press, 1971 (K–3).

YOLEN, JANE. *The Girl Who Loved the Wind*, Ed Young, illus., Crowell, 1972 (K–3).

YOUNG, MIRIAM. *Jellybeans for Breakfast*, Parents' Magazine Press, 1968 (K–3).

ZOLOTOW, CHARLOTTE. *Janey*, Ronald Himber, illus., Harper & Row, 1973 (preschool–3).

———. *William's Doll*, William Pene DuBois, illus., Harper & Row, 1972 (preschool–3).

———. *A Father Like That*, Ben Shecter, illus., Harper & Row, 1971 (K–2).

———. *Hold My Hand*, Thomas di Grazia, illus., Harper & Row, 1972 (preschool–3).

———. *The Summer Night*, Ben Shecter, illus., Harper & Row, 1974 (preschool–3).

## Fiction for the middle and older grades

ALCOTT, LOUISA M. *Little Women*, Barbara Cooney, illus., Crowell, 1955 (orig. pub. 1868–69) (5–8).

ALMEDINGEN, E. K. *Anna*, Farrar, Straus & Giroux, 1972 (8–10).

ANDERSEN, HANS CHRISTIAN. "The Snow Queen," in *It's Perfectly True and Other Stories*, trans. by Paul Leyssac, Richard Bennett, illus., Harcourt Brace Jovanovich, 1938 (6–8).

BAILY, CAROLYN. *Miss Hickory*, Ruth Gannett, illus., Viking Press, 1968, Newbery Medal (5–8).

BAUM, FRANK L. *The Wizard of Oz*, W. W. Denslow, illus., Reilly, 1956 (orig. pub. 1900) (3–6).

BAWDEN, NINA. *Carrie's War*, Lippincott, 1973 (7+).

———. *The Runaway Summer*, Lippincott, 1969 (4–6).

BELLAIRS, JOHN. *The House with a Clock in Its Walls*, Edward Gorey, illus., Dial Press, 1973 (3–7).

BENARY-ISBERT, MARGOT. *The Ark*, trans. by Clara and Richard Winston, Harcourt Brace Jovanovich, 1953 (7–9).

BOLTON, CAROL. *Never Jam Today*, Atheneum, 1971 (8–11).

BRANSCUM, ROBBIE. *Johnny May*, Charles Robinson, illus., Doubleday, 1975 (4–7).

BRINK, CAROL RYRIE. *Caddie Woodlawn*, Kate Seredy, illus., Macmillan, 1935, Newbery Medal (4–7).

BULLA, ROBERT. *Shoeshine Girl*, Leigh Grant, illus., Crowell, 1975.

BURCH, ROBERT. *Queenie Peavy*, Jerry Lazare, illus., Viking Press, 1966 (6–9).

BURNETT, FRANCES HODGSON. *The Secret Garden*, Nora S. Unwin, illus., Lippincott, 1938 (4–6).

BURTON, HESTER. *The Henchmans at Home*, Victor G. Ambrus, illus., Crowell, 1970 (5–8).

CAMERON, ELEANOR. *A Room Made of Windows*, Trina Schart Hyman, illus., Atlantic–Little, Brown, 1971 (7+).

———. *The Court of the Stone Children*, Dutton, 1973 (5+).

———. *To the Green Mountains*, Dutton, 1975.

CAMPBELL, HOPE. *No More Trains to Tottenville*, Saturday Review Press, 1971 (7+).

CANFIELD, DOROTHY. *Understood Betsy*, Thrushwood, 1970 (5–11).

CARROLL, LEWIS. *Alice's Adventures in Wonderland* and *Through the Looking Glass*, John Tenniel, illus., Heritage, 1944 (orig. pub. 1865, 1871) (5+).

CLEARY, BEVERLY. *Ramona the Pest*, Louis Darling, illus., Morrow, 1968 (3–5).

———. *Ramona the Brave*, Alan Tiegreen, illus., Morrow, 1975 (3–6).

CLEAVER, VERA, and BILL CLEAVER. *Where the Lilies Bloom*, Jim Spanfeller, illus., Lippincott, 1969 (6–9).

———, and ———. *Ellen Grae*, Ellen Raskin, illus., Lippincott, 1967 (4–6).

———, and ———. *Me Too*, Lippincott, 1973 (7–9).

———, and ———. *Dust of the Earth*, 1975 (6–10).

COOLIDGE, OLIVIA. *Come by Here*, Milton Johnson, illus., Houghton Mifflin, 1970 (5+).

CUNNINGHAM, JULIA. *Burnish Me Bright*, Pantheon Books, 1970 (5–8).

DAHL, ROALD. *The Magic Finger*, William Pene DuBois, illus., Harper & Row, 1966 (5–6).

DALGLIESH, ALICE. *The Courage of Sarah Noble*, Leonard Weisgard, illus., Scribner, 1954 (2–5).

DANZIGER, PAULA. *The Cat Ate My Gymsuit*, Dell (Delacorte Press), 1974 (5–9).

DARKE, MARJORIE. *A Question of Courage*, Crowell, 1975 (6–10).

DEGENS, T. *Transport 7-41-R*, Viking Press, 1974 (7–11).

ENGDAHL, SYLVIA. *The Far Side of Evil*, Atheneum, 1971 (7–10).

ENGELBRECHT, PATRICIA. *Under the Haystack*, Nelson, 1973 (6–10).

FIELD, RACHEL. *Calico Bush*, Allen Lewis, illus., Macmillan, 1931 (5–9).

FITZHUGH, LOUISE. *Harriet the Spy*, Harper & Row, 1964 (5–7).

———. *The Long Secret*, Harper & Row, 1965 (6–8).

FLORY, JANE. *The Liberation of Clementine Tipton*, Houghton Mifflin, 1974 (3–7).

FRANK, ANNE. *The Diary of a Young Girl*, Doubleday (Pocket Books), 1952 (8+).

GARDNER, RICHARD. *Fairy Tales For Today's Children*, Alfred Lowenheim, illus., Prentice-Hall, 1974.

GEORGE, JEAN CRAIGHEAD. *Julie of the Wolves*, Harper & Row, 1972, Newbery Medal (7+).

GODDEN, RUMER. *Impunity Jane*, Adrienne Adams, illus., Viking Press, 1954 (2–6).

GREENE, BETTY. *The Summer of My German Soldier*, Dial Press, 1973 (7+).

GREENE, CONSTANCE. *A Girl Called Al*, Byron Barton, illus., Viking Press, 1969 (4–6).

GRIPE, MARIA. *The Night Daddy*, trans. by Gerry Bothmer, Harald Gripe, illus., Dell (Delacorte Press), 1971 (4–6).

HALL, ELIZABETH. *Stand Up, Lucy*, Houghton Mifflin, 1971 (3–7).

HAMILTON, VIRGINIA. *Zeely*, Symeon Shimin, illus., Macmillan, 1967 (4–6).

HART, CAROLE. *Delilah*, Edward Frascino, illus., Harper & Row, 1972 (2–6).

HAUTZIG, ESTHER. *The Endless Steppe: Growing Up in Siberia*, Crowell, 1968 (6–10).

HOFF, SYD. *Irving and Me*, Harper & Row, 1967 (5–8).

HOWARD, MOSES. *The Ostrich Chase*, Barbara Seuling, illus., Holt, Rinehart & Winston, 1974 (5–9).

JOHNSTON, NORMA. *Of Time and of Seasons*, Atheneum, (1975+).

JORDAN, JUNE. *His Own Where*, Crowell, 1971 (7–9).

KERR, M. E. *Dinky Hocker Shoots Smack*, Harper & Row, 1972 (7+).

———. *The Son of Someone Famous*, Harper & Row, 1974 (7+).

KLEIN, NORMA. *Mom, The Wolf Man and Me*, Pantheon Books, 1972 (5+).

———. *It's Not What You Expect*, Pantheon Books, 1973 (7+).

KNUDSON, R. R. *Zanballer*, Dell (Delacorte Press), 1972 (7+).

KONIGSBURG, E. L. *Jennifer, Hecate, MacBeth, William McKinley, and Me, Elizabeth*, Atheneum, 1967 (4–6).

———. *From the Mixed-Up Files of Mrs. Basil E. Frankweiler*, Atheneum, 1967, Newbery Medal (5–7).

———. *A Proud Taste for Scarlet and Miniver*, Atheneum, 1973 (6–9).

LAWRENCE, MILDRED. *Touchmark*, Deanne Hollinger, illus., Harcourt Brace Jovanovich, 1975.

L'ENGLE, MADELEINE. *A Wrinkle in Time*, Farrar, Straus & Giroux, 1962, Newbery Medal (6–9).

LENSKI, LOIS. *Strawberry Girl*, Lippincott, 1945, Newbery Medal, (4–7).

LINDGREN, ASTRID. *Pippi Longstocking*, trans. by Florence Lanborn, Louis Glanzman, illus., Viking Press, 1950 (4–7).

———. *Pippi Goes on Board*, Viking Press, 1957.

———. *Pippi In the South Seas*, Viking Press, 1959.

LINGARD, JOAN. *The Clearance*, Nelson, 1974 (7+).

LORENZO, CAROL LEE. *Heart-of-Snowbird*, Harper & Row, 1975.

MATHIS, SHARON BELL. *Sidewalk Story*, Viking Press, 1971 (3–6).

MAZER, NORMA FOX. *A Figure of Speech*, Dell (Delacorte Press), 1973 (7+).

———. *I, Trissy*, Dell (Delacorte Press), 1971 (4–7).

MILES, BETTY. *The Real Me*, Knopf, 1974 (3–6).

MILES, MISKA. *Annie and the Old One*, Peter Parnall, illus., Little, Brown, 1971 (1–3).

MINARD, ROSEMARY (ed.). *Womenfolk and Fairy Tales*, Suzanne Klein, illus., Houghton Mifflin, 1975 (2–5).

MOSKIN, MARIETTA. *I Am Rosemarie*, Day, 1972 (7+).

MURRAY, MICHELE. *Nellie Cameron*, Leonora E. Prince, illus., Seabury Press, 1971 (4–6).

NORTON, MARY. *The Borrowers*, Beth and Joe Krush, illus., Harcourt Brace Jovanovich, 1953. This book was followed by *The Borrowers Afield* (1955), *The Borrowers Afloat* (1959), *The Borrowers Aloft* (1961) (4–7).

O'DELL, SCOTT. *Island of the Blue Dolphins*, Houghton Mifflin, 1960, Newbery Medal (6–9).

——. *Sing Down the Moon*, Houghton Mifflin, 1970 (6–9).

PEARCE, A. PHILIPPA. *Tom's Midnight Garden*, Susan Einzig, illus., Lippincott, 1958 (5–8).

PECK, RICHARD. *Representing Super Doll*, Viking Press, 1974 (7+).

PERL, LILA. *That Crazy April*, Seabury Press, 1974 (4–8).

POPE, ELIZABETH MARIE. *The Perilous Gard*, Richard Cuffari, illus., Houghton Mifflin, 1974 (11+).

RANSOME, ARTHUR. *Swallows and Amazons*, Helene Carter, illus., Lippincott, 1931 (7–8).

REISS, JOHANNA. *The Upstairs Room*, Crowell, 1972 (4–7).

RENVOIZE, JEAN. *A Wild Thing*, Atlantic–Little, Brown, 1970 (7+).

RODGERS, MARY. *Freaky Friday*, Harper & Row, 1972 (5+).

SACHS, MARILYN. *The Truth About Mary Rose*, Doubleday, 1973 (4–7).

——. *Veronica Ganz*, Louis Glanzman, illus., Doubleday, 1968 (5–7).

SAWYER, RUTH. *Roller Skates*, Valenti Angelo, illus., Viking Press, 1936, Newbery Winner (7–8).

SLOBODKIN, FLORENCE. *Sarah Somebody*, Louis Slobodkin, illus., Vanguard Press, 1970 (3–5).

SMITH, DORIS BUCHANAN. *Kick a Stone Home*, Crowell, 1974 (5+).

SNYDER, ZELPHA KEATLEY. *The Witches of Worm*, Alton Rauble, illus., Atheneum, 1973 (5–8).

——. *The Headless Cupid*, Alton Raible, illus., Atheneum, 1970 (4–6).

——. *The Egypt Game*, Alton Raible, illus., Atheneum, 1967 (4–7).

——. *The Changeling*, Alton Raible, illus., Atheneum, 1970 (5–7).

SOUTHALL, IVAN. *Josh*, Macmillan, 1971 (7+).

SPEARE, ELIZABETH GEORGE. *The Witch of Blackbird Pond*, Houghton Mifflin, 1958, Newbery Winner (9+).

SPYKMAN, E. C. *Terrible Horrible Edie*, Harcourt Brace Jovanovich, 1960 (5–8).

STREATFIELD, NOEL. *Thursday's Child*, Peggy Fortnum, illus., Random House, 1970 (4–6).

SYMONS, GERALDINE. *Miss Rivers and Miss Bridges*, Alexy Pendle, illus., Macmillan, 1972 (6–8).

——. *The Workhouse Child*, Alexy Pendle, illus., Macmillan, 1971 (5–7).

THOMAS, MARLO; STEINEM, GLORIA; and POGREBIN, LETTY COTTIN. *Free to Be You and Me*, McGraw-Hill, 1974 (all ages).

TRAVERS, P. L. *Mary Poppins*, Mary Shepard, illus., Harcourt Brace Jovanovich, 1934 (3–7).

——. *Mary Poppins Comes Back*, Mary Shepard, illus., Harcourt Brace Jovanovich, 1935 (3–7).

——. *Mary Poppins in the Park*, Mary Shepard, illus., Harcourt Brace Jovanovich, 1952 (3–7).

——. *Mary Poppins Opens the Door*, Mary Shepard and Agnes Sims, illus., Harcourt Brace Jovanovich, 1943 (3–7).

UCHIDA, YOSHIKO. *Journey to Topaz: A Story of the Japanese-American Evacuation*, Donald Carrick, illus., Scribner, 1971 (5–7).

WERSBA, BARBARA. *The Dream Watcher*, Atheneum, 1968 (6–9).

WHITE, E. B. *Charlotte's Web*, Garth Williams, illus., Harper & Row, 1952 (5+).

ZINDEL, PAUL. *The Pigman*, Harper & Row, 1968 (7–9).

Save
our planet–
save
ourselves

Industrial society is the most successful way of life mankind has ever known. Not only do our people eat better, sleep better, live in more comfortable dwellings, get around more and in far greater comfort, and—notwithstanding all the manifold dangers in the industrial way of life— live longer than ever done before. Our people are better informed than ever before. At the height of the technological revolution we are now living in a golden age of scientific enlightenment and artistic achievement.[1]

*C. E. Ayers, Economist*

The rise of our industrial nation, and with it an ever-increasing standard of living, has led us to cherish progress and growth as articles of faith. We optimistically look to science and technology as the oracles of infinite answers to present and future problems. Our complex computers, miracle drugs, powerful fertilizers, supersonic communications and transportation systems, and mass-produced products are being disseminated beyond our national boundaries to developing nations around the world.

Only slowly are Americans beginning to understand that technological progress has been made at a severe cost to our planet's delicate and intricate environmental balance. Continuous economic growth through an endless series of technological advances can no longer be assumed as our right or our future. The world's environment is finite; our power to structure our future is limited.

Among those Americans who will be most affected by the ramifications of industrial growth and technology are children and young adults. Today's children will live most of their lives in tomorrow's world, and they are increasingly sensitive to the stake they have in ensuring that the quality of life does not deteriorate over the years. The active role of a good many children in the growing but still fragile ecology movement is one example of their increased awareness of the dangers to our

# 10 Spaceship Earth: Ecology in Children's Literature

environment. From paper drives to nature walks, from wearing ecology emblems to reading nature books, children are demonstrating an increased concern about the quality of their environment.

Schools too are reflecting this concern with lessons, projects, activities, and entire units related to ecology. Moreover, the significant number of children's books about the environment that have recently been published can play an important role in the environmental education of children. One reason for their potential importance is found in the deficiencies of textbooks dealing with this topic. One study, for example, recently reviewed the treatment of ecology in fourteen popular texts ranging from mathematics to social studies. The conclusions revealed significant deficiencies.[2]

1. Most of the textbooks studied contained very limited information related to the environment, and dealt only superficially with conservation.
2. Conservation was depicted in generalities, with only one viewpoint presented.
3. A frequent theme was the ability of humans to use the environment, to apply technical and creative processes to alter the environment in the name of progress.
4. The texts studied gave the impression that we had the ability to provide a bright future, and that the environment could be successfully managed. The danger to our environment was presented as readily solvable.

The importance of ecology to our survival and the limitations of the textbooks suggest the potential significance of trade books in a child's understanding of the environment. In addition, children's books offer a dimension of involvement not found in the typical textbook. In contrast to the information-dispensing format of the textbook, children's trade books have greater power to involve children affectively and experientially in various environmental concerns. Moreover, a well-written and balanced selection of trade books can provide children with a more comprehensive and thorough understanding of the ecology issues than can a textbook. Trade books have the potential of "pulling" the reader to both a better understanding of and a more active involvement in this social concern.

In this chapter we discuss several different approaches that children's books have taken in their attempt to portray the various dimensions of the ecology movement. We also examine the quality and usefulness of these books and offer some suggestions for their evaluation and selection.

Before turning our attention to children's books in this area, it may be useful to review briefly a few salient aspects of the ecology movement.

## The dimensions of ecology

### Poisoning our environment

Perhaps the most widely known aspect of the ecology movement is concerned with halting the ever-increasing pollution of our air, water, and earth. Such contamination takes a variety of forms and is carried out by industry and government as well as by individuals. Detergents that destroy marine life, cans and packages that clutter the land, and automobile exhaust that destroys the quality of our air are examples of the pollution problem. In several instances the critical nature of this problem has become headline news. In London a few years ago an unusual air inversion that lasted for days trapped the fumes of the city, and Londoners throughout the city died. The wastes dumped into our waterways have

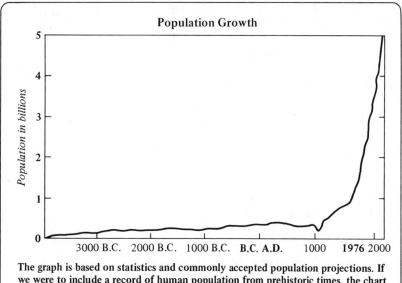

The graph is based on statistics and commonly accepted population projections. If we were to include a record of human population from prehistoric times, the chart would extend approximately 70 feet or more to the left.

reached such proportions that the ability of certain bodies of water to sustain life is virtually nil. Lake Erie, for example, is already considered dead. Pollution has provided us with deadly artifacts of the technological growth that we have always held so dear. As Senator Gaylord Nelson of Wisconsin points out, "Progress—American style—adds up each year to 200 million tons of smoke and fumes, 7 million junked cars, 20 million tons of paper, 48 billion cans and 28 billion bottles."[3]

## The population bomb

Unlike the antipollution dimension, the threat to our environment posed by population growth is less understood. Historical forces, such as famine and disease, have been somewhat neutralized by medical advances, increased longevity, and more effective distribution of food resources. The result is not only the largest world population in history, but the prediction that the population will double in twenty or thirty years, and triple in approximately sixty years. Without worldwide family planning and birth control techniques or a major catastrophe, the world's growing population will place an overwhelming burden on our planetary resources. Famine and a decrease in the world's standard of living are foreseen as the possible results of the population explosion. Others predict that nations will resort to war in order to acquire the world's limited resources.

## The attraction of nature

A greater concern for and appreciation of nature is a predictable reaction to the environmentalist's dismay at the problems created by an industrial society. This attraction to nature is represented in several ways. On one level, it is reflected in contemporary thirst for a less harried life-style, simple clothes, and organic food. But this appreciation is also evident in attempts to protect and conserve our environment. Oil spills, strip mining, and thoughtless hunting for sport or profit have destroyed the usefulness and beauty of many areas, while endangering or exterminating a variety of species. Ecologists wish to reverse this trend, to reclaim land and water areas, and to preserve endangered species. Although technology has increased the complexities of our world and has attempted to place people in control of nature, the ecologist is attracted to a more simple and natural order and strives to place humans in harmony with nature.

The concept of humanity in balance with the environment is not in itself new; rather, it is newly revived. *The Life and Strange and Surprising Adventures of Robinson Crusoe* (1719), by Daniel Defoe, is an early example of the lure of a natural, a simple, and an uncivilized environment. Originally intended for adults, *Robinson Crusoe* appealed to children as well. Robinson Crusoe escaped from the complexities and regimentation of "civilization" to the simple and pure world of nature; through the years many readers have enjoyed this escapism. The romanticism of a flight from civilization is also present in many recently published books, as the appeal of nature attracts new adherents.

These varied dimensions of the ecology movement, although far from comprehensive, do give some indication of the cost we have all paid for unplanned growth and technology. The giant advances that our technological society has made have endangered our very existence. As the French poet Paul Valéry said, "We are blind and impotent, yet armed with knowledge and power, in a world we have organized and equipped, and whose inextricable complexity we now dread."[4]

# The environment in children's books
## The nature book

One of the earlier forms of books about the environment is the nature book. Dating back to the eighteenth century, the nature book is enjoying new popularity in our ecologically oriented age. The nature book is concerned with the phenomenon of nature without the involvement, and frequently beyond the notice of most human beings. Abandoning personal value judgments, the nature writer observes and reports on life. The subject may be a raccoon, a tree, or the rhythm of the ocean's waves. The pure nature book offers an unbiased account of the balance of nature, of the world all around us.[5]

There are a great many nature books, and we shall discuss only a few in this section. Our purpose is to share a sample of such books and to alert the reader to their potential role in helping children appreciate the wonders of nature. An appreciation of nature may be a first step in a personal commitment to the ecology movement. In fact, some of the more recent nature books represent a hybrid of the traditional nature book and a call for environmental concern. This new form contains not only an account of our world, but a plea to preserve it. But whether it is this new form of the nature book or the more traditional form, the nature book written for the young child can represent a fine combination of natural wonder and literary beauty.

A long-standing advocate of environmental concern, Jean Craighead George explains that her fascination with nature grew as the intriguing research for one book led to further discoveries about the unique forms of life.[6] George cites several examples to support her attraction to the wonders of nature. For instance, the whiptailed lizard of the Southwest gives birth only to females. The species contains no males.

The sea cucumber defends itself by shooting its inners at any enemy, and then it totally collapses like a balloon. But the sea cucumber does not die in this process; it slowly regenerates itself. These incredible variations of the life cycle spurred George to write over thirty books, nature stories as well as adventure stories with a strong environmental theme.

An early example of George's nature books is *The Hole in the Tree* (1957), a book that depicts the creation and life of a simple tree hole. Created by a bark beetle's bite, the hole slowly enlarges through the activities of the woodpecker, ants, bees, birds, and other creatures who make use of the hole. The same simple yet informative approach appears in one of George's more recent books, *All Upon a Stone* (1971), a brief picture book about the numerous forms of life found on and under a rock. Inspired by the curiosity of her own children for exploring rocks, George writes of the trek of a mole cricket to locate other mole crickets. During the cricket's journey from below the rock to its top, a variety of life forms is encountered: a sowbug, beetle, salamander, fairy shrimp, and spider.

Alvin Tresselt is another popular writer of children's nature books. In *The Beaver Pond* (1970) Tresselt relates the evolutionary cycle of a pond from its creation by a beaver's dam to the causes of its disappearance. A similar cycle is explored in Tresselt's *The Dead Tree* (1972), which recounts the ways a tree serves nature even in death (see Chapter 4). The water cycle is traced from puddle to pond, from river to ocean, in Tresselt's *Rain Drop Splash* (1948). The effect of weather is explored in *White Snow, Bright Snow* (1947) and *Hide and Seek Fog* (1965). As is so frequently the case in nature books, Tresselt's books contain illustrative drawings or photographs that enhance the power of the narrative.

The devastation caused by a lightning fire in the forest is related in Evans Valens' *Wildfire* (1963). In this detailed account of the destruction of a forest, the havoc imposed on the numerous inhabitants is graphically presented in narrative and illustration. But the book concludes on an optimistic note as a new forest is reborn.

Nature books provide children with an attractive introduction to the world around them, with a fundamental appreciation of na-

---

### P.S. # "Southern California"

Today I found
A pond of tule marsh
That some farmer hadn't drained,
Plowed under long ago:
The light green reeds
Bowed and flexed, still dancing with the
Wind—that seemed to skim
Across the water in little crescent
Waves rippling
To the edges
Of the marsh: here
Was
The home of the falcon
And fox.

Now, the stands of eucalyptus
Are slaughtered on the road side;
Stumps and graying limb-wood, bear
Witness to a few decaying orange groves;
The tract houses are packed
Like eggs
In a throw away carton—
A gift of dry wall
From a master architect.

It is not far from here
That I teach
In a grey building
That has no windows.

*Kathleen Gray, Garden Grove, Calif.*
*From the* English Journal, *62, no. 4, 548*
*April 1973*

ture and of the environmental controls built into the natural cycle of life. A number of other nature books for children are cited in the bibliography to this chapter.

## The environment in fantasy

The accuracy and objectivity that are the hallmarks of the nature book provide sharp contrast to the great degree of literary license frequently found in children's fiction concerned with the environment. Books of fantasy about nature and nature's creatures often provide children with an imaginative and appealing introduction to our environment. In many instances authors take great liberty in reporting on the environment, and place greater emphasis on an appealing story and a general appreciation of nature than on an accurate reflection of the environment.

For example, one popular technique found in children's fantasy is to attribute human characteristics to animals, plants, and other living creatures. Human skills and attitudes are attributed to the many different animals in George Selden's *Tucker's Countryside* (1969), a witty book that reflects an awareness of the need to preserve natural surroundings. Tucker Mouse and Harry Cat leave their comfortable home, a sewer in the Times Square subway station in New York, to help their friend who lives in Hedley, Connecticut. The problem confronting the two city dwellers is to devise a plan to save a beloved meadow in Hedley from encroaching civilization. The difficulty of adjusting to country life, the interesting cast of human and animal characters, and the creative solution to save the meadow combine to make *Tucker's Countryside* a humorous and charming story.

Another strong appeal to preserve our environment is made in several other books as well. Betty Levin's *The Zoo Conspiracy* (1973) concerns animals who inhabit a zoo designed to preserve endangered species. The animals become jealous when they learn of the arrival of a new and extremely rare species. However, their conspiracy to exterminate the new arrival withers as they learn of the importance of the survival of all animals. In *The Seal and the Slick* (1974), by Don Freeman, a young seal ignores warnings and swims into the open ocean. The young seal is coated with oil from a spill and barely manages to survive the effects of humanity's carelessness.

The danger to our environment posed by technological growth also appears as the key theme in *The Lorax* (1971), by Dr. Seuss. Typical of the Seuss books, attractive illustrations and humorous rhyme are joined into an exciting book, one that also makes an important statement against thoughtless industrial growth. The beautiful Truffula trees are attacked by the Once-ler, who builds factories to turn them into thneeds. Once-ler insists that thneeds are incredibly useful—as socks, gloves, shirts, and hats, to name just a few. The Lorax, who speaks for the trees, protests the slaughter of the Truffula forest. But the Once-ler is greedy, and sees only profit. The fish and the birds are forced to leave, as the environment that supports them is ravaged. The Once-ler ignores all the signs of disaster, and concentrates only on "biggering." When the land is devastated, the Once-ler and his group move on. A young boy who is told this story is placed in charge of the last Truffula seed, and he learns the meaning of the single-word epitaph *unless*.

> Unless someone, like you cares
> a whole awful lot,
>   nothing is going to get better.
> It's not.[7]

A similar fantasy is presented in Bill Peet's *The Wump World* (1970), a picture book that begins with a description of lush, unspoiled land: "The Wump World was mostly grassy meadows and clumps of leafy green trees with a few winding rivers and lakes. But it was perfect for the Wumps."[8] However, natural order and beauty are endangered by an invasion of the Pollutians from the Planet Pollutus. The Pollutians rocket away from their used-up, worn-out world; with anticipation to begin anew, they arrive on the peaceful and lush *Wump World*. Meadows become roads, factories and buildings appear, and new cities are formed, all flying the Pollutians' flag. And as the landscape changes, smoke, debris, car exhaust fumes, and polluted rivers soon make even the Wump World intolerable. The Pollutians leave to find another world, and the Wumps emerge from their hiding place to reclaim their world: "In time the murky skies would clear up and the rains would wash scum from the rivers and lakes. The tall buildings would come tumbling down and the freeways would crumble away. And in time the green growth would wind its way up through the rubble. But Wump World would never be quite the same. . . ."[9]

Many of these books are well written and illustrated, and they emphasize the important ecological message of preserving our environment. Nevertheless they also are marred in

Wump
World

that they oversimplify the issue by depicting industry and growth as monolithic evils. In *The Wump World, The Lorax,* and *The Seal and the Slick,* children are treated to a polemic against all technology, with the underlying message that nature and the countryside must be preserved at all cost. This is a somewhat unrealistic appraisal, since technology will neither disappear, fade into the sunset, nor rocket out of our lives and into space. Presenting a case for ecology within a balanced story represents a real challenge for authors of children's books. The appeal of generalizing the evils of industry while extolling the virtues of nature represents a common and inviting simplification, an unfortunate simplification that detracts from the effectiveness of children's literature.

Another example of this problem appears in stories set in urban environments. To many authors who are concerned with ecology, the city becomes an example of a disrupting and dysfunctional environmental influence. Focusing on the population density, pollution, and alienation of urban life, many authors exclude any mention of the redeeming qualities of the city, offering instead a simplified presentation of the city as an enemy of a pure and clean environment.

One example of a slanted presentation of the city is Virginia Lee Burton's *The Little House* (1942).[10] This popular picture book relates the story of an attractive, pink house that leads a pleasant life in the country watching the seasons change along with the gentle daily activities of the people. The little house is curious about the lights of the city seen in the distance, but it is not until a road is built and the city begins to expand that the little house gets to experience city life firsthand. As stores and tenements are built, the little house becomes the victim of neglect. The illustrations turn muddy brown and the beautiful country-

side is lost amidst rushing people, tall buildings, dust, smoke, bright lights, and the noise of the city. The little house becomes rundown and dilapidated and takes on the appearance of a victim of a mugging. The house is saved from this fate worse than death (i.e., living in a city) and is transported back to the country. Totally renovated, the house is now happy and seems to have learned an important lesson: "Never again would she be curious about the city. . . . Never again would she want to live there. . . . The stars twinkled above her. . . . A new moon was coming up. . . . It was spring . . . and all was quiet and peaceful in the country."[11] Although this Caldecott winner is in many respects an excellent and charming picture book, it does, unfortunately, offer an overly negative and one-dimensional portrayal of city life.

*The Last Forest* (1973), by Laurie Glick, is another direct attack on the city. Urban dwellers, through growth, pollution, and neglect, have managed to destroy all the earth's forests except one. It is through the efforts of young Fern, a forest ranger, that the thoughtless denizens of the city are dissuaded from destroying the last forest. Again, the city is depicted in dreary illustrations, whereas the forest is presented as a colorful and exciting place.

Although the city is frequently treated as a scapegoat, not all children's books paint the city in negative tones. Some books reflect the diversity and assets of urban America, presenting urban problems with wit and humor. The result is a more balanced picture of the promise and problems of American cities. For example, Judith Barrett's *Old MacDonald Had an Apartment House* (1969) offers a novel and humorous response to population density. Old MacDonald is a building superintendent whose tolerance to the demands of some of his complaining tenants seems to decrease in direct

The Little
House

relation to his fondness for plants and animals. By redecorating various apartments into mini-gardens and dairy farms and changing the decor of the apartment house to "Late Vegetarian," he creates a more attractive and humane urban environment.

Jean Merrill's *The Pushcart War* (1964) also treats the problem of fast-paced urban change without denigrating the worth and viability of urban life. In this modern fantasy the wealth and influence of the large trucking companies allow them to threaten taking over the streets of the city. The pushcart operators, first to be threatened by the impersonal trucking giants,

wage an ingenious guerilla war. The pushcart peddlers' victory also marks a victory for the people, and for a less polluted, more humane, and more livable city.

Another creative response to fast paced, and potentially inhumane, industrial change is Virginia Lee Burton's *Mike Mulligan and His Steam Shovel* (1939). Although Mike Mulligan and his steam shovel, Mary Anne, are busily engaged in building roads and airports, the creation of diesel and electric shovels eventually puts them out of work. To prove once again their usefulness they wager that they can dig a cellar for a new town hall in only one day. Their success is short-lived when they discover that they have forgotten to build their exit ramp and find themselves imprisoned in the newly excavated cellar. A young boy provides the solution to the predicament by suggesting that Mary Anne be converted into the furnace for the new town hall: "Now when you go to Poppersville, be sure to go down to the cellar of the new town hall. There they'll be, Mike Mulligan and Mary Anne . . . Mike in his rocking chair smoking his pipe, and Mary Anne beside him, warming up the meetings in the new town hall."[12]

Although *Mike Mulligan and His Steam Shovel* does not directly deal with the city, it does reflect the kind of creative and positive response to technological change that is too frequently omitted from children's books about city life. It is important for teachers and librarians to recognize the negative generalizations and distortions attributed to the city in particular, and to technology in general. The problems of urban life and industrial growth are real, but the benefits of industrial progress and the joy and excitement of urban America are real also. A balanced portrayal of these topics will help children to understand better the role of technology and urban life, which is necessary to a more complete and objective awareness of environmental dangers.

## The environment in realistic fiction

An appreciation for nature and nature's creatures is a recurrent theme in children's books about the environment. Yet this affection for nature represents only one of several themes in children's books, ranging from crusading to preserve the environment to attempting to conquer nature and kill nature's creatures. The great variety of treatments of the relationship between humans and the environment in realistic fiction suggests the need for

careful analysis. The following sections reflect several of these different themes and are designed to aid the reader in helping children to sort out these various treatments and to evaluate the power and limitations of each approach.

## Loving nature and nature's creatures

One of the more popular themes in realistic fiction depicts a young protagonist who develops a special relationship with an animal or with nature. This approach is illustrated in Frederic Bell's *Jenny's Corner* (1974), a brief but involving book for elementary school children. Jenny Drury and her family settle and farm in Pennsylvania in the spring of 1856. In the difficult conditions of establishing a new home and livelihood in rustic surroundings, Jenny learns to love the beauty of nature and becomes particularly fond of the beautiful deer that roam the woods near her home. But Jonas Weaver and his sons, although friendly and helpful neighbors to the Drury family, regularly hunt the deer. Although the Weavers hunt only deer that they intend to eat, Jenny is not appeased. Her concern reaches serious proportions when she runs into the woods during a blizzard trying to help a wounded deer. She becomes ill, and recovers only after the Weavers promise to refrain from killing her beloved deer. For generations the Weavers keep hunters away from that part of the Pennsylvania countryside, known as "Jenny's Corner." *Jenny's Corner* is a brief yet appealing book that emphasizes the appreciation and love for nature felt by a young child. Although one might argue with Jenny's disapproval of even the Weaver's limited hunting for food, a rather natural function of nature's balance, the young reader nonetheless learns of Jenny's reverence for nature's creatures.

The love of nature theme is not restricted to

historical settings. Link Keller, in Keith Robertson's *In Search of a Sandhill Crane* (1973), is at first quite reluctant to leave "civilization" New Jersey style. But Link has agreed to a summer visit to a little-known aunt living in the rural Upper Peninsula of Michigan. Link's first few days in Michigan are disappointing, and he looks forward to returning to New Jersey, baseball, and television. He decides to stay just long enough to use the photographic equipment he was given and fulfill his promise of taking a picture of a sandhill crane. But getting a picture of a sandhill crane is more difficult than he anticipates. Link's stay is extended as he tries to get his picture, and his desire to return to New Jersey diminishes as he learns of the wonders of nature.

Seventeen-year-old Sam Gribley, in Jean Craighead George's *My Side of the Mountain* (1959), learns of the beauty and hardships of pioneering. Sam lives in modern America but is determined to spend a year living as his ancestors did on a farm in the Catskills in New York. Without provisions, Sam's courage and deep love for the woods bring him through a rough winter, and eventually onto the pages of a newspaper. Sam's love of nature is translated into a desire to live as a part of nature, in a simple and preindustrial relationship with the environment.

Returning to simpler times and a less complex society is a theme that also appears in Jean Craighead George's *Julie of the Wolves* (1972), a compelling story of a thirteen-year-old Eskimo girl who is caught between the traditional ways of her people and the pressures of a modern, industrial society. A 1973 Newbery winner, *Julie of the Wolves* is the story of a girl who leaves her Eskimo surroundings to begin her trek across the tundra in an attempt to reach San Francisco. She becomes lost and is adopted by a wolf pack. By learning the language and ways of the wolves,

she manages to survive and eventually reaches the coast and finds her father.

*Julie of the Wolves* is an exciting adventure story as well as a poignant account of a girl maturing to womanhood. Moreover, the powerful and engrossing descriptions of life among the wolves on the tundra add a significant environmental dimension. By learning the sky and land of the tundra, trapping and eating animals, using caribou droppings for fuel and animal skins for clothing, and communicating with her comrades, the wolves, Julie demonstrates her ability to become a part of nature's balance. She is told, "You are Eskimo. . . . And never forget it. We live as no other people can, for we truly understand the earth."[13] But times are changing and the white world is intruding on the harsh beauty of Eskimo life. When Julie's wolf friend, Kapu, is shot by a hunter from a plane, the insensitivities of this new, white civilization become crystallized.

The air exploded and she stared up at the belly of the plane. Bolts, doors, wheels, red, white, silver, and black, the plane flashed before her eyes. In that instant she saw great cities, bridges, radios, school books. She saw the pink room, long highways, T.V. sets, telephones, and electric lights. Black exhaust enveloped her, and civilization became this monster that snarled across the sky.[14]

## The cult of kill

Quite a different relationship between a youngster and nature is depicted in Marjorie Rawlings' *The Yearling* (1939). Young Jody is ordered to kill his pet deer who is destroying the family's crops. In spite of his deep love for the yearling, he follows his parents pronouncement and tracks down and kills the deer.

He found himself listening for something. It was the sound of the yearling for which he listened.

. . . He did not believe he should ever again love anything, man or woman or his own child, as he had loved the yearling. He would be lonely all his life. But a man took it for his share and went on.[15]

One of the more popular and highly acclaimed books, *The Yearling* is nevertheless cited by Jean McClure Kelty as an example of the "cult of kill."[16] The cult of kill appears in books with a protagonist, usually a boy, who must prove his maturity by performing an act of violence against an animal or the natural world. Rather than living in or loving the natural world, these characters prove their readiness for adulthood by conquering some aspect of nature. In contrast to current ecological sensitivities, books that contain the cult of kill portray nature as a hostile and alien force.

Another popular children's book, *Old Yeller* (1956), by Fred Gipson, also emphasizes the cult of kill. A beloved family dog, Old Yeller, has saved two family members from the attack of a wolf. But fear that the wolf, and now Old Yeller, may be rabid, leads to the decision that Old Yeller must be killed. And again, a young boy is assigned the task of executioner: "I reloaded my gun and called Old Yeller back from the house. I struck the muzzle of the gun against his head and pulled the trigger."[17]

Again, the killing of an animal represents a boy's initiation into manhood. Unfortunately, the cult of kill reappears in a number of books. Killing wild animals or pets occurs in Melville's *Moby Dick* (1950), Hemingway's *Old Man and the Sea* (1952), Wojciechowska's *Shadow of a Bull* (1964), and Walton's *Harpoon Gunner* (1968), to name but a few. Books that counteract this glorification of killing include Allan Eckert's *Incident at Hawk's Hill* (1971).

*Incident at Hawk's Hill*, set in Canada in 1870, is the story of the Macdonalds and their six-year-old son, Ben. Young Ben's special talents include his ability to imitate and communicate with animals. Ben's ability to befriend even the dangerous badger proves to be his salvation. Although the badger is eventually shot and killed, this wanton act is not glorified as a necessary ritual on the road to manhood. Rather, the killing is roundly criticized. *Incident at Hawk's Hill* presents a sensitive alternative to the cult of kill.

Other alternatives include Jean Craighead George's *The Summer of the Falcon* (1962) and Hal Borland's *When the Legends Die* (1963). *The Summer of the Falcon* is the story of a young girl and her sparrow hawk and their learning from one another and growth to maturity and independence. A young Indian in *When the Legends Die* has abandoned the ways of his people for the life of the rodeo. But the cruelty and killing of rodeo life become intolerable, and the young Indian finally rejects senseless violence.

Although death and brutality are in fact integral parts of life, they do not make the world a gentler and more compassionate place. Nor is brutal killing a prerequisite for adulthood. Moreover, the cult of kill suggests the need to conquer nature violently rather than live in harmony with it. This attitude contradicts the very foundations of the ecological movement.

## Crusading for ecology

Some of the more recently published books of realistic fiction feature young characters who are actively involved in a campaign to protect and preserve the environment. Jean Craighead George's *Gull Number 737* (1964) and *Who Really Killed Cock Robin? An Ecological Mystery* (1971) are at the same time informative and interesting. In *Gull Number 737*, Luke Rivers and his father, an ornithologist, spend their summers on Block Island doing research on seagulls. The tedious work of the scientist is difficult for Luke to endure, until the research proves valuable in saving the lives of passengers using Logan Airport in Boston. *Gull Number 737* emphasizes the use of modern scientific research to help resolve at least one environmental problem caused by modern technology.

In Don Moser's *A Heart to the Hawks* (1975) young Mike Harrington is an active scientist, interested in plant and animal life. When a contractor decides to replace a large natural area on the outskirts of Cleveland with a suburban development, Mike decides to fight to stop it. He loses, but not without a grand fight, and the scientifically erudite yet boyishly awkward Mike makes for a truly memorable character.

Tony Isidoro and Mary Alice are two young, ecologically knowledgeable residents of Saddleboro, in *Who Really Killed Cock Robin? An Ecological Mystery*. A local radio station announces the arrival of a robin family as a sign of spring, but the good omen backfires when the birds die; all that remains of the robin family is a deformed baby robin. The town's residents, including the flamboyant mayor, are incensed and want to discover the culprit. Tony, Mary, and a friend at the local university become the chief investigators to determine the environmental cause of the robins' deaths. Detergents, fertilizers, NASA, sewerage, mercury, and parasites are all investigated. The delicate balance of our ecosystem, and the responsibility we all have in maintaining our environment are revealed in the search to discover who killed cock robin.

*Gull Number 737*, *A Heart to the Hawks*, and *Who Really Killed Cock Robin?* are examples of books that manage to combine literary quality with an informative and active approach to environmental dangers. This ap-

proach is also found in other children's books cited in this chapter's bibliography. Although many of these books are effective in alerting children to the dangers to our environment, others sacrifice literary quality and become uneven polemics against pollution. Some criteria for the evaluation of children's books concerned with ecology are discussed in the final section.

## Evaluating ecology books

In an article published in the *School Library Journal*, Katherine Heland suggests criteria that would be useful in selecting and assessing children's books concerned with ecology.[18] In this concluding section we review these criteria and offer examples of books that illustrate each criterion.

The first criterion consists of the universal literary standards that apply to all books. Literary standards include not only the flow, beauty, and power of the prose, but the accuracy, format, and effectiveness of the entire book. Many of the nature books discussed in this chapter provide fine examples of works that meet this criterion and combine effective prose, a beautiful format, and striking illustrations.

A second criterion cited by Heland concerns the appropriateness of ideas and concepts for the age level of the intended readership. A book can fail to meet this criterion by presenting concepts that are either too difficult for children to grasp or too simple and elementary to interest the reader. This criterion is sometimes difficult to apply for two reasons. First, children even of the same age frequently exhibit a wide range of abilities and experiences. Second, critics and authors sometimes disagree as to the appropriateness of a given idea and concept.

The difference of opinion that sometimes

occurs when applying this second criterion can be seen in the reaction various individuals have to books of fantasy. For example, Marjorie Flack's *The Restless Robin* (1937) has been criticized for not fulfilling this second criterion.[19] The book is about the life of a family of robins who exhibit an astounding array of human middle-class values. Mr. and Mrs. Robin teach their offspring—Muffy, Puffy, and Buffy—middle-class values, similar to "Robins should be seen and not heard." Good manners, self-control, and sharing feelings of pride are presented as part of the robins' daily life-style.

Some critics point out that attributing a middle-class set of values to a family of robins may confuse children. They point out that in an attempt to write an interesting fantasy, Flack is simplifying the truth and presenting ideas that will confuse, misinform, or even offend young readers. Others contend that *The Restless Robin* is only fantasy and is not meant to be an honest presentation of reality. They maintain that a precise and accurate account of a robin's existence is not called for, and may in fact detract from the effectiveness of the story.

A third point of view might also be considered. It is possible that by attributing human characteristics to robins, children may be more able to identify with, understand, and respect a robin's existence. The argument can then be made that such distortions, in the long run, may serve the useful purpose of helping young children to respect and appreciate all forms of life, and thus promote an awareness of and appreciation for our environment.

These varied assessments of *The Restless Robin* suggest the difficulty that sometimes occurs in applying this second criterion to children's books. Although some books may be difficult to evaluate in relation to this criterion, other books provide clear examples of concepts and ideas that are either too simple or too difficult for the intended readership.

The third criterion cited by Heland applies more specifically to books concerned with ecology. This criterion refers to the need to be aware of and avoid proselytizing ecology books that overemphasize environmental dangers at the expense of literary standards and accuracy. Crusading and proselytizing books are as inappropriate for ecology as they are for religion and politics. Several books previously discussed in this chapter oversimplify environmental dangers and hold technology and urban America to be unmitigated evils and enemies of the environment. These crusading polemics may disturb or confuse children. Or the authors of these books may be so preoccupied with making a strong case for environmental concern that their books may lack literary merit and become propaganda rather than literature.

For example, Cynthia Chapin's *Clean Streets, Clean Water, Clean Air* (1970) is a crusading story survey of the causes of varied forms of pollution and of man's endeavor to confront them. Told through young Jack and his friends, the book lacks excitement and takes on the appearance of a Dick and Jane story, with shallow characters and an empty plot. Michael Chester's *Let's Go to Stop Water Pollution* (1969) uses heavy-handed prose in an attempt to stress the urgency of the environmental crisis. Both books are crusading polemics, uninteresting and unlikely to attract many adherents to the cause of preserving the environment.

Unfortunately, there are too many books that fail to meet these three criteria. The importance of environmental awareness and concern suggests that teachers and librarians must exercise particular care in selecting children's ecology books. By choosing books that exhibit both literary merit and an objective presentation of environmental dangers, teachers contribute to children's understanding of and concern with ecology. The role is an important one, if today's involved and informed children are to be able to resolve tomorrow's ecological problems.

## NOTES

1. C. E. Ayers quoted in Richard Falk's *This Endangered Planet: Prospects and Proposals for Human Survial*, New York, Random House (Vintage Books), 1972, p. 47.
2. Paul Fadelli, *A Study: Conservation Education and the Western Textbook*, California State Department of Education, Sacramento, Calif., 1973.
3. Senator Gaylord Nelson quoted in Falk, op. cit., p. 180.
4. Paul Valéry quoted in Falk, op. cit., p. 37.
5. Richard G. Lillard, "The Nature Book in Action," *English Journal*, 62, no. 4 (April 1973), 537–548.
6. Jean Craighead George, "The Ecology of a Book on Ecology," *Claremont Reading Confernce, 35th Yearbook*, Malcolm P. Douglass (ed.), Claremont, Calif., 1971, pp. 34–36.
7. Dr. Seuss, *The Lorax*, New York, Random House, 1971.
8. Bill Peet, *The Wump World*, Boston, Houghton Mifflin, 1970, p. 1.
9. Ibid., p. 44.
10. Katherine M. Heland, "The Little House Syndrome vs. Mike Mulligan and Mary Ann," *School Library Journal*, April, 1970; reprinted in *Issues in Children's Book Selection*, Lillian N. Gerhardt, ed., New York, Bowker, 1973, p. 142.
11. Virginia Lee Burton, *The Little House*, Boston, Houghton Mifflin, 1942.
12. Virginia Lee Burton, *Mike Mulligan and His Steam Shovel*, Boston, Houghton Mifflin, 1939.
13. Jean Craighead George, *Julie of the Wolves*, John Schoenhen, illus., New York, Harper & Row, 1972, p. 81.
14. Ibid., p. 141.
15. Marjorie Kinnan Rawlings, *The Yearling*, New York, Scribner, 1939, p. 400.
16. Jean McClure Kelty, "The Cult of Kill in Adolescent Fiction," *English Journal*, 64, no. 2, February 1975, pp. 56–61.
17. Fred Gipson, *Old Yeller*, New York, Harper & Row, 1956, p. 143.
18. Heland, op. cit., p. 143.
19. Deborah Shields Tully, "Nature Stories—Unrealistic Fiction," *Elementary English*, 51, no. 3 (March 1974), 348–352.

## BIBLIOGRAPHY

### Picture books

ARUEGO, JOSE. *Symbioses: A Book of Unusual Friendships.* Scribner, 1970 (1–3).

ASIMOV, ISAAC. *ABC's of Ecology*, Walker, 1972 (K–4).

BARRETT, JUDITH. *Old MacDonald Had an Apartment House*, Ron Barrett, illus., Atheneum, 1969 (preschool–3).

BESKOW, ELSA. *Children of the Forest*, trans. by William Jay Smith, Dell (Delacorte Press), 1965 (K–3).

BRINTOE, JULIE. *The Spider Web*, Doubleday, 1974 (K–2).

BURTON, VIRGINIA LEE. *The Little House*, Houghton Mifflin, 1942 (K–3).

———. *Mike Mulligan and His Steam Shovel*, Houghton Mifflin, 1939 (K–3).

CARRICK, DONALD. *The Tree*, Macmillan, 1971 (K–3).

CHESTER, MICHAEL. *Let's Go Stop Water Pollution*, Albert Micale, illus., Putnam, 1969 (1–3).

FLACK, MAJORIE. *The Restless Robin*, Houghton Mifflin, 1937 (K–3).

FREEMAN, DON. *Come Again Pelican*, Viking Press, 1961 (preschool–3).

———. *The Seal and the Slick*, Viking Press, 1974 (K–3).

GEORGE, JEAN CRAIGHEAD. *All Upon a Sidewalk*, Don Bolognese, illus., Dutton, 1974.

———. *All Upon a Stone*, Don Bolognese, illus., Crowell, 1971 (1–5).

———. *The Hole in the Tree*, Dutton, 1957 (1–4).

GRIFALCONI, ANN. *City Rhythms*, Bobbs-Merrill, 1965 (K–3).

GUGGENMOS, JOSEF. *Wonder Fish from the Sea*, trans. by Alvin Tresselt. Parents' Magazine Press, 1971 (K–3).

HOWELL, RUTH REA. *A Crack in the Pavement*, Atheneum, 1970 (K–2).

HURD, EDITH. *Wilson's World*, Clement Hurd, illus., Harper & Row, 1971 (K–3).

JENNINGS, GARY. *The Earth Book*, Lippincott, 1974 (K–3).

MILES, MISKA. *Apricot ABC*, Peter Parnall, illus., Atlantic–Little, Brown, 1969 (K–3).

———. *Fox and the Fire*, Little, Brown, 1966 (K–2).

———. *Nobody's Cat*, John Schoenherr, illus., Atlantic–Little, Brown, 1969 (K–3).

PEET, BILL. *The Wump World*, Houghton Mifflin, 1970 (1–4).

PRINGLE, LAURENCE. *From Field to Forest*, World, 1970 (K–3).

ROCKWELL, HARLOW. *The Compost Heap*, Doubleday, 1974 (K–2).

ROTHMAN, JOEL. *At Last to the Ocean: The Story of the Endless Cycle of Water*, Crowell-Collier, 1971 (K–3).

SCHOENHERR, JOHN. *The Barn*, Atlantic–Little, Brown, 1968 (K–3).

SEUSS, DR. *The Lorax*, Random House, 1971 (1–3).

TRESSELT, ALVIN. *The Beaver Pond*, Roger Duvoisin, illus., Lothrop, Lee & Shepard, 1970 (K–3).

———. *The Dead Tree*, Charles Robinson, illus., Parents' Magazine Press, 1972 (K–3).

———. *Hi, Mister Robin*, Robert Duvoisin, illus., Lothrop, Lee & Shepard, 1950 (K–3).

———. *Hide and Seek Fog*, Roger Duvoisin, illus., Lothrop, Lee & Shepard, 1965 (K–2).

———. *Rain Drop Splash*, Leonard Weisgard, illus., Lothrop, Lee & Shepard, 1948 (K–1).

———. *White Snow, Bright Snow*, Roger Duvoisin, illus., Lothrop, Lee & Shepard, 1947 (K–1).

VALENS, EVANS G. *Wildfire*, Clement Hurd, illus., World, 1963 (1–3).

WHITE, E. B. *Stuart Little*, Garth Williams, illus., Harper & Row, 1945 (K+).

YASHIMA, TARO. *The Village Tree*, Viking Press, 1953 (K–3).

## Books for the middle and upper grades

ANNIXTER, PAUL. *Swiftwater*, Hill & Wang, 1950 (7+).

BELL, FREDERICK. *Jenny's Corner*, Zenowij Onyshkewych, illus., Random House, 1974 (2–5).

BIXBY, WILLIAM A. *A World You Can Live In*, McKay, 1971 (5–8).

BODECKER, N. M. *The Mushroom Center Disaster*, Erik Blegved, illus., Atheneum, 1974 (3–6).

BORLAND, HAL. *When the Legends Die*, Lippincott, 1963 (10+).

BURTON, VIRGINIA LEE. *Life Story: A Play in Five Acts*, Houghton Mifflin, 1962 (3–6).

CARLSON, CARL WALTER, and BERNICE WELLS CARLSON. *Water Fit to Use*, Day, 1966 (7+).

CHAPIN, CYNTHIA. *Clean Streets, Clean Water, Clean Air*, Charles Lynch, illus., Whitman, 1970 (K–2).

CLEAVER, VERA, and BILL CLEAVER. *Where the Lilies Bloom*, Jim Spanfeller, illus., Lippincott, 1969 (6–9).

DEFOE, DANIEL. *Robinson Crusoe*, N. C. Wyeth, illus., Scribner, 1952 (6+).

DRUMMOND, A. H. *The Population Puzzle: Overcrowding and Stress Among Animals and Men.* Addison-Wesley, 1973 (6+).

ECKERT, ALLAN W. *Incident at Hawk's Hill*, John Schoenherr, illus., Dell, 1971 (7+).

ELLIOTT, SARAH M. *Our Dirty Air*, Messner, 1971 (3–6).

FOX, MICHAEL. *Sundance Coyote*, Dee Gates, illus., Coward, McCann & Geoghegan, 1974 (5–11).

GEORGE, JEAN CRAIGHEAD. *Gull Number 737*, Crowell, 1964 (7+).

———. *Julie of the Wolves*, John Schoenherr, illus., Harper & Row, 1972 (7+).

———. *My Side of the Mountain*, Scholastic, 1959 (7+).

———. *The Thirteen Moores Series*, Crowell, 1967–1970 (3–6).

———. *Who Really Killed Cock Robin? An Ecological Mystery*, Dutton, 1971 (7+).

———. *The Summer of the Falcon*, Crowell, 1962 (7+).

GIPSON, FRED. *Old Yeller*, Harper & Row, 1956 (7+).

GLICK, LAURIE. *The Last Forest*, Young Readers Press, 1973 (4–7).

HEMINGWAY, ERNEST. *The Old Man and the Sea*, Scribner, 1952 (7+).

HICKS, CLIFFORD B. *Alvin Fernald, Superweasel*, Bill Sokol, illus., Holt, Rinehart and Winston, 1974 (4–7).

HIRSCH, S. CARL. *Guardians of Tomorrow: Pioneers in Ecology*, William Steinel, illus., Viking Press, 1971 (5–9). .

HUSSEY, LOIS and CATHERINE PESSINO. *Collecting for the City Naturalist*, Barbara Neill, illus., Crowell, 1975 (4–8).

HUTCHINS, ROSS E. *Little Chief of the Mountains*, Jerome Connolly, illus., Rand McNally, 1970 (3–5).

HYLANDER, CLARENCE. *Wildlife Communities: From the Tundra to the Tropics in North America*, Houghton Mifflin, 1965 (7+).

KALENA, SIGMUND. *The House That Nature Built*, Betty Fraser, illus., Lothrop, Lee & Shepard, 1972 (7+).

KEEN, MARTIN. *The World Beneath Our Feet; The Story of Soil*, Haris Petie, illus., Messner, 1974 (4–8).

LATERROP, DOROTHY P. *Let Them Live*, Macmillan, 1954 (4–6).

LAWSON, ROBERT. *Rabbit Hill*, Viking Press, 1944 (4–6).

LAYCOCK, GEORGE. *America's Endangered Wildlife*, Norton, 1968 (5–9).

————. *Water Pollution*, Grosset, 1972 (3–6).

LEEK, SYBIL. *The Tree That Conquered the World*, Barbara Efting, illus., Prentice-Hall, 1969 (5–8).

LEVIN, BETTY. *The Zoo Conspiracy*, Marian Perry, illus., Hastings House, 1973 (4–6).

MARZANI, CARL. *The Wounded Earth: An Environmental Survey*, Young Scott Books, 1972 (7+).

MELVILLE, HERMAN. *Moby Dick*, Random House (Modern Library), 1950 (7+).

MERRILL, JEAN. *The Pushcart War*, Ronni Solbert, illus., Young Scott Books, 1964 (3–7).

MILNE, LORUS and MARGERY MILNE. *Because of a Flower*, Kenneth Gosner, illus., Atheneum, 1975.

————, and ————. *The Phoenix Forest*, Elinor Van Ingen, illus., Atheneum, 1968 (4–6).

MOSER, DON. *A Heart to the Hawks*, Atheneum, 1975 (6+).

O'DELL, SCOTT. *Island of the Blue Dolphins*, Houghton Mifflin, 1960 (7+).

PECK, ROBERT NEWTON. *A Day No Pigs Would Die*, Dell, 1972 (7+).

PENNINGTON, HOWARD. *The New Ocean Explorers*, Little, 1972 (6+).

PRINGLE, LAURENCE. *Into the Woods: Exploring the Forest Ecosystem*, Macmillan, 1973 (3–6).

————. *One Earth, Many People: The Challenge of Human Population Growth*, Macmillan, 1971 (5–8).

————. *The Only Earth We Have*, Macmillan, 1969 (5+).

RAWLINGS, MARJORIE KINNAN. *The Yearling*, Scribner, 1939 (8+).

RINGI, KJELL. *The Sun and the Cloud*, Harper & Row, 1971 (3–7).

ROBERTSON, KEITH. *In Search of a Sandhill Crane*, Richard Cuffari, illus., Viking Press, 1973 (7+).

ROTH, ARTHUR. *The Iceberg Hermit*, Four Winds Press, 1974 (7+).

RUSSELL, HELEN ROSE. *City Critters*, Marcia Erickson, illus., 1969 (4–7).

SCHUCK, ALICE. *The Peregrine Falcons*, Peter Parnall, illus., Dial Press, 1975 (3–6).

SCHWARTZ, ALVIN. *Old Cities and New Towns*, Dutton, 1968 (5–9).

SELDEN, GEORGE. *Tucker's Countryside*, Garth Williams, illus., Farrar, Straus & Giroux, 1969 (4–6).

SILVERBERG, ROBERT. *World Within the Tide Pool*, Bob Hines, illus., Weybright and Talley, 1972 (7+).

SIMON, HILDA. *Our Six-Legged Friends and Allies: Ecology in Your Back Yard*. Vanguard Press, 1972 (5–7).

SPERRY, ARMSTRONG. *Call It Courage*, Macmillan, 1940 (4–6).

VAN DERSAL, WILLIAM R. *The Land Renewed: The Story of Soil Conservation*. Walck, 1968 (7–9).

WALTON, BRYCE. *Harpoon Gunner*, Crowell, 1968 (7+).

WIER, ESTER. *The Hunting Trail*, Richard Cuffari, illus., Walck, 1974 (5–8).

WOJCIECHOWSKA, MAIA. *Shadow of a Bull*, Atheneum, 1964 (5+).

# 11
# War and Peace

To every thing there is a season, and a time
  to every purpose under the heaven:
A time to be born, and a time to die;
A time to plant, and a time to pluck up
  that which is planted;
A time to get, and a time to lose;
A time to keep and a time to cast away;
A time to rend, and a time to sow;
A time to keep silence, and a time to speak;
A time to love, and a time to hate;
A time of war, and a time of peace. . . .

*Ecclesiastes 3*

Americans younger than thirty-five cannot remember a time when their daily lives have not been shadowed by the threat of human violence: crime in the anonymity of city streets and in the familiarity of one's own neighborhood; international warfare and the specter of nuclear devastation; the violent carelessness with which humanity disregards and insults its precious natural environment. Americans today stand witness to "a widening gap between the promise of human fulfillment and the reality of human suffering arising from violence, destruction, and continuing war throughout the modern world."[1]

> The FBI's latest figures indicate that the rate of serious crime . . . was 17 percent higher in 1974 than in 1972. . . . That is the biggest increase in the 42 years the bureau has been collecting statistics. . . . Impersonal, passionless murder on the street has come to symbolize to many people the insecurity of living in crowded urban environments.
>
> *Quoted in* Parade, *May 1975.*

Although violence and war are by no means new to humankind, never has their escalation been so rapid. Even before World War II, violence in warfare was twenty-five times greater in the 1900s than in the previous century and more than 150 times greater than in the twelfth century.[2] And never before have civilian deaths become such an accepted part of war's tragedy. Although civilian casualties made up about 13 percent of the total casualties in World War I, they accounted for approximately 90 percent of the deaths in the Vietnam war.[3]

This escalation in civilian deaths has been caused, at least in part, by a change in the ground rules of warfare. War no longer consists of armies facing one another in close proximity on battlefields, intensely aware of the deadly consequences of their actions. Rather, modern technology has made death from a distance commonplace, and bombs dropped from the sky where their impact causes unknown and unwitnessed suffering has led to a bizarre desensitization to violence. The growing number of international incidents such as those in which terrorists have assassinated nonmilitary groups, from schoolchildren to athletes participating in the Olympics, is further indication of an increasing disregard for the rights and sanctity of the civilian.

Violence is seen as a solution to conflict off the battlefield as well as on; it is part of the fabric of society and enters the lives of children with the simple flick of a television dial. On the average, preschoolers watch twenty-eight-and-one-half hours of television per week, children in the six to eleven age bracket watch television for approximately twenty-four hours each week, and adolescents watch about twenty hours a week.[4] This viewing time exposes them to a world of brutality and crime where violence is often the means to resolution of conflict. A recent study of 192 hours of programing on seven Los Angeles stations showed 501 killings, 61 robberies, 394 attempted robberies, 40 kidnappings, 5 sui-

cides, and numerous murder conspiracies and acts of arson.[5] Indeed it has been estimated that the average viewer will witness about 18,000 television murders during his or her lifetime.[6] Nor are children's shows exempt from this predominance of violence. A recent study shows that of twenty-five themes studied, violence emerges as the most frequent theme in children's cartoons.[7]

Violence also comes packaged in the form of toy weapons, playthings of death that appear incongruous under the Christmas tree, the symbol of worldwide peace. Moreover, attempts to resolve conflict, both at home and at school, too often employ violence, as parents whip their offspring for disobedience, and in some schools peer violence can make a walk through the halls a dangerous experience.

There is a pervasive informal curriculum through which children and adults learn of violence and war. We also learn of war in a more formal curriculum, one taught in public schools and in institutions of higher learning. School books frequently depict history as a chronological succession of wars, and these texts may lead students to conclude that, "war is a natural and normal relationship between nations; it is dreadful but inevitable, and its horror is full of interest."[8]

Training to accept and to participate in war goes on far more overtly when public school is over. In 1970 alone, almost 16,000 foreign officers and enlisted men came to the United States to study the practice of war and of strategic and systematic killing. Some came from "countries that intended to fight one another, some from countries that use their armies for repressing social change and frustrating democracy. It is as if the Borgia family ran a school for poisoning with an open admission policy."[9]

Harold Taylor suggests there is an international system of war and a concomitant array of colleges that teach its curriculum, whereas,

### Los Angeles Station Seeks Better Broadcasting for Kids

Batman has been shot down, along with Superman and Aquaman, by Los Angeles television station KTTV. Bowing to pressure brought by the National Association for Better Broadcasting, the station chloroformed 42 shows that feature violence. . . . The station will also warn parents about 81 other violence-oriented shows it will continue to air, such as "The Man from Uncle," by playing two bongs on a soft chime before the show begins.

Instructor, *March 1974*

in contrast, there are too few places one can go to study the curriculum of peace. He asks, "Where is the peace system and its colleges? Where do politicians, scholars, diplomats and citizens go to learn how to prevent wars and stop them once they have started?"[10] And, we might add to this listing, where and how do children learn to settle conflict and to live in peace?

## The peace curriculum

Concern over contemporary society's immersion in an environment of violence and war has led to the development of a recent curricular phenomenon most often labeled "peace studies." The various interpretations of peace studies are too complex to explore in depth in this chapter. However, there seems to be agreement that peace studies are rooted in analyses of the conditions of peace and the causes of war and an attempt to determine the most satisfactory methods for peaceful resolution of conflict. Peace education is interdisciplinary, concerned with knowledge orientation and values. "Its basic purpose is to help students design strategies of action which can contribute to the shaping of a world order characterized by social justice and absence of exploitation."[11]

It was during the 1960s that courses in

peace studies were first instituted. By 1974, twenty-nine United States undergraduate institutions of higher education offered either a certificate or an academic major in peace studies. One of the most exciting aspects of this new curricular development is that courses in peace education can be found not only on college campuses, but also in a growing number of secondary and elementary schools across the country.[12] Although the field of peace education is still in its early stages, some research on its effectiveness has already been conducted. An analysis of peace studies students at six universities showed that after a semester in peace studies courses, students seek less aggressive solutions to societal problems.[13]

Given the violent nature of contemporary times, it seems that some form of peace studies must be an integral part of the elementary and secondary curricula. Children's literature should be one key aspect of this curricular development, for it offers many fine books that explore pertinent issues and evoke various images of war. By reading such books children can experience vicariously what life is like in countries ravaged by war. They can consider the various images of war that children's books convey and they can formulate their own interpretation of war, whether as a chaotic and senseless exercise, a horrible but an inevitable and necessary occurrence, or possibly even an event that may develop human potential and hold the seeds for positive social change. Reading literature concerning war and peace can help children analyze why wars occur and what conditions are necessary for people to live in peace.

Adult attitudes toward war reflect the complex moral and psychological dimensions of this issue. Some consider aggression to be an innate and unchangeable characteristic of people; war, therefore, becomes an inevitable aspect of the human condition. For others the essential nature of humanity is ultimately changeable rather than static. Since human potential is as yet barely tapped, they envision a time when war will have become obsolete as a method of resolving conflict.

The moral questions involved also engender a wide spectrum of reactions. For some, warfare is a likely and continually necessary occurrence in a hostile world of antithetical forces. For others an intense desire to avoid war's suffering must be put aside when certain principles such as individual freedom and liberty are violated. And there are those who consider no principle worth the sacrifice of human life and can envision no circumstance in which the act of war might be condoned. In the next section we review research that indicates how children feel about this ultimate and most devastating expression of human violence.

## What children think about war and peace

I hate war. Too many people get killed each year. . . .

It isn't nice to fight for nothing. That is why I don't like war. I hate war so much I wish I could stop it but I can't. . . .

War is many things to many people. To some it's a game. To others a way to money. To me it's a waste of everything we've learned. . . .

I don't think I will or my great, great, great grandchildren will ever witness complete peace in the world. . . .

There are no rules. War is war. It is in every one of us. People have been doomed to war as long as they could argue. As people's language and customs separate them, they find reasons for war. . . .[14]

As these excerpts from student's essays indicate, children's reactions to war are complex. Although these varied reactions are a challenge to researchers who attempt to make broad generalizations, studies do show us that certain key themes emerge. One significant finding is that violence appears to be a deeply rooted and integral part of the thoughts and fantasy lives of children. Evelyn Goodenough Pitcher collected and analyzed 360 stories from nursery school children. What she found most surprising was the predominance of themes of aggression, violence, death, and catastrophe.[15] Other researchers have also found that violence is the outstanding theme in the stories of children between the ages of two and five. Research also shows us that children's conceptions of war begin at a young age. Many children make their first remarks about war at the age of six; by the time they reach seven or eight, they have fairly well-defined ideas about its meaning.[16]

Herbert Tolley recently conducted one of the most thorough explorations of what children know and how they feel about war.[17] In 1971 he interviewed 2677 children in the third to eighth grades in New York, New Jersey, and Maryland. He found, as many of the preceding excerpts from children's writing suggest, that children come to think of war as horrible but inevitable. Although nearly all the children indicated that war is "very, very bad," 54 percent stated that "wars are sometimes needed." Tolley found that the oldest children in the study tended to accept war to a greater extent than did the youngest. The group that emerged as most inimical to the idea of war were children in the fifth and sixth grades. Evidently, tolerance for war decreases in the intermediate grades and then reverses and reaches its highest point in the eighth grade.

Adolescents feel far more certain than do younger children that wars will recur and that war is necessary if it is over a "good cause." For some children in Tolley's study, a good cause was the United States beating the Communists. For others defense of the nation's freedom was the primary rationale for war. As one boy explained, "We have to go to war for a purpose, to have a free country. . . . Every country has got to go to war sometime or another to defend themselves." In their conviction that wars may be necessary to protect their country, children did not, however, express unquestioning allegiance to the president. Only one-quarter of the children said they would support the president in wartime if they felt that he were wrong.

Not only do children, particularly at the upper grade levels, express their sense of war's inevitability, but they are also highly pessimistic about its eventual impact. In the early 1960s Sibylle K. Escalona and her colleagues conducted a questionnaire study in which children from the age of four to adolescence were asked what they thought the world would be like when they were grown up. More than 70 percent of the children mentioned war and nuclear disaster as likely possibilities, and a relatively large proportion, including first and second graders as well as older children, spoke pessimistically of only an even chance of survival. What makes these responses all the more disturbing is that the researchers had never mentioned war or nuclear weapons in their questions.[18]

Although children are surprisingly knowledgeable and concerned about war, they have far less tangible conceptions about the meaning of peace, and they have fewer ideas about

peace as an active process. One recent study of 2500 students attempted to ascertain how children from kindergarten through college conceptualize peace.[19] Following are some of the ways that children between five and eleven most often defined peace:

Peace means quiet in school, in church.
To be quiet, not to fight.
To be alone sitting under a tree reading a book.
No war.
Love.

Students in junior high school defined peace as follows:

Sharing and not being so greedy and selfish.
Peace is without war, demonstrations, violence.
Friendship and unity, freedom, respect, and cooperation with those in authority.
All races being able to live together.

At the junior high level, children's responses to the question "How can we have peace?" indicate their realization of the difficulty of attaining peace, and an awareness of outside actions, such as demonstrations and peace movements. Students in high school evidenced an understanding of the need to resolve conflicts peacefully, whereas college students expressed even more strongly their need for equality of opportunity and for a nonviolent system of conflict resolution.

Thus we find that children are more knowledgeable of and concerned about war than adults may realize. Research also shows that although children desire a peaceful society, they have only vaguely defined ideas about peace as an active process, perhaps because they have had less opportunity to learn about the peaceful resolution of conflict than they have about the uses of force and violence.

Ours is a society where knowledge of violence and war comes at an early age. One way children may confront war and peace is in the books they read. The following sections look at charges, countercharges, and research studies concerning the extent of violence in children's literature. Then the portrayal of war and peace in picture books, modern fantasy, and realistic fiction are discussed.

## Children's literature: a violent medium?

One parent tells of reading a fairy tale in which a young prince is threatened with a bath of boiling oil if a ship bearing proof of his identity does not arrive in time. The ship does arrive, the prince is saved, yet the child listening to the story burst into tears. When comforted with the fact that the prince did no get boiled, the child retorted that this was the very reason she was crying; she had wanted him to be boiled in oil.[20]

Such stories, although only anecdotal, make us aware that we really cannot be sure of how children will react to a book and of what they may find frightening and disturbing. Nevertheless there have been, from time to time, alarm and consternation expressed at violence in almost every aspect of children's literature, from nursery rhymes to fairy tales, from picture books to historical fiction. For example, critics have analyzed nursery rhymes to reveal that approximately half of these traditional favorites contain many forms of violence, and many rhymes that refer to whipping or death have been dropped out of anthologies or have even been rewritten. For example,

Ding dong bell, Pussy's at the well.
Who took her there? Little Johnny Hare.
Who'll bring her in? Little Tommy Wren.
What a jolly boy was that to get some milk
    for pussy cat,
Who ne'er did any harm, but played with the
    mice in his father's barn.[21]

In this rewritten version not only is the mischievous boy who tries to drown pussy reformed, but the cat is also rehabilitated, for instead of killing mice, she adopts them as playmates.

Worried adults have also attacked numerous fairy tales. Typical of these attacks is the claim that "Jack and the Beanstalk" contains thievery, murder, and with the refrain

Fee, fi, fo, fum
I smell the blood of an Englishman.
Be he alive or be he dead,
I'll grind his bones to make my bread.

even introduces youngsters to cannibalism. These critics note that the theme of one creature devouring or attempting to devour another occurs again and again in the most well-known fairy tales. In "Hansel and Gretel" the witch fattens Hansel for her dinner; the wolf repeatedly attempts to eat each of the Three Little Pigs, and the fox cleverly maneuvers the Gingerbread Boy from his back to his nose to his tummy.

In addition, picture books have not escaped occasional adult censure for depicting violence or aggression. Maurice Sendak's *Where the Wild Things Are*, winner of the 1964 Caldecott Medal, is one such book. It is about Max who puts on a wolf suit one night and makes mischief until he gets sent to bed without supper. In his room he watches a forest grow, boards a passing boat, and sails to the land of the wild things. There he becomes king of the monsters, cavorts with them, sends them to bed without their supper, and then, feeling lonely, sails back to his own room, where his supper is waiting for him. It was the vibrant, dynamic pictures of the monsters that disturbed some adults. The reviews reflected adult concern, noting that the illustrations of the wild things "may well prove frightening," or that "we should not like to have it left about where a sensitive child might find it to pore over in the twilight."[22]

Most adults scoff at the notion of rewriting nursery rhymes and dismiss the idea that "Jack and the Beanstalk" and the 'Three Little Pigs" are terrifying and harmful to children. Indeed psychologists, educators, and writers are aware that children do have violent thoughts and fantasies, and books that portray frightening ideas, without dwelling on them unnecessarily, may actually be therapeutic. Children may find such stories cathartic, realizing that they are not the only ones to feel hatred, anger, or envy. As Nicholas Tucker says, "Like Rumpelstiltskin, frightening things tend to lose a lot of their power when they are brought out into the open and named."[23] And Maurice Sendak's *Where the Wild Things Are* has proved to be a children's favorite that delights youngsters rather than terrifies them. Sendak says that children send him drawings of their own wild things that make his look like "cuddly fuzzballs" and he even receives letters that beg for directions to his wild kingdom: "How much does it cost to get to where the wild things are? If it is not too expensive my sister and I want to spend the summer there. Please answer soon."[24]

However, even those who note the therapeutic effects of depicting violent emotions agree that there are some things that are unnecessarily grotesque and that may frighten children. Hideous pictures are apparently more worrisome to children than are violent stories. Children can read or listen to a story and, through their imagination, minimize the ugliness of a witch or the size of a giant. However, a picture that portrays the hideousness of the witch in vivid detail or emphasizes the gargantuan size of the giant may become imprinted in the memory of the child and return later to haunt him.

Also, some stories dwell too vividly on horrible or bizarre details of violence. For example, it is very questionable whether a tale such as "The Juniper Tree" from the Grimm collection is appropriate for young children. In this story a mother kills her stepson by be-

Where the Wild Things Are

heading him with the heavy lid of a chest. She then remounts the head on the boy's shoulders and commands her daughter to give the boy a box on his ears. The daughter is not aware of her mother's sinister deed, and when the boy's head flies off, the girl is convinced that she has killed her brother. The mother then bakes her son in a pudding; the family eats him for supper and discards the bones. The boy emerges from the bones as a beautiful bird and avenges his murder by dropping a millstone upon his mother's head.

One might also question whether George Mendoza's picture book *The Hunter, The Tick and the Gumberoo* (1971) is suitable reading material for young children. This is the story of a hunter on the trail of the notoriously ferocious Gumberoo. During his journey the hunter finds that a lump caused by a tick has begun to grow on one side of his face. The tick insists on consuming the hunter's game until finally the lump has swollen to the size of a man. The desperate hunter points the gun at his obscenely distended face and shoots the tick. The book concludes, "Sometime later, two hunters happened to cross the ground where the body of a man lay, clutching a rifle in his hand . . . a bullet hole through the center of his head, and on the side of his face was a speck—like a brown wood tick."[25] Philip Wende's gross pictures and Mendoza's bizarre plot combine to form an unnecessarily repulsive way for the author to express to young children his condemnation of hunting.

There is also widespread agreement that if children are to handle violence and conflict in their reading, there must be some form of resolution, some way to change chaos into order, some sense that violence not only is recognized but is controlled as well. Sendak too shows a recognition of this need when he says of *Where the Wild Things Are*, "the fantasy has to be resolved. . . . If Max had stayed on the island with the wild things, a child reading the book might well have been frightened. Max, however, comes home."[26]

Some adults have been opposed to violence in literature not so much because children may be frightened as because they may attempt to imitate the violent behavior themselves. Adult worries about children's modeling aggressive behavior forms at least part of the rationale behind objections to television violence, and there is a growing body of research to indicate that children may imitate violent behavior that is exhibited by a live or filmed model. There is not, however, any such corresponding research to suggest that children who *read* about violent behavior will imitate that behavior.

Moreover, there are several other differences between violence in children's literature and violence in television programs. Gloria Blatt performed a content analysis of 170 realistic fiction books that were selected from the American Library Association Notable Books List between 1960 and 1970.[27] She found that there is more than twice as much violence on television as in children's literature. Whereas almost 26 percent of television shows focused primarily on violence, in only 8.7 percent of the children's books studied was violence central to the story. Blatt also found that picture books were almost totally lacking in violence and that historical fiction was, on the average, more than twice as violent as modern realistic fiction, a disparity due at least in part to historical fiction's more frequent portrayal of war.

Another difference between television and children's literature is that television programs often present the act of violence, but its brutal consequences are passed over without detail. In contrast, children's literature presents information concerning the effects of violence. Also, unlike television, where the bad guys are clearly just that, villains in children's literature are often multidimensional, with good as well as bad characteristics, and realistic motivation is provided for behavior. Plots in children's literature are also more complex, and neither villains nor heroes resort so readily to violence to achieve their goals.

Thus we may conclude that, with but a few exceptions, literature for children is not exceptionally violent; it certainly does not portray violent action in the brutal and simplistic terms of television. Moreover, there is widespread feeling that violent or frightening actions portrayed and resolved in children's literature can be beneficial. Such stories not only recognize the violence that is often present in children's fantasies, but they also show that violence can be controlled. In the following sections we discuss picture books, modern fantasy, and realistic fiction, to see how war, the ultimate form of violence, is portrayed.

## Picture books

Actual war is seldom portrayed in picture books. More frequently depicted are the hostility and competitiveness that temporarily mar or even destroy a once friendly relationship, an occurrence that is close to the understanding and experience of many young children. In those picture books that depict conflict between friends, gang fighting, or actual war, the assets of reconciliation and peace are heavily emphasized.

Perhaps Arnold Lobel's *Frog and Toad Are Friends* is a classic example of the many picture books that present the theme of friendship. However, one aspect of friendship not as often portrayed is that of conflict and anger that can on occasion arise between friends. Janice May Udry's *Let's Be Enemies* (1961) shows this side of friendship. Two boys, once the closest of friends, find themselves in hostile opposition as they fight over who's boss, grab each others toys, and throw sand at one another. The conflict is eventually resolved peacefully and at the close of the book, the two boys are sharing a pretzel and a pair of roller skates. Although there is no apparent justification for resolution of their feud, other than the whims of early childhood, the book is a very on-target depiction of the small irritations that can cause young children to become temporarily furious with one another.

A slightly more sophisticated statement of friendship gone awry and transformed into hatred is Charlotte Zolotow's *The Hating Book* (1969). It begins:

> I hate hated hated
>     my friend.
> When I moved over on the school bus,
> She sat somewhere else.
> When her point broke in arithmetic
>     and I passed her my pencil,
> She took Peter's instead.
> "Ask," my mother said,
> "Ask your friend why."
> But I wouldn't,
> I couldn't,
> I'd rather die.[28]

The girl finally takes her mother's advice and moves to settle the conflict by asking the cause

"GOOD-BYE!"
"GOOD-BYE!"

Let's Be Enemies

THE HATING BOOK

by CHARLOTTE ZOLOTOW

Pictures by Ben Shecter

of her friend's anger. The fight, it turns out, has been based on a misunderstood comment and is cleared up as quickly as it began. Again, the book is a beautifully accurate depiction of childhood hatred that can temporarily loom so large and then vanish so quickly and completely.

An interesting and amusing twist on the theme of peaceful resolution of conflict is offered by Susan Pearson's *Monnie Hates Lydia* (1975). Although Monnie has worked diligently to make Lydia's birthday a success, Lydia behaves in a thoroughly obnoxious manner, calling her younger sister a pain and ignoring or deriding all her well-intentioned efforts. Monnies finally reaches her satiation point, and she mashes the birthday cake right into Lydia's face. This small moment of violence clears the air, Lydia realizes she has received her just desserts, and the two sisters sit down to eat what is left of the birthday cake.

Another book, one with animal characters, that presents friends turned temporary enemies

is Natalie Savage Carlson's *Marie Louise and Christophe* (1974), the story of two friends, a snake and a mongoose, who become involved in a deadly quarrel. It is only when they are caught and urged into combat for human amusement that the two animals realize that they really do not want to fight at all.

In some picture books an unhealthy spirit of competition is presented as the primary cause for animosity between two individuals. In *The Wicked Wizard and the Wicked Witch* (1972), by Seymour Leichman, a wizard and witch compete with one another to prove who is the more wicked. After a night of casting evil spells on each other, they are exhausted, decide it really does not matter whose magic is the strongest, and join together to clean up the mess that the night of spell casting has created. Kjell Ringi's *The Winner* (1969), a brilliantly colorful picture book without words, also illustrates the ultimate absurdity of competition. Two neighbors try to outdo one another, first in their dress, then in their mode of transportation, and on and on, until one neighbor produces a fire-breathing dragon who promptly devours them both, thereby becoming the winner. A material possession, a pink shell, is the cause of the quarrel between Sam and Boris in Michael Foreman's *The Two Giants* (1967). The fight is finally resolved when the two giants remember how much happier they were when they lived in peace. A similar theme is reflected in Alan Venable's *The Checker Players* as a tinker and a carpenter find cooperation more effective than antagonism.

Picture books that present quarrels between groups rather than individuals come closer to actually dealing with the issue of war. For example, Louise Fitzhugh's *Bang, Bang You're Dead* (1969) portrays bloody fighting between street gangs. A group of friends play at "bang, bang you're dead." However, when a new group challenges them, play turns intensely serious as two groups struggle violently with one another. The stark language mirrors the physical brutality:

"Give up, puke-face. You don't have a chance," said Big Mike.

"Up your nose, you freak-out," yelled James.[29]

The intensity of the fighting stuns both sides and they decide that peaceful coexistence is better than war.

Louise Fatio's Happy Lion series has been a perennial favorite with children, and one of the books in the series, *The Happy Lion's Treasure* (1970), makes a strong statement concerning the unfortunate effect of group fighting and of the importance of peace and love. News that the Happy Lion has a secret treasure causes the zoo animals to bicker until the lion explains that the love all the animals hold for each other is the secret treasure. Then the animals stop their fighting, sing and dance, and celebrate their love for each other and for the Happy Lion.

Picture books that actually portray war are far less optimistic. Some emphasize the causes of war, and these are often satirical. For example, in Bernice Myers' *The Apple War* (1973) two kings quarrel over who is the owner of apples that fall from an apple tree, the king who owns the tree or the king on whose land the apples fall. Because of this ridiculous argument, two countries are threatened with possible war.

A petty competitiveness is shown as the cause of hostilities in Betty Baker's *The Pig War* (1969). In 1859 on an island occupied by American farmers and British traders, each side, its nationalism stirred, tries to outdo the other in the morning flag raising ceremonies. The rivalry leads to escalating animosity and the arrival of American and British troops. However, the troops eat so much that both farmers and traders decide they will be better off to send the troops away and settle their minor differences amicably.

War is again satirized in Joy Cowly's *The Duck in the Gun* (1969), a book in which an invading army finds that it cannot fire its cannon because a duck is nesting in the barrel. As the battle is postponed while everyone waits for the duck's eggs to hatch, the invading army and the beleaguered town get to know one another and decide that they would rather live in peace than wage war.

The few picture books that emphasize the effects of war rather than its causes are not so humorous or satirical. Rather, they convey the grimness of war's impact. Anita Lobel's *Potatoes, Potatoes* (1967) tells the story of a woman who builds a wall around herself, her sons, and her potato farm as protection against two warring armies. However, when the sons grow up, they are enticed by the apparent glamor of war, and one joins the army of the East, the other the army of the West. Eventually the hardships of warfare supersede its glamor, and both starving armies converge on the woman's farm, screaming for potatoes. The book's strong antiwar theme becomes most apparent as a battle breaks out that devastates the farm. Finally all the soldiers realize the futility of war. They leave for their own homes, and the woman and her sons rebuild the potato farm.

Two books that conclude with less optimism are Janosch's *Bollerbam* (1969) and Bernice Kohn's *One Sad Day* (1971). Bollerbam is a soldier whose expert marksmanship creates havoc and suffering for the opposing army. When a magic charm causes his skill to vanish, the soldier is captured and put to death by the army he once terrorized. The book concludes with the observation that such a punishment is a just retribution for one who has waged war and inflicted suffering on others.

Bernice Kohn's *One Sad Day* (1971) portrays the demise of two fine civilizations. One is the Spots, peace-loving and in tune with nature, fishing the seas and harvesting food from the land; the other is the Stripes, more technologically advanced, with magnificent buildings, schools, and museums. The Stripes decide that their less-advanced neighbors need to be educated, and in the war that breaks out both cultures are obliterated. A very strong antiwar theme pervades the book and is summarized in its concluding statement, "War kills."

In picture books the hostility that can prevent or mar a friendship is realistically portrayed. Actual war, a topic more controversial and more difficult to present to very young readers, although not out of their range of comprehension, is depicted less often and less successfully. Whether these books deal with fighting between friends, groups, or countries, they all stress the importance of living in peace rather than in war.

## Modern fantasy

### The ultimate absurdity

The topic of war is prevalent in much of the finest modern fantasy, and there are several variations on the way it is treated. Occasionally modern fantasy takes a humorous look at war, revealing it as humanity's ultimate absurdity. In Natalie Babbitt's satirical *The Search for Delicious* (1969) a civil war breaks out over an issue as minute and ridiculous as the best definition of *delicious* for the kingdom's new dictionary. Bickering spreads throughout the kingdom over what is the most delicious thing of all, and the queen's evil brother, thirsty for power, capitalizes on the unrest and turns a silly squabble into a serious conflict.

Jean Merrill says in the introduction to her unique and cleverly executed book, *The Pushcart War* (1964), "I have always believed that we cannot have peace in the world until all of us understand how wars start." In a lighthearted but sophisticated spoof written in pseudodocumentary style, Merrill offers one version of how wars start, how they are fanned into continued existence, and how their ramifications pervade various facets of society. The setting is New York in 1976, when the city has become so overrun by huge trucks that traffic is in a constant irritating jam. The heads of the three largest trucking companies decide they must redirect all the negative attention and publicity, so they begin a campaign to con-

The Pushcart War

vince the public that the pushcarts are ruining the city. The war is on, and the pushcart owners retaliate with the famous peashooter campaign, an impressive victory that results in flattened tires for over 19,000 trucks. A marvelous array of characters is introduced, including Maxie Hammerman, the Pushcart King; Frank the Flower, who becomes the public hero of the war; and elderly General Anna, who leads the colorful army of pushcart owners.

Maurice Druon's *Tistou of the Green Thumbs* (1958) is another gentle satire against the evils of war. Tistou, the son of the wealthy owner of the Mirepoil munitions factory, is different from other children, but it is Mr. Mustache, the gardener, who discovers Tistou's truly unique talent. The boy has green thumbs, and he can make flowers bloom immediately anywhere. Tistou uses his hidden talent well; he transforms a depressing prison into an arbor, and he converts Mirepoil's slums into a garden so beautiful that people pay money for admission. When Tistou learns about war, "the greatest and most horrible injustice that could happen in the world since everyone lost in it what they loved best," he manages to alleviate this social injustice too. He uses his green thumbs so that arms from the Mirepoil munitions factory are overrun by climbing and clinging plants, and, instead of firing, they flower. There is peace, and the munitions factory is changed into a flower factory that advertises with slogans such as, "Say No to War, but Say It with Flowers." It is only at the end of this imaginative satire, when Tistou climbs a ladder of flowers and vines into the sky, that his real identity is revealed.

Another trend in fantasy and science fiction is the portrayal of violent acts upon the mind. In Otfried Preussler's *The Satanic Mill* (1973), a gripping story set against the background of seventeenth-century Germany, Krabat, a fourteen-year-old beggar boy, is drawn by an irresistible force to a mill that is actually a school for black magic. He eventually learns that the only route to freedom from the power of the mill's master lies in the strength of his own will and the love of another. Robert O'Brien's *A Report from Group 17* (1972) is a compelling book focusing on a German scientist's psychological experiments conducted on a twelve-year-old girl. In books such as *Run* (1973) ond *House of Stairs* (1974) William Sleator also reflects the trend toward depiction of violence done to the human mind.

## The epic conflict

In modern fantasy that is more serious, war often emerges as a classic struggle between the forces of good and the forces of evil. This epic struggle is portrayed in the heroic fantasies of three marvelous lands: Middle-Earth, Narnia, and Prydain, each developed with superb consistency and fine detail.

J. R. R. Tolkein, an authority on philology and myth, has created Middle-Earth, and in the *Hobbit* (1938) has drawn a character that appeals to children and adults alike. Hobbits are little people, smaller than dwarves, who love peace and quiet above all else. The hero of this particular adventure is Bilbo Baggins, a sedate, respectable homebody who loves his creature comforts, but underneath there is a touch of wildness. Despite warnings from the conservative part of his nature, Bilbo joins a troop of dwarves and Gandalf, the Wizard, in their mission to win back treasure stolen by the dragon, Smaug. The book concludes with the massive Battle of Five Armies with goblins and wolves on the side of evil and elves, men and dwarves representing the forces of good. Goodness triumphs, and Bilbo returns to his comfortable home. However, his once impeccable reputation is tarnished, and his behavior is never quite the same. He writes poetry, visits elves, and reminisces about past adventures and old battles. The *Lord of the Rings,* a three-volume sequel, which is more difficult to read and therefore more appropriate for mature adolescents and adults, is also pervaded by a sense of conflict between good and evil.

C. S. Lewis' series of books beginning with *The Lion, the Witch, and the Wardrobe* (1950) creates the land of Narnia, a fantastic place that four human children enter through a wardrobe. In Narnia evil is symbolized by the White Queen, a malicious witch whose spell is upon the land, and good takes the form of the powerful but kindly lion, Aslan. Aslan, in order to save one of the children, agrees to become a sacrifice to the witch and her grotesque horde of evil spirits. However, there is deeper magic than the witch knows, and Aslan comes to life again to lead a successful battle against the witch and her followers. The four children become kings and queens on Narnia until they accidentally tumble through the wardrobe once again and pick up their own lives as though they had never been away. The chronicles of Narnia conclude with *The Last Battle* (1956), in which the evil unleashed for once appears too great to conquer, and all the humans and the Narnians who love Aslan pass through a stable door and enter a new and beautiful world. Young readers are usually unaware of the Christian symbolism that pervades the books about Narnia. Nevertheless once they pass through the wardrobe, they are soon immersed in the conflict between good and evil and are engrossed in its outcome.

The *Book of Three* (1964), the first of Lloyd Alexander's five-book cycle about the land of Prydain, introduces Taran, whose job it is to care for Hen Wen, the only oracular pig in Prydain. However, Taran would rather be winning glory in battle. Taran gets his chance in battle soon enough, for he joins Prince Gwydion in combating the Horned King, the evil representative of the lord of the land of death. During this conflict between good and evil, Taran meets many of the marvelously drawn characters who appear in the other books of the Prydain cycle: the effervescent and self-possessed Princess Eilonwy; the strange creature, Gurgi, whose rhymed whimperings mask a loyal and stout heart; and the bard, Fflewddur Flam, whose hyperbole is checked by his magic harp, on which a string breaks whenever he tells a lie. When the battle is over and the Horned King finally vanquished, Taran returns to his job as Assistant Pig-Keeper far more appreciative of the pleasures of peace. In the final book of the cycle, *The High King,* winner of the 1969 Newbery award, the conflict between good and evil takes Taran to the very door of the Land of the Dead and to his ultimate clash with the Death Lord.

In Ursula LeGuin's trilogy, *A Wizard of Earthsea* (1968), *The Tombs of Atuan* (1972), and *The Farthest Shore* (1972)—about the greatest Wizard of Gont, Sparrowhawk—evil is also associated with the land of the dead. *A Wizard of Earthsea* describes Sparrowhawk's early training as a mage and the overweening pride that causes him to unleash a vile and evil shadow from the land of the dead, one that pursues him, drains him of his power, and attempts to possess him. Only when Sparrowhawk confronts the sharow does he conquer it and the darker, evil side of his own nature as well. In *The Farthest Shore* Sparrowhawk must again confront a spirit of evil from the land of the dead. A central theme in this trilogy is that there is a basic equilibrium in nature, and only the actions of people can disrupt the balance of things. Imagery of dark and light is associated with evil and good. The text, richly complex and lyrical, is perhaps most appropriate for better readers.

Susan Cooper's series, eventually to include five books about the Old Ones, emphasizes even more heavily the imagery of dark and light to symbolize the war between evil and good. *Over Sea, Under Stone* (1965) is the story of three English children's hunt for a treasure, one that leads them into conflict with the powers of evil. They are aided by their Uncle Merry, an ancient man who seems ageless. In the dramatic and suspenseful *The Dark Is Rising* (1953), eleven-year-old Will Stanton discovers that he is the last of the Old Ones, immortals dedicated throughout the ages to the Light and to protecting the world from domination by the forces of evil, the Dark. Will begins a mystical quest for the six signs that will one day aid the Old Ones in the final battle between the Dark and the Light. In the third book in the series, *Greenwitch* (1974), mortal children join with the Old Ones, Will Stanton and Merriman, in combating a more minor and less exciting uprising of the Dark. In *The Grey King*, winner of the 1976 Newbery Medal, Will Stanton goes to the ancient hills of North Wales in quest of the harp and the six sleepers to make ready for the ultimate conflict between Dark and Light. Michael Helsop's illustrations, eerie and compelling, emphasize the sense of high magic and ancient lore that pervade this fine book.

John Christopher's science fantasies depict a twenty-first-century world in which the forces of evil attempt to subjugate humanity and to deny the individual's freedom of will. In the first book of his white mountains trilogy, *The White Mountains* (1967), the Tripods, machinelike creatures, gain control over humans by inserting steel caps in the skulls of all children when they become fourteen, a process that deprives them of freedom of will and leaves them totally subservient. Three boys—Will, Henry, and Beanpole—manage to escape being capped and join a colony of other free men who live in the mountains of Switzerland. The second volume in the trilogy, *The City of Gold and Lead* (1967), finds Will and Fritz, another boy from the colony of free men, entering the city of the Tripods as spies.

In the final book, *The Pool of Fire* (1968), the free men penetrate the cities of the masters and destroy them. The book concludes as Will, Fritz, and Beanpole realize that freedom alone is not sufficient. At a worldwide conference, delegates from different lands meet, but the conference is characterized by discord and bickering. The three disillusioned friends pledge their lives to help men live together "in peace as well as liberty."

In modern fantasies and science fiction, war is often depicted as a classic struggle of good against evil, of the powers of Light against the powers of Dark, of human freedom and self-determination against the attempt to subjugate and enslave. In these books war is necessary if evil is to be vanquished and honorable men and women allowed to live in freedom and peace. War is also seen as a testing ground that offers a hero the opportunity to grow in wisdom, maturity, and courage. In the following sections we examine the portrayal of war in modern realistic fiction and historical fiction, categories that include some of the most powerful books available to readers in the middle and upper grades.

## Realistic fiction

Realistic fiction, both contemporary and historical, reflects war's complexity and conveys various images of intense conflict. In some books, such as those by Robb White, war is the exciting arena in which a central character proves his courage and manhood. For other authors war sets forth a chain reaction of violence that causes senseless devastation and suffering. In these books a main character's romanticized view of glory and adventure is altered as he or she becomes more keenly aware of the grim suffering that war can bring. Other authors, although conveying the atmosphere of senseless killing and chaos, present the paradox of war as a necessary horror holding the seeds of better times and constructive social change.

## A war of children

Some of the books that speak most personally and intensely to young readers are not about wars between nations but, in the fashion of *Lord of the Flies*, about the cruel violence that can occur between groups of children. Warfare between rival gangs has been the topic of such widely read books as Frank Bonham's *Durango Street* (1965) and S. E. Hinton's *The Outsiders* (1967). In these two books, both for older readers, the scene of fighting is the streets, and conflict episodes are highly violent and potentially deadly. In a few more recent books gang conflict is taken out of the streets and put in the schoolroom and among the suburban middle class. Three such books are Betsy Byars' *The 18th Emergency* (1973), Judy Blume's *Blubber* (1974), and Robert Cormier's *The Chocolate War* (1974). These fine books explore a topic that can be intensely serious to elementary and secondary school children, that of intergroup violence that is both physical and psychological in nature.

*The 18th Emergency* introduces Mouse, a boy with a predilection for comic graffiti, who, after writing the name Marv Hammerman under a school picture of Neanderthal man, must face the very real fact that Hammerman, the toughest and the biggest boy in the sixth grade, has vowed to kill him. Mouse is in a state of psychological trauma; able to stand the state of perpetual dread no longer, he confronts his adversary. In a moment of insight Mouse realizes that in ridiculing Marv Hammerman, he has struck a psychological blow. He understands that their fight is a matter of honor and that Marv Hammerman must retaliate physically, which is the only way he knows.

*Blubber* too conveys the traumatic effect that potential violence, either psychological or physical, can have on elementary school children. Further, it is an exploration of the viciousness with which children can act in the presence of a cruel leader and a natural victim. The victimization of Linda, the pudgiest girl in the fifth grade, is told by a classmate, Jill Brenner. Under the leadership of the popular Wendy, a clique has formed whose main intent is to torment Linda. The group creates increasingly distasteful tortures, almost as if trying to see how much Linda will take. The clique forces Linda to say, "I am Blubber, the smelly whale of class 206," before she can use the toilet, eat lunch, or get on the bus. After a while, she says it without being forced. When Jill, who has participated in these tortures, finally takes a stand against them, she runs into direct conflict with Wendy, the clique's leader. Then she finds how easy it is to slip from the "inside" to the "outside" as she herself becomes the victim.

The theme of mob violence unleashed by a sadistic leader is even more vividly evoked in Robert Cormier's dramatic book for older readers, *The Chocolate War*. It is the story of Jerry Renault, a courageous freshman at Trinity High and of his eventual victimization by the Vigils, the school's secret club. Brother Leon, Trinity's acting head, a fanatic and cruel man, has organized a chocolate sale and is obsessed with its success. When Jerry refuses to sell chocolates, he becomes a school hero, and the success of the entire sale is jeopardized as other students begin to imitate his refusal. However, the Vigils make selling chocolates popular, the "cool" thing to do. Then Jerry goes from hero to school pariah as his classmates want to know why he will not join the group effort. He is both physically and psychologically harassed. The process of victimization reaches a devastating conclusion as the Trinity students converge to observe Jerry fight another boy and bet on the outcome of the fight with raffle tickets. The mob is furious and violent, screaming for Jerry's death. Jerry is cruelly beaten and sustains what may be serious injuries; the book ends on a pessimistic note as Jerry warns his friend, Goober

to play ball, to play football, to run, to make the team, to sell the chocolates, to sell whatever they wanted you to sell, to do whatever they wanted you to do. . . . They tell you to do your own thing, but they don't mean it. They don't want you to do your own thing, not unless it happens to be their thing too. It's a laugh, Goober, a fake. Don't disturb the universe, Goober, no matter what the posters say.[30]

*The Chocolate War* explores the psychological ramifications of clique cruelty against a selected victim who has taken an unpopular stand as a matter of conscience, and it presents the devastating effect of mob violence.

### The faces of war

Numerous children's books portray wars that have occurred in different eras and in different parts of the world. From these books a complex, multidimensional image of war emerges. Many authors emphasize the pathetic waste of life that results from the chain reaction of violence and revenge that war sets in motion.

Harry Behn, well known for his children's poetry and his sensitive translation of Japanese haiku, treats the somber theme of war's senseless waste in *The Faraway Lurs* (1963). Set in Denmark during the Bronze Age, the story tells of two lovers, Heather, who belongs to the Forest People, and Wolfstone, of the Sun People. Their two cultures are at war and the conflict results in pointless tragedy for the lovers, with the murder of Wolfstone and the eventual sacrifice of Heather by her own people.

The chain reaction of violence that war causes is also a theme in Erik Christian Haugaard's *Hakon of Rogen's Saga* (1963). The story is set during the last days of the Vikings, on the mountainous island of Rogen, land that has been in Hakon's family for generations and that is Hakon's birthright. When Hakon's father brings home a kidnapped bride, her family retaliates by attacking Rogen and

### Violence Begets Violence

When a recent writer complained of a comic strip in which two villains start to apply a cigarette lighter to the feet of a dog, Ed Dodd, creator of the strip in question, admitted that the act is sadistic and objectionable. However, he insisted, he hoped to show "how cruel some heartless people can be toward animals and—hopefully—teach a lesson . . . since, on the following day, Mark knocks the daylights out of the dog torturers." (Letters, Jan. 29)

The lesson implied—that physical violence will cure physical violence—is self-defeating. It is much like the mother screaming, "Don't you ever strike another child!" as she swats away at her own off-spring, contradicting her words and firmly implanting through action the notion that physical attack is the ultimate way to make a point. It is the notion that leads us, finally, to wars.

*Donn B. Murphy,*
*Professor of Fine Arts,*
*Georgetown University,* Washington Post, *February 1974*

killing Hakon's father. Hakon, who finds himself a captive of his treacherous uncle, manages to bide his time and eventually mounts a rebellion to regain his birthright. The book not only conveys a sense of war's devastation but also, as if in counterpoint, emphasizes the Viking credo of the mortality of man, the immortality of his deeds, and the necessity of war to maintain power.

Books about war in the United States also emphasize the senselessness of conflict and its cycle of revenge. Set during the American Revolution, Howard Fasts's *The Hessian* (1972) is a dramatic tale in which one act of violence begets another.

The theme of James Lincoln Collier and Christopher Collier's *My Brother Sam Is Dead* (1974) is also that of war's absurdity. Set during the American Revolution, it tells of the conflict between sixteen-year-old Sam, who is eager to join the rebel cause, and his father, who has antipathy to all wars and forbids Sam to go.

"Oh God, Sam fight? Is it worth war to save a few pence in taxes?"

"It's not the money, it's the principle."

"Principle, Sam? You may know principle, Sam, but I know war. Have you ever seen a dear friend lying in the grass with the top of his skull off and his brains sliding out of them like wet oats? . . .

"Have you ever heard a man shriek when he felt a bayonet go through the middle of his back? I have, Sam, I have. It was at Louisberg the year before you were born. Oh, it was a great victory. They celebrated it with bonfires all over the colonies. And I carried my best friend's body back to his mother—sewed up in a sack. Do you want to come home that way?"

Despite the opposition, Sam steals his father's gun and goes off to fight. During the course of the war there are atrocities committed on both sides. Sam's father is killed, and Sam is senselessly hanged by his own side on false charges of thievery.

Irene Hunt's superbly authenticated *Across Five Aprils* (1964) tells of the tragic impact of the Civil War on the Creighton family and their southern Illinois neighbors. The story is told from the point of view of the youngest son, Jethro, who watches his parents age as their sons join opposing sides and fight one against the other. Even happiness that comes at the war's end is tempered by the tragedy of Lincoln's assassination and the uncertainty of times that lie ahead. Again, the hopelessness and absurdity of conflict, this time the Vietnam war, is conveyed in Gail Graham's *Cross-Fire* (1972) when an American soldier and a group of Vietnamese children experience growing trust that is terminated with their brutal deaths.

Occasionally a children's book presents a protagonist who realizes that he or she must break war's chain reaction of violence and revenge. In James Houston's *The White Archer* (1967), Kungo, an Eskimo boy who has watched a raiding band of Indians kill his parents and carry off his sister, is filled with hatred and an overwhelming desire for vengeance. However, Kungo learns compassion from an elderly couple, and when he finally reaches the land of the Indians, he puts aside his desire for violent retaliation. He has learned that violence breeds violence, that if he takes his revenge the Indians take theirs, and he will be "piling hatred upon hatred like stones that might fall and kill everyone."

Other authors suggest that when the sanctity of life and liberty are threatened by an aggressive force, war becomes a terrible necessity. Rosemary Sutcliffe, considered by many critics to be the finest writer of historical fiction for children, manages to convey war's brutality and suffering. Yet there is a counterbalancing theme in her books, a sense of hopefulness and optimism that darkness, violence, and barbarism eventually will be replaced by light, peace, order, and reason. This theme is conveyed in her trilogy, *The Eagle of the Ninth* (1954), *The Silver Branch* (1958), and *The Lantern Bearers* (1959), which superbly re-create the life and times of early Britain.

The final book in the trilogy, *The Lantern Bearers*, is set during the time when the last of the Roman auxiliaries is leaving Britain to the internal strife and warfare of the invading Saxons. Aquila, a young Roman officer, returns home to watch his villa razed, his blind father killed, and his sister carried off by the Saxon invaders. He himself is taken prisoner and serves as a Saxon thrall for three years. His eventual escape is mixed with bitterness, for he learns that his sister, Flavia, has married a Saxon and has borne his child. The book demonstrates the tragedy of war, not only through the loss of human life, but also through the psychological havoc it can cause. After years of fighting with the Roman British leader, Ambrosius, Aquila is still filled with resentment. Although he has a warm and loyal British wife, Ness, and a fine son, and although he does find some measure of contentment, he has lost the joy of living he previously had, and he can never quite regain it.

*The Lantern Bearers*, however, is not a total condemnation of war. Aquila despises war and the tragedy left in its wake, but he is also fiercely committed to ridding the land of the invading Saxons. War is necessary to achieve his ends, and the book concludes with the sense that love and compassion will be the eventual outcome: "It may be that the night will close over us in the end, but I believe that morning will come again. Morning always grows again out of the darkness, though maybe not for the people who saw the sun go down."[31]

The book next published after *The Lantern Bearers* was *Dawn Wind* (1962), which begins in the midst of darkness and chaos. Fourteen-year-old Owain regains consciousness after the battle of Aquae Sulis to find that his father and brother have been killed and that he is the only British survivor of this final key battle between Saxons and Britains. After twelve years in service to the Saxons, Owain is finally able to begin a new life for himself; he feels the "dawn wind" and the hope that darkness will be replaced by light for himself and Britain.

Unfortunately, the Sutcliffe books are difficult reading for those American children who have insufficient background in early British history. However, many are still attracted to the powerful Sutcliffe novels, for they deal in the "big basic themes, comradeship between men, loyalty and treachery and divided loyalty, love and hate, the sense of property, revenge for slain kinsfolk; and of course the age-old struggle between good and evil."[32]

In other books war has tragic personal outcomes yet harbors the possibility of eventual social betterment. K. M. Peyton's the *Flambards* trilogy draws a picture of the Edwardian period and of World War I's impact on the class structure of England. In *Flambards* (1968) Christina Parsons, a young orphan, comes to the Russell estate to live with her uncle and his two sons, Mark and Will. She resents her uncle's bullying attitude toward servants, but cannot bring herself to consider Dick, a groom on the estate, as a serious suitor. She also rejects the attention of the aggressive, domineering Mark, and leaves the Flambards' estate with Will. *The Edge of the Cloud*, winner of the Carnegie Award, depicts Will and Christina's engagement and their eventual marriage. It is also a detailed account of Will's fascination with airplanes and the early days of flying. In *Flambards in Summer* (1970) the time is 1916. Will has been killed in a wartime air crash, and Christina returns to Flambards as a widow. Eventually Christina falls in love again, and it is a significant sign of a changing social structure that has emerged from World War I, that her choice is Dick, the Flambards' former groom.

Children's literature portrays wars that have occurred between many different people and cultures. In books about war the authors' values are conveyed and various perspectives are offered. Usually war is condemned. Sometimes it is condemned totally as an unnecessary, useless, and absurd waste of human life. In other books war's horror is portrayed but there is a sense that war is an unfortunate necessity in which people must participate if positive ends are to be reached. And occasionally, authors demonstrate through the actions of their protagonists how peaceful resolution of conflict can be carried out.

In the following section we look more closely at one particular war and the many fine children's books that have been written about it.

## World War II

Between 1940 and 1945 few children's books with a World War II setting were published. In the late 1950s, however, more books about World War II began to appear, and several, such as Marie McSevigan's *Snow Treasure* (1942), Claire Huchet Bishop's *Pancakes-Paris* (1947), and *Twenty and Ten* (1952), depicted children involved in some heroic act, from smuggling out a country's gold supply on sleds to hiding Jewish children from Nazi soldiers. Although these books provided an accurate sense of living conditions during the war and of the ever-present danger and threat of death, in comparison to books written later their portrayal of war is subdued and muted.

In contrast, the 1960s and early 1970s, a time when authors have been allowed greater realism, particularly when writing for older children, have given us children's books about World War II that are often beautifully writ-

ten and uniquely powerful in impact. There are a number of similarities in these later books. They often emphasize the maturing effect of war and show children placed in enormously difficult circumstances, situations that would be beyond their comprehension in time of peace. These children are asked to respond to hardship and to war's atrocity with a degree of wisdom and courage that would normally be considered far beyond the abilities of the young.[33] Several books portray nonstereotyped female characters who grow up attempting to cope with the effects of World War II, and other books convey the horrors endured by Jewish children. Many books about World War II raise complex ethical questions concerning conflict between conscience and country and the necessity of recognizing the unique humanity of all involved in war, enemy as well as friend.

## The end of innocence: children growing up in war

In many of the books about World War II, the innocence of childhood is shown to be an untenable luxury as youngsters come into harsh confrontation with the reality of war. Often children are shown without adult supervision, fending for themselves as they flee the shadow of Nazism. For example, Jane Whitbread Levin's *Star of Danger* (1966) follows the journey of two boys who leave their families in Germany and attempt to find sanctuary in Denmark. Later, when the Nazis moved to arrest Danish Jews, the boys are smuggled out of Denmark by the Danish Resistance. Based on an actual experience, the book is a tribute to Danes who risked their own safety to help Jews escape the persecution that characterized their treatment elsewhere.

Anne Holm's *North to Freedom* (1965) also presents a boy, David, traveling on his own through the chaos of war as he escapes from an Eastern European prison camp and tries to make his way to Denmark. Joseph Joffo's *A Bag of Marbles* (1974) is a poignant reminiscence of two boys' flight through Nazi-occupied France. Ian Serraillier's *The Silver Sword* (1959) is another story of families separated by war and of children fending for themselves. Ruth, Edek, and Bronia, the three children of the Balicki family, have been forcefully separated from their parents. Along with a rebellious young friend, Jan, they learn to find their own food and shelter and gradually make their way to Switzerland, where they are reunited with their family.

One of the most powerful of these books showing children traveling alone is Erik Christian Haugaard's *The Little Fishes* (1967), the story of three children and their odyssey from Naples to Cassino in 1943. Twelve-year-old Guido, whose mother and father are dead, is one of the little fishes, the starving children of Naples, who must beg to stay alive. He befriends two other orphans, eleven-year-old Anna and her four-year-old brother. Despite the tragedy he encounters, Guido refuses to hate his enemies, for then he feels his efforts would be meaningless. All the books in this group portray ordinary children in whom the needs of the times draw out previously untapped depths of courage and resourcefulness.

Other books portray the changes that Nazi occupation makes in the daily lives of children in various European countries. Colette Vivier's *The House of the Four Winds* (1969) is set in 1943, when Paris is occupied by the Germans, and it describes the effect of war on the life of young Michel, his involvement in the Resistance, and his participation in the liberation of Paris. Alki Zei's *Petros' War* shows how occupation changes the lives of ordinary citizens of Athens, and, in particular, how Petros' family is affected. The book describes the widespread starvation and the maneuvers people carried

out, some noble, some contemptible, in order to survive.

Susan Cooper's *Dawn of Fear* (1970) is set in London and is a sensitive study of the way children's perception of war can change. Three friends—Derek, Peter, and Geoff—are fascinated by war, by the German planes that fly daily over London, and by the exciting nightly trips to the air raid shelter. However, when they become involved in gang warfare with two older boys, the youngsters witness a degree of violence that they had not been aware of before. After learning of the potential magnitude of adult hatred, Derek finds that the air raid is no longer exciting and that it brings instead a strange and unfamiliar fear. When he learns that Peter and his parents have been killed in the bombing, his innocence is stripped away, and he comes into total confrontation with war's pain and fear: "His world had stopped and the world he would live in from now on would be a different world. The old one with Peter in it would never come back again."[34]

## Women and war

Many books, set in different European countries, portray young women who experience war's impact and the changes it makes in their lives. Set on a rugged Norwegian island, Margaret Balderson's *When Jays Fly to Barmbo* (1969) depicts Ingeborg, a young woman torn between her need to keep the family farm after her father's death and her desire to follow the Nomadic wanderings of her Lapp relatives. The 1940 invasion of Norway by the Germans destroys Ingeborg's world and forces her to mature quickly, to confront new problems and make significant decisions.

In England war also has its impact on the lives of ordinary citizens, as is shown in Nina Bawden's *Carrie's War* (1973). When twelve-year-old Carrie and her younger brother, Nick, are evacuated during the bombing of London, they must cope with situations that are strange to them. Carrie's main fear is that, by inadvertently causing a fire, she has harmed people who have been kind to her. It is only when she returns years later as a grown woman that she realizes she has been living with guilt needlessly. It is the story of people meeting the troubles and satisfactions of their private lives within the larger context of a war that often seems distant and removed, and essentially Carrie's war is a private one.

Hester Burton's *In Spite of All Terror* (1969) shows the impact of war on different social classes in England. Orphaned Liz Hawtin, living with a stingy, begrudging aunt, appears to have only the most menial future open to her. However, the war provides an avenue of escape as London's children are evacuated to the country, and Liz finds a new home with the wealthy and kindly Brereton family. The Brerentons too are touched by war as their son joins the fighting, and the grandfather dies during the evacuation of Dunkirk.

Some of the books about women in war emphasize not only their courageous efforts to survive, but also their struggle to rebuild when war's devastation is over. *The Ark* (1953), by Margot Benary-Isbert, is set in the desolation of postwar Germany and depicts the aftermath of war. The book portrays the lives of women and children who wait in a disrupted and wasted city, hoping for the return of their men; and while they wait, they rebuild. The Lechow family, a mother and her four children, is trying to find living quarters and to keep up something of a normal home life in a devastated city. The older children search for employment. Margaret, who loves animals, is delighted to get a job as kennel maid to Mrs. Almut, who has managed by herself to bring a prosperous farm through the war. On the Almut property is an old railroad car that

Margaret and her brother rebuild; it becomes "The Ark," a new home for the whole Lechow family.

One of the finest and most intriguing portrayals of a girl facing the devastation of war-torn Germany appears in T. Degens' *Transport 7-41-R* (1974). A bitter yet strong and resourceful German girl helps an elderly man bring his dead wife across Germany to Cologne, where she had longed to be buried. The macabre elements of the plot are submerged by the perceptive analysis of human behavior, its pettiness and its dignity in a time of severe stress and deprivation.

Jews who managed to survive the holocaust as children have come of age to write, and many of these writers are women. Often their books are stories of escape and relocation. Judith Kerr's *When Hitler Stole Pink Rabbit* (1972) tells of a family of Jewish German refugees who, because of the father's awareness of what will happen when Hitler comes to power, settles in France. The themes of survival and the courage to begin again are stressed, as they are in Sonia Levitin's *Journey to America* (1970), which depicts the struggles of the Platt family as they attempt to leave Berlin and reach the United States.

Esther Hautzig tells in *The Endless Steppe* (1968) of how she and her immediate family managed to escape the fate of so many other Jews during this period, although ironically their escape was not voluntary. Her story begins in 1941 in Vilna, Poland, where Esther felt she lived in the best of all possible worlds. She belonged to a large, loving, and prosperous family, and she did not want even the smallest detail of her life changed. But in one morning everything was swiftly and irrevocably altered. Russian soldiers entered her beloved home and herded her family onto cattle cars bound for Siberia. In Siberia Esther copes with fear, hunger, hard labor, poverty, and the isolation of the outsider in a strange land. Moreover, she must live with the devastating awareness that although, through a stroke of fortune, she has survived, many of her friends and relatives did not.

Some books tell of the Jewish children who did not manage to relocate in time and were forced instead into hiding. Marilyn Sachs's *A Pocket Full of Seeds* (1973) relates the story of Nicole Nieman, who lived in France during the time of the German occupation and whose family did not believe the Germans would do anything to harm the Jews living quietly in the town of Aix-les-Bains. One day Nicole returns from school to find that her parents have been arrested. No friends or neighbors will help her except the school mistress, who allows her to hide in the school, where she waits for the war to end and hopes for her family's return.

*In the Upstairs Room* (1972) Johanna Reiss writes of what it was like to be a Jewish child in Holland during the German occupation of World War II. Annie and her older sister, Sini, had to go into hiding together in a farmer's home, and, with only a few exceptions, they were confined to a single room. The two girls faced interminable waiting, the ever-present fear of discovery, the lack of human contact, reading material, sunshine, or exercise. For over two years they lived in a barren world circumscribed by four walls. The book is remarkable for the portrayal of Annie and her sister, who squabbled and fought but ultimately found comfort in one another, and for its finely drawn characterizations of the three members of the family who took them in. As in the previous books, there is a gentleness in the reminiscence that is in moving contrast to the horror of what is remembered.

Another Jewish girl's story of waiting and hiding during World War II, a story with a tragic ending, is the classic *The Diary of a Young Girl*, by Anne Frank. Anne went into the Secret Annex at thirteen and died before she was sixteen, only two months before the liberation of Holland. The diary has been made into a play and movie and has been translated into thirty-one languages.

A Jewish girl's experiences in a concentration camp are recounted in *I Am Rosemarie* (1972), by Marietta Moskin. Rosemarie Brenner lived a contented and happy childhood in Amsterdam until the Nazi invasion and occupation of Holland. Then tragedy strikes swiftly. The family's possessions are taken away, they are evicted from their home, and finally they are separated and sent to concentration camps. The book recounts Rosemarie's struggle for survival in Bergen-Belsen, where she has to face hunger, unbearably crowded and unsanitary living conditions, hard labor, and the torture of watching friends and relatives die. The book is a portrayal not only of a girl's determination to survive but also of her struggle for maturity and self-understanding.

Thus books with a World War II setting offer some finely drawn characterization of girls who mature early as they attempt to cope with the abhorrent conditions of war. Like their brothers, they exhibit qualities of courage, resourcefulness, and perseverance that are usually beyond the scope of childhood.

## A matter of conscience

A recent Harvard University survey concerning the My Lai massacre in Vietnam showed that 67 percent of those questioned agreed that most people who were ordered to shoot the My Lai civilians, women and children and the elderly, would have done so. Half of those responding to the survey said that they too would have shot the My Lai villagers; only 19 percent stated that they would have refused to kill.[35] Apparently, many of those surveyed could not conceive of the possibility of exercising personal choice or decision that might be in conflict with authoritative orders.

Difficult moral issues are raised during war,

and some World War II children's books touch upon these. Many of these books raise questions concerning an individual's responsibility to follow the dictates of his or her own conscience when they conflict with higher orders or laws. This issue is explored in Hans Peter Richter's *Friedrich* (1970), Martha Bennett Stiles's *Darkness over the Land* (1966), John Tunis' *His Enemy, His Friend* (1967), and James Forman's *Ceremony of Innocence* (1970). Each of these books presents a German protagonist who must determine whether to succumb to a climate he or she finds morally abhorrent or to make an individual decision to stand against the times even in the face of personal danger.

*Friedrich* is a study of the demise of a small Jewish family, the Schneiders, as seen through the eyes of a German boy and his family. During the early 1930s the German family remains friendly and sympathetic as they witness the Schneiders' change in fortunes: Herr Schneider's enforced early retirement at the age of thirty-two and Friedrich Schneider's dismissal from school. However, the German boy joins the *Jungvolk* and his father becomes a member of the Nazi party, not because he believes all its tenets but because it will be personally advantageous for him. Later the German boy participates in a pogrom of Jewish homes and businesses and finds his involvement in the destruction strangely exhilarating. During the tragic events that follow—the death of Friedrich's mother, the total impoverishment of the family, and the eventual arrest of the father—the German family remains unobtrusively helpful, surreptitiously sending Friedrich small gifts such as an electric heater and a bag of potatoes. In the book's dramatic conclusion Friedrich leaves hiding to visit the German family when an air raid is called. Afraid of causing trouble for themselves, the German family decides to leave Friedrich in their apartment rather than take him to the air raid shelter, an act of self-interest that results in the Jewish boy's death.

The German family is not drawn as cruel or vicious. They are very ordinary people who lack the strength to stand up for, or in fact, even formulate, their own convictions. It is symbolic that they are never given a name, for they represent in microcosm all those who silently observed the devastation of Jewish friends and through this quiet acquiescence became participants in the persecution.

*Darkness over the Land* also presents a German boy, Mark Eland, who struggles with the conflict between his conscience and the police of Nazi Germany. As a youngster Mark participates in the Nazi Youth movement. But as he grows older, he is repelled by Nazi actions, and he and his family quietly become involved in minor sabotage. However, he refuses to protest in a more major way, and when asked, "If you see something and do nothing, aren't you partly responsible?"[36] he is terrified and refuses to become more deeply involved. This book is less powerful than *Friedrich*. It is also a less searing condemnation of those who observed injustice and violence but did not act to stop it.

In *His Enemy, His Friend* (1967), the main character comes much closer to taking a stand based on personal decision rather than on obedience to higher authority. Feldwebel Hans, a soldier in Hitler's Third Reich, is stationed in the French village of Nogent-Plage, where he alone of all the German soldiers is liked by the town's inhabitants and adored by the children. However, when his superior is assassinated, Hans is left in charge, and his orders from Division Headquarters are to kill six townspeople. Hans is faced with a dilemma but decides not to give the order to fire because the "order to do so offended my conscience. And when conscience and the State conflict, the conscience of a man must take precedence."[37] Another soldier gives the execution order, but when the war is over, Hans is convicted and sentenced to ten years of hard labor. The last section of the book takes place years later, when Hans accidentally returns to Nogent-Plage, where he is killed by an angry mob hungry for further revenge. The book powerfully demonstrates war's cycle of violence and retribution as it explores the question of obedience to individual conscience versus obedience to authoritative orders.

*Ceremony of Innocence*, James Forman's moving account of the activities of Hans and Sophie Scholl, is a portrayal of two students who rebelled against the imperatives of the State to follow their own convictions and who were willing to accept the ultimate implications of their moral decision. The Scholls, sickened by the activities of the Nazis, began producing the famous "White Rose" leaflets denouncing Nazism and urging the German people to passive resistance. They were finally caught by the Gestapo and guillotined. Forman, in an afterword to their story, addresses himself to the moral problem involved:

They are remembered. But in terms of their objective, the overthrow of Nazi tyranny, they did not shorten Hitler's dictatorship by one day. Were their lives wasted then? . . . if their lives were squandered, there was perfection in their dying. They took nothing away with them except the unmarketable consciousness of having done what they ought to do in spite of pain and fear; that which sentimental people might degrade by calling it glory, but which is glory all the same.[38]

Thus a significant ethical question is raised in these powerful books, and the authors explore the predicament of ordinary citizens baffled about what course to take when their government commits atrocities and when resistance may mean martyrdom. Although it is clear where the admirations of authors lie, they draw the full complexity of the situation and offer no definitive answers.

## The human gesture

### The Man He Killed

Had he and I but met
By some old ancient inn,
We should have sat us down to wet
Right many a nipperkin!

But ranged as infantry,
And staring face to face,
I shot at him as he at me,
And killed him in his place.

I shot him dead because—
Because he was my foe,
Just so; my foe of course he was;
That's clear enough; although

He thought he'd 'list, perhaps,
Off-hand like—just as I—
Was out of work—had sold his traps—
No other reason why.

Yes; quaint and curious war is!
You shoot a fellow down
You'd treat if met where any bar is,
Or help to half-a-crown.

*Thomas Hardy, 1902*

The rhetoric of war can create a psychological framework by which people are robbed of individual humanity and become categorized as the "good guys" and "bad guys," as "the enemy" and "us." Some of the finest books about World War II devastate such simplistic conceptions and emphasize that no life may be held cheaply and that there must be regard for the enemy. These books portray acts of compassion that do not recognize enemy lines and that unite human beings despite the inhumanity of war.

One book, exceptional for its portrayal of this theme as well as for its sensitively developed characterizations, is Bette Greene's *Sum-*

mer of *My German Soldier* (1973). The novel is set during World War II in a small Arkansas town. When German prisoners are brought to a POW camp outside Jenkinsville, the town regards them all as hated Nazis. However, Patti Bergen, a twelve-year-old Jewish girl, develops a warm relationship with one of the soldiers, Anton, a sensitive and ethical young man. Patti helps Anton escape, and he, in turn, gives her his family ring and the realization that she is a "person of value." When Patti learns that Anton has been shot to death, she is stunned and confesses her role in his escape. The story sends shock waves throughout the Arkansas town and indeed throughout the country. To some the story of a Jewish girl harboring a Nazi casts aspersions on the loyalty of all Jews and uncovers barely concealed feelings of anti-Semitism. For others, however, the story of an act of compassion between a Jewish girl and a German boy becomes symbolic of the love that is possible even amidst the callous atrocities of war.

James Forman's *My Enemy, My Brother* (1969), set in the aftermath of World War II, portrays the strength and also the futility of bonds of friendship that strive to unite individuals separated by enemy lines. At the end of World War II, Dan, a young Jewish boy, having escaped death in a concentration camp, finds that he has nothing to return to; his parents have been killed and all their property confiscated. As an alternative to Europe, Dan makes his way to a Kibbutz in Israel called Promise of the Future. Seeking a promised land of peace, Dan finds instead that the British, Arabs, and Jews are poised on the brink of open conflict. He refuses to be drawn into the conflict and instead becomes a shepherd. When he saves the life of another shepherd, an Arab boy, Said, the two pledge their friendship. However, pressures of war appear to be more than the friendship of the Arab boy and the

Jewish boy can withstand. At one point Dan is no longer able to resist the fighting, and, in the atmosphere of chaos and violence, he mistakenly kills Said's father. Said, too, after watching the decimation of his family and townspeople, becomes filled with the desire for revenge and future war.

---

## On a Sunny Evening

On a purple, sun-shot evening
Under wide-flowering chestnut trees
Upon the threshold full of dust
Yesterday, today, the days are all like these.

Trees flower forth in beauty,
Lovely too their wood all gnarled and old
That I am half afraid to peer
Into their crowns of green and gold.

The sun has made a veil of gold
So lovely that my body aches.
Above, the heavens shriek with blue
Convinced I've smiled by some mistake.
The world's abloom and seems to smile,
I want to fly but where, how high?
If in barbed wire, things can bloom
Why couldn't I? I will not die!

*Anonymous 1944, written by the children in Barracks L318 and L417, ages ten to sixteen, in* I Never Saw Another Butterfly . . . Children's Drawings and Poems from Terezin Concentration Camp 1942–1944

---

Perhaps *Boris* (1967), by Jaap Ter Haar, most clearly depicts the act of friendship that can humanize even the most inhuman of wars. The book tells of a twelve-year-old Russian boy who lived through the 500 days of the 1942 German siege of Leningrad. Driven by hunger, Boris and his friend, Nadia, go in search of potatoes in a field outside the city, a no-man's land that is the territory between Russian and German lines. German soldiers find the children and are stunned by their deplorable condition. The Germans feed the youngsters and, under a white flag, return them to Leningrad even though it means walking straight into Russian lines. Boris halts the Russians' initial impulse to shoot the German soldiers. He makes it clear that the German soldiers are his friends, and, as they are allowed to return to their own lines, each side learns that "even in an inhuman war, people can show human feelings." At the book's conclusion Boris finds opportunity to return the act of compassion. Watching a group of German prisoners being marched through the streets of Leningrad, he is filled with pity, and convinced that he must show his fellow Russians that there are good Germans as well as bad, he runs to one of the wounded Germans and gives him a bar of chocolate.

The row halted for a moment. The German's eyes lightened. Instead of a wounded, beaten, captive animal, he looked like a man again. He looked intently at Boris and smiled his thanks.

Then he was past. But Boris would never forget their meeting. With a profound sense of gratitude he stared over the Germans. It was almost impossible, but it was so; one small bar of chocolate had given a kind of firmness to their dragging feet. Slowly Boris went back to his place, his eyes on the ground. He didn't dare to look up, but he felt a hundred reproachful eyes looking at him, and on all sides he heard disapproving voices:

"They're devils—what did you do that for?"

"Do you call yourself a Russian?"

Then Boris felt someone lay a hand on his shoulder, and in a moment of silence an old woman's voice said, for everyone to hear: "You did right, child."

Boris looked up. The old woman was looking at him. Her wrinkled face was half hidden by her black shawl, but her eyes were bright.

"You did right." She turned to the people around them. "What use is our freedom to us if we still live in hate?"

There was a pause, then most people nodded. Because those who have suffered much, can forgive much. . . .[39]

In the preceding sections we have examined conceptions that children, growing up in a violent society, have of war and peace. We have also looked at claims that children's literature is a violent medium, and we have discussed how war, the ultimate expression of violence, has been portrayed in picture books, modern fantasy, and realistic fiction. We have, in particular, emphasized some of the books written about World War II, superb books both in terms of literary quality and in the dimension and significance of the moral issues and the psychological concerns that they raise.

It is our feeling that such books should occupy a key place in the school curriculum and in the reading material offered children. It seems clear that, particularly on the affective dimension, children's literature has much to offer in the development of a curriculum concerned with peace. Through picture books such as *The Hating Book* or *Potatoes Potatoes*, even young children can gain insight into the causes and effects of conflict on both an interpersonal and an international level. Various heroic fantasies from the Prydain cycle to the books of Susan Cooper can give rise to discussions concerning the necessity of war. Realistic fiction such as *Blubber* and *The Chocolate War* may help students analyze the processes of gang scapegoating and victimization. A variety of moral and psychological issues are raised in books such as *Friedrich, Ceremony of Innocence, Summer of My German Soldier,* and *Boris*. And innumerable other children's books of high literary quality provide an experiential dimension to help children realize what it is like to live during war.

In any study of war and peace, cognitive information is not enough. The experiential and the affective dimension must be provided—as one principal recognized in a note to his teachers on the first day of the school year.

Dear Teacher:

I am a survivor of a concentration camp. My eyes saw what no man should witness:

Gas chambers built by *learned* engineers.

Children poisoned by *educated* physicians.

Infants killed by *trained* nurses.

Women and babies shot and burned by *high school* and *college* graduates.

So, I am suspicious of education.

My request is: Help your students become human. Your efforts must never produce learned monsters, skilled psychopaths, educated Eichmanns.

Reading, writing, arithmetic are important only if they serve to make our children more humane.[40]

# NOTES

1. Thornton B. Monez, "Working for Peace: Implications for Education," in *Education for Peace; Focus on Mankind*, George Hendersen, ed., Washington, D.C., Association for Supervision and Curriculum Development, 1973, p. 11.
2. Pitirim Sorokin, *Social and Cultural Dynamics*, Totowa, N.J., Bedminster Press, 1941; reprinted, 1962.
3. Monez, op. cit., p. 12.
4. Figures based on the 1970 statistics of the A. S. Neilson Media Research Division.
5. "Reporting from the World of Television and Radio," *New York Herald Tribune*, August 1964.
6. John Savage, "Jack, Janet, or Simon Barsinister," *Elementary English, 50*, no. 1 (January 1973), 133–136.
7. John Carmody, "TV Violence: Many More Victims," *Washington Post*, December 16, 1974.
8. Richard Steplieus, "Schools and War," *Teachers College Journal*, May 1967, p. 257.
9. Harold Taylor, "A Curriculum for Peace," *Saturday Review, 54*, September 4, 1971.
10. Ibid.
11. Monez, op. cit., p. 18.
12. William Boyer, "World Education: What Is It?" *Phi Delta Kappan, 56*, no. 8 (April 1975), 524–527.
13. Vincent Parrillo and Kevin Michael Marion, "Peace Studies for Students: How Effective?" *Phi Delta Kappan, 56*, no. 2 (October 1974), 146–147.
14. Norma R. Law, "Children and War," *Childhood Education, 49*, no. 5 (February 1973), 231.
15. Evelyn Goodenough Pitcher, "Values and Issues in Young Children's Literature," *Elementary English, 46*, no. 3 (March 1969), 287–294.
16. Peter Cooper, "The Development of the Concept of War," *Journal of Peace Research, 2*, 1965, 1–17.
17. Howard Tolley, Jr., *Children and War*, New York, Teachers College Press, 1973.
18. Sibylle Escalona, "Children and the Threat of Nuclear War," in *Behavioral Science and Human Survival*, M. Schwebel, ed., Palo Alto, Calif., Science and Behavior Books, 1965.
19. Juliette P. Burstermann, "Let's Listen to Our Children and Youth," in *Education for Peace: Focus on Mankind*, op. cit., 63–80.
20. Catherine Storr, "Fear and Evil in Children's Books," *Children's Literature in Education*, March 1970, pp. 22–40.
21. Nicholas Tucker, "Books That Frighten," in *Children and Literature; Views and Reviews*, ed. Virginia Haviland, Glenview, Ill., Scott, Foresman, 1973, pp. 104–109.
22. Quoted in Nat Hentoff, "Among the Wild Things," in *Only Connect: Readings on Children's Literature*, Sheila Egoff, G. T. Stubbs, and L. F. Ashley, eds., New York, Oxford University Press, 1969, pp. 323–346.
23. Nicholas Tucker, in ibid., p. 105.
24. Quoted in Hentoff, in ibid., p. 330.
25. George Mendoza, *The Hunter, the Tick, and the Gumberoo*, Philip Wende, illus., New York, Cowles, 1971.
26. Quoted in Hentoff, op. cit., p. 343.
27. Gloria Toby Blatt, "Violence in Children's Literature: A Content Analysis of a Select Sampling of Children's Literature and a Study of Children's Responses to Literary Episodes Depicting Violence," Ph.D. dissertation, Michigan State, 1972.
28. Charlotte Zolotow, *The Hating Book*, pictures by Ben Shecter, New York, Harper & Row, 1969.
29. Louise Fitzhugh, *Bang Bang You're Dead*, Sandra Scarpaletti, illus., New York, Harper & Row, 1969.
30. Robert Cormier, *The Chocolate War*, New York, Pantheon, 1974, p. 248.
31. Rosemary Sutcliff, *The Lantern Bearers*, Charles Keeping, illus., New York, Walck, 1959, pp. 250–251.
32. Rosemary Sutcliff, "History Is People," in *Children and Literature; Views and Reviews*, op. cit., p. 311.
33. Marcia Shutze and M. Jean Greenlaw, "A Study of Children's Books with World War II Settings," *Top of the News, 31*, no. 2 (January 1975).
34. Susan Cooper, *Dawn of Fear*, Margery Gill, illus., New York, Harcourt Brace Jovanovich, 1970, p. 149.

35. Aubrey Haan, "Antecedents of Violence," in *Education for Peace; Focus on Mankind*, op. cit., pp. 43–60.

36. Martha Bennett Stiles, *Darkness Over the Land*, New York, Dial Press, 1966, p. 104.

37. John Tunis, *His Enemy, His Friend*, New York, Morrow, 1967, p. 24.

38. James Forman, *Ceremony of Innocence*, New York, Hawthorne, 1970, p. 248.

39. Jaap Ter Haar, *Boris*, trans. by Martha Mearns, Rien Poortvliet, illus., Dell (Delacorte Press), 1970, pp. 148–149.

40. Quoted in *School: Pass at Your Own Risk*, Arthur Daigon and Richard Dempsey, eds., Englewood Cliffs, N.J., Prentice-Hall, 1974, p. 35.

# BIBLIOGRAPHY

## Fiction for younger grades

BAKER, BETTY. *The Pig War*, Robert Lopshire, illus., Harper & Row, 1969 (2–3).

CARLSON, NATALIE SAVAGE. *Marie Louise and Christophe*, Jose Aruego and Ariane Dewey, illus., Scribner, 1974 (K–3).

COWLEY, JOY. *The Duck in the Gun*, Edward Sorel, illus., Doubleday, 1969 (K–3).

FATIO, LOUISE. *The Happy Lion's Treasure*, Roger Duvoisin, illus., McGraw-Hill, 1970 (K–2).

FITZHUGH, LOUISE. *Bang, Bang You're Dead*, Sandra Scoppettone, illus., Harper & Row, 1969 (3–6).

FOREMAN, MICHAEL. *The Two Giants*, Pantheon Books, 1967 (K–4).

JANOSCH. *Bollerbam*, trans. by Refna Wilkin, Walck, 1969.

KOHN, BERNICE. *One Sad Day*, Barbara Kohn Isaac, illus., Third Press, 1971.

LEAF, MUNRO. *The Story of Ferdinand*, Robert Lawson, illus., Viking Press, 1936 (K–3).

LEICHMAN, SEYMOUR. *The Wicked Wizard and the Wicked Witch*, Harcourt Brace Jovanovich, 1972 (K–3).

LIONNI, LEO. *The Alphabet Tree*, Pantheon Books, 1968 (K–3).

LOBEL, ANITA. *Potatoes, Potatoes*, Harper & Row, 1967 (K–3).

MCGOWEN, TOM. *The Apple Strudel Soldier*, John E. Johnson, illus., Follett, 1968 (K–3).

MENDOZA, GEORGE. *The Hunter, the Tick, and the Gumberoo*, Philip Wende, illus., Cowles, 1971.

MYERS, BERNICE. *The Apple War*, Parents' Magazine Press, 1973 (K–3).

PEARSON, SUSAN. *Monnie Hates Lydia*, Diane Paterson, illus., Dial Press, 1975 (preschool–3).

RINGI, KJELL. *The Winner*, Harper & Row, 1969 (preschool–1).

UDRY, JANICE MAY. *Let's Be Enemies*, Maurice Sendak, illus., Harper & Row, 1961 (preschool–1).

VENABLE, ALAN. *The Checker Players*, Byron Barton, illus., Lippincott, 1973 (K–3).

WAHL, JAN. *The Animals' Peace Day*, Victoria Chess, illus., Crown, 1970 (preschool–2).

WONDRISKA, WILLIAM *The Tomato Patch*, Harper & Row, 1963 (2–4).

ZOLOTOW, CHARLOTTE. *The Hating Book*, Ben Shecter, illus., Harper & Row, 1969 (K–2).

## Fiction for the middle and the upper grades

ALEXANDER, LLOYD. *The Black Cauldron*, Holt, Rinehart and Winston, 1965 (6–8).

———. *The Book of Three*, Holt, Rinehart and Winston, 1964 (6–8).

———. *The Castle of Llyr*, Holt, Rinehart and Winston, 1966 (5–8).

———. *Taran Wanderer*, Holt, Rinehart and Winston, 1967 (6–8).

———. *The High King*, Holt, Rinehart and Winston, 1968, Newbery Medal (6–8).

ARNOLD, ELLIOTT. *A Kind of Secret Weapon*, Scribner, 1969 (5–8).

BABBITT, NATALIE. *The Search for Delicious*, Farrar, Straus & Giroux, 1969 (4–6).

BALDERSON, MARGARET. *When Jays Fly to Barmbo*, Victor G. Ambrus, illus., World, 1969 (6–9).

BAWDEN, NINA. *Carrie's War*, Lippincott, 1966 (7+).

BEHN, HARRY. *The Faraway Lurs*, World, 1963 (7–10).

BENARY-ISBERT, MARGOT. *The Ark*, trans. by Clara and Richard Winston, Harcourt Brace Jovanovich, 1953 (7–9).

BENCHLEY, NATHANIEL, *A Necessary End: A Novel of World War II*, Harper & Row, 1976 (7–11).

BERNA, PAUL, *They Didn't Come Back*, Pantheon Books, 1968 (7+).

BEZDEKOVA, ZDENKA. *They Called Me Leni*, paintings by Eva Bednaroxa, trans. and adapted by Stuart Amos, Bobbs-Merrill, 1973.

BISHOP, CLAIRE HUCHET. *Pancakes-Paris*, Georges Schreiber, illus., Viking Press, 1947 (3–7).

———. *Twenty and Ten*, as told by Janet Joly, William Pene du Bois, illus., Viking Press, 1964 (3–7).

BLUME, JUDY. *Blubber*, Bradbury Press, 1974 (4–6).

BONHAM, FRANK. *Durango Street*, Dutton, 1965 (9+).

BRANCATO, ROBIN. *Don't Sit Under the Apple Tree*, Knopf, 1975 (5+).

BRUCKNER, KARL. *The Day of the Bomb*, Van Nostrand, 1972 (7+).

BURCH, ROBERT. *Hut School and the Wartime Home-Front*, Viking Press, 1974 (8–12).

BURCHARD, PETER. *Jed*, Coward, McCann & Geoghegan, 1960 (5–8).

———. *Rat Hell*, Coward, McCann & Geoghegan, 1971 (5–8).

———. *North by Night*, Coward, McCann & Geoghegan, 1962 (12+).

BURTON, HESTER. *Beyond the Weir Bridge*, Victor G. Ambrus, illus., Crowell, 1969 (7–10).

———. *In Spite of All Terror*, Victor G. Ambrus, illus., World, 1969 (6–9).

BYARS, BETSY. *The 18th Emergency*, Robert Grossman, illus., Viking Press, 1973 (6+).

CHRISTOPHER, JOHN. *Beyond the Burning Lands*, Macmillan, 1971 (6–9).

———. *The City of Gold and Lead*, Macmillan, 1967 (6–9).

———. *The Guardians*, Macmillan, 1970 (6–9).

———. *The Lotus Caves*, Macmillan, 1969 (6–9).

———. *The Pool of Fire*, Macmillan, 1968 (6–9).

———. *The Prince in Waiting*, Macmillan, 1970 (6–9).

———. *The White Mountains*, Macmillan, 1967 (6–9).

COLLIER, JAMES LINCOLN, and CHRISTOPHER COLLIER. *My Brother Sam Is Dead*, Four Winds Press, 1974 (7+).

———. *The Bloody Country*, Four Winds Press, 1976 (7+).

COOPER, SUSAN. *Over Sea, Under Stone*, Margery Gill, illus., Harcourt Brace Jovanovich, 1965 (4–6).

———. *The Dark Is Rising*, Alan E. Cober, illus., Atheneum, 1973 (4–9).

———. *Greenwitch*, Michael Helsop, illus., Atheneum, 1974 (4–7).

———. *Dawn of Fear*, Margery Gill, illus., Harcourt Brace Jovanovich, 1970 (5–6).

———. *The Grey King*, Michael Helsop, illus., Atheneum, 1975, Newbery Medal (4–7).

CORMIER, ROBERT. *The Chocolate War*, Pantheon Books, 1974 (7+).

CROSBY, ALEXANDER. *One Day for Peace*, Little, Brown, 1971 (6–10).

DEGENS, T. *Transport 7-41-R*, Viking Press, 1974 (7+).

DEJONG, MEINDERT. *The House of Sixty Fathers*, Maurice Sendak, illus., Harper & Row, 1956 (6–8).

DIXON, PAIGE. *Promises to Keep*, Atheneum, 1974 (6+).

DRUON, MAURICE. *Tistou of the Green Thumbs*, Jacqueline Duheme, illus., Scribner, 1958 (4–6).

ENRIGHT, ELIZABETH. *Tatsinda*, Irene Haas, illus., Harcourt Brace Jovanovich, 1963 (4–7).

FAST, HOWARD. *The Hessian*, Morrow, 1972 (9+).

FORBES, ESTHER. *Johnny Tremain*, Lynd Ward, illus., Houghton Mifflin, 1943, Newbery Medal (7–9).

FORMAN, JAMES. *The Skies of Crete*, Farrar, Straus & Giroux, 1963.

———. *Horses of Anger*, Farrar, Straus & Giroux, 1967 (9+).

———. *My Enemy, My Brother*, Meredith, 1969 (7–12).

———. *The Traitors*, Farrar, Straus & Giroux, 1968 (8+).

———. *Ceremony of Innocence*, Hawthorn, 1970 (7+).

FRANK, ANNE. *The Diary of a Young Girl*, Doubleday (Pocket Books), 1952.

GARDAM, JANE. *A Long Way from Verona*, Macmillan, 1972 (6–8).

GRAHAM, GAIL. *Cross-Fire*, Pantheon Books, 1972 (7+).

GRAHAME, KENNETH. *The Reluctant Dragon*, Ernest H. Shepard, illus., Holiday, 1953 (4–6).

GREENE, BETTY. *Summer of My German Soldier*, Dial Press, 1973 (7+).

HAUGAARD, ERIK CHRISTIAN. *Hakon of Rogen's Saga*, Leo and Diane Dillon, illus., Houghton Mifflin, 1963 (6–9).

———. *Orphans of the Wind*, Houghton Mifflin, 1966 (5–7).

———. *The Little Fishes*, Milton Johnson, illus., Houghton Mifflin, 1967 (7+).

———. *The Rider and His Horse*, Leo and Diane Dillon, illus., Houghton Mifflin, 1968 (7–12).

HAUTZIG, ESTHER. *The Endless Steppe: Growing Up in Siberia*, Crowell, 1968 (6–10).

HENTOFF, NAT. *I'm Really Dragged but Nothing Gets Me Down*, Simon & Schuster, 1968 (9–12).

HINTON, S. E. *The Outsiders*, Viking Press, 1967 (8–10).

———. *Rumble Fish*, Dell (Delacorte Press), 1975 (7+).

HOLM, ANNE. *North to Freedom*, trans. by L. W. Kingsland, Harcourt Brace Jovanovich, 1965 (6–8).

HOUSTON, JAMES. *The White Archer: An Eskimo Legend*, Harcourt Brace Jovanovich, 1967 (5–7).

———. *Ghost Paddle: A Northwest Coast Indian Tale*, Harcourt Brace Jovanovich, 1972 (4–6).

HUNT, IRENE. *Across Five Aprils*, Follett, 1964 (12+).

JOFFO, JOSEPH. *A Bag of Marbles*, Houghton Mifflin, 1974 (7+).

JONES, WEYMAN. *The Edge of Two Worlds*, J. C. Kocsis, illus., Dial Press, 1968 (5–8).

KEITH, HAROLD. *Rifles for Watie*, Crowell, 1957, Newbery Medal (7–11).

KENDALL, CAROL. *The Gammage Cup*, Erik Blegvad, illus., Harcourt Brace Jovanovich, 1959 (5–8).

KERR, JUDITH. *When Hitler Stole Pink Rabbit*, Coward, McCann & Geoghegan, 1972 (4–7).

KNOWLES, JOHN. *A Separate Peace*, Macmillan, 1960 (7+).

KRUMGOLD, JOSEPH. *Henry 3*, Alvin Smith, illus., Atheneum, 1967 (6–9).

LEGUIN, URSULA. *A Wizard of Earthsea*, Ruth Robbins, illus., Parnassus, 1968 (6–8).

———. *The Tombs of Atuan*, Gail Garraty, illus., Atheneum, 1972 (6–8).

———. *The Farthest Shore*, Gail Garraty, illus., Atheneum, 1972 (6–8).

L'ENGLE, MADELEINE. *A Wrinkle in Time*, Farrar, Straus & Giroux, 1962, Newbery Medal (6–9).

LEVITON, SONIA. *Journey to America*, Charles Robinson, illus., Atheneum, 1970 (5–7).

LEVIN, JANE WHITHEAD. *Star of Danger*, Harcourt Brace Jovanovich, 1966 (7–10).

LEWIS, CLIVE STAPLES. *The Last Battle*, Pauline Baynes, illus., Macmillan, 1956 (3–7).

———. *The Lion, the Witch and the Wardrobe*, Pauline Baynes, illus., Macmillan, 1950 (3–7).

———. *Prince Caspian*, Pauline Baynes, illus., Macmillan, 1951 (3–7).

———. *The Silver Chair*, Pauline Baynes, illus., Macmillan, 1953 (3–7).

———. *Horse and His Boy*, Pauline Baynes, illus., Macmillan, 1954 (3–7).

LINDGARD, JOAN. *The Twelfth Day of July*, Nelson, 1970 (6+).

———. *Across the Barricades*, Nelson, 1972 (7+).

———. *Into Exile*, Nelson, 1973 (8+).

MANN, PEGGY. *The Street of the Flower Boxes*, Peter Burchard, illus., Coward, McCann & Geoghegan, 1966 (4–6).

MCSEVIGAN, MARIE. *Snow Treasure*, Mary Reardon, illus., Dutton, 1942 (3–7).

———. *All Aboard for Freedom*, E. Harper Johnson, illus., Dutton, 1954 (5–9).

MERRILL, JEAN. *The Pushcart War*, Ronni Solbert, illus., Scott, Foresman–Addison, 1964 (5–7).

MILES, MISKA. *Hoagie's Rifle-Gun*, John Schoenherr, illus., Little, Brown, 1970 (1–3).

MONJO, FERDINAND. *The Vicksburg Veteran*, Douglas Gorsline, illus., Simon & Schuster, 1971 (2–5).

MOSKIN, MARIETTA. *I Am Rosemarie*, Day, 1972 (7–12).

NURENBERG, THELMA. *The Time of Anger*, Abelard-Schuman, 1975 (7–11).

O'BRIEN, ROBERT. *A Report from Group 17*, Atheneum, 1972 (7–11).

PEYTON, K. M. *The Edge of the Cloud*, Victor G. Ambrus, illus., World, 1970 (7–10).

———. *Flambards*, Victor G. Ambrus, illus., World, 1968 (7–10).

———. *Flambards in Summer*, Victor G. Ambrus, illus., World, 1970 (7–10).

PLOWMAN, STEPHANIE. *My Kingdom for a Grave,* Houghton Mifflin, 1971 (8+).

POLLAND, MADELEINE. *To Tell My People,* Richard M. Powers, illus., Holt, Rinehart and Winston, 1968 (6–8).

PREUSSLER, OTFRIED. *The Satanic Mill,* trans. by Anthea Bell, Macmillan, 1973 (7–11).

REISS, JOHANNA DE LEEUW. *The Upstairs Room,* Crowell, 1972 (4–7).

RICHTER, HANS PETER. *Friedrich,* trans. by Edite Kroll, Holt, Rinehart and Winston, 1970 (6–9).

RINALDO, C. L. *Dark Dreams,* Harper & Row, 1974 (7+).

SACHS, MARILYN. *A Pocket Full of Seeds,* Ben Stahl, illus., Doubleday, 1973 (4–7).

SERRAILLIER, IAN. *The Silver Sword,* C. Walter Hodges, illus., Criterion Books, 1959 (7–9).

SINGER, ISAAC BASHEVIS. *The Fools of Chelm,* Uri Shulevitz, illus., Farrar, Straus & Giroux, 1973 (4–6).

SLEATOR, WILLIAM. *Run,* Dutton, 1973 (7–11).

———. *House of Stairs,* Dutton, 1974 (7–11).

SPEARE, ELIZABETH. *The Bronze Bow,* Houghton Mifflin, 1961, Newbery Medal (6–10).

STEELE, WILLIAM O. *The Perilous Road,* Paul Galdone, illus., Harcourt Brace Jovanovich, 1958 (6–8).

STILES, MARTHA BENNETT. *Darkness Over the Land,* Dial Press, 1966 (8+).

SUHL, YURI. *On the Other Side of the Gate,* Watts, 1975.

———. *Uncle Misha's Partisans,* Four Winds Press, 1973 (5–10).

SUTCLIFF, ROSEMARY. *Dawn Wind,* Charles Keeping, illus., Walck, 1962 (7+).

———. *The Eagle of the Ninth,* C. Walter Hodges, illus., Walck, 1954 (8+).

———. *The Lantern Bearers,* Charles Keeping, illus., Walck, 1959 (8+).

———. *The Shield Ring,* C. Walter Hodges, illus., Walck, 1957 (8+).

———. *The Silver Branch,* Charles Keeping, illus., Walck, 1958 (8+).

TAYLOR, THEODORE. *The Children's War,* Doubleday, 1971 (7–10).

TER HAAR, JAAP. *Boris,* trans. by Martha Mearns, Rien Poortvliet, illus., Dell (Delacorte Press), 1970 (5–7).

TOLKIEN, JOHN R. R. *The Hobbit,* Houghton Mifflin, 1938 (5–8).

TUNIS, JOHN. *His Enemy, His Friend,* Morrow, 1967 (7–10).

———. *Silence Over Dunkerque,* Morrow, 1962 (7–10).

TURNBULL, ANN. *The Frightened Forest,* Gillian Gaze, illus., Seabury, 1975 (4–7).

UCHIDA, YOSHIKO. *Journey to Topaz: A Story of the Japanese-American Evacuation,* Donald Carrick, illus., Scribner, 1971 (5–7).

VAN STOCKUM, HILDA. *The Borrowed House,* Farrar, Straus & Giroux, 1975 (7+).

———. *The Winged Watchman,* Farrar, Straus & Giroux, 1962 (5–7).

VIVIER, COLETTE. *The House of the Four Winds,* trans. and edited by Miriam Morton, Doubleday, 1969 (6–9).

WATSON, SIMON. *The Partisan,* Macmillan, 1975 (4–7).

WHITE, ROBB. *Up Periscope,* Doubleday, 1956 (7–9).

———. *The Frogmen,* Doubleday, 1973 (7–12).

———. *Torpedo Run,* Doubleday, 1962 (8–10).

———. *Silent Ship, Silent Sea,* Doubleday, 1967 (8–10).

———. *The Survivor,* Doubleday, 1964 (8–10).

WIBBERLY, LEONARD. *John Treegate's Musket,* Farrar, Straus & Giroux, 1959 (7–10).

———. *Peter Treegate's War,* Farrar, Straus & Giroux, 1960 (7–10).

———. *Sea Captain from Salem,* Farrar, Straus & Giroux, 1961 (7–10).

———. *Treegate's Raiders,* Farrar, Straus & Giroux, 1962 (7–10).

———. *Leopard's Prey,* Farrar, Straus & Giroux, 1971 (6–9).

WOODFORD, PEGGY. *Backwater War,* Farrar, Straus & Giroux, 1975 (6–9).

ZEI, ALKI. *Wildcat Under Glass,* trans. by Edward Fenton, Holt, Rinehart and Winston, 1968 (5–7).

———. *Petros' War,* trans. by Edward Fenton, Dutton, 1972 (5–7).

# 12

# Room for Laughter

David Copperfield is a little Dickens
Robin was a Hood
The first western settler was the sun
The palmist has red hands
Tree surgeons are branching out

Is the third day of the week
pronounced Wednesday or Wedsday?
It's pronounced Tuesday.

What gets wetter as it dries?
A towel

Knock, knock
Who's there?
A little old lady
A little old lady who?
I didn't know you could yodel.

On what side of the pitcher is the handle?
on the outside

Why did the moron salute the refrigerator?
Because it was a General Electric.

## What's so funny?

What can I do about this ringing in my ears?
*Get an unlisted number.*

Where was the Declaration of Independence signed?
*At the bottom.*

If Harry Albright, the butcher, is 6 feet tall, has blue eyes and red hair, lives in the Bronx, and owns three suits, what does Harry weigh?
*Meat.*

Alice is about to be married to a ninety-year-old millionaire, what should she be married in?
*A hurry.*

You may find some, all, or none of the preceding riddles funny, for a sense of humor is a unique attitude, and adults vary greatly on what they consider funny. But humor for children is quite a different matter. Young children frequently find the same things funny, and laugh aloud as adults look on in bewilderment. What is funny to most children is often not funny to adults, and vice versa. Yet understanding the humor of children and being familiar with books that children find funny is important for several reasons.

"Can you find me a book that is funny?" ask children of teachers, librarians, and parents, for amusement is high on the list of reasons given by children in explaining why they like to read.[1] Being able to select books children find amusing is important because it can "turn on" children to the world of books and the joy of reading. Humor provides children with enjoyment and pleasure, and books that can be read and reread provide children with hours of happiness. Humor in children's literature is important for both the reading habits it can lead to in the future and the joy it brings in the present.

Yet despite this interest in funny books, many adults have maintained that children, especially young children, do not possess a sense of humor. In fact, scholars have made statements such as, "humor does not appeal to small children,"[2] or, "humor is the product of the mature, and the highest types are found among the most mentally acute. The appreciation of it begins about the time of adolescence."[3]

One reason that some adults have made such statements is that children frequently miss those points of humor that adults find funny. However, this is not because children lack a sense of humor; rather it is due to their very unique sense of humor. In fact, current research suggests that children may have a sense of humor before they develop any significant language skills; that is, before the age of two years. New parents, for example, prove this point when they make ridiculous faces and outrageous sounds bringing smiles and laughter (and some consternation, no doubt) to their two- and three-month-old children.

To understand the impact of a humorous children's book one must appreciate the kind of humor enjoyed by children. Several researchers have attempted to analyze the nature of this humor, and they have concluded that an important factor is the concept of incongruity.[4] Children laugh at characters, ideas, words, and events that do not fit, that are illogical and unnatural. But in order to appreciate the incongruity of a given situation, the child must understand the natural order, and therefore see the comedy in the grouping of incompatibles. Since children are generally much more limited in experience and background than adults, they are able to see fewer incongruities. Therefore their sense of humor is somewhat different and more limited than that of adults. For example, children do not find subtle forms of verbal humor funny until they can master and understand the finer uses of the language. On the other hand, a nose so big that it gets caught in doorways is funny to children (if not to the bearer of the nose) because they understand the normal size of a nose, and can appreciate the humor in the exaggeration.

Katherine Hull Kappas has developed a comprehensive set of categories that children find funny.[5]

1. *Exaggeration*—wild overstatement or understatement in relation to size, number, events, feelings, facts, experience, proportions, and so on.
2. *Surprise*—unexpected happenings create humor, and in a more subtle form, the unexpected becomes irony.
3. *Slapstick*—loud, fast, and wild physical activity, sometimes accompanied by rowdy verbal humor.
4. *The absurd*—irrational, ridiculous, prepos-

terous nonsense, which may also be whimsical.

5. *Human predicaments*—situations in which characters appear foolish, silly, tricked, or beaten by someone else or by life itself.

6. *Ridicule*—a mockery of adults, society, human foibles, or oneself that can be either playful or hostile and in its more sophisticated form becomes satire.

7. *Defiance*—rebelling against and violating accepted conventions, such as violating adult authority or expressing forbidden ideas.

8. *Violence*—releasing hostility through the expression of sudden or extreme violence, such as the beatings characteristic of "Punch and Judy" puppet shows.

9. *Verbal Humor*—humor through language in the form of jokes, sarcasm, wit, and name calling that differs from the other categories in that it is not a situational form of humor but a verbal form. (During the early elementary years verbal humor is quite simple, and examples of it are interspersed throughout this chapter.)

10. *Incongruity*—although elements of incongruity can be found in most of these categories, pure incongruity does provide a category unto itself.

The majority of these categories are concerned with broad, unsophisticated, and frequently visual forms of humor. Robert Bateman,[6] in attempting to determine what makes children between six and eleven years old laugh, identified fewer categories, but they were similar to those of Kappas. Bateman determined that children found visual humor amusing, whether a funny incident was described or merely suggested. Superiority and misfortune also caused mirth, as did nonsense sounds.[7] But again, verbal humor, unless quite simple in nature, frequently went unappreciated and unnoticed.

A commonly accepted explanation of the difference between adult and children's humor is that humor is developmental in nature. As children mature they develop a greater potential for appreciating humor. A five-year-old is generally knowledgeable about home and family life, but with no real conception of time or abstract ideas, he or she possesses relatively few potential areas of humor. What the five-year-old finds funny is his or her own attempts at coordination and physical activity, slapstick and simple surprise, defiance of parents, and very simple jokes. But many other potential areas for humor are not considered funny and are not even fully understood. At five the child is quite egocentric and humor directed at his or her own predicaments or failings is more likely to create an outburst or set up a defense mechanism than to be appreciated as a form of humor.

By the fourth grade, children are generally enjoying more sophisticated and varied examples of humor. Nine-year-olds have developed the capacity to laugh at themselves because they have a more complete and objective view of their place in the world than do five-year-olds. Nine-year-olds can also appreciate more subtle jokes and riddles, for they have attained a greater mastery over language. Yet the visual humor enjoyed by five-year-olds can still be enjoyed by the older child.

By the eighth grade, children are beginning to appreciate verbal wit more than visual comedy. With a greater ability for self-appraisal and critical judgment of others, the fourteen-year-old is better able to use humor to express negative and positive emotions. The fourteen-year-old is on the verge of assuming an adult sense of humor.

Those who support a developmental explanation for humor do not contend that all individuals go through all these stages and arrive at the same level. To the contrary, children and adults enjoy different perceptions of what is or is not funny, for a number of factors affect the development of a sense of humor.[8] Boys and girls, for example, sometimes find different things funny, undoubtedly because of differing cultural expectations.[9] In general, a greater intelligence suggests a greater appreciation of humor.[10] Cultural background and personality also bear on the development of one's sense of humor. Studies indicate that a higher cultural level frequently results in a greater appreciation of satire and whimsy over slapstick and the absurd.[11] Personality differences, for example, between introverts and extroverts, also result in different tastes in humor.[12] Some adults always appreciate the slapstick humor they enjoyed as children, whereas others find pie-in-the-face humor silly or irritating. Individual factors as well as developmental stages create adults with widely differing senses of humor, as anyone who has ever told a favorite joke to a crowd responding with serious silence well knows.

There are several ways in which the results of these studies are useful to teachers and others working with children. First, these results suggest that an adult evaluating a book in terms of humor is likely to reach a judgment quite different from that reached by a child. The best guide to choosing humorous children's books is to heed the sound of children's laughter. Children are not only the best judges of funny children's books; sometimes they are the only judges. And with experience adults can learn about the elements of books that amuse and entertain children.

Second, not all children will enjoy the humor of a given situation. Different factors, such as background, personality, age, sex, and intelligence, to name but a few, create individuals with differing ideas about what is funny. Teachers therefore would find it useful to be familiar with a wide variety of humorous children's books; with these they can help each child find a book that he or she finds funny,

and they can introduce children to the joy of reading.

## What tickles the fancy

When you compare the components of modern fantasy and the characteristics that children find funny, it becomes obvious why so much of modern fantasy is considered humorous. Modern fantasy stretches or partially removes the boundaries of reality; it makes chaos of the orderly and inexorable passage of time; it gives animals speech and inanimate objects life; it opens the doorway so that strange characters may enter and upset the patterns of normal routine; it laughs at human conventions and foibles; it is characterized by the ridiculous, the nonsensical, the absurd. In the following sections we discuss some of the modern fanciful stories that give children the pleasure of laughter.

### The fairy tale revisited

Modern authors have playfully twisted the forms and motifs of the traditional fairy tale to create their own humorous tales that are often more in tune with contemporary times. Phyllis McGinley's *The Plain Princess* (1945) tells of the transformation of Esmeralda, a spoiled princess who owns the world's finest two-wheeled bicycle. However, a visit to Dame Goodwit and her five daughters gives Esmeralda greater perspective on her own importance, and she grows more helpful and less selfish. As her character changes for the better, so does her appearance, and she becomes beautiful both within and without.

Jay Williams and Friso Hensta are an author illustrator team who blithely ignore the former stereotyped princesses characterized by pretty passivity. They create some resourceful, plucky young women who rely not on princes to solve their problems but on their own wits. *The*

*Practical Princess* (1969), eighteen-year-old Bedelia, uses her common sense to slay a dragon and rescue a prince. *Petronella* (1973) is a princess who sets out to rescue a prince, but when she discovers he is not worth the bother, she brings home an enchanter as her prospective husband. *The Silver Whistle* (1971) tells the story of Prudence, who was cheerful, homely, and plain. When all eligible maidens go to the palace because the prince is going to select a bride, he chooses Prudence. After all, he never said he wanted to marry the most beautiful maiden in the kingdom; he just wanted the one who suited him the best. Joseph Schrank also spoofs the fairy tale genre in *The Plain Princess and the Lazy Prince* (1958), a tale in which the king and queen must advertise for a dragon, and traditional roles are again reversed as the princess rescues the prince.

Occasionally, one particular fairy tale is satirized, as in Raymond Briggs' *Jim and the Beanstalk* (1970). In this modernized version of the famous Jack story, the giant is much older, a victim of the passing years. Instead of stealing from the giant, Jim tries to help him by providing giant-sized eyeglasses, false teeth, and a wig, all fitted with the aid of a huge tape measure.

James Thurber is a humorist who has created some popular modern fairy tales with subtle changes in the traditional pattern. In *Many Moons* (1943) the Princess Lenore is sick, and she flatly states that she must be given the moon if she is to get better. The excitable king is driven to ever greater heights of frenzy by the preposterous suggestions of his foolish wise men. Finally it is the princess herself, from the unique perspective of childhood, who solves the problem of obtaining the moon. *Many Moons*, illustrated by Louis Slobodkin, received the 1944 Caldecott Medal. *The Great Quillow* (1944) is about a clever toy maker who saves his village from a giant with an

enormous appetite; it also presents a clever spoof on the rigid rules of parliamentary procedure. Thurber's *The 13 Clocks* (1950) is another clever fairy tale but one that requires a more sophisticated audience.

In one of his earlier books Dr. Seuss creates a delightful fairy tale in *The 500 Hats of Bartholemew Cubbins* (1938). Young Bartholemew is as lowly and insignificant as the king is mighty and important. He has no intention of defying his monarch, but every time he respectfully removes his hat, a new one appears in its place. The baffled and enraged monarch calls in wise men, magicians, and executioners, but no one can rid Bartholemew's head of the persistently emerging hats. At last the final hat appears, a masterpiece so splendid that the king's own crown pales into insignificance beside it. The monarch and the boy strike a bargain: the king gets the hat and Bartholemew gets his life spared and 500 gold pieces as well. In typical Seuss fashion, the pictures are wildly hilarious, a contrast to the more sober moments of the plot, and a constant assurance that all will turn out well in the end.

Nicholas Stuart Gray is a Scottish actor and author who has created modern fairy tales with amusingly real princes and princesses who are consistently falling in and out of trouble. *Over the Hills to Fabylon* (1970) is set in a mythical kingdom that protects itself from invaders by a spell through which the king can instantly remove his kingdom to a site beyond the mountains whenever he becomes alarmed. This is all well and good unless a nervous monarch is on the throne, and then life becomes a bit unpredictable for the citizenry. Although the current ruler is only mildly excitable, the kingdom is still shaken up frequently, so that one man complains, "out and back three times since Christmas."

The king's three children are primary causes for the king's excitability. Sixteen-year-old

Rosetta, charming and vivacious, likes to put on an apron and wander about the kingdom as a shepherdess or a milkmaid. This does not worry the king overly because everyone in the kingdom recognizes Rosetta and makes sure she meets no harm. The monarch is more troubled by the crown prince, Conrad, a young man so concerned about the responsibility of the spell that he has schooled himself from childhood to study the art of being calm. He locks himself up in a tower with weighty books and concentrates on keeping himself aloof from all emotion. The most amusing of the king's children is Alaric, who is handsome, charming, and incurably romantic. He falls hopelessly in love with every girl he meets, a characteristic that can lead him to offer several marriage proposals before lunch time. Fortunately, he is saved from the consequences of his actions because no one takes him seriously.

Witty dialogue and humorous characterization are complemented by absurd creatures and happenings, a 3-inch loathly worm who is very defensive about his height; a bewitched door that chases the captain of the king's cavalry through town; an ambitious sorcerer who lacks the talent to pull off his wicked intentions; and a cross witch with a propensity for turning royalty into thunderstorms. Behind the wit and the nonsense is the theme of self-understanding, of being true to one's own nature, as the essentially compassionate Conrad finally learns.

## Funny folk

Incongruity is one of the basic elements of humor, so it is little wonder that many of the books children themselves refer to as funny include incongruous characters, people who do not fit in our everyday world. When these characters, with their own unique set of behaviors, bump into the conventions that char-

acterize ordinary, day-to-day life, hilarious situations often result.

*Pippi Longstocking* (1950), created by the Swedish author Astrid Lindgren, is a superchild who remains true to her own code despite the attempts of societal institutions to restrict her zany behavior. She washes the kitchen floor by skating over it with two scrubbing brushes tied to her feet. Wash dishes? Not she! She tumbles the plates and cups off the table and stuffs them into a wood box. When two policemen try to take her to an orphanage, she picks them up bodily and deposits them out the door. She decides to go to school because she is upset at missing Christmas and Easter vacation, but her collision with school rules and regulations is so volatile that both she and the teacher decide that one day is more than enough. Children love the exaggeration, the surprise, and the slapstick, and they delight in watching Pippi calmly dismiss accepted convention and adult authority. The adventures of this superchild are continued in *Pippi Goes on Board* and *Pippi in the South Seas.*

Absurdity characterizes Wilson Gage's *Miss Osborne-the-Mop* (1963). The summer promises to be dull until Jody discovers that she has magic for turning people and objects into something new and then turning them back into themselves. Jody has great fun creating cakes and motorcycles until she changes a dust mop into a skinny creature bearing a striking resemblance to her fourth-grade teacher. Miss Osborne proves to be tirelessly adept at creating difficult situations, and she is perseverant too, as Jody learns when Miss Osborne refuses to be turned once again into a controllable dust mop.

Eccentric *Mrs. Piggle-Wiggle* (1947), created by Betty MacDonald, has her own unique life-style, not quite in tune with the rest of the town. She lives in an upside-down house, and in her backyard there is buried treasure, left over from the days when her husband, the pirate, was alive. She is a friend to every child in the neighborhood, and she also has a rich source of antidotes to combat such children with problem behavior as "the won't pick up toys," "the answer-backer," "the selfishness," and the "never-want-to-go-to-bedder." Her popularity with young readers suggests that the essential humor of this character saves the book from being dismissed as an extended lecture on good behavior.

The well-loved *Mary Poppins* (1934), by P. L. Travers, also takes a no-nonsense approach to children's behavior. Blown in by an east wind to care for the Banks children, Michael and Jane, she emerges with her carpet bag, her parrot-handled umbrella, and her strange powers. There is, however, no danger in the magic that Mary Poppins brings, but only pleasure and adventure. Although Michael and Jane want to talk about their adventures, Mary Poppins refuses to acknowledge her magic, and she serves up touches of enchantment in the mundane world of the nursery with all the stringency of the more ordinary adult giving out candy.

Children find exaggeration, both overstatement and understatement, amusing, and perhaps because they must view the world not at eye level but always looking up, they seem to find lilliputian characters particularly intriguing. One of the most enduring fantasies about miniscule people is *The Borrowers* (1953), by Mary Norton. The clock family of Borrowers—Homily, Pod, and Arietty—live in an old grandfather's clock in the hall and set up snug housekeeping with a bedroom made out of a cigar box, a child's block for a worktable, and a safety pin to bolt the door. Even the family's aesthetic needs are met, with a handwritten letter for wallpaper, a piece from a chess set for sculpture, and a postage stamp as a wall portrait of the queen.

Each of the three members of the clock fam-

ily is a finely developed character. Homily is a loving but slightly frazzled and excitable mother. Pod is stolid and brave, with a touch of the philosopher about him; and Arietty is sheer optimism, always ready for adventure. Her trusting nature allows her not only to be seen by one of the formidable "human beans," a boy, but even to form a friendship with him.

The gentle warmth and humor that pervades the book is paralleled by a real sense of danger. Borrowing is a risky business, and although some humans are kindly, others bring disaster as the clock family's snug home is attacked and destroyed by dogs, poison gas, and the ferret. However, the resourceful Borrowers will not be overcome, and their adventures are continued in *The Borrowers Afield*, *The Borrowers Afloat*, and *The Borrowers Aloft*.

The preceding characters bring their strange ways and their magic into the ordinary world. In *Finn Family Moomintroll* (1965) and other books, Tove Jansson, winner of the 1966 Hans Christian Andersen Prize, has created the strange yet endearing Moomintroll and his family. The Moominfamily are pudgy creatures with comfortably rounded snouts and long tails, and they look something like cheerful hippopotamuses. They love sunshine and warmth, and they hibernate all winter long. Moomintroll's equally strange friends include the vain snork maiden, whose only claim to beauty is her fluffy fringe of hair; the stamp-collecting Hemulin; the restless snufkin, with a call to wander; the irritable muskrat, who reads books on the uselessness of everything; and Thingumy and Bob, who speak in spoonerisms and have an innocent predeliction for taking things. Throughout the tales of Moominland, these creatures remain true to their characterizations, and despite their peculiar appearances set against the backdrop of strange settings, they sometimes seem to be quite a bit like the normal, ordinary people you might meet next door.

There are also unfriendly folk in Moominland; the horrible Hattifatteners and the grim and terrible groke, who freezes the ground on which she sits as she waits forever. However, reputedly dangerous characters are, in reality, not nearly as formidable as their reputations suggest. For example, the hobgoblin is said to ride a black panther in hunt for treasure. His house is without doors or windows; it has no roof and the clouds that pass over it are blood red with the reflection of hoarded rubies. The hobgoblin's eyes are red too and they shine in the dark as he searches ceaselessly for the king's ruby, as big as the panther's head and as red as leaping flames. When the hobgoblin finally emerges, he is not frightening at all. He turns out to be a rather friendly, if melancholy sort, and he pleases everyone by granting their wishes.

The creatures from Moominland take adversity in their stride and have that most significant ability of viewing any partially filled glass of water as half full rather than half empty. For example, when Moomintroll's house gets strangled by a thick growth of jungle vines, the family matter-of-factly breaks its way through and pays the chaos no mind, while imperturbably eating jungle fruit and playing Tarzan and Jane. In short, as Tove Jansson says of Moomintroll and his friends: "Everyone did what they liked and seldom worried about tomorrow. Very often, unexpected and disturbing things used to happen, but nobody ever had time to be bored, and that is always a good thing."[13]

## Things that bump around in the night

An' all us other childern, when the supper-things is done,
We set around the kitchen fire an' has the mostest fun
A-list'nin' to the witch tales 'at Annie tells about,

An' the Gobble-uns 'at git you
　if you
　　don't
　　　watch
　　　　out!

*From "Little Orphan Annie,"*
*by James Whitcomb Riley*

A group of youngsters gather around a night fire to listen with shivery anticipation as a storyteller weaves an eerie spell with a ghost tale. This is a familiar scene, one in which, perhaps, many of us have participated. There is little doubt that children regard goblins, witches, ghosts, and other supernatural creatures with intense fascination. This interest seems to encompass conflicting emotions, horror and dread for potentially dangerous creatures and also affection and empathy for more likable, good-natured beings from that mysterious "other" world. On one night a child may be terrified of going to bed and demand that the light be kept on to ward off the weird creature lurking under the bed or in the closet. The next night the same child may cheerfully wrap himself or herself in a white sheet and join a group of spooky-looking friends as they go trick-or-treat on Halloween. In this section we discuss some of the children's books that respond to the warmer, more positive feelings children have for goblins, ghosts, and other weird creatures and that create a humorous vision of the world of the occult.

Two characters, one a ghost, the other a witch, have become special favorites of younger children. Robert Bright's *Georgie* (1944) is a shy, pudgy, marshmallow–like ghost who lives in Mr. and Mrs. Whittaker's house, where he is very content creaking the stairs and squeaking the parlor door. But when Mr. Whittaker oils the door and hammers a nail into the loose board on the stairs, things just are not the same for Georgie. He leaves to live in an old cow barn and does not resume his friendly haunt until a long winter returns the Whittaker house to its former creaky state. Other Georgie books include his adventures with Halloween, a noisy ghost, robbers, and a magician. Georgie is a harmless, lovable fellow, a ghost that many children want to comfort and protect.

In Dorrie, Patricia Coombs has created a little witch with whom youngsters can identify. Dorrie's room is untidy, her hat is always on crooked, and her stockings never match. In *Dorrie and the Weather Box* (1966) the trouble-prone little witch creates an indoor storm and discovers the perils of dabbling in Big Witch's magic. *Dorrie and the Goblin* (1972) finds her facing the impossible task of goblin sitting. However, in *Dorrie and the Blue Witch* (1964) she emerges triumphant and wins a medal for singlehandedly capturing Mildred, the mean and grumpy blue witch. Other stories about friendly witches include Janice May Udry's *Glenda* (1969) and Wende and Harry Devlin's old witch stories, such as *The Old Witch Rescues Halloween* (1972).

For children in the intermediate and upper grades there is Penelope Lively's *The Ghost of Thomas Kempe* (1973), about a zany, trouble-making spirit. The Harrisons find much to be puzzled over in their new home. Archaic messages mysteriously appear, doors bang, objects vanish, the alarm clock goes off at odd hours of the night; and James, with a much-deserved reputation as a prankster, gets the blame. Actually the mischief is caused by the ghost of Thomas Kempe, a seventeenth-century sorcerer who wants to enlist James as his latest apprentice. Thomas Kempe's mischief lands James into many hilarious predicaments. But in the end the spirit proves his heart is in the right place, and he finally departs.

Another madcap adventure with a supernatural creature is George Selden's *The Genie of Sutton Place* (1973). In order to save his dog, Sam, young Tim Farr releases a genie who has been trapped in a museum carpet. The resulting

adventures include the unconventional medium Madam Sostros, the dog Sam, who becomes a man, and the well-meaning Dooley, who eventually chooses to become human rather than to remain a powerful but imprisoned genie.

John Bellairs' *The House with a Clock in the Walls* (1973) provides a finely developed contrast of good and evil spirits. Lewis enjoys living in a large stone mansion, and he takes pleasure in the friendship of Uncle Jonathan and Mrs. Zimmerman, both of whom are skilled in the art of good magic. However, suspense mounts as Lewis learns that the house was previously owned by an evil sorcerer, Isaac Izard, who has hidden a deadly clock within its walls, one that ticks away the minutes until Doomsday. Lewis foolishly dabbles in magic himself and, in an eerie cemetery scene, allows Selena Izard, Isaac's wife, to escape from her grave. The frightening situation that results is lightened by the humorous characterization of the good magicians, Uncle Jonathan and Mrs. Zimmerman.

Another humorous story of a ghost's intrusion into contemporary time is William Mac-Kellar's *Alfie and Me and the Ghost of Peter Stuyvesant* (1974). The Staten Island ferry provides the setting for the meeting between Billy Carpenter and the now gentle ghost of the once irascible Peter Stuyvesant. From that point on Billy and his pal, Alfie, are involved in madcap adventures that include uncovering lost treasure buried beneath Times Square and at least partially fulfilling the ghost's dream of having a bridge named after him.

In these books creatures from the mysterious other world enter the world of reality. Nicholas Stuart Gray's *Grimbold's Other World* (1963) differs in that the safe daytime world of shepherds and farmers has gaps through which humans can slip to the mysterious night world of magic. Muffler is led into the world of magic by the cat, Grimbold, who warns him, "If the opportunity occurs for you to return to this world . . . think twice before doing it. So far no harm is done. But the knowledge of magic and mystery may change your life if you let it."[14] Muffler does return to the world of magic, where, among other adventures, he meets a lost baby dinosaur, gets involved in a generation gap between a sorcerer and his son, and rescues a weirdie's canary. The weirdie expresses her gratitude by giving him a silver ring of which she says, "A small reward. But, if ever you are bored—rub the stone. Nothing will happen, but it whiles away the time."[15] Any world, even a mysterious magic one, that has witches giving such advice, can't be all that dangerous.

## On the bumpy road to high adventure

The hardship, the violence, and the sheer bravado of an early America spawned the larger-than-life heroes Paul Bunyan, Pecos Bill, Mike Fink, John Henry, and Captain Stormalong, whose gigantic stature and enormous escapades still delight elementary school children. The overriding characteristic of these tall tales is wild exaggeration, and the more whopping the lie, the better—providing it is told with a poker straight face that blithely ignores any suggestion that the tale is not true. These phenomenal he-men were born and bred in various regions across the country—the New England coast, the South, the lumber camps, the mighty Mississippi, the western plains—and their braggadocio is a tribute to the optimism of earlier times, when man could tackle any situation and win.

There are several skillful modern authors who continue to write in the tall tale tradition of American folklore. In *Daniel Boone's Echo* William Steele presents the terrified Aaron Adamsale, who joined Daniel Boone on his trip to Kentucky. How Daniel helps Aaron conquer his fears of the one-horned Summple

and the sling-tailed Galoatis makes for hilarious reading. In *Davy Crockett's Earthquake* the hero's tame plans for bear hunting are modified when he meets and masters a comet and an earthquake. The tall tale adventures of Andy Jackson and his friend Chief Ticklepitcher are recorded in *Andy Jackson's Water Well.*

Sid Fleischman has become outstandingly adept in his ability to relate tall tale adventures.

"Ladies and gentlemen." Pa smiled. "Gentlemen and ladies. Boys and girls, and girls and boys. We present for your amusement, edification and jollification our traveling temple of mysteries! A program of wonders and marvels for young and old! Feats of legerdemain and tricks of prestidigitation! Behold! Magic, mirth, and music!"[16]

So opens the magic show of *Mr. Mysterious and Company* (1962), in reality, Mr. Andrew Perkins and family, who travel across the country and stop in frontier towns to put on magic shows. There are adventures along the way, such as the incident in which Ma terrifies a band of Indians with a magic lantern show, and the time when the family captures the Badlands Kid right in the middle of their sphinx act. But always the outstanding figure is Pa, kindly, and able to handle every situation no matter how difficult or dangerous. *By the Great Horn Spoon* (1963) presents an even grander tall tale hero, Mr. Praiseworthy, the butler, who is indeed a man for all times and all seasons. He and young Jack Flagg join the California gold rush in hopes of recouping sagging family fortunes. There they meet adventure and obstacles, and Praiseworthy, looking less like a butler every day, becomes known as the cleverest and toughest miner in California, one who can win a fortune and then, without batting an eye, lose it all.

In Fleischman's *The Ghost in the Noonday Sun* (1965) the competent hero is Oliver Finch, a young lad who, shanghaied by the dreadful Captain Scratch, has the unenviable task of uncovering the elusive ghost of the pirate, Gentleman Jack. The adventure is heightened by a band of cutthroat pirates who are equally ready to walk the plank, mutiny, or leave Oliver stranded on a tropical isle. Shysters and tall tale tellers emerge in *Chancy and the Grand Rascal* (1966), in which orphaned Chancy sets off to find his long lost sister, Indiana. Along the way he runs into his Uncle Will and a series of marvelously improbable adventures.

In his stories about McBroom and his amazing one-acre farm, Fleischman has created a tall tale hero who delights younger independent readers and also provides a grand vehicle for storytelling and reading aloud. The McBroom farm must combat grasshoppers who would eat anything green, including McBroom's socks, a wind so powerful that it blows McBroom's eleven children into the sky, and a winter so cold that sounds freeze and are not heard until they thaw out in the spring.

In *The Smartest Man in Ireland* (1963) and *Thomas and the Warlock* (1967) Mollie Hunter captures the essence of Irish and Scottish legends and creates two appealing, larger-than-life heroes. The spirited Patrick Kentigern Keenan boasts that he's the "smartest man in Ireland," and to prove it he makes repeated attempts to outwit the fairies. His boast involves him in humorous antics and a suspenseful conclusion in which he travels to the fairies' underground cavern to rescue his young son, Kiernon. In *Thomas and the Warlock* the mischievous, likable Thomas Thompson, a blacksmith in a little village in the Scottish lowlands, poaches in the woods of the fearsome warlock, Hugo Gifford. The essential humor and bravery of the protagonist lighten the frightening nature of his escapades.

Joan Aiken is a master at creating some of the most marvelously suspenseful and outlandish tall tales imaginable. Told in the Gothic tradition, *The Wolves of Willoughby Chase* (1962) places young Bonnie and her cousin in the brutal hands of their governess, Miss Slighcarp, whose evil ambitions include a scheme to take over the wealthy estate of Willoughby Chase. *Black Hearts in Battersea* (1964) is a Dickensian mystery set in nineteenth-century London, where fifteen-year-old Simon uncovers a plot against King James and the Duke and Duchess of Battersea. The zany adventures include combatting a wild pack of wolves with a croquet mallet, riding over England in a balloon, and a series of coincidences and mistaken identities.

*Nightbirds on Nantucket* (1966) returns some of the characters from former adventures, plucky, resourceful Dido Twite and the sinister Miss Slighcarp. This gallivanting, anything-goes burlesques involves a Hanoverian plot against the English king, one in which Miss Slighcarp and her cohorts in crime plan to blow up the king's palace via a Nantucket-based cannon. The day is saved by an obliging pink whale who tows the cannon, with Miss Slighcarp clinging to the gun carriage, over a cliff's edge into the white foam below. *Smoke from Cromwell's Time and Other Stories* (1970) is a robustly humorous collection of fanciful tales, and *The Whispering Mountain* (1969) is an outlandish burlesque that includes a dour grandfather, a magic harp, gypsies, a foreign potentate, a cruel marquess, a breed of little men living inside a mountain, and fractured Welsh dialect as well.

Aiken's stories of tall tale adventure perch on the slim borderline between the real and the fantastic. With Lloyd Alexander, however, there is no doubt that his fine contemporary books are at the heart of modern fantasy. His five-book chronicle of Prydain conveys significant themes in a style lightened by humor.

Humor also characterizes *The Marvelous Misadventure of Sebastian*, winner of the 1971 National Book Award. This is the story of a young fiddler, who, unjustly dismissed from his position, optimistically sets out to make his way on the road to fame and fortune—and finds it bumpier than he had expected. En route he meets a collection of humorous characters who teach him that things are not always what they appear. There is the cat accused of being a witch; the bear who turns out to be an extravagant theatrical performer; the scrawny lad who is actually the Princess Irene, a solemn young lady predisposed to formal circumlocution; and the deceptive Nicholas, whose pudgy, complacent exterior conceals surprising skill and courage. But most important of all, there is the marvelous fiddle, reputedly an instrument of evil spells; but its exquisite melodies allow Sebastian to triumph over a despotic monarch and to discover what his life is meant to be about. In the more broadly absurd *The Cat Who Wished to Be a Man* (1973) an enchanter turns his cat, Lionel, into a man. In the town of Brighton, Lionel learns about the foibles and vices of humanity and also of the drama and emotion that come with being human.

## Word magic

Some children never see anything funny in books that rely on word play for their humor. Others, however, more intrigued with words and the way they are used, are delighted by literal-minded Amelia Bedelia and the inventive verbal games of James Thurber, Norton Juster, and Lewis Carroll.

Peggy Parrish created *Amelia Bedelia* (1963), a maid who follows her employer's instructions to the letter. When told to draw the drapes, Amelia Bedelia gets out her art supplies, and when instructed to dress the chicken, she cheerfully puts needle and thread to work. Her absurd adventures with words are continued in *Thank You, Amelia Bedelia.*

James Thurber's *The Wonderful O* (1957)

offers more sophisticated play with words and therefore requires an audience of greater verbal fluency and maturity. In this tale an evil pirate who has hated the letter *o* ever since his mother became wedged in a porthole, banishes all use of words beginning with *o* as well as all objects they represent. When the people of the island use four words containing *o*—*hope, love, valor,* and *freedom*—the pirate is vanquished and *o* is returned to its rightful place.

Many readers are daunted by the verbal gymnastics displayed in Norton Juster's *The Phantom Tollbooth* (1961), yet the book has a devoted following and is still a favorite in many college bookstores. Milo and his companions Tock and Humbug travel through the rival cities of Dictionopolis and Digitopolis, through the Valley of Sound and the Forest of Sight to rescue two princesses from the Castle-in-Air. Along the way Milo eats a light meal (one consisting of lights); visits a spelling bee (a bee who spells); attends a banquet where people eat their words; and runs into other odd and diverse dangers. Milo finally rescues the two princesses, Sweet Rhyme and Pure Reason, and with their return vanquishes chaos and confusion.

In Lewis Carroll's *Alice's Adventures in Wonderland* (1865) and *Through the Looking Glass* (1871) characters gravely converse in the most absurd nonsense imaginable, but their disjointed conversation sometimes cloaks perceptive truths. Those children who enjoy characters who speak in riddles and nonsequiturs will learn by heart the nonsense verses of "The Walrus and the Carpenter," "The Lobster Quadrille," "Father William," and "Jabberwocky"; they will be intrigued by Carroll's creation of such portmanteau words as *slithy* and *chortle,* and they will delight in the inane Mad-Tea-Party and the know-it-all Cheshire Cat, grinning at questions and answers beyond normal comprehension.

Currently, a significant number of children's

books are being published that focus exclusively on word humor. Puns, riddles, and jokes fill the pages of books by such authors as Alvin Schwartz. For example, in Schwartz's *Whoppers: Tall Tales and Other Lies Collected from American Folklore* (1975) the reader is informed that at one time the heat was so bad that farmers were forced to feed their hens cracked ice in order to prevent them from laying hard-boiled eggs. The bibliography at the end of this chapter identifies several books of jokes, puns, and riddles for children who enjoy word humor.

### The detective spoof

Both realistic fiction and fantasy contain amusing mystery stories for children fascinated by the "whodunit" genre. Some of the most popular of these books feature children as detectives. William Pene Du Bois' *The Alligator Case* (1965), characterized by slapstick, tells of a young detective's attempts to solve a circus theft, not an easy challenge when the suspects are concealed among some fifty circus alligators. Du Bois' *The Case of the Gone Goose* features twelve-year-old Inspector Tearle, known as the "boy bloodhound" and the "noisiest kid in town." The ingeniously preposterous plot of Ellen Raskin's *The Tattooed Potato and Other Clues* (1975) involves Dickory Dock and Garson, two unconventional sleuths, in such mysteries as "The Case of the Horrible Hairdresser" and "The Case of the Confusing Corpus."

Donald Sobel has created one of the most popular of the young detective set in *Encyclopedia Brown, Boy Detective* (1963). Leroy Brown, known to everyone in Idaville as Encyclopedia Brown because his mind is crammed with facts and figures as though it were an encyclopedia, is the enterprising son of the chief of police. He is responsible for solving most of Idaville's crimes. When Encyclopedia

goes into the detective business for himself, the reader is asked to unravel the crimes along with the boy detective and then check his or her success with the solutions recorded in the back of the book. Although Encyclopedia is himself a rather flat character, the interest revolves around the story riddles in which he is involved.

Mystery in fantasy often highlights animal detectives, many of these from the mouse family. Eve Titus has created Basil, a mouse modeled after Sherlock Holmes, and his adventures are recorded in *Basil of Baker Street* (1963) and *Basil and the Lost Colony* (1964). Julia Cunningham's *Dear Rat* is a grand parody on the hard-boiled detective story. It features Andrew, a rat of Wyoming origin, whose tough exterior is the façade that conceals a tender heart. Pitted against Croge, evil leader of an underworld mob, Andrew finds himself involved in a jewel robbery and a fast-moving chase through the sewers of Paris.

Another spoof on the detective story centers around the Pott family's amazing car, *Chitty-Chitty-Bang-Bang* (1964). The plot involves a hidden cave, a kidnapping, and a collection of mobsters, such as Joe the Monster, Man-Mountain, Fink, and Blood-Money Banks. But the marvelous car can become an airplane or boat and can operationalize her fantastic radar scanner, so she is a sure match for any set of gangsters. The author of *Chitty-Chitty-Bang-Bang*, Ian Flemming, is also the creator of the well-known gadget-oriented spy, agent 007, James Bond.

### Unscientific science fiction

What science fiction has been doing for the last forty years is to shake up people's thinking, make them skeptical of dogma, get them used to the idea of change, let them dare to want new things. Nobody will ever know for sure how much effect these stories have had, but it is almost impossible to believe they have had none.[17]

(S)cience fiction differs from fantasy not in subject matter but in aim, and its unique aid is to suggest real hypotheses about mankind's future or the nature of the universe.[18]

As these quotes indicate, science fiction has its avid supporters who are convinced of the worth and importance of this genre. And indeed, some fine writers for older children—Madeleine L'Engle, Ben Bova, Peter Dickinson, John Christopher, Andre Norton, Sylvia Louise Engdahl, Robert Heinlein, and others—convey significant themes in their writing. Such authors consider the impact of technology on human society, its development and values. They hypothesize about the future of humanity, and they envision fascinating possibilities, all the more intriguing because they are logical extensions of contemporary knowledge.

Science fiction written for younger children is, however, a very different matter. It is frequently characterized by playful planet hopping and often provides little more than a unique setting for a conventional adventure story. Despite limitations and inaccuracies, the following science fiction offerings can provide amusement and laughter for young children.

The easy-to-read, amusing adventures of Marty the Martian and his friend Eddie Blow, who lives on earth, are recounted in Louis Slobodkin's *The Space Ship Under the Apple Tree* (1952). Felsen's *The Boy Who Discovered the Earth,* also for younger readers, is another entertaining book about interplanetary friendship. Texson and his family, on a space voyage from the planet Feor, are forced to land on earth for space ship repairs. There Texson befriends an earthling, Tommy Taplinger, and the two almost switch places, until Tommy decides that it is more fun to be a child on earth than on Feor. John M. Schealer's books also depict friendly relationships between earth people and creatures from other planets. In *Zip-Zip and His Flying Saucer* (1956), Zip-

*Zip Goes to Venus* (1958), and *Zip-Zip and the Red Planet* (1961) the Kiddle family helps a Martian obtain a steam shovel, locate his father, and defeat the barbaric Tubars.

The eccentric Miss Pickerell, created by Ellen MacGregor, is still a favorite with children in the middle elementary grades. In *Miss Pickerell Goes to Mars* (1951) the elderly lady is enraged to find a spaceship perched in her pasture. She boards the vehicle with intent to complain and, in the resulting confusion, finds herself a passenger en route to Mars. Children who enjoy this character can also follow her adventures in *Miss Pickerell and the Geiger Counter, Miss Pickerell Goes Undersea,* and *Miss Pickerell Goes to the Arctic.*

Ruthven Todd's Flyball, the *Space Cat* (1954) is another humorous early example of the interplanetary traveler as created for children. In this series a variety of astral bodies provide comic settings for the escapades of Flyball and his human master.

Eleanor Cameron has written a convincing series about the people who visit Basidium, the Mushroom Planet. *The Wonderful Flight to the Mushroom Planet* (1956) suggests that children may be better able than adults to help beings from other planets. Two boys from California, Chuck and David, save the people of Basidium by restoring an essential food to their diet.

In Jerome Beatty, Jr.'s series about Matthew Looney, the humor is even broader and turns into science fiction satire. For example, in Matthew Looney's *Voyage to the Earth* (1961) Matt's initial arrival on earth leads him to conclude that the planet is lifeless because, under the assumption that the earth's white areas will be more habitable than its blue and green regions, the space ship has landed in the Antarctic.

These stories hold interest and laughter for young science fiction buffs. Nevertheless, we would also hope for the emergence of a more

> As the elephant was dipping his trunk in the water, an alligator came by and bit off the elephant's trunk. The elephant glared at the alligator, stamped his feet and shouted "Berry Puddy."
>
> Did you know that it takes three sheep to make one sweater? *No. I didn't even know they could knit!*
>
> The grasshopper went into a bar for a drink. The amazed bartender said, "Do you know that we have a drink named after you?" The grasshopper responded, "You have a drink named 'Irving'?"
>
> One goat found a can of a movie film, opened it and began eating the film. A second goat passed by and asked, "How is it?" "Not bad," was the reply, "but I liked the book better."

serious vein of science fiction for younger readers, stories that are more grounded in scientifically accurate information and that take as their charge a more meaningful exploration of what the future holds and what its impact on humanity may be.

## Funny animals

Humorous children's books are frequently populated by animal characters. Perhaps this is in part because children show a special affinity for animals, an affection that they may express by coaxing parents to give them a pet or take them on a trip to the zoo. Children will even imitate animals, and any nursery or kindergarten class room offers the sight of children pretending to be lumbering elephants, scary tigers or strong bears. Animal characters also provide children with a fantasy existence when these characters defy authority, get into mischief, and have wild adventures.

Many representatives from a wide array of animal species amuse children while conveying, through their antics and interactions, aspects of life that are integral to the world of childhood. For example, the theme of friendship permeates the brief episodes in James Marshall's *George and Martha* (1972) and

*George and Martha Encore* (1973), those two adorable if somewhat heavy hippopotamuses. Much of the humor is visual, and adults will also enjoy the pictures, such as the one of a hippopotamus dressed in very stylish leotards and learning the fine art of dance. The give and take that is part of friendship is skillfully conveyed in Arnold Lobel's *Frog and Toad*

George and Martha

Frog and Toad Are Friends

*Are Friends* (1970) and *Frog and Toad Together* (1972), and it is reassuring to watch these two likable characters take such obvious pleasure in one another's company. In these two books, as in the stories of George and Martha, the humor is visual. However, it is also subtle and dependent on the more involved narrative.

Two stories written in the folktale style also deal with aspects of the theme of friendship. One applauds the virtues of sharing and cooperation; the other is a gently humorous admonition of what happens without them.

In Will and Nicholas' *Finders Keepers* (1951), a Caldecott Medal winner, we are introduced to Nap and Winkle, two dogs whose friendship perches perilously on the outcome of a bone dispute. One dog saw the wayward bone first, but the other touched it first. In order to resolve the bone's ownership, Nap and Winkle seek the advice of a farmer, a goat, and a barber whose philosophy of life seems to revolve around the premise that, "Hair that is neat is better than meat." But all these consultations are to no avail. However, when a large dog attempts to resolve the conflict by assuming full ownership of the bone, Nap and Winkle learn the meaning and advantages of sharing. *Finders Keepers* is an example of the use of a predicament as the basis for a humorous story line, and the difficulties of sharing is a common problem for children in their first years of school.

Wanda Gag's *Millions of Cats* (1928) concerns an old man and an old woman who want a cat. Unable to choose which cat, the old man returns home with "hundreds of cats, thousands of cats, millions and billions and trillions of cats." The selfish cats are unable to coexist in harmony, and they destroy each other. Only one weak, skinny cat survives, and eventually thrives. The enduring quality of this book is the direct simplicity, conveyed by both text and illustrations. There is also its compelling rhythmical quality; adults as well as children enjoy reading the refrain "hundreds of cats, thousands of cats, millions and billions and trillions of cats."

Some humorous animal books express the day-to-day situations, the fears, the troubles, the pleasures that characterize the young child's world. The books about *Little Bear* (1957), by Else Holmelund Minarik, feature a realistic bear; that is, very real from the point of view of children. As he interacts with friends and relatives, plays "let's pretend," and feels the need for the warmth of a hug or of a reassuring comment, he is clearly one of their own. In *Little Bear's Visit* (1961), illus

Millions of Cats

trated by Maurice Sendak, Little Bear enjoys visiting Grandmother and Grandfather Bear and hearing stories of his mother when she was a little bear. Little Bear also enjoys pretending to be asleep, so that he can overhear the grown-ups talking, a trick not unfamiliar to human children.

Russell Hoban, in his stories about the small badger Frances, creates with understanding humor those small difficulties (small to an adult, that is) that can loom so large in the young child's world. In *Bedtime for Frances* (1969) Frances prepares for bedtime in a procedure all too familiar to parents. Singing the alphabet, Frances unsuccessfully attempts to fall asleep. Then the fears begin: Are there tigers lurking about to get Frances? Is that a

coat on a chair or is it a giant? Are those spiders emerging from those suspicious cracks in the ceiling? The fears finally are put to rest, and so is Frances. Other familiar childhood situations are the topics of such books as *A Baby Sister for Frances* (1964), *Best Friends for Frances* (1969), and *Frances Makes a Bargain* (1970).

Ellen MacGregor's *Theodore Turtle* (1955) shows that adults too can become involved in minor difficulties. Theodore is a professorial, pipe-smoking, and somewhat forgetful turtle. Looking for his four rubbers in order to go out in the rain, Theodore manages to forget one. When he goes to retrieve it, he forgets where the other three are. After a series of cases of mini-amnesia—a trail of forgotten items, a

dog with black spots. Like many children we know, Harry is fond of playing all about and getting good and dirty. And like many children, Harry was born with a natural inclination to avoid the bathtub. Unfortunately, Harry becomes so dirty that he soon resembles a black dog with white spots, and he is not recognized until a bath reveals his true identity. A similar fate befalls Harry in Zion's *Harry by the Sea* (1965) when Harry is covered by seaweed thoughtlessly deposited on him by the ocean waves. His appearance as a four-legged, scampering sea monster is short-lived, and Harry, the lovable white dog with black spots, is once again reunited with his family.

Little Bear

minor fire, and major exhaustion—Theodore finally manages to round up all four rubbers and walks outside into the bright sunshine.

Sometimes the depiction of predicaments is more broadly humorous, as the child, disguised as an animal, is more actively mischievous. The Angus stories by Marjorie Flack, published almost forty years ago, are still popular with children. Angus is a young and curious Scottish terrier who manages to get into a series of adventures and misadventures. In *Angus and the Ducks* (1930) Angus' curiosity leads him under a hedge and into the midst of some neighborhood ducks. The quacking and pecking of the ducks temporarily cures the Scottish terrier of his curiosity, and "For exactly THREE minutes, by the clock, Angus was NOT curious about anything at all."

In Gene Zion's *Harry the Dirty Dog* (1956) an amusing predicament is heightened by the exaggerated visual humor. This popular children's book concerns Harry, a lovable white

Petunia Takes A Trip

Roger Duvoisin's *Petunia* (1950) is a goose who collides with trouble not because she is mischievous, but because at times she is just plain silly. Finding a book, naive Petunia imagines that wisdom is hers. Without the ability to read, she nonetheless freely dispenses such insightful advice as the roosters' red comb is plastic; six chicks are considerably more than nine chicks; and f-i-r-e-c-r-a-c-k-e-r-s spells candy. That last bit of advice literally knocks some sense into boastful Petunia and her animal friends. In *Petunia Takes a Trip* (1953) we are treated to a goose attempting to adjust to New York City but finally returning to her familiar farm surroundings.

Disobedience is the flaw in Peter's character in that classic childhood favorite by Beatrix Potter, *The Tale of Peter Rabbit* (1903). Children can readily identify with this rabbit, who ignores his mother's wise advice and slips into Mr. MacGregor's enticing but dangerous cabbage patch. The suspense mounts as he is chased about the garden and into a watering can; finally, there is happy satisfaction as Peter returns to his mother's reproaches and the security of his own bed. This well-loved character was created almost by chance. In 1893, Beatrix Potter wrote letters to an invalid child, and to cheer him up she included the adventures of Peter Rabbit. Since then the story has cheered and engrossed countless other children as well.

The Curious George series by H. A. Rey is a favorite with young children and features a monkey who is not only disobedient, but at times appears to have singlehandedly invented and popularized the phrase *monkey business*. George's curiosity led to his capture in the jungle, and curiosity leads him into a series of humorous misadventures, from which he is

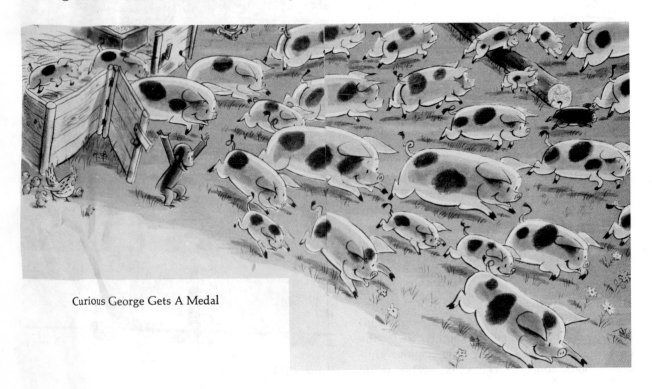

Curious George Gets A Medal

continually rescued by the man in the yellow hat. In books such as *Curious George Gets a Medal* (1957), *Curious George Learns the Alphabet* (1963), and *Curious George Flies a Kite* (1958) Curious George involves himself in a variety of predicaments that seem to entertain and amuse young children.

For somewhat older children we have the delightful antics of *A Bear Called Paddington* (1958), by Michael Bond. A stowaway from Peru, Paddington is adopted into the Brown family, and he manages to keep things from getting dull in London. In *Paddington Helps Out* (1960) he gets into trouble in the kitchen as well as in a movie theater, where, from balcony height, he accidentally drops some choice ice-cream scoops on several selected patrons. Although in *Paddington Abroad*

An Anteater Named Arthur

Lyle, Lyle Crocodile

(1972) he has trouble waking up ("I think my lids are stuck"), Paddington does manage to plan an "eyetinnery" for the Brown's vacation in France, a vacation spiced with a generous dose of Paddington's antics.

Not all humorous animal characters are involved in comic antics that create chaos. Some other amusing animals not only are in control of themselves but also manage to keep things together for the other animals and humans around them.

More successful at urban life than Paddington is Lyle, a crocodile residing on East 88th Street in New York. *Lyle, Lyle Crocodile* (1965) by Bernard Waber is one of several books about Lyle, a rather polite and useful member of the Primm family (a liberal interpretation of the extended family concept). A real New Yorker, Lyle enjoys ice skating, antiquing, and sidewalk superintending. In spite of some unfriendly neighbors, who exist even in New York, Lyle proves through a brave act that even (especially?) crocodiles can thrive in the hustle-bustle of urban America.

Another funny book by Waber is *An Ant-eater Named Arthur* (1967). Young Arthur may be an anteater but most children can readily identify with his actions. These range from being a fussy eater preferring black ants to red) to avoiding school by forgetting his pencil case, his sneakers, and a kiss for his mother.

*The Happy Lion* (1954), written by Louise Fatio and illustrated by Roger Duvoisin, presents a lion who lives in a small French park where his friends include the zoo keeper's little boy. When the happy lion leaves his cage, he is amazed at people's frightened responses, and he allows himself to be quietly led back by his young friend. In *The Happy Lion's Treasure* (1970) he manages to quell the squabbling of the zoo animals as he teaches them that a real treasure is the ability to live in harmony.

Anatole

Leo Lionni's *Swimmy* (1963) features a resourceful and practical tiny black fish. After surviving a feast by a large tuna that devours his friends, Swimmy convinces his new equally tiny fish friends to swim in formation. The formation is that of a large fish, and the tiny fish are no longer in continual danger of being a meal on fins. The meek have inherited the sea, if not the earth.

But for cleverness few animals could surpass *Anatole* (1956), a tiny French mouse created by Eve Titus. When Anatole overhears humans decrying the behavior of mice who freeload off human food, the little mouse's pride is stung. Determined to make his own way, Anatole sneaks into a cheese factory, tastes all the cheeses, and leaves behind his own concise reviews, such as "specially good" and "no good." Anatole, the unofficial cheese taster, is known to humans only by the messages he leaves behind, but the success of the cheese factory is evidence enough that Anatole is earning his own way. In *Anatole and the Cat* (1957), the presence of Anatole's traditional enemy unnerves the mouse and causes a series of poor cheese reviews: "mix in pistachio ice cream," "use six moldy marshmallows," "use crushed jelly beans." The problem is eventually resolved by a creative cat trap, and Anatole's stature in his mouse-sized Parisian community remains intact.

For somewhat older children there is another admirable and accomplished member of the animal world, *Miss Bianca* (1962), who resides in an embassy. Margery Sharp has created a genteel yet courageous and clever mouse who solves mysteries and rescues prisoners in the Orient, the Antarctic, the salt mines, the Black Castle, and even in her own embassy. Danger, mystery, and gentle humor are the elements of stories in which Miss Bianca, along with the faithful Bernard, meets and takes charge of any situation.

Some books create a replica of human society populated almost exclusively by animals, animals who wear human clothing and possess human personalities. Although human characters may enter these animal civilizations, they must keep their place as minor members of the society.

The Babar series is a case in point. In *The Story of Babar, the Little Elephant* (1933), young Babar leaves the forest after his mother is killed, and he lives in the city where an elderly woman becomes his patroness. Outfitted in a stunning new wardrobe, Babar soon becomes "citified," learning about schooling, exercises, and bathtubs. When Babar eventually returns to the forest (via automobile, of course) he brings the wonders of human society to his elephant associates. The society Babar creates is on a par with human civilization, and the nation of elephants contains domesticated pets, urban renewal, a class structure, and a clear set of occupational roles from shoemaker to doctor. In *Babar Comes to America* (1965) we witness official recognition of Babar as legitimate ruler of a foreign nation when the president extends an official invitation for Babar to visit the United States. The Babar series was created by Jean de Brunhoff and has been continued by Laurent de Brunhoff.

Any discussion of the humorous societies populated by animals must include the perennial favorites *Winnie-the-Pooh* (1926) and *The House at Pooh Corner* (1928), by A. A. Milne. These stuffed but very much alive animal

The Story
of Babar

characters inhabit the Hundred Acre Wood and seem to exist for young Christopher Robin. Winnie-the-Pooh is a lovable bear with very little brain, a characteristic borne with admirable humility. Winnie-the-Pooh's world consists of, among others, small Piglet, a natural follower; uppity Owl; sad Eeyore; and shrewd (of sorts) Rabbit. In and out of minor tragedies, the citizens of the Hundred Acre Wood weave a path to eventual resolution, if not success. The simple world of Pooh consists of chapters of minor mishaps, such as the mistaken identity of Eeyore's tail for a door ringer, or equally minor schemes that inevitably go awry, such as Pooh's attempt to disguise himself as a cloud in order to reach his much desired honey. A frequent promoter of these schemes is Rabbit. With natural followers like Pooh, Rabbit is able to pull failure out of the jaws of success and create complexity out of simplicity. There was, for example, the time Rabbit devised a scheme to rid the Hundred Acre Wood of a baby kangaroo. To provide you with an insight into Pooh's world, Rabbit's sophisticated and destined-to-fail plan is duly reported:

PLAN TO CAPTURE BABY ROO[19]

1. *General Remarks.* Kanga runs faster than any of Us, even Me.
2. *More General Remarks.* Kanga never takes her eye off Baby Roo, except when he's safely buttoned up in her pocket.
3. *Therefore.* If we are to capture Baby Roo, we must get a Long Start, because Kanga runs faster than any of Us, even Me. (see 1)
4. *A Thought.* If Roo had jumped out of Kanga's pocket and Piglet had jumped in, Kanga wouldn't know the difference, because Piglet is a Very Small Animal.
5. Like Roo.
6. But Kanga would have to be looking the other way first, so as not to see Piglet jumping in.
7. See 2.
8. *Another Thought.* But if Pooh was talking to her very excitedly, she *might* look the other way for a moment.
9. And then I could run away with Roo.
10. Quickly.
11. *And Kanga wouldn't discover the difference until afterwards.*

For older children a unique and exciting animal society can be found in Kenneth Grahame's long-time favorite *The Wind in the Willows* (1908). The incidental creation of this animal world is itself an interesting story. Grahame was born in Scotland in 1859 and became a successful banker as well as a noted author. *The Wind in the Willows* was not written for publication, but to fulfill a promise to Grahame's son, Alastair, whom he affectionately called Mouse. Mouse was so fond of listening to his father create the adventures of Mole, Rat, Badger, and Toad that he once refused to go on a trip to the seaside for fear of not being able to hear the continuation of these adventures. Grahame agreed to mail him a daily account of the activities in this animal fantasy, and these letters, preserved by the boy's governess, eventually became the much-celebrated *The Wind in the Willows*.

The animals in this book provide a study in contrasts: the foolish, boastful Toad and the wise old Badger; the sensitive, innocent Mole and the knowledgeable and friendly Water Rat. Each chapter relates an adventure concerning these four characters, yet each chapter stands alone as a complete story. The adventures include the Toad's travels, the Mole's great adventure, simple picnics, and minor tragedies. But the beauty and power of the book resides in the effective and sensitive prose that brings the senses alive and stimulates the imagination of adults as well as children.

Imaginative characters and stories are the stock and trade of Dr. Seuss, whose numerous books are quite different from *The Wind in the Willows*. Dr. Seuss (pseudonym for Theodor Seuss Geisel) has been a prolific and successful writer of humorous children's books for the past forty years, since the publication of his first book *And to Think That I Saw It on Mulberry Street* (1937). Dr. Seuss's characters live in entirely animal societies as well as in societies of animals and people. But common to both types of Dr. Seuss books are rhyme, nonsense sounds, creative illustrations, surprise, and slapstick. For example, in *If I Ran the Zoo* (1950) we are treated to a parade of Dr. Seuss's creatures congregating to form a most unusual zoo. Young Gerald McGrew daydreams of his ideal zoo, which would include an elephant-cat, a mulligatawny, an iota, thwerlls, a tizzle-topped tufted mazurka, nerds galore, proos, preeps, and, of course, last but not least, an It-Kutch.

Other Dr. Seuss books include *Yertle the Turtle, How the Grinch Stole Christmas, Green Eggs and Ham, The Cat and the Hat,* and *Horton Hears a Who!* The longevity of Dr. Seuss's zany animal characters attests to the appreciation of these well-written, well-illustrated, funny stories.

The final book that we discuss in this section is also a fanciful view of the animal world. Beatrice Schenk de Regniers' *May I Bring a Friend?* (1964), illustrated by Beni Montresor, is a Caldecott award winner about a young boy invited to join the king and queen for tea. He requests that a friend join them.

> The King and Queen
> Invited me
> To come to their house
> On Sunday for tea.
> I told the Queen
> And the Queen told the King
> I had a friend
> I wanted to bring
> The King told the Queen
> "My dear, my dear,
> Any friend of our friend
> Is welcome here."[20]

The friends are in fact a succession of animals —a giraffe, a hippopotamus, monkeys, an elephant, a seal—so many, in fact, that the royal couple and their young friend decide to move closer to their guests. The regal tea is reconvened at the zoo.

## Growing up absurd

A royal visit is also the subject of Uri Shulevitz's *One Monday Morning* (1967). "One Monday morning the king, the queen, and the little prince came to visit me. But I wasn't home."[21] As each day passes, an even larger entourage of the royal court climbs the stairs of the apartment house looking for the young boy, until finally they locate him. After they say hello their needs are met, and they vanish back into the deck of cards with which the boy has been playing. *One Monday Morning* is an example of a humorous book that features a child, rather than an animal, as the central character. In this section we discuss some fanciful books and some realistic ones as well, books that present with a generous dose of humor those embarrassments, fears, and triumphs that children meet on the way to adulthood.

It is particularly difficult for young children, given their limited appreciation of the various forms of humor, to enjoy the funny side of their own mistakes and problems. The ability to laugh at oneself is not fully developed in the early elementary school years, and this is probably one reason for the popularity of humorous books featuring animal characters. Young children can better appreciate humorous books that may be related to their own behavior, if there is a touch of fantasy or exaggeration to ensure that the child character is in total command of the situation.

A good example of such an approach is Maurice Sendak's *Where the Wild Things Are* (1963). When Max does not obey his parents, he is sent to his room as punishment. His room soon becomes a forest, and he sails away to the land where the wild things are. The ghoulish and ghastly monsters who inhabit this land are no match for Max, who becomes king of them all. Eventually Max returns home to his own room where things are back to normal, and his dinner is waiting for him. When *Where the Wild Things Are* was first published, adults feared that these monsters would frighten young children, but they did not. This book serves as a good example of the power of fantasy and the resilience of children.

Monsters and weird people also inhabit the world of Iris Fogel in Ellen Raskin's *Spectacles* (1969). These monsters are not the creations of a fantasy world, as in *Where the Wild Things Are*, but the result of poor vision. Iris' hesitancy to wear glasses is finally overcome when she finds a pair that make her look intelligent. She also appreciates being able to see things as they are (except for a weird monster still appearing every now and then when she removes her spectacles).

A surrealistic and macabre type of humor is demonstrated to an even greater degree by such authors as Frank Asch. In *Rebecka* (1972) a young boy explores the possibility of marrying his dog, but dietary incompatibility and the potential offspring of such a union dissuade him. In *I Met a Penguin* (1972) unrequited romance is again the theme as a lion learns that it is better to have loved and lost a penguin than never to have loved at all. Other strangely humorous tales by Asch include the weird mental visions of a teddy bear, *In the Eye of the Teddy* (1973) and a story about *Linda* (1969), a girl not above saying "good morning" to cars, mattresses, debris, and the night.

The awkward moments, those self-doubts on the way to adulthood, provide the humor for children's books such as *Alexander and the Terrible, Horrible, No Good, Very Bad Day* (1973), by Judith Viorst. Alexander is experiencing one of those days when getting out of bed is the initial mistake, and things deteriorate steadily from there. His gum becomes wedged in his hair, his lunch box does not have his usual dessert, the shoe store has only a plain white sneaker in his size, he spills ink all over his father's desk, his cat refuses to sleep with him, he bites his tongue, and his Mickey Mouse night light burns out. Young children, uninhibited by the social norms that suggest that it is inappropriate to laugh at the misfortunes of others, are happily pleased with Alexander's horrendous day.

The humor of superiority is also basic to Bernard Waber's *Nobody Is Perfick* (1971). This book presents Peter Perfick, that kind of terrific kid we have all known and hated as children. Peter is always polite, eats all his food, sits straight, has sharpened pencils in school, and never scuffs his shoes. Fortunately there is a large wind-up key protruding from his mechanical body, so that young readers may be confirmed in their belief that "nobody is perfick."

Peter and Alexander provide humorous escape valves for children who fall short of adult expectations and their own expectations as well. Waber's *Ira Sleeps Over* (1972) also contains this theme as young Ira, delighted at being invited to spend the night at his friend's house, is filled with doubt as to whether or not he should bring his teddy bear. Although he needs his teddy bear in order to go to sleep, he is worried about his friend's reaction to his "childish" need. But when his friend takes a teddy bear to bed, the predicament is resolved, and the needs of small children are confirmed as legitimate and appropriate.

The lazy behavior of some children provides the basis for the fantastic exaggeration of William Pene Du Bois' *Lazy Tommy Pumpkinhead* (1966). Lazy Tommy has all his needs cared for by a *really* all-electric house which wakes, washes, dresses, and feeds him. But a power failure causes Tommy to sleep for two days, get doused in a cold bathtub, get dressed upside down, and have a delicious, plentiful breakfast fed into his feet.

"In an old house in Paris that was covered with vines lived twelve little girls in two straight lines."[22] Such is the tightly structured environment of *Madeline* (1939), created by Ludwig Bemelmans. Although Madeline, her eleven friends, and the steadfast Miss Clavel walk a narrow line between fantasy and reality, Madeline has become as real as any friend to many young readers. In this series Madeline manages to upset her well-ordered world by falling into the Seine, having an appendicitis attack, and, along with Pepito, being carried off by gypsies. The Madeline books, with their strikingly handsome watercolors, are popular with young children. One of these lightly humorous tales, *Madeline's Rescue* (1953), won the Caldecott Medal.

A frequent approach to humor for the elementary school reader is through fact and fantasy creations of children whose active curiosity and initiative seem continually to land them in hot water. These characters are usually boys who have good hearts but manage nonetheless to create a continuing series of minor catastrophes.

Obadiah, a young Quaker boy in Brinton Turkle's *The Adventures of Obadiah* (1972), has a difficult time containing his curiosity and his imagination. At the annual sheep shearing on the island of Nantucket, Obadiah's stories of fire-eating Indians, fortunetellers, and a pig performing tricks are initially discounted as run-of-the-mill, Obadiah-type fibs. Yet they turn out to be true. Charley Cornett, in Rebecca Caudill's *Did You Carry the Flag Today, Charley?* (1966), exhibits the kind of energetic curiosity that gets Obadiah into trouble. In a rainstorm Charley curls up on the ground in an attempt to determine how a rock feels. In a classroom experiment he manages to get himself and his teacher wet. But on one proud day Charley's behavior is exceptional, and he is rewarded with the honor of carrying the flag for his classmates in their small Appalachian school. *Did You Carry the Flag Today, Charley?* is a touching as well as an amusing book.

Astrid Lindgren has created a wildly mischievous character in her Emil series, set in Sweden. Emil's mother keeps a written record of Emil's activities in little blue notebooks that tell of such events as a trick that hobbled his father's foot, an auction through which Emil seemingly cornered the market on worthless junk, and a series of clever schemes to pull out his sister's aching tooth. Some of Emil's mischief is even too upsetting to be recorded in these private notebooks. But in spite of Emil's pranks, it is made clear that he is basically a good and even courageous boy. Emil is simply going through a "difficult phase" on the road to adulthood, more difficult for his family and friends than for Emil himself.

*Homer Price* (1943), by Robert McCloskey, is not a prankster, but excitement seems to follow him. Homer lives in Centerburg, a typical midwestern city with an atypical assortment of adventures. For example, Homer and his pet skunk, Aroma, capture four robbers, one of whom explains, "Our early environment is responsible for our actions." But the sheriff is quick to recognize a "smell job of swelling, I mean a swell job of smelling!" When Super Duper from Cosmic Comics comes to Centerburg to promote his new film, Homer is delighted to be able to see and talk to his idol. He is delighted, that is, until a car accident reduces Super Duper to an average guy, with scratches on his body and his super powers abated. A doughnut machine gone berserk, a musical mousetrap, and a cord ball contest provide other exciting adventures for the irrepressible Homer Price.

A more contemporary Super Duper hero is found in Clifford Hicks' *Alvin Fernald, Superweasel* (1974). Young Alvin responds to a class ecology project with unusual fervor. He decides to fight polluters in the disguise of a caped crusader, Superweasel. Superweasel climbs tall chimneys in a slow but steady bound, tosses dead fish into swimming pools with his bare hands, and, disguised as Alvin Fernald, typical elementary school student, fights a never-ending battle for truth, clean air, and the American way. Young Alvin takes on the powerful but polluting chemical company, the smoking chimney of a foundry, and the most prevalent polluter of them all, the litterbug. In his fight against the evil polluters, Superweasel is aided by his Magnificent Brain, a clever voice in Alvin's head that never lets him down, although once old M. B. did manage to let down Alvin's pants. *Alvin Fernald, Superweasel* is but one of the several books about Alvin's adventures.

Although Alvin Fernald seeks out adventure, Henry Reed, in *Henry Reed, Inc.* (1958), by Keith Robertson, seems to find adventure stalking his every move. On a summer visit to his aunt and uncle in New Jersey, Henry establishes his own pure and applied research company. Along with his partner, Midge, Henry manages to create a traffic jam, find an old, valuable pot while looking for truffles, find an abandoned oil tank while looking for water, and quite accidentally Henry gets a grouchy neighbor's cat stranded on a roof while getting his own pet dog stranded aloft in a balloon.

Oliver Butterworth's *The Enormous Egg* (1956) is a humorous fantasy about the havoc that follows young Nate Twitchell after his hen lays an enormous egg. But the trouble really begins when the egg hatches and a dinosaur, thought to be extinct for millions of years, emerges. Nate is offered a large sum of money for his pet Triceratops by a luggage company that wants the dinosaur's hide for its new line of dinosaur skin luggage. And some very funny political satire emerges in the form of Senator Granderson, who, after making a careful study of the situation, decides that the dinosaur should not be allowed in the National

Zoo. The reason is obvious—the dinosaur is clearly foreign and un-American.

Many other books draw a gently humorous portrait of more ordinary children who confront the pleasures and problems of day-to-day living. In the middle elementary years children are ready for the illustrated story in which text rather than illustrations becomes of major importance. Frequently in these stories a young boy or girl of about ten or eleven becomes involved in familiar yet humorous situations.

Carolyn Haywood has written two series of books that touch the concerns of young children: the Betsy series and the Little Eddie books. *B Is for Betsy* (1939) relates the concerns of a young girl, including getting a dog, and the first-day-of-school jitters. There are pranks at school and the typical mistakes and accidents that are part of growing up. *Little Eddie* (1947) is an avid collector of valuable items that adults would generally classify as junk. Although Eddie manages to turn his collecting instincts into a profit, his family must endure Gardenia the goat, an entire telephone pole suitable for chopping into firewood, and a frenzied attempt to outswap a rival collector. The Little Eddie and the Betsy series provide a warm and humorous insight into childhood.

Another author who is successful at creating a humorous vision of childhood is Beverly Cleary. In *Henry Huggins* (1950) Henry attempts to keep a stray dog, and in *Henry and Beezus* (1952) he valiantly attempts to convert $50 worth of Beauty Shoppe permanent waves and facials into a new bicycle. In *Beezus and Ramona* (1955) Beatrice (Beezus) Quimby's biggest problem is her younger sister, Ramona. Children with younger siblings readily recognize the obstacles created by this four-year-old who has staked out the living room as a special freeway designed explicitly for her tricycle. In *Ramona the Pest* (1968) four-year-old Ramona continues to create her own special brand of anarchy, and in *Ramona the Brave* (1975) she emerges as a slightly older child who must face the task of coping with life. Ramona, now a first grader, faces the loneliness of a room of her own, the boredom of those endless school workbook exercises, the inevitable clashes with her teacher, and the self-doubt as she wonders if she is "failing at the job of growing up."

Honesty of characterization gives the Moffat series by Eleanor Estes depth as well as humor. *The Moffats* (1941), *The Middle Moffat*

Ramona the Pest

(1942), and *Rufus M.* (1943) include many funny episodes of various members of the Moffat family, and are admirably illustrated by Louis Slobodkin. For example, in one episode Janey carries on the role of the middle bear in a play of "The Three Bears," but unfortunately she misplaces her bear's head. For most of the performance she is in only half a costume, but toward the end of the play the bear's head is retrieved just in time for her to put it on—backward.

Ellen Conford has written penetrating and witty stories about those difficult intermediate years. In *Dreams of Victory* (1973) Conford describes the real-world failures and ensuing daydreams of Victory Benneker. Victory believes she has been woefully misnamed, that a more appropriate name would be Defeat Benneker. She is unable to stay vertical on ice skates, is terrified of the Ferris Wheel, manages to get only six votes out of twenty-six in the class election for president, and, as a final insult, is cast as Litter instead of Clean Air in the ecology play at school. Through it all, these defeats are neutralized by Victory's daydreams, visions of being the first woman President, the first female astronaut on the moon, an Olympic ice skater, and a movie star. But in the end Victory's imagination proves to be a real asset, as her composition is chosen as the most creative in the entire class. The sweet successes of Victory's daydreams are finally matched by a sweet success in the real world. The book is touchingly illustrated by Gail Rockwell.

*Felicia the Critic* (1973) is about the very astute Felicia, who possesses an uncanny and unnerving ability to criticize. After several uncomfortable situations, Felicia attempts to follow her mother's advice and become a constructive critic. But even this role has its dangers, as Felicia discovers at her cousin's wedding. While jotting down her constructive suggestions, both the bride's mother and the groom's mother become curious, grab the paper, and, against Felicia's will, read her comments.

Don't put children's table right under band. They will go deaf. Have a Coke instead of funny tasting punch in dolphin. Have microphones in chapel so you can hear the wedding. No pea soup. Let the ushers sit with who they want. Have more time before the wedding so people can eat the canapes and things. Don't let accordian player sing. Smaller dinner so people have room for baked Alaska.[23]

After effectively dampening the happiest day for the happy couple's formerly happy parents, Felicia slowly learns the power of her critical eye and attempts to be a more judicious critic. Another fine, humorous book about another girl with a harshly critical eye is Louise Fitzhugh's *Harriet the Spy* (1964).

Another author who writes with humorous understanding of the trials of the burgeoning adolescent is Judy Blume. In *Are You There God? It's Me, Margaret* (1970) Margaret Simon is concerned with her developing sexuality, or more precisely, her lack of developing sexuality. In her talks with God she prays for something to put in her bra, and for months she practices with the appropriate equipment, preparing for her first period. Tony Miglione in Blume's *Then Again, Maybe I Won't* (1971) is concerned with his erotic dreams, his urge to peep into the bedroom window of the cheerleader next door, and the developing crass materialism of his parents.

The problems confronting characters like Felicia, Victory, Margaret, and Tony, problems related to self-understanding and the quest for acceptance, are typical and sometimes critical issues during early adolescence. The older teenager also faces a difficult and demanding period of maturation. On the verge of adulthood, the adolescent must deal with a growing awareness of sexuality, decisions about future adult roles, and perhaps friction with parents and other adults. Although portraying these problems with sensitivity and humor presents a great challenge, it is a challenge that several authors have successfully met. Certainly one of the earliest and most influential of these books is J. D. Salinger's *The Catcher in the Rye* (1951).

In many ways *The Catcher in the Rye* set a precedent for the humorous adolescent novel. Holden Caulfield's interaction with society uncovers artificial and phony adults holding empty values. The book is written in the first person, with candor and humor, and although it was not originally written for adolescents, they have taken it as their own. The penetrating honesty, the unmasking of societal pretense, and the first-person narrative of a teenager are characteristics that have made *The Catcher in the Rye* immensely popular with teenagers, the object of widespread censorship, and an influential precedent for other authors.

Another more contemporary author who deals with the problems of high-school-age adolescents is M. E. Kerr. Her first book, *Dinky Hocker Shoots Smack* (1972), is about bright, witty, obese Dinky Hocker and her mother, who is so busy being the community's good Samaritan, that she neglects her own daughter. In *If I Love You Am I Trapped Forever?* (1973) Kerr writes of the strain in adolescent relationships and the come-from-behind popularity of the initially very uncool Duncan Stein. The generation gap leads to funny as well as serious incidents in Kerr's *The Son of Someone Famous* (1974), a story about the search for identity of a boy who happens to be the son of a very famous father.

There are many other humorous versions of the hiatus between parent and child. A kind of reverse generation gap exists in Hope Campbell's *Why Not Join the Giraffes?* (1968). Suzie Henderson is rebelling against her parents because they are too unconventional and non-conforming. Mary Rodgers' *Freaky Friday* (1972) manages to bridge the generation gap when thirteen-year-old Annabel Andrews wakes up in her mother's body. In the sequel to *Freaky Friday, A Billion for Boris* (1974), Rodgers continues her humorous account of parent-teenager difficulties with the attempts of fastidious, earnest Boris to convert his artistic, carefree mother into a down-to-earth, responsible, checkbook-balancing parent. In this effort Boris is aided by a television set that telecasts the next day's programs and by Annabel and her young brother who is known as the mechanical wizard, Ape Face.

In these books we see the use of humor to soften the harsh realities of adolescence. Frequently these stories concern topics formerly considered taboo, and they still raise the ire of some adults who see them not as humorous but as threats to their values. But as we indicated in the introduction to this chapter, adults and children do not always appreciate each other's humor.

The books we have discussed provide a humorous insight into the lives of children. However, as you may have noticed, these are mainly stories of white, middle-class suburban families. Unfortunately, there are not many well-written humorous portrayals of the different racial and cultural groups in America. Currently the creation of sensitive yet humorous books about our pluralistic society remains more a goal to be reached than an accomplishment already achieved.

One recent humorous book that does offer finely developed characterization of two black children in the upper elementary grades is Bette Greene's *Philip Hall Likes Me. I Reckon Maybe* (1974). Intelligent, vivacious eleven-year-old Beth Lambert has a crush on Philip Hall, the cutest, smartest boy in class, and the book relates the ups and downs of their relationship. Some of the "downs" happen when

Philip does not invite Beth to his birthday party because he is afraid of being tagged a sissy and when Beth beats Philip in the county fair calf-raising contest. But the "ups" prevail and, the book's conclusion suggests, so will the friendship of Philip Hall and Beth Lambert.

## From Dagwood to Doonesbury: the world of the comic strip

No popular art, whatever medium, is so pervasive and persistent in American society as the comics. Studies have continuously shown that they reach about half the total population more or less regularly. The comic strip since its beginnings has produced from eight to twelve million drawings, by far the largest body of materials of any popular art.

*From Russel Nye's* The Unembarrassed Muse: The Popular Arts in America, *New York, Dial Press, 1970*

The comic strip has been described as a base and crude literary form. Many educators and many children's literature texts try to avoid the topic or give it at most passing attention, hoping perhaps that children will instead read better literature and Superman will be reduced to a powerless, unattractive, two-dimensional character. Not likely. Comic strips and comic books enjoy a far higher readership than all the Newbery and Caldecott winners combined. To avoid exploring this aspect of children's reading represents a serious omission.

Two hundred million people in at least sixty nations around the world are regular readers of some American comic strip.[24] Of these, 100 million American adults and children are avid comic strip followers. An estimated breakdown of the readership suggests that 60 percent of the readers are above eighteen years of age, 15 percent are in the twelve- to seventeen-year-old category, and 25 percent are under twelve.[25] A study of 1000 schoolchildren in

Massachusetts revealed that 97 percent of the girls and 99 percent of the boys read one or more comic strips printed in the daily or Sunday newspaper.[26] Seventy-five percent of those questioned stated that they discussed the comics with their friends. And, despite prevalent stereotypes, a college graduate is twice as likely to read the comic strips of a newspaper as is an adult with an eighth-grade education.[27] In fact, comics enjoy a higher readership than any other newspaper feature except for the front page headlines, with three times as many people reading the comics as the important daily news.[28]

Why are the comics so appealing? One obvious reason for the popularity of comic strips is their fast-paced, easy-to-read format. Another factor must be the quick reinforcement of one's effort. In other words, spending just ten or twenty seconds involved in easy reading brings a quick and satisfying reward. In addition, a reader can choose from an incredible variety of comic strips: there are the superbeings, cops and robbers, slapstick jokes, family disputes, children speaking with the wisdom of the generations, and adults speaking with the foolishness of children. A reader can select the fantasy of his choice, and in a few seconds, on a daily basis, be rewarded and entertained. In fact, most readers from decade to decade, nation to nation, and generation to generation explain that their addiction to the funnies derives from the enjoyment and entertainment they provide.[29]

The beginning of newspaper comics can be traced to February 16, 1896, when Joseph Pulitzer's *New York World* published "Yellow Kid." Since that time the comic strip has undergone several changes in style and content and was extended to magazine form with the emergence of the comic book. The comic strip, the comic book, and animated cartoons have enjoyed considerable success in the twentieth century, and although they are all designed to amuse, they are not devoid of underlying cultural significance.

Almost any comic strip that has been around for some time will probably lend itself to a fruitful study of its reflection of cultural mores. Kurtzman, in an article in *Esquire* entitled "Takin' the Lid Off the Id," offers a pictorial survey of the societal trends reflected in the comic strips:[30]

*1920's*—the comics reflected a delicate balance between individuals. The society at large and the family unit in particular were undergoing stress and change. As society attempted to cope with these changes, the comics mirrored these adjustments.

*1930's and 1940's*—A violent struggle for supremacy between hostile individuals or special interest groups appeared in the comic strips during this period. For example, the police struggled with criminals and the Americans fought the Japanese.

*Recent comic strips*—The struggles between individuals and special interest groups have been replaced by the fantasies and personal visions of the cartoonists.

The popularity of the comic strip and its reflection of societal trends have not secured it a place in American culture. On the contrary, the comics have attracted numerous and outspoken critics, including parents, educators, and psychiatrists. Frederic Wertham, a New York psychiatrist, contended that the comic book promotes illiteracy, unwholesome states of mind, and delinquent behavior.[31] Upon publication of Dr. Wertham's views in the early 1950s, the National Education Association designated Wertham's book as the "most important book of 1954" and strongly suggested that educators "see that it is widely read and that the community take steps to protect children from the menace it describes."[32]

Critics point out that comics appeal to the immature mind, to those who believe that life is a simple adventure, that love, money, and strength can solve most if not all of life's challenges. Readers of comic strips learn that people are either all good or all bad, and that their physical appearance proclaims their role in life. Moreover, comic strip fans are encouraged to accept the notion that the ends justify the means and that if a criminal's head is severed from his body by the Batmobile, then justice has been served. Such misconceptions, the critics maintain, serve to distort reality and encourage deviant behavior.

Just the opposite point of view is taken by George Newton Gordon in his support of the comics.[33] Gordon asserts that post-Victorian sentimentality, Dewey's educational philosophy, utopian liberal thinking, and Americanized psychoanalytic theory have given us a false image of children as pure and good. This romanticized version of the nature of the child clashes with reality. Real children, Gordon maintains, are incompatible with their portrayal in magazines, television, or children's books. For example, "Kids in comics are ugly, delightfully ugly."[34] Although there are some sentimental exceptions, most comic strip children can be sloppy, cruel, fresh, interesting, and spontaneously wise in an anti-intellectual sort of way. The characters in *Peanuts*, for example, illustrate these realistic if not always positive qualities. And children as well as many adults prefer comic strip characters because they, if not the critics, recognize these realistic qualities. "Comics speak realistically *for* and *of* children with warmth, not coldly about them. . . . Let cartoonists keep up their quiet rebellion against middle class pressures that produce those photographs of the pretty little bastards on the covers of *Good Housekeeping* and *Woman's Day*. Fakes, every one of them."[35]

Those who are critical of comics wish to move children's reading habits away from them to fine children's books. Those who hold the comics in a more positive light find reading them useful in itself. But both camps acknowledge the amazing popularity of the comics and the fact that children, uncoaxed by adults, seek out this form of reading on their own. Whether your own evaluation is on the positive or negative side, the comics are a literary phenomenon that cannot and should not be ignored.

Although comic strips have thrived for three-quarters of a century, in recent years the number of comic strips has been reduced. "Today there are some 400 syndicated strips running in U.S. papers—twenty percent fewer than during pre-TV days—and most of the casualties have been adventure serials. . . . The perennially successful funnies are those that are—well—funny: self-contained, gag-a-day strips."[36]

Many of the adventure strips like *Smilin' Jack* and *Terry and the Pirates* have fallen victim to the unpopularity of the Vietnam war. About 60 percent of today's comic strips are concerned with humor, much of it directed to and understood by children.[37] The humor of the comics is frequently appreciated by children on both verbal and pictorial levels. Archie's waffle iron hair and Jughead's dumb expression are enjoyed along with the joke lines.

Although many of the funnies consist of a daily series of unrelated events, continuity is provided by a stable and firm setting. In "Archie" it is the social and academic world of the teenager. In "Nancy," "Dennis-the-Menace," and "Henry" it is the world of the small (but clever, and in Dennis' case, mischievous) child. "Superman," "Popeye" and "Joe Palooka" have a talent at being winners, through special but distinctly American powers. We admire these superheroes while at the same time laughing at Dagwood in "Blondie" and at "Andy Capp." Both Dagwood and Andy are henpecked bumblers, and we enjoy the humor of our superiority and their hopeless antics.

Murat Young, the creator of "Blondie,"

An example of the cultural influence of the comic strip is illustrated in the words and phrases which, introduced in comic strips, have become part of our language.[39]

"the long and the short of it," "fall guy," "got his goat," "piker," "inside stuff."
*From Bud Fisher's "Mutt and Jeff"*

"apple-sauce," "ball and chain," "yes, we have no bananas," "you said it," "twenty-three skiddoo."
*From cartoonist T. A. Dorgan*

"let George do it."
*From George McManus' "Maggie and Jiggs"*

"jeep," and a variety of burger delicacies.
*From Elzie Crisler Segar's "Popeye"*

"hardbird," "hot mama," "heebie-jeebies," "horse-feather," "time's a-wastin'."
*From Billy DeBeck's "Barney Google"*

"dingbat."
*From George Herriman's "The Dingbat Family"*

writes, "I stick to three basic ideas . . . eating, sleeping and raising a family. Readers all over the world are able to identify with those activities."[38] "Mutt and Jeff," originally involved in the life of carefree, gambling bachelorhood, joined the henpecked, suburban story line. Jokes about marital disharmony now provide the mainstay for "Mutt and Jeff."

A particularly popular comic strip, "Peanuts," by Schultz, deserves special attention. Unlike the slapstick, one-liners that dominate most humorous comic strips, "Peanuts" holds up a psychological mirror to contemporary America.[40] In "Peanuts" we laugh at our hang-ups and fears, at ourselves and at the people we know. The characters in "Peanuts" are representative of our psychologically conscious society. In Charlie Brown we see reflected our own insecurities and fears of failure. Charlie is probably the worst baseball player to set foot on the field. He is equally inept at checkers and marbles. When Charlie attempts to get a kite aloft, the only dangerous places to be are on the ground and in a tree. Round, lovable, nondescript Charlie Brown is the bumbler we have all been or fear being.

Lucy, on the other hand, is a somewhat snobbish young lady, much taken with her own fine educational background (i.e., nursery school). She is a fussbudget of the worst sort, and she almost always gets her way. If her powerful sulk does not convince you, a screaming temper tantrum will literally knock you off your feet. If she could only win over Schroeder, the world would be hers.

The humor of "Peanuts" is the humor of identification, which is why so many people send relevant "Peanuts" cartoons to their friends and/or enemies and post them on walls and doors in offices, schools, and homes. "Peanuts" is a sign of our time; related artifacts—lunch boxes, greeting cards, wall decorations—have become a multimillion-dollar enterprise.

The psychologically oriented humor of "Peanuts" is a relatively recent addition to the comics, but the socially conscious humor of the type portrayed in the popular "Doonesbury" was preceded by the political satire of such comics as "Pogo" and "Lil Abner." Doonesbury provides a frontal attack on the foibles of our political and social world, an approach that is currently quite appealing to disenchanted adolescents and adults.[41]

Megaphone Mark is the professional, dedicated campus radical. B.D. is an ex-football jock who has never abandoned his helmet. He is also the Vietnam veteran who has not forgotten his Vietcong friend, Phred. B.D. has relevant comments to make about current political concerns and still finds time to give his plants a pep talk. The Reverend W. S. Sloan, Jr. (strikingly similar to Yale's former chaplain, William Sloan Coffin, Jr.) is an outspoken opponent of the administration. Reverend Sloan is accompanied by his Irish setter, "Unconditional Surrender," and his cat, "Kent State." Clyde, on the other hand, is a black dude, heavily "into comfort" and large, expensive, unaffordable cars.

The cutting satire of "Doonesbury" is a welcome escape valve for the frustrations and anxieties that come with the social and political stresses of our times. As with "Peanuts," people can understand and identify with the characters; they become real. In fact, when Joannie Caucus, an almost liberated woman of "Doonesbury" decided to return to school and become a lawyer, four real law school deans sent her actual application forms for admission.

"Doonesbury," "Peanuts," and other comic strip characters permeate the literary lives of many children and adults. The elements of humor, easy reading, and exciting illustrations combine to make the comic strip world a force to be reckoned with. Teachers, librarians, and parents who understand the attraction of comic strips will have a better grasp of the humor that appeals to and is enjoyed by tens of millions of children.

From the funnies to animal stories, from the crises of growing up to wild fantasies and science fiction, the many forms of humor provide children with enjoyment and satisfaction. A command of humorous children's books can help you open the world of books and touch the lives of children.

## NOTES

1. Clifford Woody, *Reading Interest of Pupils in the Public Schools of Michigan*, Bureau of Educational Reference and Research, Bulletin No. 158, Ann Arbor: School of Education, University of Michigan, May 1, 1948. See also Paul Witty, Ann Coomer, and Dilla McBean, "Children's Choices of Favorite Books: A Study Conducted in Ten Elementary Schools," *Journal of Educational Psychology*, 37 (May 1945), 266–278.
2. Kopple C. Friedman and Claude L. Nemzek, "A Survey of Reading Interest Studies," *Education*, LVII (September 1936), 51–56.
3. Clark Wissler, "The Interests of Children in the Reading Work of the Elementary Schools," *Pedagogical Seminary*, V (October 1898), 538.
4. Katherine H. Kappas, "A Developmental Analysis of Children's Responses to Humor," *The Library Quarterly*, 37, no. 1 (January 1967), 67–77.
5. Ibid.
6. Robert Bateman, "Children and Humorous Literature," *School Librarian and School Library Review*, 15 (July 1967), 153–156.
7. See also Sylvia Lee Tibbetts, "What's So Funny? Humor in Children's Literature," *California Journal of Educational Research*, 24, no. 1 (January 1973), 42–46.
8. Katherine Hull Kappas, "A Study of Humor in Children's Books" (unpublished M.A. dissertation, University of Chicago, 1965), p. 46.
9. Carney Landis and John W. H. Ross, "Humor and Its Relation to Other Personality Traits," *Journal of Social Psychology*, 4 (1933), 156–175.
10. Ibid.
11. Ruth E. Wells, "A Study of Tastes in Humorous Literature Among Pupils of Junior and Senior High Schools," *Journal of Educational Research*, 28 (1934), 88.
12. Landis and Ross, op. cit., pp. 156–175.
13. Tove Jansson, *Finn Family Moomintroll*, New York, Walck, 1965, p. 16.
14. Nicholas Stuart Gray, *Grimbold's Other World*, ill. by Charles Keeping, Des Moines, Iowa, Meredith, 1963, p. 22.
15. Ibid.
16. Sid Fleischman, *Mr. Mysterious & Company*, ill. by Kurt Werth, New York, Norton, 1967, p. 82.
17. Damon Knight, ed., in the introduction to *Worlds to Come*, New York, Harper & Row, 1967, p. xi.
18. Sylvia Louise Engdahl, "The Changing Role of Science Fiction in Children's Literature," *How Book*, 47 (October 1971), 450.
19. A. A. Milne, *Winnie-the-Pooh*, New York, Dutton, 1926, pp. 93–94.
20. Beatrice Schenk de Regnier, *May I Bring a Friend*, ill. by Beni Montresor, New York, Atheneum, 1964.

21. Uri Shulevitz, *One Monday Morning*, New York, Scribner, 1967.
22. Ludwig Bemelmans, *Madeline*, New York, Viking Press, 1939, p. 1.
23. Ellen Conford, *Felicia the Critic*, ill, by Avis Stewart, Boston, Little, Brown, 1973, pp. 105, 107.
24. David Manning White and Robert H. Abel, eds., *The Funnies, An American Idiom*, New York, Free Press, 1963, p. vii.
25. Fred Dickenson, "The Fascinating Funnies," *Reader's Digest*, 99 (November 1971), 201–204T.
26. Edward J. Robinson and David Manning White, "Who Reads the Funnies—and Why?" in White and Abel, op. cit., pp. 179–189.
27. Ibid.
28. White and Abel, op. cit., p. 3.
29. Ibid., p. 23.
30. Harvey Kurtzman, *"Takin' the Lid Off the Id,"* *Esquire*, LXXV, no. 6 (June 1971), 128–137.
31. Frederic Wertham quoted by Dwight Burton, "Comic Books: A Teacher's Analyses," *Elementary School Journal*, 56 (October 1955), 73–75.
32. Ibid.
33. George Newton Gordon, "Can Children Corrupt Our Comics," in White and Abel, op. cit., pp. 158–166.
34. Ibid., p. 161.
35. Ibid., p. 166.
36. "New Look at the Funny Pages," *Newsweek*, 81 (March 5, 1973), 76–77.
37. Francis Barcus, "The World of Sunday Comics," in White and Abel, op. cit., pp. 190–218.
38. Dickenson, op. cit., p. 203.
39. White and Abel, op. cit., p. 19.
40. Martin Jezer, "Quo Peanuts?" in White and Abel, op. cit., pp. 167–176.
41. "Trudeaumania," *Newsweek*, 85 (January 17, 1975), 49.

# BIBLIOGRAPHY

## Books for younger readers

ASCH, FRANK. *I Met A Penguin*, McGraw-Hill, 1972 (preschool–3).

———. *In the Eye of the Teddy*, Harper & Row, 1973 (preschool–3).

———. *Linda*, McGraw-Hill, 1969 (preschool–3).

———. *Rebecka*, Harper & Row, 1972 (preschool–2).

BEMELMANS, LUDWIG. *Madeline*, Viking Press, 1939 (K–2).

———. *Madeline's Rescue*, Viking Press, 1959 (K–2).

BERENSTAIN, STAN, and JANICE BERENSTAIN. *Bear Scouts*, Random House, 1967 (K–3).

BRIDWELL, NORMAN. *Clifford the Big Red Dog*, Scholastic, 1966 (K–3).

BRIGGS, RAYMOND. *Jim and the Beanstalk*, Coward, McCann & Geoghegan, 1970 (preschool–2).

BRIGHT, ROBERT. *Georgie*, Doubleday, 1944 (K–2). See also, *Georgie and the Noisy Ghost, Georgie and the Magician, Georgie and the Robbers, Georgie to the Rescue, Georgie's Halloween*.

BURNINGHAM, JOHN. *Mr. Gumpy's Outing*, Holt, Rinehart and Winston, 1971 (4 yr.–2nd grade).

CAUDILL, REBECCA. *Did You Carry the Flag Today, Charley?*, Nancy Grossman, illus., Holt, Rinehart and Winston, 1966 (K–2).

COOMBS, PATRICIA. *Dorrie and the Weather-Box*, Lothrop, Lee & Shepard, 1966 (preschool–2).

———. *Dorrie and the Goblin*, Lothrop, Lee & Shepard, 1972 (preschool–2).

———. *Dorrie and the Blue Witch*, Lothrop, Lee & Shepard, 1964 (preschool–2).

DE BRUNHOFF, JEAN. *Babar Comes to America*, trans. by M. Jean Craig, Random House, 1965 (K–3).

———. *Babar the King*, trans. by Merle S. Haas, Random House, 1935 (K–3).

———. *The Story of Babar, the Little Elephant*, trans. by Merle S. Haas, Random House, 1933, 1960 (K–3).

DE REGNIERS, BEATRICE SCHENK. *May I Bring a Friend?*, Beni Montresor, illus., Atheneum, 1964 (K–2).

DEVLIN, WENDE, and HARRY DEVLIN. *Old Witch Rescues Halloween*, Parents' Magazine Press, 1972 (K–3).

DU BOIS, WILLIAM PENE. *Lazy Tommy Pumpkinhead*, Harper & Row, 1966 (1–4).

DUVOISIN, ROGER. *Petunia*, Knopf, 1950 (K–3).

———. *Petunia Takes a Trip*, Knopf, 1953 (K–3).

FATIO, LOUISE. *The Happy Lion in Africa*, Roger Duvoisin, illus., McGraw-Hill, 1955 (K–3).

———. *The Happy Lion Roars*, Roger Duvoisin, illus., McGraw-Hill, 1957 (K–3).

———. *The Happy Lion's Treasure*, Roger Duvoisin, illus., McGraw-Hill, 1970 (K–2).

———. *The Three Happy Lions*, Roger Duvoisin, illus., McGraw-Hill, 1959 (K–3).

FLACK, MARJORIE. *Angus and the Cat*, Doubleday, 1931 (K–2).

——. *Angus and the Ducks*, Doubleday, 1930 (K–2).

——. *Angus Lost*, Doubleday, 1932, 1941 (K–2).

——. *Ask Mr. Bear*, Macmillan, 1932, 1958 (K–2).

GAG, WANDA. *Millions of Cats*, Coward, McCann & Geoghegan, 1928 (K–3).

HAYWOOD, CAROLYN. *B Is for Betsy*, Harcourt Brace Jovanovich, 1939 (1–3).

HEIDE, FLORENCE PARRY. *The Shrinking of Treehorn*, Edward Gorey, illus., Holiday, 1971 (K–3).

HOBAN, RUSSELL. *A Baby Sister for Frances*, Lillian Hoban, illus., Harper & Row, 1964 (K–1).

——. *A Bargain for Frances*, Harper & Row, 1970 (K–3).

——. *Bedtime for Frances*, Garth Williams, illus., Harper & Row, 1969 (K–1).

——. *Best Friends for Frances*, Lillian Hoban, illus., Harper & Row, 1969 (K–2).

——. *Bread and Jam for Frances*, Harper & Row, 1964 (K–3).

——. *How Tom Beat Captain Najork and His Hired Sportsmen*, Quentin Blake, illus., Atheneum, 1974 (K–3).

HOFF, SYD. *The Horse in Harry's Room*, Harper & Row, 1970 (K–1).

——. *Syd Hoff's Joke Book*, Putnam, 1972 (K–3).

KENT, JACK. *The Egg Book*, Macmillan, 1975 (K–2).

KRAHN, FERNANDO. *Who's Seen the Scissors?*, Dutton, 1975 (preschool–1).

LEAF, MUNRO. *The Story of Ferdinand*, Robert Lawson, illus., Viking Press, 1936 (K–3).

LIONNI, LEO. *Alexander and the Wind-up Mouse*, Pantheon Books, 1969 (K–1).

——. *Swimmy*, Pantheon Books, 1963 (preschool–2).

LOBEL, ARNOLD. *Frog and Toad Are Friends*, Harper & Row, 1971 (K–3).

——. *Frog and Toad Together*, Harper & Row, 1972 (K–3).

——. *The Man Who Took the Indoors Out*, Harper & Row, 1974 (K–3).

LORD, JOHN VERNON. *The Giant Jam Sandwich*, verses by Janet Burroway, Houghton Mifflin, 1972 (K–3).

MACGREGOR, ELLEN. *Theodore Turtle*, Paul Galdone, illus., McGraw-Hill, 1955 (K–3).

MAHOOD, KENNETH. *Why Are There More Questions Than Answers, Grandad?*, Bradbury Press, 1974 (K–3).

MARSHALL, JAMES. *George and Martha*, Houghton Mifflin, 1972 (K–2).

——. *George and Martha Encore*, Houghton Mifflin, 1973 (K–2).

MCCLOSKEY, ROBERT. *Make Way for Ducklings*, Viking Press, 1941 (K–3).

MCLEOD, EMILE WARREN. *The Bear's Bicycle*, David McPhail, illus., Atlantic Monthly Press, 1975 (K–2).

MINARIK, ELSE HOLMELUND. *Little Bear's Visit*, Maurice Sendak, illus., Harper & Row, 1961 (K–2).

NESS, EVALINE. *Yeck Eck*, Dutton, 1974 (K–2).

OAKLEY, GRAHAM. *The Church Mice and the Moon*, Atheneum, 1974 (K–3).

POTTER, BEATRIX. *The Tale of Peter Rabbit*, Warne, 1903 (K–3).

PROVENSEN, ALICE, and MARTIN PROVENSEN. *My Little Hen*, Random House, 1974 (K–3).

RASKIN, ELLEN. *Spectacles*, Atheneum, 1969 (K–2).

REY, HANS A. *Curious George*, Houghton Mifflin 1941 (K–3).

——. *Curious George Gets a Medal*, Houghton Mifflin, 1957 (K–4).

——. *Curious George Learns the Alphabet*, Houghton Mifflin, 1963 (K–3).

SCARRY, RICHARD. *The Great Pie Robbery*, Random House, 1969 (K–4).

SEGAL, LORE. *Tell Me a Mitzi*, Harriet Pincus, illus., Farrar, Straus & Giroux, 1970 (K–2).

SENDAK, MAURICE. *In the Night Kitchen*, Harper & Row, 1970 (K–2).

——. *Chicken Soup with Rice*, Harper & Row, 1962 (K–3).

——. *Where the Wild Things Are*, Harper & Row, 1963 (K–2).

SEUSS, DR. (pseud. for Theodor Seuss Geisel). *ABC*, Random House, 1963 (K–1).

——. *And to Think That I Saw It on Mulberry Street*, Vanguard, 1937 (K–3).

——. *Did I Ever Tell You How Lucky You Are?*, Random House, 1973 (K–3).

————. *Horton Hatches the Egg*, Random House, 1940 (K–3).

————. *Horton Hears a Who!*, Random House, 1954 (K–3).

————. *If I Ran the Zoo*, Random House, 1950 (K–3).

————. *Marvin K Mooney, Will You Please Go Now!*, Random House, 1972 (K–3).

————. *McElligot's Pool*, Random House, 1947 (K–3).

————. *The Cat in the Hat*, Random House, 1957 (K–3).

————. *The Cat in the Hat Comes Back!*, Random House, 1958 (K–3).

————. *The King's Stilts*, Random House, 1939 (K–3).

SHULEVITZ, URI. *One Monday Morning*, Scribner, 1967 (K–2).

SLOBODKIN, LOUIS. *The Space Ship Under the Apple Tree*, Macmillan, 1952 (K–3).

STEIG, WILLIAM. *Amos & Boris*, Farrar, Straus & Giroux, 1971 (K–2).

————. *Farmer Palmer's Wagon Ride*, Farrar, Straus & Giroux, 1974 (K–3).

————. *Roland the Minstrel Pig*, Windmill Books, 1968 (K–3).

————. *C D B!*, Simon & Schuster, 1968 (K–5).

THAYER, JANE. *Gus Was a Christmas Ghost*, Seymour Fleishman, illus., Morrow, 1969 (K–3).

TITUS, EVE. *Anatole*, Paul Galdone, illus., McGraw-Hill, 1956 (K–3).

————. *Anatole and the Cat*, Paul Galdone, illus., McGraw-Hill, 1957 (K–3).

————. *Anatole and the Thirty Thieves*, Paul Galdone, illus., McGraw-Hill, 1969 (K–3).

TOBIAS, TOBI. *The Quitting Deal*, Trina Schart, illus., Hyman. Viking Press, 1975 (K–3).

TURKLE, BRINTON. *The Adventures of Obadiah*, Viking Press, 1972 (K–2).

UNGERER, TOMI. *Crictor*, Harper & Row, 1958 (K–3).

UDRY, JANICE MAY. *Glenda*, Marc Simont, illus., Harper & Row, 1969 (K–3).

VIORST, JUDITH. *Alexander and the Terrible, Horrible, No Good, Very Bad Day*, Ray Cruz, illus., Atheneum, 1973 (K–2).

WABER, BERNARD. *Also Lovable Lyle*, Houghton Mifflin, 1965 (K–2).

————. *An Anteater Named Arthur*, Houghton Mifflin, 1967 (K–3).

————. *Ira Sleeps Over*, Houghton Mifflin, 1972 (K–3).

————. *Lovable Lyle*, Houghton Mifflin, 1969 (K–3).

————. *Lyle and the Birthday Party*, Houghton Mifflin, 1966 (K–3).

————. *Lyle Finds His Mother*, Houghton Mifflin, 1974 (K–3).

————. *Lyle, Lyle Crocodile*, Houghton Mifflin, 1965 (K–3).

————. *Nobody Is Perfick*, Houghton Mifflin, 1971 (K–3).

————. *The House on East 88th Street*, Houghton Mifflin, 1965 (K–3).

WILL AND NICOLAS (pseud. for William Lipkind and Nicolas Mordvinoff). *Finders Keepers*, Harcourt, 1951 (K–3).

WILLIAMS, JAY. *The Silver Whistle*, Friso Henstra, illus., Parents' Magazine Press, 1971 (K–3).

ZION, GENE. *Harry by the Sea*, Margaret Bloy Graham, illus., Harper & Row, 1965 (K–2).

————. *Harry the Dirty Dog*, Margaret Bloy Graham, illus., Harper & Row, 1956 (K–2).

## Books for the middle and upper grades

AIKEN, JOAN. *The Wolves of Willoughby Chase*, Pat Marriott, illus., Doubleday, 1962 (5–9).

————. *Smoke from Cromwell's Time: And Other Stories*, Doubleday, 1970 (5–7).

————. *The Whispering Mountain*, Frank Bozzo, illus., Doubleday, 1969 (5–9).

ALEXANDER, LLOYD. *The Cat Who Wished to Be a Man*, Dutton, 1973 (4–7).

————. *The Foundling and Other Tales of Prydain*, Holt, Rinehart and Winston, 1973 (2–6).

————. *The Marvelous Misadventures of Sebastian*, Dutton, 1970 (4–7).

————. *The Truthful Harp*, Evaline Ness, illus., Holt, Rinehart and Winston, 1967 (3–4).

ANDERSEN, HANS CHRISTIAN. *The Emperor's New Clothes*, Virginia Lee Burton, illus., Houghton Mifflin, 1949 (K–5).

————. *The Nightingale*, trans. by Eva La Gallienne, Nancy Ekholm Burhert, illus., Harper & Row, 1965 (3+).

———. "The Princess and the Pea," in *Seven Tales*, trans. by Eva La Gallienne, Maurice Sendak, illus., Harper & Row, 1959 (2+).

ATWATER, RICHARD, and FLORENCE ATWATER. *Mr. Popper's Penguins*, Robert Lawson, illus., Little, Brown, 1938 (3–6).

BABBITT, NATALIE. *The Devil's Storybook*, Farrar, Straus & Giroux, 1974 (3–6).

———. *The Search for Delicious*, Farrar, Straus & Giroux, 1969 (3+).

BEATTY, JEROME, JR. *Matthew Looney and the Space Pirates*, Young Scott Books, 1972 (4–7).

BELLAIRS, JOHN. *The House with a Clock in Its Walls*, Edward Gorey, illus., Dial Press, 1973 (4–7).

BENCHLEY, NATHANIEL. *Feldman Fieldmouse*, Hilary Knight, illus., Harper & Row, 1971 (3–5).

BLUME, JUDY. *Are You There God? It's Me, Margaret*, Bradbury Press, 1970 (5–7).

———. *It's Not the End of the World*, Bradbury Press, 1972 (5–8).

———. *Then Again, Maybe I Won't*, Bradbury Press, 1971 (5–7).

BODECKER, NIM. *Let's Marry Said the Cherry and Other Nonsense Poems*, Atheneum, 1974 (4+).

BOND, MICHAEL. *A Bear Called Paddington*, Peggy Fortnum, illus., Houghton, Mifflin, 1960 (4–6).

———. *Paddington Abroad*, Peggy Fortnum, illus., Houghton Mifflin, 1972 (3–7) .

———. *Paddington Helps Out*, Peggy Fortnum, illus., Houghton Mifflin, 1960 (3–7).

BRIDWELL, NORMAN. *How to Care for Your Monster*, Scholastic, 1970 (3–6).

BROOKS, WALTER R. *Freddy and the Dragon*, Knopf, 1958 (4–7).

BUTTERWORTH, OLIVER. *The Enormous Egg*, Louis Darling, illus., Little, Brown, 1956 (3–7).

CAMPBELL, HOPE. *Why Not Join the Giraffes?*, Dell, 1968 (5–8).

CARROLL, LEWIS. *Alice's Adventures in Wonderland* and *Through the Looking Glass*, John Tenniel, illus., Heritage, 1944 (orig. pub. 1865, 1871) (5+).

CLEARY, BEVERLY. *Beezus and Ramona*, Louis Darling, illus., Morrow, 1955 (3–7).

———. *Ellen Tebbits*, Louis Darling, illus., Morrow, 1951 (3–7).

———. *Emily's Runaway Imagination*, Beth and Joe Krush, illus., Morrow, 1961 (4–6).

———. *Fifteen*, Beth and Joe Krush, illus., Morrow, 1956 (7–10).

———. *Henry Huggins*, Louis Darling, illus., Morrow, 1950 (3–5).

———. *Mitch and Amy*, George Porter, illus., Morrow, 1967 (4–6).

———. *Ramona the Brave*, Morrow, 1975 (3–7).

———. *Ramona the Pest*, Louis Darling, illus., Morrow, 1968 (3–7).

———. *Ribsey*, Louis Darling, illus., Morrow, 1964 (4–6).

CLEMENS, SAMUEL (MARK TWAIN). *A Connecticut Yankee in King Arthur's Court*, Dodd, Mead, 1960 (5+).

CONFORD, ELLEN. *Dreams of Victory*, Gail Rockwell, illus., Little, Brown, 1973 (4–7).

———. *Felicia the Critic*, Arvis Stewart, illus., Little, Brown, 1973 (4–6).

———. *The Luck of Pokey Bloom*, Bernice Lowenstein, illus., Little, Brown, 1975 (4–7).

CORCORAN, BARBARA. *Meet Me at Tamerlane's Tomb*, Charles Robinson, illus., Atheneum, 1975 (5–9).

DAHL, ROALD. *Charlie and the Chocolate Factory*, Joseph Schendelman, illus., Knopf, 1964 (5–6).

DOTY, ROY. *Q's Are Weird O's: More Puns, Quips, and Riddles*, Doubleday, 1975.

DU BOIS, WILLIAM PENE. *The Alligator Case*, Harper & Row, 1965 (4–6).

———. *The Twenty-One Balloons*, Viking Press, 1947, Newbery Medal (5–7).

ESTES, ELEANOR. *The Middle Moffat*, Louis Slobodkin, illus., Harcourt Brace Jovanovich, 1944 (4–6).

———. *The Moffats*, Louis Slobodkin, illus., Harcourt Brace Jovanovich, 1941 (4–6).

———. *Rufus M*, Harcourt Brace Jovanovich 1943 (4–6).

FITZHUGH, LOUISE. *Harriet the Spy*, Harper & Row, 1964 (4–7).

FLEISCHMAN, SID. *McBroom and the Big Wind*, Kurt Werth, illus., Norton, 1967 (4–6).

———. *McBroom's Ear*, Kurt Werth, illus., Norton, 1969 (3–6).

———. *Mr. Mysterious & Company*, Eric Von Schmidt, illus., Little, Brown, 1962 (5–7).

———. *By the Great Horn Spoon*, Eric Von Schmidt, illus., Little, Brown, 1963 (5–7).

———. *McBroom's Ghost*, Robert Frankenberg, illus., Grosset & Dunlap, 1971 (3–6).

———. *McBroom Tells the Truth*, Kurt Werth, illus., Grosset, 1966 (2–5).

———. *The Ghost in the Noonday Sun*, Warren Chappell, illus., Little, Brown, 1965 (5–7).

FLEMING, IAN. *Chitty-Chitty-Bang-Bang: The Magical Car*, John Burningham, illus., Random House, 1964 (5–6).

GAGE, WILSON. *Miss Osborne-the-Mop*, Paul Galdone, illus., World, 1963 (4–6).

GRAHAME, KENNETH. *The Reluctant Dragon*, Ernest H. Shepard, illus., Holiday, 1938 (2–5).

———. *The Wind in the Willows*, Ernest H. Shepard, illus., Scribner, 1933, 1961 (4+).

GRAY, NICHOLAS STUART. *Grimbold's Other World*, Charles Keeping, illus., Meredith, 1963 (3–6).

———. *Over the Hills to Fabylon*, Charles Keeping, illus., Hawthorn, 1970 (3–6).

GREEN, BETTE. *Philip Hall Likes Me. I Reckon Maybe*, Charles Lilly, illus., Dial Press, 1974 (4–7).

HALE, LUCRETIA P. *The Peterkin Papers*, Harold Brett, illus., Houghton Mifflin, 1960 (5–7).

HAYWOOD, CAROLYN. *B Is for Betsy*, Harcourt Brace Jovanovich, 1939 (1–5).

———. *Eddie and His Big Deals*, Morrow, 1953 (3–5).

———. *Eddie's Happenings*, Morrow, 1971 (3–5).

———. *Eddie's Pay Dirt*, Morrow, 1953 (3–5).

———. *Little Eddie*, Morrow, 1947 (3–5).

HICKS, CLIFFORD B. *Alvin Fernald, Superweasel*, Bill Soko, illus., Holt, Rinehart and Winston, 1974 (4–7).

HUNTER, MOLLIE. *The Smartest Man in Ireland*, Charles Keeping, illus., Funk & Wagnalls, 1963 (4–6).

———. *Thomas and the Warlock*, Joseph Cellini, illus., Funk & Wagnalls, 1967 (6–8).

HUTCHINS, PAT. *The House That Sailed Away*, Laurence Hutchins, Greenwillow, 1975 (3–6).

JUSTER, NORTON. *The Phantom Tollbooth*, Jules Fieffer, illus., Random House, 1961 (6–8).

KELLER, CHARLES (compiler). *Ballpoint Bananas and Other Jokes for Kids*, David Barrios, illus., Prentice-Hall, 1973 (4–6).

KERR, M. E. *Dinky Hocker Shoots Smack!*, Harper & Row, 1972 (7+).

———. *If I Love You, Am I Trapped Forever?*, Harper & Row, 1973 (7+).

———. *The Son of Someone Famous*, Harper & Row, 1974 (7+).

KIPLING, RUDYARD. *Just So Stories*, Nicolas, illus., Doubleday, 1952 (orig. pub. 1902) (3–7).

———. *Just So Stories*, J. M. Gleeson, illus., Doubleday, 1946 (orig. pub. 1912) (3–7).

KONIGSBURG, E. L. *From the Mixed-Up Files of Mrs. Basil E. Frankweiler*, Atheneum, 1967 (5–7).

LINDGREN, ASTRID. *Emil and Piggy Beast*, Bjorn Berg, illus., Follett, 1973 (2–6).

———. *Emil's Pranks*, Bjorn Berg, illus., Follett, 1966 (2–6).

———. *Pippi Longstocking*, trans. by Florence Lamborn, Louis S. Glanzman, illus., Viking Press, 1950 (4–7).

LIVELY, PENELOPE. *The Ghost of Thomas Kempe*, Anthony Mailland, illus., Dutton, 1973 (3–6).

LOFTING, HUGH. *The Story of Dr. Dolittle*, Lippincott, 1920 (4–7).

———. *The Voyages of Dr. Dolittle*, Lippincott, 1922 (4–7).

LOW, JOSEPH. *Five Men Under One Umbrella and Other Ready-to-Read Riddles*, Macmillan, 1975 (2–5).

MACDONALD, BETTY. *Mrs. Piggle-Wiggle*, Hilary Knight, illus., Lippincott, 1947 (K–4).

MACGREGOR, ELLEN. *Miss Pickerell Goes to Mars*, Paul Galdone, illus., McGraw-Hill, 1951 (3–6).

———, and DORA PANTELL. *Miss Pickerell Goes on a Dig*, Whittlesay House, 1966 (3–6).

MACKELLAR, WILLIAM. *Alfie and Me and the Ghost of Peter Stuyvesant*, David K. Stone, illus., Dodd, Mead, 1974 (5–9).

MCCLOSKEY, ROBERT. *Homer Price*, Viking Press, 1943 (3–7).

———. *Lentil*, Viking Press, 1940 (2–6).

MCGINLEY, PHYLLIS. *The Plain Princess*, Helen Stone, illus., Lippincott, 1945 (2–5).

MERRILL, JEAN. *The Pushcart War*, Ronni Solbert, illus., Scott, Foresman–Addison, 1964 (5–7).

———. *The Toothpaste Millionaire*, Houghton Mifflin, 1974 (3–6).

MILNE, A. A. *The World of Pooh*, E. H. Shepard, illus., Dutton, 1957 (3–5). Contains both *Winnie-the-Pooh* and *The House at Pooh Corner*.

MONJO, F. N. *Poor Richard in France*, Brinton Turkle, illus., Holt, Rinehart and Winston, 1973 (3+).

NESBIT, EDITH. *The Story of the Treasure Seekers*, Coward, McCann & Geoghegan, 1958 (3–6).

———. *Five Children and It*, J. S. Goodall, illus., Looking Glass Library, Random House, 1948 (3+).

———. *The Phoenix and the Carpet*, J. S. Goodall, illus., Looking Glass Library, Random House, 1948 (3+).

NORTON, MARY. *The Borrowers Afield*, Beth and Joe Krush, illus., Harcourt Brace Jovanovich, 1955 (4–7).

———. *The Borrowers*, Beth and Joe Krush, illus., Harcourt Brace Jovanovich, 1953 (4–7).

———. *The Borrowers Aloft*, Beth and Joe Krush, illus., Harcourt Brace Jovanovich, 1961 (4–7).

O'BRIEN, ROBERT C. *Mrs. Frisby and the Rats of NIMH*, Zena Bernstein, illus., Atheneum, 1971 (4–6).

PANTELL, DORA. *Miss Pickerell and the Weather Satellite*, Whittlesay House, 1971 (3–6).

PARISH, PEGGY. *Amelia Bedelia*, Fritz Seibel, illus., Harper & Row, 1963 (3–6).

RASKIN, ELLEN. *The Tattooed Potato and Other Clues*, Dutton, 1975 (3–7).

ROBERTSON, KEITH. *Henry Reed's Big Show*, Robert McCloskey, illus., Viking Press, 1970 (5–7).

———. *Henry Reed, Inc.*, Robert McCloskey, illus., Viking Press, 1958 (6–8).

RODGERS, MARY. *A Billion for Boris*, Harper & Row, 1974 (5+).

———. *Freaky Friday*, Harper & Row, 1972 (5+).

ROTH, ARNOLD. *A Comick Book of Sports*, Scribner, 1974.

SALINGER, J. D. *The Catcher in the Rye*, Little, Brown, 1951 (7+).

SCHEALER, JOHN M. *Zip-Zip and His Flying Saucer*, Dutton, 1956 (2–5).

———. *Zip-Zip Goes to Venus*, Dutton, 1958 (2–5).

———. *Zip-Zip and the Red Planet*, Dutton, 1961 (2–5).

SCHRANK, JOSEPH. *The Plain Princess and the Lazy Prince*, Vasiliv, illus., Day, 1958 (6+).

SCHWARTZ, ALVIN (compiler). *Whoppers: Tall Tales and Other Lies Collected from American Folklore*, Glen Rounds, illus., Lippincott, 1975.

SELDEN, GEORGE. *The Cricket in Times Square*, William Garth, illus., Farrar, Straus & Giroux, 1960 (4–7).

———. *The Genie of Sutton Place*, Farrar, Straus & Giroux, 1973 (5–7).

———. *Harry Cat's Pet Puppy*, Garth Williams, illus., Farrar, Straus & Giroux, 1974 (3–7).

SENDAK, MAURICE. *Higglety Pigglety Pop! or There Must Be More to Life*, Harper & Row, 1967 (3–5).

SEUSS, DR. *The 500 Hats of Bartholomew Cubbins*, Vanguard Press, 1938 (1–5).

SHARP, MARGERY. *Miss Bianca: A Fantasy*, Garth Williams, illus., Little, Brown, 1962 (7+).

———. *Miss Bianca and the Bridesmaid*, Erik Blegvad, illus., Little, Brown, 1972 (5+).

SLOBODKIN, LOUIS. *Round Trip Space Ship*, Macmillan, 1968 (3–5).

———. *The Space Ship Under the Apple Tree*, Macmillan, 1952 (3–5).

———. *The Space Ship in the Park*, Macmillan, 1972 (3–5).

SOBOL, DONALD. *Encyclopedia Brown*, Leonard Shortall, illus., Nelson, 1963 (2–6). See also *Encyclopedia Brown and the Case of the Secret Pitch, Encyclopedia Brown Finds the Clues, Encyclopedia Brown Gets His Man, Encyclopedia Brown Solves Them All, Encyclopedia Brown Keeps the Peace, Encyclopedia Brown Saves the Day, Encyclopedia Brown Tracks Them Down.*

STEELE, WILLIAM O. *Andy Jackson's Water Well*, Michael Ramus, illus., Harcourt Brace Jovanovich, 1959 (4–8).

STEIG, WILLIAM. *Dominic*, Farrar, Straus & Giroux, 1972 (4–6).

TERRIS, SUSAN. *The Pencil Families*, Greenwillow, 1975 (3–7).

THURBER, JAMES. *The Great Quillow*, Doris Lee, illus., Harcourt Brace Jovanovich, 1944 (3–6).

———. *Many Moons*, Louis Slobodkin, illus., Harcourt Brace Jovanovich, 1943 (2–5).

———. *The Thirteen Clocks*, Marc Simont, illus., Simon & Schuster, 1950 (6–7).

———. *The Wonderful O*, Marc Simont, illus., Simon & Schuster, 1957 (5+).

TITUS, EVE. *Basil and the Lost Colony*, Paul Galdone, illus., McGraw, 1964 (4–6).

———. *Basil of Baker Street*, Paul Galdone, illus., McGraw, 1963 (3–6).

TODD, RUTHVEN. *Space Cat*, Paul Galdone, illus., Dutton, 1954 (3–5).

———. *Space Cat Meets Mars*, Paul Galdone, illus., Scribner, 1957 (3–5).

TRAVERS, P. L. *Mary Poppins*, Mary Shepard, illus., Harcourt Brace Jovanovich, 1934 (3–7).

———. *Mary Poppins Comes Back*, Mary Shepard, illus., Harcourt Brace Jovanovich, 1935 (3–7).

———. *Mary Poppins in the Park*, Mary Shepard, illus., Harcourt Brace Jovanovich, 1952 (3–7).

———. *Mary Poppins Opens the Door*, Mary Shepard, illus., Harcourt Brace Jovanovich, 1943 (3–7).

WELLS, ROSEMARY. *Noisy Nora*, Dial Press, 1973 (3–6).

WHITE, E. B. *Charlotte's Web*, Harper & Row, 1952, 1973 (K–6).

YOUNG, MIRIAM. *Truth and Consequences*, Diane de Groat, illus., Four Winds Press, 1975 (4–7).

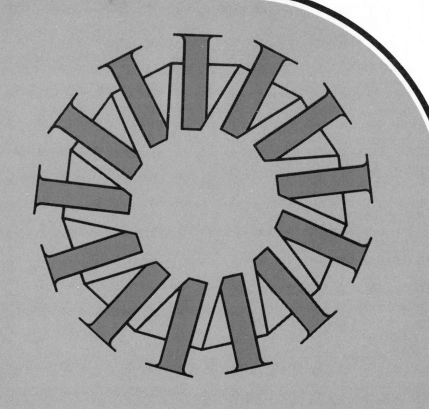

# Approaches
# to working
# with children
# and books

## The it-can't-happen-to-me syndrome

Probably one of the most common misconceptions teachers have regarding censorship is that it is limited to only a few controversial books. Teachers gain a sense of security believing that if they avoid *The Quotations of Mao-tse Tung* or *Children's Guide to Sexual Experimentation* they will remain untouched by criticism and censorship. The following books have been attacked by censors at one time or another, and support our first contention about censorship: *Any book is a potential target of censorship. There are no totally safe, universally accepted, uncontroversial books.*

George Eliot's *Silas Marner:* "You can't prove what that dirty old man is doing with that child between chapters."

Plato's *Republic:* "This book is un-Christian."

Jules Verne's *Around the World in Eighty Days:* "Very unfavorable to Mormons."

Shakespeare's *Macbeth:* "Too violent for children."

Fydor Dostoevsky's *Crime and Punishment:* "Serves as a poor model for young people."

Herman Meville's *Moby Dick:* "Contains homosexuality."[1]

Such criticisms are not confined to the "uncontroversial" classics. Much of modern fiction has come under the censor's eye, especially that which speaks directly to contemporary concerns of children.

Susan Hinton's *The Outsiders:* "A glorification of violence and gangs."

Ann Head's *Mr. and Mrs. Bo Jo Jones:* "Teenagers are too young to learn about pregnancy."

Robert Lipsyte's *The Contender:* "Pro-black, and boxing is a foul racket to talk about with young people."

# 13
# The Censorship Controversy

Nat Hentoff's *I'm Really Dragged but Nothing Gets Me Down:* "Vietnam is too controversial for any classroom, and the novel is anti-American."[2]

These selections are but a few of the books that have been the object of censorship. The more relevant and realistic the book, the more likely it will attract the censor's attention. But any book is a potential target, and teachers too often grow complacent about the scope of the censor's interest.

The sources and subjects of censorship vary greatly, but probably the most commonly censored subject is sexuality. In Caldwell Parish, Louisiana, for example, most of the community and the librarians believe that "nudity is wrong." When Maurice Sendak's *In the Night Kitchen* (1970) was acquired by the Caldwell Parish public libraries, an embarrassing situa-

In The Night Kitchen

tion developed. Sendak's book is an imaginative and beautifully illustrated story of a small boy's dream of an escapade from baker's batter to the milky way. It was not the story, however, that upset the librarians; rather the illustration of a naked boy caused the controversy. However, the librarians conquered the problem posed by Mickey's exposed genitals; they painted tempera diapers to cover the formerly naked boy.[3]

During the 1940s and 1950s some of the strongest pressures toward censorship emanated from citizens committed to racial segregation. These pressures continue today, as can be seen in the case of an irate white mother from Mississippi who published a letter in a local newspaper denouncing a Little Golden Book of Mother Goose rhymes. She was upset with the verse concerning three babies in a basket: "one was yellow and one was black/ And one had eyes of blue." To make matters worse, the rhyme was illustrated. Her letter read:

I bought one of the Little Golden Books entitled *Counting Rhymes.* I was horrified when I was reading to my innocent young child, and, behold, on page 15 there was actually the picture of three small children in a basket together . . . and one was a little Negro! I put my child and the book down and immediately called the owner of the drugstore and told him he would not have any more of my business (and I buy a lot of drugs, for I am sick a lot) if he didn't take all the rest of his copies of that book off his shelves.[4]

Undaunted, the mother hotly pursued this basket case of forced integration of children and stated that she got in touch with the author. The author (Mother Goose?) explained that the black child:

was aware that he didn't belong there, and he was looking down in shame because somebody (a symbol for the outside meddling Yankees) has placed him in the same basket with the white child, where he didn't really want to be. Also he was looking down at the mouse as if he recognized some kinship to animals.[5]

This incident represents outlandish censorship practiced by prejudiced citizens. But censorship has been attempted, and with success, by established and respectable individuals, in the interest of what they believe to be sincere and worthy motives. Two groups that have promoted censorship are the International Conference of Police Associations (ICOPA) and The National Association for the Advancement of Colored People (NAACP).

Police organizations became upset with William Steig's Caldecott award winning book *Sylvester and the Magic Pebble* (1969). Sylvester is a young donkey who is confronted by a dangerous lion, and, using a magic pebble, he wishes that he were a rock. The magic of the pebble works and Sylvester is transformed into a rock, but he is unable to hold the pebble and wish himself back to a donkey. Luckily, when Sylvester's parents are picnicking, the father places the pebble on the rock and Sylvester wishes himself back to his original form. Although the story seems innocuous, it has been criticized on at least two counts.

When Sylvester disappears, his parents go to the police station to seek help. The police are drawn as pigs. Needless to say, policemen in contemporary America are quite sensitive to the police-as-pig image. In a number of cities, police organizations attempted to pressure libraries to halt circulation of *Sylvester and the Magic Pebble* on the grounds that it portrayed a negative picture of policemen. The police expressed their fear that such an illustration was particularly harmful for young children who need to trust and respect the police.

Another criticism of *Sylvester and the Magic Pebble* was launched by Dr. David

Davis in 1972. Davis suggested that the book was an allegorical "trip," and that Sylvester's turning into a stone was symbolic for "getting stoned," and therefore the book alluded to the drug scene. Both these criticisms received notice, and police pressure did result in some success when, for example, the Toledo (Ohio) Board of Education removed the book from the school libraries.[6]

This example of censorship from a respected, conservative organization can be balanced with an example of censorship from a respected, liberal organization. The NAACP is one of the liberal organizations attempting to censor *The Story of Little Black Sambo*, written by Helen Bannerman in 1899. The story concerns a dark-skinned boy who gives away his prized clothes to a series of hungry tigers, a sacrifice which results in success; the young hero escapes the tigers and watches them furiously race after each other until they turn into butter. The NAACP cites the book as racist, contending that the characters' names—Mumbo, Jumbo, and Sambo—are demeaning and therefore racist. The silly names of Mumbo and Jumbo are bad enough, but Sambo has acquired a negative connotation from minstrel shows, where Sambo was the commonly used name for a simple and ignorant Negro character. The gaudy clothes and unattractive illustrations in some editions are also criticized as contributing to the negative stereotype. *The Story of Little Black Sambo* is cited as providing a negative black image to children who have too few good black picture books available. The NAACP believes that the book has a negative psychological impact on children and that it should be banned.

The NAACP has met with some success in its efforts. The Montgomery County school system in suburban Maryland, outside of Washington, D.C., considered this issue, and a special committee ruled to remove all books, filmstrips, and records of *Little Black Sambo* from the public school libraries. A spokesperson declared, "The decision is not to be construed as book burning, but rather as book selection." The issue then moved to the county's public libraries, which also pulled *Little Black Sambo* off the shelves, available for circulation but well out of view.[7]

The attempts to ban *Sylvester and the Magic Pebble* and *Little Black Sambo* have been led by responsible groups who are interested in serving the needs of children, as they view those needs. Many would concur with the aims of these groups: to treat all individuals as individuals, not to taunt police with the epithet *pig* or to promote racist actions and attitudes. But the method of achieving these ends is one we find difficult to accept.

These books do not present serious threats to the development of children's attitudes. In *Sylvester and the Magic Pebble* the pigs used to portray policemen are also used to portray other characters. The police illustration is incidental to the story line, and there are no negative characteristics or actions attributed to the police. Moreover, the main character and his parents are portrayed as donkeys (i.e., jackasses), an equally unflattering illustration. The animal characters present an interesting way to "people" the story. They are simply enjoyed by children, not analyzed for deeper sociological meanings.

*Little Black Sambo* is more widely criticized than *Sylvester*. In our experience, however, children have responded in a positive way to the humorous story line and to Sambo's success in overcoming obstacles. The name Sambo and its historically negative connotations are lost on many children, too young to be aware of any negative connotations. The gaudy clothes stereotype and the nature of the illustrations are so subtle that young children are totally unaware of any negative meanings. To some children, however, *Little Black Sambo* may be offensive. Also, some psychologists suggest that a "delayed effect" may occur, and the racist undertones of *Little Black Sambo* may emerge at a later date. Teachers who use the book may choose to focus on the stereotypes and explain that the book is a product of the social milieu of the last century. The book itself may thus become a tool in reducing racism. Or teachers may choose not to use the book in their classroom. But to ban it from school and public libraries, to deny the book to all children, does seem to be an overreaction.

It is interesting to note that other books that more directly depict negative characterizations of blacks and of police have not received as much attention as *Sylvester* and *Sambo*. For example, *Soul Brothers and Sister Lou* (1968) and *Listen for the Fig Tree* (1974) paint a negative picture of the police as ruthless and brutal. *Mary Poppins* (1934), *Dr. Dolittle* (1920), and *Charlie and the Chocolate Factory* (1964) do an equally effective job of stereotyping black people. Yet these books and others have received less criticism for more negative treatment of these groups. Should we ban these books too, and analyze all books in order to censor racist or antipolice passages?

In referring to another case of NAACP censorship, a librarian in California wrote, "It is ironic . . . that the NAACP, which has fought so valiantly against the suppression of ideas regarding the contributions of black citizens to American History is now cast in the role of suppressor of ideas with which [that] organization disagrees."[8]

It is a sign of the attraction of censorship that it can be aimed at books as different as *Sylvester* and *Sambo* and be promoted by groups as different as the NAACP and police organizations. These examples illustrate that almost any organization might resort to pressure to prevent children from reading any material it believes to be offensive.

In spite of these numerous and often irrational attempts at censorship, teachers often are unaware and unprepared to meet censorship pressures. Too often teachers treat censorship in the same way some people treat serious illness or a serious accident, as a regrettable tragedy most likely to affect someone else. This it-can't-happen-to-me syndrome makes the teacher a prime target and a likely victim of censorship pressures.

This chapter is intended to prepare teachers to meet and overcome unfair censorship attempts. We analyze the arguments for and against censorship, the profile of the typical censor, and procedures available to teachers to avoid unfair censorship pressures. Included in the chapter are examples of children's books that have been attacked by censors in different communities. These examples include comments made by censors and are designed to alert the reader to the breadth and danger of censorship, and to help extinguish the it-can't-happen-to-me syndrome.

Hersey's *Hiroshima:* "pacifist"

Keyes' *Flowers for Algernon:* "dirty, filthy book about a sex pervert"

Golding's *Lord of the Flies:* "impure"

Anne Frank's *Diary of a Young Girl:* "Obscene and blasphemous"[9]

## Background to the censorship controversy

The activities of the censor can be traced from ancient China and the attempt to suppress the writings of Confucius to the 1970s attempt of the Nixon administration to prevent publication of the *Pentagon Papers* in the *New York Times*. Although the targets and techniques of censorship have changed, the attempt to censor is a recurrent theme in history. The censorship of children's books in America is, however, a fairly recent event, dating back to the nineteenth century.

Various churches in the 1800s organized committees to review and evaluate children's books. Probably the most influential group was the Ladies Commission on Sunday School Books, founded in 1865 in Boston and affiliated with the Unitarian church. Its criteria for evaluating children's books were explicitly presented in an article the group published in the *Unitarian Review*. The commission's position closely followed the advice of St. Paul:

> Whatsoever things are true,
> whatsoever things are honest,
> whatsoever things are just,
> whatsoever things are lovely,
> whatsoever things are of good
> report, "write" on those things.[10]

If the results are any indication, the commission seems to have strictly adhered to its standards. Between 1867 and 1873, 4042 books were reviewed and only 1087 were rated as acceptable.[11] The work of the Ladies Commission on Sunday School Books brings us to a pertinent question: When, if ever, is censorship appropriate?

Today, as in years past, teachers, principals, and librarians are subject to complaints about the books they have selected or approved, and they must decide which, if any, of the complaints are valid. For whatever selections are made, some of the books are likely to face objections from those who consider them too liberal or too conservative, too realistic or too phony, racist, sexist, anti-Semitic, pornographic, or without literary or educational merit. Some of these complaints may contain valid points, well worth considering, and others may represent charges and blatant attempts at censorship. Without a rational policy for considering objections to books, teachers will face difficulty in separating legitimate complaints from groundless ones, and they may find themselves the victims of pressures that cause them to lose their freedom to select the most appropriate books for their students. Censorship pressures exist in many schools and often result in the loss of a teacher's right to teach and a student's right to learn.

Obviously unfair attempts at censorship are those that are in conflict with the meaning and direction of America. To censor a book because one disagrees with the politics of the author or to ban a book because black or Jewish characters are included are clearly incompatible with the American ethic and represent unacceptable attempts at censorship.

Although many of the objections lodged against books are unjustified attempts at suppression, not all objections can be generalized this way. For example, educators may receive complaints that indicate errors or omissions in their process of book selection. These are *legitimate complaints* and may indicate that a book selected for use is outdated and that more current information is available in a book that was not considered. Or perhaps such legitimate complaints may indicate books that provide a more insightful treatment of an issue or one that is finer in terms of literary quality than the book originally chosen. Educators should have a policy for considering such complaints and for incorporating changes that will improve the reading program of their students.

Some complaints are made against books because individuals do not believe that a certain topic or treatment is appropriate for children. Such issues as violence, pornography, racism, and sexism, for example, have been criticized as having the potential for psychological damage to children. Those who are concerned about the effect of such books on children advocate *preadult censorship*, which applies to certain topics and pertains only to children's reading materials. They support the notion that it is better, for example, to prevent impressionable children from reading racist books than to permit them to acquire racist attitudes. The pros and cons of preadult censorship are discussed in the following sections.

## The right to read: the argument against preadult censorship

Although Americans enjoy relatively free access to all kinds of reading material, the Supreme Court has consistently restricted that freedom in relation to a certain group of Americans: those under eighteen. The Court has recognized that children are a special group, with limited experience and impressionable minds. Although limited students' civil rights have been affirmed in a variety of cases, many times the Court has granted the right to censor children's books to parents, school boards, and school administrators. Court decisions are not always predictable, and they do vary, depending on individual cases, court membership, and social trends. But as of this writing, the courts have ruled that on issues such as pornography, certain adults have the right to censor the reading material of those under eighteen.[12]

This position is not universally accepted by all Americans or, in fact, by all the Supreme Court justices. Justice Douglas dissented from an opinion that let stand a decision in New York City granting a school board the right to censor Piri Thomas' *Down These Mean Streets* (1967). The reason for banning this autobiography of a Puerto Rican growing up in New York City was that the book contained "obscene" words. In his dissent Justice Douglas wrote: "What else can the School Board now decide it does not like? How else will its sensibilities be offended? Are we sending children to be educated by the norms of the School Board or are we educating our youth to shed the prejudices of the past, to explore all forms of thought, and to find solutions to our world's problems."[13]

The American Civil Liberties Union agrees with Justice Douglas, as do a variety of organizations, including the American Library Association. The ALA is committed to the idea that the responsibility for determining a child's reading habits is best left to the child and his parents and that such decisions are not to be determined by librarians, teachers, or governmental or community groups. One reason for this policy is explained in the ALA's *Newsletter on Intellectual Freedom:*

In today's world, children are exposed to adult life much earlier than in the past. They read materials and view a variety of media on the adult level at home and elsewhere. Current emphasis upon early childhood education has also increased opportunities for young people to learn and to have access to materials and has decreased the validity of using chronological age as an index to the use of libraries. . . . The American Library Association holds that it is the parent—and only the parent—who may restrict his children—and only his children—from access to library materials and services. The parent who would rather his child not have access to certain materials should so advise the child.[14]

The arguments against any censorship of children's books are far-ranging. In "The

Fear of Books," John Henry Merryman of San-ford School of Law points out that there is no scholarly basis for the assumption that reading controversial books leads to undesirable be-havior. In contrast, Merryman maintains that there are more persuasive arguments to the contrary. Studies of juvenile delinquency, for example, show that those who get into trouble are far less likely to be active readers than those who do not become delinquents. Sheldon and Eleanor Glueck, leading authorities on juvenile delinquency, have identified ninety factors that might lead to or explain delinquent behavior. Reading matter was not one of the ninety. Moreover, some psychiatrists believe that reading material may serve as an escape valve, dissipating aggression that might other-wise injure society.[15] Other researchers have disputed this and have suggested that there may be a relationship between reading and be-havior. But in any event, at this point we sim-ply do not have conclusive evidence that read-ing affects behavior; therefore any grounds for censorship based on a relationship between reading and behavior is purely speculative.

Those who oppose any censorship of chil-dren's books go beyond this denial of the po-tential evil effects of certain books, and they cite the negative effect of censorship itself. At the heart of the issue is one's definition of educa-tion. If one believes that education is designed to pass on from generation to generation a pre-scribed, accepted, and limited body of informa-tion, then one can make a case for censoring material that is taboo and that is not included in the prescribed body of knowledge. If, on the other hand, one believes that the purpose of education is to teach children to be problem solvers, to determine their own positions, to establish new procedures, and to gain new in-sights, then censorship is more difficult to sup-port. Such inquiry requires freedom, not con-straint.

However, children currently are not offered this choice. Adults determine whether children are to be restricted in their educational aims or encouraged to explore many alternatives.

Children constitute one of the largest and most vulnerable minority groups. They have no voice in the political process. They participate directly in no lobbies on their own behalf. At a time when they are particularly weak and easily intimidated and manipulated, their rights are particularly vulnerable to infringement, perhaps at least as often by those who disclaim that they act in the children's regard.[16]

It is an adult's right to decide if a particular book is offensive, unacceptable, or unwhole-some. It is also an adult's right to question whether a book should be read by a child, and then to discuss the point with the child. But it is a totally different matter for an adult to say that a certain book cannot be read by others and then proceed to prevent schoolchildren from reading it; this is philosophically out of step with a democratic society. Those who op-pose censorship on these philosophical grounds can find support in the comments of Milton, Franklin, Jefferson, President Kennedy, and a host of noted authors. The idea of one individual imposing his or her views on another is anath-ema to our way of life. Those who would cen-sor are mortals, with no special insight into truth, and should not be granted the privilege of restricting the freedom of others. If most members of a community believe one way, they still do not have the right to enforce their views on a minority. This philosophical stand by those opposed to censorship is nicely put by John Stuart Mill in *On Liberty:* "If all mankind were of one opinion, and only one person were of the contrary opinion, mankind would be no more justified in silencing one person than he, if he had the power, would be justified in silencing mankind."

Finally, those opposed to censorship point to practical considerations, emphasizing the fact that censorship simply does not work.

> Zindel's *My Darling, My Hamburger*: "perverted and filthy book"
>
> Donovan's *I'll Get There. It Better Be Worth the Trip*: "degenerate sex"
>
> White's *Charlotte's Web*: "morbid picture of death"
>
> Stevenson's *Treasure Island*: "you know what men are like and what they do when they've been away from women that long"[17]

Children usually can obtain books censored in schools from other sources. Frequently the fact that a particular book has been censored in-read the book because of the controversy. The creases a student's interest; the student may result might be a wider audience for a sup-posedly censored book.

Before we present some of the arguments in favor of selective censorship of children's books, it might be useful to review the points of those opposed to censorship of children's books.

1. There is no definitive evidence that reading certain pornographic or controversial books leads to disruptive behavior. Evidence can be found to suggest such reading does not adversely affect behavior.
2. Censorship limits free inquiry and therefore limits the intellectual development of children; it inhibits learning.
3. To enforce one's beliefs on another, to tell children what they can and cannot read, is anathema to the very idea of a free society.
4. Censorship does not work. Children can obtain censored books with relative ease, and censorship controversy often encourages them to do so.

## The right to censor: the argument for preadult censorship

Throughout this chapter we are including groups of books that have been under the censor's attack, in order to demonstrate that no book is safe. But the arguments made by those who support some degree of censorship of children's books is not always as specious or outrageous as these examples suggest. The proponents of preadult censorship make strong points well worth considering.

The most fundamental assumption by these advocates is that young children are impressionable and intellectually vulnerable, and with the limited experience and knowledge that children have, they can be profoundly influenced in these formative years. To permit children to read certain books may negatively affect their intellectual or moral development. Norman Thomas, candidate for the presidency six times on the Socialist party ticket, has emphasized this position when he stated:

I do not think the First Amendment gives any guarantee to men to seduce the innocent and to exploit the kind of uninformed mind and uninformed emotions of children and adolescents. I think there is a great deal of dangerous nonsense in this appeal to the First Amendment and to the freedom of the press when one is dealing with this kind of thing. . . . I think it is nonsense to say that we are bound by a very extreme interpretation of the freedom of the press that we cannot act.[18]

The importance of these early, impressionable years has been emphasized by a variety of disparate sources.

Train up a child in the way that he should go; and when he is old he will not depart from it.

*Proverbs XXII, 6*

Give me a child for the first seven years, and
you may do what you like with him afterwards.

*Jesuit saying*

Give us a child for the first eight years, and it
will be a Bolshevist forever.          *Lenin*[19]

The responsibility to select reading materials for these young, impressionable children
often falls to teachers and librarians. When
teachers and librarians sift through all the potential books they might order, they must employ some criteria, some process of selection.
Some books are of higher literary quality than
others, some books are more related to specific
children's needs than others, but some books
and authors are also less controversial than
others in language and theme. Advocates of
some form of censorship believe that professional judgment should be used in obtaining
the best, most appropriate, and least offensive
books. In fact, teachers and librarians often
use the selection process to acquire books that
are appropriate to student needs as well as to
the norms and values of a community.

The concept of professional responsibility is
frequently defined to include the selection of
appropriate and nonoffensive materials for children. Teachers and librarians have been asked
to exercise such professional judgment, as have
school boards. For example, in a recent case in
New York, a book about ghetto life used in a
school district contained candid four-letter
words and created a furor among parents, who
requested that the school board exert its professional responsibility and ban the book. The
school board did precisely that, and was taken
to a court by the parents, teachers, and a librarian who objected to the action. In support
of their censorship of the book the school
board submitted an affidavit by a psychiatrist:
"If youngsters are steeped in the literature of
violence, lawlessness, sexual promiscuity and
perversion at this time of life, it cannot but

influence their development adversely, no matter how significant the underlying purpose of
the book."[20] The courts ruled in favor of the
ban and stated that "school officials should be
given wide discretion in administering their
schools."[21]

Another argument used for censorship for
children is that absolute and total freedom is
the sign of a doctrinaire, unthinking liberal and
that such a purist stand is impractical and
could be damaging to children. The idea, for
example, that all interests and views are acceptable is simplistic, dangerous, and not socially responsible. Is bigotry just another point
of view? Are anti-Semitism, racism, and sexism acceptable and socially responsible alternatives to which children should be introduced. Should books advocating violence or
even murder be given children as a possible
avenue for them to pursue? Is a handbook on
rape acceptable reading? The answer, say the
advocates of some form of control, is clearly
no. Pure freedom—the freedom to read how
to hate, to hurt, to kill—is simply not acceptable in a responsible society. Rational limits
are needed because some things are right and
some things are wrong; it is as simple as that.

To sum up some of the arguments for preadult censorship:

1. Young children comprise a group of citizens
   unlike any other, and some censorship is required to ensure that these individuals at
   an impressionable and vulnerable age are
   not misled, corrupted, confused, or psychologically damaged.
2. Educators have a responsibility to select
   children's reading materials, at least as far
   as school work is concerned. When they
   exercise their professional judgment, they
   should make certain that their choices do
   not contain obscene or in any way damaging and inappropriate material. This is the

responsibility the community expects school boards, principals, teachers, and librarians to exercise.

3. There are some areas that are antihuman, hurtful as well as harmful, and not legitimate options for children to consider. Racism, sexism, anti-Semitism, violence, murder are some of these areas that are irrational avenues of intellectual pursuit.

Censorship, therefore, is not a simple and clear-cut issue, and even the laws concerning the censorship of books for children are continually in flux as courts attempt to determine how much freedom is appropriate for children.

As you weigh these arguments for and against preadult censorship, you can develop your own position on the issue. But whichever position you finally accept, you very well may be involved in a censorship controversy in your own school, one in which you believe your rights or the rights of a colleague are being challenged. In order to establish and maintain your freedom to teach, and to be able to select truthful and effective books for your students, you must be prepared to meet the censor and withstand irrational attempts to ban books.

## Meeting the censor

Consider yourself teaching in a school and location you always hoped for. Your classes are going well, you are enjoying your job, and you are particularly excited about a new book you are using. Your students are enjoying the book and your class discussions are lively, animated, and successful. As you pick up your morning mail you notice a memo from the principal.

Dear Mr./Ms. _____:
        (Fill in your name)

Mr. Torro called me last evening with a serious complaint about the book his daughter is reading for your class. He said it was "filled with filth" and is "racist and communistic." He's called for a special meeting of the Parent Teachers Association. I've asked him to meet me in my office at 3 this afternoon. I'd like you to be there too—and bring the book.

*Bertrand C. Forte*
Principal

Are you ready to meet with Mr. Forte and Mr. Torro? If you have always assumed that such a confrontation would never happen to you, then you may be in for some very difficult times. Without having taken some simple but important steps in your adoption of the book in question, you may find yourself fighting a lonely, frustrating battle. Teachers should be prepared to review objections to a book, considering the merits of the complaint. But teachers must also be prepared to ward off groundless and prejudicial attacks and to de-

---

Hunter's *Soul Brothers and Sister Lou:* "biased about black people."

Dahl's *Charlie and the Chocolate Factory:* "racist."

Edmonds' *The Matchlock Gun:* "Stereotypes of cruel and savage Indians."

Sterling's *Mary Jane:* "Do we have to fill our children's minds with sociological non-literature like this?"

Rodgers' *Freaky Friday:* "Makes fun of parents and parental responsibility."[22]

fend their books with courage, foresight, and clarity.

## Profile of a censor

The first prerequisite to any defense of a book is to understand who the potential censor is and how he or she is likely to operate. As we have seen in the previous section, any organized group—liberal, conservative, or middle of the road—has the potential of exerting pressures to discredit and ban books. Since organizations often represent significant numbers of citizens and since they often command financial, legal, and public relations resources, they can prove formidable adversaries. Individual citizens, speaking for themselves or for the interests of their children, comprise another group of potential censors. Once a school board or school superintendent decides to remove a book, it is usually beyond the teacher's power to reverse such a decision. Often it is beyond the will of the courts to reverse such decisions as well.

School districts vary greatly in their will or ability to halt censorship. Some systems adhere to established procedures and are rarely affected by outside pressure. Most schools, however, are quite vulnerable to such pressures. Schools in liberal communities are more prone to censor books that offend liberals, and schools in conservative communities are more apt to ban books that offend conservative philosophy. Some citizens believe it is the duty of schools to respond to community pressure, based on the facts that it is their taxes that support schools and their children who are attending the schools. The superintendent of schools in North Little Rock in the early 1960s agreed with this position. When a group of parents objected to a book *Great American Negroes* because it contained essays about Ralph Bunche and Langston Hughes, the

> **Tolkein's** *The Hobbitt:* "Subversive elements."
>
> **Patton's** *Good Morning, Miss Dove:* "The wood cuts of the dove are proof positive of the influence of the international Communist conspiracy."
>
> **Stolz's** *A Love, or a Season:* "A nice girl should never admit she could feel anything sexual until after she's married."[24]

superintendent obligingly banned the book. He stated it was the board's policy to remove any book that was objectionable to parents. If the superintendent did adhere to this policy, it is difficult to imagine what books might be left in his school libraries.[23]

Some individuals and some organizations spend much of their energy promoting censorship. George Sloan, in "Censorship in Historical Perspective," indicates that those heavily involved in censorship movements exhibit one or more of the traditional characteristics of the censor. They attempt to edit that with which they disagree, they espouse secrecy, and they set themselves up as judges for what is morally or politically acceptable.[25]

In an article in *Publishers' Weekly* Peter Jennison writes,

No scientifically precise psychological profile has ever been drawn of the typical censor, but if one were, it would reveal almost equal strains of fear, insecurity, ignorance and arrogance. The censor is prey to the disease of bibliophobia: he is afraid of books and fearful of their corrupting influence on those more impressionable than he. He is anxious about the social and political upheavals and the insecurities of the age: get rid of "dirty" books and juvenile delinquency would disappear; get rid of books which do not assail the United Nations and the international Communist conspiracy will wither and die. And finally, "Big Brother" knows best what his neighbors should and should not read and buy.[26]

These uncomplimentary profiles of individuals committed to censorship come to life in numerous censorship cases. For instance, there is the case of an individual who organized a campaign to ban Griffin's *Black Like Me*, a story about a white man who literally changes skin colors to experience firsthand prejudice and racism. This potential censor won substantial support by basing his complaint on the "obscene" language used in the book. His cloak of respectability, however, would have been severely tarnished if his followers had known of his general crusade against "those goddamned niggers and kikes."[27]

Of course not all those who oppose a book are as vile or as irresponsible as the individual in this case. Sometimes the complaints are well founded, in which case the books should be re-evaluated. But it is important for teachers to recognize that some members in their community are likely to be full-time, "professional" censors, attempting to repress that with which they disagree, and not above resorting to subterfuge or using any argument to achieve their end.

## We have met the enemy—and it is us

We have yet to look at the most effective censor, the one who most often succeeds in banning books and limiting children's reading. We are that censor—teachers, principals, and librarians, comprise the most active group of censors affecting the reading habits of school-children. Through self-censorship, educators attempt to forestall conflict and controversy. By avoiding the use of books that may be objectionable to some organizations or individuals in their community, educators attempt to

avoid censorship problems. The result itself is a serious censorship problem. Self-censorship, quietly practiced in classrooms and libraries across the nation, is frequently more severe than any censorship that might be imposed from outside the school.

Librarians frequently resort to self-censorship, while supplying themselves with an escape route. In Montgomery County, Maryland, a child browsing through the book shelves of the public library would not find a copy of *Little Black Sambo*. If you ask the librarian why it is being censored, she will politely explain it is not being censored, but is located on the "closed shelf." The "closed shelf" is a device by which libraries can continue to own a book while at the same time effectively discouraging children from reading it. Sometimes the "closed shelf" is behind the librarian's desk. In one case we have found the shelf safely locked in the supply closet, next to the cleaning detergents.

Many teachers, like librarians, practice self-censorship:

We could have many complaints, but most of our teachers, myself included, steered clear of books that might offend.

When they hire English teachers in my town, they make sure that the English teachers are either cowards or pliable. Those that are cowards present no threat to anything (especially good literature or kids). Those that are pliable are brainwashed. Nobody here ever taught anything remotely worth censoring.[28]

Several investigators have documented the extent of self-censorship. In 1969 James Symula surveyed incidents of censorship in high schools and found that the most-censored book was J. D. Salinger's *Catcher in the Rye*, a humorous and candid story of the world as perceived by a teenage boy. Most of the complaints aimed at *Catcher in the Rye* came from teachers.[29] Burress and Cole, in another study, found that 78 percent of complaints from within a school were granted, whereas only 50 percent of complaints from individuals outside the school were granted.[30] Self-censorship is not only widespread; it is also effective.

Teachers should be prepared to deal with censorship pressures, whether the source be the teacher's own fears, pressures from within the school, or complaints from the community. To be ready to deal with censorship challenges, teachers must use a professional process for book selection.

## Criteria for selecting trade books

Using criteria to choose children's books is useful in establishing an objective and fair procedure for book selection. By carefully considering books according to both literary and educational merit, the teacher can help to ensure a worthwhile experience for students. A second benefit of applying criteria to book selection is that it provides the first line of defense against ill-conceived attempts to reconsider or ban a book. It is important that teachers consider a variety of factors in choosing children's books; we present two different sets of criteria to facilitate an effective selection procedure.

1. Literary Quality

   Teachers can acquire a sense of the effectiveness of a book by reading reviews of it in various periodicals or other reference sources. The best way to determine a book's effectiveness, however, is to read the book and assess its impact on your students. The teacher is generally the best judge of a book's effectiveness for the students. One will need to ask oneself whether the students will understand and enjoy the book. In evaluating a book's literary worth, teach-

ers may wish to consider the following areas:[31]

   a. *Setting.* Is the setting authentic and clear? Does the setting add or detract from the book? Will the students understand and enjoy the setting?
   b. *Point of View.* Who tells the story? Is it done effectively?
   c. *Characters.* Who are the characters? Are they believable? Are they consistent? Can children relate to these characters?
   d. *Plot.* What is the story about? Is the plot well developed? Are the actions believable and interesting to children?
   e. *Theme.* What is the meaning, purpose, or main idea of the story? Is the theme appropriate and effectively presented for your students?
   f. *Style.* How is the story written? How does the author use words, imagery, sentence structure, and rhythm to convey the story? Is the dialogue realistic?

A book might fall short in one or more of these categories and still be a fine book. But these categories do provide a framework for teachers to analyze the literary quality of children's books.

2. Educational Criteria

   Teachers must also select books in relation to educational standards. Three useful educational criteria are the following:

   a. *Subject.* Does the book bring deeper understanding of the topics and issues being studied? What new insights regarding the subject are presented? How does the book supplement other curricular materials?
   b. *Student.* Is the book helpful in the development of student knowledge or attitudes? Does it meet a particular need for an individual student or the

class as a whole? How might students benefit from reading this book? Is the book written on an appropriate reading level?

c. *Society.* Does the book contribute to the understanding of important concerns confronting our society? Does the book relate to the needs or goals of our society? In what way will reading this book help students to become better citizens in their neighborhoods, communities, and the nation at large?

Few books fill all three criteria, but many that relate to only one criterion still possess sound educational reasons for its use. The nature of the content being taught, the needs and aspirations of both individual students and the society at large provide general yet pertinent areas of educational concerns by which to evaluate and select books.

When you carefully apply literary and educational criteria, you feel more comfortable with the quality of the books you select, and probably more aware of their educational purposes in your classroom. This is a rational and professional approach to book selection, and it is the first step to resisting censorship pressures.

When evaluating books according to literary and educational criteria, it is helpful to write out a rationale for the book finally selected and to retain a copy of that rationale. In addition, if you send a copy of the rationale to the principal, you will have not only attended to a professional courtesy, but earned a potential ally in any possible censorship dispute because the principal will now be prepared to respond to inquiries or complaints about the book.

Kenneth Donelson, in his article "Censorship in the 1970's: Some Ways to Handle It When It Comes (and It Will)," writes that such rationales should include answers to at least five questions:

1. Why has this book been chosen to use with a particular class?
2. What are the teacher's objectives in using this book?
3. How will the book be used to reach these objectives?
4. What problems of style, tone or theme might be grounds for censorship, and how will the teacher plan to meet these problems?
5. Assuming that the objectives are met, how will the students change or grow because of their reading of this book?[32]

In order to answer the last point you might want to consider several of the general advantages of any reading program. These include the ability of books

1. To provide the enjoyment of reading in and of itself.
2. To help children understand themselves and their problems.
3. To help children understand others.
4. To provide vicarious experiences to extend one's knowledge of other people and other places.
5. To help compare, alter, or strengthen one's values and behaviors by reading about individuals and groups with different beliefs and practices.
6. To provide experience of other times, to help children see the imperfect but real world as it is, as it was, and as it might be.

The criteria and rationale we have discussed are useful when selecting children's trade books, but different circumstances exist when we consider the adoption of textbooks. Textbooks affect the selection and use of trade books, and comprise a major component of a student's total reading program. For these reasons we briefly consider some of the concerns and issues involved in the selection and use of textbooks.

## Criteria for selection of textbooks

Textbooks have long been the mainstay of elementary and secondary teachers. Although recent trends toward the open classroom and individualized instruction have dealt some harsh blows to the textbook industry, the textbook is still treated in many classrooms as the repository for truth. Yet textbooks have severe limitations, and selecting one is often a difficult task.

For hundreds of years textbooks have been the source of moralization and propaganda. *McGuffey's Eclectic Primer* (1881) provided children with equal doses of reading instruction and lessons on the proper and righteous way to live one's life. Social studies textbooks have also been a source of continual propaganda since the nation's very beginning. Although all subject areas have been affected by pressures to propagandize, reading and social studies texts have been prime targets. To simplify our discussion we focus on social studies textbooks, but much of what we write can be generalized to other subjects as well.

Understanding the purpose of a textbook publisher is central to understanding the major problems inherent in the textbook itself. A textbook company produces a textbook designed to contain the major areas of information of a subject while appealing to the largest possible audience. A successful textbook is not necessarily well written, insightful, creative, or even comprehensive, although it may be all of these. To most companies a successful textbook is one that sells. In order to sell, it must appeal to the greatest number of potential customers: school boards, state textbook adoption committees, school administrators, and teachers. Attractive illustrations and authoritative authors, although helpful, are not enough to sell a text;

the book must also not offend any powerful groups. Therefore textbooks tend to reflect the mores, attitudes, and conventional wisdom of the time. They tend to skirt difficult issues while avoiding controversial ones completely. Unfortunately, the difficult and controversial issues are ones that students need to learn about. The pressures on textbook companies to avoid such topics are severe, for if they do not write an inoffensive book, they face a potential economic loss. To understand the nature of the pressure faced by publishers, consider the following criticisms that have been leveled against textbooks.

During the 1950's, a member of Indiana's Textbook Commission (without the commission's approval, no school in the State of Indiana could use the book) charged that "there is a Communist directive in education now to stress the story of Robin Hood" because he took from the rich and gave to the poor (an obvious Communist activity).[33]

E. Merrill Root, a long time critic of textbooks, scorned the "liberal" leaning textbook authors who gloat over America's past ills while missing our nation's greatness. For example, he cites a social studies textbook in which "steady, patient, deeply-rooted Herbert Hoover, whose stature grows with the decades, is given only 67 lines as compared with Wilson's 110 and Roosevelt's 151!"[34]

The Daughters of the American Revolution published a pamphlet entitled "Textbook Study" which is used as a guide in several school districts. Most of the 412 texts reviewed were rated as objectionable, usually because they were too liberal, and in some cases because they contained references to a single "left-of-center" writer.[35]

Although we have generally focused on conservative criticisms, liberal groups also evaluate texts and pressure publishers, as do local organizations and individual citizens. Textbook companies respond in a variety of ways. Some books are totally revised so that no one is offended, and little is learned. This "balanced" approach has many problems; as sociologist Sol M. Elken points out, "Presenting the pros and cons of slavery . . . is just not acceptable any longer."[36]

Some companies respond to the pressure by publishing different versions of the same book. Southern states receive a book with scant treatment of racial issues and with segregated illustrations. Northern states receive a version of the same book emphasizing the contributions of a variety of ethnic groups to American history. In Massachusetts children read about America's first Thanksgiving, at Plymouth. In Virginia the children read about America's first Thanksgiving, at Jamestown. No issue is too great or too small to be altered, and some of the less scrupulous publishers make their profits by pandering to local views and attitudes of the past and present.

In selecting texts, the following criteria should be useful:

Does the book present opposing views, conflict and controversy, or does it emphasize a single interpretation of events?

Does the book simplify information to the point that little is said other than bland generalizations?

Is the textbook well written and readable?

Are minority groups and women cited for their roles in society and their contributions to America?

Are unpopular ideas and movements, like Communism, or Fascism, objectively defined and treated?

Does the text avoid controversial topics such as sexism, racism, and other real issues confronting our society?

Who wrote the book? What are the author's credentials? Can you detect the author's attitudes?

What issues are omitted, given scant coverage, or distorted?

Would other materials be more effective than the textbook (trade books, independent study, and so on)?

Textbooks must meet a demanding standard of objectivity, and some of the criteria used for textbook evaluation would be inappropriate when applied to trade books. Unlike trade books, the text is often the single source of information for the class on numerous topics, and it is often required reading. Although students might select from a variety of trade books, they usually must read from a single textbook. If a text is not fair or complete in its treatment, then that error is passed on to students. A comprehensive and objective textbook is an important part of a student's total reading program.

One of the primary concerns of educators currently involved in text evaluation is the issue of minority and female representation. The traditional writer of textbooks, a white, middle-class male, has for too long omitted from the pages of textbooks the contributions of such groups as women, blacks, Jews, native Americans, and white ethnic, Asian, Hispanic Americans, as well as others. Yet all these groups combined account for the majority of our population. (The female population alone constitutes a majority.) The history we have been reading of a white, male, Christian society has been a history of a small part of our entire society. The same is true for other textbooks, such as readers, which have presented a generally white world dominated by male characters. Many publishers are responding to these omissions with new editions that include minority and female representation, and many school systems are focusing their attention on examining textbooks in terms of this issue. One approach used to assess textbooks is to consider the following questions:

Does this textbook or learning material in both its textual content and illustrations:[37]

|                                                                                                                                                                                                                                                                                                                                                 | Yes | No |
| --- | --- | --- |
| 1. Evidence on the part of writers, artists, and editors a sensitivity to prejudice, to stereotypes, to the use of material which would be offensive to women or to any minority group? | ☐ | ☐ |
| 2. Suggest, by omission or commission, or by overemphasis or underemphasis, that any sexual, racial, religious, or ethnic segment of our population is more or less worthy, more or less capable, more or less important in the mainstream of American life? | ☐ | ☐ |
| 3. Utilize numerous opportunities for full, fair, accurate, and balanced treatment of women and minority groups? | ☐ | ☐ |
| 4. Provide abundant recognition for women and minority groups by placing them frequently in positions of leadership and centrality? | ☐ | ☐ |
| 5. Depict both male and female adult members of minority groups in situations which exhibit them as fine and worthy models to emulate? | ☐ | ☐ |
| 6. Present many instances of fully integrated human groupings and settings to indicate equal status and nonsegregated social relationships? | ☐ | ☐ |
| 7. Make clearly apparent the group representation of individuals—Caucasian, Afro-American, Indian, Chinese, Mexican American, etc.—and not seek to avoid identification by such means as smudging some color over Caucasian facial features? | ☐ | ☐ |
| 8. Give comprehensive, broadly ranging, and well-planned representation to women and minority groups—in art and science, in history and mathematics and literature, and in all other areas of life and culture? | ☐ | ☐ |
| 9. Delineate life in contemporary urban environments, so that today's city children can also find significant identification for themselves, their problems and challenges, and their potential for life, liberty, and the pursuit of happiness? | ☐ | ☐ |
| 10. Portray sexual, racial, religious, and ethnic groups in our society in such a way as to build positive images—mutual understanding and respect, full and unqualified acceptance, and commitment to ensure equal opportunity for all? | ☐ | ☐ |

If you decide to use a textbook and if you find one that meets most of the criteria we have suggested, you will probably still need supplementary reading materials. Many of the children's books discussed in other chapters of this book will provide useful sources to supplement textbooks, especially since many of them relate to issues crucial to children yet avoided in textbooks.

Your selection of either trade or textbooks, no matter how carefully done, may lead to responsible or irresponsible objections. Suggestions for handling such disputes are offered in the final section.

## What to do when the censor comes

Before we begin, it would be useful to review several of our assumptions about the nature of censorship in schools:

1. Any book is vulnerable to censorship.
2. The more contemporary the book, the more likely target it is for criticism and possible censorship.
3. Criticism of books can come from both liberal and conservative groups as well as from individual citizens acting on their own.
4. The most effective censors are within the school, for self-censorship among educators is widely practiced.
5. Criticism of a book may be justified and should be considered.

Governor Lester Maddox of Georgia urged the dismissal of a white Georgia High School English teacher for using Elizabeth Kata's *A Patch of Blue,* a story about a romance between a white girl and a Negro man.

*Arizona Republic,*
*June 14, 1964*

6. Rational literary and educational criteria should be applied when selecting and evaluating books.
7. The nature of textbooks suggests the need for careful and comprehensive assessment procedures.
8. Although censorship is widespread, most teachers and librarians do not believe it will affect them. Being unprepared to respond to a censorship challenge, they become vulnerable to it.

To prepare teachers to respond to censorship when it does occur, we outline some procedures intended to aid teachers both to consider justified criticism and to defend books from unjustified criticism. A more complete description of these procedures can be found in *The Students' Right to Read* (published by the National Council of Teachers of English) and Kenneth Donelson's "What to Do When the Censor Comes" (*Elementary English,* March 1974). Moreover, the Library Bill of Rights and the School Library Bill of Rights (published by the ALA) provide useful statements in support of academic freedom.

The first step is to select books using professional judgment and established standards. We have already discussed some of the criteria that could be applied when evaluating books; in most cases this procedure would work best in a group setting. By considering the merits and deficiencies of various books in an open and free exchange, teachers are able to share their perceptions of and experiences with various books. By writing a rationale for each book to be used, teachers become involved in a process of reconsidering the book, their educational goals, and the potential problems in using the book. Such rationales require an investment of time but serve to ensure that attention and forethought are given to each book. These rationales provide the school administration and the community with evidence that teachers have chosen their books with care.

But a careful selection process is not enough; teachers cannot afford to rest on their rationales. Schools should establish a standing committee to open lines of communication with the community. This committee could be composed of teachers, parents, students, and other community leaders who would inform the community of the school objectives, activities, and book selection process. Parent-teacher meetings or meetings of other community organizations could serve as the forums for these discussions. Too often educators are naive about the political process and the allies and friends they have in the community. By informing the community of school goals and precedures *before* a controversy, teachers can win community support early and make the efforts of a potential censor an uphill struggle.

The same committee can also serve as a review panel to consider complaints against particular books. These complaints may be lodged by individuals who are sensitive to a book's language, who are intolerant of its philosophy or theme, or who express other criticisms. Whatever the source and whatever the reason, each complaint should be considered individually, for any blanket approval or dismissal of complaints will nullify the value of the committee in the community's eyes, and probably deservedly so. The committee must carefully consider each complaint and explain the reasons for committee decisions.

Another advantage of such a standing com-

# Citizen's Request for
# Reconsideration of a Work

HARDCOVER ——————

Author ————————————————————————— PAPERBACK ——————

Title ———————————————————————————————

Publisher (if known) ———————————————————————

Request initiated by ————————————————————————

Telephone ———————— Address ——————————————

City ———————————— Zip Code ——————————————

Complainant represents
———— himself
———— (name organization) ————————————————————
———— (identify other group) ———————————————————

1. To what in the work do you object? Please be specific; cite pages. ————————
   ———————————————————————————————————

2. What of value is there in this work? ——————————————————
   ———————————————————————————————————

3. What do you feel might be the result of reading this work? ———————————
   ———————————————————————————————————

4. For what age group would you recommend this work? —————————————
   ———————————————————————————————————

5. Did you read the entire work? ———————— What pages or sections? ——————
   ———————————————————————————————————

6. Are you aware of the judgment of this work by critics? ——————————————
   ———————————————————————————————————

7. Are you aware of the teacher's purpose in using this work? —————————————
   ———————————————————————————————————

8. What do you believe is the theme or purpose of this work? ————————————
   ———————————————————————————————————

9. What would you prefer the school do about this work?
   ———— Do not assign or recommend it to my child.
   ———— Withdraw it from all students.
   ———— Send it back to the English department for revaluation.

10. In its place, what work of equal value would you recommend that would convey
    as valuable a picture and perspective of a society or a set of values? ——————
    ———————————————————————————————————

————————————————————————
*(Signature of Complainant)*

mittee is that it represents an accepted policy for processing complaints. Teachers and administrators need not feel alone and defenseless, ready to capitulate to demands and threats of individual citizens or groups. Challenges to books can be directly channeled through the committee, and the committee's decision can then be forwarded to the superintendent and the board of education, who legally bear the responsibility for book selection and who may have to make the final judgment.

A useful technique for receiving complaints is to ask the individual to explain the criticism fully on a standard form. This serves to indicate to the responsible objector that the complaint will be considered and will go through the appropriate channels. This will also serve to compel the irresponsible objector to formalize the complaint, which may well discourage him or her from taking further action, or to indicate in the written comments that the complaint lacks substance.

A suggested format for such complaints is provided by the National Association of Teachers of English and the American Library Association, and is presented on p. 380.

Educators who are prepared to respond to citizen's objections can be both sensitive to legitimate community complaints and vigilant to unfair attempts at censorship. The teacher's freedom to teach and the student's right to learn depend on such vigilance. Unfortunately, too many teachers are unwilling to confront the threat of censorship. In a study conducted by John Farley in New York, only 29 percent of the schools studied had a formal book selection procedure, and 50 percent of the school librarians felt that the school administration would not defend a work if it received complaints.[38]

Only if we plan and work for freedom from unfair pressures will we succeed in fully and freely educating children in the important issues of the day. Great ideas and great societies are the products of such free inquiry.

Somebody in Washington wants to put Mr. DuBois in jail. Somebody in France wanted to put Voltaire in jail. Somebody in Franco's Spain sent Lorca, their greatest poet, to death before a firing squad. Somebody in Germany under Hitler burned the books, drove Thomas Mann into exile, and led their Jewish scholars to the gas chamber. Somebody in Greece long ago gave Socrates the hemlock to drink. Somebody at Golgotha erected a cross and somebody drove the nails into the hands of Christ. Somebody spat on his garments. No one remembers their names.

*Langston Hughes, defending
W. E. B. DuBois in the 1950s*[39]

## NOTES

1. Kenneth L. Donelson, editor, *The Students' Right to Read*, Urbana, Ill., National Council of Teachers of English, 1972, p. 1.
2. Ibid., p. 2.
3. James A. Harvey, "Acting for the Children," *Library Journal*, 98, no. 4 (February 15, 1973), 602–605.
4. Nancy Larrick, "The All-White World of Children's Books," *Saturday Review*, September 11, 1965, p. 65.
5. Ibid.
6. Harvey, op. cit.
7. "'Sambo' Banned by Montgomery County Schools," *Library Journal*, 96, no. 16 (September 15, 1971), 2213–2214.
8. "NAACP v. Epaminondas," *The Wilson Library Bulletin*, 45 (April 1971), 718.
9. Kenneth L. Donelson, "A Few Safe Assumptions About Censorship and the Censor," *Peabody Journal of Education*, 50, no. 3 (April 1973), 235–244.
10. Richard Darling, "Censorship—An Old Story," *Elementary English*, 51, no. 5 (May 1974), 691–696.
11. Ibid.
12. Alan H. Levine, "'Impressionable Minds' . . . 'Forbidden Subjects': A Case in Point," *Library Journal*, 98, no. 4 (February 15, 1973), 595–601.
13. U.S. Supreme Court Justice William O. Douglas, quoted in Levine op. cit., p. 595.
14. *Newsletter on Intellectual Freedom*, September 1972, p. 125.
15. John Henry Merryman, "The Fear of Books," *Stanford Today*, Autumn 1966, reprinted in *Censorship and the English Teacher, Arizona English*

*Bulletin, 11,* no. 2 (February 1969), 5–8.

16. Mary Kohler quoted in Harvey, op. cit.

17. Kenneth L. Donelson, "What To Do When the Censor Comes," *Elementary English, 51,* no. 3 (March 1974), 403–409.

18. Norman Thomas quoted in Richard Kuh, "Obscenity, Censorship, and the Non-doctrinaire Liberal," *Wilson Library Bulletin, 42,* no. 9 (May 1968), 902–909.

19. Quoted in Sheila Egoff, "If That Don't Do No Good, That Won't Do No Harm: The Uses and Dangers of Mediocrity in Children's Books," *School Library Journal, 97* (October 1972).

20. Levine, op. cit., p. 597.

21. Ibid., p. 599.

22. Donelson, "What To Do When the Censor Comes," op. cit., 403–404.

23. "Freedom to Read Bulletin," March 1962, quoted in "Censorship and the English Teacher," *Arizona English Bulletin, 11,* no. 2 (February 1969), p. 53.

24. Kenneth L. Donelson, "White Walls and High Windows: Some Contemporary Censorship Problems," *English Journal, 61,* no. 8 (November 1972), 1191–1198.

25. George Sloan quoted in Clifford A. Hardy, "Censorship and the Curriculum," *Educational Leadership, 31,* no. 1 (October 1973), 10–11, 13.

26. Peter Jennison, "Censorship: Strategy for Defense, *Publishers' Weekly,* March 2, 1964, pp. 58–61.

27. Donelson, "White Walls and High Windows: Some Contemporary Censorship Problems," op. cit., p. 1194.

28. Donelson, "What to Do When the Censor Comes," op. cit., p. 405.

29. James F. Symula, "Censorship of High School Literature: A Study of the Incidents of Censorship Involving J. D. Salinger's *Catcher in the Rye,*" unpublished Ed.D dissertation, SUNY-Buffalo, April 1969.

30. Lee A. Burress, Jr., and Georgia Cole, "Censorship Report," unpublished tentative report of AASL-NCTE Joint Commission on Book Selection, November 1966.

31. For a complete discussion of literary criteria, see Mary Hill Arbuthnot and Zena Sutherland, *Children and Books,* 4th ed., Glenview, Ill., Scott, Foresman, 1972, Chapter 2.

32. Kenneth L. Donelson, "Censorship in the 1970's: Some Ways to Handle It When It Comes (and It Will)," *English Journal, 63,* no. 2 (February 1974).

33. Allan J. Dyson, "Ripping Off Young Minds: Textbooks, Propaganda, and Librarians," *Wilson Library Bulletin, 46,* no. 3 (November 1971), 261.

34. Ibid.

35. Ibid.

36. Sol M. Elkin, "Minorities in Textbooks," *Teachers College Record, 66* (March 1965), 506.

37. Max Rosenberg, "Evaluate Your Text books for Racism, Sexism," *Educational Leadership* (November 1973), pp. 107–109.

38. John J. Farley, "Book Censorship in the Senior High School Libraries of Nassau County, N.Y.," unpublished Ph.D. dissertation, New York University, 1964.

39. Langston Hughes quoted in Milton Meltzer "Four Who Locked Horns with the Censor," *Wilson Library Bulletin, 44,* no. 3 (November 1969), 278–286.

It is the opening day of school, and the very first time that you have a class of your own. Of course you have observed many school classes in your college education courses. And you have had an opportunity to do what you consider to be some "real teaching" during the eight weeks of your student teaching assignment. Even then, however, it was not really your class or your students. You were more like a visitor on an extended stay, one who had to fit into already established norms and expectations. And if you wanted to vary the routine, you had to check with your cooperating teacher to make sure that your proposed innovation would not seriously violate his or her educational philosophy and teaching style.

To be sure, those eight weeks were enormously helpful. They had given you the chance at last to put into practice some of the theoretical knowledge and the strategies you had flopped (and sometimes you did), there was discussed in your courses. But when you your cooperating teacher with an experienced shoulder to cry on and the skill to put the jumbled pieces back together. And if things really got bad, your college instructors and/or supervisor were only an SOS telephone call away.

But starting today you are on your own. There may be other members of an instructional team to help you, but it is your name on the name plate outside the door and essentially it is you who must take responsibility for guiding the learning of the twenty-six students you see before you.

You pretend to be engrossed in organizing the "first day of school papers" that have already littered your desk, but actually you study the twenty-six faces. There is the fidgety boy in the third seat who is rapping on his desk the beat of some music that only he hears. You wonder a little nervously whether he will stop when you start the class or if he will persist in maintaining a rhythmical accompaniment to

# 14
# Creative Teaching with Literature

your lesson. There is the knot of students talking animatedly in the right corner. Are they a clique, you wonder. What are they so engrossed in discussing? There is a well-developed girl in the back of the room who is already experimenting with makeup and sophisticated hair styles. Can she really belong in this class? Beside her the other children look like babies. There is the pudgy boy near the front of the room, alone in the midst of the groups that have formed, trying to look as though he does not mind being by himself in a crowd.

You feel a sense of anticipation and worry as you wonder what these students, your class, will be like. You know that the only thing you can safely assume at this point is that each child will emerge as an individual, different in his or her own way from the other students. Will you be able to "reach" these students? Will you in some way be able to make an impact on this class?

You will need to draw on every possible resource within yourself and within the school environment. The eventual result, whether you succeed or fail, will rest with you—your creativity, your charisma, your own unique way of relating, making contact, establishing rapport, organizing content, creating structure and pattern out of potential chaos and disorder.

Fortunately, there is an invaluable resource outside of yourself upon which you can draw, and that is the array of children's books within your school or classroom library. The individuals in your class can travel to wonderful lands by opening the pages of *The Book of Three* or *The Wizard of Oz*. They can meet book children who emerge from their pages with all the dimension and reality of classroom neighbors. And your students can test their own concerns and problems against those of children as close to home as the struggling adolescents in the books of M. E. Kerr and Judy Blume or as far away as the young protagonists in Maia Woj-

ciechowska's *Shadow of a Bull* or Armstrong Sperry's *Call It Courage*. Your students can clarify their values concerning themselves and society as they ponder the universal questions literature asks, those that explore people's relationships with nature, their families, the other sex, and people of different racial and national groups.

If you can help the members of your class come into contact with these book children and explore some of the crucial issues that literature raises, you indeed will have an impact. How will you construct the necessary bridges? How will you help them connect?

In the following pages we suggest some skills and strategies for making the connection between children and books. We discuss and provide exercises for the acquisition of pertinent teaching skills. We also describe related areas such as creative dramatics and creative writing, and we suggest ways for these to be joined with the study of literature. Further, we describe some affective or humanistic teaching skills that may help you work with students as they, through involvement with literature, begin to express and clarify emotions and values of their own.

## Presenting literature to children

### Reading aloud

One way of presenting literature to children and of motivating them to turn to other books is that of reading aloud. Younger children, whose reading skills are not yet developed, take special delight in having stories read to them. However, a teacher who reads aloud to middle and upper elementary school students can also provide them with a source of pleasure and enjoyment. Reading aloud can fill the still existing discrepancy between what these students are capable of reading and what interests and intrigues them.

A regularly scheduled period for reading aloud can provide a quiet, relaxing time during the day for both younger and older students. Also, reading aloud can fill the gap created by some minor emergency in the regular teaching schedule such as a guest speaker who fails to arrive or a lesson that in the lesson plan book was supposed to take thirty minutes but in the reality of the classroom took only ten. Moreover, for children of all ages, listening to stories read aloud helps develop skills of aural comprehension, an ability that is very important in today's world of sound bombardment.

One of the most important reasons for reading aloud is that this activity can create a unique bond between a teacher and the members of his or her class. Here is how one teacher describes the experience of reading E. B. White's *Charlotte's Web* aloud to her class.

The group lived together (vicariously, to be sure, but eights are beginning to be quite able to live some life vicariously) through some of the major problems of life. We laughed till we wept, together, and we struggled to hold back tears of sadness with pride that we all could do so. Then, together, we faced death and accepted it maturely, recognizing the continuity of life. Finally, at the end of the book, the members of the group were closer to one another than they had ever been.[1]

It is recommended that teachers create a warm, comfortable environment when reading to their students. Young children can be gathered together to form a story circle in a carpeted area of the room, perhaps one adjacent to the library center. The teacher should be seated on a low chair close to the children so that they can see the illustrations and also the expression conveyed by the teacher's face. By holding the book perpendicularly to one side, the teacher can read the words and allow the children to see the pictures at all times.

Through changes in voice tone and pitch, the teacher can convey the author's meaning and express the varying moods that the story may evoke. If a story contains dialect, it may be helpful to practice the dialect before reading the story to children.

The length of time that one can read to children is, to a large extent, determined by age level. Younger children usually demand a selection that can be completed in a single session. There can be greater flexibility when reading to middle and upper elementary school children, but it is usually wise to complete one incident or chapter during a single period.

## Storytelling

During storytelling there is no book to separate the teacher from the students. This more direct eye contact allows for greater facial expression and also enables the teacher to attend to the students and be alert to fidgeting and other signs of flagging attention. Moreover, storytelling is a more flexible experience in that a story may be modified to meet varying age levels, interests, and needs, and difficult words or concepts can be explained as the need arises within the context of the story. In short, a teacher can create more intimate contact and rapport through telling stories than through reading them.

There are a number of considerations to take into account when selecting a story to tell to your class. First you, as the storyteller, must find the story interesting and entertaining. It will be difficult to transmit enthusiasm about a story if you find it boring and without appeal. The story should also fit your personality and storytelling ability. If, for example, you have great difficulty mastering dialect, you should probably avoid stories that are comprised of extensive amounts of dialect.

Another factor to consider is the time involved in preparing a story. A teacher's day is often hectic and tiring, and time is a precious commodity. If one story takes an inordinate amount of time to prepare, perhaps another story should be selected. In addition, before learning a new story it is wise to assess whether the story adds greater variety and contrast to the repertoire of stories you already have available.

A primary consideration is, of course, that the story fit the age and ability levels of the students as well as meet their particular interests and concerns. Stories with considerable action and dialogue usually have great appeal, and young listeners, in particular, are bored or confused by stories that include lengthy descriptive passages or too many events and characters.

Finally, you should determine whether the story you are considering is indeed one that is better told than read aloud. In some cases a great deal of charm is lost if the exact words of the original story are not used. For example, to omit phrases such as the "great grey-green, greasy Limpopo River all set about with fever trees" from Kipling's story, *The Elephant Child,* would detract from the story. Since memorization of several phrases would be necessary, a story such as this one should probably be read rather than told. Also picture books in which the illustrations are a necessary part of the whole should be read. Children should be treated to the visual humor of characters such as H. A. Rey's *Curious George* or Bemelmans' *Madeline,* and they should experience the form and rhythm of books such as Virginia Burton's *The Little House.*

When adapting a story or an incident from a longer book, it is helpful for the storyteller to outline and become thoroughly familiar with the characters and sequence of events. Although careful preparation is necessary, memorization is usually not recommended.

When telling a story, good diction and a sincere, natural manner are essential. The mood of the story can be conveyed by vocal expression as well as by physical gesture, but these should not be distracting. It should be remembered that the object of storytelling is to focus attention not on the storyteller but on the story.

Some storytellers believe that use of any visual aid detracts from the story. However, teachers who are in daily contact with children realize that such devices are often important ingredients in maintaining interest by varying the stimulus. Flannel boards are one popular way of varying the storytelling routine. As a story is told, figures and scenery cut from flannel, felt, or paper are attached to the board. Stories told with the flannel board should not be too complex, for a large cast of characters and detailed settings are too difficult to portray through this medium. Accumulative tales, such as the Caldecott winner, *One Fine Day,* in which one detail or character is added at a time, are particularly effective when re-created through the flannel board story.

Storytelling is an art that has been carried down since the time of the early minstrels. As Dewey Chambers notes, it is a skill that has been employed by the world's greatest teachers:

Jesus used it, as did Plato, Confucius, and other great philosophers and teachers. It is an instructional technique that did not belong only in the past. It has relevance for today's teacher as well. The modern teacher who employs this technique as a teaching tool is using an ancient method that is as modern as tomorrow.[2]

## Related learning activities

Select a picture book and read it aloud to a small group of elementary school students in a microteaching setting. Microteaching affords you the opportunity to teach between four and ten students for approximately five minutes while you concentrate on a single skill, in this case the skill of reading aloud. A supervisor and/or a group of your peers can be invaluable in enabling you to evaluate your performance. Also an audio or videotape recording of the session can give you further insight into the nature and quality of your performance. When you feel you are ready, try reading aloud in an elementary or secondary school classroom.

Select a story, either a folktale, myth, or incident or chapter from a longer book, and prepare it for storytelling. Then try out your storytelling skills in a microteaching situation. When you think you are ready, try telling a story in an elementary or secondary school classroom.

## Questioning skills

The student teacher was attractive and composed. She quickly dispensed with the administrative details of classroom organization, attendance records and homework assignments. Then the classroom chatter about the Saturday night dance and the upcoming football game subsided as the tenth grade students settled into their seats. The students liked this teacher, for she had the knack of mixing businesslike attention to academic content with a genuine interest in her students. As the principal of Madison High walked by her room, he paused to watch the students settle into a discussion of Shakespeare's *Hamlet.* Classroom operation appeared to be running smoothly, and he made a mental note to offer Ms. Ames a contract when her eight weeks of student teaching were over.

Had he stayed a little longer to hear the discussion—and had he been somewhat sophisticated in the quality of verbal interaction, he would not have been so satisfied.

MS. AMES: I would like to discuss your reading assignment with you. As the scene begins, three clowns are on stage. What are they doing?

CHERYL: They are digging a grave.

MS. AMES: Right. Who is about to be buried, Jim?

JIM: Ophelia.

MS. AMES: Yes. One of the grave diggers uncovers the skull of Yorick. What occupation did Yorick once have? Donna?

DONNA: He was the king's jester.

MS. AMES: Good. A scuffle occurs by Ophelia's graveside. Who is fighting? Bill?

BILL: Laertes and Hamlet.

MS. AMES: That's right. In what act and scene does Ophelia's burial occur, Tom?

TOM: Scene 1, Act 5.

Throughout the forty-five minute English class, Ms. Ames asked a series of factual questions, received a series of one and two word replies—and Shakespeare's play was transformed into a bad caricature of a television quiz show.[3]

Research tells us that the ineffective questioning pattern that this teacher demonstrated is one that frequently occurs in classrooms across the country, at all grade levels, from kindergarten through high school. The first major study of classroom questioning was conducted in 1912. The findings disclosed that although 80 percent of classroom talk was devoted to asking, answering, and reacting to questions, almost all the questions teachers asked demanded student responses that called only for memory and a superficial understanding of the material.[4] Unfortunately, over sixty years later, things have not changed much, and studies in the 1970s show that the vast majority of questions asked still require only rote memorization for a correct response.[5]

Of course questions that call for students to demonstrate their acquisition of factual knowledge are important in the study of literature. Through responses to such *who, what, where,* and *when* questions, teachers can assess whether students have gained a basic knowledge regarding who the characters are, what the sequence of the events or plot is, what the setting is, and where and when the story takes place. However, once this basic knowledge is gained, it is important that teachers ask questions that demand a higher level of student thought.

Benjamin Bloom, in *The Taxonomy of Educational Objectives*, indicates that there is a six-level hierarchy of cognitive processes toward which teachers can address their questions.[6] Following are the six levels on which questions can be formulated.

1. *Knowledge.* A question on the knowledge level requires students to repeat information exactly as memorized. Such questions ask students to respond with previously memorized facts, figures, names, places and definitions, and they often begin with the words *who, what, where,* and *when.* As noted, these questions are the ones teachers ask most frequently.

2. *Comprehension.* Comprehension questions ask students to go beyond memorization in showing that they have a basic grasp or understanding of the material under discussion. Such questions often ask students to explain a main idea, to compare and contrast, and to rephrase previously learned information, to "put it in their own words." Questions that call for students to demonstrate basic comprehension frequently begin with such words or phrases as *describe, compare, contrast, rephrase, put in your own words,* and *explain the main idea.*

3. *Application.* Application questions ask students to apply previously learned information to determine a single correct answer. They often begin with such words or phrases as *apply, classify, choose, employ, write an example, solve.*

4. *Analysis.* Analysis questions are exceptionally important in the study of literature, particularly to the understanding of characterization. These questions ask students to identify motives or causes, draw conclusions, or derive evidence. These are the questions that ask students *why;* they also may begin with such words as *support, analyze,* or *conclude.*

5. *Synthesis.* Questions at the synthesis level call for the most creative thinking. They ask students to make predictions, produce original communications, or solve problems that have more than one correct answer. They often begin with such words or phrases as *predict, produce, write, design, develop, construct, what happens if, how can we solve,* and *how can we improve.* Such questions are particularly important in stimulating student thought and creativity in the areas of creative writing, art, and music.

6. *Evaluation.* Evaluation questions are at the heart of literary criticism. They ask students to offer opinions and make judgments, and they often begin with such words or phrases as *judge, argue, validate, assess, which is better,* and *give your opinion.*

To teach literature effectively to children and to fulfill the purpose of the literature program, it is crucial that teachers ask questions on all six levels of the taxonomy. Knowledge, comprehension, and application questions can lead to children's familiarity with specific selections of literature, with noted authors and illustrators, and with pertinent genres and types of literature. Analysis and evaluation questions are crucial in the study of characterization and literary criticism, whereas synthesis questions are invaluable for stimulating creative activities in the related areas of writing, art, music, and drama.

Following are some sample questions on each of the six levels of the taxonomy:

*Knowledge*

1. Where does C. S. Lewis' *The Lion, the Witch and the Wardrobe* take place?
2. What is the plot of Marguerite Henry's *King of the Wind?*
3. Who is the main character in Armstrong Sperry's *Call It Courage?*

*Comprehension*

1. Explain the main idea of Kate Seredy's *The Good Master.*

2. In your own words summarize Arthur Ransome's *Swallows and Amazons*.

3. Compare Don Freeman's *Dandelion* with Gene Zion's *Harry the Dirty Dog*.

*Application*

1. Would you classify E. B. White's *Stuart Little* as fantasy or realism?

2. Give an example of a contemporary animal story.

3. Select an illustrator of children's books whose art work is influenced by cubism.

*Analysis*

1. What conclusions can you make about the German family in Hans Peter Richter's *Friedrich?*

2. Support or refute the following sentence using specific examples from the text: "Madeleine Pollard's *To Tell My People* makes a pessimistic statement about the ability of human beings to live in peace with one another."

3. Analyze the language in June Jordan's *His Own Where* to determine how it helps fulfill the author's overall intent or purpose.

*Synthesis*

1. Write a sequel to Beatrix Potter's *The Tale of Peter Rabbit*.

2. Develop a modern dance that conveys the mood of Maurice Sendak's *The Moon Jumpers*.

3. How might Judith Viorst's *The Tenth Good Thing About Barney* be used in explaining death to children?

*Evaluation*

1. Which book do you think includes the more finely developed portrayal of old age, Carol Lorenzo's *Mama's Ghosts* or Miska Miles' *Annie and the Old One?*

2. In your opinion is Paula Fox's *Slave Dancer* a racist book?

3. In your judgment what role does censorship play in the selection of children's reading material?

The six taxonomic levels described are designed to elicit cognitive responses from students. However, since the teaching of literature includes areas in the affective domain, such as the enjoyment and appreciation of literature, and the ability to feel empathy for others through vicarious experience, it is important for teachers to ask affective questions as well as cognitive ones. An affective question is one that elicits emotional responses from students. Following are some sample affective questions that relate to the study of children's literature.

1. How do you imagine Alice felt after falling through the rabbit hole?

2. When you read *Charlotte's Web*, how did you feel when Charlotte's children were born?

3. Which of the books that you read gave you the most pleasure?

In conducting a discussion regarding literature, it is not only the nature of the questions that is important but their timing as well. Research shows us that teachers ask an enormous number of questions—on the average, between two and three per minute, and it is not at all unusual to find a teacher asking as many as seven to ten questions in a single minute. Ironically, although teachers ask many questions, they often show little tolerance in waiting for student response. In fact, studies show that the mean amount of time a teacher waits after asking a question is approximately *one second*.[7] Typically, if the student is not able to come up with an answer within that second, the teacher will repeat or rephrase the question, call on another student, or ask a different question.

It is very important that teachers learn to increase the time they can wait for a student response, particularly after asking a question that engenders an emotional response or one that is designed to stimulate higher levels of cognitive thinking. When teachers learn to increase the time they wait after asking a question from one second to three or more, the effect in the classroom is most positive. For example, students give longer and more appropriate answers, and failures to respond are less frequent. Moreover, students appear to be more confident about their comments; student comments on the levels of analysis and synthesis increase; and students ask more questions.

The final result of increased teacher wait time, that of students asking more questions, is of great importance if the study of literature is to be vital and dynamic. Unfortunately, student-initiated questions are rare in classrooms. In fact, in one study of high-school classrooms, the researcher found an average of one student question per pupil per month.[8] When an elementary school girl was asked why she did not ask questions in school, her response was, "I never thought about asking questions. It never occurred to me that I should."

"Literature transmits the accumulated wisdom of mankind, and continues to ask universal questions about the meaning of life and man's relationships with nature and other men."[9] For children truly to contemplate what literature has to offer, they must be stimulated by questions that are both cognitive and affective. They must be given time to consider their responses, and they must be encouraged to ask questions of their own. Of course students should not be questioned and probed every time they interact with a selection of literature. Consistently reacting to a battery of questions might indeed be counterproductive and actually be detrimental to the development of appreciation for and love of literature. However, there should be occasional questioning associated with the reading of literature, and this ques-

tioning should encourage students to respond at a variety of cognitive and affective levels.

## Related learning activities

1. Select one of the following books and construct questions on all six levels of Bloom's *Taxonomy* as they pertain to the particular book:

*In the Night Kitchen*, by Maurice Sendak
*The Barn*, by John Schoenherr
*The Yearling*, by Marjorie Kinnan Rawlings
*A Grass Rope*, by William Mayne
*Then Again Maybe I Won't*, by Judy Blume
*My Darling, My Hamburger*, by Paul Zindel
*Strawberry Girl*, by Lois Lenski
*The Dead Bird*, by Margaret Wise Brown
*Pedro, the Angel of Olvera Street*, by Leo Politi
*Harriet the Spy*, by Louise Fitzhugh

*Your Questions*

_____

_____

_____

_____

_____

_____

_____

_____

_____

If you like, work on developing these questions with a small group of your classmates. If this exercise gives you trouble, try the next one for further practice.

2. The following passage is from Madeleine L'Engle's *A Wrinkle in Time*. Read the passage and construct six questions pertaining to

the passage so that all six levels of the *Taxonomy* are represented. Then compare the questions you have developed with the sample questions on page 392.

In search of their father, Meg and Charles Wallace, along with their friend Calvin, are about to enter the town of Camzotz:

Below them the town was laid out in harsh angular patterns. The houses in the outskirts were all exactly alike, small square boxes, painted gray. Each had a small, rectangular plot of lawn in front, with a straight line of dull-looking flowers edging the path to the door. Meg had a feeling that if she could count the flowers there would be exactly the same number for each house. In front of all the houses children were playing. Some were skipping rope, some were bouncing balls. Meg felt vaguely that something was wrong with their play. It seemed exactly like children playing around any housing development at home, and yet there was something different about it. She looked at Calvin, and saw that he, too, was puzzled.

"Look!" Charles Wallace said suddenly. "They're skipping and bouncing in rhythm! Everyone's doing it at exactly the same moment."

This was so. As the skipping rope hit the pavement, so did the ball. As the rope curved over the head of the jumping child, the child with the ball caught the ball. Down came the ropes. Down came the balls. Over and over again. Up. Down. All in rhythm. All identical. Like the houses. Like the paths. Like the flowers.

Then the doors of all the houses opened simultaneously, and out came women like a row of paper dolls. The print of their dresses was different, but they all gave the appearance of being the same. Each woman stood on the steps of her house. Each clapped. Each child with the ball caught the ball. Each child with the skipping rope folded the rope. Each child turned and walked into the house. The doors clicked shut behind them.[10]

*Your Questions*

—————————————————————

—————————————————————
—————————————————————
—————————————————————
—————————————————————
—————————————————————
—————————————————————
—————————————————————

Obviously your questions will not be exactly the same as the sample questions. However, the sample questions should give you an idea of the kinds of questions you might have asked on each of the six levels of the *Taxonomy*.

3. Discuss a children's book of your choice with your classmates, a group of children in a microteaching situation or, if possible, a group of children in an elementary or secondary school classroom. During the discussion concentrate on your question-asking skills. Analyze your performance with the help of your instructor, your peers, and/or a videotape recorder. The checklist on page 393 may aid you in evaluating your questioning performance. It will probably be helpful if you plan out your questioning strategy ahead of time rather than relying on extemporaneous brilliance.

## Creative ideas for experiencing literature

The preceding sections have briefly delineated a few key skills that you as a teacher can develop and refine as you present literature to children. There are also many related creative activities that can be structured to enrich the literary experience, to allow students greater personal involvement, and to encourage creative and divergent thinking in the classroom. Following are activities in the areas of creative drama and creative writing that can be inte-

## Sample Questions

*Knowledge*
1. What color were all the houses painted?
2. What puzzled Meg about the children's play?

*Comprehension*
1. Describe the town of Camzotz.
2. Compare Camzotz with the town in which you live.

*Application*
1. Given the information in the passage, would you classify the town of Camzotz as (a) individualistic or (b) conforming.
2. Give an example of a situation in your country that stresses everyone doing the same thing at the same time.

*Analysis*
1. What conclusions can you make about the people of Camzotz?
2. Analyze the writing in the final paragraph to discover how it conveys the atmosphere of Camzotz.

*Synthesis*
1. Why do you suppose the people of Camzotz were behaving in this manner?
2. Draw a picture of Camzotz.
3. What do you think life would be like if everyone did the same thing at the same time?

*Evaluation*
1. Which do you think is better—a country that is highly individualistic or one that is highly conforming?
2. This year we have read other books about civilizations of automatons. In your opinion which book is the best?

grally tied to the literature program. The activities discussed are representative rather than inclusive, but they do provide a means to begin connecting literature to related creative activities.

## Creative drama

Have you ever watched a five-year-old play "Let's pretend?" Perhaps he or she has a birthday party or a tea party and invites a conglomeration of dolls or a single imaginary friend. Or a group of young children may turn out the lights; their room then becomes a "spook house" and they turn into skeletons, witches, and goblins. Or a child may lumber about slowly, arms extended and clasped together before his or her face and ask, "Can you guess what animal I am?"

These are examples of dramatic play, the

| Type of question | Number asked | Example |
|---|---|---|
| Knowledge Questions | | |
| Comprehension Questions | | |
| Application Questions | | |
| Analysis Questions | | |
| Synthesis Questions | | |
| Evaluation Questions | | |

**Approximate length of wait time:**

**Areas in which questioning skills appear to be most effective:**

**Areas related to questioning that are most in need of improvement:**

free play of the young child through which he or she tries on the roles of friends and neighbors and expresses feelings through movements and words. It is a primary way through which the child explores, interprets, reacts to and learns about the world.

Winifred Ward has noted, "Drama comes in the door of every school with the child."[11] And by extending and building upon children's experience with and love of dramatic play, teachers can help them move into the areas of creative dramatics, role play, and puppetry.

Creative drama goes beyond dramatic play in that it makes use of a complete story with a beginning, middle, and end. However, whether or not it is based on a well-known story or an original plot, lines are never memorized. It is improvised drama and dialogue is created extemporaneously.

## Pantomime

An excellent way to begin creative dramatics is through pantomime, which is expression, action, and gesture without words. For many five- and six-year-olds, pantomime is a natural means of expression, and for older children it stimulates use of the whole body and relieves participants of the added skill of having to think of dialogue. Nellie McCaslin suggests that an effective way for beginning pantomime is to have the children handle a small object such as a box or an eraser as though it were a diamond bracelet, a kitten with soft fur, a dirty and empty wallet, a knife, a full glass of water.[12]

There are three basic areas around which pantomime can be developed: (1) activities, (2) mood and feeling, and (3) characterization.

Pantomiming activities involved with making or doing something proves to be effective with children of all ages. Children can pantomime getting dressed for a party, doing homework, playing tennis, ice-skating, or baking a cake. Other activities can be based on the five senses; students can pantomime looking for a hat in a dark room, hearing an explosion, smelling cookies baking in the oven, eating a hot fudge sundae, or touching a hot stove. These are but a few suggestions; a wealth of other pantomime activities can be developed around the five senses.

Feelings will probably emerge to some extent as students pantomime activities; therefore pantomimes focused specifically on mood and feeling will soon be appropriate. For such pantomimes children have to concentrate on their emotions and get in touch with how they feel when they are angry, sad, lonely, worried, excited, happy, and so on. From the pantomiming of feelings, children can move toward characterization and attempt to combine expression, gesture, and movement to create a believable character or personality.

## Creative dramatics

After work with pantomime the teacher can determine when children are ready to improvise dialogue. Initially creative drama can be stimulated by situations or objects. For example, the scene can be a toy shop on Christmas Eve, and on the stroke of midnight the toys can come alive. The children must determine which toy they will be and by their actions and conversation must show who they are and why they were not sold. Any object, such as a broom, briefcase, cane, or straw hat, can serve as a springboard for creative dramatics. Costumes too can stimulate improvisation, and the wise teacher will have available a supply of hats, shoes, capes, jewelry, shawls, and so on.

The most popular and the most effective form of creative drama is that based on literature. Fairy tales and legends provide fine material for creative dramatics, particularly for children up to the ages of ten or eleven. Older children often prefer adventure and stories of real life; these, because of their length, often have to be shortened or rearranged. Here the teacher's role is crucial, for he or she must help the children isolate the main events and arrange them in logical order. The teacher must also help with visualizing scenes and characters and with room arrangement or staging. Once the drama is in progress, the teacher should remain in the background but be ready to offer assistance if the creative drama appears to be in danger of faltering.

To be adapted to creative drama, literature should have highly developed action and vivid characterization. The following are a few of the books for younger children that are particularly appropriate for creative drama.

*Curious George* books, by H. A. Rey
*The Happy Lion* books, by Louise Fatio
*Frog and Toad Are Friends,* by Arnold Lobel
*Drummer Hoff,* by Barbara Emberly
*One Fine Day,* by Nonny Hogrogian
*Little Tim and the Brave Sea Captain,* by Edward Ardizzone
*Play with Me,* by Marie Hall Ets
*Mr. Penny,* by Marie Hall Ets
*Arrow to the Sun,* by Gerald McDermott
*Finders Keepers,* by William & Nicolas
*William's Doll,* by Charlotte Zolotow
*The Bears on Hemlock Mountain,* by Alice Dalgliesh
*Where the Wild Things Are,* by Maurice Sendak

Some books that contain episodes or incidents appropriate for creative drama with children in the middle or the upper grades are the following:

*It's Not the End of the World*, by Judy Blume
*Philip Hall Likes Me. I Reckon Maybe*, by Bette Greene
*Homer Price*, by Robert McCloskey
*Ramona the Pest*, by Beverly Cleary
*Henry Huggins*, by Beverly Cleary
*Tom Sawyer*, by Mark Twain
*The Upstairs Room*, by Johanna Reiss
*Alice's Adventure in Wonderland*, by Lewis Carroll
*A Wrinkle in Time*, by Madeleine L'Engle
*Rass*, by Bernice Rabe
*Where the Lilies Bloom*, by Vera and Bill Cleaver
*Blubber*, by Judy Blume
*That Crazy April*, by Lila Perl
*The 18th Emergency*, by Betsy Byars
*From the Mixed Up Files of Mrs. Basil E. Frankweiler*, by E. L. Konigsberg

The teacher can work with the students in evaluating a creative drama that emerges from a particular selection of literature. Such evaluation can lead to fine, succeeding performances and greater personal growth for the individuals involved in the creative drama.

## Role playing

Role play makes use of drama to solve particular social or emotional problems. It is somewhat related to therapy but differs vastly in degree and intensity. "Role playing may be considered preventive in that it provides an opportunity for all children in a group to develop sensitivity toward the feelings of others, and encourages changes of attitude through understanding."[13]

In the classroom the purpose of role playing is not therapeutic but educative. It provides a way for children to get "into another's shoes" and gain greater understanding and tolerance for how other people feel in different situations. Classroom role plays are usually based on fam-

ily or school situations. The discussion following the role play allows opportunity for the expression and clarification of attitudes and values.

Many of the books discussed in the previous chapters can provide material for a variety of role plays. For example, Judy Blume's *Blubber* or Robert Cormier's *The Chocolate War* could be the springboard for a role play involving cliques and how "in groups" and "out groups" feel. Lila Perl's *That Crazy April* generates a good deal of material for role-playing family or peer situations involving sex role stereotyping. Yet other children's books, such as Paula Fox's *Slave Dancer* or Yoshiko Uchida's *Journey to Topaz*, can stimulate role plays that provide understanding for human emotion and suffering involved in various historical incidents.

One specific form of role play, called the alter ego role play, is particularly effective in helping students gain awareness of the complexity and multidimensionality of human interaction. In the alter ego role play, two children are necessary to play each single character. One plays the outer behavior and speech of the character, his or her public self; the other plays the character's inner self, and speaks his or her private thoughts and feelings. We have used the alter ego role play with great effectiveness in demonstrating how a newcomer feels when trying to break into already established cliques that do not want to open their barriers. When fifth graders did a role play of this situation, the child playing the newcomer's public voice met each rebuff with nonchalance and an "I don't care" attitude whereas the newcomer's private voice expressed hurt, anger, and frustration. The role play was well done, and it stimulated a frank discussion in which children talked about how they feel when they are on the outside of the "in group."

Alter ego role play can also be used as a

modification of creative drama based on litera-ture. In one class the students put on a very effective creative drama of the scene in Long-fellow's *The Courtship of Miles Standish* in which John Alden comes to court Priscilla Mul-lins for Miles Standish, when in reality he loves her himself. This scene, in which inner motivation is so directly opposed to surface reality, was a fine vehicle for an alter ego situation, and the students showed a sophisti-cated awareness of the multidimensionality of human interaction.

## Puppetry

Place a puppet on the hand of a child and things begin to happen. He or she will wriggle the puppet and speak for it or to it, assuming a voice or accent other than their normal one. These spon-taneous reactions springing from the dynamics of puppetry can be used creatively to motivate chil-dren to read, discuss, enact, create, and enjoy literature.[14]

There is little doubt that activities involving puppetry are extremely popular and enjoyable. Puppetry provides an outlet for different kinds of creativity; children not only develop and participate in the drama but construct the pup-pets as well. A great deal of imagination is re-quired to dress and decorate the puppets, for each puppet must become a unique individual through costume and the way character is ex-pressed in the puppet's features. Puppetry is particularly valuable for shy or timid children who find it difficult to express themselves in creative drama. "The puppet, an extension of the self, serves as a mask, enabling the player to gain a freedom which he or she cannot achieve when acting a part. Behind the puppet stage, the timid child can lose inhibitions and enter into the drama without self-conscious-ness."[15]

The creation of puppets can be a complex undertaking and therefore appears formidable to the inexperienced teacher. Fortunately, there are a variety of imaginative puppets that are so simple to make that even very young chil-dren can be involved in their creation. Follow-ing are brief descriptions of some puppet types that are simple and still allow for much cre-ativity and imagination.[16]

### Ball puppets

Either a hollow rubber ball or a styrofoam ball may be used to construct a ball puppet. A hole must be cut or a depression hollowed out that is sufficiently large for the index finger to be inserted. Paint or glued felt pieces can be used to make features on a rubber ball, and colored thumb tacks are appropriate for making features on the styrofoam ball puppet. The puppet's costume can be made by draping a handkerchief or similar piece of material over the puppeteer's hand and twisting a rub-ber band over the third finger and thumb.

### Fruit and vegetable puppets

Fruit and vegetable puppets are created by inserting a stick into carrots, potatoes, turnips, peas, apples, or oranges. Features can be hol-lowed out or pasted on, or such items as thumb tacks, pins, or paper reinforcers can be in-serted. For a costume the stick can be pushed through a small hole in a handkerchief before it is placed inside the fruit or vegetable. Al-though these puppets obviously do not last forever, they are great fun to make and often result in a vividly comic cast of characters.

### Cylinder puppets

A 3-inch section is cut from a tube of paper toweling to form the cylinder puppet. Hair, features, and clothing can be drawn or painted or pieces of felt, yarn, and colored paper can be glued in place. When the child inserts his or her index and third fingers inside the cylinder, the puppet moves and bends forward.

### Stick puppets

Pictures cut from magazines or children's art work can be pasted on thin cardboard and then cut out again. These sturdy shapes are taped to a plastic straw or a stick and when the child, hidden behind the screen or stage, moves the stick, the puppet appears to glide unassisted through space.

### Paper bag puppets

In making a paper bag puppet the puppet's face is drawn or painted on the folded end of a closed paper bag. The upper part of the mouth is drawn on this folded end; the bottom part of the mouth is drawn on the actual body of the bag. The puppeteer's hand is placed inside the bag with the fingers inside the folded end. When the fingers move up and down, the puppet's mouth opens and closes.

### Box puppets

To make a box puppet two small boxes are taped together, and the face is drawn or painted on the upper box, with the mouth divided between the upper and lower box. The child's fingers go in the upper box, the thumb in the lower one; as the fingers and thumb move apart and together, the puppet's mouth opens and closes.

### Sock puppets

To make a sock puppet an oval cardboard 3 by 5 inches is inserted into the foot of a sock extending from the toe to the heel. When the cardboard is folded across the center, the upper and lower jaws of the puppet are formed. The child places his or her hand inside the sock with the fingers above the top fold of the cardboard and the thumb under the bottom fold. As the fingers and thumb are brought together and then apart, the puppet's mouth opens and closes. Hair, features, and clothing can be made by pasting on colored paper, yarn, and felt.

These are some of the basic puppet types that can be made easily in the classroom. When creating their puppets, children should be allowed to forget about accurately duplicating nature; instead they can exaggerate and put all their powers of whimsy and imagination to work.

### The puppet stage

A puppet stage can be created simply by turning a table on its side. Another kind of puppet stage can be made by extending a sheet or a large piece of cardboard across a doorway to conceal the action of the puppeteers.

### Selecting the story

Folktales provide action, conflict, and lively dialogue and thus make fine material to be adapted for puppet plays. Familiar tales such as *The Three Bears, Henny Penny, The Pancake, The Three Billy Goats Gruff, Little Red Riding Hood, The Three Little Pigs,* and *Rumpelstiltskin* are particularly suitable for primary grade children. Virginia Haviland's collections provide an exciting variety of material reflecting folktales of diverse ethnic origins. Also children enjoy creating and watching puppet shows about favorite characters such as the following:

*Curious George,* by H. A. Rey
*George and Martha* and *George and Martha Encore,* by James Marshall
*Amelia Bedelia,* by Peggy Parish
*Sylvester and the Magic Pebble,* by William Steig
*Roland, the Minstrel Pig,* by William Steig
*Anatole,* by Eve Titus
*Ask Mr. Bear,* by Marjorie Flack
*Madeline,* by Ludwig Bemelmans
*The Funny Little Woman,* retold by Arlene Mosel

Modern fanciful stories with unique characters offer material that can be adapted to create some stunning puppet shows. Children love creating wild puppet monsters for Maurice Sendak's *Where the Wild Things Are. The Borrowers,* by Mary Norton, and *The Return of the Twelves,* by Pauline Clark, also offer intriguing material for the creation of puppet plays.

## Related learning activities

1. Most children bring experience with dramatic play into the classroom with them. Make a conscious effort to observe young children and how they participate in dramatic play. Watch younger brothers and sisters or children for whom you babysit. Observe children playing in the neighborhood or at a day-care center or nursery school.

In what types of activities are they involved?
What roles do they assume?
For what length of time are they able to participate in dramatic play?

Share your observations with your classmates.

2. Before asking children to participate in an activity it is wise to try it yourself first. Try pantomiming the characters involved in the following situation:

You go into a fancy restaurant to order a meal.

Do it as

a. A fat woman who loves to eat but who lately has been attending Weight Watchers and is determined to take off 20 pounds.
b. A finicky child who only likes peanut butter and jam sandwiches and cannot find them on the menu.
c. A poor elderly man who is hungry, but whose ability to select is severely limited by his pocketbook.

Create some other situations for pantomime and try your skill. Then experiment with pantomime in a microteaching situation or a class-

room. Evaluate the experience with your instructor, your peers, and the videotape recorder.

3. We have suggested a short list of books that are particularly suitable to creative drama. Compile a list of some other books that you feel could be readily adapted for creative drama. Discuss your choices with your classmates and assess their reactions. With a group of classmates try developing a creative drama from one of your selections. In a microteaching situation or an elementary school classroom, help a group of children develop a creative drama based on one of your selections. What questions will you ask to generate ideas for the creative drama session? What problems will you perhaps encounter? How will you meet them? Evaluate the creative drama session with the help of your instructor, peers, and/or videotape recorder.

4. Create a puppet based on a well-known character from children's literature. Use one of the puppet types described previously. Which puppet type is most suitable for creating your particular character and why?

5. Make your puppet act

a. nervous because he or she is about to enter a haunted house; nervous because he or she is about to be reprimanded by a parent.
b. happy because it is a beautiful day; happy because he or she is bringing home an all-A report card.
c. sad because a best friend is moving away; sad because there is no more ice cream left in the refrigerator.

Help a group of children make their puppets express different emotions stimulated by different events and resulting in varying degrees of intensity.

6. Which Caldecott Medal books and Caldecott Honor books include characters that could develop into exciting puppets? Explain reasons for your choices.

## Creative writing

Robin, at the age of five, is not yet a facile word expert who thoughtlessly turns out slickly turned phrases and cliches. Instead she fumbles with words, struggling to find her own perfect language to communicate her observations, her reality. She spots a dragon fly over the lake and calls attention to the "bizzer bird." She is enchanted by the sparks on the hearth and lovingly calls them her "drops of fire." She tries on a new pair of shoes and proudly shows off her "shining feet." And when a summer storm is ended, she softens its violence by comparing it to everyday things, calling thunder "a loud voice" and rain "her warm shower."

Many parents, teachers, and writers find delight in the way children's language is still in touch with the "freshness, deep-down things." James Smith says, "When children begin to coin words, when they manipulate and explore them, when they begin to draw analogies, when they see relationships in their environment and draw comparisons in word experiences, when they paint word pictures and become unique and novel in expressing themselves, we have creative writing."[17] Kenneth Koch in *Wishes, Lies, and Dreams* records his experiences in helping elementary school students write poetry and tells of his pleasure in the spontaneity and natural creativity that was released.

The classroom environment can help children express themselves with freshness and spontaneity; it can foster a natural creativity and render it even more fine. But for this to occur there must be a tone and a feeling that tells children that their language, both spoken and written, is valuable and worthy of respect. Smith comments further:

Each child needs to come to appreciate the beauty of language itself, the effective use of words and

the creative ways they may help him express his own original thoughts.

This is the study of language for language's sake. It is loving the rhythm of certain words; it is delighting in the way words are put together; it is using words and phrases to paint pictures. It includes the creative: the job of sorting, deciding and choosing the right word for the right spot. It means children evaluate according to what they can do to make language forceful and effective. It means children write their own literature and recognize beauty in the writing of others. It is the building of appreciation for authors, poets, and composers. It is knowledge of that which lifts language from the commonplace to the beautiful.[18]

As Smith further notes, one way to encourage creativity in children is to help them become knowledgeable and appreciative of the creativity of others. All the following activities are a good way to begin: give children experiences with literature, storytelling, reading aloud; question, raising the level of discussion from the literal and the factual to the interpretive and the analytic; communicate a love and respect for the way author and illustrator interpret and clarify experience. There are also a wealth of language arts activities that, as a parallel and a complement to the literature program, can preserve and uncover the "freshness, deep-down things." Numerous books have been written on language experience and creative writing. It is our purpose in the next few pages to highlight some of those activities we have found most effective in working with children, language, and books.

### Word play

Playing with words, experimenting with them, and manipulating them encourage enjoyment of language and stimulate and refine creative writing skills.

Word charts posted around the room or stored in envelopes and folders in a creative writing center may encourage delight in and experimentation with words. For example,

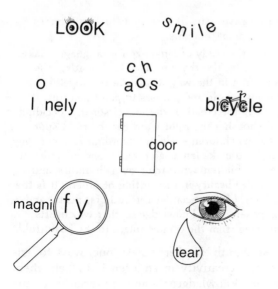

there might be a chart for *Dy No Mite Words*, selected for a variety of reasons—sound, appearance, length, the way they convey meaning. These can be defined, discussed, used in sentences and writing activities. Another word chart or activity for a creative writing center is one in which children complete similes such as: *as warm as, as gentle as, as hard as,* and *as lonely as.* Although these similes may initially invite clichés, a teacher and class can work together in sharpening responses.

Charles Shultz's *Happiness Is a Warm Puppy* is probably responsible for the widespread use of an exercise that asks children to personalize abstract concepts. For example, one class of first graders wrote:

Happiness is jumping in a pile of leaves.
Happiness is buying new crayons.
Happiness is picking apples from a tree.
Happiness is shaking President Ford's hand.
Happiness is having a dog around the house.
Happiness is getting a present for no reason at all.
Happiness is having the boys liking you.

Happiness is having my brother and sister come home from college.
Happiness is to have a car.

Other abstract words such as *freedom, loneliness, peace, and sadness* can be used in a similar manner.

Children of all ages enjoy a strategy in which they toy with the visual aspect of words, relating the word's appearance to its meaning. Here is what one group of elementary students came up with.

Hinky Pinkies, sometimes called Terse Verse, provide practice with rhyming, with word meanings, and synonyms, and in general, they offer a great deal of fun. To make a hinky pinky, a "daffynition" is given and the students must provide two rhyming words that fit the descriptions; for example;

| | |
|---|---|
| a shy male | coy boy |
| "with it" fish | mod cod or cool school |
| attractive feline | pretty kitty |
| white monkey | vanilla gorilla |
| clean jewelry | speckless necklace |

Do not worry if your store of hinky pinkies runs out. Once the students get some practice in this activity, they will enthusiastically create their own.

Palindromes are another source of enjoyment for children. These are words, phrases, and sentences that read the same both backward and forward. *Mom, dad, wow,* and *pop* are a few easy ones to start with. Students will really be amazed when you show them some of the more complex creations, such as *Rise to vote sir* or *Madam I'm Adam.* Some of the brighter students will be able to create complex palindromes of their own.

William Gordon devised a problem-solving model called synectics that develops creativity through the use of analogy. Originally used by industry, synectics has been adapted to the classroom with fascinating results. Although too complex to be described comprehensively here, synectics essentially stretches the mind by two types of analogies, personal and direct. Following are examples of direct analogies that encourage children to relate what at first appears to be two unlike things.

A picket fence is like a dragon's tail
because _____
A steam roller is like what animal? Why? _____
Which is louder, a smile or a frown? _____

A personal analogy demands that the student become personally involved in the comparison. For example:

Imagine that you are a boy's pencil. He uses you in school, and he uses you to do his homework. Be the thing! You are a pencil; your feet are a sharp point; your head is an eraser.

How do you feel when the boy grinds away at you in the pencil sharpener?
Would you rather have a long or a short point? Why?
Every time you are sharpened you grow smaller. How do you feel?[19]

This situation encouraged one rather chubby student to write the following response.

Zoom. Around and around in the pencil sharpener. How all the excess weight flies off and I become sleek and thin and svelte.

Oh, make me a long point. Gone is that short, stubby look. I'll become lean and thin and then maybe end up on the cover of *Vogue*.

So what if I don't last long this way. The world might not be here tomorrow.

### Poetry

Word play should lead to keener student awareness of words and a sharper sense of when a word or a phrase goes beyond cliché and communicates to the reader or listener in a uniquely fresh and vivid way. Such word play is a good warm-up activity to stimulate the writing of poetry and narrative.

There are numerous books in which teachers tell of their experiences in working with children and poetry. These report techniques that failed and those that had stunning results. Kenneth Koch, for example, found that wishes, lies, and dreams were topics that stimulated students to write with both lighthearted spontaneity and serious candor. He found stressing repetition to be particularly effective and suggested, for example, one poetry form in which students begin every line with a phrase such as *I wish*. Other teachers have found success in using specific poetry forms, such as haiku, tanka, cinquain, and septain.

Haiku, a form of Japanese poetry, provides children with the following structure: three lines with five syllables in the first line, seven syllables in the second line, and five syllables in the third line. Haiku does not rhyme and it usually conveys a beautiful image that pertains to nature and the seasons. However, teachers seem to have differing points of view concerning topics for haiku. Some report highly successful experiences in which children have written haiku on a wide variety of topics whereas others insist that to depart from the theme of nature violates the essential purpose and beauty of this poetic form.

Haiku can be written by students at almost any age level, although it is more difficult for students who not yet understand syllabication. Following is a haiku written by a student in a college children's literature course and then one written by a sixth grader.

Flowers in the breeze
Dancing like Ballerinas,
Swaying to and fro.
    *Lynn Ellenger, student, American University*
Small ponds are quiet;
Water glistens in sunlight;
Others are wavy.

    *Don Bell, sixth grade*

There are many fine books of haiku compiled for children. Harry Behn, for example, has sensitively translated haiku in *Cricket Songs* and *More Cricket Songs*. Both books are illustrated by reproductions of paintings by Japanese artists.

Tanka is an extension of the haiku form. It

consists of five lines with five syllables in the first line, seven syllables in the second, five syllables in the third, and seven syllables in each of the two remaining lines. Again, tanka may be used with many age levels, as the following examples indicate.

> Mothers and fathers,
> Doing the "best they know how,"
> Sometimes hurt children
> Because they often forget
> that maturity takes time.
>
> *Janice Polizzi, student, American University*
>
> Death is close to all.
> It is all around the world;
> Striking someone now.
> Why did it pick that person?
> Hopefully it will pass me.
>
> *Cheryl Knebel, student, American University*
>
> The caterpillar,
> Taking all the time he wants
> To walk by my house,
> Seeing all the things we miss
> When we're in such a hurry.
>
> *Majorie Hughes, sixth grade*

Cinquain is another poetry form that allows children creativity within structure. When presenting cinquain, particularly to young children, it may be helpful to provide dittoed sheets marked as follows:

————— (Word)
————— ————— (Two adjectives or describing words)
————— ————— ————— (Three words that express action)
————— ————— ————— ————— (A four-word statement about the topic)
————— (A synonym for the first word or an adjective that describes it)

> Wars
> Violent ugly
> Vicious bloody painful
> They are not inevitable
> hell
>
> *Janice Polizzi*
> *student, American University*

Another form of cinquain consists of five lines with each succeeding line containing one word less than the line above it.

> Hope I never grow old
> People won't like me
> They turn cold
> Leaving me
> Rejected
>
> *Genie Morrissy, student, American University*

The structure of septain poetry is a bit more difficult and is not appropriate for most primary-grade children. However, it can be used at the higher elementary levels and on up with successful results. Again it may be helpful to provide an explanatory dittoed sheet.

————— (Noun)
————— ————— (Two words describing line 1)
————— ————— ————— (Three characteristics or verbs describing line 1)
————— ————— ————— ————— (Transition line)
————— ————— ————— (Three characteristics or verbs describing line 7)
————— ————— (Two words describing line 7)
————— (One noun that is the opposite of line 1)

Following is an example of septain written by a sixth grader.

> Valley
> green warm
> descending growing rolling
> flowers animals boulders rocks
> snowing ascending climbing
> cold rough
> Mountain
>
> *John Dorn, sixth grade*

We have found that some of our most exciting experiences with creative writing have occurred as a result of using mosaic poetry. As its name implies, a mosaic poem is comprised of a composite of words and phrases contributed by many different individuals. Members of the class contribute words, phrases, and sentences that a specific topic brings to mind. Then, working in small groups, the class rearranges the disparate contributions to form a poem. Occasionally, prepositions, conjunctions, and other small phrases can be added; if possible, each student's contribution should be used. When working with children in the primary and even intermediate grades, the teacher rather than the students will probably have to unite the words and phrases into coherent whole.

One class given the topic of war contributed the following words and phrases:

| | |
|---|---|
| living in fear | oppressed |
| why do we fight | countries destroyed |
| thousands of people involved | who profits |
| | death |
| conflict between groups | peace |
| homeless, thousands | hatred |
| stupid | handicapped |
| prisoners of war | people killed |
| constant motion | where is peace |
| hunger | marches |
| victims | riots |

and then compiled these words and phrases into the following poem:

WAR

People killed
Thousands of people involved in conflict between
    groups,
The constant stupid motion of marches and riots.
Hunger everywhere, victims oppressed, countries
    destroyed,
Prisoners of war, handicapped, homeless.
Who profits from this living in fear, this death?
    Why do we fight?
    Where is peace?

Another class, given the topic of a day at the beach, created a mosaic poem with an ecological theme:

Whose ocean this is, I know;
    It belongs to the people.
Crowds and crowds and crowds
    Own the ocean.
They envelop it with transistor radios,
With french fried board walks.
They surround it with oil slick bodies,
With couples kissing under striped umbrellas;
They cover it with sailboats,
With frisbees that mock the gliding seagulls,
While white creamed, muscled life guards
    Play god over all
Night comes—reflects the moon.
Rolling waves swallow man made sand castles,
Leave broken shells and thrashing foam.
Who owns the ocean—never ending, tranquil,
    empty.
No one owns the ocean—but the ocean.

We have discussed some techniques for encouraging word play and for generating poetry through the use of several specific poetry forms. In the following Related Learning Activities there are suggestions, using these techniques and others, for encouraging creative writing that is directly related to children's literature.

*Related learning activities*

1. Children can write cinquain poetry about a favorite character from children's literature. In a storytelling session one group of primary-grade children listened to *The Story of Ferdinand* and carefully studied Robert Lawson's pictures. The story of the iconoclast bull who wanted to smell the flowers rather than become a bullring hero amused the children and fired their imaginations. They learned the rules for cinquain poetry, and then they formed groups to write cinquain about this character. Here is one cinquain written by a group of first graders:

Ferdinand
    gentle quiet
    hates to fight
    he likes to smell
        flowers.

Try writing a cinquain about a favorite character so that you will have a better feeling for what you will be asking your students to do. Then, after reading aloud or telling a story to a small group of students, teach them the cinquain form and work with them to develop a cinquain about the story's central character. If possible, have a peer, a supervisor, and/or a videotape recorder to help you evaluate your lesson.

2. Students can also write mosaic poetry to convey the images and feelings a particular book, character, or setting elicits. In a micro-teaching or classroom situation, teach a lesson similar to the preceding one, but work with mosaic instead of cinquain poetry. Do you find one form more effective than the other in generating creative writing? Why?

3. Septain can be effective when children have read a book or several books that include contrasting characters. An upper elementary student expressed her view of the opposing sides in Jean Merrill's *The Pushcart War* through septain.

Pushcarts
colorful, picturesque
aesthetic, slow, peaceful
personal, quiet, big-time movers
rushing, honking, noisy
huge, oppressive
Mack Trucks

Join with a group of students from your class and write a septain about two contrasting characters, either from the same book or from two different books. Share your septain with other members of your class.

4. There are several exquisite picture books with nature or ecological themes. After reading a book such as Tresselt's *The Dead Tree* or Alice Goudy's *Houses from the Sea*, try writing a haiku to capture the mood or theme of the book. After you have tried this activity yourself, you might want to incorporate it into

a lesson for elementary or secondary school students.

5. Even very young children delight in Mary O'Neal's *Hailstones and Halibut Bones*, and this book often inspires children to write various forms of color poetry. The following color poems were written by primary-grade children at the Beauvoir School in Washington, D.C.:

GREEN
Green is my favorite color—
Green is a chair, grass, a pear.
Green is a shoe, a sweat shirt, too.
An apple is green, or a watermelon skin,
Or a chalkboard, or a banana that is really thin.

*Brandy Strauss*

PURPLE
Purple is a night color that strolls through
                    dark corners
And is allowed to go everywhich way.
It comes at evening and at dawn.
People go through city streets and
                look down at things.
All they see is purple.

*Peter Cook*

PINK
Pink is pretty stones.
A bride's dress, a flower girl's dress
            and a communion dress.
Pink is the loveliness of spring.
Pink is gentle.
It's soft.
It's powder.

*Cecilia Calvo*

Try developing a color poetry lesson using *Hailstones and Halibut Bones* as a springboard. Teach it to members of your class or to a group of elementary school students. This activity lends itself naturally to work in other creative areas such as art and music.

6. Although Edward Lear did not invent the limerick, he was certainly a master of this form and responsible for increasing its popularity.

Children enjoy writing limericks about some of the more humorous characters in literature, and we have found Dr. Seuss characters to be particularly effective in generating nonsense verse and limericks. After trying your hand at a few limericks, develop a creative writing lesson using this form. Before expecting students to write limericks, be sure that they understand the structure of this five-line verse with its a/a/b/b/a rhyme scheme.

7. Rather than assigning a global topic for children to write stories or themes about, many teachers have found that giving students a vivid beginning or concluding sentence is often more effective in generating creative writing. Many such opening and ending sentences can be garnered from children's books.

Joan Aiken is a master craftsperson in setting an eerie, suspenseful mood, and her books often open with sentences or paragraphs that capture the reader's attention. Students can use the following to develop some spine tinglers of their own.

It had been raining all day. Even in good weather the park around Midnight Court was not a cheerful place.[20]
(From *Midnight Is a Place*)

It was dusk—winter dusk. Snow lay white and shining over the pleated hills, and icicles hung from the forest trees.[21]
(From *The Wolves of Willoughby Chase*)

Madeleine L'Engle's *A Wrinkle in Time* also provides a suspenseful opening:

It was a dark and stormy night. In her attic bedroom Margaret Murray, wrapped in an old patchwork quilt, sat on the foot of her bed and watched trees tossing in the frenzied lashing of the wind. Every few moments the moon ripped through them, creating wraith-like shadows that raced along the ground.[22]

The books of Sid Fleishman, a writer skilled in the art of the tall tale, frequently begin and end with lines that can stimulate student creativity. The opening lines of *Mr. Mysterious and Company* are effective in generating student writing:

It was a most remarkable sight. Even the hawks and buzzards sleeping in the blue Texas sky awoke in mid-air to glance down in wonder.[23]

We have also used the opening and closing sentences of *McBroom's Ghost*, with imaginative student writing as the result.

*Opening:* Ghosts? mercy, yes—I can tell you a thing or three about ghosts. As sure as my name's Josh McBroom a haunt came lurking about our wonderful one-acre farm.[24]

*Closing:* Well, that's the truth about our prairie winters and McBroom's ghost—as sure as I'm a truthful man.[25]

We have also found that the concluding line of Collier and Collier's *My Brother Sam Is Dead* generates some provocative themes about war from older students.

But somehow, even fifty years later, I keep thinking that there might have been another way, beside war, to achieve the same end.[26]

Analyze a variety of children's books to select what you think are effective opening and closing lines. By sharing these with other students in your class, you can develop a pool of theme generators. Try them out with small groups of elementary and secondary school students to see if they are indeed effective in stimulating creative writing.

8. Dr. Seuss is a highly inventive writer when it comes to creating nonsensical names and words. So is A. A. Milne. Walter Petty and Mary Bowen in *Slithery Snakes and Other Aids to Children's Writing* suggest that children also love to invent nonsense and write about nonsense language. If you provide chil-

dren with nonsense titles, such as "The Day I Tricked a Flooble" or "All About Aunt Josephine's Glug," you may be delighted with the results.

Make up a few such titles and try them out with elementary school children. You probably will find that students can help you increase your collection, for many can invent their own nonsense titles.

9. An effective way to generate writing is to encourage students to identify with an inanimate object and write a story from the point of view of that object. We have seen some uniquely inventive stories told from the point of view of a penny, a piece of bubble gum, an old school desk, or a pair of shoes. Since many children's books are written about inanimate objects, they can provide a wealth of different perspectives. For stories about dolls try Rumer Godden's *The Dolls' House, Impunity Jane,* or *Miss Happiness and Miss Flower.* There is also Margery Williams Bianco's *The Velveteen Rabbit;* Rachel Field's *Hitty, Her First Hundred Years;* Carolyn Sherwin Bailey's *Miss Hickory;* or Carlo Lorenzini's *The Adventures of Pinocchio.* Books incorporating the point of view of other inanimate objects include Hardie Gramaty's *Little Toot;* Wilson Gage's *Miss Osborne-the-Mop;* or Virginia Burton's *Mike Mulligan and His Steam Shovel, The Little House, Choo Choo,* and *Katy and the Big Snow.*

With your classmates compile a list of other children's books about inanimate objects. Read one of these books to a group of elementary or secondary school students, and then encourage them to write their own stories from the perspective of objects of their choosing. Share the results with your classmates. By the way, this same approach is also effective using the point of view of animals instead of objects, and there are innumerable animal stories to help generate such writing.

10. Stories about one form of inanimate ob-

ject, the machine, can be effective in another way. For example, after reading Ian Fleming's *Chitty Chitty Bang Bang* or William Pène du Bois' *The Twenty-one Balloons,* childern may want to write about their own fantastic traveling machine.

Make up a list of your own marvelous machines, such as the Tipsey Topsy Machine, the Mover Groover Machine, the Dandy Candy Machine, the Half-Baked Machine. Try out your collection with a group of elementary students to see what kinds of stories they generate. Share the results with other students in your class.

11. Children often enjoy writing sequels to stories about their favorite characters. Fairy tale characters such as Rumpelstiltskin, Sleeping Beauty, or Cinderella are often favorites for this activity, but children will also be eager to write about many others, such as Robert McCloskey's *Homer Price,* Donald Sobol's *Encyclopedia Brown,* Beverly Cleary's *Ramona,* Marjorie Flack's *Ping the Duck,* Ludwig Bemelmans's *Madeline,* and Astrid Lindgren's *Pippi Longstockings,* to name just a few.

Develop and teach a creative writing lesson in which your objective is for students to write the further adventures of a particular character. Before you try this, consider what questions you may want to ask the students about the nature of the character and his or her previous escapades. Share the results of this creative writing lesson with your classmates.

12. Following is a partial listing of creative writing ideas that students from our children's literature classes have developed. They come from various books and magazines, from other teachers, and from their own work with children, writing, and books. Join with members of your class to see how many ideas you can add to the list.

a. Use music as a backdrop to creative writing.

b. Use evocative pictures to stimulate writing.

c. Give students a list of anywhere from three

to ten words, such as:

(balloon)  (octopus)  (riddle)

and ask them to write a story incorporating those words.

d. After students have read Rudyard Kipling's *Just So Stories*, ask students to make up pourquoi stories of their own, such as "Why does the octopus have eight legs?"

e. Use newspaper headlines to generate stories.

f. Use plot synopses from *T.V. Guide* to generate stories.

g. Use brief plot summaries of books, such as those provided by publishers for advertising, to generate stories.

h. Read a story, stop at a crucial point, and let students finish the story. Then compare their endings to the author's.

i. Use various forms of the traveling story. For example, one student begins telling a story, and at a sign from the teacher, the first student stops and another begins. This goes on until several students have participated, and the story has worked its way to a conclusion.

j. Have two inanimate objects talk to one another. For example, "What might the log say to the fire?" or "What might lightning say to thunder?"

k. Captalize on field trips to a zoo, a farm, an aquarium, a museum, and so on, to generate student writing.

## Other aesthetic experiences

The seventh-grade class had just finished reading Conrad Richter's *The Light in the Forest*, the story of True Son, a white boy captured and reared by the Indians and forced as an adolescent to return to white society. It is essentially the story of a boy who is on the edge of two cultures and who cannot find a place for himself in either society. The class had become deeply involved in and moved by the novel and, with the teacher's guidance, de- termined to interpret True Son's dilemma through a series of aesthetic activities. The class divided into groups, with each group having the responsibility of expressing the novel through either drama, art, music, or dance.

This class had previous work in creative drama, and the drama group enthusiastically began selecting scenes and characters. They determined to play three key scenes in the novel—the highly emotional scene in which True Son is forced to leave his Indian family; the revulsion True Son feels when a crass white relative denounces the boy's "barbaric" past; and the final scene, when True Son realizes that he belongs to neither the white nor the Indian culture and that he has no place to go. The art group worked with the drama group in the selection of these three scenes and then developed them into a vibrant, wall-length mural to form a backdrop against which the creative drama was played out. The class had worked on mural making before; like the creative drama group, this group of children had little difficulty in becoming involved in the activity.

The other students, however, had not had any previous background in creating music or dance, and their inexperience showed. At first the music group just played around with the instruments the music teacher had brought in —drums, cymbals, triangles, xylophones, and recorders. However, after a period of experimentation, the children began to improvise a score to convey the mood and theme of the novel. For example, xylophones and recorders expressed the sense of peace True Son found with his Indian family, and drums and cymbals became the predominant instruments when True Son was feeling torn between the two cultures, not knowing where to turn.

The ten girls in the dance group were initially the most reluctant of all, almost fearful of using their bodies to convey the mood of the novel. However, when they did manage to break out of their inhibited pattern, the results were at times stunning. The dance they finally created was a mixture of literal and symbolic interpretation. Often they merely pantomimed the scenes, but on a few rare moments they reached the level of dancing out the story's mood and theme.

In this project teachers from various aesthetic areas joined together to make this work of literature come alive through different artistic forms. It is but one example of how literature can be joined with other arts to stimulate student creativity.

*Related learning activities*

1. Creative aesthetic experiences can occur when children have been excited or moved by a good story, when art and music materials are available, and when children have sufficient time and space to manipulate and experiment with the materials.

Select a book and help interpret its mood and theme through musical instruments. You will have to provide instruments such as cymbals, drums, recorders, and xylophones, and it may be necessary to enlist the aid of a music teacher or somone skilled in the use of these instruments.

2. A variety of art activities can function as a powerful corollary to the literature program.

a. Mural making. To make murals children need a long strip of wrapping or shelf paper, tempera paint, and large brushes. A literary selection upon which a mural is to be based should be one that conveys vivid mental images, for the art work should be vibrant and bold, with a minimum of tiny detail. To avoid later confusion children should have a cohesive plan for the composition of their mural before they begin to paint.

b. Frieze making. A frieze is a long, thin decorative border. In the classroom children can cut out objects and figures and paste them on a long, narrow strip of paper. Accumulative tales in which characters or events are added one at a time make particularly good subjects for frieze construction.

c. Collage. A collage is made by gluing materials of different texture and shape onto a flat surface. Such material may consist of paper, cloth, yarn, buttons, seeds, rice, different shapes of macaroni, and a wide variety of other materials that have intriguing colors, shapes, patterns, or textures. Since collages lend themselves to abstract design, they are effective for showing children that art need not always be literal and realistic.

d. Easel painting. Painting with tempera paint at an art easel is a common activity in elementary school classrooms, and a very significant one. Ofter children are happy with large splashes of color, but at other times they want to paint a particular picture, often about a character, scene, or event from their literature.

Select a book such as John Burningham's *Mr. Gumpy's Outing* or Wanda Gàg's *Millions of Cats,* and help a group of elementary school children construct a frieze or mural based on the story.

Characters from modern fantasy often make good subjects for collages. Work with a group of elementary students in developing collage characters from a fanciful tale of their choice.

## Literature and the affective experience

Involvement with literature is both a cognitive and an affective experience for children. On the cognitive side children must, for example, understand plot development and character development and the way theme relates to the story. They must comprehend, analyze, synthesize, and evaluate. But literature also, perhaps more than any other area of the curriculum, has the ability to stimulate an affective or emotional response in children. In this section we discuss pertinent teaching skills and value clarification strategies that help students express, reflect upon, and clarify the feelings and values that a literary selection may evoke.

## Interpersonal communication skills

The loud shrill of the bell sounds, but the students continue chatting with their friends and walking around the room. The teacher, Ms. Miller, urges them to settle down.

MS. MILLER: Allright class, settle down. We have a good deal of material to cover today.

Slowly the students take their seats and clear the miscellaneous materials off their desks. The noise subsides.

MS. MILLER: Today we will discuss the book you just finished, Hans Peter Richter's *Friedrich.* What's the story about, Susan?

SUSAN: Well, Friedrich is a Jewish boy living in Germany during World War II. He makes friends with a German boy, but the Nazis make it difficult for Friedrich and his parents to do anything—work, go to school, even go to the park. Friedrich's father refuses to believe that the Germans could be so cruel, and the German family really doesn't help. Finally Friedrich and his parents are killed.

MS. MILLER: Good summary, Susan. How exactly was Friedrich killed? Jack?

JACK: Actually, he was killed by Allied bombs because the Germans refused to let him into the air raid shelter.

MS. MILLER: That's right. Why didn't Hans and his family hide Friedrich?

ROBIN: Because they were frightened at what might happen to them if they were caught hiding a Jew.

MS. MILLER: Very fine. You seem to have really gotten the main points of the story. This book will be included in the theme paper you will be asked to write later this semester.

(*There is an audible collective groan.*)

Classroom interactions similar to this one occur in more extended form in schools across the nation. Many teachers view the mastery of cognitive information that pertains to a story as the most crucial material to be learned, and certainly the easiest to test. Think back to your own years in elementary and secondary school. How often were you asked to recount the plot and identify which character did what to whom? Or perhaps you were asked to write a book report to conform to an outline similar to the one following:

First paragraph: Include title, author, publishing company, year of publication, and why you chose to read this book.
Middle paragraphs: Describe the main points of the story.
Concluding paragraphs: Did you like the book? Why? Would you recommend it to others?

Although an understanding of the story line is a necessary step to enjoying a book, it is not the final step. Indeed teachers who restrict the study of literature to this level of understanding ignore the real power of books to move children. Books have an emotional impact. They can affect the development of attitudes and values. They help to create or reduce prejudice. They can alter, for better or worse, a reader's view concerning a given issue, or concerning society at large.

Unfortunately, too often educators do not effectively deal with the power of books to affect the feelings, attitudes, and values of young readers. No doubt this is partially due to the fact that teachers generally receive no training in techniques that can help students share their attitudes and values and clarify them. It is also due to the belief held by some that teachers should not concern themselves with value laden issues and the expression of concerns and feelings that they may generate. "Stick to the facts. Leave values out of it. Be objective!"

Such a position is ultimately untenable, for education has always touched the attitudes and values of children. Although this impact is usually not reflected in lesson plans and the official curriculum, it has always occurred incidentally as part of what has become known as the "hidden curriculum." In informal discussions and interactions in school corridors, on the playground, wherever children assemble together, attitudes are expressed and perhaps altered. However, by bringing such discussions into the classroom and by using pertinent interpersonal communication skills and values clarification strategies, teachers can help students become aware of their feelings and values and realize the consequent effect of these feelings and values on the way they behave and act.

Education that disassociates itself from the affective concerns and emotions of children is meaningless, or even worse, dangerous. Germany, for example, had a superior technical education system before World War II and managed to run very efficient concentration camps. In the United States a "high government official," a graduate of some of the nation's finest schools, became deeply involved in the Watergate scandal and explained on his way to prison that he had "lost his ethical compass." Our educational process must help today's children and tomorrow's citizens reflect and clarify as they develop their personal value systems.

The question that naturally follows is, "In which direction should our student's ethical compasses point?" What values should be taught? Obviously it would be in itself immoral to impose a fixed and singular set of values on children. However, we are suggesting that value issues and related children's books, like many of those explored in this text, should be vital components of the curriculum. We believe that children should confront issues that will affect their lives and society at large

and that this exploration should take place in a free and open school environment. In such an environment children can be encouraged to share their values, analyze them, and when they consider it appropriate, alter or modify them.

In this chapter we suggest several techniques that do not impose a particular set of values on students but rather encourage them to express what they feel and reflect upon what they care about. Although the books discussed in this text provide a beginning for values discussions, educators cannot assume that reading alone will result in acquisition of self-knowledge and the ability to reflect upon and clarify values. However, there are teaching skills and strategies that can aid students in this process. In the last section of this chapter we offer a series of values clarification exercises that pertain to selected children's books and deal with the various topics discussed in this book. But first we briefly outline some skills through which educators can encourage values discussions in a classroom environment.[27]

The initial step in dealing with children's feelings, attitudes, and values is to establish open lines of communication. Children and adults must feel comfortable and at ease if they are to disclose their feelings and values honestly. Following are descriptions of selected teaching skills that can be used to encourage free and open communication and that, in conjunction with the study of literature, can help students become aware of their feelings and values, and share them, and reflect upon them and the effect they may have on behavior.

## Attending behavior

Did you ever speak to someone whose eyes seemed to be zeroed in on some object approximately one foot to your right? Or have you ever become somewhat disappointed when the person that you were conversing with reacts to your comments with a response that indicates he has heard or understood nothing of what you said? Unless you attend to your students' comments, unless they perceive you as a good listener, there is little chance that they will discuss their feelings and values with you. Good listeners encourage sharing; poor listeners do not. The skill of attending behavior is fundamental and not particularly difficult. Good eye contact, a nod of your head now and then, and short verbal encouragers like *uh uh* or *I see* are simple physical demonstrations that you are paying attention, that you are listening. In addition, a cognitive demonstration of your understanding of what is said can be accomplished by briefly summarizing the main points expressed by the speaker. Such summaries should be extremely brief but indicate to the speaker that you are indeed following what is said.

Naturally you need to practice this skill and the other skills in this section in order to develop and improve them. But good attending behavior is fundamental to the success of the other skills and is an important factor in interpersonal communications of any sort. It must be stressed that this is not a mechanical process; rather, underlying effective attending behavior must be a sincere interest in what your students have to say.

## Inventory questions

Research has indicated that an extremely small percentage of teacher-pupil interactions is concerned with the vital areas of values and feelings. One reason for this is the fact that teachers frequently do not ask questions in this area. Inventory questions can help to remedy this situation. Inventory questions ask the students to take a self-inventory, to share values or feelings related to a certain issue, and to identify the thoughts, feelings, and actions with which they characteristically respond to specific stimuli that they may encounter in their lives or in the books they read. Inventory questions also help students identify discrepancies between what they value and how they behave or between what their value system currently is and what they ideally would like it to be. For example, in Virginia Hamilton's *The Planet of Junior Brown*, a teacher might ask, "How would you feel if you were Junior Brown? What sentences are running through your head as Junior is carrying the body out of the apartment? Do you think he was doing the right thing by keeping those boys in his 'family'? How would you feel being a member of his family? When Junior became frightened, he stopped talking and seemed to go into his own little world. What do you do when you feel frightened? What part of your body is most affected by fear? Are there characteristic ways with which you typically respond when you are afraid? Do these responses serve you well, or would you, in some way, like to change your behavoir?"

Inventory questions turn the focus on to the students and ask them to share their feelings and values. Literature can stimulate such questions by providing situations and issues that serve as good topics for exploration.

## Reflection

Long a skill used in counseling, reflection may be used by teachers to help students clarify their values. Reflecting holds a mirror up to students and gives them information about the way their verbal and nonverbal messages are being received. When reflecting, teachers may simply repeat the main thought or idea in a student's comment. They may also describe the nonverbal messages a student is transmitting. A more complex form of reflecting requires that the teacher make an inference concerning what thoughts or feelings may underlie a student's verbal or nonverbal message.

These three types of reflecting offer the student the opportunity to become more aware of what he or she has said and to take a moment to consider the feelings and values that were expressed.

## Modifying behavior

Since values serve as guides to behavior, modifying or changing values should be reflected in modified or changed behaviors. For example, a student who verbally has come to understand the ramifications of sexism should be encouraged to demonstrate this new attitude in his or her behavior. Teacher and students could brainstorm and suggest ways that this newly integrated value can be reflected in behavior. Perhaps everyday activities could be modified or activities with just one person could be altered to reflect this new sensitivity. Or perhaps a commitment could be made to read related literature. Even small steps are significant, since behavior change is a slow process. But reflecting in behavior those values that have been expressed and clarified verbally is a critical step. It provides students with the opportunity to demonstrate new behaviors that may be more congruent with changing attitudes or values, and it brings reality into the classroom and the literature program.

We have briefly described some interpersonal communication skills that encourage student expression and clarification of feelings and values. Let us now look again at the opening scenario to see how such skills could have been used in the discussion of *Friedrich*.

> The loud shrill of the bell sounds, but the students continue chatting with their friends and walking around the room. The teacher, Ms. Miller, urges them to settle down.
>
> Slowly the students take their seats and clear the miscellaneous materials off their desks. The noise subsides.

MS. MILLER: Today we will discuss the book you just finished, Hans Peter Richter's *Friedrich*. What's the story about, Susan?

SUSAN: Well, Friedrich is a Jewish boy living in Germany during World War II. He makes friends with a German boy, but the Nazis make it difficult for Friedrich and his parents to do anything—work, go to school, even go to the park. Friedrich's father refuses to believe that the Germans could be so cruel, and the German family and his parents are killed.

MS. MILLER: Good summary, Susan. How exactly was Friedrich killed? Jack?

JACK: Actually, he was killed by Allied bombs because the Germans refused to let him into the air raid shelter.

MS. MILLER: That's right. Why didn't Hans and his family hide Friedrich?

ROBIN: Because they were frightened at what might happen to them if they were caught hiding a Jew.

MS. MILLER (inventory question): How would you have felt if you were a member of the German family? Dennis?

DENNIS: I would have been frightened, but I hope I wouldn't have acted like they did.

MS. MILLER (reflection): So what you are saying is that you hope you would have enough courage to stand up for what you believe and help others—even if the result might be personal danger.

DENNIS: Yes. That's how I feel about it.

MS. MILLER (inventory question): How would you have felt if you were a member of the German family, Sally?

SALLY: I would have been very worried and anxious. I know the position of that family was wrong, but, realistically, I don't see how they could have done anything else.

MS. MILLER (reflection): You're saying that you, also, would have been very worried, and, perhaps, if you were in the position of that family, you might have acted as they did.

SALLY: Well, I guess maybe I would have acted as they did.

MS. MILLER (reflection): I can see by the puzzled look on your face that you would find this a difficult moral problem to wrestle with and you feel uncomfortable with how you might have behaved in that situation.

SALLY: Yes.

MS. MILLER (inventory): Sally, let's change the focus for a minute. How would you feel if you were in Friedrich's situation?

SALLY: Totally frustrated. And very frightened and helpless. Through no fault of his own, simply because he was Jewish, he lost everything—even his life.

MS. MILLER (reflection and inventory): You mentioned that if you were the German family you would be worried and confused and that if you were Friedrich you would feel very frightened. Where in your body do you feel worry and where do you feel fear? Are the feelings in the same place or in different places?

SALLY: Very different. I feel worry in my head, maybe in the place between my eyes. But fear I feel in my stomach and my heart and it's a much stronger, much tenser feeling.

MS. MILLER: Well, class, our discussion is touching the heart of what *Friedrich* is about. We have a German family that was unwilling to give help in the face of possible danger and a Jewish family that was destroyed as the result.

You know that you will be asked to write a paper concerning *Friedrich* later in the semester. Think about the following questions for potential inclusion in this theme.

(Inventory): Has there ever been a time when you had to consider taking a personal, moral stand that you knew would result in consequences that would jeopardize you in some way? How did you feel in that situation? How did you act? As you look back upon the situation, are you satisfied with your behavior or do you wish that you could, in some way, change the way you acted?

(Inventory): As you review the story for the theme and unit test, Sally, I'd like you to think a little more about how the German family and how Friedrich felt in their respective situations, and

reflect again on how you would behave if you were in the position of the German family.

This classroom interaction is a brief sample of how some interpersonal communication skills can be used in the classroom. By using inventory questions and reflections, Ms. Miller was able to raise the discussion above mere plot summary and even to carry it beyond a cognitive analysis of the story's theme. She helped students identify with the characters, and she used the story's situation to encourage students to express and clarify their feelings and values. Through interpersonal communication skills, this teacher elicited affective comments and intensified the potential of literature to have an impact on children.

The value clarification strategies in the next section provide you with practical classroom strategies that encourage students to share their values. The exercises help students to clarify their positions, and some exercises suggest ways that students can act on their values. These value clarification strategies are related to the issues and themes found in many of the children's books we have discussed. Used in conjunction with related literature and with the skills described in this section, these exercises provide you with a practical technique for dealing with substantive issues in your classroom.

## Values clarification strategies

The first comprehensive explication of values clarification was presented by Raths, Harmin, and Simon in *Values and Teaching* (1966).[28] Since then many other books and articles have emerged to discuss values clarification and expand the exercises that can be used in this process. Values clarification is not concerned with the content of people's values but rather with their process of valuing. Its aim is not that of values inculcation but rather that of helping students clarify both those values that have already been formed and those that are still emerging. Some of the exercises are simply designed to encourage students to express their feelings on these issues. Others ask them to analyze and clarify their attitudes and values. Still others may help students identify incongruities, such as, for example, a potential discrepancy between an individual's stated value and his or her actual behavior.

Following are a few key values clarification strategies that could be used to help children explore their values and attitudes concerning issues raised in children's books. In each case we briefly describe a values clarification exercise and then apply it directly to a book discussed in this text, to illustrate how these strategies can be used in making a children's literature program responsive to the affective impact of children's books.

*Values sheets*

Values sheets are comprised of thought-provoking statements or quotes. These are followed by questions that ask students to express their values concerning the statement or quotation that they have just read. A values sheet based on Nicholasa Mohr's *Nilda* could be constructed as follows:

Mrs. Ramirez, Nilda's dying mother, gives her the following advice:

Do you have that feeling, honey? That you have something all yours . . . you must . . . like when I see you drawing sometimes, I know you have something all yours. Keep it . . . hold on, guard it. Never give it to nobody . . . not to your lover, not to your kids. . . . We are all born alone . . . and we all die alone. And when I die, Nilda, I know I take nothing with me that is only mine.[29]

1. Do you think that it is important to "have something all yours," something that you would never share? Why?

2. Do you have something special, some talent or interest that marks you as an individual with something of your very own? What is it? Why is it special to you?

3. How can you preserve a place of your own, a talent or interest or purpose that is uniquely yours in the years ahead?

4. Mrs. Ramirez gave her time and efforts totally to her family, and she died with nothing of her own. Do you think these sacrifices are more likely to be made by women than by men? Why? Can you identify any women or men who you think are making the same kind of sacrifice as that made by Mrs. Ramirez?

5. If you were a reporter on a local newspaper, what would you write for Mrs. Ramirez' obituary?

6. If you were asked to explain how you were special or unique, or to describe some accomplishment that you were particularly proud of, what would you say?

*Values voting*

The teacher reads aloud a sentence beginning, "How many of you . . . ?" Those who respond affirmatively raise their hands; those who respond negatively point their thumbs down; those who are undecided or wish to pass fold their arms. This strategy gives students the opportunity to take a position on an issue and also to view the spectrum of opinion on that issue. If they wish, students can explain why they have voted a particular way on a given issue.

For example, Sharon Bell Mathis' *The Hundred Penny Box* is a sensitive exploration of the aging process and of the bond between young and old. "Values voting" questions such as the following could help students express their response to this book and to clarify their feelings and values about what it means to grow old.

How many of you

1. Think that Michael's mother should throw away the Hundred Penny Box?
2. Think that Aunt Dew, as she is portrayed in the illustrations, is ugly? Is beautiful?
3. Have ever known an old person who you thought was beautiful?
4. Think that Aunt Dew would be better off in a nursing home?
5. Would want one of your grandparents to move in with your family?
6. Have ever been inside a nursing home?
7. Have had a close relationship with a grandparent?
8. Have ever thought about what it would be like to be old—perhaps as old as Aunt Dew?
9. Think that the United States should spend more money to improve the quality of life for its elderly citizens?

### Unfinished sentences

The teacher gives the students incomplete sentences, which the students are asked to finish. The students' responses can be shared or they may remain private. For example, unfinished sentences could be constructed around the issues in Charlotte Zolotow's *William's Doll*, a brief but effective picture book about a boy who wants a doll but encounters a good deal of opposition. After reading this book, elementary students could participate in completing "unfinished sentences" such as the following:

1. I think William should/should not be given a doll because _____
2. I would/would not want William for a friend because _____
3. When I see a five-year-old girl playing with a doll, I _____
4. When I see a five-year-old boy playing with a doll, I _____
5. When I see Rosey Greer doing needlepoint, I _____

6. To me women's liberation _____
7. I think that a nonsexist book is _____

### Rank orders

The teacher asks the class a question and suggests three or four potential answers to the question. The students then rank-order their choices as to their first preference, second preference, and so on. The students can discuss their preferences in small groups or as a total class. This strategy helps students to choose from competing alternatives and to share and discuss the values that helped them to make their choices.

The following rank orders could generate a values discussion based on William Sleator's *House of Stairs*, a gripping story of a bizarre experiment in psychological conditioning and of violent intrusion on the human mind.

1. Rank-order the five characters in *House of Stairs* according to which you most admire: Peter, Lola, Blossom, Abigail, Oliver.
2. Which do you think the greater evil: torture of the human body or torture of the human mind?
3. If you had been placed in the House of Stairs, which decision do you think you would have made: to defy the machine no matter how devastating the consequences (Lola and Peter) or to succumb to the machine in order to survive (Blossom, Oliver, and Abigail)?
4. It is the responsibility of a government to strive to achieve the best goals for all its citizens. In reaching these goals a government may have to deprive some of its citizens of their rights and their freedom, as demonstrated in Sleator's *House of Stairs*.
   a. This is always a right of government.
   b. This is often a right of government.
   c. This is a function of government that should only be exercised on rare occasions.

d. Under no circumstances may government deprive its law abiding citizens of their rights.

*Values continuum*

The teacher draws a line or continuum on the blackboard. Polar positions are written on either end of the continuum, and each student goes to the blackboard and places a mark on the continuum that indicates his or her position on the issue. The student can then give some of the reasons for the position taken. The more extreme the polar positions are, the greater the number of options available to students.

In the sample continuum shown below, polar positions A and B were written by the teacher; the other positions—1, 2, 3, and 4—were offered by students.

In *Journey to Topaz*, by Uchida, or in Katushima's *A Child in Prison Camp* we learn about the deprivations suffered by Japanese citizens of America and Canada during World War II. Both books explore the relocation of the Japanese to camps based not on their loyalty or disloyalty to Canada or the United States, but only on the fact that they were Japanese. Here are some examples of how the values continuum could be applied to *Journey to Topaz* to help children identify their own position on the treatment of Japanese-Americans.

*Sample Continuum*

Issue: Do you believe in capital punishment?

Choose a point on each of the following continuums on page 417. Then describe what that point stands for. What specifically is your position on this issue?

*Related learning activities*

1. Select two books discussed in the chapter "Facing the Reality of Death in Children's Literature." For each book construct at least one rank order that explores the issue of death.

2. Ask your students to respond to the rank orders. Ask them to explain *why* they held preferences for certain choices. As your students respond to the rank orders, try to use the interpersonal communication skills. See how many skills you can use comfortably, and over time, try to increase your repertoire and include the following: attending behavior, inventory questions, reflection, and modifying behavior.

3. Construct a values sheet for *Grandmother Didn't Wave Back*, by Rose Blue. Try to choose a paragraph or quote that reflects an important area of concern. Formulate at least five or six questions that are related to the excerpt from the book and ask your students to give serious and personal thought to the issue.

4. Construct a values voting exercise for Alice Childress' *A Hero Ain't Nothin' But a Sandwich*. Try to incorporate a number of

| A | 1 | 2 | 3 | 4 | B |
|---|---|---|---|---|---|
| All criminals for any offense should be executed on the day of their conviction. | All those convicted of murder should be executed. | Those convicted only of premeditated murder should be executed. | Those convicted of mass murder only should be executed. | No executions ever, but no bonuses either. | No criminal should ever be executed. Ex-convicts should be paid "reform bonuses" as a way of deterring their desire or need to commit a crime. |

*Continuum I.* If you were a Japanese-American interned at Topaz, Utah, which position would you take?

Mr. Kurihara:
When the war
is over, go
back to Japan.
_____

Ken's friend:
Join the U.S.
Army and
demonstrate
your loyalty,
even if it
costs your
life.

*Continuum II.* During World War II all Japanese-Americans should have been

brought to
trial, jailed,
or deported
because of
Japan's
attack on the
United States.
_____

put into
positions
of power
because
they better
understand
the enemy
and would
help achieve
a U.S. victory

*Continuum III.* After World War II all imprisoned Japanese-Americans should have

written a
letter of
thanks to the
government
for the free
food and
lodging and
humane care
they received.
_____

received
reparation
for lost
income and
lost freedom
and also
received a
personal
letter of
regret
from the
President.

the different perceptions reflected in the book.

5. Develop a series of unfinished sentences based on Robert Peck's *Fawn*. Try the sentences in class and see which ones seem to be the most effective. Analyze the results and try to identify the qualities of an effective unfinished sentence.

6. After reading one or both of the following paperbacks: *Values and Teaching*, by Raths, Harmin, and Simon, and *Values Clarification*, by Simon, Kirchenbaum, and Howe,

ask your students to continue the values clarification exercises and develop rank orders, values voting, and so on, on their own. Start a file of the most effective exercises developed by yourself and your students.

These selected values clarification strategies represent but a sample of the number and variety of strategies available to teachers. When used in conjunction with the interpersonal communication skills, they can provide a useful vehicle for clarifying and building on the values issues explored in many contemporary children's books.

As James Miller noted at the 1966 Anglo-American Conference at Dartmouth College, "teachers of literature should select books embodying the diverse visions of life and beliefs about values, and then question, discuss, and explore them with the students; this would lead to an awareness of moral complexity, ambiguity, and paradox."[30] Values clarification and interpersonal communication skills provide an approach for this exploration to take place.

The purpose of this chapter has been to suggest creative classroom ideas, to delineate cognitive and affective teaching skills, and to offer examples of values clarification strategies that will aid adults as they explore with children the rich world of children's books. We hope that these ideas will help you to establish creative, sensitive, and productive classroom environments. Effective teachers and the power of children's literature can provide young readers with a deeper, keener, more sensitive, and more tolerant vision, one encompassing all the ambiguity and paradox of life itself. As the noted children's author, Eleanor Cameron, says,

I think that a good many persons . . . feel that bookish people allow reading to take the place of experience, that we are afraid of or want something to substitute for life. But I have always found that far from substituting for it, my reading enlarges life, intensifies the flavor of it, intensifies my seeing, that it deepens each experience by giving me echoes and reverberations and bridges, compelling me always to obey E. M. Forster's precept, "Connect—only connect!"[31]

# NOTES

1. Lucy Nulton, "Eight-Year-Olds Tangled in 'Charlotte's Web,'" *Elementary English*, 31 (January 1954), 16.

2. Dewey W. Chambers, *Literature for Children: Storytelling and Creative Drama*, Dubuque, Iowa, Brown, 1970, p. 43.

3. David Sadker and Myra Sadker, "Everything You Always Wanted to Know About Questions but Were Afraid to Ask," in *Handbook of Teaching Skills*, James Cooper, ed., Lexington, Mass., Heath, 1976.

4. Romiett Stevens, "The Question as a Measure of Classroom Practice," *Teachers College Contributions to Education*, no. 48, New York, Teachers College, Columbia University, 1912.

5. O. L. Davis and Drew Tinsley, "Cognitive Objectives Revealed by Classroom Questions Asked by Social Studies Teachers and Their Pupils," *Peabody Journal of Education*, 44 (July 1967), 21–26. Also, see O. L. Davis and Francis P. Hunkins, "Textbook Questions: What Thinking Processes Do They Foster?" *Peabody Journal of Education*, 43 (March 1966), 285–292.

6. Benjamin Bloom et al., *Taxonomy of Educational Objectives. Handbook I: Cognitive Domain*, New York, McKay, 1956.

7. Mary Budd Rowe, "Wait-Time and Rewards as Instructional Variables: Their Influence on Language, Logic, and Fate Control," paper presented at the National Association for Research in Science Teaching, Chicago, April 1972.

8. G. L. Fahey, "The Questioning Activity of Children," *Journal of Genetic Psychology*, 60 (1942), 337–357.

9. Charlotte S. Huck and Doris Young Kuhn, *Children's Literature in the Elementary School*, 2nd ed., New York, Holt, Rinehart & Winston, 1968, p. 652.

10. Madeleine L'Engle, *A Wrinkle in Time*, New York, Farrar, Straus & Giroux, 1962, pp. 103–104.

11. Winifred Ward, *Drama with and for Children*, Washington, D.C., U.S. Department of Health, Education and Welfare, Bulletin #30, 1960, p. 1.

12. Nellie McCaslin, *Creative Dramatics in the Classroom*, New York, McKay, 1968.

13. Ibid., p. 8.

14. Hans J. Schmidt, "A Creative Approach to Puppetry and Literature," in Sam Leaton Sebesta and William J. Iverson, *Literature for Thursday's Child*, Chicago, Science Research Associates, 1975, p. 487.

15. McCaslin, op. cit., p. 59.

16. These suggestions are based on Betty Coody, *Using Literature with Young Children*, Dubuque, Iowa, Brown, 1973, pp. 52–56.

17. James Smith, *Creative Teaching of the Language Arts in the Elementary School*, 2nd ed., Boston, Allyn & Bacon, 1973, p. 199.

18. Ibid., pp. 38. 39.

19. Adapted from Synectics, Inc., New York, *Making It Strange*, Harper & Row, 1968.

20. Joan Aiken, *Midnight Is a Place*, New York, Viking Press, 1974, p. 9.
21. Joan Aiken, *The Wolves of Willoughby Chase*, ill. by Pat Marriott, Garden City, N.Y., Doubleday, 1962, p. 7.
22. Madeleine L'Engle, *A Wrinkle in Time*, New York, Farrar, Straus & Giroux, 1962, p. 3.
23. Sid Fleishchman, *Mr. Mysterious & Company*, ill. by Eric Von Schmidt, Boston, Little, Brown, 1962, p. 3.
24. Sid Fleischman, *McBroom's Ghost*, ill. by Robert Frankenberg, New York, Grosset & Dunlap, 1971.
25. Ibid.
26. James Lincoln Collier & Christopher Collier, *My Brother Sam Is Dead*, New York, Four Winds, 1974, p. 211.
27. David Sadker and Myra Sadker, "Microteaching for Affective Skills," *Elementary School Journal*, November, 1975.
28. Louis Raths, Merrill Harmin, Sidney Simon, *Values and Teaching*, Columbus, Ohio, Merrill, 1964.
29. Nicholasa Mohr, *Nilda*, New York, Harper & Row, 1973, p. 277.
30. James Miller as quoted in Herbert J. Muller, *The Uses of English*, New York, Holt, Rinehart and Winston, 1967, p. 93.
31. Eleanor Cameron, "McLuhan, Youth, and Literature," *The Horn Book*, 48, no. 5 (October 1972), 433.

# ADULT REFERENCES

ANDERSON, PAUL S. *Language Skills in Elementary Education*, Macmillan, 1964.

———. *Flannelboard Stories for Primary Grades*, Denison, 1962.

ANDERSON, WILLIAM, and PATRICK GROFF. *A New Look at Children's Literature*, Wadsworth, 1972.

APPLEGATE, MAUREE. *Freeing Children to Write*, Harper & Row, 1963.

ARBUTHNOT, MAY HILL, and ZENA SUTHERLAND. *Children and Books*, 4th ed., Scott, Foresman, 1972.

ARNSTEIN, FLORA J. *Poetry in the Elementary Classroom*, Appleton-Century-Crofts, 1962.

———. *Children Write Poetry: A Creative Approach*, Dover, 1967.

BAIRD, BIL. *The Art of the Puppet*, Macmillan, 1965.

BATCHELDER, MARJORIE H., and VIRGINIA COMER. *Puppets and Plays: A Creative Approach*, Harper & Row, 1956.

BLOOM, BENJAMIN, et al. *Taxonomy of Educational Objectives. Handbook 1: Cognitive Domain*, McKay, 1956.

CARLSON, RUTH KEARNEY. *Enrichment Ideas*, 2d. ed., Brown, 1976.

CHAMBERS, DEWEY W. *Children's Literature in the Curriculum*, Rand McNally, 1971.

CIANCIOLO, PATRICIA. *Illustrations in Children's Books*, 2d ed., Brown, 1976.

COODY, BETTY. *Using Literature With Young Children*, Brown, 1973.

COOPER, JAMES, ed. *Handbook of Teaching Skills*, Heath, 1976.

CULLUM, ALBERT. *Push Back the Desks*, Citation, 1968.

GREENE, HARRY A., and WALTER T. PETTY. *Developing Language Skills in the Elementary Schools*, Allyn & Bacon, 1971.

HUCK, CHARLOTTE. *Children's Literature in the Elementary School*, 3rd ed., Holt, Rinehart and Winston, 1976.

KRATHWOHL, DAVID, et al. *Taxonomy of Educational Objectives. Handbook II: Affective Domain*, McKay, 1964.

KOCH, KENNETH. *Wishes, Lies, & Dreams: Teaching Children to Write Poetry*, Chelsea House, 1970.

———. *Rose, Where Do You Get That Red?*, Random House, 1973.

LARRICK, NANCY. *A Parent's Guide to Children's Reading*, 4th ed., Bantam Books, 1975.

LEWIS, SHARI. *Making Easy Puppets*, Dutton, 1967.

LONSDALE, BERNARD J., and HELEN K. MACINTOSH. *Children Experience Literature*, Random House, 1973.

LUKENS, REBECCA. *A Critical Handbook of Children's Literature*, Scott, Foresman, 1976.

MCCASLIN, NELLIB. *Creative Dramatics in the Classroom*, McKay, 1968.

MEARNS, HUGHES. *Creative Power: The Education of Youth in the Creative Arts*, rev. ed., Dover, 1954.

PETTY, WALTER T., and MARY BOWEN. *Slithery Snakes and Other Aids to Children's Writing*, Appleton-Century-Crofts, 1967.

RANDALL, ARNE. *Murals for Schools*, Davis, 1956.

RATHS, LOUIS, MERRILL HARMIN, and SIDNEY SIMON. *Values and Teaching*, Merrill, 1964.

REID, VIRGINIA, ed. *Reading Ladders for Human Re-*

*lations*, 5th ed., Washington, D.C., American Council on Education, 1972.

RUDMAN, MASHA. *Children's Literature: An Issues Approach*, D. C. Heath, 1976.

SAWYER, RUTH. *The Way of the Storyteller*, rev. ed., Viking Press, 1962.

SEBESTA, SAM LEATON, and WILLIAM J. IVERSON. *Literature for Thursday's Child*, Science Research Associates, 1975.

SHAFTEL, FANNIE R., and GEORGE SHAFTEL. *Role-Playing for Social Values*, Prentice-Hall, 1967.

SIKS, GERALDINE B. *Children's Literature for Dramatization*, Harper & Row, 1964.

SMITH, JAMES. *Creative Teaching of the Language Arts in the Elementary School*, 2d ed., Allyn & Bacon, 1973.

SUTHERLAND, ZENA (ed.). *The Best in Children's Books*, The University of Chicago Press, 1973.

TIEDT, IRIS, and SIDNEY TIEDT. *Contemporary English in the Elementary School*, 2d ed., Prentice-Hall, 1975.

TOOZE, RUTH. *Storytelling*, Prentice-Hall, 1959.

TORRANCE, PAUL. *Guiding Creative Talent*, Prentice-Hall, 1962.

WALTER, NINA WILLIS. *Let Them Write Poetry*, Holt, Rinehart and Winston, 1966.

WARD, WINIFRED. *Playmaking with Children*, Appleton-Century-Crofts, 1947.

WHITEHEAD, ROBERT. *Children's Literature: Strategies of Teaching*, Prentice-Hall, 1968.

WILLEK, RENE, and AUSTIN WARREN. *Theory of Literature*, Harcourt Brace Jovanovich, 1956.

# Appendixes

# Appendix A

# Annotated Bibliography of Books Depicting the Handicapped*

One of the major characters in Harper Lee's *To Kill a Mockingbird* is never seen or heard. He is the retarded, grown son who lives next door. Messages are exchanged with him, and he saves the young protagonist from a fierce attack. Everyone in town knows about the man, everyone talks about him, yet everyone pretends that he does not exist.

Art mirrors life, and Harper Lee was portraying the handling of the mentally handicapped as she had known it. To have a child "like that" was a blot on the family name, it meant bad genes. So the child was hidden; life was ended before it began. Although the child might live to old age, it was never more than a "vegetable."

To have a child who was physically handicapped was not necessarily such a shameful burden for a parent to bear. However, such a child was often left to become a burden for society, because no one knew what to do for the child, how to train that young person to become a contributing member of society. Think of the loss to the world if Helen Keller's loving, well-meaning parents had had their way with her. Their love would have left her a prisoner in a dark, silent, wildly terrifying world. Annie Sullivan's love for Helen showed itself in a stern, disciplined way, opened Helen's prison of herself, and gave her the world and her to the world.

Ask any librarian about books that cannot be kept on the shelf, and Helen Keller's autobiography will be at the top of the list. Children who are not particularly good readers take out that book, a long and difficult one to read, and pore over it. Marie Killilea's inspired book about her daughter, *Karen,* is nearly as popular, a book showing a family's loving fight against tremendous odds to provide communication and mobility for Karen, born with cerebral palsy.

* This bibliography was compiled and annotated by Abby Campbell Hunt. She is the book review editor for *Children's House Magazine* and has taught Children's Literature at American University.

Today the handicapped are demanding their long-neglected rights, and society is trying to make their lives easier. States have commissions on the handicapped, with the handicapped themselves in charge. Museums, libraries, and other public facilities are providing ramps and wider doors for wheelchairs, braille floor signs in the elevators, and special tours and displays for the handicapped, much of which has been done by the handicapped themselves. The media are recognizing problems faced by the handicapped. And children's literature now offers some fine portrayals of the struggles, concerns, goals, and hopes of those who happen to be handicapped.

Often the best books in this area are nonfiction; therefore this bibliography is not restricted to fiction. These books, such as E. G. Valens' *The Other Side of the Mountain*, have the wonderful ring of truth. They speak to young readers and offer them a vision of great hope and courage. During National Handicap Week, the blind musician Ray Charles was interviewed on the radio. Here are some of the things he said: "I hate the word *handicap*. A person can have obstacles in his way. Everybody has handicaps. I don't want anybody to feel that he is different because of a handicap. Your neighbor has something he has to live with. . . . O.K., I'm blind. But whatever I do, you can be sure I'm going to do the best I can. . . . Whatever I do, my blindness has nothing to do with it. . . . Cancel that word *handicap*. Tell me that I'm good at whatever I do."

Perhaps by bringing the struggles and the goals of our neighbors out of the closet, we can help to cancel that word *handicap* and help us focus on what every person *can* do, not on what he or she cannot.

## Picture books

BACH, ALICE. *The Smartest Bear and His Brother Oliver*, Steven Kellogg, illus., Harper & Row, 1975 (K–3). Oliver prefers to stuff himself in preparation for hibernation, whereas Ronald wants to spend the winter finishing Volume 5 of the encyclopedia.

BEMELMANS, LUDWIG. *Madeline*, Viking Press, 1939 (Pre–3). Madeline's stay at the hospital, after an attack of appendicitis, is so successful that all of her little friends develop stomachaches.

CAUDILL, REBECCA. *A Certain Small Shepherd*, William Pene du Bois, illus., Holt, Rinehart and Winston, 1965 (2–6). Jamie, mute, grows up angry and frustrated at his handicap. His father's understanding and the birth of a baby on Christmas morning combine to create the miracle of speech for the boy.

HEIDE, FLORENCE P. *Sound of Sunshine, Sound of Rain*, Kenneth Longtemps, illus., Parents, 1970 (K–3). Beautiful illustrations for this book about a blind boy.

KEATS, EZRA JACK. *Apt. 3*, Macmillan, 1971 (K–4). One rainy day two young boys hear harmonica music. When they find the blind harmonica player they talk with him and discover they have made a new friend.

KRAUS, ROBERT. *Leo the Late Bloomer*, Jose Aruego, illus., Dutton, 1973 (Pre–2). Leo is a slow learner. Eventually he catches up with the others, as his mother knew he would.

LIONNI, LEO. *Tico and the Golden Wings*, Pantheon Books, 1964 (1–3). A beautiful tale of a wingless bird. His wish for wings results in golden wings, so that he is still an oddity. He gives his feathers to the poor, and they are replaced by black feathers—a gift of love.

NESS, EVALINE. *The Girl and the Goatherd or This and That and Thus and So*, Dutton, 1970 (K–3). The girl is so very ugly that only the goatherd will have her. Granted beauty by magic, she learns that beauty is not everything and marries the goatherd, who truly loved her all the time.

PEET, BILL. *Fly, Homer, Fly*, Houghton Mifflin, 1969 (K–3). Injured on his return from a visit to the city, Homer is assisted by his sparrow friends.

QUIGLEY, LILLIAN. *The Blind Man and the Elephant*, Janice Holland, illus., Scribner, 1959 (K–4). What an elephant is like depends on one's point of view.

REY, MARGARET, and H. A. SMITH. *Curious George Goes to the Hospital*, Houghton Mifflin, 1966 (Pre–3). George swallows a piece of a jigsaw puzzle and goes to the hospital to have it removed. Although told with great hilarity, this story could be used to acquaint a child with hospital procedure.

ROBINSON, BARBARA. *The Fattest Bear in First Grade*, Random House, 1969 (K–3). The endearing story of a little girl bear who finds out that life is not much fun when you are much too fat. She learns to say, "No, thank you," to the delicious but fattening things she loves to eat, which are served in abundance at her house. Inspired by her success in losing weight, her whole family joins in saying, "No, thank you."

STEIN, SARA BENNETT. *About Handicaps*, photos by Dick Frank, Danbury Press, 1974 (Pre +). This series, designed to be used by adults and children simultaneously, has parallel texts for adult and child facing each full-page photo.

———. *A Hospital Story*, photos by Dick Frank, Danbury Press, 1974 (Pre–2).

WEBER, ALFONS, M.D. *Elizabeth Gets Well*, Jacqueline Blass, illus., Crowell, 1969 (K–3). In school Elizabeth gets a stomachache that turns out to be a bad appendix. A realistic trip to the hospital for surgery, told with great charm.

WHITE, ALICEN. *Walter in Love*, Rosekrans Hoffman, illus., Lothrop, 1973 (K–4). An amusing tale of love between Walter and Tita. Love overcomes Walter's problem of dyslexia.

WILLIAMS, JAY. *Stupid Marco*, Frinso Henstra, illus., Parents, 1970 (Pre–3). Although Marco is "cheerful, good-hearted and handsome," he is not very bright. Sylvia is bright and learns to love Marco because he rescues her from boredom.

## Books for the middle and upper grades

AIKEN, JEAN. *The Mooncusser's Daughter*, Arvis Stewart, illus., Viking Press, 1973 (7+). A fascinating play with some marvelous theatrical effects. One character is the blind mother, honest and innocent, who sees and understands much that those with sight cannot.

ALCOTT, LOUISA MAY. *Jack and Jill*, Louisa May Alcott Library, 1971 (5–9). The third downhill run on a treacherous slope ends in an accident for Jack and Jill. Jack's leg is broken, but it is feared that Jill's back injury may leave her a permanent invalid. Family and friends keep them happily occupied until both are fully recuperated.

———. *Little Men*, Macmillan, 1963 (4–9). Among Jo's "Little Men" are Dick, with the crooked back, who says, "My soul is straight, if my back isn't"; Dolly, who stutters; Billy, whose father drove him to a nervous breakdown; and spoiled, fat Stuffy. Jo and her dear Professor Bhaer help them all with love and understanding. Sequel: *Jo's Boys*.

ALDRIDGE, JAMES. *Sporting Proposition*, Little, Brown, 1973 (7+). Scott, a desperately poor Australian boy, has caught and tamed a wild pony, which then disappears. Soon thereafter, Suzie, rich but crippled with polio, chooses the missing wild pony to draw her pony cart. Both children claim the pony, and the book is the gripping story of their conflict.

ANDERSON, C. W. *The Blind Connemara*, Collier, 1971 (4–6). Rhoda loves a horse that goes blind. It is her task to become the pony's eyes and to gain its trust. She succeeds and is able to enter the blind horse in competition in its class.

ARTHUR, RUTH M. *Portrait of Margarita*, Margery Gill, illus., Atheneum, 1968 (6–8). Margarita knows the pain of discrimination. She finds solace and strength in teaching mentally disturbed children.

BOWDEN, NINA. *Carrie's War*, Lippincott, 1973 (4–6). Evacuated from London during the war, Carrie and her brother are drawn to Hepzibah and Mr. Johnny Gotobed, the "idiot" man she takes care of.

———. *The Witch's Daughter*, Lippincott, 1966 (4–6). A mystery story, set on a remote Scottish island, dealing with a botanist and his family, two jewel robbers, and a blind girl, the witch's daughter.

BECKMAN, GUNNELL. *Admission to the Feast*, Holt, Rinehart and Winston, 1972 (7+). A nineteen-year-old girl discovers she has leukemia. The book deals with her deliberation over her past life and what lies ahead.

———. *The Girl Without a Name*, Borghild Reed, illus., Harcourt Brace Jovanovich, 1967 (4–6). Gunilla is the name chosen for an Iranian orphan whose family and memory were destroyed in an earthquake. Adopted and brought to Sweden, her memory is jolted by personal violence and a frightening storm reminiscent of the earthquake.

BEEKS, GRAYDON. *Hosea Globe and the Fantastical Peg-Legged Chu*, Carol Nicklaus, illus., Atheneum, 1975 (4–6). An amusing spy spoof with fat, not too bright Hosea Globe and smart, three-legged, talking Mr. Chu (a dog of uncertain origin) as its heroes.

BERTOL, ROLAND. *Sundiata: The Epic of the Lion King*, Gregorio Prestopino, illus., Crowell, 1970 (5+). A tale from Mali. Sundiata is the youngest son of a king. He is ugly, mute, and so weak he must crawl along the ground. When he becomes king, he gains strength from the scepter. He rids his country of the leader who killed his ten brothers. A tale of good conquering evil.

BLAND, E. NESBIT. *Harding's Luck*, H. R. Millar, illus., Coward, McCann & Geoghegan, 1961 (6+). When a poor, crippled orphan becomes involved in time travel, he discovers that he is a lord and that when he is in the past he is no longer lame.

BROWN, CHRISTY. *My Left Foot*, Simon & Schuster, 1955 (7+). The lively, moving autobiography of a writer whose only controllable limb was his left foot.

BROWN, ROY. *Escape the River*, Seabury Press, 1972 (6+). Paul is the only one in the family who seems to care for his older brother, Kenny, who is quite retarded. He decides to run away with Kenny and very nearly gets into bad trouble with a tough young delinquent.

————. *Flight of Sparrows*, Macmillan, 1973 (5–8). Set in London, this story involves four young boys living in the basement of a condemned building. Two have escaped from reform school; one is a runaway who takes up with a small mute boy with no history. They have a few brief days together and then are scattered.

BURCH, ROBERT. *Renfroe's Christmas*, Rocco Negri, illus., Viking Press, 1968 (2–5). Reform has always had trouble with sharing. This Christmas he seems especially conscious of his thoughtlessness. Finally he gives his precious Christmas watch to "Crazy Nathan," who is to go to an institution.

————. *Simon and the Game of Chance*, Fermin Rocker, illus., Viking Press, 1970 (6+). After Simon's mother has a nervous breakdown and is sent to an institution, the father and six children adjust as best they can. When the eldest sister's fiance is killed hours before their wedding, Simon fears her depression will develop into a breakdown.

BURNETT, FRANCES HODGSON. *The Secret Garden*, Tasha Tudor, illus., Lippincott, 1962 (first pub. in 1909) (4–9). Colin, an invalid who has spent his life sheltered and hidden away, begins to gain strength as the secret garden progresses. This old classic is still loved by today's children.

BUTLER, BEVERLEY. *Feather in the Wind*, Dodd, Mead, 1965 (7+). Five-year-old Julie, orphaned during an Indian massacre, went blind at that time. A brutal attack upon the two people she loves and trusts fires her anger and restores her sight.

————. *Light a Single Candle*, Dodd, Mead, 1966 (6–9). The author herself lost her sight at fourteen. This book deals with Cathy, whose eyesight is already failing. After surgery she finds herself totally blind. Although at times embarrassingly adolescent, this book and its sequel are admirable for portraying a blind girl's attempt to live a normal life. Sequel: *Gift of Gold*, Dodd, Mead, 1972 (4–8).

BYARS, BETSY. *After the Goat Man*, Ronald Himler, illus., Viking Press, 1974 (5–9). Fat Harold V. Coleman is a wonderful character, laughing at himself with tears in his eyes. Luckily he has pluck and stamina, and Ada for a friend, all of which he needs in his encounter with Figgy and the goatman. A tale told with love, humor, and sensitivity.

————. *The Summer of the Swans*, Ted CoConis, illus., Viking Press, 1970 (5–7). Sara is devoted to her extremely retarded younger brother. His running off alone in the night to view the swans brings Sara hours of terror, but also provides her with an enemy who becomes a friend. Newbery.

BYERS, IRENE. *Mystery at Mappins*, Victor Ambrus, illus., Scribner, 1964 (5–8). Major Clevedon, injured in the war and permanently confined to a wheelchair, has bought Mappins. Now he needs an estate manager. Because he is so disagreeable, the post has not been filled. When Mr. Meredith and his family are taken on for a trial month, their industry and love of Mappins cause good changes in both the estate and the major.

CANTY, MARY. *The Green Gate*, Vera Bock, illus., McKay, 1965 (4–6). Through reading about this eight-year-old's adjustment, the reader can learn about problems faced by the blind.

CARPELAN, BO. *Bow Island*, Dell (Delacorte Press),

1968 (6+). The climax of this book comes when Marvin, a retarded young man, overcomes his terror to go through a raging storm to bring help for his friend, Johan. Although slow-moving, the tale shows the effects that both cruelty and kindness can have on the retarded. Sequel: *Dolphins in the City*, Dell (Delacorte Press), 1975.

CHARLIP, REMY, and MARY BETH. *Handtalk: An ABC of Finger Spelling and Sign Language*, photos by George Ancona. Parents, 1974 (1+). A delightful book, all photos and humor, depicting the finger alphabet and short cuts of sign language. A pleasant way to learn.

CHRISTOPHER, MATT. *Long Shot for Paul*, Foster Caddell, illus., Archway, 1974 (2–6). Younger boys interested in basketball might like this book about Glen Marlette's attempts to make a basketball player out of his retarded older brother.

CLEAVER, VERA, and BILL CLEAVER. *Me Too*, Lippincott, 1973 (5–7). A heartbreaking story about Lydia and her mirror twin, Lornie—with the exception that Lornie is severely mentally retarded. The story deals with one summer they spend together with Lornie in Lydia's care. So much time, love, and imagination go into Lydia's teaching. The only time it appears to have worked is once when Lornie lashes out in anger at Lydia.

———. *The Mimosa Tree*, Lippincott, 1970 (7+). One of Marvella's greatest concerns in fighting the dreary and frightening Chicago slum is caring for and protecting her blind father.

CLEWES, DOROTHY. *Storm over Innish*, Nelson, 1973 (8+). When a young man, injured and unconscious, is washed ashore on their island, the Ward family relives the death of fourteen-year-old Charlie Ward, who had washed up in the same spot four years ago. The young man's amnesia provides a mystery that must be unraveled, thread by thread.

CLIFFORD, ETH. *The Year of the Three-Legged Deer*, Richard Cuffari, illus., Houghton Mifflin, 1971 (3–7). The three-legged deer brings joy to Philili, who has a special way with animals. The deer's escape leads to Philili's death, however, and the breakup of the dead girl's family. A fascinating tale of life on the border of Indian country, 1819–1820.

CONE, MOLLY. *Simon*, Marvin Friedman, illus., Houghton Mifflin, 1970 (5–8). Many portrayals of handicaps: Simon, who has withdrawn from the world; a blind man; and a mentally retarded girl.

COOLIDGE, OLIVIA. *Tales of the Crusades*, Houghton Mifflin, 1970 (7+). Chapter "The Heir"—Prince Balwin, a child of great promise, wins a match of pinching. When he exposes the pinched arm, we learn that he has leprosy. Unhappy that a prince of such great promise faces an early and horrible death, the king's counselors resignedly state, "The King must have another son."

CORCORAN, BARBARA. *A Dance to Still Music*, Charles Robinson, illus., Atheneum, 1974 (5–8). Newly enclosed in her silent world, Margaret learns the loneliness and abuse suffered by the deaf. She runs away and finds comfort, acceptance, and finally encouragement to return to the outside world. One of Barbara Corcoran's better books.

CRANE, CAROLINE. *A Girl Like Tracy*, McKay, 1966 (7–9). Kathy's older sister, Tracy, is beautiful and retarded. In taking care of her, Kathy realizes that Tracy must have professional help. Her parents finally agree, and Tracy goes to a special school.

CRAWFORD, CHARLES. *Three-Legged Race*, Harper & Row, 1974 (7+). Brent, with a broken back, Kirk, with chronic bone problems, and Amy, who presumably has leukemia share the summer in a hospital. Although there are marvelous moments of insight into the problems of youth and of warmth and delight, Kirk's grating personality and language make this a difficult book.

CUNNINGHAM, JULIA. *Burnish Me Bright*, Pantheon Books, 1971 (4–6). The tale of a friendship between an elderly mime and a mute boy.

D'AMELIO, DAN. *Taller than Bandai Mountain*, Fred Banbury, illus., Viking Press, 1968 (3–7). A fictionalized biography of Dr. Hideyo Noguchi. Poor and with a hand crippled from a bad burn, Noguchi became a doctor, skilled in bacteriological research.

DANZIGER, PAULA. *The Cat Ate My Gym Suit*, Dell (Delacorte Press), 1974 (5+). Marcy Lewis is a female Harold V. Coleman (Byars, *After the Goatman*). Bright but shy because there is so much of her, she alternately laments and laughs at her condition. The firing of a popular teacher fires Marcy into action. As she opens her mouth to speak up more often, she opens it less often to eat.

DE ANGELI, MARGUERITE. *The Door in the Wall,* Doubleday, 1949 (4–6). Robin, left alone and crippled in plague-stricken London, is rescued and taken to a monastery by Brother Luke. There he learns to get about on rude crutches. Though he will never walk again, it is he who is responsible for the lifting of a siege on the Welsh castle where he is a squire. Newbery.

DE JONG, MEINDERT. *Journey from Peppermint Street,* Emily Arnold McCully, illus., Harper & Row, 1968 (5+). Grandfather takes Siebren to visit his great aunt and uncle, who is a deaf mute. This uncle greets the boy with humor and interest, and Siebren's fear of the huge, silent man quickly vanishes.

DIXON, PAIGE. *May I Cross Your Golden River?,* Atheneum, 1975 (8+). A tremendously moving book about Jordan Phillips, who at eighteen discovers that he has "Lou Gehrig's disease," a degenerative, fatal disease. His discussions with his wonderful family and his actions during the few months left to him should start any reader thinking about living his life and about our mortality and immortality.

DUNCAN, JANE. *Camerons at the Castle,* Victor Ambrus, illus., St. Martin's Press, 1964 (4–6). Nink is the youngest of the four Cameron children. Sent to spend the summer with their aunt, they go to Castle Vannich and help its owner prepare it for summer guests. Nink, severely retarded, finds two of the castle's missing treasures in a secret room. Sequel: *Camerons in the Hills.*

ELLIS, ELLA THORPE. *Celebrate the Morning,* Atheneum, 1972 (5–9). Although the mental illness of April's mother is not described too specifically, this book relates two haunting visits April and her mother have at the state asylum after the mother's breakdown.

FASSLER, JOAN. *One Little Girl,* M. Jane Smyth, illus., Human Sciences, 1975 (K–4). When Laurie's parents and teachers stop thinking and saying that she is slow and begin emphasizing her abilities, Laurie responds positively.

FISHER, AILEEN. *Skip,* Scholastic, 1972 (4–6). Krissy fights to keep her dog Skip after he goes blind.

FORBES, ESTHER. *Johnny Tremain,* Lynn Ward, il-lus., Houghton Mifflin, 1943 (7–9). Johnny Tremain's pride is directly responsible for his fall. Deliberately handed a faulty mold, Johnny finds his career as a silversmith ended when the mold breaks, drenching his hand in molten silver. The Revolution and Johnny's conquering spirit complete the tale. Newbery.

FRIIS-BAASTAD, BABBIS. *Don't Take Teddy,* Scribner, 1967 (5–7). It is too bad that the bulk of this book is so extremely tedious, for it could and should be a useful and interesting work. Its value lies in several tremendously painful scenes showing the mocking cruelty often inflicted on the mentally retarded and the frustrations experienced by those who love and want to help them.

GALLICO, PAUL. *The Snow Goose,* Knopf, 1963 (7+). This beautiful and brief story takes place on a small English Channel isle during World War II. A deformed hermit, kind to animals, painter of his world, is brought a wounded snow goose by a frightened girl. It is only as this man sets out on his final sail, to rescue the troops at Dunkirk, that the girl, now a woman realizes that she loves him.

GARFIELD, JAMES B. *Follow My Leader,* Robert Greiner, illus., Viking Press, 1957 (4–6). Jimmy Carter, blinded by a firecracker, is able to train to get Leader, a guide dog. With Leader, Jimmy is able to resume many of his old activities, even going on overnight hikes with the Boy Scouts.

GARFIELD, LEON. *Black Jack,* Anthony Maitland, illus., Pantheon Books, 1969 (7+). Black Jack, returned to life after being hanged, takes up with an orphan boy, Tolly, and an "insane" girl, Belle. After many adventures Black Jack rescues the two youths, helps them stow away on a ship bound for New England, and rows out of their lives.

————, and EDWARD BLISHEN. *The God Beneath the Sea,* Zevi Blum, illus., Pantheon Books, 1971 (9+). A retelling of tales of the gods, centering around ugly, misshapen Hephaestus, firstborn of Zeus and Hera.

GILBERT, NAN. *A Dog for Joey,* Harper & Row, 1967 (5+). Joey gets off to a bad start in a new community; however, the responsibility and love involved in raising and training a future guide dog get Joey on the right track.

GOLD, PHYLLIS. *Please Don't Say Hello,* photos by Carl Baker, Human Sciences, 1975 (4–7). Mrs.

Gold, the mother of an autistic child, writes of the problems the Mason family faces in introducing their autistic child and a new neighborhood.

GREISE, ARNOLD A. *At the Mouth of the Luckiest River*, Glo Coalson, illus., Crowell. (3–6). Tatlek, born with a crippled foot, has incurred the anger of the tribe's medicine man. Knowing he cannot become a great warrior, Tatlek dreams of becoming a medicine man who "would be kind to all his people and would always use his yegas to help them."

GRIFFITHS, HELEN. *The Mysterious Appearance of Agnes*, Voctor Ambrus, illus., Holiday, 1975 (5+). A mute child arrives in a remote English village, where she is eventually accused of being a witch.

———. *The Wild Horse of Santander*, Doubleday, 1965 (5–7). Although temporarily blind, a young Spanish boy is able to save and train a mare.

GROSKOPF, BERNICE. *Shadow in the Sun*, Atheneum, 1975 (7+). Fran Phillips, spending a month on Cape Cod, is hired as a companion to Wilma, who is confined to a wheelchair. Bright and frustrated, Wilma strikes out verbally at anyone around her. The climax is a nearly fatal accident for Wilma.

HAMILTON, VIRGINIA. *The Planet of Junior Brown*, Macmillan, 1971 (6–9). Throwaway boys, misfits, those nobody wants or cares about. This very strange books deals with a whole underground network of such boys, including Junior Brown, grotesquely fat and emotionally disturbed.

HATHAWAY, KATHERINE B. *The Little Locksmith*, Coward, McCann & Geoghegan, 1942 (7+). Katherine Butler was stricken with a spinal disease, for which the treatment was being strapped to a board for months. When she arose she was fragile and a hunchback. Her loving, overly protective mother assumed a normal life was not for Katherine. The daughter asserted her independence, made a home, and eventually found her own love. An inspiring autobiography.

HENRY, MARGUERITE. *King of the Wind*, Wesley Dennis, illus., Rand McNally, 1948 (4–6). From birth Sham's adventures are shared by his young, mute Moroccan groom, Agba. Although Sham never races, he sires three winners at Newmarket and becomes known as the Godolphin Arabian, great-great-grandsire of Man O' War.

———. *Mustang, Wild Spirit of the West*, Robert Lougheld, illus., Rand McNally, 1971 (4–6). Crippled by polio, Wild Horse Annie takes up the cause of the wild mustangs. Because of her work, the Department of the Interior creates in 1962 the first wild horse refuge in America.

HODGES, C. WALTER. *The Namesake*, Coward, Mc-Cann & Geoghegan, 1964 (5–7). Alfred, the One-Legged, struggles to save his country from the Danes. Sequel: *The Marsh King*, Coward, McCann & Geoghegan, 1967 (6–3).

HOLLAND, ISABELLE. *Heads You Win, Tails I Lose*, Lippincott, 1973 (7+). A frightening book involving the effects on a child of ever-quarreling parents. In order to lose weight quickly, Melissa steals and takes her mother's diet and sleeping pills.

HUGGINS, ALICE MARGARET and HUGH LAUGHLIN ROBINSON. *Wan Fu*, Longmans, 1957 (4–6). After her blind father is killed, Wan Fu is taken to a hospital where her crippled leg is repaired with surgery and where she learns to read and write. A striking picture of China's poor before the war.

HUNT, IRENE. *Up a Road Slowly*, Follett, 1966 (7+). A most beautiful book about Julia, who is sent to live with an aunt on the death of her mother. Two sad sequences involve those with handicaps. One is the death of a schoolmate who is not only mentally retarded but so dirty she smells. The other involves a lovely woman gone mad, who is always mentally far away and is often violent and unreasonable. Julia is involved in and changed by both experiences. Newbery

HUNTER, EDITH F. *Sue Ellen*, Bea Holmes, illus., Houghton Mifflin, 1969 (3–7). Sue Ellen, the product of a poor home environment, suffers learning difficulties. She is enrolled in a special class and begins to enjoy school as she learns.

HUNTER, MOLLIE. *The Stronghold*, Harper & Row, 1974 (7+). This fascinating book grew from the author's interest in a large network of ancient towers in the northern Scottish islands. Coll, a cripple, can never be a success by primitive standards. But it is he who designs and oversees the building of the Stronghold, which saves his people from periodic Roman attacks.

ISH-KISHOR, SULAMITH. *Our Eddie*, Pantheon, 1969 (6+). The sad observation of Eddie and his mother, both of whom suffer from multiple sclerosis.

JEWETT, ELEANORE M. *The Hidden Treasure of Glaston*, Frederick T. Chapmans, illus., Viking Press, 1946 (5–9). An interesting theory about what happened to King Arthur and his treasure. Twelve-year-old Hugh is left by his father at Glastonbury. There he finds some of Arthur's treasure, and his lame leg is cured by a miracle related to the Holy Grail.

JOHNSTON, NORMA. *Of Time and of Seasons*, Atheneum Press, 1975 (7+). A most interesting family at the time when the Civil War is erupting. Eighteen-year-old Bedelia is beautiful, but an accident when she was two caused brain damage. Since then she has been "an innocent" who speaks in rhyme. A midnight raping leaves her terrified and mute. Much is made of her family's constant refusal to send her away.

KELLER, HELEN. *The Story of My Life*, photos, Doubleday, 1902 (6+). Although this is a long book with small print, it continues to be popular with readers both young and old.

KERR, M. E. *Dinky Hocker Shoots Smack*, Harper & Row, 1972 (7+). The night of the banquet honoring her mother for her work in drug rehabilitation, poor fat Dinky Hocker plasters the neighborhood with signs, "Dinky Hocker Shoots Smack!" Dinky's only date, P. J. Knight, also bright and overweight, has weight-watched himself thin. This proves to be such a shock to Dinky that it brings on her painted plea for help.

———. *Is That You, Miss Blue?*, Harper & Row, 1975 (7+). Sent to Charles School, Flanders Brown makes friends slowly. One is her hall-mate, Agnes Thatcher, gorgeous but a deaf mute. Flanders, Agnes, and two other girls band together in defense of Miss Blue, a wonderful science teacher, but too engrossed in her religion to suit the school.

KILLILEA, MARIE. *Karen*, Prentice-Hall, 1952 (6+). An inspiring book about life with a victim of cerebral palsy. Told by doctors that Karen is a vegetable, that it would have been better if she had died at birth, Karen's parents refuse to abandon her to a life of hopelessness. They finally find a helpful doctor, and one by one vari-

ous hurdles are overcome. This book is so powerful because it is true.

KNIGHT, RUTH A. *Brave Companions*, Doubleday, 1959 (7–9). Tom, blinded, finds comfort in Joey, the puppy of his K-9 dog. Tom's adjustment to blindness is difficult until he receives a seeing-eye dog.

KONIGSBURG, E. L. *Altogether, One at a Time*, Atheneum, 1975 (5–7). Four short stories—one about a "fat farm" where two of the young "campers" are visited and inspired to lose weight by an artist who, it turns out, is long dead.

———. *(George)*, Atheneum, 1970 (4–9). In this amusing and unusual book, George lives inside Benjamin, talks to him a great deal of the time, and is brilliant at science, which is a help at school. Trouble only ensues when Benjamin's step-mother hears him and George talking to each other one night and sends him (them?) to a psychiatrist.

LAMPMAN, EVELYN SIBLEY. *Cayuse Courage*, Harcourt Brace Jovanovich, 1970 (6–9). *Cayuse Courage* is a quite successful description of the events leading to the massacre of the Whitman family in Oregon in the 1800s. Dr. Whitman amputates the gangrenous arm of Samuel, a Cayuse boy, thus rendering him a misfit by Cayuse standards. Samuel then observes life in both the Indian and white worlds, showing why the Indians resented the whites.

———. *Rattlesnake Cave*, Pamela Johnson, illus., Atheneum, 1974 (4–7). Eleven-year-old Jamie, sent to his Montana relatives because of his asthma, befriends an old Indian and his grandson. Jamie relives the battle of The Little Big Horn, partly from books and friends, partly from the magic of an Indian medicine bag, which he finds in the Rattlesnake Cave.

LAWRENCE, MILDRED. *Touchmark*, Deanne Hollinger, illus., Harcourt Brace Jovanovich, 1975 (5+). Nabby is taken into the Boston home of a pewterer to care for Emily, the crippled daughter. Nabby invents a wheelchair from a barrel and wheels, which enables the girls to explore the city and to be involved in some Revolutionary activities. She also encourages Emily to use her artistic talent on her father's pewter.

LEE, MILDRED. *The Skating Rink*, Seabury Press, 1969 (6–8). The only observer of his mother's accidental drowning, Tuck begins to stutter. Finding his speech a source of amusement for others, the boy becomes silent and withdrawn, able to express himself on paper, unwilling to share his thoughts in speech. The owner of a new skating rink becomes a friend for Tuck, who is then taught artistic skating. The confidence gained and skating money earned help Tuck and enable him to help his family.

L'ENGLE, MADELEINE. *The Young Unicorns*, Farrar, Straus & Giroux, 1968 (7+). A robbery, which includes the blinding of a young girl, involves the characters in a hair-raising mystery revolving about the rough area around the Cathedral of St. John the Divine in New York City.

LEVINE, EDNA S. *Lisa and Her Soundless World*, George Kamen, illus., Human Sciences, 1974 (3–5). A very nicely presented book about the problems a deaf child faces and some solutions. Should be read with an adult.

LINDQUIST, JENNIE D. *The Golden Name Day*, Garth Williams, illus., Harper & Row, 1955 (3–7). Four little girls befriend a boy who must spend his days in a wheelchair. They form a club and thoroughly enjoy their small-town life. The first of a warm, wonderful series. Sequels: *The Little Silver House*, Harper & Row, 1959. *The Crystal Tree*, Harper & Row, 1966.

LITTLE, JEAN. *From Anna*, Jean Sanden, illus., Harper & Row, 1972 (4–6). Anna is the youngest of five children, the awkward, stupid one of the family. When the family emigrates from Germany to Canada, it is learned that Anna's eyesight is terribly bad. She is given glasses, put in a special class where she finally learns to read and to become adept with her hands.

———. *Mine for Keeps*, Little, Brown, 1962 (3–7). Sal has cerebral palsy and returns home after three years away at a special school. She is slow at making friends until she gets a dog, and several children and dogs form the Pooch Academy to train their dogs together.

———. *Spring*, Little, Brown, 1966 (3–7). Meg, the youngest daughter, is failing in school. Part of her problem involves having to share a room with her crippled sister.

———. *Take Wing*, Little, Brown, 1968 (3–7). Laurel works to protect her mentally retarded brother, though some of her family try to deny his condition.

MATHIS, SHARON BELL, *Listen for the Fig Tree*, Viking Press, 1974 (8+). Muffin is blind. Her father was murdered a year ago, and since then Muffin's mother has been an unattractive drunk. Muffin is an admirable and likable character because of her determination not to be handicapped by her blindness, her poverty, or her mother's drinking.

MAZER, HARRY. *Dollar Man*, Dell (Delacorte Press), 1974 (5–7). Marcus Rosenbloom is fat, fatherless and has only one friend. He has developed some insight at the end of the book, but it is difficult to care.

MICKLISH, RITA. *Sugar Bee*, Ted Lewin, illus., Dell (Delacorte Press), 1972 (3–7). Because of her good grades Sugar Bee, poor and black, is chosen to visit a white family in the country. When she arrives she finds that Rosemary, the daughter, is blind. Sugar Bee learns "if Rosemary could find beauty without eyes to see, then she could find beauty too."

MOE, BARBARA. *The Ghost Wore Knickers*, Nelson, 1975 (5+). Five incredibly unattractive students go on an overnight hike with a teacher. One, Wally, is fat and asthmatic. Theoretically, all the young people "grow" from the experience, but not noticeably.

MULOCK, DINAH M. *The Little Lame Prince*, Jon Nielsen, illus., Collins, 1946 (4–6). On the day of his christening Prince Dolor is dropped, which makes him lame. And his mother dies. Soon thereafter his father dies, and his regent uncle banishes him. His fairy godmother guards him, and he is restored to his kingdom.

NAKAMOTO, HIROKO. *My Japan: 1930–1951*, McGraw-Hill, 1970 (5+). A young woman tells of her experiences as a victim of the bombing of Hiroshima.

NORRIS, GUNILLA. *The Top Step*, Richard Cuffari, illus., Atheneum, 1970 (2–6). An inconsequential book about Michael, an asthma victim, who is afraid to do too many things. The title refers to a seventh step from which he finally has the courage to jump.

NORTH, BROWNING. *Help Me, Charlie Buoy*, Coward, 1974 (5+). Charlie Buoy has run away to find a friend and inadvertently gets involved with the kidnapping of a blind girl. Not a great book, but children will probably love it, as it is full of action.

O'DELL, SCOTT. *Sing Down the Moon*, Houghton Mifflin, 1970 (5–8). This is a story of the tragic

"Long Walk" the Navajos were forced to make from the Canyon de Chelly in Arizona to Fort Sumner. The heroine and Tall Boy, who has a permanently paralyzed arm, escape from the fort and make their way back to the canyon to live.

PARKER, RICHARD. *Three by Mistake*, Nelson, 1974 (9–12). A timely book about three youngsters kidnapped by terrorists for ransom. Two are the children of the ambassador of an unnamed Middle Eastern country. The third, taken only because he happens to be with his friends, is an asthmatic child. Although the children are well treated, they figure that they will eventually have to be killed. After a couple of unsuccessful escape attempts, the three manage to overcome their captors just as rescuers arrive.

PECK, RICHARD. *Dreamland Lake*, Avon, 1974 (3–7). A strange book involving Brian and Flip, who find a dead body, and Elvan, lonely, fat, obsessed with a love of Nazism. Elvan falls through a railroad bridge to his death.

PERL, LILA. *Me and Fat Glenda*, Simon & Schuster, 1973 (5+). A hippie family moves next door to fat Glenda Waite. A Typical teen tale.

PHIPSIN, JOAN. *Good Luck to the Rider*, Margaret Horder, illus., Harcourt Brace Jovanovich, 1968 (4–6). Weakened by a childhood bout with typhoid, Barbara has been pampered by her family and has always been timorous. She conquers her fear of horses when she adopts a wild colt and trains him herself.

POTTER, BRONSON. *Antonio*, Ann Grifalconi, illus., Atheneum, 1968 (2–6). A small village in Portugal. A boy with a crippled hand saves the fishing fleet during a storm.

PYLE, HOWARD. *Otto of the Silver Hand*, Random House, 1960 (5–9). The victim of his father's cruelty to others, young Otto has his right hand severed in an act of vengeance. Ever gentle, the favorite of a "simple" monk, Otto believes that it is better to rule with a hand of silver than of iron.

RICK, LOUISE. *Three of a Kind*, William M. Hutchinson, illus., Watts, 1970 (4–6). Sally Gray, a "State Kid," has lived on Star Island with Rhoda and Ben for a year and a half. Rhoda dotes on Benji, her four-and-a-half-year-old grandson. Benji appears to be autistic. Rhoda asks if Benji can stay with them for a while.

Slowly Benji begins to come out of himself, and Sally comes to love and cherish him.

RINALDO, C. L. *Dark Dreams*, Harper & Row, 1974 (6+). *Dark Dreams* is a good name for this depressing book. Carlo is twelve and has had rheumatic fever. Because he must rest, the neighborhood toughs taunt him. He finds companionship with a retarded man, Joey, who is finally put into an institution, where he dies. Carlo's heart improves, but he misses Joey.

RINHOFF, BARBARA. *The Watchers*, Knopf, 1972 (5–7). The reader never knows exactly what is wrong with ten-year-old Sanford Townsend. He is obviously brain-damaged, which affects his motor ability. His mother is overprotective. His relationship with Chris Blake opens new worlds to him, such as loud sport shirts, food from street vendors, and running off to Central Park instead of going to school. All this gives him the self-confidence he has badly needed.

ROBINSON, VERONICA. *David in Silence*, Victor G. Ambrus, illus., Lippincott, 1966 (5–7). David is deaf. This book can be used to help a child understand what it means to be deaf.

ROOS, AUDREY and WILLIAM. *The Mystery Next Door*, Ingrid Fetz, illus., Scribner, 1972 (4–6). The day Fatso Adele socks her neighbor, Puny Wayne, on the chin, things begin to happen. The two children rescue their invalid neighbor, Mrs. Smallwood, at the same time as they become less fat and less puny, respectively. Fun to read.

SACHS, MARILYN. *Amy and Laura*, Tracy Sugarman, illus., Doubleday, 1966 (4–6). An auto accident. Months in the hospital. Finally Amy's and Laura's mother can come home. Everyone is eager to treat Mama like an invalid until she finally asserts herself, and life begins to get back to normal. An interesting treatment of the wide-reaching effects this situation can have.

———. *The Bears' House*, Louis Glanzman, illus., Doubleday, 1971 (4–7). Fran Ellen's real world includes a mother who is mentally ill. She "escapes" to life in a doll's house.

SAVITZ, HARRIET MAY. *The Lionhearted*, Day, 1975 (6–8). A motorcycle accident leaves Rennie paralyzed from the waist down. Combined with her struggle of wheelchair versus braces and crutches is the plot of her overweight friend's struggle to lose weight. The message is better than the plot.

SKURZYNSKI, GLORIA. *The Poltergeist of Jason Morey,* Dodd, Mead, 1975 (6+). After he is orphaned, Jason is possessed by a poltergeist, which is apparently the energy of his hostility. His behavior is suspect, until an aunt and uncle provide love and security for Jason but no home for the poltergeist.

SLOTE, ALFRED. *Hang Tough, Paul Mather,* Lippincott, 1973 (5+). Paul, a whiz of a Little League pitcher, has leukemia. When he moves to a new town, he sneaks out to pitch for the local team. Most of the story involves his experiences thereafter in the hospital. This fine book is especially popular with boys.

SMITH, DORIS BUCHANAN. *Kelly's Creek,* Alan Tiegreen, illus., Crowell, 1975 (3–5). Young Kelly O'Brien has a learning disability, which affects his coordination. His love for and knowledge of the natural life of his creek bring him praise and consolation.

SMITH, EMMA. *Out of Hand,* Anthony Maitland, illus., Harcourt Brace Jovanovich, 1964 (5–7). When Polly breaks her leg, four cousins help amuse her.

SMITH, GENE. *The Hayburners,* Ted Lewin, illus., Dell (Delacorte Press), 1974 (4–6). A hayburner is a horse who eats a lot but brings no financial return to its owner. It appears that Will's 4-H calf and Joey, the mentally retarded handyman Will's family has taken from the local institution for the summer, are two hayburners. Joey's loving ways and determination prove both assumptions wrong. A lovely book.

SOBOL, HARRIET LANGSAM. *Jeff's Hospital Book,* photos by Patricia Agree, Walck, 1975 (3+). Jeff Langsam was born with crossed eyes. Now about eight years old, he goes to the hospital for eye surgery. In words and photographs this is the story of that hospitalization. Useful for any child about to undergo surgery.

SOMERFELT, AIMEE. *The Road to Agra,* Ulf Aas, illus., Criterion, 1961 (4–6). India. Lalu hears of a hospital in Agra where eye diseases can be cured. He takes his small sister on the long, dangerous journey to save her sight. If this happens she can go to school and then teach him to read and write.

SOUTHALL, IVAN. *Let the Balloon Go,* Ian Ribbons, illus., St. Martin's Press, 1968 (5–9). A twelve-year-old spastic boy, left alone for the day, climbs a tree, symbolically declaring his desire for independence.

SPENCE, ELEANOR. *The Nothing Place,* Harper & Row, 1973 (5+). Although this book is incredibly slow, it does describe the attempts of a deaf boy to hide his condition and his resentment of outside help. There are some very nice scenes between the boy, Glen, and Reggie, an old vagrant.

SPYRI, JOHANNA. *Heidi,* Greta Elgaard, illus., Macmillan, 1962 (first pub. in 1884) (4–6). Heidi has many adventures in this classic. Much of the tale involves her relationship with Clara, who is crippled and confined to her home in Frankfurt. When Clara is allowed to visit Heidi and her grandfather and share their simple, healthy mountain life, her health improves a great deal, and she eventually learns to walk.

STINEHORF, LOUISE A. *A Charm for Paco's Mother,* Joseph Escourido, illus., Day, 1965 (3–6). A small Mexican boy wants to help his mother regain her eyesight.

STORR, CATHERINE. *Thursday,* Harper & Row, 1972 (7+). Bee, recovering from mononucleosis, learns that her friend Thursday has been missing for a week. Although hampered by her weakness, Bee searches for and finds Thursday, who is strangely withdrawn. A great deal is made of fairies and changelings. Using this lore, Bee is able to "save" Thursday from "them" on Midsummer's Eve. The cure is hard to swallow!

SUTCLIFF, ROSEMARY. *Warrior Scarlet,* Walch, 1966 (8+). Sutcliff always tells a good tale. This one is set in Bronze Age Britain. Orem succeeds in getting his wolf on the second chance, despite his lame arm.

———. *The Witch's Brat,* Walch, 1970 (7–9). Lovell, crippled, finds meaning for his life in Winchester Monastery.

TATE, JOAN. *Ben and Annie,* Judith Gwyn Brown, illus., Doubleday, 1974 (5–7). Annie is an invalid whose life is drab and confined until she meets Ben. Ben expands her world, even taking her on outings with his boyfriends. In the midst of one ecstatic roughhouse, a well-intentioned man misunderstands Annie's delighted screams. All adults accept it as fact that the boys were torturing Annie. The children are never allowed to explain, and the relationship and Annie's progress are finished. A disturbing ending.

TAYLOR, THEODORE. *The Cay*, Doubleday, 1969 (5–9). Timothy, an old black man, and young white Philip are shipwrecked on a deserted cay (an island). Philip is temporarily blind. Fearing that they may never be found, Timothy trains the boy to be totally self-sufficient. Almost a classical tragic hero, Timothy gives his life to save Philip. After his rescue, Philip knows that he can never again share his mother's antiblack prejudice.

————. *Teetoncey*, Richard Cuffari, illus., Doubleday, 1974 (5–7). Life on the Outer Banks has long involved men, the sea, and shipwrecks. During a terrible storm, Ben finds the only survivor of a wreck, a child terrified into amnesia. Ben and his mother take her in. It is only during the next storm that the child, named Teetoncey by Ben's mother, regains her memory. The first of a trilogy.

TERRIS, SUSAN. *The Drowning Boy*, Doubleday, 1972 (6–9). In this strange book, Jason is a "misunderstood" boy, which is easy to understand, for he is truly a difficult person to relate to, much less like. He finally relates to Buddy, a six-year-old, who is severely disturbed.

THRASHER, CRYSTAL. *The Dark Didn't Catch Me*, Atheneum, 1975 (5–9). The story of a desperately poor family during the Depression. The girl who relates the tale has a ten-year-old epileptic brother. He has a seizure during a storm, falls into the creek, and drowns. This is a powerful book with a hopeful ending.

TREASE, GEOFFREY. *The Red Towers of Granada*, Charles Keeping, illus., Vanguard Press, 1965 (6–7). Thirteenth-century Spain. A young boy is thought to be a leper. His illness (not leprosy) is cured by a Jewish doctor.

TREECE, HENRY. *The Dream Time*, Charles Keeping, illus., Hawthorn Books, 1968 (6–8). An allegory about a cripple, cast out of his tribe in prehistoric Britain.

TURNBULL, AGNES SLIGH. *The White Lark*, Nathan Goldstein, illus., Houghton Mifflin, 1968 (3–6). Short stories revolving around Suzy and Mr. Prettyford, who is crippled.

UNKLEBACH, KURT. *The Dog Who Never Knew*, Four Winds, 1968 (6–9). A girl trains a dog who has lost one eye.

UNDERHILL, RUTH M. *Antelope Singer*, Peter Barrett, illus., Puffin, 1961 (3–6). Nummer, a Painte boy, has the measles. The Hunt family, left by a wagon train, nurses the Indian back to health. Because Nummer has a withered hand, he wishes to die. The Hunts encourage him to show his worth, and he becomes an Antelope Singer.

VALENS, E. G. *The Other Side of the Mountain*, Warner, 1975 (7+). The inspiring story of skier Jill Kinmont, who became a quadraplegic after a ski accident.

VAN ITERSON, SINY ROSE. *Pulga*, Morrow, 1971 (6–9). Pulga is a desperately poor child of Bogata's slums. Two weeks as a truck driver's assistant show him a way out for himself and his crippled brother. A good look at the real life of Latin America.

VAN STOCKUM, HILDA. *The Cottage at Bantry Bay*, Viking Press, 1938 (4–6). Francie, a sprightly five-year-old, in spite of a crippled foot, makes life constantly interesting for his quiet twin brother.

————. *Mogo's Flute*, Robin Jacques, illus., Viking Press, 1966 (4–6). Kenya. Mogo, one of many children, is never allowed to help his parents because of his weakness. He learns to strengthen himself gradually and is honored by the tribe when he saves the tribe's goats during a fearful storm.

VINSON, KATHRYN. *Run with the Ring*, Harcourt Brace Jovanovich, 1965 (7+). Accidentally blinded, Mark learns how to compete in track by learning to run with the ring.

WATSON, SALLY. *Other Sandals*, Holt, Rinehart and Winston, 1966 (5–9). Set in Israel, Haifa and a Kibbutz. Two cousins are swapped for the vacation. Devra, the Kibbutzim, anti-Arab, a stammerer, acts without thinking. Eytan is bitter over his lame leg. Devra makes friends with an Arab girl and learns to hold her tongue a bit. Eytan, surly at first, decides to act pleasantly and even helps another girl overcome her peevishness.

WATSON, SIMON. *The Partisan*, Macmillan, 1975 (7+). A weird book about a group of boys who gather around Dom, a cripple, and play strange games in which Dom is the chief. New tough boys break into the group and destroy the group and the good times.

WEIK, MARY HAYS. *The Jazz Man*, Ann Grifalconi,

illus., Atheneum, 1966 (3+). A strange but effective story about a boy with a lame leg who stays inside his tenement apartment, observing life from the windows. Zeke's parents leave, the Jazz Man across the way leaves. Zeke gets into bed, and dreams all have returned. When he awakens, they have.

WEIS, ROSEMARY. *Three Red Herrings*, Nelson, 1972 (6+). Eva, Midge, and Willie are the Three Red Herrings, who form a singing troup after their father, the Great McGowan, dies. After a bout with diphtheria, Eva loses her voice.

WIGGEN, KATE DOUGLAS. *The Bird's Christmas Carol* Houghton Mifflin, 1886 (3–6). An overly sentimental story about Carol, sickly, saintly. She invites the many Ruggles children to share her Christmas dinner and dies as the Christmas bells ring.

WILDER, LAURA INGALLS. *Little Town on the Prairie*, Garth Williams, illus., Harper & Row, 1941 (4–8). In this volume of the extremely popular *Little House* series, Laura's older sister, Mary, goes blind. Later she is able to go to a school for the blind.

WILLARD, BARBARA. *The Iron Lily*, Dutton, 1973 (7–9). One of a fine series dealing with a family secret that is handed down to one member of each succeeding generation. Lilias is the Iron Lily, so named by her ironmonger husband as he lies dying. Although alone and a hunchback, Lilias becomes Master of the forge and makes strong allies.

————. *Three and One to Carry*, Douglas Hall, illus., Harcourt Brace Jovanovich, 1964 (6+). Arthur, with his broken leg, is another stray taken in by the family at Winterpicks. The period of recuperation changes him so that the family is almost sorry to see him go.

WITHERIDGE, ELIZABETH. *Dead End Bluff*, Charles Geer, illus., Atheneum, 1966 (3–7). Guy, who has been blind all his life, must prove his capabilities to his father.

WOLF, BERNARD. *Don't Feel Sorry for Paul*, photos. Lippincott, 1974 (8–12). The reader will not easily forget this glimpse into the life of Paul Jockimo and his family. Although healthy and hearty, seven-year-old Paul must wear three prostheses, one each on his arms and one on a leg. He runs, plays football, rides horseback. Although he faces hardships, his strength is in family and close friends who do not pity him and who encourage and even push him to try everything.

WOJCIECHOWSKA, MAIA. *A Single Light*, Harper & Row, 1968 (5+). Born deaf and mute, a Spanish girl is rejected by her family. She is taken in by the priest and works in the church. There she finds a hidden statue of the baby Jesus, which she loves and caresses as if it were real. The baby is stolen, and mob violence follows. From this violence the priest is sure love and acceptance of the girl will come.

WRIGHTSON, PATRICIA. *A Racecourse for Andy*, Margaret Horder, illus., Harcourt Brace Jovanovich, 1968 (4–6). Andy, retarded, thinks he has bought a racecourse. Understanding adults help him.

YATES, ELIZABETH. *Amos Fortune, Free Man*, Nora S. Unwin, illus., Dutton, 1950 (7+). Born the son of an African king, Amos is captured at fifteen and sent to Boston, where he is brought up by a Quaker and learns a trade. Once he is free he saves his money to free three women, each of whom is crippled. He does this because he cannot forget his beloved younger sister, who was crippled. He dies a fairly wealthy, respected, loved man. Newbery.

YEP, LAWRENCE. *Sweetwater*, Julia Noonan, illus., Harper & Row, 1973 (5+). Science fiction. The planet Harmony, where there is no longer harmony. Tyree wants only to make music and is taught to play the flute by Amadeus, a spider-like creature. Tyree has a blind sister who loves all forms of beauty.

YOLEN, JANE. *The Transfigured Hart*, Donna Diamond, illus., Crowell, 1975 (6–8). Because of a rheumatic heart Richard spent much time alone reading his father's books. When forced to go out he discovers an albino hart, which he thinks is a unicorn. The boy, animal, and a girl share a magical moment.

# Appendix B

# Publishers' Addresses

## A

Abelard-Schuman, Ltd., 257 Park Ave. S., N.Y., N.Y. 10010.

Abingdon Press, 201 8th Ave. S., Nashville, Tenn. 37203.

Harry N. Abrams, Inc., 110 E. 59th St., N.Y., N.Y. 10022.

Academic Press Inc., 111 5th Ave., N.Y., N.Y. 10003.

Ace Publishing Corp. (See Charter Communications, Inc.).

Addison-Wesley Pub. Co., Reading, Mass. 01867.

C. W. Alban Co., 901 S. Grand Blvd., St. Louis, Mo. 63103.

Aldine-Atherton, Inc., 529 S. Wabash Ave., Chicago, Ill. 60605.

Allyn and Bacon, Inc. Rockleigh, N.J. 07647.

American Accounting Assn., 653 S. Orange Ave., Sarasota, Fla. 33577.

American Bible Society, 1865 Broadway, N.Y., N.Y. 10023.

American Book Co. (See Van Nostrand Reinhold).

American Continental Publishing Corp., Box 13265, Fort Worth, Tex. 76118.

American Elsevier Publ. Co., Inc., 52 Vanderbilt Ave., N.Y., N.Y. 10017.

American Heritage Press (See McGraw-Hill Book Co.).

American Inst. of Certified Public Accountants, 666 Fifth Ave., N.Y., N.Y. 10019.

American Law Institute, 4025 Chestnut St., Philadelphia, Pa. 19104.

American Library Assn., 50 E. Huon St., Chicago, Ill. 60611.

American Map Co., Inc., 3 W. 61st St., N.Y., N.Y. 10023.

American RDM Corp. (See Study *Master).

American Veterinary Publications, Inc., 114 N. West St., Wheaton, Ill. 60187.

Apollo Editions, 666 Fifth Ave., N.Y., N.Y. 10019.

Appleton-Century-Crofts, Inc., 440 Park Ave. S., N.Y., N.Y. 10016.

Architectural Book Pub. Co., Inc. (See Hastings House).

Arco Pub. Co., Inc., 219 Park Ave. S., N.Y., N.Y. 10003.

Association Press, 291 Broadway, N.Y., N.Y. 10007.

Atheneum Publishers, 122 E. 42nd St., N.Y., N.Y. 10017.

Theo. Audel & Co. (See Howard Sams & Co., Inc.).

Augsburg Pub. House, 426 S. 5th St., Minneapolis, Minn. 55415.

The AVI Pub. Co., PO Box 831, Westport, Conn. 06880.

Avon Book Div.—The Hearst Corp., 959 Eighth Ave., N.Y., N.Y. 10019.

# B

Ballantine Books, Inc., 101 Fifth Ave., N.Y., N.Y. 10003.

Banks-Baldwin Law Pub. Co., 1904 Ansel Rd., Cleveland, Ohio 44106.

Bantam Books, Inc., 666 Fifth Ave., N.Y., N.Y. 10019.

A. S. Barnes & Co., Box 421, Cranbury, N.J. 08512.

Barnes & Noble Publications (See Harper & Row).

Barron's Educational Series, Inc., 113 Crossways Park Dr., Woodbury, N.Y. 11797.

Bartell Media Corp., 205 E. 42nd St., N.Y., N.Y. 10017.

Basic Books, Inc., 404 Park Ave. S., N.Y., N.Y. 10016.

The Beacon Press, 25 Beacon St., Boston, Mass. 02108.

Matthew Bender & Co., Inc., 1275 Broadway, Albany, N.Y. 12201.

W. A. Benjamin, Inc., Reading, Mass. 01867.

Chas. A. Bennett Co., 809 W. Detwiler Dr., Peoria, Ill. 61614.

Berkley Pub. Corp., 200 Madison Ave., N.Y., N.Y. 10016.

The Bethany Press, 2640 Pine Blvd., PO Box 179, St. Louis, Mo. 63166.

Binfords & Mort Publishers, 2505 S.E. 11th Ave., Portland, Oregon 97242.

Blaisdell Publishing Co. (See Xerox College Publishing.)

Bloch Pub. Co., 915 Broadway, N.Y., N.Y. 10010.

The Bobbs-Merrill Co., 4300 W. 62nd St., Indianapolis, Ind. 46268.

Boosey & Hawkes, Inc., Oceanside, N.Y. 11572.

Boston Music Co., 116 Boylston St., Boston, Mass. 02116.

R. R. Bowker Co., 1180 Ave. of the Americas, N.Y., N.Y. 10036.

Charles T. Branford Co., P.O. Box 41, Newton Centre, Mass. 02159.

George Braziller, Inc., 1 Park Ave., N.Y., N.Y. 10016.

Broadman Press, 127 9th Ave. N., Nashville, Tenn. 37203.

The Brookings Institution, 1775 Mass. Ave. N.W., Washington, D.C. 20036.

Wm. C. Brown Publishers, 2460 Kerper Ave., Dubuque, Iowa 52001.

The Bruce Pub. Co., 8701 Wilshire Blvd., Beverly Hills, Cal. 90211.

Burgess Pub. Co., 426 S. Sixth St., Minneapolis, Minn. 55415.

# C

Callaghan & Co., 6141 N. Cicero Ave., Chicago, Ill. 60646.

Cambridge Univ. Press, 32 E. 57th St., N.Y., N.Y. 10022.

The Catholic Univ. of America Press, Inc., 620 Michigan Ave. N.E., Washington, D.C. 20017.

The Caxton Printers, Ltd., 312 Main St., Caldwell, Idaho 83605.

Chandler Publishing Co. (See Intext).

Charter Communications, Inc., 1120 Ave. of the Americas, N.Y., N.Y. 10036.

Chelsea Publishing Co., 159 East Tremont Ave., Bronx, N.Y. 10453.

Chilton Book Co., 401 Walnut St., Philadelphia, Pa. 19106.

Christopher Publishing House, 53 Billings Rd., N. Quincy, Mass. 02171.

The Citadel Press, 120 Enterprise Ave., Secaucus, N.J. 07094.

Clark Boardman Co., Ltd., 435 Hudson St., N.Y., N.Y. 10014.

Cliff's Notes, P.O. Box 80728, Lincoln, Neb. 68501.

College Notes and Texts, Inc., 280 Madison Ave., Suite 709, N.Y., N.Y. 10016.

Collier Books (See Macmillan Publishing Co., Inc.).

Wm. Collins Sons & Co., Ltd., 215 Park Ave. South, N.Y., N.Y. 10003.

Columbia Univ. Press, 562 W. 113th St., N.Y., N.Y. 10025.

Commerce Clearing House, Inc., 4025 W. Peterson Ave., Chicago, Ill. 60646.

Comm. for Economic Development, 477 Madison Ave., New York, N.Y. 10022.

Concordia Publishing House, 3558 S. Jefferson Ave., St. Louis, Mo. 63118.

Congressional Quarterly, Inc., 1735 K St., N.W., Washington, D.C. 20006.

Cornell Maritime Press Inc., Box 109, Cambridge, Md. 21613.

Cornell University Press (Also Comstock Pub. Assoc.), 124 Roberts Pl., Ithaca, N.Y. 14850.

Cowles Book Co., Inc., 114 W. Illinois St., Chicago, Ill. 60610.

George F. Cram Co., Inc., 301 S. LaSalle St., Indianapolis, Ind. 46206.

Criterion Books, Inc., 257 Park Ave. S., N.Y., N.Y. 10010.

Thomas Y. Crowell Co., 201 Park Ave. S., N.Y., N.Y. 10003.

Crown Publishers, 419 Park Ave. S., N.Y., N.Y. 10016.

Cummings Publishing Co., South St., Reading, Mass. 01876.

## D

Dance Horizons, Inc., 1801 E. 26th St., Brooklyn, N.Y. 11229.

Data-Guide, Inc., 154–01 Barclay Ave., Flushing, N.Y. 11355.

Davis Publications, Inc., 50 Portland St., Worcester, Mass. 01608.

F. A. Davis Co., 1915 Arch St., Phila., Pa. 19103.

Dell Pub. Co., Inc., 750 Third Ave., N.Y., N.Y. 10017.

Delmar Publishers, Inc., Albany, N.Y. 12205.

Dennis & Co., Inc., 251 Main St., Buffalo, N.Y. 14203.

Denoyer-Geppert Co., 5235 Ravenswood Ave., Chicago, Ill. 60640.

The Devin-Adair Co., 1 Park Ave., Old Greenwich, Conn. 06870.

DeVorss & Co., Inc., 1641 Lincoln Blvd., Santa Monica, Cal. 90404.

The Dial Press and Delacorte Press, 750 Third Ave., N.Y., N.Y. 10017.

D. C. Divry, Inc., 293 Seventh Ave., N.Y., N.Y. 10001.

Dodd, Mead & Co., Inc., 79 Madison Ave., N.Y., N.Y. 10016.

M. A. Donohue & Co. (See Hubbard Press).

Dorrance & Co., 1809 Callowhill St., Phila., Pa. 19130.

Dorsey Press, 1818 Ridge Rd., Homewood, Ill. 60430.

Doubleday & Co., Inc., 501 Franklin Ave., Garden City, N.Y. 11531.

Dover Publications, Inc., 180 Varick St., N.Y., N.Y. 10014.

Duke University Press, College Station, Box 6697, Durham, N.C. 27708.

E. P. Dutton & Co., Inc., 201 Park Ave. S., N.Y., N.Y., 10003.

## E

J. W. Edwards, Publisher, Inc., 2500 S. State St., Ann Arbor, Mich. 48104.

Wm. B. Eerdmans Publishing Co., 255 Jefferson Ave., S.E., Grand Rapids, Mich. 49502.

Eliot Books, Inc., 35–53 24th St., Long Island City, N.Y. 11106.

Encyclopaedia Britannica, Inc., 425 N. Mich. Ave., Chicago, Ill. 60611.

Engineering Technology, Inc., 503 E. Main St., Mahomet, Ill. 61853.

Expression Co., Publishers, P.O. Box 11, Magnolia, Mass. 01930.

## F

Fairchild Pubs., 7 E. 12th St., New York, N.Y. 10003.

Family Serv. Assoc. of Amer., 44 E. 23rd, N.Y., N.Y. 10010.

Farrar, Straus & Giroux, 19 Union Sq. W., N.Y., N.Y. 10003.

Fawcett Publications, Inc., Fawcett Place, Greenwich, Conn. 06830.

Fearon Publishers, Inc., 6 Davis Dr., Belmont, Calif. 94002.

Frederick Fell, Inc., 386 Park Ave. S., N.Y., N.Y. 10016.

Field Museum of Natural History, Roosevelt Rd. & Lake Shore Dr., Chicago, Ill. 60605.

Follett Pub. Co., 1010 W. Washington Blvd., Chicago, Ill. 60607.

Fordham University Press, 441 E. Fordham Rd., Bronx, N.Y. 10458.

Foreign Policy Ass'n, Inc., 345 E. 46th St., N.Y., N.Y. 10017.

Forest Press, Inc., 85 Watervliet Ave., Albany, N.Y. 12206.

Fortress Press, 2900 Queen Lane, Philadelphia, Pa. 19129.

Four Continent Book Corporation, 156 Fifth Ave., N.Y., N.Y. 10010.

Free Press (See Macmillan Publishing Co., Inc.).

W. H. Freeman & Co., 660 Market St., San Francisco, Calif. 94104.

French & European Publications, Inc., 610 Fifth Ave., N.Y., N.Y. 10020.

Samuel French, Inc., 25 W. 45th St., N.Y., N.Y. 10036.

French Book Guild, 11–03 46th Ave., Long Island City, N.Y. 11101.

Friendship Press, 475 Riverside Dr., N.Y., N.Y. 10027.

Funk & Wagnalls, 201 Park Ave. S., N.Y., N.Y. 10003.

## G

General Learning Corp., Morristown, N.J. 07960.

The Geological Society of America, Inc., 3300 Penrose Pl., Boulder, Colo. 80301.

Ginn & Co. (See Xerox College Publishing).

Glencoe Press, 8701 Wilshire Blvd., Beverly Hills, Calif. 90211.

Golden Press, Inc. (See Western Publishing Co.).

Goodheart-Willcox Co., Inc., 123 W. Taft Dr., S. Holland, Ill. 60473.

Goodyear Publishing Co., 15115 Sunset Blvd., Pacific Palisades, Cal. 90272.

Gregg Div., McGraw-Hill Book Co., 1221 Ave. of The Americas, N.Y., N.Y. 10036.

Grosset & Dunlap, Inc., 51 Madison Ave., N.Y., N.Y. 10010.

Grove Press, Inc., 53 E. 11th St., N.Y., N.Y. 10003.

Grune & Stratton, Inc., 111 Fifth Ave., N.Y., N.Y. 10003.

## H

Hafner Pub. Co., Inc., 866 Third Ave., N.Y., N.Y. 10022.

Hammond, Inc., 515 Valley St., Maplewood, N.J. 07040.

Harcourt Brace Jovanovich, Inc., 757 Third Ave., N.Y., N.Y. 10017.
Branch
　1372 Peachtree Street, N.E., Atlanta, Georgia 30309.
　7555 Caldwell Avenue, Chicago, Illinois 60648.
　Polk and Geary, San Francisco, California 94109.

Harper & Row Publishers, Inc., 10 E. 53rd St., N.Y., N.Y. 10022.

Harvard University Press, 79 Garden St., Cambridge, Mass. 02138.

Hastings House, Publishers, Inc., 10 E. 40th St., N.Y., N.Y. 10016.

Hayden Book Cos., 116 W. 14th St., N.Y., N.Y. 10011.

D. C. Heath and Co., Div. Raytheon Educ. Co., 125 Spring St., Lexington, Mass. 02173.
Branch
　2700 N. Richardt Ave., Indianapolis, Ind. 46219.
　1731 Commerce Dr., N.W., Atlanta, Ga. 30318.
　Suite 510, Stemmons Tower East, Dallas, Tex. 75207.

Hebrew Pub. Co., 79 Delancey St., N.Y., N.Y. 10002.

W. S. Heinman, Imported Books, 1966 Broadway, N.Y., N.Y. 10023.

Herald Press, 616 Walnut Ave., Scottdale, Pa. 15683.

Herder and Herder, Inc., 232 Madison Ave., N.Y., N.Y. 10016.

Hill & Wang, Inc. (See Noonday Press).

Holden-Day, Inc., 500 Sansome St., San Francisco, Cal. 94111.

A. J. Holman Co., Box 956, E. Washington Sq., Phila., Pa. 19105.

Holt, Rinehart & Winston, Inc., 383 Madison Ave., N.Y., N.Y. 10017.
Branch
　2121 Toughy Ave., Centex Park, Elk Grove Village, Ill. 60004.
　Crocker Park, Valley Rd., Brisbane, Cal. 94005.

Horizon Press, Inc., 156 Fifth Ave., N.Y., N.Y. 10010.

Houghton Mifflin Co., 110 Tremont St., Boston, Mass. 02107.
Branch
　666 Miami Circle, N.E., Atlanta, Ga. 30324.
　6626 Oakbrook Blvd., Dallas, Texas 75235.
　1900 S. Batavia Ave., Geneva, Ill. 60134.
　53 W. 43rd St., New York, N.Y. 10036.
　777 California Ave., Palo Alto, Calif. 94304.

Hubbard Press, 2855 Shermer Rd., Northbrook, Ill. 60062.

Human Science Press, Div. of Behavioral Publications, Inc., 72 Fifth Ave., N.Y., N.Y. 10011.

Humanities Press, Inc., 303 Park Ave. S., N.Y., N.Y. 10010.

Bruce Humphries, 68 Beacon St., Sommerville, Mass. 02143.

Hutchins Oriental Books, 1034 Mission St., South Pasadena, Cal. 91030.

## I

Indiana University Press, 10th & Morton St., Bloomington, Ind. 47401.

The Industrial Press, 200 Madison Ave., N.Y., N.Y. 10016.

Inor Pub. Co., Inc., 203–205 Lexington Ave., Sweet Springs, Mo. 65351.

International City Management Ass'n, 1140 Conn. Ave., N.W., Washington, D.C. 20036.

International Publishers Co., Inc., 381 Park Ave. S., N.Y., N.Y. 10016.

International Universities Press, Inc., 239 Park Ave. S., N.Y., N.Y. 10003.

Interscience Publishers, Inc. (See John Wiley & Sons, Inc.).

The Interstate Printers and Publishers, 19–27 N. Jackson St., Danville, Ill. 61832.

Intext Educational Publishers, Scranton, Pa. 18515.

Iowa State University Press, Ames, Iowa 50010.

Richard D. Irwin, Inc., 1818 Ridge Rd., Homewood, Ill. 60430.

## J

The Johns Hopkins Press, Baltimore, Md. 21218.

Marshall Jones Co., Francestown, N.H. 03043.

## K

P. J. Kenedy & Sons, 866 Third Ave., N.Y., N.Y. 10022.

Alfred A. Knopf, Inc. (See Random House).

John Knox Press, 801 E. Main St., Richmond, Va. 23209.

## L

Landsford Publishing Co., 2516 Landsford Ave., San Jose, Cal. 95125.

Lane Magazine and Book Co., Menlo Park, Calif. 94025.

Lange Medical Publications, Drawer "L", Los Altos, Calif. 94022.

Larousse & Co., 572 Fifth Ave., N.Y., N.Y. 10036.

The Lawyers Co-operative Pub. Co., Aqueduct Bldg., Rochester, N.Y. 14603.

Lea & Febiger, 600 S. Washington Sq., Phila., Pa. 19106.

Liberal Arts Press, Inc. (See Bobbs-Merrill Co.).

J. B. Lippincott Co., E. Washington Sq., Phila., Pa. 19105.

Little, Brown & Co., Inc., 34 Beacon St., Boston, Mass. 02106.

Littlefield, Adams & Co., 81 Adams St., Totowa, N.J. 07512.

Liveright Pub. Corp., 386 Park Ave. S., N.Y., N.Y. 10016.

Louisiana State University Press, Hill Memorial Bldg., Louisiana State Univ., Baton Rouge, La. 70803.

Loyola University Press, 3441 N. Ashland Ave., Chicago, Ill. 60657.

## M

MacFadden-Bartell (See Bartell Media Corp.).

Mack Pub. Co., 20th & Northampton Sts., Easton, Pa. 18042.

Macmillan Publishing Co., Inc., 866 Third Ave., N.Y., N.Y. 10022.

Markham Publishing Co., 3322 W. Peterson Ave., Chicago, Ill. 60645.

McCormick-Mathers Pub. Co., Inc., Div. of Litton Ind., 300 Pike St., Cincinnati, Ohio 45202.

McGraw-Hill Book Co., 1221 Ave. of the Americas, N.Y., N.Y. 10020.

Branch
  Princeton Rd., Hightstown, N.J. 08520.
  Manchester Road, Manchester, Missouri 63011.
  8171 Redwood Highway, Novato, California 94947.

David McKay Co., Inc., 750 Third Ave., N.Y., N.Y. 10017.

McKnight & McKnight Pub. Co., P.O. Box 854, Bloomington, Ill. 61701.

Merck & Co., Inc., 126 E. Lincoln Ave., Rahway, N.J. 07065.

G. & C. Merriam Co., 47 Federal St., Springfield, Mass. 01101.

Chas. E. Merrill Publ. Co., 1300 Alum Creek Dr., Columbus, Ohio 43216.

Michigan State University Press, Box 550, E. Lansing, Mich. 48823.

M.I.T. Press, 28 Carleton St., Cambridge, Mass. 02142.

The Military Service Pub. Co. (See Stackpole Books).

Modern Language Ass'n., 62 Fifth Ave., N.Y., N.Y. 10011.

Modern Library, Inc., 201 E. 50th St., N.Y., N.Y. 10022.

Monarch Press (See Simon & Schuster).

Moody Press, 820 LaSalle St., Chicago, Ill. 60610.

The Morrison Pub. Co., R.R. No. 3, Claremont, Ont., Can.

William Morrow & Co., Inc., 105 Madison Ave., N.Y., N.Y. 10016.

The C. V. Mosby Co., 3301 Washington Blvd., St. Louis, Mo. 63103.

Muhlenberg Press (See Fortress Press).

# N

National Council of Teachers of English, 1111 Kenyon Rd., Urbana, Ill. 61801.

National Education Assn., 1201 16th St., N.W., Washington, D.C. 20036.

National Geographic Society, Washington, D.C. 20036.

National Press Books, 850 Hansen Way, Palo Alto, Cal. 94304.

National Textbook Co., 8259 Niles Center Rd., Skokie, Ill. 60076.

Thomas Nelson, Inc., 407 Seventh Ave. S., Nashville, Tenn. 37202.

The New American Library, Inc., 1301 Avenue of the Americas, New York, N.Y. 10019.

New Directions (See J. B. Lippincott Co.).

New York Graphic Society Publishers, Ltd., 140 Greenwich Ave., Greenwich, Conn. 06831.

New York University Press, Washington Sq., N.Y., N.Y. 10003.

Newbury House, Publishers, 66 Middle Rd., Rowley, Mass. 01969.

The Newman Press (See Paulist/Newman Press).

Noonday Press, Inc., 19 Union Sq. W., N.Y., N.Y. 10003.

Northwestern University Press, 1735 Benson, Evanston, Ill. 60201.

W. W. Norton & Co., Inc., 55 Fifth Ave., N.Y., N.Y. 10003.

# O

Oceana Publications, Dobbs Ferry, N.Y. 10522.

The Odyssey Press (See Bobbs-Merrill Co.).

Ohio State University Press, 2070 Neil Ave., Columbus, Ohio 43210.

Open Court Pub. Co., Box 599, LaSalle, Ill. 61301.

Oxford Book Co., 387 Park Ave. S., N.Y., N.Y. 10016.

Oxford University Press, Inc., 16–00 Pollitt Dr., Fair Lawn, N.J. 07410.

# P

Paris Book Center (See Larousse & Co.).

Paulist/Newman Press, 1865 Broadway, N.Y., N.Y. 10023.

F. E. Peacock Publishers, Inc., 401 W. Irving Park Rd., Itasca, Ill. 60143.

Pegasus (See Bobbs-Merrill Co.).

Penguin Books, Inc., 7110 Ambassador Rd., Baltimore, Md. 21207.

Pergamon Press, Inc., Maxwell House, Fairview Park, Elmsford, N.Y. 10523.

Peter Pauper Press, 629 MacQuesten Pkwy., Mt. Vernon, N.Y. 10552.

Philosophical Library, 15 E. 40th St., N.Y., N.Y. 10016.

Pitman Pub. Corp., 6 E. 43rd St., N.Y., N.Y. 10017.

Pocket Books, Inc., 630 Fifth Ave., N.Y., N.Y. 10020.

Popular Library Inc., 355 Lexington Ave., N.Y., N.Y. 10017.

Charles T. Powner Co., 407 S. Dearborn St., Chicago, Ill. 60605.

Praeger Publishers, Inc., 111 Fourth Ave., N.Y., N.Y. 10003.

Prentice-Hall, Inc., Englewood Cliffs, N.J. 07632.
Branch
    4700 South 5400 West, Salt Lake City, Utah 84118.

Press of Case Western Reserve Univ., Frank Adgate Quail Bldg., Cleveland, Ohio 44106.

Princeton University Press, Princeton, N.J. 08540.

Pruett Publishing Co., P.O. Box 1560, Boulder, Colo. 80302.

The Psychological Corp., 304 E. 45th St., N.Y., N.Y. 10017.

Public Affairs Pamphlets, 381 Park Ave. S., N.Y., N.Y. 10016.

Public Affairs Press, 419 New Jersey Ave., S.E., Washington, D.C. 20003.

G. P. Putnam's Sons, 200 Madison Ave., N.Y., N.Y. 10016.

Pyramid Publications, Inc., 919 Third Ave., N.Y., N.Y. 10022.

# Q

Quadrangle Books, Inc., 10 E. 53rd St., N.Y., N.Y. 10022.

# R

Rand McNally & Co., Box 7600, Chicago, Ill. 60680.

Random House, Inc., 201 E. 50th St., N.Y., N.Y. 10022.

Henry Regnery Co., 114 W. Illinois St., Chicago, Ill. 60610.

Reinhold Pub. Corp. (See Van Nostrand Reinhold Co.).

Fleming H. Revell Co., Old Tappan, N.J. 07675.

The Ronald Press Co., 79 Madison Ave., N.Y., N.Y. 10016.

The H. M. Rowe Co., 624 N. Gilmor St., Baltimore, Md. 21217.

# S

St. Martin's Press, Inc., 175 Fifth Ave., N.Y., N.Y. 10010.

Albert Saifer: Publisher, Box 56. Town Center, W. Orange, N.J. 07050.

Howard W. Sams & Co., Inc., 4300 W. 62nd St., Indianapolis, Ind. 46206.

W. B. Saunders Co., W. Washington Sq., Philadelphia, Pa. 19105.
Branch
   900 Stierlin Rd., Mountain View, Cal. 94040.

Schaum Publishing Co. (See McGraw-Hill).

G. Schirmer, Inc., 4 E. 49th St., N.Y., N.Y. 10017.

Schocken Books, Inc., 200 Madison Ave., N.Y., N.Y. 10016.

Schoenhof's Foreign Books, Inc., 1280 Mass. Ave., Cambridge, Mass. 02138.

Science Research Associates, Inc., 1540 Page Mill Rd., Palo Alto, Calif. 94304.

Scott, Foresman & Co., 1900 E. Lake Ave., Glenview, Ill. 60025.
Branch
   1955 Montreal Rd., Tucker, Ga. 30084.
   1900 E. Lake Ave., Glenview, Ill. 60025.
   11310 Gemini Lane, Dallas, Texas 75229.
   99 Bauer Drive, Oakland, New Jersey 07436.
   855 California Avenue, Palo Alto, California 94304.

Charles Scribner's Sons, 597 Fifth Ave., N.Y., N.Y. 10017.

Seabury Press, 815 Second Ave., N.Y., N.Y. 10017.

Sheed & Ward, Inc., 64 University Pl., N.Y., N.Y. 10003.

Sheridan House, Inc., P.O. Box 254, South Sta., Yonkers, N.Y. 10705.

Silver Burdett Co. (See General Learning Corp.).

Simmons-Boardman Pub. Corp., 350 Broadway, N.Y., N.Y. 10013.

Simon & Schuster, Inc., 630 Fifth Ave., N.Y., N.Y. 10020.

Skira Art Books (See World Publishing Co.).

Peter Smith, 6 Lexington Ave., Gloucester, Mass. 01931.

Social Science Research Council, 230 Park Ave., N.Y., N.Y. 10017.

Southern Illinois Univ. Press, Carbondale, Ill. 62901.

Southern Methodist University Press, Southern Methodist University, Dallas, Texas 75222.

South-Western Pub. Co., 5101 Madison Rd., Cincinnati, Ohio 45227.
Branch
   5001 West Harrison St., Chicago, Ill. 60644.
   512 North Ave., New Rochelle, N.Y. 10802.
   11310 Gemini Lane, Dallas, Texas 75229.
   11 Guittard Rd., Burlingame, Calif. 94010.

Springer Pub. Co., Inc., 200 Park Ave. S., N.Y., N.Y. 10003.

Springer-Verlag New York, Inc., 175 Fifth Ave., N.Y., N.Y. 10010.

Stackpole Books, Cameron & Kelker Sts., Harrisburg, Pa. 17105.

Stanford University Press, Stanford, Calif. 94305.

Sterling Pub. Co., Inc., 419 Park Ave. S., N.Y., N.Y. 10016.

Study*Master Pubs., 311 Crossways Park Dr., Woodbury, N.Y. 11797.

Sunburst Books (See Farrar, Straus and Giroux, Inc.).

The Superintendent of Documents, U.S. Government Printing Office, Washington, D.C. 20402.

Swallow Press, 1139 S. Wabash, Chicago, Ill. 60605.

Syracuse University Press, Box 8, University Station, Syracuse, N.Y. 13210.

# T

Taplinger Publishing Co., Inc., 200 Park Ave. E., N.Y., N.Y. 10003.

Teachers College Press, 1234 Amsterdam Ave., N.Y., N.Y. 10027.

Theatre Arts Books, 333 Sixth Ave., N.Y., N.Y. 10014.

Paul Theobald & Co., 5 N. Wabash Ave., Chicago, Ill. 60602.

Charles C Thomas, Publisher, 301–327 E. Lawrence Ave., Springfield, Ill. 62703.

Thomas Law Book Co., 1909 Washington Ave., St. Louis, Mo. 63103.

Time-Life Books, Rockefeller Center, N.Y., N.Y. 10020.

Tudor Publishing Co. (Harlem Book Co., Penn Prints), 221 Park Ave. S., N.Y., N.Y. 10003.

Charles E. Tuttle Co., 28 S. Main St., Rutland, Vt. 05701.

The Twentieth Century Fund, 41 E. 70th St., N.Y., N.Y. 10021.

## U

Frederick Ungar Pub. Co., Inc., 250 Park Ave. S., N.Y., N.Y. 10003.

Union of American Hebrew Congregations, 838 Fifth Ave., N.Y., N.Y. 10021.

United Nations, Rm. LX2312, New York, N.Y. 10017.

U.S. Naval Institute, Annapolis, Md. 21402.

Universe Books, Inc., 381 Park Ave. S., N.Y., N.Y. 10016.

University Books, Inc., Div. of Lyle Stuart, Inc., 120 Enterprise Ave., Secaucus, N.J. 07094.

Univ. of Alabama Press, Mail Drawer 2877, University, Ala. 34586.

Univ. of California Press, 2223 Fulton St., Berkeley, Calif. 94720.

Univ. of Chicago Press, 5801 Ellis Ave., Chicago, Ill. 60637.

Univ. of Florida Press, 15 N.W. 15th St., Gainesville, Fla. 32601.

Univ. of Georgia Press, U. of Ga., Athens, Ga. 30601.

Univ. of Illinois Press, Urbana, Ill. 61801.

Univ. of Miami Press, P.O. Drawer 9088, Coral Gables, Fla. 33124.

Univ. of Michigan Press, Ann Arbor, Mich. 48106.

Univ. of Minnesota Press, 2037 University Ave. S.E., Minneapolis, Minn. 55455.

Univ. of Nebraska Press, 901 N. 17th St., Lincoln, Nebr. 68508.

The Univ. of New Mexico Press, Albuquerque, N.M. 87106.

Univ. of North Carolina Press, Box 2288, Chapel Hill, N.C. 27514.

Univ. of Notre Dame Press, Notre Dame, Ind. 46556.

Univ. of Oklahoma Press, 1005 Asp Ave., Norman, Okla. 73069.

Univ. of Pennsylvania Press, 3933 Walnut St., Philadelphia, Pa. 19104.

Univ. of Pittsburgh Press, 127 N. Bellefield Ave., Pittsburgh, Pa. 15213.

Univ. of South Carolina Press, Columbia, S.C. 29208.

Univ. of Tennessee Press, Communications Bldg., Knoxville, Tenn. 37916.

Univ. of Texas Press, P.O. Box 7819, Austin, Texas 78712.

Univ. of Toronto Press, Front Campus, Univ. of Toronto, Toronto 181, Can.

Univ. of Washington Press, Seattle, Wash. 98105.

Univ. of Wisconsin Press, P.O. Box 1379, Madison, Wis. 53701.

Univ. Press of Hawaii, 535 Ward Ave., Honolulu, Hawaii, 96814.

Univ. Press of Kansas, 366 Watson Library, Lawrence, Kansas 66044.

Univ. Press of Kentucky, Lexington, Ky. 40506.

Univ. Press of Washington, D.C., Suite 321, 1010 Vermont Ave., N.W., Washington, D.C. 20005.

## V

Van Nostrand Reinhold Co., 450 W. 33rd St., N.Y., N.Y. 10001.

Vanderbilt University Press, Nashville, Tenn. 37203.

Vanguard Press, 424 Madison Ave., N.Y., N.Y. 10017.

S. F. Vanni, 30 W. 12th St., N.Y., N.Y. 10011.

Vantage Press, Inc., 516 W. 34th St., N.Y., N.Y. 10001.

The Viking Press, Inc., 625 Madison Ave., N.Y., N.Y. 10022.

Vintage Books, Inc., 201 E. 50th St., N.Y., N.Y. 10022.

## W

Wadsworth Publishing Co., Inc., Belmont, Calif. 94002.

Frank R. Walker Co., 5030 N. Harlem Ave., Chicago, Ill. 60656.

Frederick Warne & Co., Inc., 101 Fifth Ave., N.Y., N.Y. 10003.

Watson-Guptill Publications, 165 W. 64th St., N.Y., N.Y. 10036.

Franklin Watts, Inc., 845 Third Ave., New York, N.Y. 10022.

Wayne State University Press, 5980 Cass Ave., Detroit, Mich. 48202.

Wesleyan Univ. Press, 100 Riverview Center, Middletown, Conn. 06457.

Western Pub. Co., Inc., 1220 Mound Ave., Racine, Wis. 53404.

The Westminster Press, Witherspoon Bldg., Phila., Pa. 19107.

John Wiley & Sons, Inc., 605 Third Ave., N.Y., N.Y. 10016.
Branch
   1530 S. Redwood Rd., Salt Lake City, Utah 84104.

The Williams & Wilkins Co., 428 E. Preston St., Baltimore, Md. 21202.

Willis Music Co., 7380 Industrial Rd., P.O. Box 433, Florence, Ky. 41042.

Wittenborn & Co., 1018 Madison Ave., N.Y., N.Y. 10021.

World Book Co. (See Harcourt Brace Jovanovich.)

World Publishing Co., Inc., 2080 W. 117th St., Cleveland, Ohio 44111.

The Writer, Inc., 8 Arlington St., Boston, Mass. 02116.

Writer's Digest, 22 E. 12th St., Cincinnati, Ohio 45210.

# Y

Yale University Press, 92 A Yale Station, New Haven, Conn. 06520.

Year Book Medical Pub., Inc., 35 E. Wacker Dr., Chicago, Ill. 60601.

# Z

Zondervan Pub. House, 1415 Lake Dr. S.E., Grand Rapids, Mich. 49506.

## The Newbery Medal

As a tribute to John Newbery (1713–1767), the first English publisher of books for children, Frederic G. Melcher named and donated the Newbery Medal. Beginning in 1922, the Newbery Medal has been awarded by the Children's Services Division of the American Library Association to the author of the most distinguished contribution to literature for children published in the United States during the preceding year. The award, which is announced in January, is limited to United States citizens or residents.

**1976** *The Grey King*, by Susan Cooper (Atheneum/McEldery)
**Honor Books:** *The Hundred Penny Box*, by Sharon Bell Mathis (Viking); *Dragonwings* by Laurence Yep (Harper)
**1975** *M. C. Higgins the Great* by Virginia Hamilton (Macmillan)
**Honor Books:** *My Brother Sam Is Dead*, by James Lincoln Collier and Christopher Collier (Four Winds); *The Perilous Gard*, by Elizabeth Marie Pope (Houghton); *Philip Hall Likes Me. I Reckon Maybe*, by Bette Greene (Dial); *Figgs & Phantoms* by Ellen Raskin (Dutton)
**1974** *The Slave Dancer*, by Paula Fox (Bradbury)
**Honor Book:** *The Dark Is Rising*, by Susan Cooper (Atheneum)
**1973** *Julie of the Wolves*, by Jean Craighead George (Harper)
**Honor Books:** *Frog and Toad Together*, by Arnold Lobel (Harper); *The Upstairs Room*, by Johanna Reiss (Crowell); *The Witches of Worm*, by Zilpha Keatley Snyder (Atheneum)
**1972** *Mrs. Frisby and the Rats of NIMH*, by Robert C. O'Brien (Atheneum)
**Honor Books:** *Annie and the Old One*, by Miska Miles (Atlantic-Little); *The Headless Cupid*, by Zilpha Keatley Snyder (Atheneum); *Incident at Hawk's Hill*, by Allan W. Eckert (Little); *The Planet of Junior Brown*, by Virginia Hamilton (Macmillan); *The Tombs of Atuan*, by Ursula K. LeGuin (Atheneum)
**1971** *Summer of the Swans*, by Betsy Byars (Viking)
**Honor Books:** *Knee-Knock Rise*, by Natalie Babbitt (Farrar); *Enchantress from the Stars*, by Sylvia Louise Engdahl (Atheneum); *Sing Down the Moon*, by Scott O'Dell (Houghton)
**1970** *Sounder*, by William H Armstrong (Harper)
**Honor Books:** *Our Eddie*, by Sulamith Ish-Kishor (Pantheon); *The Many Ways of Seeing:*

# Appendix C
# Children's Book Awards

*An Introduction to the Pleasures of Art*, by Janet Gaylord Moore (World); *Journey Outside*, by Mary Q. Steele (Viking)

**1969** *The High King*, by Lloyd Alexander (Holt)
**Honor Books:** *To Be a Slave*, by Julius Lester (Dial); *When Shlemiel Went to Warsaw & Other Stories*, by Isaac Bashevis Singer (Farrar)

**1968** *From the Mixed-Up Files of Mrs Basil E. Frankweiler*, by E. L. Konigsburg (Atheneum)
**Honor Books:** *Jennifer, Hecate, Macbeth, William McKinley, and Me, Elizabeth*, by E. L. Konigsburg (Atheneum); *The Black Pearl*, by Scott O'Dell (Houghton); *The Fearsome Inn*, by Isaac Bashevis Singer (Scribner's); *The Egypt Game*, by Zilpha Keatley Snyder (Atheneum)

**1967** *Up a Road Slowly*, by Irene Hunt (Follett)
**Honor Books:** *The King's Fifth*, by Scott O'Dell (Houghton); *Zlateh the Goat and Other Stories*, by Isaac Bashevis Singer (Harper); *The Jazz Man*, by Mary H. Weik (Atheneum)

**1966** *I, Juan de Pareja*, by Elizabeth Borten de Treviño (Farrar)
**Honor Books:** *The Black Cauldron*, by Lloyd Alexander (Holt); *The Animal Family*, by Randall Jarrell (Pantheon); *The Noonday Friends*, by Mary Stolz (Harper)

**1965** *Shadow of a Bull*, by Maia Wojciechowska (Atheneum)
**Honor Book:** *Across Five Aprils*, by Irene Hunt (Follett)

**1964** *It's Like This, Cat*, by Emily Cheney Neville (Harper)
**Honor Books:** *Rascal*, by Sterling North (Dutton); *The Loner*, by Ester Wier (McKay)

**1963** *A Wrinkle in Time*, by Madeleine L'Engle (Farrar)
**Honor Books:** *Thistle and Thyme*, by Sorche Nic Leodhas (Holt); *Men of Athens*, by Olivia Coolidge (Houghton)

**1962** *The Bronze Bow*, by Elizabeth George Speare (Houghton)
**Honor Books:** *Frontier Living*, by Edwin Tunis (World); *The Golden Goblet*, by Eloise McGraw (Coward); *Belling the Tiger*, by Mary Stolz (Harper)

**1961** *Island of the Blue Dolphins*, by Scott O'Dell (Houghton)
**Honor Books:** *America Moves Forward*, by Gerald W. Johnson (Morrow); *Old Ramon*, by Jack Schaefer (Houghton); *The Cricket in Times Square*, by George Seldon (Farrar)

**1960** *Onion John*, by Joseph Krumgold (Crowell)
**Honor Books:** *My Side of the Mountain*, by Jean George (Dutton); *America Is Born*, by Gerald W. Johnson (Morrow); *The Gammage Cup*, by Carol Kendall (Harcourt)

**1959** *The Witch of Blackbird Pond*, by Elizabeth George Speare (Houghton)
**Honor Books:** *The Family under the Bridge*, by Natalie S. Carlson (Harper); *Along Came a Dog*, by Meindert DeJong (Harper); *Chucaro: Wild Pony of the Pampa*, by Francis Kalnay (Harcourt); *The Perilous Road*, by William O. Steele (Harcourt)

**1958** *Rifles for Watie*, by Harold Keith (Crowell)
**Honor Books:** *The Horsecatcher*, by Mari Sandoz (Westminster); *Gone-Away Lake*, by Elizabeth Enright (Harcourt); *The Great Wheel*, by Robert Lawson (Viking); *Tom Paine, Freedom's Apostle*, by Leo Gurko (Crowell)

**1957** *Miracles on Maple Hill*, by Virginia Sorenson (Harcourt)
**Honor Books:** *Old Yeller*, by Fred Gipson (Harper); *The House of Sixty Fathers*, by Meindert DeJong (Harper); *Mr. Justice Holmes*, by Clara Ingram Judson (Follett); *The Corn Grows Ripe*, by Dorothy Rhoads (Viking); *Black Fox of Lorne*, by Marguerite de Angeli (Doubleday)

**1956** *Carry on, Mr. Bowditch*, by Jean Lee Latham (Houghton)
**Honor Books:** *The Secret River*, by Marjorie Kinnan Rawlings (Scribner's); *The Golden Name Day*, by Jennie Lindquist (Harper); *Men, Microscopes, and Living Things*, by Katherine Shippen (Viking)

**1955** *The Wheel on the School*, by Meindert DeJong (Harper)
**Honor Books:** *The Courage of Sarah Noble*, by Alice Dalgliesh (Scribner's); *Banner in the Sky*, by James Ullman (Lippincott)

**1954** *And Now Miguel*, by Joseph Krumgold (Crowell)
**Honor Books:** *All Alone*, by Claire Huchet Bishop (Viking); *Shadrach*, by Meindert DeJong (Harper); *Hurry Home Candy*, by Meindert DeJong (Harper)

**1953** *Secret of the Andes*, by Ann Nolan Clark (Viking)
**Honor Books:** *Charlotte's Web*, by E. B. White (Harper); *Moccasin Trail*, by Eloise McGraw (Coward); *Red Sails to Capri*, by Ann Weil (Viking); *The Bears on Hemlock Mountain*, by Alice Dalgliesh (Scribner's); *Birthdays of Freedom, Vol. 1*, by Genevieve Foster (Scribner's)

**1952** *Ginger Pye*, by Eleanor Estes (Harcourt)
**Honor Books:** *Americans before Columbus*, by Elizabeth Baity (Viking); *Minn of the Mississippi*, by Holling C. Holling (Houghton); *The Defender*, by Nicholas Kalashnikoff (Scribner's); *The Light at Tern Rocks*, by Julia Sauer (Viking); *The Apple and the Arrow*, by Mary and Conrad Buff (Houghton)

**1951** *Amos Fortune, Free Man*, by Elizabeth Yates (Aladdin)

**Honor Books:** *Better Known as Johnny Apple-seed,* by Mabel Leigh Hunt (Lippincott); *Gandhi, Fighter without a Sword,* by Jeanette Eaton (Morrow); *Abraham Lincoln, Friend of the People,* by Clara Ingram Judson (Follett); *The Story of Appleby Capple,* by Anne Parrish (Harper)

1950 *The Door in the Wall,* by Marguerite de Angeli (Doubleday)
**Honor Books:** *Tree of Freedom,* by Rebecca Caudill (Viking); *The Blue Cat of Castle Town,* by Catherine Coblentz (Longmans); *Kildee House,* by Rutherford Montgomery (Doubleday); *George Washington,* by Genevieve Foster (Scribner's); *Song of the Pines,* by Walter and Marion Havighurst (Winston)

1949 *King of the Wind,* by Marguerite Henry (Rand)
**Honor Books:** *Seabird,* by Holling C. Holling (Houghton); *Daughter of the Mountains,* by Louise Rankin (Viking); *My Father's Dragon,* by Ruth S. Gannett (Random); *Story of the Negro,* by Arna Bontemps (Knopf)

1948 *The Twenty-One Balloons,* by William Pène du Bois (Viking)
**Honor Books:** *Pancakes—Paris,* by Claire Huchet Bishop (Viking); *Li Lun, Lad of Courage,* by Carolyn Treffinger (Abingdon); *The Quaint and Curious Quest of Johnny Longfoot,* by Catherine Besterman (Bobbs); *The Cow-Tail Switch, and Other West African Stories,* by Harold Courlander (Holt); *Misty of Chincoteague,* by Marguerite Henry (Rand)

1947 *Miss Hickory,* by Carolyn Sherwin Bailey (Viking)
**Honor Books:** *Wonderful Year,* by Nancy Barnes (Messner); *Big Tree,* by Mary and Conrad Buff (Viking); *The Heavenly Tenants,* by William Maxwell (Harper); *The Avion My Uncle Flew,* by Cyrus Fisher (Appleton); *The Hidden Treasure of Glaston,* by Eleanore Jewett (Viking)

1946 *Strawberry Girl,* by Lois Lenski (Lippincott)
**Honor Books:** *Justin Morgan Had a Horse,* by Marguerite Henry (Rand); *The Moved-Outers,* by Florence Crannell Means (Houghton); *Bhimsa, the Dancing Bear,* by Christine Weston (Scribner's); *New Found World,* by Katherine Shippen (Viking)

1945 *Rabbit Hill,* by Robert Lawson (Viking)
**Honor Books:** *The Hundred Dresses,* by Eleanor Estes (Harcourt); *The Silver Pencil,* by Alice Dalgliesh (Scribner's); *Abraham Lincoln's World,* by Genevieve Foster (Scribner's); *Lone Journey: The Life of Roger Williams,* by Jeanette Eaton (Harcourt)

1944 *Johnny Tremain,* by Esther Forbes (Houghton)
**Honor Books:** *These Happy Golden Years,* by Laura Ingalls Wilder (Harper); *Fog Magic,* by Julia Sauer (Viking); *Rufus M.,* by Eleanor Estes (Harcourt); *Mountain Born,* by Elizabeth Yates (Coward)

1943 *Adam of the Road,* by Elizabeth Janet Gray (Viking)
**Honor Books:** *The Middle Moffat,* by Eleanor Estes (Harcourt); *Have You Seen Tom Thumb?,* by Mabel Leigh Hunt (Lippincott)

1942 *The Matchlock Gun,* by Walter D. Edmonds (Dodd)
**Honor Books:** *Little Town on the Prairie,* by Laura Ingalls Wilder (Harper); *George Washington's World,* by Genevieve Foster (Scribner's); *Indian Captive: The Story of Mary Jemison,* by Lois Lenski (Lippincott); *Down Ryton Water,* by Eva Roe Gaggin (Viking)

1941 *Call It Courage,* by Armstrong Sperry (Macmillan)
**Honor Books:** *Blue Willow,* by Doris Gates (Viking); *Young Mac of Fort Vancouver,* by Mary Jane Carr (Crowell); *The Long Winter,* by Laura Ingalls Wilder (Harper); *Nansen,* by Anna Gertrude Hall (Viking)

1940 *Daniel Boone,* by James Daugherty (Viking)
**Honor Books:** *The Singing Tree,* by Kate Seredy (Viking); *Runner of the Mountain Tops,* by Mabel Robinson (Random); *By the Shores of Silver Lake,* by Laura Ingalls Wilder (Harper); *Boy with a Pack,* by Stephen W. Meader (Harcourt)

1939 *Thimble Summer,* by Elizabeth Enright (Rinehart)
**Honor Books:** *Nina,* by Valenti Angelo (Viking); *Mr. Popper's Penguins,* by Richard and Florence Atwater (Little); *"Hello the Boat!,"* by Phyllis Crawford (Holt); *Leader by Destiny: George Washington, Man and Patriot,* by Jeanette Eaton (Harcourt); *Penn,* by Elizabeth Janet Gray (Viking)

1938 *The White Stag,* by Kate Seredy (Viking)
**Honor Books:** *Pecos Bill,* by James Cloyd Bowman (Little); *Bright Island,* by Mabel Robinson (Random); *On the Banks of Plum Creek,* by Laura Ingalls Wilder (Harper)

1937 *Roller Skates,* by Ruth Sawyer (Viking)
**Honor Books:** *Phoebe Fairchild: Her Book,* by Lois Lenski (Stokes); *Whistler's Van,* by Idwal Jones (Viking); *Golden Basket,* by Ludwig Bemelmans (Viking); *Winterbound,* by Margery Bianco (Viking); *Audubon,* by Constance Rourke (Harcourt); *The Codfish Musket,* by Agnes Hewes (Doubleday)

1936 *Caddie Woodlawn,* by Carol Brink (Macmillan)
**Honor Books:** *Honk, the Moose,* by Phil Stong (Dodd); *The Good Master,* by Kate Seredy (Viking); *Young Walter Scott,* by Elizabeth Janet

Gray (Viking); *All Sail Set*, by Armstrong Sperry (Winston)

1935 *Dobry*, by Monica Shannon (Viking)

**Honor Books:** *Pageant of Chinese History*, by Elizabeth Seeger (Longmans); *Davy Crockett*, by Constance Rourke (Harcourt); *Day on Skates*, by Hilda Van Stockum (Harper)

1934 *Invincible Louisa*, by Cornelia Meigs (Little)

**Honor Books:** *The Forgotten Daughter*, by Caroline Snedeker (Doubleday); *Swords of Steel*, by Elsie Singmaster (Houghton); *ABC Bunny*, by Wanda Gág (Coward); *Winged Girl of Knossos*, by Erik Berry (Appleton); *New Land*, by Sarah Schmidt (McBride); *Big Tree of Bunlahy*, by Padraic Colum (Macmillan); *Glory of the Seas*, by Agnes Hewes (Knopf); *Apprentice of Florence*, by Anne Kyle (Houghton)

1933 *Young Fu of the Upper Yangtze*, by Elizabeth Foreman Lewis (Winston)

**Honor Books:** *Swift Rivers*, by Cornelia Meigs (Little); *The Railroad to Freedom*, by Hildegarde Swift (Harcourt); *Children of the Soil*, by Nora Burglon (Doubleday)

1932 *Waterless Mountain*, by Laura Adams Armer (Longmans)

**Honor Books:** *The Fairy Circus*, by Dorothy P. Lathrop (Macmillan); *Calico Bush*, by Rachel Field (Macmillan); *Boy of the South Seas*, by Eunice Tietjens (Coward); *Out of the Flame*, by Eloise Lownsbery (Longmans); *Jane's Island*, by Marjorie Allee (Houghton); *Truce of the Wolf and Other Tales of Old Italy*, by Mary Gould Davis (Harcourt)

1931 *The Cat Who Went to Heaven*, by Elizabeth Coatsworth (Macmillan)

**Honor Books:** *Floating Island*, by Anne Parrish (Harper); *The Dark Star of Itza*, by Alida Malkus (Harcourt); *Queer Person*, by Ralph Hubbard (Doubleday); *Mountains Are Free*, by Julia Davis Adams (Dutton); *Spice and the Devil's Cave*, by Agnes Hewes (Knopf); *Meggy Macintosh*, by Elizabeth Janet Gray (Doubleday); *Garram the Hunter*, by Herbert Best (Doubleday); *Ood-Le-Uk the Wanderer*, by Alice Lide and Margaret Johansen (Little)

1930 *Hitty, Her First Hundred Years*, by Rachel Field (Macmillan)

**Honor Books:** *Daughter of the Seine*, by Jeanette Eaton (Harper); *Pran of Albania*, by Elizabeth Miller (Doubleday); *Jumping-Off Place*, by Marian Hurd McNeely (Longmans); *Tangle-Coated Horse and Other Tales*, by Ella Young (Longmans); *Vaino*, by Julia Davis Adams (Dutton); *Little Blacknose*, by Hildegarde Swift (Harcourt)

1929 *The Trumpeter of Krakow*, by Eric P. Kelly (Macmillan)

**Honor Books:** *Pigtail of Ah Lee Ben Loo*, by John Bennett (Longmans); *Millions of Cats*, by Wanda Gág (Coward); *The Boy Who Was*, by Grace Hallock (Dutton); *Clearing Weather*, by Cornelia Meigs (Little); *Runaway Papoose*, by Grace Moon (Doubleday); *Tod of the Fens*, by Elinor Whitney (Macmillan)

1928 *Gayneck, the Story of a Pigeon*, by Dhan Gopal Mukerji (Dutton)

**Honor Books:** *The Wonder Smith and His Son*, by Ella Young (Longmans); *Downright Dencey*, by Caroline Snedeker (Doubleday)

1927 *Smoky, the Cowhorse*, by Will James (Scribner's)

**Honor Books:** No Record

1926 *Shen of the Sea*, by Arthur Bowie Chrisman (Dutton)

**Honor Book:** *Voyagers*, by Padraic Colum (Macmillan)

1925 *Tales from Silver Lands*, by Charles Finger (Doubleday)

**Honor Books:** *Nicholas*, by Anne Carroll Moore (Putnam's); *Dream Coach*, by Anne Parrish (Macmillan)

1924 *The Dark Frigate*, by Charles Hawes (Atlantic-Little)

**Honor Book:** No Record

1923 *The Voyages of Doctor Dolittle*, by Hugh Lofting (Lippincott)

**Honor Book:** No Record

1922 *The Story of Mankind*, by Hendrik Willem van Loon (Liveright)

**Honor Books:** *The Great Quest*, by Charles Hawes (Little); *Cedric the Forester*, by Bernard Marshall (Appleton); *The Old Tobacco Shop*, by William Bowen (Macmillan); *The Golden Fleece and the Heroes Who Lived before Achilles*, by Padraic Colum (Macmillan); *Windy Hill*, by Cornelia Meigs (Macmillan)

## The Caldecott Medal

As a tribute to Randolph Caldecott (1846–1886), the acclaimed English illustrator, Frederic G. Melcher named and donated the Caldecott Medal. Since 1938 the Caldecott Medal has been awarded by the Children's Services Division of the American Library Association to the illustrator of the most distinguished picture book for children published in the United States during the preceding year. The award, which is announced in January, is limited to United States citizens or residents.

1976 *Why Mosquitoes Buzz in People's Ears, A West African Tale*, retold by Verna Aardema, illus. by Leo and Diane Dillon (Dial)
   **Honor Books:** *Strega Nona*, retold and illus. by Tomie de Paola (Prentice-Hall); *The Desert Is Theirs*, by Byrd Baylor, illus. by Peter Parnall (Scribner)

1975 *Arrow to the Sun, A Pueblo Indian Tale*, adapted and illus. by Gerald McDermott (Viking)
   **Honor Book:** *Jambo Means Hello, Swahili Alphabet Book*, by Muriel Feelings, illus. by Tom Feelings (Dial)

1974 *Duffy and the Devil*, by Margot Zemach (Farrar)
   **Honor Books:** *Three Jovial Huntsmen*, adapted and illus. by Susan Jeffers (Bradbury); *Cathedral: The Story of Its Construction*, by David Macaulay (Houghton)

1973 *The Funny Little Woman*, retold by Arlene Mosel, illus. by Blair Lent (Dutton)
   **Honor Books:** *Anansi the Spider*, adapted and illus. by Gerald McDermott (Holt); *Hosie's Alphabet*, by Hosea, Tobias, and Lisa Baskin, illus. by Leonard Baskin (Viking); *Snow White and the Seven Dwarfs*, translated by Randall Jarrel, illus. by Nancy Ekholm Burkert (Farrar); *When Clay Sings*, by Byrd Baylor, illus. by Tom Bahti (Scribner)

1972 *One Fine Day*, by Nonny Hogrogian (Macmillan)
   **Honor Books:** *Hildilid's Night*, by Cheli Durán Ryan, illus. by Arnold Lobel (Macmillan); *If All the Seas Were One Sea*, by Janina Domanska (Macmillan); *Moja Means One*, by Muriel Feelings, illus. by Tom Feelings (Dial)

1971 *A Story, a Story*, by Gail E. Haley (Atheneum)
   **Honor Books:** *The Angry Moon*, by William Sleator, illus. by Blair Lent (Atlantic-Little); *Frog and Toad Are Friends*, by Arnold Lobel (Harper); *In the Night Kitchen*, by Maurice Sendak (Harper)

1970 *Sylvester and the Magic Pebble*, by William Steig (Windmill/Simon & Schuster)
   **Honor Books:** *Goggles*, by Ezra Jack Keats (Macmillan); *Alexander and the Wind-Up Mouse*, by Leo Lionni (Pantheon); *Pop Corn & Ma Goodness*, by Edna Mitchell Preston, illus. by Robert Andrew Parker (Viking); *Thy Friend, Obadiah*, by Brinton Turkle (Viking); *The Judge*, by Harve Zemach, illus. by Margot Zemach (Farrar)

1969 *The Fool of the World and the Flying Ship*, by Arthur Ransome, illus. by Uri Shulevitz (Farrar)
   **Honor Book:** *Why the Sun and the Moon Live in the Sky*, by Elphinstone Dayrell, illus. by Blair Lent (Houghton)

1968 *Drummer Hoff*, by Barbara Emberley, illus. by Ed Emberley (Prentice)

   **Honor Books:** *Frederick*, by Leo Lionni (Pantheon); *Seashore Story*, by Taro Yashima (Viking); *The Emperor and the Kite*, by Jane Yolen, illus. by Ed Young (World)

1967 *Sam, Bangs, and Moonshine*, by Evaline Ness (Holt)
   **Honor Book:** *One Wide River to Cross*, by Barbara Emberley, illus. by Ed Emberley (Prentice)

1966 *Always Room for One More*, by Sorche Nic Leodhas, illus. by Nonny Hogrogian (Holt)
   **Honor Books:** *Hide and Seek Fog*, by Alvin Tresselt, illus. by Roger Duvoisin (Lothrop); *Just Me*, by Marie Hall Ets (Viking); *Tom Tit Tot*, by Evaline Ness (Scribner)

1965 *May I Bring a Friend?*, by Beatrice Schenk de Regniers, illus. by Beni Montresor (Atheneum)
   **Honor Books:** *Rain Makes Applesauce*, by Julian Scheer, illus. by Marvin Bileck (Holiday); *The Wave*, by Margaret Hodges, illus. by Blair Lent (Houghton); *A Pocketful of Cricket*, by Rebecca Caudill, illus. by Evaline Ness (Holt)

1964 *Where the Wild Things Are*, by Maurice Sendak (Harper)
   **Honor Books:** *Swimmy*, by Leo Lionni (Pantheon); *All in the Morning Early*, by Sorche Nic Leodhas, illus. by Evaline Ness (Holt); *Mother Goose and Nursery Rhymes*, illus. by Philip Reed (Atheneum)

1963 *The Snowy Day*, by Ezra Jack Keats (Viking)
   **Honor Books:** *The Sun Is a Golden Earring*, by Natalia M. Belting, illus. by Bernarda Bryson (Holt); *Mr. Rabbit and the Lovely Present*, by Charlotte Zolotow, illus. by Maurice Sendak (Harper)

1962 *Once a Mouse . . .*, by Marcia Brown (Scribner's)
   **Honor Books:** *The Fox Went Out on a Chilly Night*, illus. by Peter Spier (Doubleday); *Little Bear's Visit*, by Else Holmelund Minarik, illus. by Maurice Sendak (Harper); *The Day We Saw the Sun Come Up*, by Alice E. Goudey, illus. by Adrienne Adams (Scribner)

1961 *Baboushka and the Three Kings*, by Ruth Robbins, illus. by Nicholas Sidjakov (Parnassus)
   **Honor Book:** *Inch by Inch*, by Leo Lionni (Astor-Honor)

1960 *Nine Days to Christmas*, by Marie Hall Ets and Aurora Labastida, illus. by Marie Hall Ets (Viking)
   **Honor Books:** *Houses from the Sea*, by Alice E. Goudey, illus. by Adrienne Adams (Scribner); *The Moon Jumpers*, by Janice May Udry, illus. by Maurice Sendak (Harper)

1959 *Chanticleer and the Fox*, adapted from Chaucer, and illus. by Barbara Cooney (Crowell)
   **Honor Books:** *The House That Jack Built*, by Antonio Frasconi (Harcourt); *What Do You Say,*

*Dear?,* by Sesyle Joslin, illus. by Maurice Sendak (Scott); *Umbrella,* by Taro Yashima (Viking)

**1958** *Time of Wonder,* by Robert McCloskey (Viking)

**Honor Books:** *Fly High, Fly Low,* by Don Freeman (Viking); *Anatole and the Cat,* by Eve Titus, illus. by Paul Galdone (McGraw)

**1957** *A Tree Is Nice,* by Janice May Udry, illus. by Marc Simont (Harper)

**Honor Books:** *Mr. Penny's Race Horse,* by Marie Hall Ets (Viking); *1 Is One,* by Tasha Tudor (Walck); *Anatole,* by Eve Titus, illus. by Paul Galdone (McGraw); *Gillespie and the Guards,* by Benjamin Elkin, illus. by James Daugherty (Viking); *Lion,* by William Pène du Bois (Viking)

**1956** *Frog Went A-Courtin',* ed. by John Langstaff, illus. by Feodor Rojankovsky (Harcourt)

**Honor Books:** *Play with Me,* by Marie Hall Ets (Viking); *Crow Boy,* by Taro Yashima (Viking)

**1955** *Cinderella, or the Little Glass Slipper,* by Charles Perrault, trans. and illus. by Marcia Brown (Scribner)

**Honor Books:** *Book of Nursery and Mother Goose Rhymes,* illus. by Marguerite de Angeli (Doubleday); *Wheel on the Chimney,* by Margaret Wise Brown, illus. by Tibor Gergely (Lippincott); *The Thanksgiving Story,* by Alice Dalgliesh, illus. by Helen Sewell (Scribner)

**1954** *Madeline's Rescue,* by Ludwig Bemelmans (Viking)

**Honor Books:** *Journey Cake, Ho!,* by Ruth Sawyer, illus. by Robert McCloskey (Viking); *When Will the World Be Mine?,* by Miriam Schlein, illus. by Jean Charlot (Scott); *The Steadfast Tin Soldier,* by Hans Christian Andersen, illus. by Marcia Brown (Scribner); *A Very Special House,* by Ruth Krauss, illus. by Maurice Sendak (Harper); *Green Eyes,* by A. Birnbaum (Capitol)

**1953** *The Biggest Bear,* by Lynd Ward (Houghton)

**Honor Books:** *Puss in Boots,* by Charles Perrault, illus. and trans. by Marcia Brown (Scribner); *One Morning in Maine,* by Robert McCloskey (Viking); *Ape in a Cape,* by Fritz Eichenberg (Harcourt); *The Storm Book,* by Charlotte Zolotow, illus. by Margaret Bloy Graham (Harper); *Five Little Monkeys,* by Juliet Kepes (Houghton)

**1952** *Finders Keepers,* by Will, illus. by Nicolas (Harcourt)

**Honor Books:** *Mr. T. W. Anthony Woo,* by Marie Hall Ets (Viking); *Skipper John's Cook,* by Marcia Brown (Scribner); *All Falling Down,* by Gene Zion, illus. by Margaret Bloy Graham (Harper); *Bear Party,* by William Pène du Bois (Viking); *Feather Mountain,* by Elizabeth Olds (Houghton)

**1951** *The Egg Tree,* by Katherine Milhous (Scribner)

**Honor Books:** *Dick Whittington and His Cat,* by Marcia Brown (Scribner); *The Two Reds,* by Will, illus. by Nicolas (Harcourt); *If I Ran the Zoo,* by Dr. Seuss (Random); *The Most Wonderful Doll in the World,* by Phyllis McGinley, illus. by Helen Stone (Lippincott); *T-Bone, the Baby Sitter,* by Clare Newberry (Harper)

**1950** *Song of the Swallows,* by Leo Politi (Scribner)

**Honor Books:** *America's Ethan Allen,* by Stewart Holbrook, illus. by Lynd Ward (Houghton); *The Wild Birthday Cake,* by Lavinia Davis, illus. by Hildegard Woodward (Doubleday); *The Happy Day,* by Ruth Krauss, illus. by Marc Simont (Harper); *Bartholomew and the Oobleck,* by Dr. Seuss (Random); *Henry Fisherman,* by Marcia Brown (Scribner)

**1949** *The Big Snow,* by Berta and Elmer Hader (Macmillan)

**Honor Books:** *Blueberries for Sal,* by Robert McCloskey (Viking); *All Around the Town,* by Phyllis McGinley, illus. by Helen Stone (Lippincott); *Juanita,* by Leo Politi (Scribner); *Fish in the Air,* by Kurt Wiese (Viking)

**1948** *White Snow, Bright Snow,* by Alvin Tresselt, illus. by Roger Duvoisin (Lothrop)

**Honor Books:** *Stone Soup,* by Marcia Brown (Scribner); *McElligot's Pool,* by Dr. Seuss (Random); *Bambino the Clown,* by George Schreiber (Viking); *Roger and the Fox,* by Lavinia Davis, illus. by Hildegard Woodward (Doubleday); *Song of Robin Hood,* ed. by Anne Malcolmson, illus. by Virginia Lee Burton (Houghton)

**1947** *The Little Island,* by Golden MacDonald, illus. by Leonard Weisgard (Doubleday)

**Honor Books:** *Rain Drop Splash,* by Alvin Tresselt, illus. by Leonard Weisgard (Lothrop); *Boats on the River,* by Marjorie Flack, illus. by Jay Hyde Barnum (Viking); *Timothy Turtle,* by Al Graham, illus. by Tony Palazzo (Welch); *Pedro, the Angel of Olvera Street,* by Leo Politi (Scribner); *Sing in Praise: A Collection of the Best Loved Hymns,* by Opal Wheeler, illus. by Marjorie Torrey (Dutton)

**1946** *The Rooster Crows* (traditional Mother Goose), illus. by Maud and Miska Petersham (Macmillan)

**Honor Books:** *Little Lost Lamb,* by Golden MacDonald, illus. by Leonard Weisgard (Doubleday); *Sing Mother Goose,* by Opal Wheeler, illus. by Marjorie Torrey (Dutton); *My Mother Is the Most Beautiful Woman in the World,* by Becky Reyher, illus. by Ruth Gannett (Lothrop); *You Can Write Chinese,* by Kurt Wiese (Viking)

**1945** *Prayer for a Child,* by Rachel Field, illus. by Elizabeth Orton Jones (Macmillan)

**Honor Books:** *Mother Goose,* illus. by Tasha Tudor (Walck); *In the Forest,* by Marie Hall Ets (Viking); *Yonie Wondernose,* by Marguerite de

Angeli (Doubleday); *The Christmas Anna Angel*, by Ruth Sawyer, illus. by Kate Seredy (Viking)

**1944** *Many Moons*, by James Thurber, illus. by Louis Slobodkin (Harcourt)
**Honor Books:** *Small Rain: Verses from the Bible*, selected by Jessie Orton Jones, illus. by Elizabeth Orton Jones (Viking); *Pierre Pigeon*, by Lee Kingman, illus. by Arnold E. Bare (Houghton); *The Mighty Hunter*, by Berta and Elmer Hader (Macmillan); *A Child's Good Night Book*, by Margaret Wise Brown, illus. by Jean Charlot (Scott); *Good Luck Horse*, by Chin-Yi Chan, illus. by Plao Chan (Whittlesey)

**1943** *The Little House*, by Virginia Lee Burton (Houghton)
**Honor Books:** *Dash and Dart*, by Mary and Conrad Buff (Viking); *Marshmallow*, by Clare Newberry (Harper)

**1942** *Make Way for Ducklings*, by Robert McCloskey (Viking)
**Honor Books:** *An American ABC*, by Maud and Miska Petersham (Macmillan); *In My Mother's House*, by Ann Nolan Clark, illus. by Velino Herrera (Viking); *Paddle-to-the-Sea*, by Holling C. Holling (Houghton); *Nothing at All*, by Wanda Gág (Coward)

**1941** *They Were Strong and Good*, by Robert Lawson (Viking)
**Honor Book:** *April's Kittens*, by Clare Newberry (Harper)

**1940** *Abraham Lincoln*, by Ingri and Edgar d'Aulaire (Doubleday)
**Honor Books:** *Cock-a-Doodle Doo*, by Berta and Elmer Hader (Macmillan); *Madeline*, by Ludwig Bemelmans (Viking); *The Ageless Story*, illus. by Lauren Ford (Dodd)

**1939** *Mei Li*, by Thomas Handforth (Doubleday)
**Honor Books:** *The Forest Pool*, by Laura Adams Armer (Longmans); *Wee Gillis*, by Munro Leaf, illus. by Robert Lawson (Viking); *Snow White and the Seven Dwarfs*, by Wanda Gág (Coward); *Barkis*, by Clare Newberry (Harper); *Andy and the Lion*, by James Daugherty (Viking)

**1938** *Animals of the Bible*, by Helen Dean Fish, illus. by Dorothy P. Lathrop (Lippincott)
**Honor Books:** *Seven Simeons*, by Boris Artzybasheff (Viking); *Four and Twenty Blackbirds*, by Helen Dean Fish, illus. by Robert Lawson (Stokes)

## National Book Award, Children's Book Category

Since March, 1969, the National Book Awards have included a prize in the category of children's books. Contributed by the Children's Book Council and administered by the National Book Committee, this award is presented annually to a juvenile title that a panel of judges considers the most distinguished written by an American citizen and published in the United States in the preceding year.

**1975** *M. C. Higgins The Great*, by Virginia Hamilton (Macmillan)

**1974** *Court of the Stone Children*, by Eleanor Cameron (Dutton)

**1973** *The Farthest Shore*, by Ursula K. LeGuin (Atheneum)

**1972** *The Slightly Irregular Fire Engine*, by Donald Barthelme (Farrar)

**1971** *The Marvelous Misadventures of Sebastian*, by Lloyd Alexander (Dutton)

**1970** *A Day of Pleasure: Stories of a Boy Growing Up in Warsaw*, by Isaac Bashevis Singer (Farrar)

**1969** *Journey from Peppermint Street*, by Meindert DeJong (Harper)

## Council On Interracial Books For Children Award

Since 1968 the Council on Interracial Books for Children Award has been given annually to encourage the publication of children's books by minority authors. The number of award categories has been expanded, and, beginning in 1973, the Council on Interracial Books for Children has offered five awards for unpublished manuscripts by writers who are black, Chicano, American Indian, Puerto Rican, and Asian-American and who have not yet published a book for children. The selections below reflect those manuscripts that have been or will soon be published.

**1974** African American: *Simba, Midnight (the Stallion of the Night) and Mweusi*, by Aishah S. Abdullah; Chicano: *My Father Hijacked a Plane*, by Abelardo B. Delgado; Puerto Rican: *Yari*, by Antonia A. Hernandez

**1973** African American: *Song of the Trees*, by Mildred D. Taylor; American Indian: *Morning Arrow*, by Nanabah Dee Dodge; *Grandfather's Bridge*, by Michele P. Robinson; Asian American: *Eyak*, by Dorothy Tomiye Okamoto; Puerto

Rican: *El Pito De Plato De Pito*, by Jack Aqueros

**1971–1972** Asian-American: *Morning Song*, by Min-fong Ho; black: *The Rock Cried Out*, by Florenz Webbe Maxwell; Puerto Rican: *The Unusual Puerto Rican*, by Theodore Laquer-Franceschi

**1970** American Indian: *Jimmy Yellow Hawk*, by Virginia Driving Hawk Sneve (Holiday); black: *Sneakers* (orig. title *Warball*), by Ray Anthony Shepard (Dutton); Chicano: *I Am Magic*, by Juan Valenzuela (Indian Historian Press)

**1969** Ages three to six: *ABC: The Story of the Alphabet*, by Virginia Cox (Wayne State U.); Ages seven to eleven: *Sidewalk Story*, by Sharon Bell Mathis (Viking); ages twelve to sixteen: *Letters from Uncle David: Underground Hero*, by Margot S. Webb

**1968** Ages three to six: *Where Does the Day Go?*, by Walter N. Myers (Parents'); ages seven to eleven: no award; ages twelve to sixteen: *The Soul Brothers and Sister Lou*, by Kristin Hunter (Scribner)

## The Hans Christian Andersen Prize

Established in 1956 by the International Board on Books for Young People, the Hans Christian Andersen Prize is given biennially to one author and one illustrator (since 1966) who, by his or her entire body of work, has made an important international contribution to children's literature.

**1974** Author: Maria Gripe (Sweden); Illustrator: Farshid Nesghali (Iran)

**1972** Author: Scott O'Dell (U.S.A.); Illustrator: Ib Spang Olsen (Denmark)

**1970** Author: Gianni Rodari (Italy); Illustrator: Maurice Sendak (U.S.A.)

**1968** Authors: James Krüss (Germany), José Maria Sanchez-Silva (Spain); Illustrator: Jiri Trnka (Czechoslovakia)

**1966** Author: Tove Jansson (Finland); Illustrator: Alois Carigiet (Switzerland)

**1964** René Guillot (France)

**1962** Meindert DeJong (U.S.A.)

**1960** Erich Kästner (Germany)

**1958** Astrid Lindgren (Sweden)

**1956** Eleanor Farjeon (Great Britain)

## Laura Ingalls Wilder Award

Begun in 1954, the Laura Ingalls Wilder Award, administered by the American Library Association, Children's Services Division, is now given every five years (since 1960) in recognition of an author or illustrator whose books are published in the United States and have made an important contribution to children's literature over a period of years.

**1975** Beverly Cleary
**1970** E. B. White
**1960** Clara Ingram Judson
**1954** Laura Ingalls Wilder

## Carnegie Medal

Awarded annually since 1937, the Carnegie Award has been presented by the British Library Association to the outstanding children's book written by a British author and published in England during the year prior to the award.

**1975** *The Stronghold* by Mollie Hunter (Hamilton)

**1974** *The Ghost of Thomas Kempe*, by Penelope Lively (Dutton)

**1973** *Watership Down*, by Richard Adams (Rex Collings)

**1972** *Josh*, by Ivan Southall (Angus & Robertson)

**1971** *The God Beneath the Sea*, by Leon Garfield and Edward Blishen (Longmans)

**1970** *The Edge of the Cloud*, by Kathleen Peyton (Oxford)

**1969** *The Moon in the Cloud*, by Rosemary Harris (Faber)

**1968** *The Owl Service*, by Alan Garner (Collins)

**1967** No Award

**1966** *The Grange at High Force*, by Philip Turner (Oxford)

**1965** *Nordy Bank*, by Sheena Porter (Oxford)

**1964** *Time of Trial*, by Hester Burton (Oxford)

**1963** *The Twelve and the Genii*, by Pauline Clarke (Faber)

**1962** *A Stranger at Green Knowe*, by Lucy Boston (Faber)

**1961** *The Making of Man*, by I. W. Cornwall (Phoenix House)

**1960** *The Lantern Bearers*, by Rosemary Sutcliff (Oxford)

**1959** *Tom's Midnight Garden*, by Philippa Pearce (Oxford)

**1958** *A Grass Rope*, by William Mayne (Oxford)

**1957** *The Last Battle*, by C. S. Lewis (Bodley Head)

**1956** *The Little Bookroom*, by Eleanor Farjeon (Oxford)

**1955** *Knight Crusader*, by Ronald Welch (Oxford)

**1954** *A Valley Grows Up*, by Edward Osmond (Oxford)

**1953** *The Borrowers*, by Mary Norton (Dent)

**1952** *The Wool-Pack*, by Cynthia Harnett (Methuen)

**1951** *The Lark on the Wing*, by Elfrida Vipont Foulds (Oxford)

**1950** *The Story of Your Home*, by Agnes Allen (Transatlantic)

**1949** *Sea Change*, by Richard Armstrong (Dent)

**1948** *Collected Stories for Children*, by Walter de la Mare (Faber)

**1947** *The Little White Horse*, by Elizabeth Goudge (Brockhampton Press)

**1946** No Award

**1945** *The Wind on the Moon*, by Eric Linklater (Macmillan)

**1944** No Award

**1943** *The Little Grey Men*, by B. B. (Eyre & Spottiswoode)

**1942** *We Couldn't Leave Dinah*, by Mary Treadgold (Penguin)

**1941** *Visitors from London*, by Kitty Barne (Dent)

**1940** *Radium Woman*, by Eleanor Doorly (Heinemann)

**1939** *The Circus Is Coming*, by Noel Streatfield (Dent)

**1938** *The Family from One End Street*, by Eve Garnett (Muller)

**1937** *Pigeon Post*, by Arthur Ransome (Cape)

## Kate Greenaway Medal

Established in 1955 by the British Library Association, the Kate Greenaway Medal is given annually to the most distinguished illustrated book for children published in the United Kingdom during the preceding year.

**1975** *The Wind Blew*, by Pat Hutchins (Bodley Head)

**1974** *Father Christmas*, by Raymond Briggs (Coward)

**1973** *The Woodcutter's Duck*, by Krystyna Turska (Hamilton)

**1972** *The Kingdom under the Sea*, by Jan Pienkowski (Cape)

**1971** *Mr. Gumpy's Outing*, by John Burningham (Cape)

**1970** *The Quangle-Wangle's Hat*, by Edward Lear, illus. by Helen Oxenbury (Heinemann); *Dragon of an Ordinary Family*, by Margaret Mahy, illus. by Helen Oxenbury (Heinemann)

**1969** *Dictionary of Chivalry*, by Grant Uden, illus. by Pauline Baynes (Longmans)

**1968** *Charlie, Charlotte & the Golden Canary*, by Charles Keeping (Oxford)

**1967** *Mother Goose Treasury*, by Raymond Briggs (Hamilton)

**1966** *Three Poor Tailors*, by Victor Ambrus (Hamilton)

**1965** *Shakespear's Theatre*, by C. W. Hodges (Oxford)

**1964** *Borka*, by John Burningham (Cape)

**1963** *Brian Wildsmith's ABC*, by Brian Wildsmith (Oxford)

**1962** *Mrs. Cockle's Cat*, by Philippa Pearce, illus. by Antony Maitland (Longmans)

**1961** *Old Winkle and the Seagulls*, by Elizabeth Rose, illus. by Gerald Rose (Faber)

**1960** *Kashtanka and a Bundle of Ballads*, by William Stobbs (Oxford)

**1959** No Award

**1958** *Mrs. Easter and the Storks*, by V. H. Drummond (Faber)

**1957** *Tim All Alone*, by Edward Ardizzone (Oxford)

**1956** No Award

# Indexes

# Subject Index

# Title Index